Mike Holt's Illustrated Guide to

Changes to THE NEC® 2011

Mike Holt Enterprises, Inc.
888.NEC.CODE (632.2633) • www.MikeHolt.com • Info@MikeHolt.com

NOTICE TO THE READER

Mike Holt's Illustrated Guide to Changes to the NEC® 2011

First Printing: October 2010

Technical Illustrator: Mike Culbreath
Cover Design: Madalina Iordache-Levay
Layout Design and Typesetting: Cathleen Kwas

ISBN 978-1-932685-61-9

For more information, call 888.NEC.CODE (632.2633), or E-mail Info@MikeHolt.com.

I dedicate this book to the
Lord Jesus Christ,
my mentor and teacher.
Proverbs 16:3

ONE TEAM

To Our Instructors and Students:

We're committed to providing you the finest product with the fewest errors, but we're realistic and know that there'll be errors found and reported after the printing of this book. The last thing we want is for you to have problems finding, communicating, or accessing this information. It's unacceptable to us for there to be even one error in our textbooks or answer keys. For this reason, we're asking you to work together with us as One Team.

Students: Please report any errors you may find to your instructor.

Instructors: Please communicate these errors to us.

Our Commitment:

We'll continue to list all of the corrections that come through for all of our textbooks and answer keys on our Website. The most up-to-date answer keys will always be available to instructors to download from our instructor Website. We don't want you to have problems finding this updated information, so we're outlining where to go for all of this below:

To view textbook and answer key corrections: Students and instructors go to our Website, www.MikeHolt.com, click on "Books" in the sidebar of links, and then click on "Corrections."

To download the most up-to-date answer keys: Instructors go to our Website, www.MikeHolt.com, click on "Instructors" in the sidebar of links and then click on "Answer Keys." On this page you'll find instructions for accessing and downloading these answer keys.

If you're not registered as an instructor you'll need to register. Your registration will be sent to our educational director who in turn will review and approve your registration. In your approval E-mail will be the login and password so you can have access to all of the answer keys. If you have a situation that needs immediate attention, please contact the office directly at 888.NEC.CODE (632.2633).

Call 888.NEC.CODE (632.2633) or visit us online at www.MikeHolt.com

Table of CONTENTS

INTRODUCTION

Mike Holt's Illustrated Guide to Changes to the NEC® 2011

Mike Holt's Illustrated Guide to Changes to the NEC® 2011 is intended to provide you with the tools necessary to understand the changes made to the 2011 National Electrical Code® (NEC). There were over 5,000 proposals to change the NEC, and hundreds of Code rules have changed that will affect us all.

The writing style of this textbook, and in all of Mike Holt's products, is meant to be informative, practical, useful, informal, easy to read, and applicable for today's electrical professional. Just like all of Mike Holt's textbooks, this book contains hundreds of full-color illustrations to help you see the safety requirements of the *National Electrical Code* in practical use, helping you visualize the *Code* in today's electrical installations.

This illustrated textbook contains cautions regarding possible conflicts or confusing *NEC* requirements, tips on proper electrical installations, and warnings of dangers related to improper electrical installations. In spite of this effort, some rules may seem to be unclear or need additional editorial improvement.

We can't eliminate confusing, conflicting, or controversial *Code* requirements, but we do try to put them into sharper focus to help you understand their intended purpose. Sometimes a requirement is so confusing nobody really understands its actual application. When this occurs, this textbook will point the situation out in an upfront and straightforward manner. We apologize in advance if that ever seems disrespectful, but our intention is to help the industry understand the current *NEC* as best as possible, point out areas that need refinement, and encourage *Code* users to be a part of the change process that creates a better *NEC* for the future.

The *Code* is updated every three years to accommodate new electrical products and materials, changing technologies, improved installation techniques, and to make editorial refinements to improve readability and application. While the uniform adoption of each new edition of the *NEC* is the best approach for all involved in the electrical industry, many inspection jurisdictions modify the *Code* when it's adopted. To further complicate this situation, the *NEC* allows the authority having jurisdiction, typically the "Electrical Inspector," the flexibility to waive specific *Code* requirements, and to permit alternative wiring methods contrary to the *NEC* requirements. This is only allowed when he or she is assured the completed electrical installation is equivalent in establishing and maintaining effective safety [90.4].

Keeping up with requirements of the *Code* should be the goal of everyone involved in the safety of electrical installations. This includes electrical installers, contractors, owners, inspectors, engineers, instructors, and others concerned with electrical installations.

About the 2011 *NEC*

The actual process of changing the *Code* takes about two years, and it involves thousands of individuals making an effort to have the *NEC* as current and accurate as possible. Let's review how this process works:

Step 1. Proposals—November, 2008. Anybody can submit a proposal to change the *Code* before the proposal closing date. Over 5,000 proposals were submitted to modify the 2011 *NEC*. Of these proposals, over 300 rules were revised that significantly effect the electrical industry. Some changes were editorial revisions, while others were more significant, such as new articles, sections, exceptions, and Informational Notes.

Step 2. *Code*-Making Panel(s) Review Proposals—January, 2009. All *Code* proposals were reviewed by *Code*-Making Panels. There were 19 panels in the 2011 *Code* process who voted to accept, reject, or modify them.

Step 3. Report on Proposals (ROP)—July, 2009. The voting of the *Code*-Making Panels on the proposals was published for public review in a document called the "Report on Proposals," frequently referred to as the "ROP."

Step 4. Public Comments—October, 2009. Once the ROP was available, public comments were submitted asking the *Code*-Making Panel members to revise their earlier actions on change proposals, based on new information. The closing date for "Comments" was October, 2009.

Step 5. Comments Reviewed by *Code* Panels—December, 2009. The *Code*-Making Panels met again to review, discuss, and vote on public comments.

Step 6. Report on Comments (ROC)—April, 2010. The voting on the "Comments" was published for public review in a document called the "Report on Comments," frequently referred to as the "ROC."

Step 7. Electrical Section—June, 2010. The NFPA Electrical Section discussed and reviewed the work of the *Code*-Making Panels. The Electrical Section developed recommendations on last-minute motions to revise the proposed *NEC* draft that would be presented at the NFPA annual meeting.

Step 8. NFPA Annual Meeting—June, 2010. The 2011 *NEC* was voted by the NFPA members to approve the action of the *Code*-Making Panels at the annual meeting, after a number of motions (often called "floor actions") were voted on.

Step 9. Standards Council Review Appeals and Approves the 2011 *NEC*—July, 2010. The NFPA Standards Council reviewed the record of the *Code*-making process and approved publication of the 2011 *NEC*.

Step 10. 2011 *NEC* Published—September, 2010. The 2011 *National Electrical Code* was published, following the NFPA Board of Directors review of appeals.

> **Author's Comment:** Proposals and comments can be submitted online at the NFPA Website (www.nfpa.org). From the homepage, click on "Codes and Standards" at the top of the page, then from the Codes and Standards page click on "Proposals and Comments" in the box on the right-hand side of the page. The deadline for proposals to create the 2014 *National Electrical Code* is November 5, 2011. If you would like to see something changed in the *Code*, you're encouraged to participate in the process.

The Scope of This Textbook

This textbook, *Illustrated Guide to Changes to the NEC 2011*, covers those installation requirements that we consider to be of critical importance, and is based on the following conditions:

1. Power Systems and Voltage. All power-supply systems are assumed to be one of the following, unless identified otherwise:

2-wire, single-phase, 120V
3-wire, single-phase, 120/240V
4-wire, three-phase, 120/240V Delta
4-wire, three-phase, 120/208V or 277/480V Wye

2. Electrical Calculations. Unless the question or example specifies three-phase, they're based on a single-phase power supply. In addition, all amperage calculations are rounded to the nearest ampere in accordance with Section 220.5(B).

3. Conductor Material. Conductors are considered copper, unless aluminum is identified or specified.

4. Conductor Sizing. Conductors are sized based on a THHN/THWN copper conductor terminating on a 75°C terminal in accordance with 110.14(C), unless the question or example identifies otherwise.

5. Overcurrent Device. The term "overcurrent device" refers to a molded-case circuit breaker, unless specified otherwise. Where a fuse is specified, it's a single-element type fuse, also known as a "one-time fuse," unless the text specifies otherwise.

NEC Changes Library

To understand the changes in greater detail, watch Mike explain how the *NEC* changes might affect you. Order the 2011 *NEC* Changes DVDs by calling 888.NEC.CODE (632.2633).

Mike Holt's Detailed *Code* Library

If you want to really understand the 2011 *National Electrical Code*, then Mike Holt's Detailed *Code* Library is ideal for you. Mike explains in great detail the history of the rule, the reason for the rule, and how to apply the *Code*. This program covers general installation requirements, branch circuits, feeders, services and overcurrent protection, grounding and bonding, conductors, cables and raceways, boxes, panels, motors, transformers, and much more. Summary questions are included in all books to help you test your knowledge.

This program includes 3 textbooks and 10 DVDs:

- *Understanding the National Electrical Code Volume 1* textbook
- *Understanding the National Electrical Code Volume 2* textbook
- *NEC Exam Practice Questions* book
- General Requirements Part 1 DVD and Part 2 DVD
- Grounding vs. Bonding Part 1 DVD and Part 2 DVD
- Wiring Methods Part 1 DVD and Part 2 DVD
- Equipment for General Use DVD
- Special Occupancies DVD
- Special Equipment DVD
- Limited Energy and Communication Systems DVD

Order the Mike Holt's Detailed *Code* Library by calling 888.NEC.CODE (632.2633).

About This TEXTBOOK

This textbook is to be used along with the *NEC*, not as a replacement for it, so be sure to have a copy of the 2011 *National Electrical Code* handy. Compare what we are explaining in this book to what the *Code* book says, and discuss any topics that you find difficult to understand with others.

You'll notice that in this book, a great deal of the *NEC* wording has been paraphrased, and some of the article and section titles appear different from the wording in the actual *Code*. Mike believes doing so makes it easier to understand the content of the rule, so keep this in mind when comparing this textbook against the actual *Code*.

We hope that as you read through this textbook, you'll allow sufficient time to review the text along with the outstanding graphics and examples, which are invaluable to your understanding.

Textbook Format

This textbook follows the *NEC* format, but it doesn't cover every *Code* requirement. For example, it doesn't include every article, section, subsection, exception, or Informational Note. So don't be concerned if you see the textbook contains Exception 1 and Exception 3, but not Exception 2.

Informational Notes. Informational Notes contained in the *NEC* will be identified in this textbook as "Note," except when that phrase is used in the change summary (gray background) or analysis (yellow background).

Important Features for the 2011 Edition of This Textbook

In order to better meet the needs of our customers, we have improved the layout of this textbook with some new feaures, in addition to the features from the 2008 edition which were so successful. These features include:

- Each *Code* section which contains a change includes a summary of the change, followed by a paraphrase of the *NEC* text affected by the change. Any specific change is denoted by <u>underlined text and in the corresponding chapter color</u>. For example, Chapter 1 the change text will be red and underlined; Chapter 2 the change text will be cyan and underlined, etc.
- Graphics that contain a 2011 *Code* change will have a green border with a green 2011 CC icon next to the heading.
- Any *NEC* changes will be in green underlined text. If you see a green bordered graphic with no green underlined text, it most likely indicates that the *Code* change is the removal of some text. Graphics without a color border support the concept being discussed, but nothing in the graphic was affected by a change for 2011.
- After each *Code* section, summary, and paraphrase is a yellow "sticky note" containing an analysis of the change.
- Additional information to better help you understand a concept is identified with light green shading.

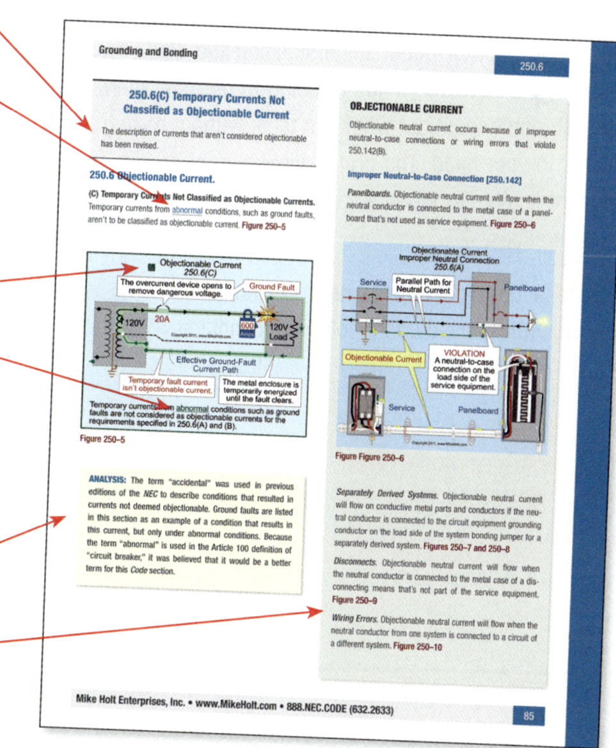

Grounding and Bonding 250.6

250.6(C) Temporary Currents Not Classified as Objectionable Current

The description of currents that aren't considered objectionable has been revised.

250.6 Objectionable Current.

(C) Temporary Currents Not Classified as Objectionable Currents. Temporary currents from <u>abnormal</u> conditions, such as ground faults, aren't to be classified as objectionable current. Figure 250–5

Figure 250–5

ANALYSIS: The term "accidental" was used in previous editions of the *NEC* to describe conditions that resulted in currents not deemed objectionable. Ground faults are listed in this section as an example of a condition that results in this current, but only under abnormal conditions. Because the term "abnormal" is used in the Article 100 definition of "circuit breaker," it was believed that it would be a better term for this *Code* section.

OBJECTIONABLE CURRENT

Objectionable neutral current occurs because of improper neutral-to-case connections or wiring errors that violate 250.142(B).

Improper Neutral-to-Case Connection [250.142]

Panelboards. Objectionable neutral current will flow when the neutral conductor is connected to the metal case of a panelboard that's not used as service equipment. Figure 250–6

Figure Figure 250–6

Separately Derived Systems. Objectionable neutral current will flow on conductive metal parts and conductors if the neutral conductor is connected to the circuit equipment grounding conductor on the load side of the system bonding jumper for a separately derived system. Figures 250–7 and 250–8

Disconnects. Objectionable neutral current will flow when the neutral conductor is connected to the metal case of a disconnecting means that's not part of the service equipment. Figure 250–9

Wiring Errors. Objectionable neutral current will flow when the neutral conductor from one system is connected to a circuit of a different system. Figure 250–10

Mike Holt Enterprises, Inc. • www.MikeHolt.com • 888.NEC.CODE (632.2633) 85

Cross-References. This textbook contains several *NEC* cross-references to other related *Code* requirements to help you develop a better understanding of how the *NEC* rules relate to one another. These cross-references are indicated by *Code* section numbers in brackets, an example of which is "[90.4]."

Author's Comments. Hundreds of "Author's Comments" are intended to help you understand the *NEC* material, and to bring to your attention things of which you should be aware.

Difficult Concepts

As you progress through this textbook, you might find that you don't understand every explanation, example, calculation, or comment. Don't become frustrated, and don't get down on yourself. Remember, this is the *National Electrical Code* and sometimes the best attempt to explain a concept isn't enough to make it perfectly clear. If you're still confused, visit www.MikeHolt.com, and post your question on the *Code* Forum for help.

Different Interpretations

Some electricians, contractors, instructors, inspectors, engineers, and others enjoy the challenge of discussing the *NEC* requirements, hopefully in a positive and productive manner. This give-and-take is important to the process of better understanding the *Code* requirements and application. However, if you're going to get into an *NEC* discussion, please don't spout out what you think without having the actual *Code* book in your hand. The professional way of discussing an *NEC* requirement is by referring to a specific section, rather than talking in vague generalities.

Textbook Errors and Corrections

Humans develop the text, graphics, and layout of this textbook, and since currently none of us are perfect, there may be a few errors. This can occur because the *NEC* is dramatically changed each *Code* cycle; new articles are added, some are deleted, some are relocated, and many are renumbered. We take great care in researching the *NEC* requirements to ensure this textbook is correct. If you believe there's an error of any kind in this textbook (typographical, grammatical, technical, or anything else), no matter how insignificant, please let us know.

Any errors found after printing are listed on our Website, so if you find an error, first check to see if it's already been corrected. Go to www.MikeHolt.com, click on the "Books" link, and then the "Corrections" link (www.MikeHolt.com/bookcorrections.htm).

If you don't find the error listed on the Website, contact us by sending an E-mail to Corrections@MikeHolt.com. Be sure to include the book title, page number, and any other pertinent information.

How to Use the *National* ELECTRICAL CODE

The *National Electrical Code* is written for persons who understand electrical terms, theory, safety procedures, and electrical trade practices. These individuals include electricians, electrical contractors, electrical inspectors, electrical engineers, designers, and other qualified persons. The *Code* isn't written to serve as an instructive or teaching manual for untrained individuals [90.1(C)].

Learning to use the *NEC* is like learning to play the game of chess; it's a great game if you enjoy mental warfare. When learning to play chess, you must first learn the names of the game pieces, how the pieces are placed on the board, and how each piece moves.

Once you understand the fundamentals of the game, you're ready to start playing the game. Unfortunately, at this point all you can do is make crude moves, because you really don't understand how all the information works together. To play chess well, you'll need to learn how to use your knowledge by working on subtle strategies before you can work your way up to the more intriguing and complicated moves.

Not a Game

Electrical work isn't a game, and it must be taken very seriously. Learning the basics of electricity, important terms and concepts, as well as the basic layout of the *NEC* gives you just enough knowledge to be dangerous. There are thousands of specific and unique applications of electrical installations, and the *Code* doesn't cover every one of them. To safely apply the *NEC*, you must understand the purpose of a rule and how it affects the safety aspects of the installation.

NEC Terms and Concepts

The *NEC* contains many technical terms, so it's crucial for *Code* users to understand their meanings and their applications. If you don't understand a term used in a *Code* rule, it will be impossible to properly apply the *NEC* requirement. Be sure you understand that Article 100 defines the terms that apply to two or more *Code* articles. For example, the term "Dwelling Unit" is found in many articles; if you don't know what a dwelling unit is, how can you apply the requirements for it?

In addition, many articles have terms unique for that specific article and definitions of those terms are only applicable for that given article. For example, Section 250.2 contains the definitions of terms that only apply to Article 250—Grounding and Bonding.

Small Words, Grammar, and Punctuation

It's not only the technical words that require close attention, because even the simplest of words can make a big difference to the application of a rule. The word "or" can imply alternate choices for equipment wiring methods, while "and" can mean an additional requirement. Let's not forget about grammar and punctuation. The location of a comma "," can dramatically change the requirement of a rule.

Slang Terms or Technical Jargon

Electricians, engineers, and other trade-related professionals use slang terms or technical jargon that isn't shared by all. This makes it very difficult to communicate because not everybody understands the intent or application of those slang terms. So where possible, be sure you use the proper word, and don't use a word if you don't understand its definition and application. For example, lots of electricians use the term "pigtail" when describing the short conductor for the connection of a receptacle, switch, luminaire, or equipment. Although they may understand it, not everyone does.

NEC Style and Layout

Before we get into the details of the *NEC*, we need to take a few moments to understand its style and layout. Understanding the structure and writing style of the *Code* is very important before it can be used and applied effectively. The *National Electrical Code* is organized into ten major components.

1. Table of Contents
2. Article 90 (Introduction to the *Code*)
3. Chapters 1 through 9 (major categories)
4. Articles 90 through 840 (individual subjects)
5. Parts (divisions of an Article)
6. Sections and Tables (*Code* requirements)
7. Exceptions (*Code* permissions)
8. Informational Notes (explanatory material)

9. Annexes (information)
10. Index

1. Table of Contents. The Table of Contents displays the layout of the chapters, articles, and parts as well as the page numbers. It's an excellent resource and should be referred to periodically to observe the interrelationship of the various *NEC* components. When attempting to locate the rules for a particular situation, knowledgeable *Code* users often go first to the Table of Contents to quickly find the specific *NEC* Part that applies.

2. Introduction. The *NEC* begins with Article 90, the introduction to the *Code*. It contains the purpose of the *NEC*, what's covered and what isn't covered along with how the *Code* is arranged. It also gives information on enforcement and how mandatory and permissive rules are written as well as how explanatory material is included. Article 90 also includes information on formal interpretations, examination of equipment for safety, wiring planning, and information about formatting units of measurement.

3. Chapters. There are nine chapters, each of which is divided into articles. The articles fall into one of four groupings: General Requirements (Chapters 1 through 4), Specific Requirements (Chapters 5 through 7), Communications Systems (Chapter 8), and Tables (Chapter 9).

Chapter 1 General
Chapter 2 Wiring and Protection
Chapter 3 Wiring Methods and Materials
Chapter 4 Equipment for General Use
Chapter 5 Special Occupancies
Chapter 6 Special Equipment
Chapter 7 Special Conditions
Chapter 8 Communications Systems (Telephone, Data, Satellite, Cable TV and Broadband)
Chapter 9 Tables–Conductor and Raceway Specifications

4. Articles. The *NEC* contains approximately 140 articles, each of which covers a specific subject. For example:

Article 110 General Requirements
Article 250 Grounding and Bonding
Article 300 Wiring Methods
Article 430 Motors and Motor Controllers
Article 500 Hazardous (Classified) Locations
Article 680 Swimming Pools, Fountains, and Similar Installations
Article 725 Remote-Control, Signaling, and Power-Limited Circuits
Article 800 Communications Circuits

5. Parts. Larger Articles are subdivided into parts.

Because the parts of a *Code* article aren't included in the section numbers, we have a tendency to forget what "part" the *NEC* rule is relating to. For example, Table 110.34(A) contains working space clearances for electrical equipment. If we aren't careful, we might think this table applies to all electrical installations, but Table 110.34(A) is located in Part III, which only contains requirements for "Over 600 Volts, Nominal installations." The rules for working clearances for electrical equipment for systems 600V, nominal, or less are contained in Table 110.26(A)(1), which is located in Part II—600 Volts, Nominal, or Less.

6. Sections and Tables.

Sections. Each *NEC* rule is called a "*Code* Section." A *Code* section may be broken down into subsections by letters in parentheses (A), (B), and so on. Numbers in parentheses (1), (2), and so forth, may further break down a subsection, and lowercase letters (a), (b), and so on, further break the rule down to the third level. For example, the rule requiring all receptacles in a dwelling unit bathroom to be GFCI protected is contained in Section 210.8(A)(1). Section 210.8(A)(1) is located in Chapter 2, Article 210, Section 8, Subsection (A), Subsubsection (1).

Many in the industry incorrectly use the term "Article" when referring to a *Code* section. For example, they say "Article 210.8," when they should say "Section 210.8." Section numbers in this book are shown without the word "Section," unless they begin a sentence. For example, Section 210.8(A) is shown as simply 210.8(A).

Tables. Many *Code* requirements are contained within tables, which are lists of *NEC* requirements placed in a systematic arrangement. The titles of the tables are extremely important; you must read them carefully in order to understand the contents, applications, limitations, and so forth, of each table in the *Code*. Many times notes are provided in or below a table; be sure to read them as well since they're also part of the requirement. For example, Note 1 for Table 300.5 explains how to measure the cover when burying cables and raceways, and Note 5 explains what to do if solid rock is encountered.

7. Exceptions. Exceptions are *Code* requirements or permissions that provide an alternative method to a specific requirement. There are two types of exceptions—mandatory and permissive. When a rule has several exceptions, those exceptions with mandatory requirements are listed before the permissive exceptions.

Mandatory Exceptions. A mandatory exception uses the words "shall" or "shall not." The word "shall" in an exception means that if you're using the exception, you're required to do it in a particular way. The phrase "shall not" means it isn't permitted.

Permissive Exceptions. A permissive exception uses words such as "shall be permitted," which means it's acceptable (but not mandatory) to do it in this way.

8. Informational Notes. An Informational Note contains explanatory material intended to clarify a rule or give assistance, but it isn't a *Code* requirement.

9. Annexes. Annexes aren't a part of the *NEC* requirements, and are included in the *Code* for informational purposes only.

Annex A. Product Safety Standards
Annex B. Application Information for Ampacity Calculation
Annex C. Raceway Fill Tables for Conductors and Fixture Wires of the Same Size
Annex D. Examples
Annex E. Types of Construction
Annex F. Critical Operations Power Systems (COPS)
Annex G. Supervisory Control and Data Acquisition (SCADA)
Annex H. Administration and Enforcement
Annex I. Recommended Tightening Torques

10. Index. The Index at the back of the *NEC* is helpful in locating a specific rule.

Changes to the *NEC* since the previous edition(s), are identified by shading, but rules that have been relocated aren't identified as a change. A bullet symbol "•" is located on the margin to indicate the location of a rule that was deleted from a previous edition. New articles contain a vertical line in the margin of the page.

How to Locate a Specific Requirement

How to go about finding what you're looking for in the *Code* depends, to some degree, on your experience with the *NEC*. *Code* experts typically know the requirements so well they just go to the correct rule without any outside assistance. The Table of Contents might be the only thing very experienced *NEC* users need to locate the requirement they're looking for. On the other hand, average *Code* users should use all of the tools at their disposal, including the Table of Contents and the Index.

Table of Contents. Let's work out a simple example: What *NEC* rule specifies the maximum number of disconnects permitted for a service? If you're an experienced *Code* user, you'll know Article 230 applies to "Services," and because this article is so large, it's divided up into multiple parts (actually eight parts). With this knowledge, you can quickly go to the Table of Contents and see it lists the Service Equipment Disconnecting Means requirements in Part VI.

Author's Comment: The number 70 precedes all page numbers because the *NEC* is NFPA Standard Number 70.

Index. If you use the Index, which lists subjects in alphabetical order, to look up the term "service disconnect," you'll see there's no listing. If you try "disconnecting means," then "services," you'll find that the Index specifies that the rule is located in Article 230, Part VI. Because the *NEC* doesn't give a page number in the Index, you'll need to use the Table of Contents to find the page number, or flip through the *Code* to Article 230, then continue to flip through pages until you find Part VI.

Many people complain that the *NEC* only confuses them by taking them in circles. As you gain experience in using the *Code* and deepen your understanding of words, terms, principles, and practices, you'll find the *NEC* much easier to understand and use than you originally thought.

Customizing Your *Code* Book

One way to increase your comfort level with the *Code* is to customize it to meet your needs. You can do this by highlighting and underlining important *NEC* requirements, and by attaching tabs to important pages. Be aware that if you're using your *Code* book to take an exam, some exam centers don't allow markings of any type.

Highlighting. As you read through this textbook, be sure you highlight those requirements in the *Code* that are the most important or relevant to you. Use yellow for general interest and orange for important requirements you want to find quickly. Be sure to highlight terms in the Index and the Table of Contents as you use them.

Underlining. Underline or circle key words and phrases in the *NEC* with a red pen (not a lead pencil) and use a 6-inch ruler to keep lines straight and neat. This is a very handy way to make important requirements stand out. A small 6-inch ruler also comes in handy for locating specific information in the many *Code* tables.

Tabbing the *NEC*. By placing tabs on *Code* articles, sections, and tables, it will make it easier for you to use the *NEC*. However, too many tabs will defeat the purpose. You can order a set of *Code* tabs designed by Mike Holt online at www.MikeHolt.com, or by calling 1.888.NEC.CODE (632.2633).

About the **AUTHORS**

Mike Holt—Author

Mike Holt worked his way up through the electrical trade from an apprentice electrician to become one of the most recognized experts in the world as it relates to electrical power installations. He was a journeyman electrician, master electrician, and electrical contractor. Mike came from the real world, and he has a unique understanding of how the *NEC* relates to electrical installations from a practical standpoint. You'll find his writing style to be simple, nontechnical, and practical.

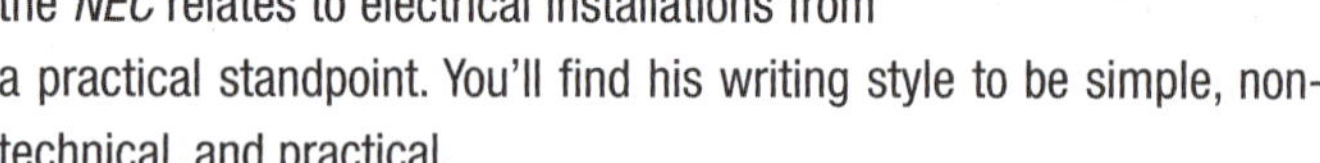

Did you know that he didn't finish high school? So if you struggled in high school or if you didn't finish it at all, don't let this get you down, you're in good company. As a matter of fact, Mike Culbreath, master electrician, who produces the finest electrical graphics in the history of the electrical industry, didn't finish high school either. So two high school dropouts produced the text and graphics in this textbook! However, realizing success depends on one's continuing pursuit of education. Mike immediately attained his GED (as did Mike Culbreath) and ultimately attended the University of Miami's Graduate School for a Master's degree in Business Administration (MBA).

Mike Holt resides in Central Florida, is the father of seven children, and has many outside interests and activities. He's a five-time National Barefoot Water-Ski Champion (1988, 1999, 2005, 2006, and 2007), has set many national records, and continues to train year-round at a World competition level [www.barefootwaterskier.com].

What sets him apart from some is his commitment to living a balanced lifestyle; he places God first, then family, career, and self.

Ryan Jackson—Author

Ryan Jackson is a combination inspector in the Salt Lake City, Utah, area. He began his career as a carpenter while in high school, and began doing electrical work at the age of 18. At the age of 23 Ryan landed his first job as an electrical inspector, and subsequently became certified in building, plumbing, and mechanical inspection (commercial and residential), as well as building and electrical plan review. Two years after becoming an inspector, he was approached by a friend in the area asking him to fill in at an electrical seminar for him. After his first class he was hooked, and is now a highly sought-after seminar instructor. Ryan has taught in several states, and loves helping people increase their understanding of the *Code*.

In 2005, Ryan met Mike Holt in Salt Lake City, and they became friends immediately. He helped Mike with his *Understanding the NEC, Volume 2* videos and began editing his books as well. Ryan believes that there are only a small handful of opportunities that change a person's life and career, and meeting Mike was one of them.

When Ryan isn't working, he can often be found in his garage turning wood on his lathe, and in the autumn you'll find him at as many University of Utah football games as he can attend, which is typically all of them. Ryan married his high school sweetheart, Sharie, and they have two beautiful children together: Kaitlynn and Aaron.

Mike Holt—Special Acknowledgments

First, I want to thank God for my godly wife who's always by my side and my children, Belynda, Melissa, Autumn, Steven, Michael, Meghan, and Brittney.

A special thank you must be sent to the staff at the National Fire Protection Association (NFPA), publishers of the *NEC*—in particular Jeff Sargent for his assistance in answering my many *Code* questions over the years. Jeff, you're a "first class" guy, and I admire your dedication and commitment to helping others understand the *NEC*. Other former NFPA staff members I would like to thank include John Caloggero, Joe Ross, and Dick Murray for their help in the past.

A personal thank you goes to Sarina, my long-time friend and office manager. It's been wonderful working side-by-side with you for over 25 years nurturing this company's growth from its small beginnings.

Ryan Jackson—Special Acknowledgments

I want to first thank my amazing wife and my children for putting up with me for all of these years, which is often a difficult task, particularly when I'm writing.

Professionally, I'm indebted to Gary Beckstrand for getting me started in my teaching career, and Noel Williams who inspired me to do it in the first place. Mark Ode is one of the finest men that I've ever met, and he has always been there for me. Dick Loyd and Mike Johnston have always been patient with me when I've had a question for them, and I appreciate it very much.

Last, and most certainly not least, I want to thank my mother, Donna Jackson. She was one of the very first certified electrical inspectors in the state of Utah, and she did an amazing job raising three boys on her own. Mom, I love you very much, and I wouldn't have made it very far without you.

Mike Holt
ENTERPRISES TEAM

Graphic Illustrator

Mike Culbreath devoted his career to the electrical industry and worked his way up from an apprentice electrician to master electrician. While working as a journeyman electrician, he suffered a serious on-the-job knee injury. With a keen interest in continuing education for electricians, he completed courses at Mike Holt Enterprises, Inc. and then passed the exam to receive his Master Electrician's license. In 1986, after attending classes at Mike Holt Enterprises, Inc., he joined the staff to update material and later studied computer graphics and began illustrating Mike Holt's textbooks and magazine articles. He's worked with the company for almost 25 years and, as Mike Holt has proudly acknowledged, has helped to transform his words and visions into lifelike graphics.

Technical Editorial Director

Steve Arne has been involved in the electrical industry since 1974 working in various positions from electrician to full-time instructor and department chair in technical postsecondary education. Steve has developed curriculum for many electrical training courses and has developed university business and leadership courses. Currently, Steve offers occasional exam prep and continuing education *Code* classes. Steve enjoys helping others as they learn and experience new insights. His goal is to help others understand more of the technological marvels that surround us. Steve thanks God for the wonders of His creation and for the opportunity to share it with others.

Steve and his lovely wife Deb live in Rapid City, South Dakota where they're both active in their church and community. They have two grown children and five grandchildren.

Editorial Team

I want to thank **Toni Culbreath** and **Barbara Parks** who worked tirelessly to proofread and edit the final stages of this publication. Their attention to detail and dedication to this project is greatly appreciated.

Production Team

I want to thank **Cathleen Kwas** who did the layout and production of this book. Her desire to create the best possible product for our customers is greatly appreciated.

Video Team Members

Steve Arne, Mike Culbreath, and Ryan Jackson (members of the Mike Holt Enterprises Team) were video team members, along with the following highly qualified professionals.

Eric Stromberg
Electrical Engineer/Instructor
Dow Chemical
Lake Jackson, TX

Eric started in the Electrical field by working as a journeyman electrician for a small contractor in the Houston area while going to college pursuing a degree in Electrical Engineering. After graduation, in 1982, Eric worked as an electronic technician where he installed and maintained life safety control systems in high rise buildings. In 1989, Eric went to work for Dow Chemical where he designed power distribution systems for major industrial complexes in the U.S., Spain, Brazil, and Germany. Eric was very involved in both creating Electrical standards and procedures as well as checking existing standards and procedures for alignment with national standards. He also worked as a Construction Manager where he ensured Code compliancy of installations as well as provided field engineering support. Eric currently has his own business and spends a good deal of time teaching classes in both the National Electrical Code and electrical circuits. He is also a member of the Electrical Safety and Licensing Advisory Board for the State of Texas.

Eric lives in Lake Jackson, Texas, with his wife Jane. They have three children: Ainsley, Austin, and Brieanna. Ainsley is a teacher in Boston who will be getting married in the summer of 2011. Austin will be enlisting in the Air Force, and Brieanna will be starting college in the Fall of 2010.

John Travers
Electrical Inspector and Instructor,
Electric *Code* Class
Hialeah, FL
http://electriccodeclass.com

John Travers completed the Joint NECA/IBEW Apprenticeship-Training program in 1977, after a tour of duty in the Air Force. He worked at various jobsites in the South Florida and Illinois areas until becoming a contractor in 1984. He began his career as an inspector in 1985 serving Hialeah Gardens. In 1988, he added the Town of Medley to his responsibilities, and became a full-time Chief Electrical Inspector for the City of Hialeah in 1990. He served in that position until 2005. He now serves as the Director of Community Development for Hialeah. His responsibilities include managing the Building, Zoning, Code Compliance and Occupational License Divisions of the City of Hialeah.

He joined the IAEI in June of 1988 and was the project chairman for the 1996 Annual Meeting in Key West, Florida. He currently serves as the Treasurer and Director of Codes & Education for the Miami-Dade Division. John oversees an aggressive Continuing Education program for the electrical industry in the South Florida area, where he is a certified Education Sponsor for electrical contractors, inspectors, engineers and tradesmen. In 2003, he began teaching nationwide, assisting the I.C.C. with seminars in Denver and Salt Lake City.

John is a family man, who has been married to Barbara for over 35 years, with three children and seven grandchildren. His hobbies include fishing, diving, philately, golf and photography. He is a martial artist in GOJU Karate, where he received his third degree black belt in 2006.

NOTES

Introduction to the *NATIONAL ELECTRICAL CODE*

INTRODUCTION TO ARTICLE 90—INTRODUCTION TO THE *NATIONAL ELECTRICAL CODE*

Many *NEC* violations and misunderstandings wouldn't occur if people doing the work simply understood Article 90. For example, many people see *Code* requirements as performance standards. In fact, the *NEC* requirements are bare minimums for safety. This is exactly the stance electrical inspectors, insurance companies, and courts take when making a decision regarding electrical design or installation.

Article 90 opens by saying the *NEC* isn't intended as a design specification or instruction manual. The *National Electrical Code* has one purpose only, and that's the "practical safeguarding of persons and property from hazards arising from the use of electricity." It goes on to indicate that the *Code* isn't intended as a design specification or instruction manual. The necessity to carefully study the *NEC* rules can't be overemphasized, and the role of textbooks such as this one is to help in that undertaking. Understanding where to find the rules in the *Code* that apply to the installation is invaluable. Rules in several different articles often apply to even a simple installation.

Article 90 then describes the scope and arrangement of the *NEC*. A person who says, "I can't find anything in the *Code*," is really saying, "I never took the time to review Article 90." The balance of Article 90 provides the reader with information essential to understanding those items you do find in the *NEC*.

Typically, electrical work requires you to understand the first four chapters of the *Code* which apply generally, plus have a working knowledge of the Chapter 9 tables. That knowledge begins with Article 90. Chapters 5, 6, and 7 make up a large portion of the *NEC*, but they apply to special occupancies, special equipment, or other special conditions. They build on, modify, or amend the rules in the first four chapters. Chapter 8 contains the requirements for communications systems, such as telephone systems, antenna wiring, CATV, and network-powered broadband systems. Communications systems aren't subject to the general requirements of Chapters 1 through 4, or the special requirements of Chapters 5 through 7, unless there's a specific reference in Chapter 8 to a rule in Chapters 1 through 7.

90.2(B)(5) Not Within the Scope of the *NEC*

The areas in which utility installations aren't covered has been revised to address federal lands, Native American reservations, state agencies, military bases, and similar locations.

90.2 Scope of the *NEC*.

(B) What Isn't Covered. The *NEC* doesn't apply to:

(5) Electric Utilities. The *NEC* doesn't apply to installations under the exclusive control of an electric utility where such installations:

a. Consist of service drops or service laterals and associated metering. Figure 90–1

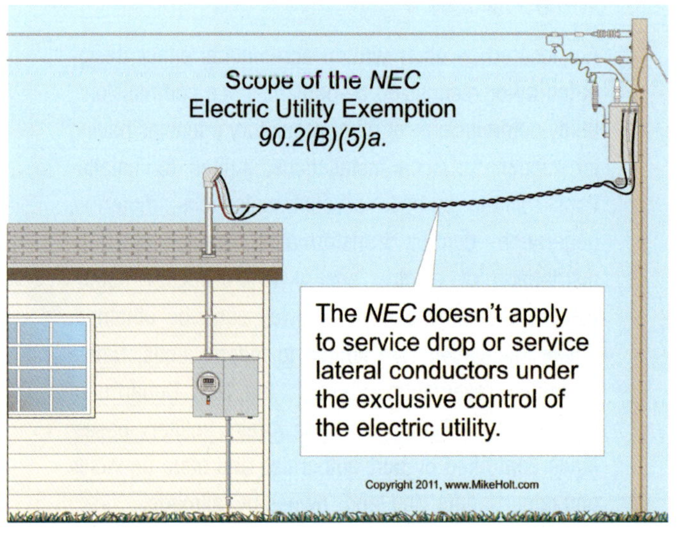

Figure 90–1

b. Are on property owned or leased by the electric utility for the purpose of generation, transformation, transmission, distribution, or metering of electric energy. **Figure 90–2**

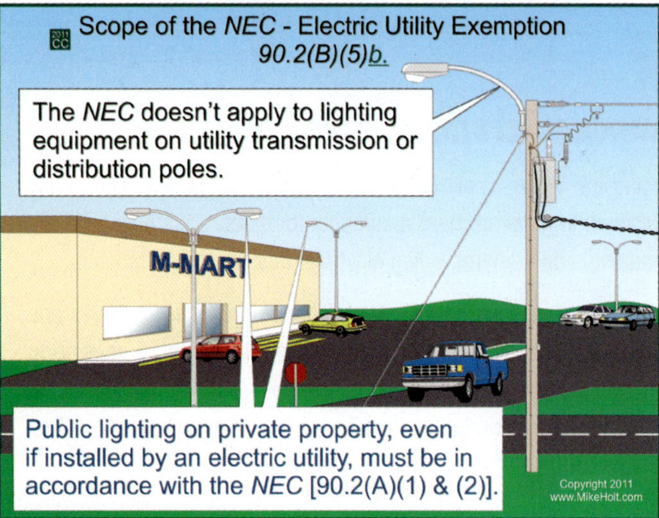

Figure 90–2

Author's Comment: Luminaires located in legally established easements, or rights-of-way, such as at poles supporting transmission or distribution lines, are exempt from the *NEC*. However, if the electric utility provides site and public lighting on private property, then the installation must comply with the *Code* [90.2(A)(4)]. See **Figure 90–2**

c. Are located on legally established easements, or rights-of-way. **Figure 90–3**

d. Are located by other written agreements either designated by or recognized by public service commissions, utility commissions, or other regulatory agencies having jurisdiction for such installations; limited to installations for the purpose of communications, metering, generation, control, transformation, transmission, or distribution of electric energy where legally established easements or rights-of-way can't be obtained. These installations are limited to federal lands, Native American reservations through the U.S. Department of the Interior Bureau of Indian Affairs, military bases, lands controlled by port authorities and state agencies and departments, and lands owned by railroads.

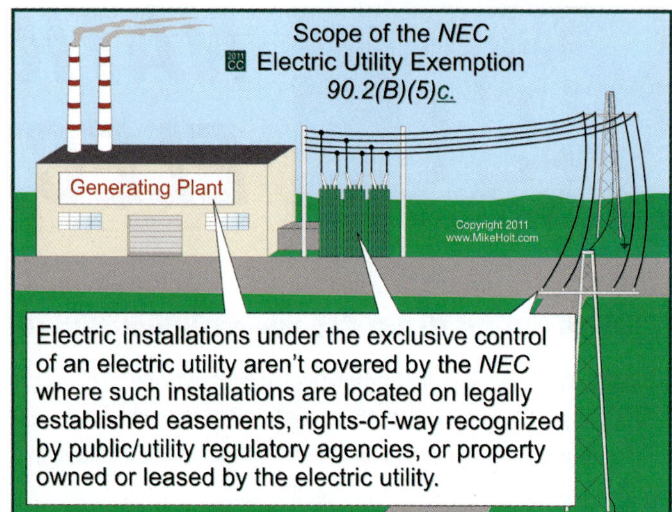

Figure 90–3

Note to 90.2(B)(4) and (5): Utilities include entities that install, operate, and maintain communications systems (telephone, CATV, Internet, satellite, or data services) or electric supply (generation, transmission, or distribution systems) and are designated or recognized by governmental law or regulation by public service/utility commissions. Utilities may be subject to compliance with codes and standards covering their regulated activities as adopted under governmental law or regulation.

ANALYSIS: A change was made in the 2008 edition of the *NEC* that eliminated "other agreements" from the list of ways that utilities could be exempted from *Code* compliance. An unintended result of this change was the removal of installations on Native American reservations, federal lands, and similar areas from *NEC* exemption. This change now gives the AHJ a means to exempt utility wiring in these areas.

90.5 Mandatory Requirements and Explanatory Material

The term "Fine Print Note" has been changed to "Informational Note." Also, the term "Annex" is now "Informative Annex."

90.5 Mandatory Requirements and Explanatory Material.

(C) Explanatory Material. References to other standards or sections of the *NEC*, or information related to a *Code* rule, are included in the form of Informational Notes. Such notes are for information only and aren't enforceable as a requirement of the *NEC*.

For example, Informational Note 4 in 210.19(A)(1) recommends that the voltage drop of a circuit not exceed 3 percent. This isn't a requirement; it's just a recommendation.

Author's Comment: For convenience and ease of reading, in this textbook, I will identify Informational Note simply as "Note," except when that phrase is used in the change summary (gray background) or analysis (yellow background).

(D) Informative Annexes. Nonmandatory information annexes contained in the back of the *Code* book are for information only and aren't enforceable as a requirement of the *NEC*.

ANALYSIS: The term "fine print" doesn't describe the function of a sentence or provision, it simply refers to the size of the text. By changing the term to "Informational Note," the *Code* makes it quite clear that these notes are intended to provide information and nothing else. The same logic applies to the change to "Informative Annexes." The style and layout of these notes and annexes haven't changed, nor has the intent.

NOTES

GENERAL

INTRODUCTION TO CHAPTER 1—GENERAL

A young child doesn't begin reading and writing until they have an understanding of some of the basic words of the language. Similarly, you must be familiar with a few basic rules, concepts, definitions, and requirements that apply to the rest of the *NEC* and you must maintain that familiarity as you continue to apply the *Code*.

Chapter 1 consists of two topics. Article 100 provides definitions so people can understand one another when trying to communicate about *Code*-related matters and Article 110 provides the general requirements needed to correctly apply the rest of the *NEC*.

Time spent learning this general material is a great investment. After understanding Chapter 1, some of the *Code* requirements that seem confusing to other people—those who don't understand Chapter 1—will become increasingly clear to you. The requirements will strike you as being "common sense," because you'll have the foundation from which to understand and apply them. When you read the *NEC* requirements in later chapters, you'll understand the principles upon which many of them are based, and not be surprised at all. You'll read them and feel like you already know them.

- **Article 100—Definitions.** Part I of Article 100 contains the definitions of terms used throughout the *Code* for systems that operate at 600V, nominal, or less. The definitions of terms in Part II apply to systems that operate at over 600V, nominal.

  Author's Comment: This textbook covers the requirements for systems that operate at 600V, nominal, or less.

Definitions of standard terms, such as volt, voltage drop, ampere, impedance, and resistance, aren't listed in Article 100. If the *NEC* doesn't define a term, then a dictionary suitable to the authority having jurisdiction should be consulted. A building code glossary might provide better definitions than a dictionary found at your home or school.

Definitions located at the beginning of an article apply only to that specific article. For example, the definition of a "Swimming Pool" is contained in 680.2, because this term applies only to the requirements contained in Article 680—Swimming Pools, Fountains, and Similar Installations. As soon as a defined term is used in two or more articles, its definition is included in Article 100.

- **Article 110—Requirements for Electrical Installations.** This article contains general requirements for electrical installations for the following:
  - PART I. GENERAL
  - PART II. 600V, NOMINAL, OR LESS

NOTES

ARTICLE 100 DEFINITIONS

INTRODUCTION TO ARTICLE 100—DEFINITIONS

Have you ever had a conversation with someone, only to discover that what you said and what he or she heard were completely different? This often happens when people in a conversation don't understand the definitions of the words being used, and that's why the definitions of key terms are located right at the beginning of the *NEC* (Article 100), or at the beginning of each article.

If we can all agree on important definitions, then we speak the same language and avoid misunderstandings. Because the *Code* exists to protect people and property, it's very important to know the definitions presented in Article 100.

Now, here are a couple of things you may not know about Article 100:

Article 100 contains many, but not all, of the terms defined by the *NEC*. In general, only those terms used in two or more articles are defined in Article 100. Those terms used only within one article are located within that article, often near the beginning of the article.

- Part I of Article 100 contains the definitions of terms used throughout the *Code* for systems that operate at 600V, nominal, or less.
- Part II of Article 100 contains only terms that apply to systems that operate at over 600V nominal.

How can you possibly learn all of these definitions? There seem to be so many. Here are a few tips:

- Break the task down. Study a few words at a time, rather than trying to learn them all at one sitting.
- Review the graphics in the textbook. These will help you see how a term is applied.
- Relate them to your work. As you read a word, think about how it applies to the work you're doing. This will provide a natural reinforcement to the learning process.

Article 100—Ampacity

The definition of ampacity has been changed to become more technically accurate.

Ampacity. The maximum current, in amperes, a conductor can carry continuously, where the temperature of the conductor won't be raised in excess of its insulation temperature rating. Figure 100–1

Author's Comment: See 310.10 and 310.15 for details and examples.

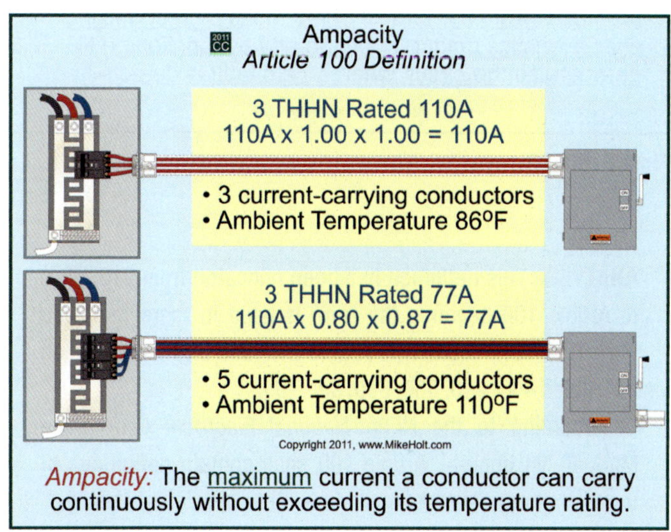

Figure 100–1

ANALYSIS: The ampacity of a conductor is the maximum current that a conductor can carry (under the conditions of use), continuously, without exceeding its temperature rating. Previous editions of the *Code* didn't include the word "maximum" in the definition, although it seemed rather obvious that this was the intent. This small change corrects that omission.

Article 100—Arc-Fault Circuit Interrupter (AFCI)

The definition of Arc-Fault Circuit Interrupter (AFCI) has been moved from 210.12(A) to Article 100.

Arc-Fault Circuit Interrupter (AFCI). An arc-fault circuit interrupter is a device intended to de-energize the circuit when it detects the current waveform characteristics unique to an arcing fault. **Figures 100–2 and 100–3**

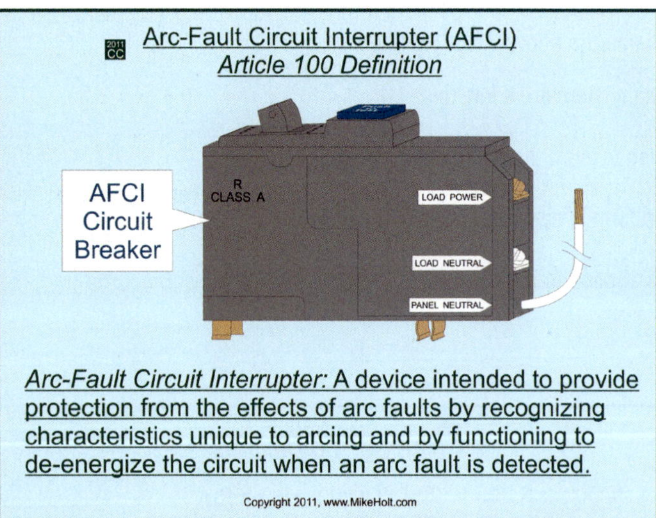

Figure 100–2

ANALYSIS: This definition has been relocated from 210.12(A) to Article 100 because the term is used in more than one *Code* Article. In addition to Article 210, this term is also used in Articles 406, 440, 550, 690, and 760.

According to the NFPA *National Electrical Code* Style Manual, "In general, Article 100 shall contain definitions of terms that appear in two or more other articles of the *NEC*" [2.2.2.1].

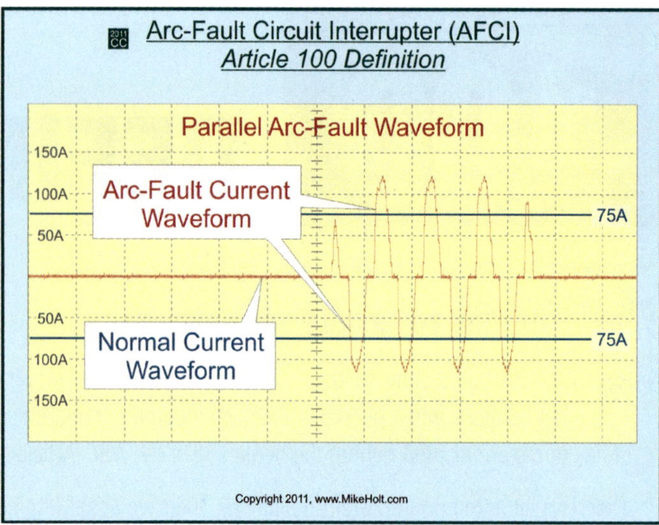

Figure 100–3

Article 100—Automatic

The term "automatic" was revised for consistency purposes.

Automatic. Functioning without the necessity of human intervention.

ANALYSIS: The term "automatic" is used in several NFPA documents, such as the *NEC*, NFPA 70E, 96, 99, 101, 101B, 550, and 901. This definition was revised to create consistency with those documents.

In addition to that, the changed definition is much shorter, more direct, and also more understandable. This should result in *Code* language that's more easily understood.

Article 100—Bathroom

Changes have been made to the definition to assist in uniform interpretation.

Bathroom. A bathroom is an area that includes a basin as well as one or more of the following: a toilet, urinal, tub, shower, bidet, or similar plumbing fixture. **Figure 100–4**

Author's Comment: All 15A and 20A, 125V receptacles located in bathrooms must be GFCI protected [210.8(A)(1)].

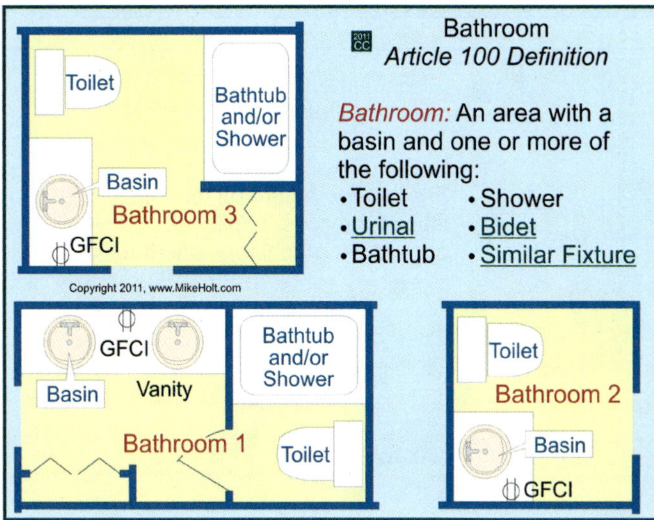

Figure 100–4

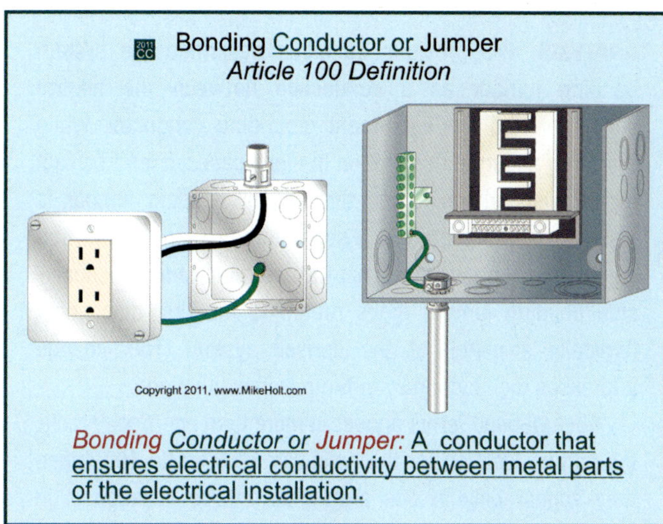

Figure 100–5

ANALYSIS: As plumbing fixtures such as urinals and bidets are becoming more common, this definition needed updating. It's now very clear that a room or space containing only a basin and a urinal, or a basin and a bidet is considered a bathroom. This change should result in a *Code* that's more uniformly interpreted throughout the industry.

Article 100—Bonding Conductor or Jumper

A change to the title of this term results in a more accurate description.

Bonding Conductor or Jumper. A conductor that ensures electrical conductivity between metal parts of the electrical installation. **Figure 100–5**

ANALYSIS: The 2008 *NEC* (and previous editions) referred only to "bonding jumpers," which seems to imply a very short length of conductor used to bond things together. Although this may often be the case, they also may be much longer. For example, bonding conductors that connect grounding electrodes together can vary in length from a few inches to several feet. Bonding jumpers for communications systems electrodes may be longer than 20 feet in length.

This revised title removes the implied meaning of a short conductor, and uses a more accurate description.

Article 100—Bonding Jumper, System

The definition of system bonding jumper was changed to provide a more accurate definition, and to incorporate new terms used in the *Code*. It was also relocated to Article 100.

Bonding Jumper, System. The connection between the neutral conductor and the supply-side bonding jumper or equipment grounding conductor, or both at a separately derived system. **Figure 100–6**

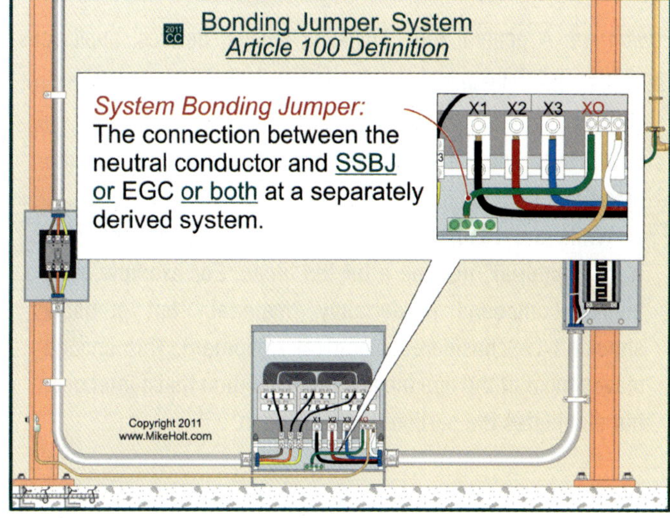

Figure 100–6

ANALYSIS: The previous definition described the system bonding jumper as a connection between the neutral conductor and the equipment grounding conductor. While this is an accurate description in many cases, it isn't correct for all installations. When the system bonding jumper is installed at the source of a separately derived system, the connection is between the neutral conductor and the supply-side bonding jumper that's routed to the first disconnect (typically a panel) of the derived system. This change addresses the inaccuracy of the previous language.

When defined terms appear in more than one *Code* article, the correct location for the definition is in Article 100. When they appear only in one article, the correct location is in the "xxx.2" section of the article in which the term is used. Because this term is used in more than just Article 250 (Article 708 for example), it's been moved from 250.2 to Article 100.

Author's Comment: The system bonding jumper provides a low-impedance fault current path to the power supply to facilitate the clearing of a ground fault by opening the circuit overcurrent device. For more information, see 250.4(A)(5), 250.28, and 250.30(A)(1).

Article 100—Equipment

The word "material" has been removed from the list of items that are considered "equipment."

Equipment. A general term including fittings, devices, appliances, luminaires, machinery, and the like. Figure 100–7

ANALYSIS: The definition of "equipment" might be the broadest definition in the entire *NEC*.

While the vastness of the definition is intentional, the word "material" may be a bit too broad. For example, wire pulling compound is certainly "material," but probably shouldn't be considered electrical equipment. This change leaves most of the openness of the definition that's intended, but eliminates the portion that's too open.

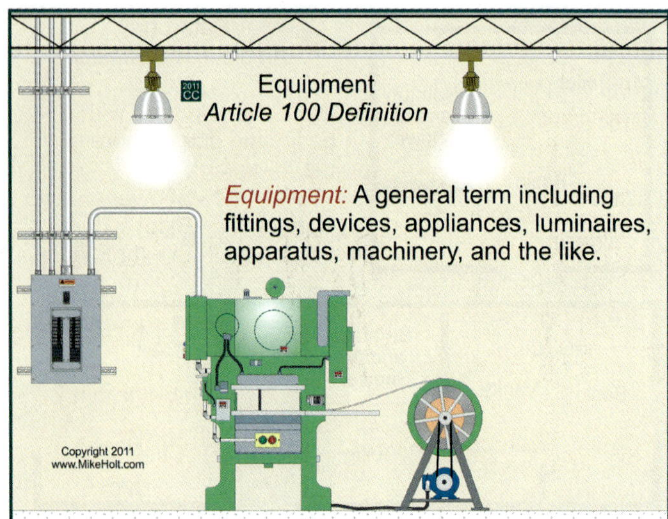

Figure 100–7

Article 100—Explosionproof Equipment

The term "Explosionproof Apparatus" has been changed to "Explosionproof Equipment."

Explosionproof Equipment. Equipment capable of withstanding an explosion that may occur within it, and of preventing the ignition of gas or vapor surrounding the enclosure by sparks, flashes, or an explosion within, and that operates at such an external temperature that surrounding flammable atmosphere won't be ignited by its heat. Figure 100–8

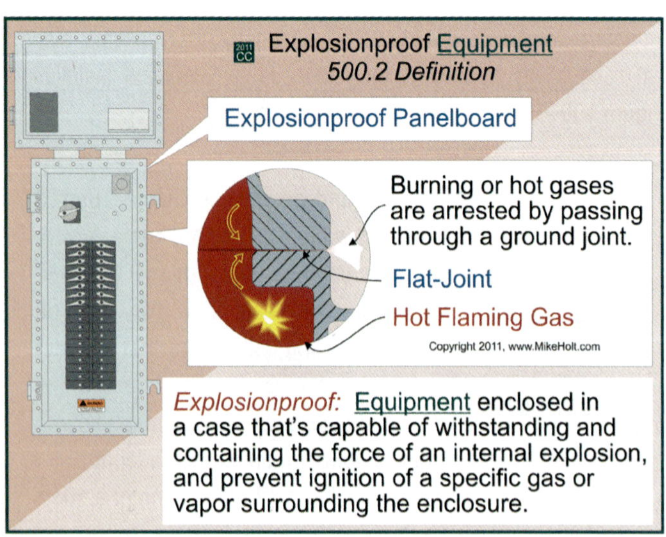

Figure 100–8

ANALYSIS: The term "equipment" is clearly defined in Article 100, however "apparatus" isn't. This change (and changes in Article 500) helps to provide simplicity in the *Code* language. It change also recognizes that the term "apparatus" isn't used by the typical user of the *NEC*, where the term "equipment" is.

Article 100—Ground Fault

The defined term "Ground Fault" has been moved to Article 100 from 250.2.

Ground Fault. An unintentional electrical connection between an ungrounded conductor and the metal parts of enclosures, raceways, or equipment. Figure 100–9

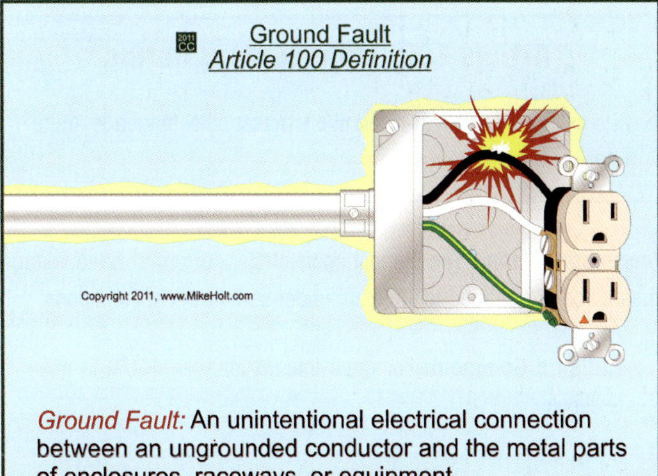

Figure 100–9

ANALYSIS: This definition has been relocated from 250.2 to Article 100 because the term is used in more than one *Code* article.

Author's Comment: According to the NFPA *National Electrical Code* Style Manual, "In general, Article 100 shall contain definitions of terms that appear in two or more other articles of the *NEC*" [2.2.2.1].

Article 100—Grounding Conductor

The term "grounding conductor" has been removed from the *Code*.

ANALYSIS: Recent revisions to Articles 100 and 250 have made this term obsolete. The definition of "grounding conductor" has become nearly identical to the definition of "grounding electrode conductor," resulting in confusion for *Code* users. The two terms have also been (incorrectly) used interchangeably in past *NEC* editions. For example, in the 2008 *Code*, 250.64 refers to the installation of "grounding electrode conductors," yet 250.64(A) refers to "grounding conductors," not "grounding electrode conductors."

Author's Comment: The use of more accurate and more specific terms, such as "grounding electrode conductor," "bonding jumper," or "bonding conductor," in place of "grounding conductor" will provide a clearer understanding of the intention of the *NEC* in each particular application.

Article 100—Grounding Conductor, Equipment (EGC)

A subtle change to the definition of "Equipment Grounding Conductor" has been made.

Grounding Conductor, Equipment (EGC). The conductive path(s) that connect metal parts of equipment to the system neutral conductor, to the grounding electrode conductor, or both [250.110 through 250.126]. Figure 100–10

Note 1: The circuit equipment grounding conductor also performs bonding.

Author's Comment: To quickly remove dangerous touch voltage on metal parts from a ground fault, the equipment grounding conductor must be connected to the system neutral conductor at the source, and have low enough impedance so that fault current will quickly rise to a level that will open the branch-circuit overcurrent device [250.2 and 250.4(A)(3)].

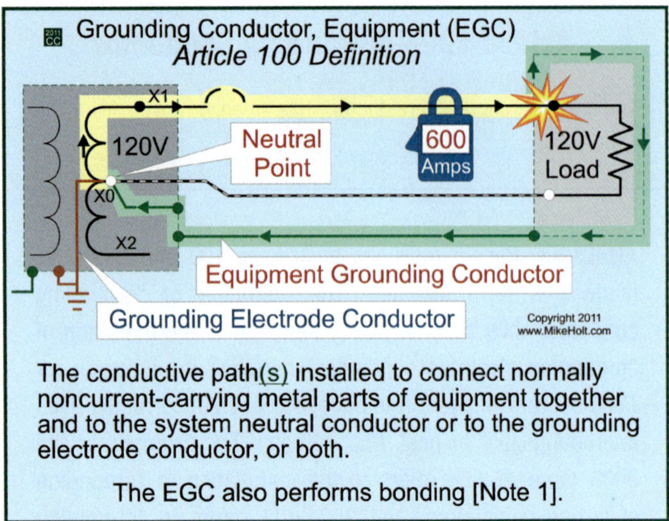

Figure 100–10

Note 2: An equipment grounding conductor can be any one or a combination of the types listed in 250.118. **Figure 100–11**

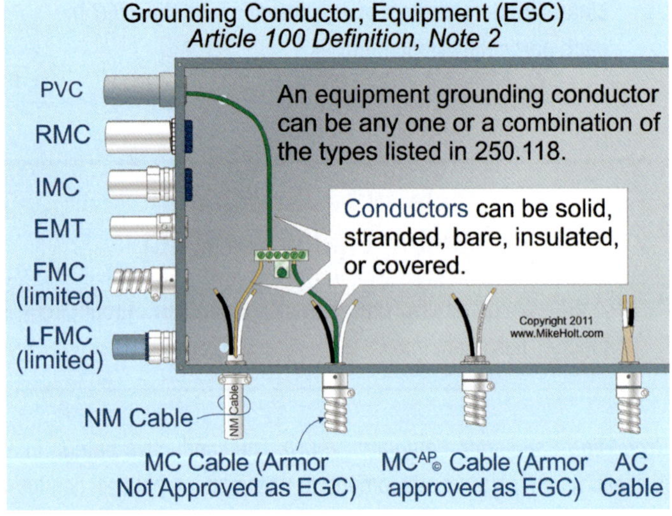

Figure 100–11

Author's Comment: Equipment grounding conductors include:

- A bare or insulated conductor
- Rigid Metal Conduit
- Intermediate Metal Conduit
- Electrical Metallic Tubing
- Listed Flexible Metal Conduit as limited by 250.118(5)
- Listed Liquidtight Flexible Metal Conduit as limited by 250.118(6)
- Armored Cable
- Copper metal sheath of Mineral Insulated Cable
- Metal-Clad Cable as limited by 250.118(10)
- Metallic cable trays as limited by 250.118(11) and 392.60
- Electrically continuous metal raceways listed for grounding
- Surface Metal Raceways listed for grounding

ANALYSIS: The 2008 *Code* inadvertently removed the concept of multiple paths being used for equipment grounding conductor purposes. This change corrects the error by using the plural form of the word "path."

An example of multiple paths for equipment grounding is patient care areas within a health care facility. Section 517.13 requires that patient care areas be provided with two equipment grounding conductors, which obviously create multiple "paths" for ground fault current.

Article 100—Interrupting Rating

A small change to the definition makes the language more consistent in the *Code*.

Interrupting Rating. The highest short-circuit current at rated voltage the device is identified to interrupt under standard test conditions.

Author's Comment: For more information, see 110.9 in this textbook.

ANALYSIS: The previous definition of interrupting rating referred to a device that's "intended" to interrupt current. This change uses the word "identified" in place of the word "intended" in order to use defined terms instead of undefined terms. This change isn't intended to be technical in nature.

Article 100—Intersystem Bonding Termination

This definition has been greatly simplified.

Intersystem Bonding Termination. A device that provides a means to connect bonding conductors for communications systems to the grounding electrode system, in accordance with 250.94. **Figure 100–12**

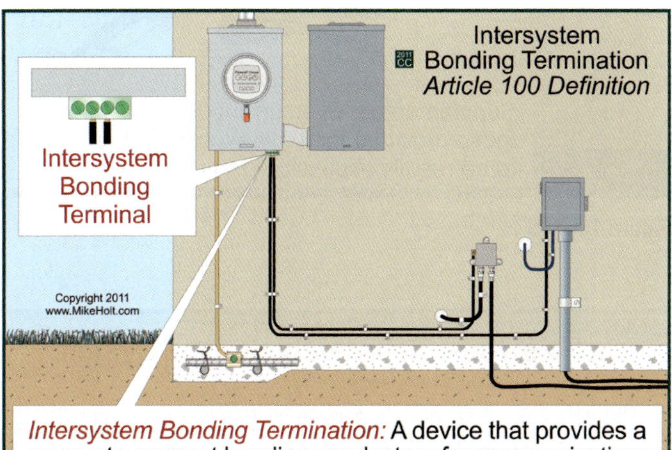

Figure 100–12

ANALYSIS: The previous definition of intersystem bonding termination included descriptions of where this device was to be located (at the service equipment). This resulted in a requirement inside of definition, which is never a good idea, and isn't allowed by the NFPA *NEC Manual of Style.* This revision simplifies the definition by providing a straight-forward description of the device, and leaving the requirements in Article 250.

Article—100 Kitchen

A small change to the definition of "Kitchen" to provide consistency with other *Code* rules and definitions has been made.

Kitchen. An area with a sink and permanent provisions for food preparation and cooking. **Figure 100–13**

Figure 100–13

ANALYSIS: Previous editions of the *NEC* referred to "permanent facilities" for food preparation and cooking. This resulted in inconsistent language in comparison to the definition of "dwelling unit," which uses the term "permanent provisions" for cooking. This change also recognizes that while appliances such as ranges which are cord connected aren't permanent, they do occupy a dedicated location that's provided for them, as opposed to portable appliances like a small microwave.

Article 100—Nonautomatic

A simplification to this definition has been made.

Nonautomatic. Requiring human intervention to perform a function.

ANALYSIS: The term "automatic" was revised in Article 100 to correlate with other NFPA documents. This change harmonizes the terms "automatic" and "nonautomatic."

Article 100—Overcurrent Protective Device, Supplementary

A small usability change to the title of the definition has been made.

Overcurrent Protective Device, Supplementary. A device intended to provide limited overcurrent protection for specific applications and utilization equipment, such as luminaires and appliances. This limited protection is in addition to the required protection provided in the branch circuit by the branch-circuit overcurrent device. **Figure 100–14**

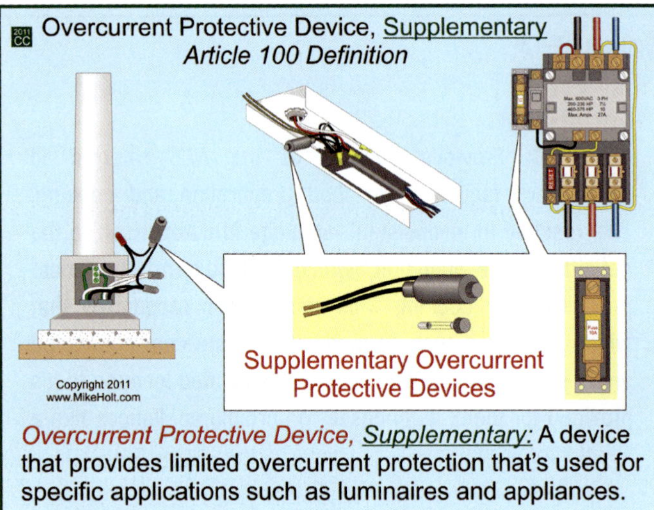

Figure 100–14

Author's Comment: Supplementary overcurrent devices are often mounted in luminaires or equipment where they may be difficult to access. Accordingly, they aren't required to be readily accessible [240.10 and 240.24(A)(2)]. **Figure 100–15**

ANALYSIS: Changes to the terms "Branch-Circuit Overcurrent Device" and "Supplementary Overcurrent Device" to "Overcurrent Protective Device, Branch-Circuit" and "Overcurrent Protective Device, Supplementary" allows them to be placed next to each other in Article 100. This allows for logical grouping of the terms, and a more user friendly document.

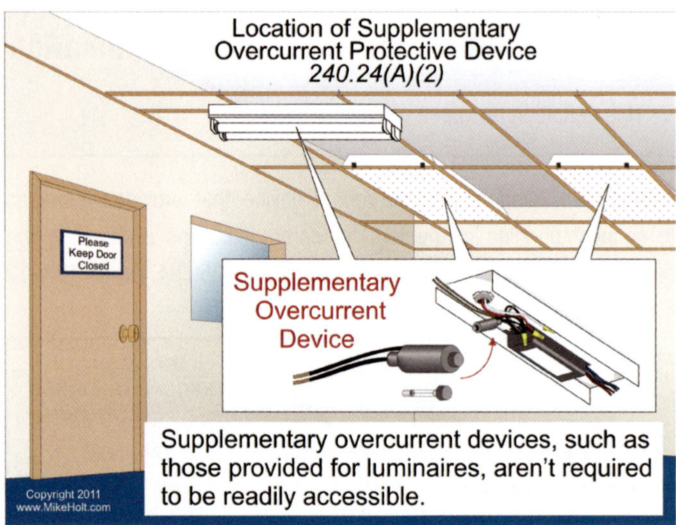

Figure 100–15

Article 100—Separately Derived System

The definition of separately derived system has been modified to allow incidental interconnections between systems.

Separately Derived System. A wiring system whose power is derived from a source of electric energy or equipment other than the electric utility service. This includes a generator, a battery, a solar photovoltaic system, a transformer, or a converter winding, where there's no direct electrical connection from circuit conductors of one system to circuit conductors of another system, other than connections through the earth, metal raceways, or equipment grounding conductors. **Figure 100–16**

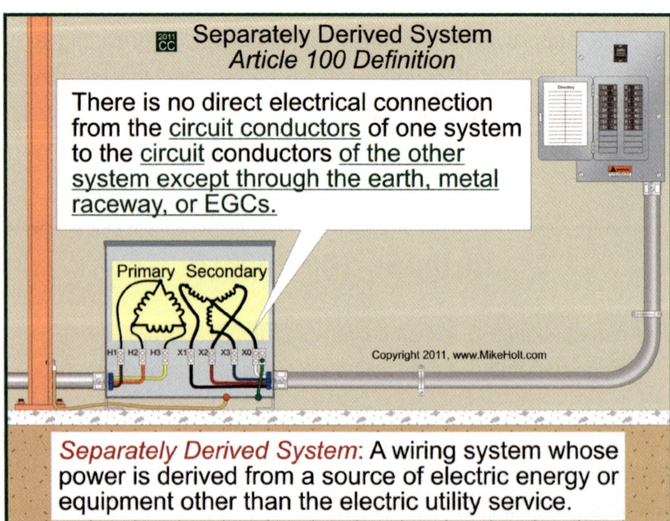

Figure 100–16

Author's Comments:

- This definition clarifies that separately derived systems also include equipment such as transformers, converters, and inverters, which might not be considered sources of energy.
- Separately derived systems are actually a lot more complicated than the above definition suggests, and understanding them requires additional study. For more information, see 250.30.

ANALYSIS: Previous editions of the *NEC* stated that a separately derived system must not have any connections between the separately derived system and another system (such as the utility supply). While this makes good sense, it isn't really possible in all applications. Connections between systems occur through the earth via grounding electrodes, and also through metallic enclosures, raceways, and similar equipment. This change clarifies that incidental interconnections such as these are permitted.

Article 100—Service Conductors, Overhead

A new term, "Service Conductors, Overhead" was added.

Service Conductors, Overhead. Overhead conductors between the service point and the first point of connection to the service-entrance conductors at the building/structure. Figure 100–17

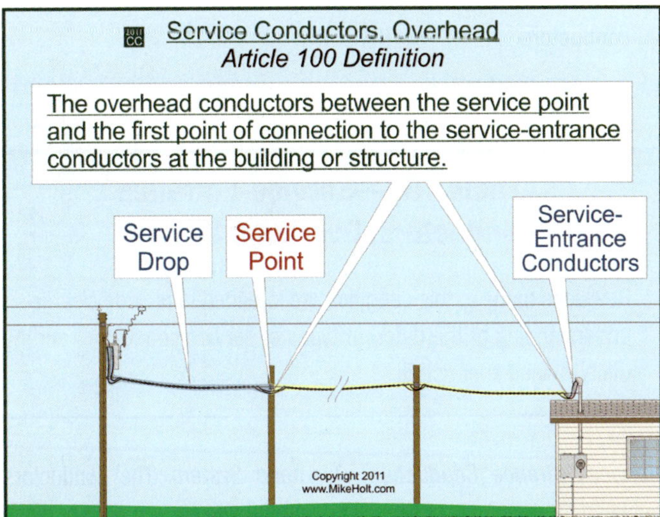

Figure 100–17

Author's Comment: These conductors fall within the requirements of Article 230, since they aren't under the exclusive control of the electric utility.

ANALYSIS: This is the first of many changes to service and service conductor related terms. Although this definition seems rather obvious, this change and the changes to many other terms are part of a collective effort to help the *Code* user understand the subtle differences between the many different types of service conductors.

Author's Comment: As you study the changes made in the definitions regarding the various service conductors, be sure to acquaint yourself with the location of the "service point," which is the point where the serving utility ends and the premises wiring begins.

Article 100—Service Conductors, Underground

A new term, "Service Conductors, Underground" was added.

Service Conductors, Underground. Underground conductors between the service point and the first point of connection to the service-entrance conductors in a terminal box, meter, or other enclosure, inside or outside the building wall. Figure 100–18

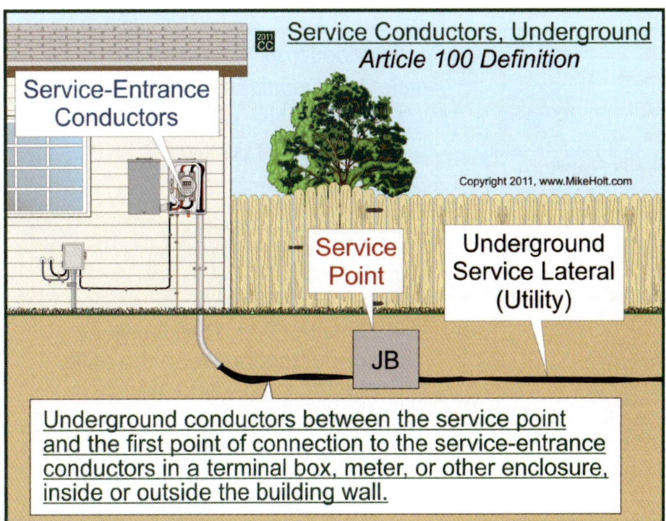

Figure 100–18

Author's Comment: These conductors fall within the requirements of Article 230, since they aren't under the exclusive control of the electric utility.

Note: Where there's no terminal box, meter, or other enclosure, the point of connection is the point of entrance of the service conductors into the building.

ANALYSIS: This new term is intended to clearly separate service lateral conductors from other service conductors that are installed underground. Underground service conductors are installed on the customer side of the service point, whereas service laterals (also installed underground) are installed on the utility side of the service point.

This new definition also contains an Informational Note that clarifies what the "point of connection" is in installations without a meter, other terminal box, or other enclosure.

Article 100—Service Drop

Revisions made to this definition are intended to provide clearer understanding of the different types of service conductors and utility-owned conductors.

Service Drop. Overhead conductors between the utility electric supply and the service point. **Figures 100–19 and 100–20**

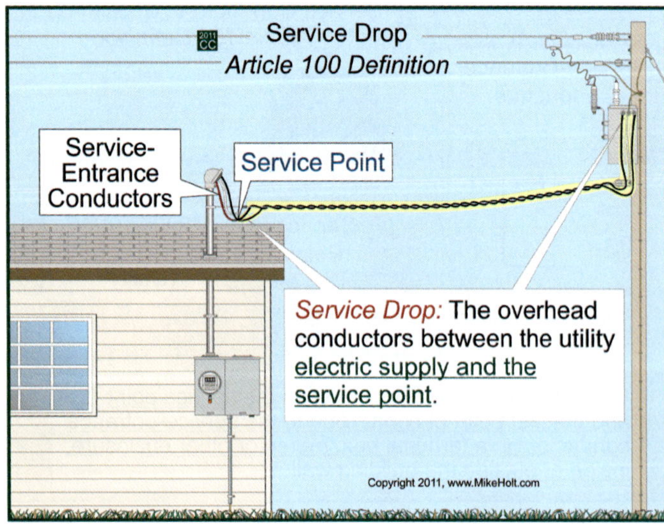

Figure 100–19

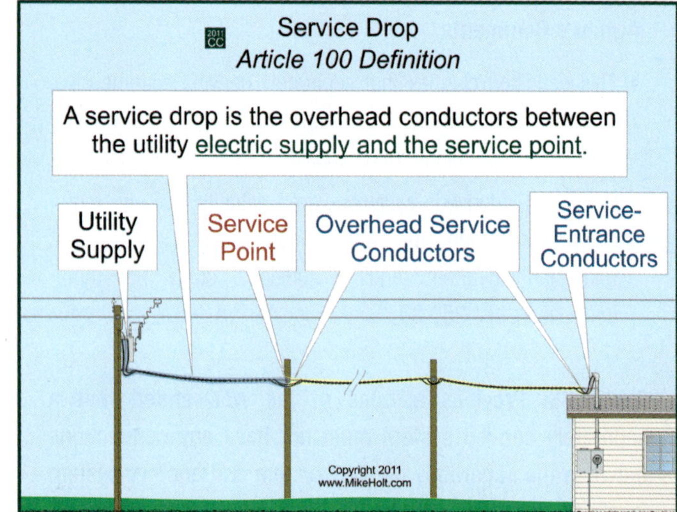

Figure 100–20

Author's Comment: These conductors don't fall within the requirements of Article 230, since they're under the exclusive control of the electric utility.

ANALYSIS: This term has been revised to clarify that only overhead conductors on the utility side of the service point are considered a service drop. Conductors that are on the customer side of the service point and are installed overhead will now be called overhead service conductors.

It's very important to notice that the definition of "service conductors" states that only conductors on the customer side of the service point are considered service conductors, so the term "service conductor" isn't used in this term.

Because of this, a service drop *does not* contain service conductors.

Article 100—Service-Entrance Conductors, Overhead System

Revisions made to this definition are intended to provide clearer understanding of the different types of service conductors and utility-owned conductors.

Service-Entrance Conductors, Overhead System. The conductors between the terminals of service equipment and service drop or overhead service conductors. **Figure 100–21**

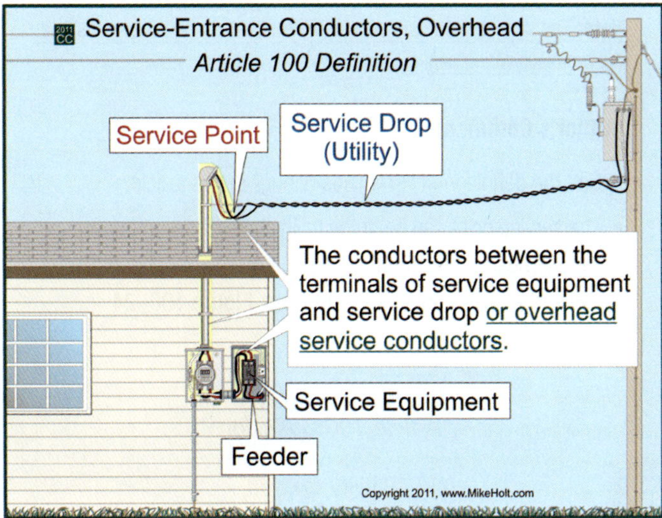

Figure 100–21

Author's Comment: These conductors fall within the requirements of Article 230, since they aren't under the exclusive control of the electric utility.

ANALYSIS: The change to this definition clarifies that overhead service-entrance conductors begin at the end of the service drop or at the end of customer-owned overhead service conductors. These conductors end at the service equipment.

Because these conductors are installed on the customer side of the service point, they're *service conductors.*

Article 100—Service-Entrance Conductors, Underground System

Revisions made to this definition are intended to provide clearer understanding of the different types of service conductors and utility-owned conductors.

Service-Entrance Conductors, Underground System. The conductors between the terminals of service equipment and service lateral or underground service conductors.

Author's Comment: These conductors fall within the requirements of Article 230, since they aren't under the exclusive control of the electric utility.

ANALYSIS: The change to this definition clarifies that underground service entrance conductors begin at the end of the utility's service lateral or at the end of customer owned underground service conductors. These conductors end at the service equipment.

Because these conductors are installed on the customer side of the service point, they're *service conductors.*

Article 100—Service Lateral

Revisions made to this definition are intended to provide clearer understanding of the different types of service conductors and utility owned conductors.

Service Lateral. Underground conductors between the utility electric supply and the service point. Figure 100–22

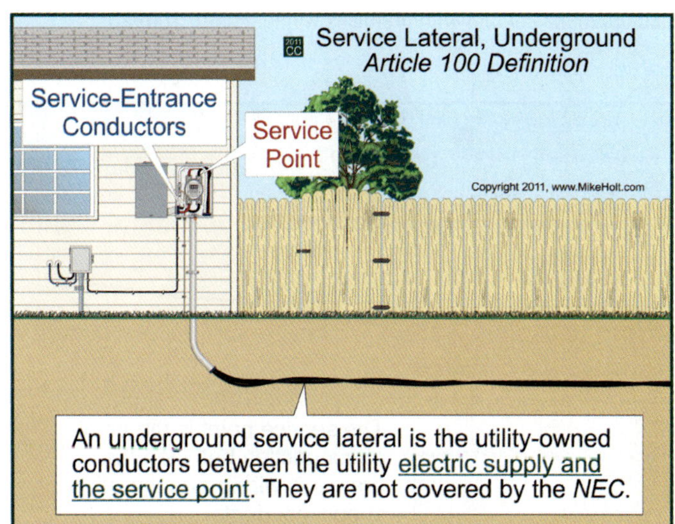

Figure 100–22

Author's Comment: These conductors don't fall within the requirements of Article 230, since they're under the exclusive control of the electric utility.

ANALYSIS: This term has been revised to clarify that only underground conductors on the utility side of the service point are considered a service lateral. Conductors that are on the customer side of the service point and are installed underground will now be called underground service conductors.

It is very important to notice that the definition of "service conductors" states that only conductors on the customer side of the service point are considered service conductors, so the term "service conductor" isn't used in this term.

Article 100—Service Point

A new Informational Note was added regarding where the service point ends.

Service Point [Article 230]. The point where the electrical utility conductors make contact with premises wiring. **Figure 100–23**

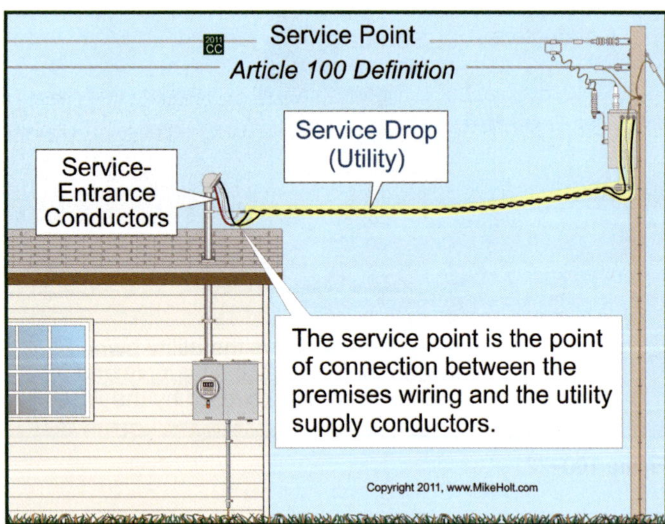

Figure 100–23

Note: The service point is the point where the serving utility ends and the premises wiring begins.

Author's Comments:

- See the definition of "Premises Wiring" in this article.
- The service point can be at the utility transformer, at the service weatherhead, or at the meter socket enclosure, depending on where the utility conductors terminate. **Figure 100–24**

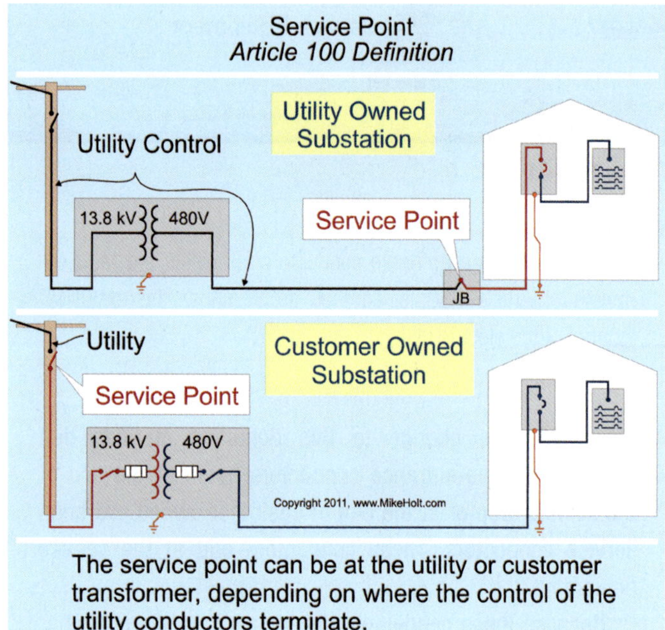

Figure 100–24

ANALYSIS: The term "service point" is a very important definition. It's also such a simple one that it isn't always fully understood. This new Informational Note should help people realize not only what the service point is, but also who controls it and where it's located.

Requirements for ELECTRICAL INSTALLATIONS

INTRODUCTION TO ARTICLE 110—REQUIREMENTS FOR ELECTRICAL INSTALLATIONS

Article 110 sets the stage for how you'll implement the rest of the *NEC.* This article contains a few of the most important and yet neglected parts of the *Code.* For example:

- How should you terminate conductors?
- What kinds of warnings, markings, and identification does a given installation require?
- What's the right working clearance for a given installation?
- What do the temperature limitations at terminals mean?
- What are the *NEC* requirements for dealing with flash protection?

110.3 Guidelines for Approval of Equipment

Additions to the Informational Note provided guidance on suitability of equipment use.

110.3 Examination, Identification, Installation, and Use of Equipment.

(A) Guidelines for Approval. The authority having jurisdiction must approve equipment. In doing so, consideration must be given to the following:

(1) Suitability for installation and use in accordance with the *NEC*

Note: Suitability of equipment use may be identified by a description marked on or provided with a product to identify the suitability of the product for a specific purpose, environment, or application. Special conditions of use or other limitations may be marked on the equipment, in the product instructions, or appropriate listing and labeling information. Suitability of equipment may be evidenced by listing or labeling.

(2) Mechanical strength and durability

(3) Wire-bending and connection space

(4) Electrical insulation

(5) Heating effects under all conditions of use

(6) Arcing effects

(7) Classification by type, size, voltage, current capacity, and specific use

(8) Other factors contributing to the practical safeguarding of persons using or in contact with the equipment

(B) Installation and Use. Equipment must be installed and used in accordance with any instructions included in the listing or labeling requirements. Figure 110–1

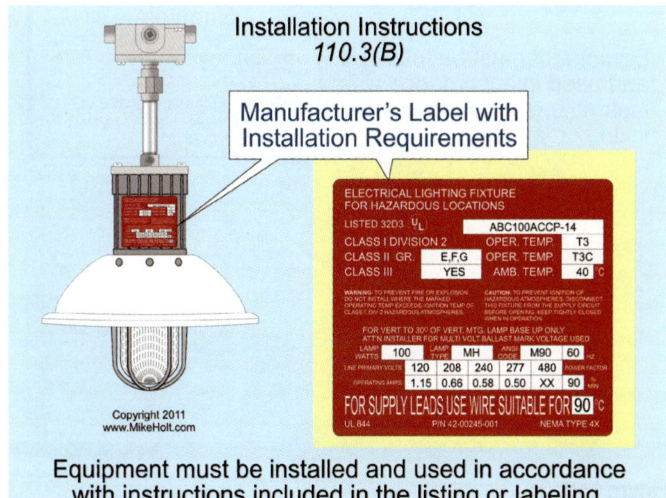

Figure 110–1

Author's Comments:

- See the definitions of "Labeling" and "Listing" in Article 100.
- Failure to follow product listing instructions, such as the torquing of terminals and the sizing of conductors, is a violation of this *Code* rule. **Figure 110–2**

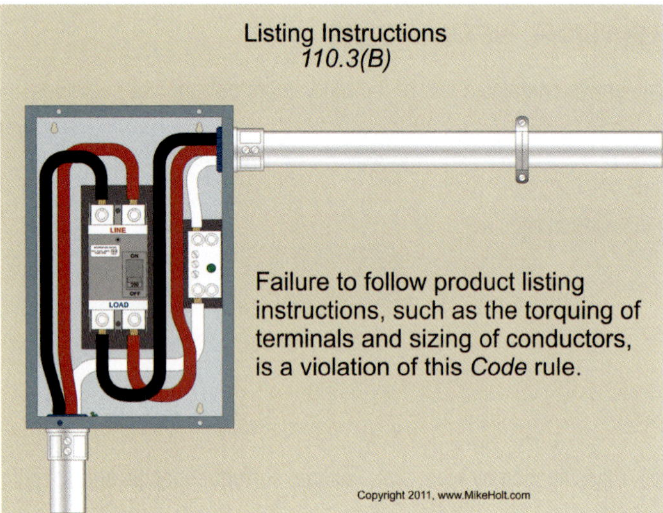

Figure110–2

- When an air conditioner nameplate specifies "Maximum Fuse Size," one-time or dual-element fuses must be used to protect the equipment. **Figure 110–3**

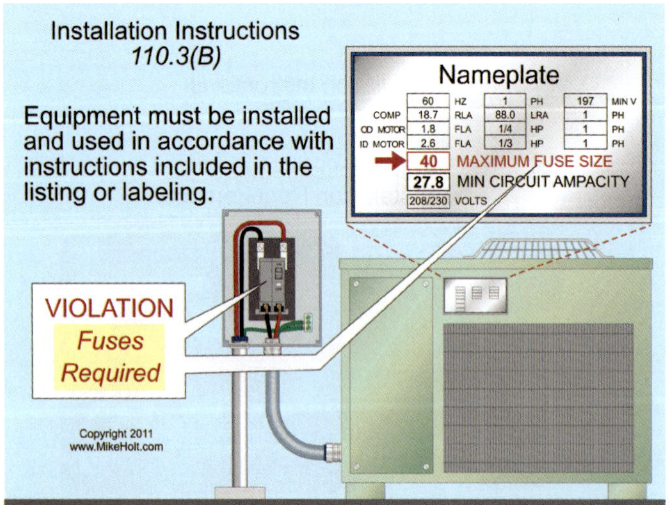

Figure 110–3

ANALYSIS: Some pieces of electrical equipment have special requirements, such as limitations on elevation, ambient temperature correction, power quality requirements, or specific types of overcurrent devices. This information may be marked on equipment, it may be in the product literature, or in the listing and labeling information. This rule helps to make all users of electrical equipment aware of these special conditions.

110.9 Interrupting Rating

A change to this section creates a more enforceable and less ambiguous requirement.

110.9 Interrupting Protection Rating. Overcurrent devices such as circuit breakers and fuses are intended to interrupt the circuit, and they must have an interrupting rating not less than the nominal circuit voltage and the current that's available at the line terminals of the equipment. **Figure 110–4**

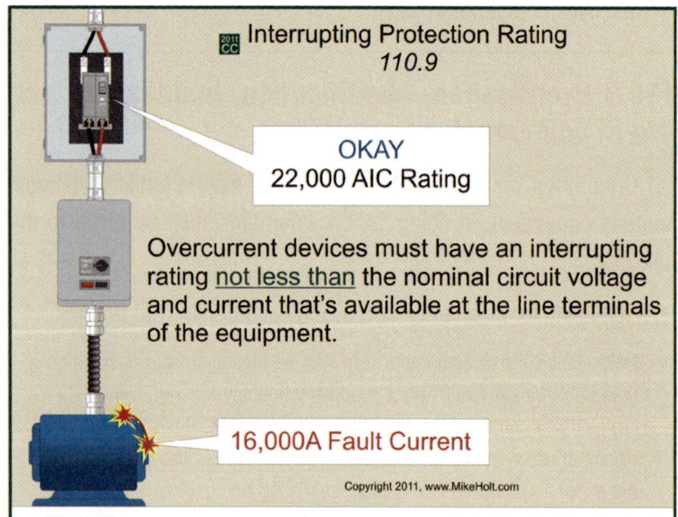

Figure 110–4

Author's Comments:

- See the definition of "Interrupting Rating" in Article 100.
- Unless marked otherwise, the ampere interrupting rating for circuit breakers is 5,000A [240.83(C)], and for fuses it's 10,000A [240.60(C)(3)]. **Figure 110–5**

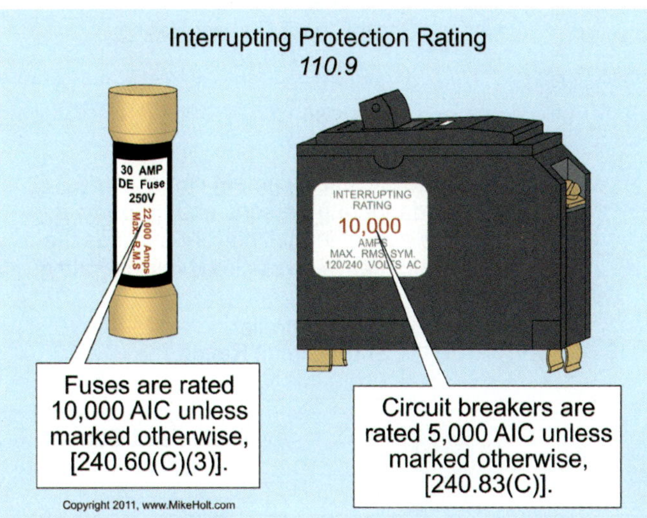

Figure 110–5

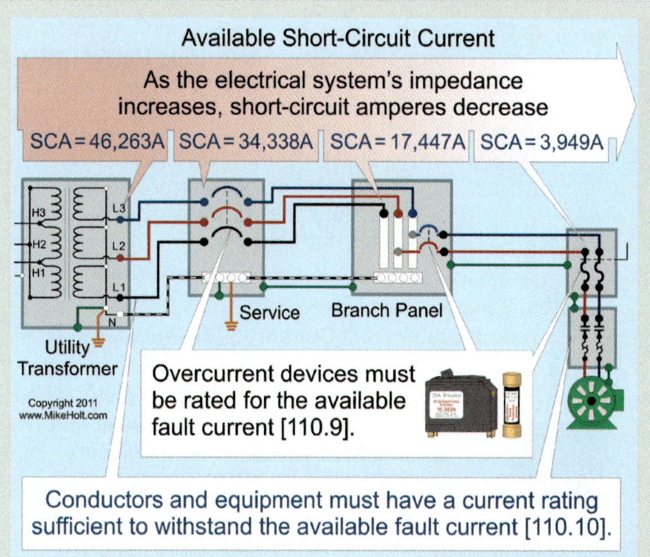

Figure 110–6

ANALYSIS: Previous editions of the *NEC* stated that equipment intended to interrupt current at fault levels must have a rating that's "sufficient" for the voltage and current. The term "not less than" provides a statement that's much clearer and less subject to misunderstanding.

This change not only makes the language more enforceable for the inspection community, but it also makes the requirement more understandable for many users of the *Code*, particularly those just beginning to study it.

AVAILABLE SHORT-CIRCUIT CURRENT

Available short-circuit current is the current, in amperes, available at a given point in the electrical system. This available short-circuit current is first determined at the secondary terminals of the utility transformer. Thereafter, the available short-circuit current is calculated at the terminals of service equipment, then at branch-circuit panelboards and other equipment. The available short-circuit current is different at each point of the electrical system. It's highest at the utility transformer and lowest at the branch-circuit load.

The available short-circuit current depends on the impedance of the circuit, which increases moving downstream from the utility transformer. The greater the circuit impedance (utility transformer and the additive impedances of the circuit conductors), the lower the available short-circuit current. **Figure 110–6**

The factors that affect the available short-circuit current at the utility transformer include the system voltage, the transformer kVA rating, and the circuit impedance (expressed in a percentage on the equipment nameplate). Properties that have an impact on the impedance of the circuit include the conductor material (copper versus aluminum), conductor size, conductor length, and motor-operated equipment supplied by the circuit.

Author's Comment: Many people in the industry describe Amperes Interrupting Rating (AIR) as "Amperes Interrupting Capacity" (AIC).

DANGER: *Extremely high values of current flow (caused by short circuits or ground faults) produce tremendously destructive thermal and magnetic forces. If the circuit overcurrent device isn't rated to interrupt the current at the available fault values at its listed voltage rating, it can explode while attempting to open the circuit overcurrent device resulting from a short circuit or ground fault, which can cause serious injury or death, as well as property damage.* **Figure 110–7**

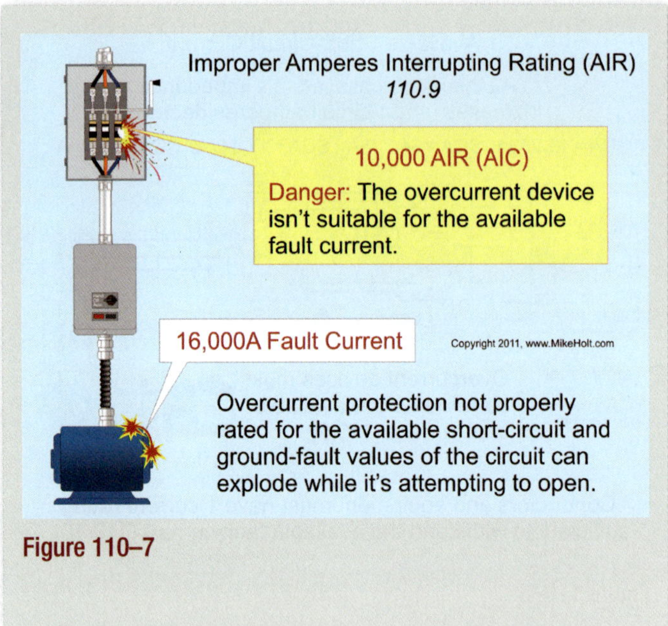

Figure 110–7

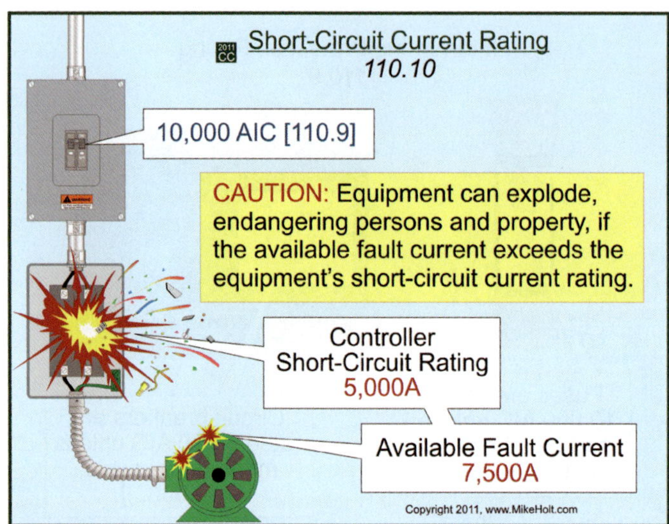

Figure 110–8

110.10 Circuit Impedance, Short-Circuit Current Ratings, and Other Characteristics

Changes to the title and text were made to clarify what "other characteristics" might mean.

110.10 Circuit Impedance, Short-Circuit Current Rating, and other characteristics. Electrical equipment must have a short-circuit current rating that permits the circuit protective device to open from a short circuit or ground fault without extensive damage to the electrical equipment of the circuit. This fault is assumed to be either between two or more of the circuit conductors or between any circuit conductor and the equipment grounding conductor(s) permitted in 250.118. Listed equipment applied in accordance with their listing is considered to have met the requirements of this section.

Author's Comment: For example, a motor controller must have a sufficient short-circuit rating for the available fault current. If the fault exceeds the controller's 5,000A short-circuit current rating, the controller can explode, endangering persons and property. Figure 110–8

ANALYSIS: In addition to the impedance of the circuit, the short-circuit current rating of equipment is a vital part of determining whether or not a system or circuit can withstand the effects of a short circuit or ground fault. Specific examples of the types of things that warrant consideration are always better than referring to "other characteristics."

The wording was also changed slightly to replace the term "grounding conductors" in this section with "equipment grounding conductors," which is a term with a more specific meaning.

110.11 Deteriorating Agents

A change to this section clarifies the type of damage to equipment that must be avoided during construction.

110.11 Deteriorating Agents. Electrical equipment and conductors must be suitable for the environment and conditions of use. Consideration must also be given to the presence of corrosive gases, fumes, vapors, liquids, or other substances that can have a deteriorating effect on the conductors or equipment. Figure 110–9

Author's Comment: Conductors must not be exposed to ultraviolet rays from the sun unless identified for the purpose [310.10(D)].

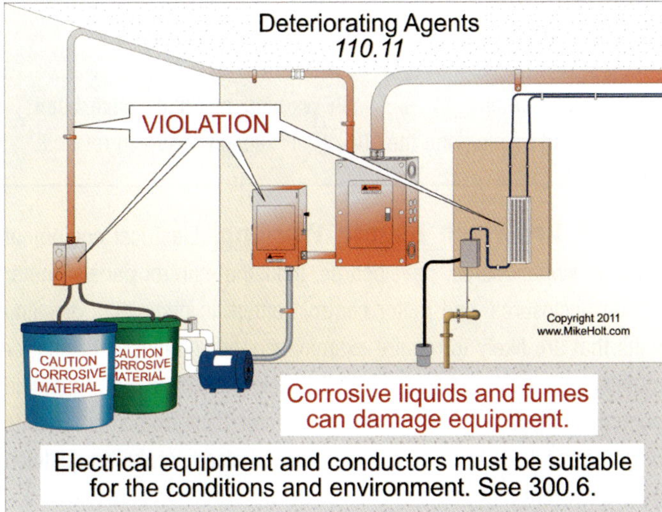

Figure 110–9

Note 1: Raceways, cable trays, cablebus, cable armor, boxes, cable sheathing, cabinets, elbows, couplings, fittings, supports, and support hardware must be of materials that are suitable for the environment in which they're to be installed, in accordance with 300.6.

Author's Comment: See the definition of "Raceway" in Article 100.

Note 2: Some cleaning and lubricating compounds contain chemicals that can cause deterioration of the plastic used for insulating and structural applications in equipment.

Equipment not identified for outdoor use and equipment identified only for indoor use must be protected against damage from the weather during construction.

Note 3: See *NEC* Table 110.28 for appropriate enclosure-type designations.

ANALYSIS: Previous editions of the *Code* didn't allow indoor equipment to be permanently damaged during the course of construction. This change clarifies that any damage to equipment during the course of construction isn't allowed.

Author's Comment: This rule requires indoor-use equipment to be protected against damage during construction from the weather, such as moisture entering an enclosure that isn't suitable for use in damp or wet locations.

110.14 Electrical Connections

Provisions for finely stranded conductors have been added.

110.14 Conductor Termination and Splicing. Conductor terminal and splicing devices must be identified for the conductor material and they must be properly installed and used. Figure 110–10

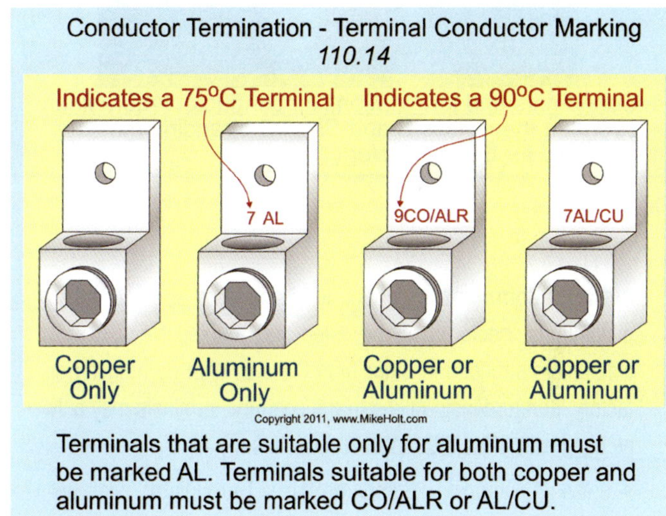

Figure 110–10

CAUTION: *When the insulation is stripped from an aluminum conductor and the conductor is exposed to air, an insulating film (aluminum oxide) immediately forms on the conductor. This film can create a poor connection and overheating at terminations. Unless the terminal or the device is manufactured with the right contacts designed to break through the film and ensure a good connection, overheating may occur. An oxide inhibiting paste can be applied to aluminum conductors at terminations to help improve the connection, but this isn't required.*

Connectors and terminals for conductors more finely stranded than Class B and Class C, as shown in Table 10 of Chapter 9, must be identified for the conductor class. Figure 110–11

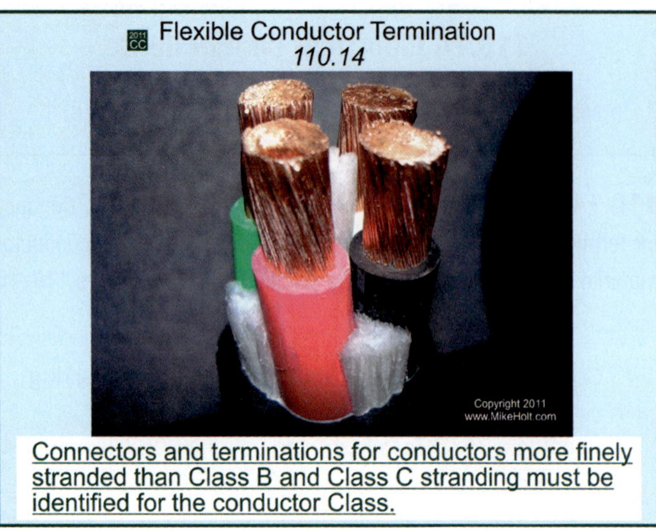

Figure 110–11

Author's Comment: According to UL Standard 486 A-B, a terminal/lug/connector must be listed and marked for use with conductors stranded in other than Class B. With no marking or factory literature/instructions to the contrary, terminals may only be used with Class B stranded conductors.

- Class B stranding (Standard) has 7 strands of wire per conductor in sizes 18-2 AWG, 19 strands in sizes 1-4/0 AWG, and 37 strands in sizes 250-500 kcmil.
- Class C stranding has 19 strands of wire per conductor in sizes 18-2 AWG, 37 strands in sizes 1-4/0 AWG, and 61 strands in sizes 250-500 kcmil.
- Class D stranding has 37 strands of wire per conductor in sizes 18-2 AWG, 61 strands in sizes 1-4/0 AWG, and 91 strands in sizes 250-500 kcmil.

ANALYSIS: Fine-stranded cables and conductors are a fairly new option in the *NEC* (2008 Article 690). The use of these cables has increased, but awareness of the special termination provisions for them has not. Now that installers are using these cables in more and more applications, the *Code* has recognized the need to alert *NEC* users to specific terminations that are required for these fine stranded conductors and cables.

The termination of finely stranded conductors is of the utmost importance when using them. Due to this, a new Table (Table 10 in Chapter 9) was added to the *Code*. The new language in this section refers to that table, making its provisions enforceable by the AHJ.

110.16 Arc Flash Hazard Warning

The requirements for arc flash warning markings have been increased (again), and the title of this section has been revised.

110.16 Arc Flash Hazard Warning. Electrical equipment such as switchboards, panelboards, industrial control panels, meter socket enclosures, and motor control centers in other than dwelling units that are likely to require examination, adjustment, servicing, or maintenance while energized must be field-marked to warn qualified persons of the danger associated with an arc flash from short circuits or ground faults. The field-marking must be clearly visible to qualified persons before they examine, adjust, service, or perform maintenance on the equipment. Figure 110–12

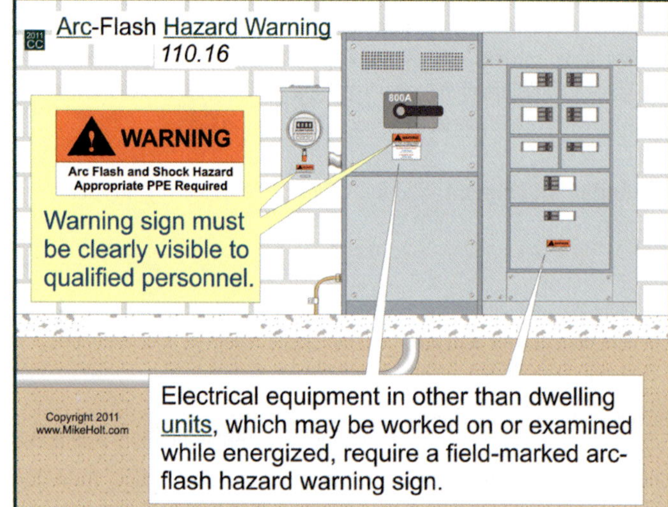

Figure 110–12

Author's Comments:

- See the definition of "Qualified Person" in Article 100.
- This rule is meant to warn qualified persons who work on energized electrical systems that an arc flash hazard exists so they'll select proper personal protective equipment (PPE) in accordance with industry accepted safe work practice standards.

Note 1: NFPA 70E, *Standard for Electrical Safety in the Workplace*, provides assistance in determining the severity of potential exposure, planning safe work practices, and selecting personal protective equipment.

ANALYSIS: The 2008 *NEC* used the term "other than dwelling occupancies" in this section. Due to this, the warnings required by this section didn't apply to multifamily dwellings, despite the fact that they might have remarkably larger services than some nondwelling occupancies. The *Code* has been changed to require the marking on multifamily dwellings, but not the individual dwellings of a multifamily dwelling unit building to address that issue.

The title of this section was also revised. This section doesn't provide any "protection" as the previous title (flash protection) implied. Rather, it provides for a warning against the hazards associated with an arc flash.

110.22(C) Tested Series Combination Systems

The existing Informational Note to this subsection has been incorporated into the *Code* text.

110.22 Identification of Disconnecting Means.

(C) Tested Series Combination Systems. Tested series-rated installations must be legibly field-marked, in accordance with 240.86(B), to indicate the equipment has been applied with a series combination rating.

ANALYSIS: In an effort to reduce the amount of Informational Notes, the former Fine Print Note referring the *Code* user to 240.86(B) is now part of the rule.

110.24 Available Fault Current

A new section requires some equipment to be marked with the available fault current and requires updating of that marking if modifications of the electrical system occur.

110.24 Available Fault Current.

(A) Field Marking. Service equipment in other than dwelling units must be legibly field-marked with the maximum available fault current, including the date the fault current calculation was performed and be of sufficient durability to withstand the environment involved. Figure 110–13

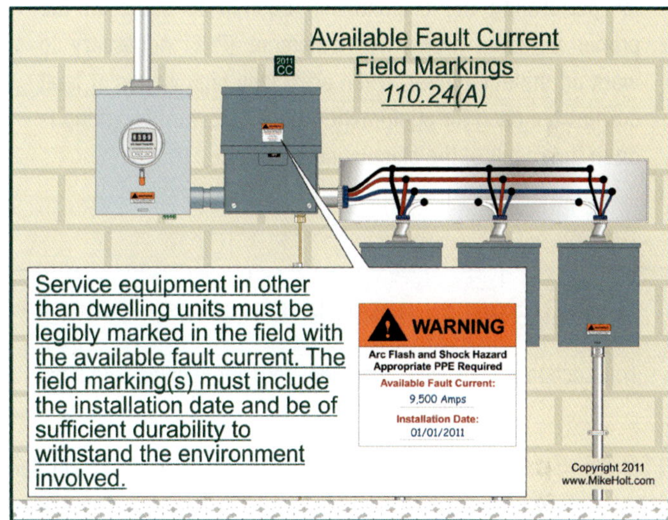

Figure 110–13

(B) Modifications. When modifications to the electrical installation affect the maximum available fault current at the service, the maximum available fault current must be recalculated to ensure the service equipment ratings are sufficient for the maximum available fault current at the line terminals of the equipment. The required field marking(s) in 110.24(A) must be adjusted to reflect the new level of maximum available fault current.

Exception: Field markings aren't required for industrial installations where conditions of maintenance and supervision ensure that only qualified persons service the equipment.

ANALYSIS: All equipment must have an interrupting rating or short-circuit current rating that's equal to or greater than the available fault current [110.9 and 110.10]. As premises wiring systems age, utilities may change transformers in an effort to become more efficient, or to increase capacity. When this occurs, the available fault current increases, many times resulting in noncompliant (and dangerous) wiring systems. This *NEC* change is intended to alert *Code* users to the fact that when utilities change transformers (or when emergency or standby systems are installed), the ratings of equipment must be reevaluated.

Opponents of this *NEC* change argue that oftentimes the ratings of equipment are based on a "worst case" basis. While this is suitable for designing a system, it isn't suitable for performing the calculations required to establish the proper personal protective equipment (PPE) necessary to work on the equipment. When artificially high values of fault current are used for equipment ratings, a lower PPE rating is often the result of the calculations.

110.26 Spaces About Electrical Equipment

This section was revised to provide more enforceable language.

110.26 Spaces About Electrical Equipment. For the purpose of safe operation and maintenance of equipment, access and working space must be provided about all electrical equipment.

ANALYSIS: Previous editions of the *Code* used the term "sufficient" to describe the access required by this section. Because the word "sufficient" is a vague and unenforceable term, it's been removed from this *NEC* rule.

110.26(A)(3) Height of Working Space

This subsection was revised to include all of the height requirements found in the section. A new exception for meters in meter sockets was added as well.

110.26 Spaces About Electrical Equipment.

(A) Working Space.

(3) Height of Working Space (Headroom). The height of the working space in front of equipment must not be less than 6½ ft, measured from the grade, floor, platform, or the equipment height, whichever is greater. **Figure 110–14**

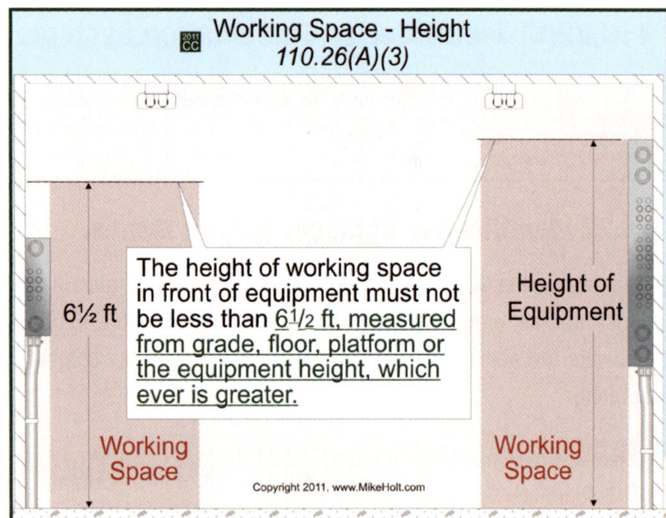

Figure 110–14

Equipment such as raceways, cables, wireways, cabinets, panels, and so on, can be located above or below electrical equipment, but must not extend more than 6 in. into the equipment's working space. **Figure 110–15**

Ex 1: The minimum headroom requirement doesn't apply to service equipment or panelboards rated 200A or less located in an existing dwelling unit.

Author's Comment: See the definition of "Dwelling Unit" in Article 100.

Ex 2: Meters are permitted to extend beyond the other equipment.

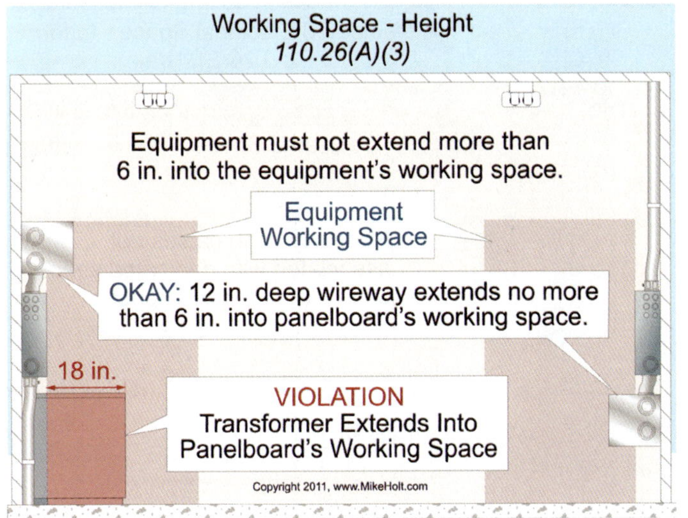

Figure 110–15

ANALYSIS: In previous *Code* editions, 110.26(A)(3) and 110.26(E) both contained provisions regarding the height of the working space described in this section. Because there's no reason to have two subsections giving similar provisions, 110.26(E) was deleted, and the text was incorporated into the existing 110.26(A)(3). The remaining subsections have also been renumbered to address the change.

Meters are obviously installed inside the working space discussed in this section, and in previous editions of the *NEC* have been allowed only to protrude up to 6 in. into the clear work space. With this change, meters that extend more than 6 in. into the work space are allowed.

110.26(D) Illumination

A clarification to the illumination requirements near electrical equipment has been made.

110.26 Spaces About Electrical Equipment.

(D) Illumination. Service equipment, switchboards, panelboards, as well as motor control centers located indoors must have illumination located indoors and must not be controlled by automatic means only. Figure 110–16

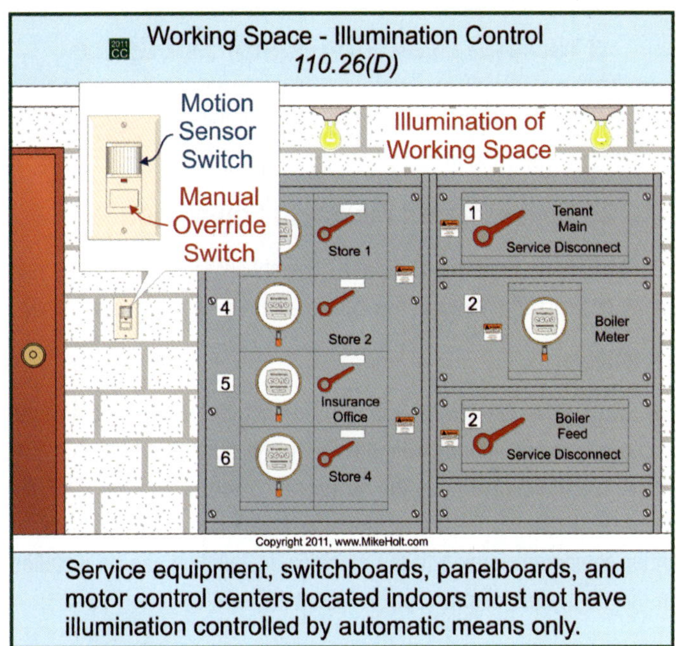

Figure 110–16

Author's Comment: The *Code* doesn't provide the minimum foot-candles required to provide proper illumination. Proper illumination of electrical equipment rooms is essential for the safety of those qualified to work on such equipment.

ANALYSIS: This change is to clarify that the required illumination for switchboards, panelboards, and motor control centers must not be switched by automatic means only. In previous editions of the *NEC*, this requirement applied only to electrical rooms, regardless of the fact that equipment addressed by this rule is often installed in spaces that aren't "electrical rooms."

110.26(E) Dedicated Equipment Space

The term "distribution board" has been deleted.

110.26 Spaces About Electrical Equipment.

(E) Dedicated Equipment Space. Switchboards, panelboards, and motor control centers must have dedicated equipment space as follows:

(1) Indoors.

(a) Dedicated Electrical Space. The footprint space (width and depth of the equipment) extending from the floor to a height of 6 ft above the equipment or to the structural ceiling, whichever is lower, must be dedicated for the electrical installation. No piping, ducts, or other equipment foreign to the electrical installation can be installed in this dedicated footprint space. **Figure 110–17**

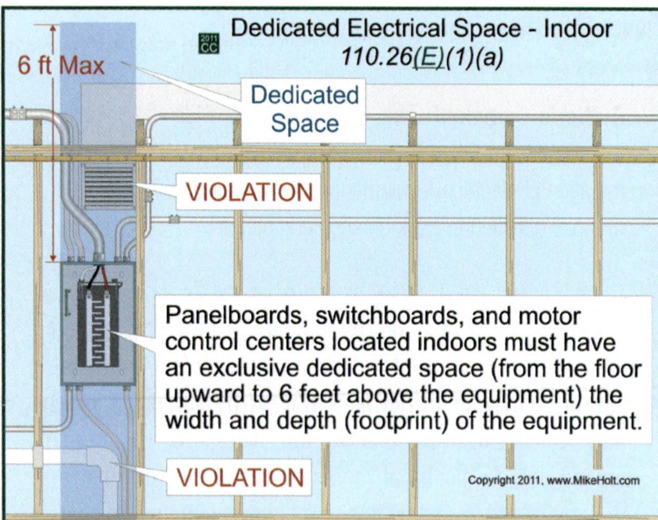

Figure 110–17

Ex: Suspended ceilings with removable panels can be within the dedicated footprint space [110.26(E)(1)(d)].

> **Author's Comment:** Electrical raceways and cables not associated with the dedicated space can be within the dedicated space. These aren't considered "equipment foreign to the electrical installation." **Figure 110–18**

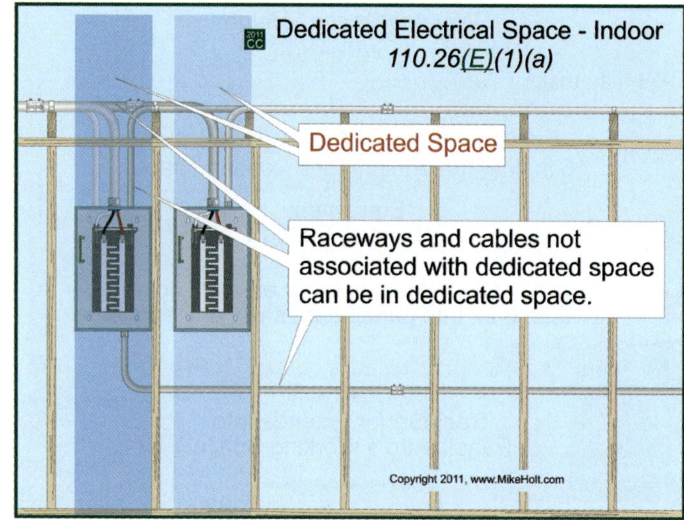

Figure 110–18

(b) Foreign Systems. Foreign systems can be located above the dedicated space if protection is installed to prevent damage to the electrical equipment from condensation, leaks, or breaks in the foreign systems, which can be as simple as a drip-pan. **Figure 110–19**

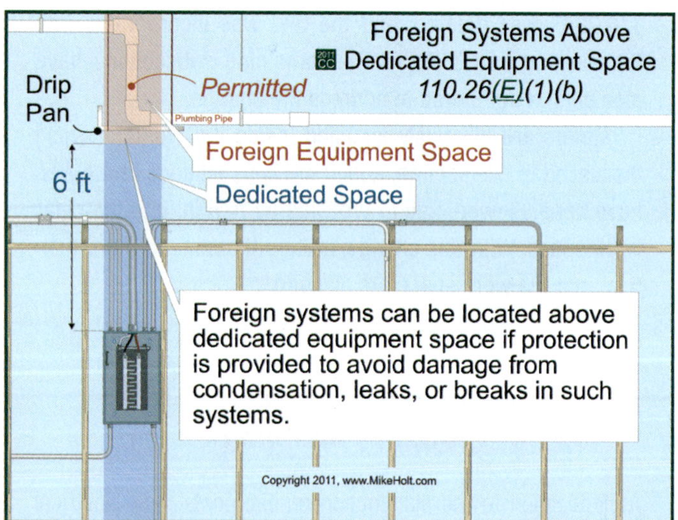

Figure 110–19

(c) Sprinkler Protection. Sprinkler protection piping isn't permitted in the dedicated space, but the *NEC* doesn't prohibit sprinklers from spraying water on electrical equipment.

(d) Suspended Ceilings. A dropped, suspended, or similar ceiling isn't considered a structural ceiling.

ANALYSIS: The term "distribution board" is an outdated phrase that's no longer used in the industry. The term isn't defined, and, due to this, many inspectors disagree on what a distribution board really is. The easiest and best solution for the *Code*-Making Panel was to simply delete the term and avoid any misunderstandings and disagreements.

110.28 Enclosure Types

The list of equipment that's required to be marked by type has been increased, and the location of the requirement in the *NEC* has been changed. A new Informational Note has also been added.

110.28 Enclosure Types. Enclosures must be marked with an enclosure-type number and be suitable for the location in accordance with Table 110.28.

The enclosures aren't intended to protect against condensation, icing, corrosion, or contamination that might occur within the enclosure or that enters via the raceway or unsealed openings.

Note: Raintight enclosures include Types 3, 3S, 3SX, 3X, 4, 4X, 6, and 6P; rainproof enclosures are Types 3R, and 3RX; watertight enclosures are Types 4, 4X, 6, and 6P; driptight enclosures are Types 2, 5, 12, 12K, and 13; and dusttight enclosures are Types 3, 3S, 3SX, 3X, 5, 12, 12K, and 13.

ANALYSIS: The list of items that was required to carry an enclosure-type number in the 2008 *Code* was quite small. This change adds several new pieces of equipment to the list, and helps to satisfy the intent of this rule. This rule was also relocated to Part II of the article so that it applies only to equipment operating at 600V or less.

Lastly, a new Informational Note was added that refers to an ANSI/NEMA standard which addresses ingress protection ratings that are afforded by different types of enclosures. This information may be found in ANSI/NEMA 60529, *Degrees of Protection Provided by Enclosures.*

NOTES

CHAPTER

2

WIRING AND PROTECTION

INTRODUCTION TO CHAPTER 2—WIRING AND PROTECTION

Chapter 2 provides general rules for wiring and the protection of conductors. The rules in this chapter apply to all electrical installations covered by the *NEC*—except as modified in Chapters 5, 6, and 7 [90.3].

Communications Systems (Chapter 8 systems) aren't subject to the general requirements of Chapters 1 through 4, or the special requirements of Chapters 5 through 7, unless there's a specific reference in Chapter 8 to a rule in Chapters 1 through 7 [90.3].

As you go through Chapter 2, remember its purpose. Chapter 2 is primarily concerned with correctly sizing and protecting circuits. Every article in Chapter 2 deals with a different aspect of this purpose. This differs from the purpose of Chapter 3, which is to correctly install the conductors that make up those circuits.

Chapter 1 introduced you to the *NEC* and provided a solid foundation for understanding the *Code*. Chapters 2 (Wiring and Protection) and 3 (Wiring Methods and Materials) continue building the foundation for applying the *NEC*. Chapter 4 applies the preceding chapters to general equipment. It's beneficial to learn the first four chapters of the *Code* in a sequential manner because each of the first four chapters builds on the preceding chapter. Once you've mastered the first four chapters, you can learn the next four in any order you wish.

- **Article 200—Use and Identification of Grounded Conductors.** This article contains the requirements for the use and identification of the neutral conductor and its terminals.

  Author's Comment: Because the neutral conductor of a solidly grounded system is always grounded to the earth, it's both a "grounded conductor" and a "neutral conductor." To make it easier for the reader of this textbook, we'll refer to the "grounded conductor" as the "neutral conductor."

- **Article 210—Branch Circuits.** Article 210 contains the requirements for branch circuits, such as conductor sizing, identification, GFCI protection of receptacles, and receptacle and lighting outlet requirements.
- **Article 215—Feeders.** This article covers the requirements for the installation, minimum size, and ampacity of feeders.
- **Article 220—Branch-Circuit, Feeder, and Service Calculations.** Article 220 provides the requirements for calculating the minimum size for branch circuits, feeders, and services. This article also aids in determining related factors such as the number of receptacles on a circuit in nondwelling installations, and the minimum number of branch circuits required.
- **Article 225—Outside Branch Circuits and Feeders.** This article covers the installation requirements for equipment, including conductors located outside that run on or between buildings, poles, and other structures on the premises.
- **Article 230—Services.** Article 230 covers the installation requirements for service conductors and equipment. It's very important to know where the service begins and ends when applying Article 230.

Author's Comment: Conductors from a battery, uninterruptible power supply, solar photovoltaic system, generator, or transformer aren't considered service conductors; they're feeder conductors.

- **Article 240—Overcurrent Protection.** This article provides the requirements for overcurrent protection and overcurrent devices. Overcurrent protection for conductors and equipment is provided to open the circuit if the current reaches a value that will cause an excessive or dangerous temperature on the conductors or conductor insulation.
- **Article 250—Grounding and Bonding.** Article 250 covers the grounding requirements for providing a low-impedance path to the earth to reduce overvoltage from lightning, and the requirements for a low-impedance fault current path necessary to facilitate the operation of overcurrent devices in the event of a ground fault.
- **Article 285—Surge Protective Devices (SPDs).** This article covers the general requirements, installation requirements, and connection requirements for surge protective devices (SPDs) permanently installed on both the line side and load side of service equipment.

Use and Identification of GROUNDED CONDUCTORS

INTRODUCTION TO ARTICLE 200—USE AND IDENTIFICATION OF GROUNDED CONDUCTORS

This article contains the requirements for the identification of the neutral conductor and its terminals.

Author's Comment: Because the neutral conductor of a solidly grounded system is always grounded to the earth, it's both a "grounded conductor" and a "neutral conductor." To make it easier for the reader of this textbook, we'll refer to the "grounded conductor" as the "neutral conductor." **Figure 200–1**

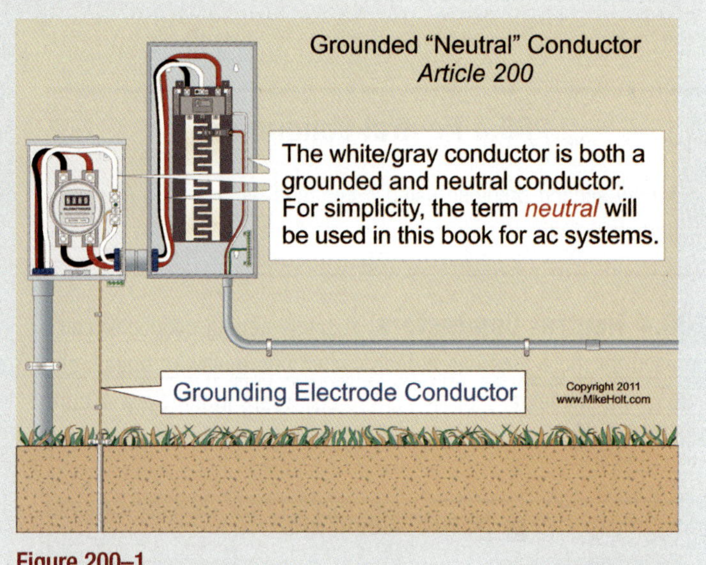

Figure 200–1

PART I. GENERAL

200.2(B) Continuity

A new Informational Note was added to this section.

200.2 General.

(B) Continuity. The continuity of the neutral conductor isn't permitted to be dependent on metal enclosures, raceways, or cable armor. Figure 200–2

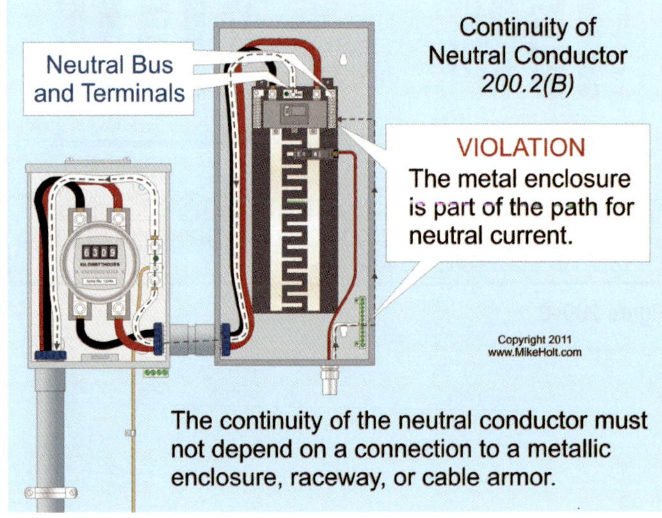

Figure 200–2

Note: See 300.13(B) for the requirements relating to the continuity of the neutral conductor on multiwire branch circuits.

Author's Comment: This requirement prohibits the practice of terminating the neutral conductor on the enclosure of a panel or other equipment, rather than on the neutral terminal bar. This ensures the metallic panelboard, raceway, or cable armor doesn't carry neutral current. Some panelboards have two terminal bars, one on either side of the panelboard with a strap connecting the terminal bars together. Caution must be taken to terminate the neutral conductor to the neutral terminal, not to the equipment grounding conductor terminal.

ANALYSIS: Because 200.2(B) and 300.13(B) both relate to the continuity of the neutral conductor, this Informational Note was added to alert *Code* users to 300.13(B). Oftentimes the *NEC* has two sections that both apply to similar requirements, and often the *Code* user will find one requirement and stop looking, not expecting a similar provision elsewhere in the *NEC*.

200.4 Neutral Conductors

A new section prohibits using a common neutral for multiple branch circuits.

200.4 Neutral Conductors. A single neutral conductor can't be used for more than one branch circuit, one multiwire branch circuit, or one feeder, except as allowed elsewhere in the *Code*. **Figure 200–3**

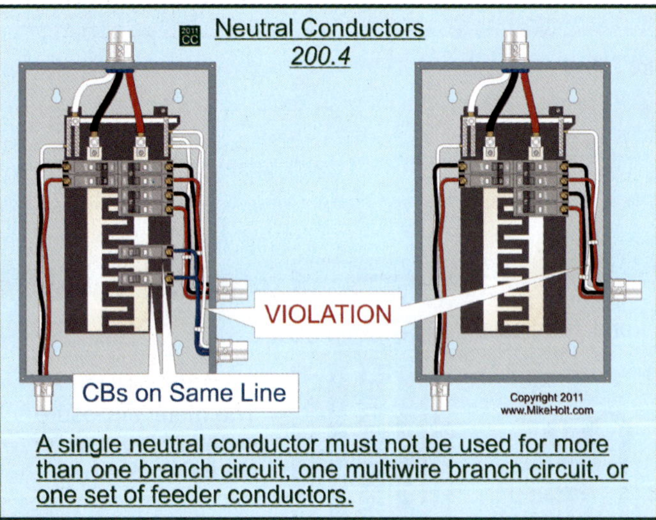

Figure 200–3

ANALYSIS: This new section was added to address the seldom used (but previously legal) practice of having one neutral conductor for multiple ungrounded conductors of the same phase or line. In previous editions of the *NEC*, there was no rule that specifically prohibited this poor practice. For example, two 12 AWG conductors of different circuits (but the same phase or line) could share a common neutral conductor, provided that the neutral conductor was sized to carry the neutral current [210.19(A)(1)]. With this change, such an installation will be in violation of this section. This practice is currently allowed in 215.4(A) and 225.7(B) for feeder circuits.

Author's Comment: A multiwire branch-circuit is considered a single circuit [Article 100].

200.6 Means of Identifying Grounded Conductors

This section has been reorganized into a list format.

200.6 Neutral Conductor Identification.

(A) 6 AWG or Smaller. Neutral conductors 6 AWG and smaller must be identified by one of the following means: **Figure 200–4**

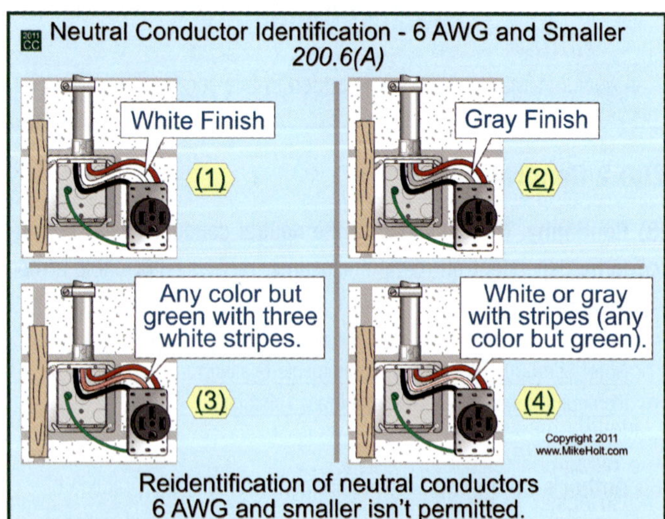

Figure 200–4

(1) By a continuous white outer finish.

(2) By a continuous gray outer finish.

(3) By three continuous white stripes along its entire length on other than green insulation.

(4) Wires that have their outer covering finished to show a white or gray color but have colored tracer threads in the braid identifying the source of manufacture are considered to meet the provisions of this section.

Author's Comment: The use of white tape, paint, or other methods of identification isn't permitted for neutral conductors 6 AWG or smaller.

(6) A single-conductor, sunlight-resistant, outdoor-rated cable used as the neutral conductor in photovoltaic power systems as permitted by 690.31(B) can be identified by distinctive white marking at all terminations. Figure 200–5

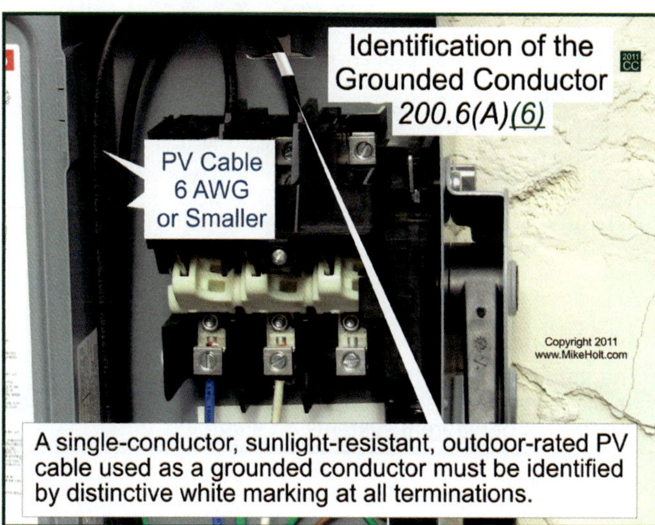

Figure 200–5

ANALYSIS: This section contains eight possible ways to identify the neutral conductor, yet the section was written in a paragraph format. The list format is easier to read, and is also easier to understand. *Code* users will likely appreciate this change.

200.6(B) Sizes Larger Than 4 AWG

This section has been rewritten into a correct list format, and the term "larger than 6 AWG" has been changed.

200.6 Neutral Conductor Identification.

(B) Size 4 AWG or Larger. Neutral conductors 4 AWG or larger must be identified by one of the following means: Figure 200–6

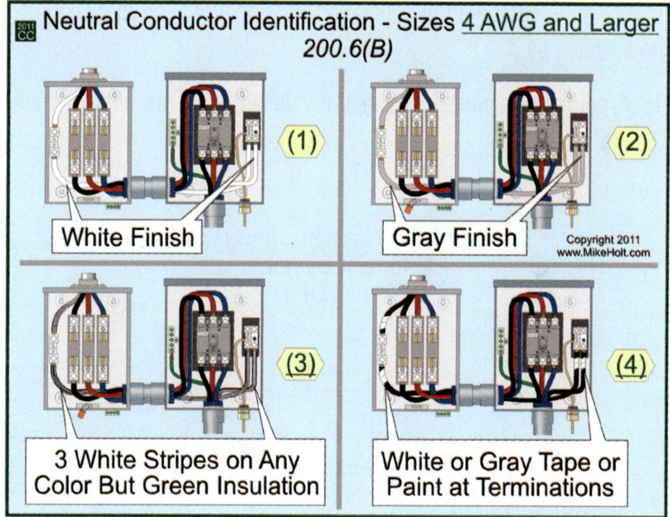

Figure 200–6

(1) A continuous white outer finish along its entire length.

(2) A continuous gray outer finish along its entire length.

(3) Three continuous white stripes along its length.

(4) White or gray tape or markings at the terminations.

ANALYSIS: Of the four methods allowed by this section to identify larger neutral conductors, only three of the methods were written in list format. This change provides uniformity in Section 200.6 by incorporating all methods of identification into lists.

This rule applies to any conductor that's 4 AWG or larger. This change clarifies that fact, and it also makes for an easier requirement to understand. For whatever reason, most people tend to agree that "4 AWG and larger" is easier to understand and visualize than "larger than 6 AWG." This change will be a welcome one for most *NEC* users.

200.6(D) Neutral Conductors of Different Systems

The text of this requirement has been revised to correlate with the requirements for ungrounded conductors.

200.6 Neutral Conductor Identification.

(D) Neutral Conductors of Different Systems. If neutral conductors of different voltage systems are installed in the same raceway, cable, or enclosure, each neutral conductor must be identified to distinguish the systems by:

(1) A continuous white or gray outer finish along its entire length. **Figure 200–7**

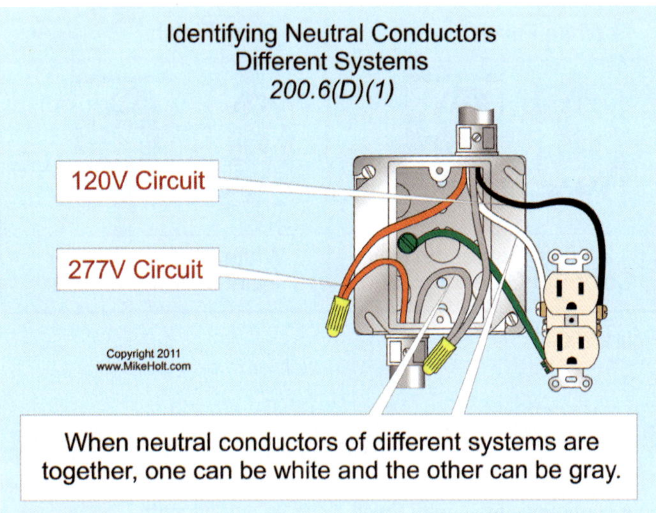

Figure 200–7

(2) The neutral conductor of the other system must have a different outer covering of continuous white or gray outer finish along its entire length or by an outer covering of white or gray with a readily distinguishable color stripe (other than green) along its entire length. **Figure 200–8**

(3) Other identification allowed by 200.6(A) or (B) that distinguishes the neutral conductor from other systems.

The means of identification must be documented in a manner that's readily available or be permanently posted where the conductors of different systems originate. **Figure 200–9**

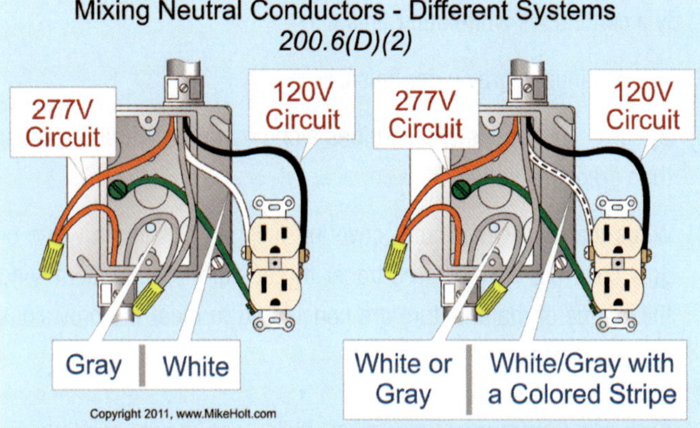

Figure 200–8

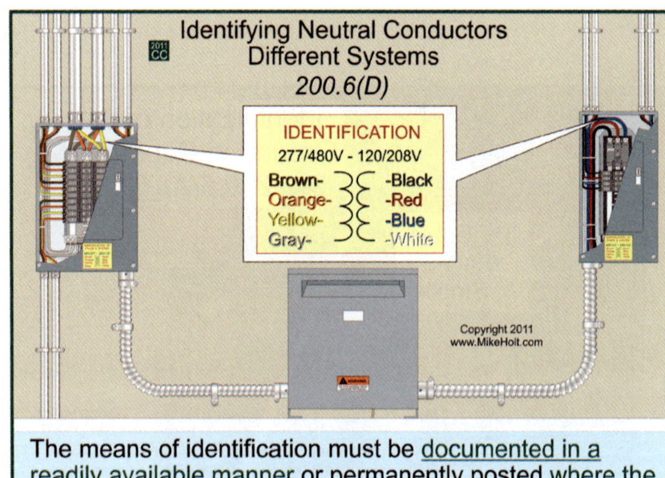

Figure 200–9

Author's Comment: If a premises wiring system has circuits supplied from more than one voltage system, each ungrounded conductor must be identified by phase or line and system [210.5(C) and 215.12(C)].

ANALYSIS: 210.5(C) and 215.12(C) both have an allowance for documenting the identification scheme used "in a manner that's readily available." Because the identification of the neutral conductor will likely be at the same location as the documentation for the ungrounded conductors, it makes sense to have the same allowance for the neutral conductor.

200.7(C) Circuits of 50 Volts or More

The rules covering the use of white wires used as ungrounded conductors have been editorially revised.

200.7 Use of White or Gray Color.

(C) Circuits of 50V or More. A conductor with white insulation can only be used for the ungrounded conductor as follows:

(1) Cable Assembly. The white conductor within a cable can be used for the ungrounded conductor, if permanently reidentified by marking tape, painting, or other effective means at each location where the conductor is visible to indicate its use as an ungrounded conductor. Identification must encircle the insulation and must be a color other than white, gray, or green. Figure 200–10

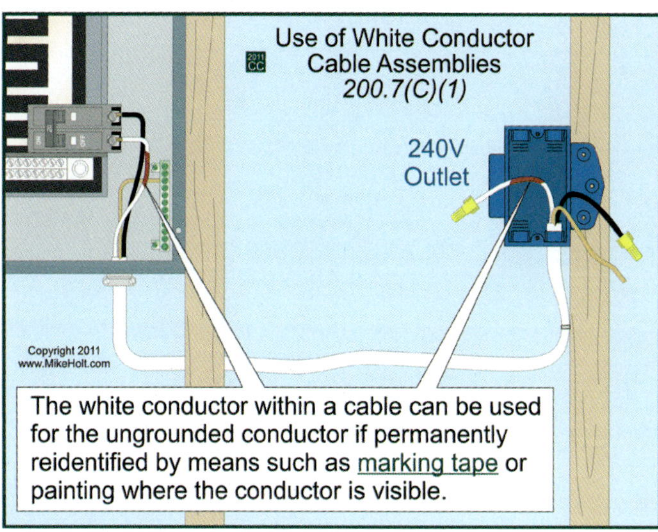

Figure 200–10

The white conductor within a cable can be used to supply power to single-pole, 3-way, and 4-way switch loops, as well as travelers for 3-way and 4-way switching if permanently reidentified at each location where the conductor is visible to indicate its use as an ungrounded conductor. Figures 200–11 and 200–12

(2) Flexible Cord. The white conductor within a flexible cord can be used for the ungrounded conductor for connecting an appliance or equipment as permitted by 400.7.

Note: Care should be taken when working on existing systems because a gray insulated conductor may have been used in the past as an ungrounded conductor.

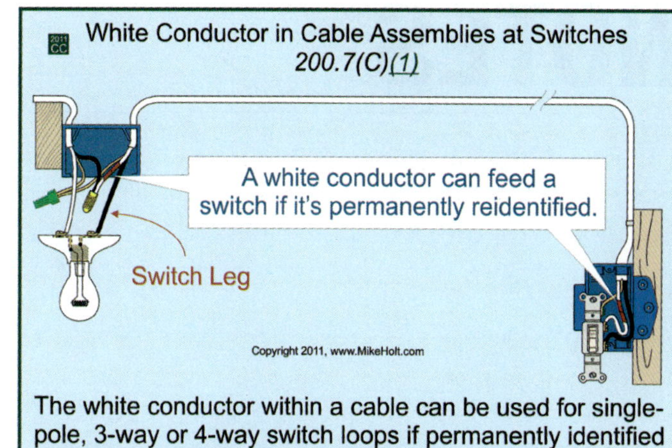

Figure 200-11

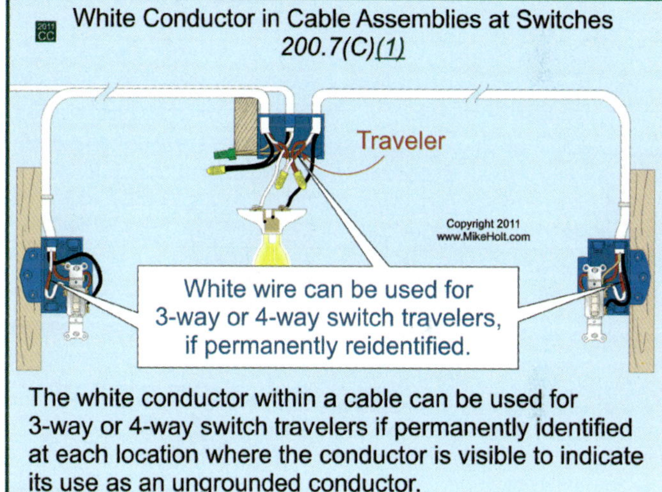

Figure 200-12

ANALYSIS: At first glance, this change seems to remove the allowance of using the white conductor of a cable assembly as an ungrounded conductor in a switch loop. A careful reading of 200.7(C)(1), however, shows that this practice is (and technically has always been) allowed. Because of that, 200.7(C)(2) was removed, as it really didn't provide any allowances that weren't already included in (C)(1).

Some nontechnical changes were also made to provide consistency with other *Code* sections.

NOTES

ARTICLE

210 Branch CIRCUITS

INTRODUCTION TO ARTICLE 210—BRANCH CIRCUITS

This article contains the requirements for branch circuits, such as conductor sizing and identification, GFCI protection, and receptacle and lighting outlet requirements. It consists of three parts:

- PART I. GENERAL PROVISIONS
- PART II. BRANCH-CIRCUIT RATINGS
- PART III. REQUIRED OUTLETS

Table 210.2 of this article identifies specific-purpose branch circuits. The provisions for branch circuits that supply equipment listed in Table 210.2 amend or supplement the provisions given in Article 210 for branch circuits, so it's important to be aware of the contents of this table.

The following sections contain a few key items on which to spend extra time as you study Article 210:

- **210.4—Multiwire Branch Circuits.** The conductors of these circuits must originate from the same panel. Multiwire branch circuits can supply only line-to-neutral loads.
- **210.8—GFCI Protection.** Crawl spaces, unfinished basements, and boathouses are just some of the many locations that require GFCI protection.
- **210.11—Branch Circuits Required.** With three subheadings, 210.11 gives summarized requirements for the number of branch circuits in certain situations, states that a load calculated on a VA per area basis must be evenly proportioned, and covers some minimum branch circuit rules for dwelling units.
- **210.12—Arc-Fault Circuit-Interrupter Protection.** An arc-fault circuit interrupter is a device intended to de-energize a circuit when it detects the current waveform characteristics unique to an arcing fault. The purpose of an AFCI is to protect against a fire hazard, whereas the purpose of a GFCI is to protect people against electrocution.
- **210.19—Conductors—Minimum Ampacity and Size.** This section covers the basic rules for sizing branch-circuit conductors, including continuous and noncontinuous loads.
- **210.21—Outlet Devices.** Outlet devices must have an ampere rating at least as large as the load to be served, as well as following the other rules of this section.
- **210.23—Permissible Loads.** This is intended to prevent a circuit overload from occurring because of improper design and planning of circuitry.
- **210.52—Dwelling Unit Receptacle Outlets.** There are some specific receptacle spacing rules and branch-circuit requirements for dwelling units that don't apply to other occupancies.

Mastering the branch-circuit requirements in Article 210 will give you a jump-start toward completing installations that are free of *Code* violations.

210.4(B) Disconnecting Means

A new Informational Note was added to alert users of requirements in Article 240.

210.4 Multiwire Branch Circuits.

(B) Disconnecting Means. Each multiwire branch circuit must have a means to simultaneously disconnect all ungrounded conductors at the point where the branch circuit originates. **Figure 210–1**

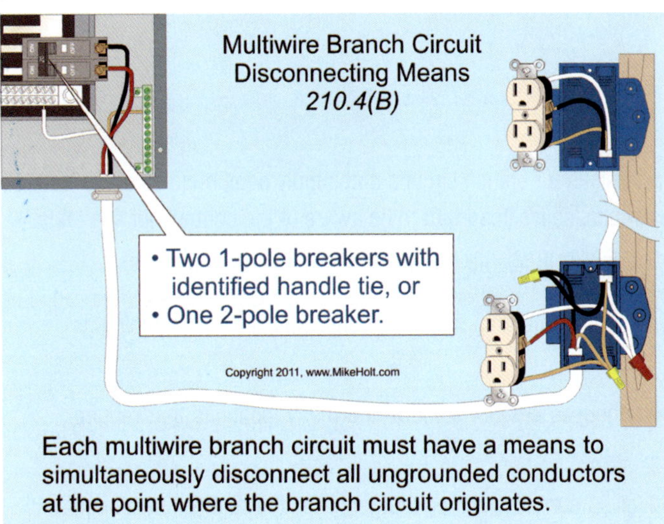

Figure 210–1

Note: Individual single-pole circuit breakers with handle ties identified for the purpose, or a breaker with a common internal trip, can be used for this application. See 240.15(B)(1).

CAUTION: *This rule is intended to prevent people from working on energized circuits they thought were disconnected.*

ANALYSIS: Section 210.4(B) requires that all multiwire branch circuits have a means to simultaneously disconnect the ungrounded conductors at the point of origination. While single-pole breakers with identified handle ties will typically satisfy this requirement, there are instances where a 2- or 3-pole breaker will be required. An example of this is where the branch circuit supplies both line-to-neutral and line-to-line loads [210.4(C) Ex 2 and 240.15(B)(1)]. The new Informational Note directs the *NEC* user to 240.15(B) in an effort to provide easier *Code* navigation.

210.4(D) Grouping

The term "wire ties" was changed to "cable ties" in this subsection.

210.4 Multiwire Branch Circuits.

(D) Grouping. The ungrounded and neutral conductors of a multiwire branch circuit must be grouped together by cable ties or similar means at the point of origination. **Figure 210–2**

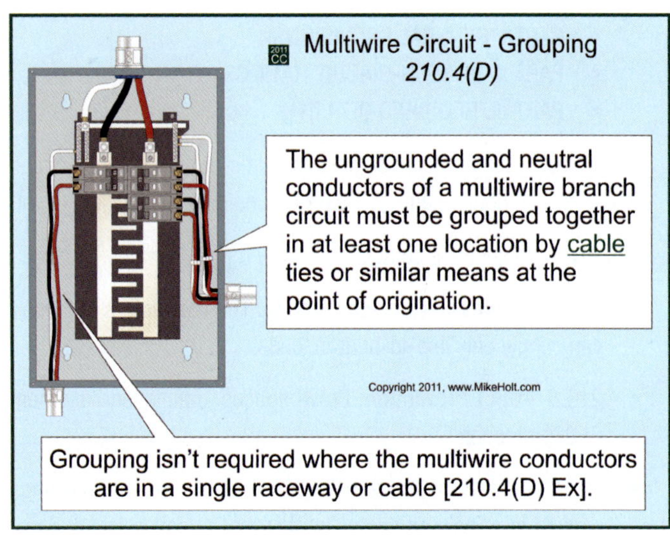

Figure 210–2

Ex: Grouping isn't required where the circuit conductors are contained in a single raceway or cable unique to that circuit that makes the grouping obvious.

Author's Comment: Grouping all associated conductors of a multiwire branch circuit together by cable ties or other means within the point of origination makes it easier to visually identify the conductors of the multiwire branch circuit. The grouping will assist in making sure that the correct neutral is used at junction points and in connecting multiwire branch-circuit conductors to circuit breakers correctly, particularly where twin breakers are used. If proper diligence isn't exercised when making these connections, two circuit conductors can be accidentally connected to the same phase.

CAUTION: *If the ungrounded conductors of a multiwire circuit aren't terminated to different phases or lines, the currents on the neutral conductor won't cancel, but will add, which can cause an overload on the neutral conductor.* Figure 210–3

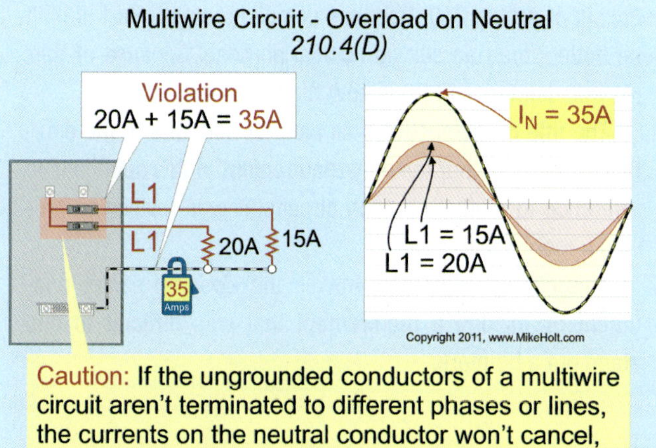

Figure 210–3

ANALYSIS: This change replaces the term "wire ties" with the more appropriate term "cable ties." Cable ties are referred to in several locations in the *Code*, and the meaning of the term is widely understood by the industry. Wire ties, however, is a less specific term that may even include the ties that come with a loaf of bread!

210.5(C) Identification of Ungrounded Conductors

The requirements for the identification of ungrounded conductors have been reorganized into a list format.

210.5 Identification for Branch Circuits.

(C) Identification of Ungrounded Conductors—More Than One Voltage System. Ungrounded conductors must be identified as follows: Figure 210–4

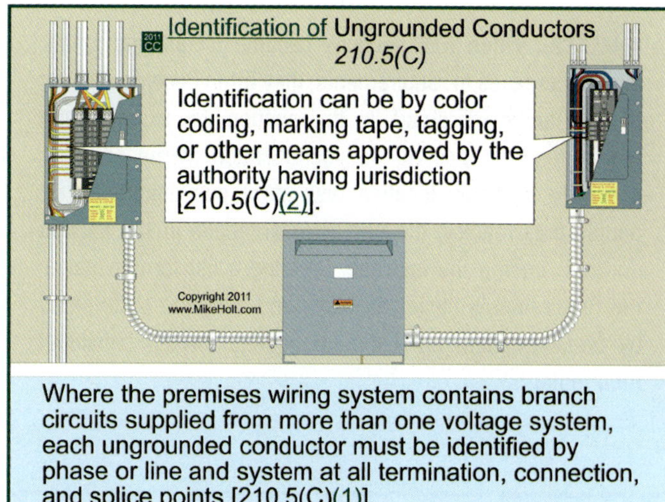

Figure 210–4

(1) Application. If the premises wiring system contains branch circuits supplied from more than one voltage system, each ungrounded conductor must be identified by phase and system at all termination, connection, and splice points.

(2) Means of Identification. Identification can be by color coding, marking tape, tagging, or other means approved by the authority having jurisdiction.

(3) Posting. The method of identification must be documented in a manner that's readily available or permanently posted at each branch-circuit panelboard.

Conductors with insulation that's green or green with one or more yellow stripes can't be used for an ungrounded or neutral conductor [250.119].

Author's Comment: Although the *NEC* doesn't require a specific color code for ungrounded conductors, electricians often use the following color system for power and lighting conductor identification:

- 120/240V, single-phase—black, red, and white
- 120/208V, three-phase—black, red, blue, and white
- 120/240V, three-phase—black, orange, blue, and white
- 277/480V, three-phase—brown, orange, yellow, and gray; or, brown, purple, yellow, and gray

ANALYSIS: When *NEC* sections become longer and longer due to increases in requirements, they often become difficult to read and understand. In this section, for example, the requirement for posting the identification at the panel or a readily available location was often overlooked due to people only reading the first two sentences of the section and not reading the last one. Creating a list format makes the requirements easier to follow and easier to understand by breaking them up and adding titles for the individual requirements.

210.7 Multiple Branch Circuits

This section was revised to omit needless information and more aptly describe the requirement.

210.7 Multiple Branch Circuits. If two or more branch circuits supply devices or equipment on the same yoke, a means to disconnect simultaneously all ungrounded conductors that supply those devices or equipment is required at the point where the branch circuit originates. **Figure 210–5**

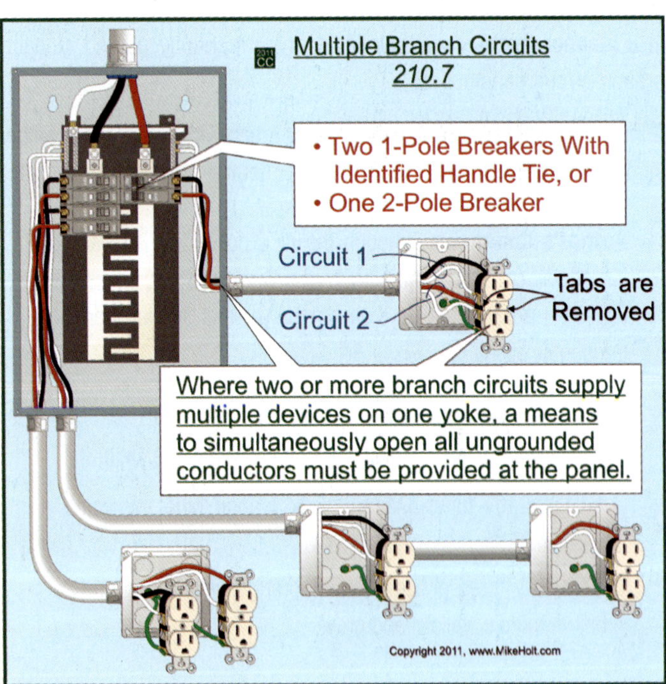

Figure 210–5

Author's Comment: Individual single-pole circuit breakers with handle ties identified for the purpose, or a circuit breaker with a common internal trip, can be used for this application [240.15(B)(1)].

ANALYSIS: Formerly this section was divided into subparts (A) and (B), with (A) requiring that *Code* users comply with Part III of Article 210. Because compliance with Part III isn't an option, the rule served no real purpose. Because of this, (A) was deleted, and (B) is now the text in the rule.

The title of the section was also revised, due to the deletion of (A). Now that the only requirement in this section is in reference to multiple branch circuits, it was revised to provide a more accurate title.

This change ultimately makes the *Code* an easier document by making a requirement that was difficult to find stand out a bit more.

210.8 GFCI Protection

A new requirement addresses the accessibility of the test and reset functions of GFCI devices.

210.8 GFCI Protection. Ground-fault circuit interruption for personnel must be provided as required in 210.8(A) through (C). The Ground-fault circuit-interrupter device must be installed at a readily accessible location. **Figure 210–6**

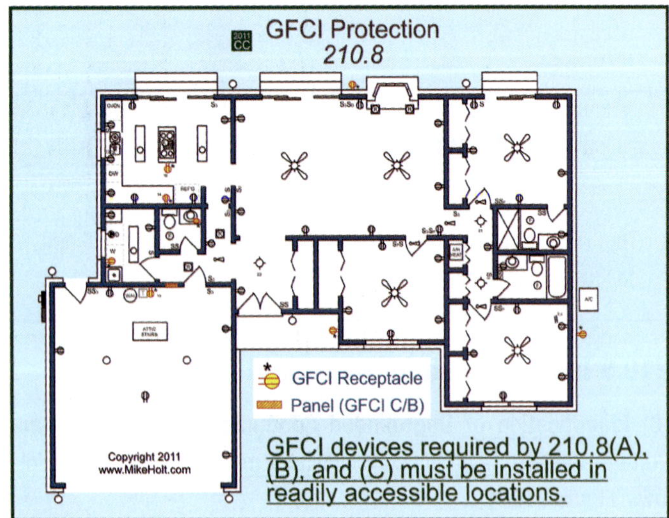

Figure 210–6

ANALYSIS: The *Code* previously didn't address the accessibility of the test and reset functions of GFCI devices. This presents two problems: First, building owners are subjected to the inconvenience of using ladders (or less safe devices) to reach the reset button should a GFCI device trip. Secondly, the listing standards of GFCIs require that they be tested on a monthly basis. While it's true that many people don't test their GFCI devices, some who would perform such tests won't go through the extra effort of finding a ladder to access these devices if they aren't readily accessible.

This change will require GFCIs in obvious locations such as bathrooms and dwelling unit garages to have their test and reset buttons readily accessible, but it also applies to less obvious locations, such as receptacles on rooftops and in soffits for holiday lighting.

210.8(A)(3) Exception, GFCI Protection Outdoor Receptacles

A new allowance for ground-fault protection of equipment for pipeline and vessel heating equipment was added.

210.8 GFCI Protection.

(A) Dwelling Units.

(3) Outdoors. All 15A and 20A, 125V receptacles located outdoors of dwelling units, including receptacles installed under the eaves of roofs, must be GFCI protected. Figure 210–7

Author's Comments:

- Each dwelling unit of a multifamily dwelling that has an individual entrance at grade level must have at least one GFCI-protected receptacle outlet accessible from grade level located not more than 6½ ft above grade [210.52(E)(2)].
- Balconies, decks, and porches that are attached to the dwelling unit and are accessible from inside the dwelling must have at least one GFCI-protected receptacle outlet accessible from the balcony, deck, or porch [210.52(E)(3)].

Ex: GFCI protection isn't required for a receptacle that's supplied by a branch circuit dedicated to fixed electric snow-melting or deicing or pipeline and vessel heating equipment, if the receptacle isn't readily accessible and the equipment or receptacle has ground-fault protection of equipment (GFPE) [426.28 and 427.22]. Figure 210–8

Figure 210–7

Figure 210–8

ANALYSIS: While the general rule of 210.8(A)(3) and (B)(4) requires GFCI protection for all 15A and 20A, 125V receptacles located outdoors, the *NEC* recognizes that some types of equipment need GFPE protection rather than Class A GFCI protection [Article 100]. For quite some time, this *Code* exception has applied to receptacle outlets used for snow-melting and deicing equipment [426.28], but it didn't address pipeline and vessel heating that's required to have GFPE by 427.22. This revision resolves the dilemma of which type of protection is allowed for these products.

This *NEC* revision also changes the term "dedicated branch circuit" to "branch circuit dedicated to." Many *Code* users interpreted the phrase "dedicated branch circuit" as meaning that the circuit couldn't have more than one outlet on it. The revision clarifies that as long as the circuit serves only the equipment specified in this section, it can have as many outlets as necessary.

210.8(A)(7) GFCI Protection—Receptacles Near Sinks

This revision clarifies and expands the type of sinks where GFCI protection is required for receptacles.

210.8 GFCI Protection.

(A) Dwelling Units.

(7) Sinks. For other than kitchen sinks, GFCI protection is required for all 15A and 20A, 125V receptacles located within an arc measurement of 6 ft from the outside edge of the sink. **Figures 210–9 and 210–10**

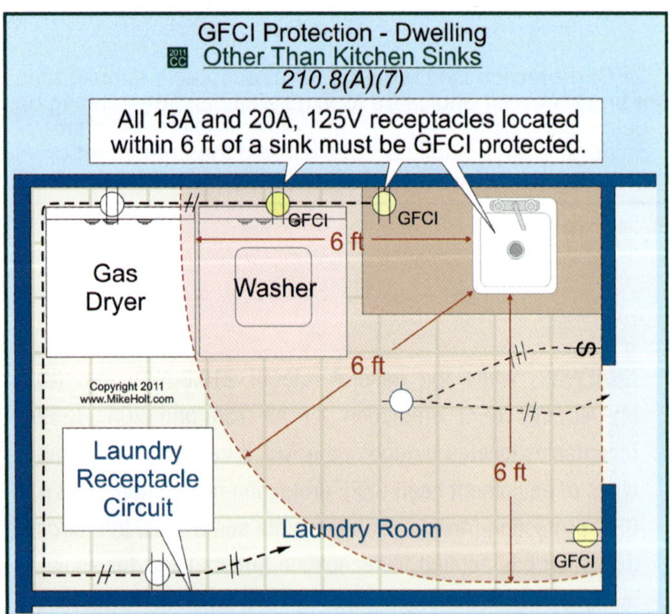

Figure 210–9

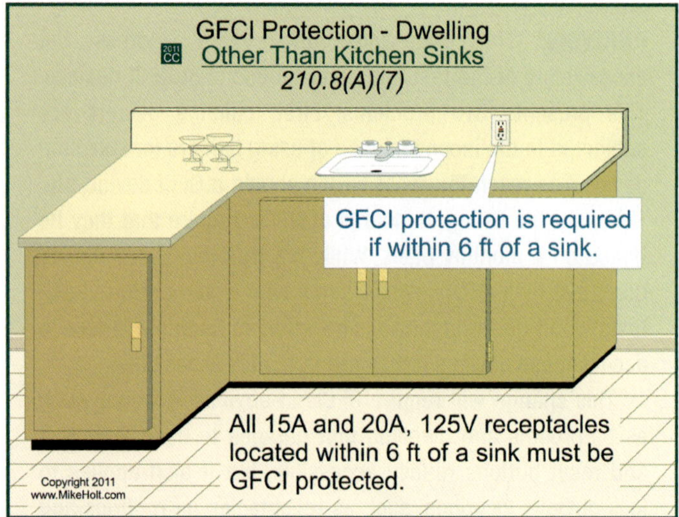

Figure 210–10

ANALYSIS: The list of "laundry, utility, and wet bar sinks" previously contained in this section left out other types of sinks found in a dwelling unit (such as mop sinks). This revision clarifies that GFCI protection is required within 6 ft of all sinks in dwelling units except kitchen sinks, which are already addressed in 210.8(A)(6).

210.8(B)(3) Exceptions, GFCI Protection Rooftop Receptacles

A new allowance for ground-fault protection of equipment for pipeline and vessel heating equipment was added.

210.8 GFCI Protection.

(B) Other than Dwelling Units.

(3) Rooftops. All 15A and 20A, 125V receptacles installed on rooftops must be GFCI protected. **Figure 210–11**

> **Author's Comment:** A 15A or 20A, 125V receptacle outlet must be installed within 25 ft of heating, air-conditioning, and refrigeration equipment [210.63].

(4) Outdoors. All 15A and 20A, 125V receptacles installed outdoors must be GFCI protected. **Figure 210–12**

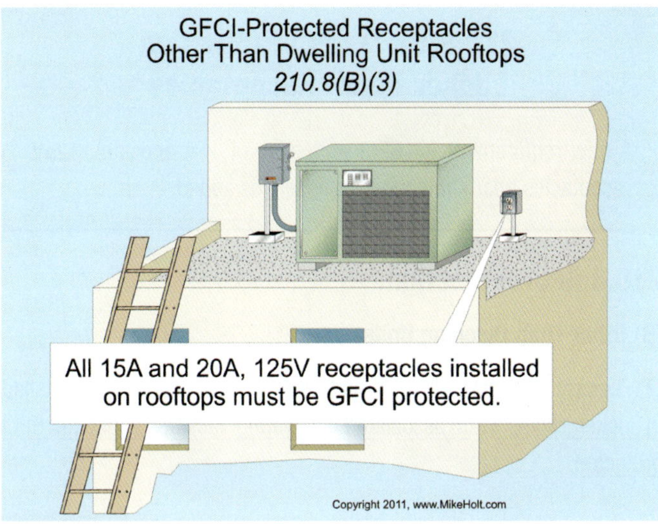

Figure 210–11

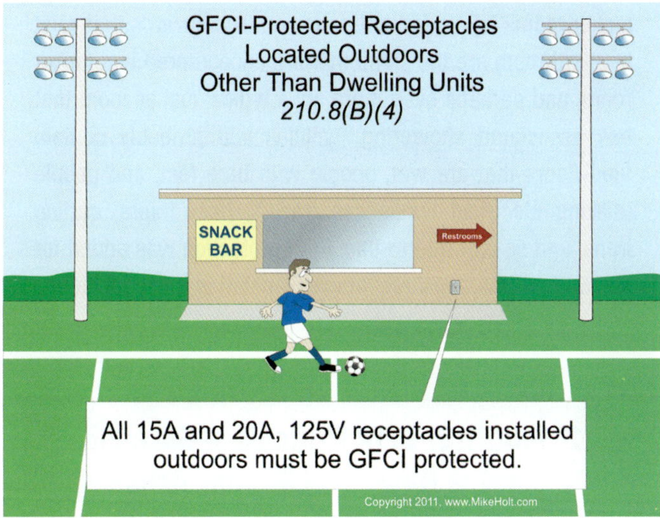

Figure 210–12

Ex 1 to (3) and (4): GFCI protection isn't required for a receptacle that's supplied by a branch circuit dedicated to fixed electric snow-melting or deicing or pipeline and vessel heating equipment, if the receptacle isn't readily accessible and the equipment or receptacle has ground-fault protection of equipment (GFPE) [426.28 and 427.22].

ANALYSIS: While the general rule of 210.8(A)(3) and (B)(4) requires GFCI protection for all 15A and 20A, 125V receptacles located outdoors, the *NEC* recognizes that some types of equipment need GFPE protection rather than Class A GFCI protection [Article 100]. For quite some time this *Code* exception has applied to receptacle outlets used for snow-melting and deicing equipment, but it didn't address pipeline and vessel heating that's required to have GFPE by 427.22. This revision resolves the dilemma of which type of protection is allowed for these products.

This *NEC* revision also changes the term "dedicated branch circuit" to "branch circuit dedicated to." Many *Code* users interpreted the phrase "dedicated branch circuit" as meaning that the circuit couldn't have more than one outlet on it. The revision clarifies that as long as the circuit serves only the equipment specified in this section, it can have as many outlets as necessary.

210.8(B)(5) Exception, GFCI Protection Receptacles Near Sinks

A revision to this requirement increases the locations of GFCI-protected outlets in patient care areas of health care facilities.

210.8 GFCI Protection.

(B) Other Than Dwelling Units.

(5) Sinks. All 15A and 20A, 125V receptacles installed within 6 ft of the outside edge of a sink must be GFCI protected. Figure 210–13

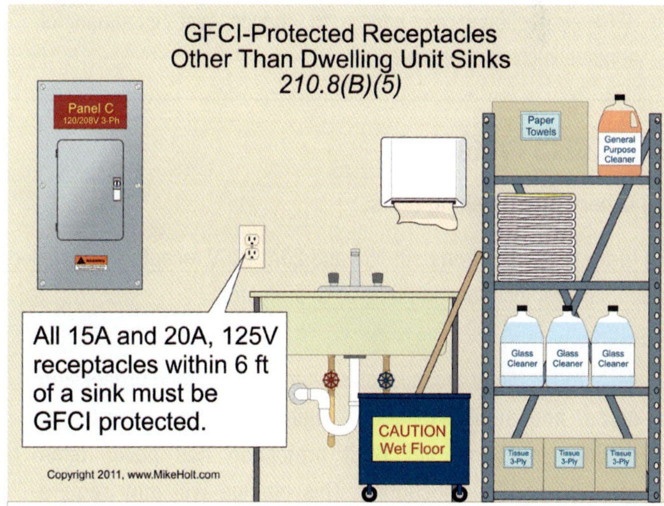

Figure 210–13

Ex 1: In industrial laboratories, receptacles used to supply equipment where removal of power would introduce a greater hazard aren't required to be GFCI protected.

Ex 2: Receptacles located in patient bed locations of general care or critical care areas of health care facilities aren't required to be GFCI protected.

ANALYSIS: A change to the 2008 *NEC* required GFCI protection near all sinks in nondwelling occupancies. One of the concerns raised by this change was the need for life support equipment to be supplied by an outlet that isn't GFCI protected. Due to this, an exception was written that exempted all receptacles in patient care areas (other than bathrooms). While this certainly took care of the life support issue, it also removed GFCI protection from all other equipment that isn't life safety oriented. For example, the many sinks found in a dental office were exempt, despite the fact that the patient is often very vulnerable to electric shock due to the invasive nature of many dental procedures. This change more accurately expresses the concerns of the medical community, while adding protection to equipment that isn't essential to life support.

210.8(B)(6) GFCI Protection Receptacles Indoor Wet Location

GFCI protection was added to indoor wet locations of nondwelling occupancies.

210.8 GFCI Protection.

(B) Other Than Dwelling Units.

(6) Indoor wet locations. All 15A and 20A, 125V receptacles installed indoors in wet locations must be GFCI protected.

ANALYSIS: Many areas, such as car washes, food processing areas, and similar locations share the same hazards as outdoor locations, yet GFCI protection has never been required in these locations. This change will now require that these areas receive the same protection against electric shock as required for outdoor locations.

It's worth noting that this change was accepted without any documented incidents cited.

210.8(B)(7) GFCI Protection Locker Room Receptacles

A new requirement for GFCI protection of 15A and 20A, 125V receptacles near showering facilities was added.

210.8 GFCI Protection.

(B) Other Than Dwelling Units.

(7) Locker Rooms. All 15A and 20A, 125V receptacles installed in locker rooms with associated showering facilities must be GFCI protected.

ANALYSIS: Requirements for GFCI protection of receptacles in bathrooms have been in place for a very long time. In Article 100, a bathroom is very clearly defined, and not all locker rooms fall under that definition. The hazards that exist in a bathroom are the same that are encountered in a locker room, and perhaps even more so. A typical locker room that has associated showering facilities will probably contain tiled floors that are wet, people with bare feet, and people utilizing electrical appliances (razors, hair dryers, curling irons, and so on). Due to this, GFCI protection was added for all 15A and 20A, 125V receptacles located in these facilities.

210.8(B)(8) GFCI Protection Garages, Service Bays, and Similar Areas

A new requirement adds GFCI protection for receptacles located in nondwelling unit garages that don't fall under the scope of Article 511.

210.8 GFCI Protection.

(B) Other Than Dwelling Units.

(8) Garages. All 15A and 20A, 125V receptacles installed in garages, service bays, and similar areas where electrical diagnostic equipment, electrical hand tools, or portable lighting equipment are to be used must be GFCI protected. Figure 210–14

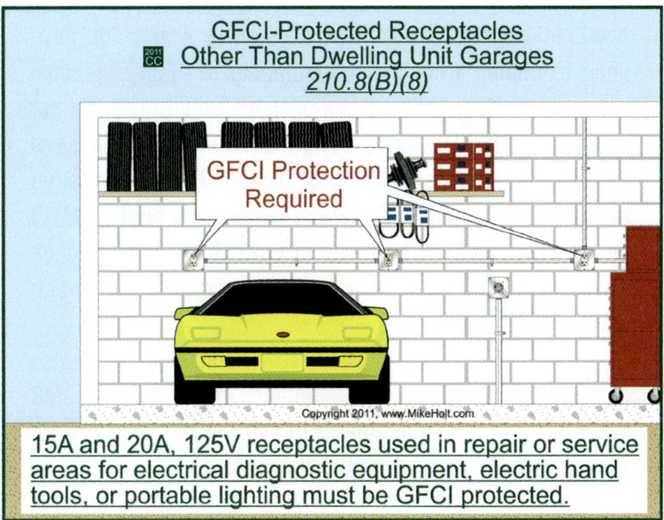

Figure 210–14

ANALYSIS: This change expands GFCI protection requirements to all commercial garages. Article 511 applies only to those garages "in which volatile flammable liquids or flammable gases are used for fuel or power." A facility that repairs only diesel powered vehicles doesn't fall under the requirements of Article 511, because diesel fuel is a combustible liquid, not a flammable liquid. Although the same electric shock hazards exist regardless of the fuel type employed, areas that use only diesel fuel didn't require GFCI protection in previous editions of the *Code*.

210.12 Arc-Fault Circuit-Interrupter Protection for Dwelling Units

Changes have been made to this section to address fire alarm circuiting, Type MC Cables, concrete-encased raceways, and branch circuit extensions or modifications.

210.12 Arc-Fault Circuit-Interrupter Protection for Dwelling Units.

Author's Comment: The combination AFCI is a circuit breaker that protects downstream branch-circuit wiring as well as cord sets and power-supply cords; an outlet branch circuit AFCI (receptacle) is installed as the first outlet in a branch circuit to protect downstream branch-circuit wiring, cord sets, and power-supply cords.

(A) Where Required. All 15A or 20A, 120V branch circuits in dwelling units supplying outlets in family rooms, dining rooms, living rooms, parlors, libraries, dens, bedrooms, sunrooms, recreation rooms, closets, hallways, or similar rooms or areas must be protected by a listed AFCI device of the combination type. **Figure 210–15**

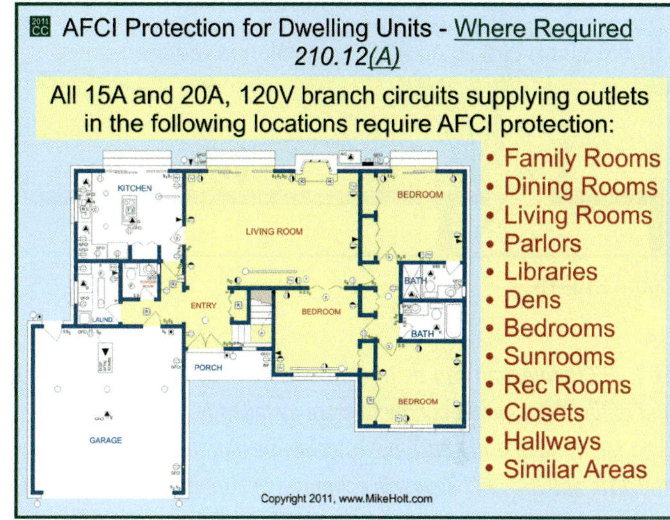

Figure 210–15

Author's Comment: The 120V circuit limitation means AFCI protection isn't required for equipment rated 230V, such as a baseboard heater or room air conditioner. For more information, visit www.MikeHolt.com, click on the "Search" link, and search for "AFCI."

Note 3: See 760.41(B) and 760.121(B) for power-supply requirements for fire alarm systems.

Author's Comment: Smoke alarms connected to a 15A or 20A circuit of a dwelling unit must be AFCI protected if the smoke alarm is located in one of the areas specified in 210.12(A). The exemption from AFCI protection for the "fire alarm circuit" contained in 760.41(B) and 760.121(B) doesn't apply to the single- or multiple-station smoke alarm circuit typically installed in dwelling unit bedroom areas. This is because a smoke alarm circuit isn't a fire alarm circuit as defined in NFPA 72, *National Fire Alarm Code*. Unlike single- or multiple-station smoke alarms, fire alarm systems are managed by a fire alarm control panel. **Figure 210–16**

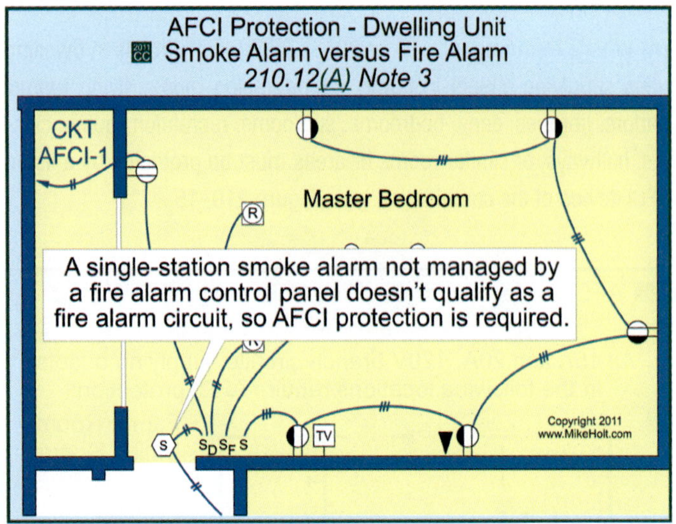

Figure 210–16

Ex 1: AFCI protection can be of the branch-circuit type located at the first outlet if the circuit conductors are installed in RMC, IMC, EMT, or Type MC or steel armored Type AC cable meeting the requirements of 250.118, and the AFCI device is contained in a metal outlet or junction box.

Ex 2: Where a listed metal or nonmetallic conduit or tubing is encased in not less than 2 in. of concrete for the portion of the branch circuit between the branch-circuit overcurrent device and the first outlet, an outlet branch-circuit AFCI at the first outlet is permitted to provide protection for the remaining portion of the branch circuit.

Ex 3: AFCI protection can be omitted for an individual branch circuit to a fire alarm system in accordance with 760.41(B) and 760.121(B), if the circuit conductors are installed in RMC, IMC, EMT, or steel sheath Type AC or MC cable that qualifies as an equipment grounding conductor in accordance with 250.118, with metal outlet and junction boxes.

(B) Branch-Circuit Extensions or Modifications—Dwelling Units. Where branch-circuit wiring is modified, replaced, or extended in any of the areas specified in 210.12(A), the branch circuit must be protected by:

(1) A listed combination AFCI located at the origin of the branch circuit; or

(2) A listed outlet branch circuit AFCI located at the first receptacle outlet of the existing branch circuit.

ANALYSIS: Fire alarm systems covered by Article 760 have been exempted from the requirements of AFCI protection, but the circuiting of the those systems was previously not addressed. This inadvertently left a loophole for installers to incorporate other outlets in areas specified by 210.12 on the same circuit as the fire alarm system and omit the AFCI protection required for circuits in those areas. This change also includes MC cable as a permitted wiring method when employing this exception.

Section 210.12 Ex 1 has been revised to allow MC cables as one of the allowable wiring methods in the exception. MC cable meeting the requirements of 250.118 has been proven safe, so this allowance seems fair enough.

New to the *NEC* is 210.12(A) Ex 2. Concrete encased raceways obviously provide an increased level of protection for circuit conductors, so a new exception was added to allow such raceways to be installed without AFCI protection at the source, provided that there's an outlet type AFCI installed at the first outlet of the circuit.

Also new to the *NEC* is subsection (B), dealing with branch-circuit extensions or modifications in existing buildings. The question of what to do with existing buildings in regard to AFCI protection has been prevalent ever since AFCI requirements were added to the *Code* in 1999. With this change it's clear that when branch-circuit wiring is extended or modified, some level of AFCI protection will be required.

PART II. BRANCH-CIRCUIT RATING

210.19(A)(1) Branch-Circuit Sizing

The exception allowing smaller neutral conductors for continuous loads was removed.

ANALYSIS: The 2008 *NEC* introduced an allowance for grounded conductors to be sized at 100 percent of the continuous load, as opposed to the traditional 125 percent for both feeder circuits and branch circuits. Because this allowance applied to conductors that are grounded and not necessarily neutral, it could have resulted in a smaller grounded conductor in a corner grounded system than is typically required. The exception allowing this oddity has been removed.

210.25(B) Common Area Branch Circuits

Editorial revisions to the rule regarding common area branch circuits have been made.

210.25 Branch Circuits in Buildings with Multiple Occupancies.

(B) Common Area Branch Circuits. Branch circuits installed for public or common areas of a multi-occupancy building aren't permitted to originate from equipment that supplies an individual dwelling unit or tenant space.

Author's Comment: This rule prohibits common area branch circuits from being supplied from an individual dwelling unit or tenant space to prevent common area circuits from being turned off by tenants or by the utility due to nonpayment of electric bills.

ANALYSIS: The 2008 *NEC* specified that branch circuits required for common purposes of multifamily or multi-occupancy buildings (burglar alarm, central lighting, communications, and so forth) must be supplied from a panel that serves only similar functions. The use of the word "required" made some *Code* users believe that only circuits required by the *NEC* or other legal requirements fell under the requirements of this section. The word "required" has therefore been replaced with "installed" to remedy this issue.

PART III. REQUIRED OUTLETS

210.52(A) Dwelling Unit Receptacle Outlet Requirements

A change to the wall spacing requirements has been made to address fixed cabinets, and the wall spacing requirements have been clarified.

210.52 Dwelling Unit Receptacle Outlet Requirements.

(A) General Requirements—Dwelling Unit. A receptacle outlet must be installed in every kitchen, family room, dining room, living room, sunroom, parlor, library, den, bedroom, recreation room, and similar room or area in accordance with (1), (2), and (3): Figure 210–17

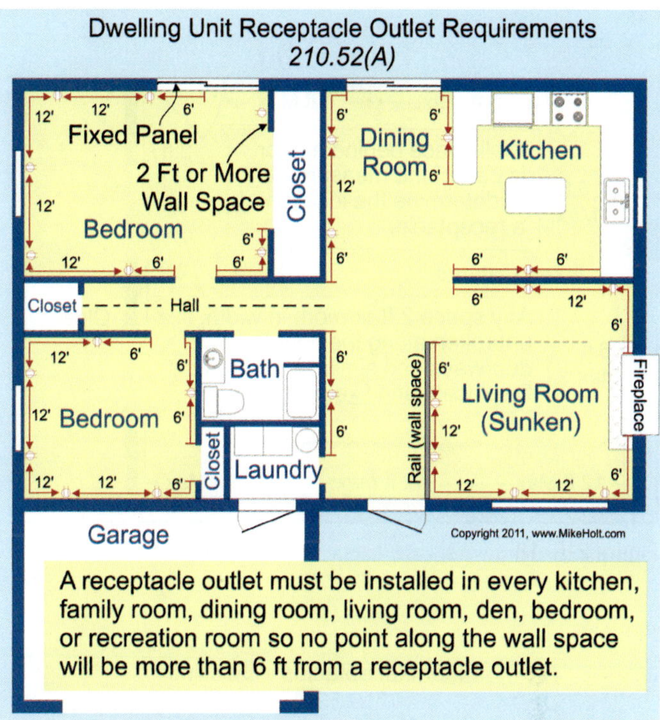

Figure 210–17

(1) Receptacle Placement. A receptacle outlet must be installed so that no point along the floor line of any wall is more than 6 ft, measured horizontally along the floor line, from a receptacle outlet.

Author's Comment: The purpose of this rule is to ensure that a general-purpose receptacle is conveniently located to reduce the chance that an extension cord will be used.

(2) Definition of Wall Space.

(1) Any space 2 ft or more in width, unbroken along the floor line by doorways and similar openings, fireplaces, and fixed cabinets. Figure 210–18

(2) The space occupied by fixed panels in exterior walls.

(3) The space occupied by fixed room dividers, such as freestanding bar-type counters or guard rails.

(3) Floor Receptacle Outlets. Floor receptacle outlets aren't counted as the required receptacle wall outlet if they're located more than 18 in. from the wall. Figure 210–19

(4) Countertop Receptacles. Receptacles installed for countertop surfaces as required by 210.52(C), can't be used to meet the receptacle requirements for wall space as required by 210.52(A). Figure 210–20

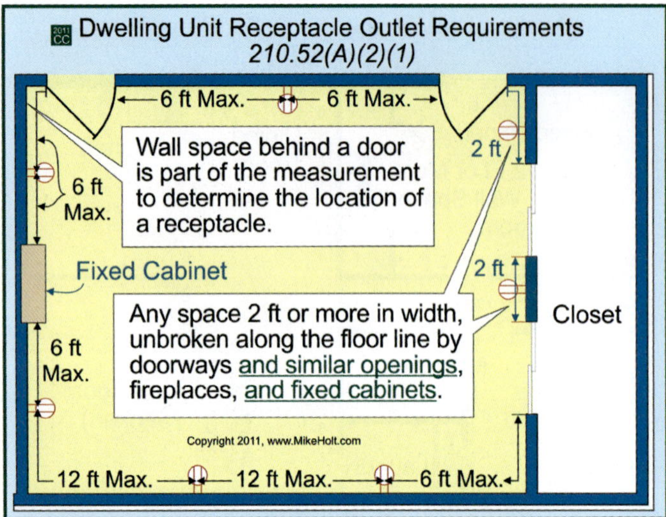

Figure 210–18

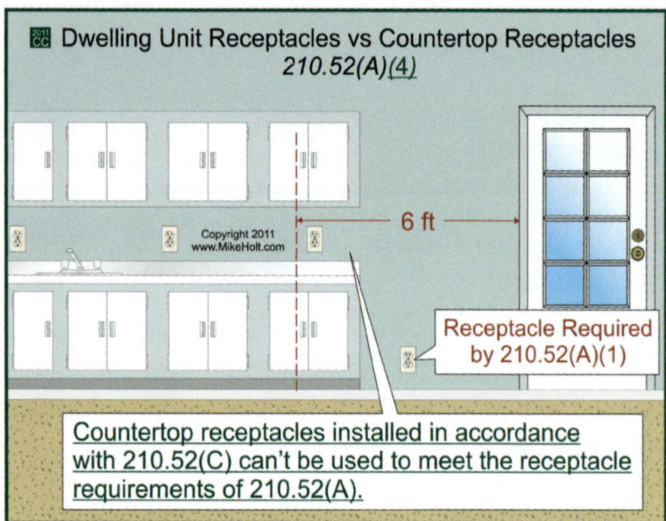

Figure 210–20

Figure 210–19

ANALYSIS: The substantiation for the change to (A)(2)(1) is to deal with kitchen cabinets. Obviously the *Code* doesn't expect a receptacle installed in front of lower kitchen cabinets to satisfy the wall space receptacles of this section. While this makes sense, and seems to be a clarification that's worth making, it also brings with it technical changes as well. For example, built-in book cases often consume entire walls in dwelling unit libraries, studies, offices, and similar rooms. With this change, it seems receptacles are no longer required in such book cases.

Changes made to 210.52(A)(4) have been made to address a fairly odd situation. It's quite common for a kitchen peninsular or island countertop to create a "wall" between the kitchen and dining room (or other room). When this occurs, 210.52(A)(1) requires receptacles on the back of the peninsula or island in order to accommodate the dining area. In previous *NEC* editions, the required countertop receptacle could be used to satisfy this requirement, provided the receptacle wasn't higher than 5½ ft above the floor [210.52(4)]. This made for a *Code* compliant installation, but also an invitation to have cords stretched across the dining room in order to reach the elevated receptacle. This change eliminates that loophole from the *NEC*, and clearly states that the required countertop receptacles required by 210.52(C) are in addition to any receptacles required in other parts of 210.52(A).

210.52(C) Countertop Receptacles

Multiple changes have been made to this section, which deals with dwelling unit kitchen countertop receptacle requirements. Among others were a reorganization of the section, and added provisions for receptacles installed *in* a countertop, as opposed to *above* a countertop.

210.52 Dwelling Unit Receptacle Outlet Requirements.

(C) Countertop Receptacles. In kitchens, pantries, breakfast rooms, dining rooms, and similar areas of dwelling units, receptacle outlets for countertop spaces must be installed according to (1) through (5) below.

(1) Wall Countertop Spaces. A receptacle outlet must be installed for each kitchen and dining area countertop wall space 1 ft or wider, and receptacles must be placed so that no point along the countertop wall space is more than 2 ft, measured horizontally, from a receptacle outlet. Figure 210–21

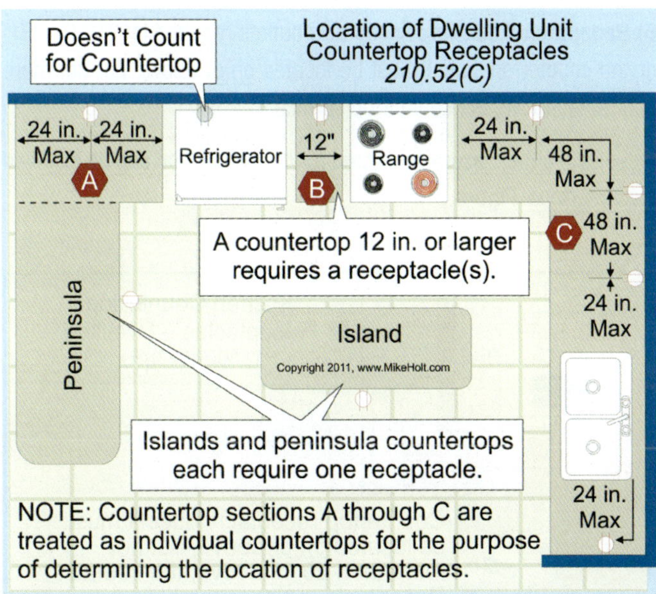

Figure 210–21

Ex: A receptacle outlet isn't required on a wall directly behind a range, counter-mounted cooking unit, or sink, in accordance with Figure 210.52(C)(1) in the NEC. Figure 210–22

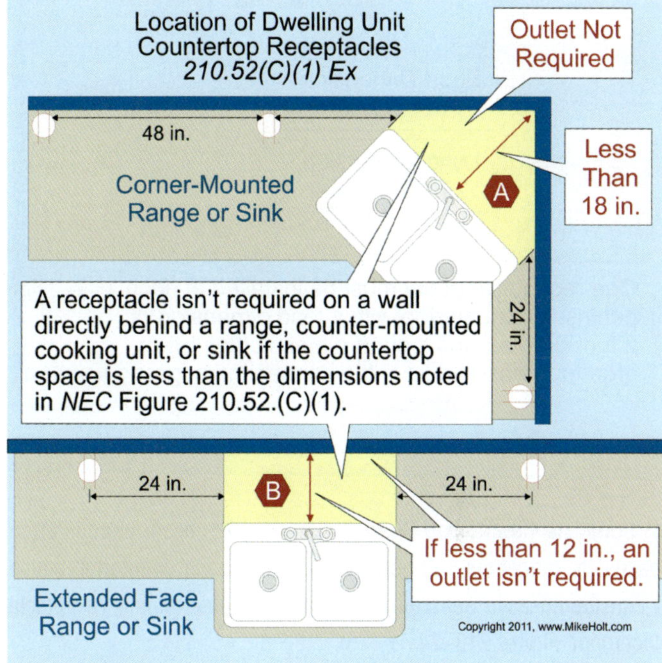

Figure 210–22

Author's Comment: If the countertop space behind a range or sink is larger than the dimensions noted in Figure 210.52(C)(1) of the *NEC*, then a GFCI-protected receptacle must be installed in that space. This is because, for all practical purposes, if there's sufficient space for an appliance, an appliance will be placed there.

(2) Island Countertop Spaces. At least one receptacle outlet must be installed at each island countertop space with a long dimension of 2 ft or more, and a short dimension of 1 ft or more.

(3) Peninsular Countertop Spaces. At least one receptacle outlet must be installed at each peninsular countertop with a long dimension of 2 ft or more, and a short dimension of 1 ft or more, measured from the connecting edge. Figure 210–23

Author's Comment: The *Code* doesn't require more than one receptacle outlet in an island or peninsular countertop space, regardless of the length of the countertop, unless the countertop is broken as described in 210.52(C)(4).

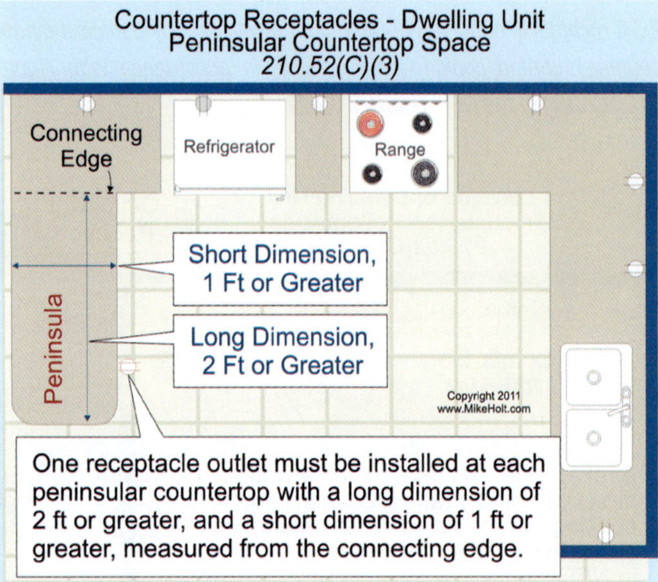

Figure 210–23

(4) Separate Countertop Spaces. When breaks occur in countertop spaces for rangetops, refrigerators, or sinks, each countertop space is considered as a separate countertop for determining receptacle placement. Figure 210–24

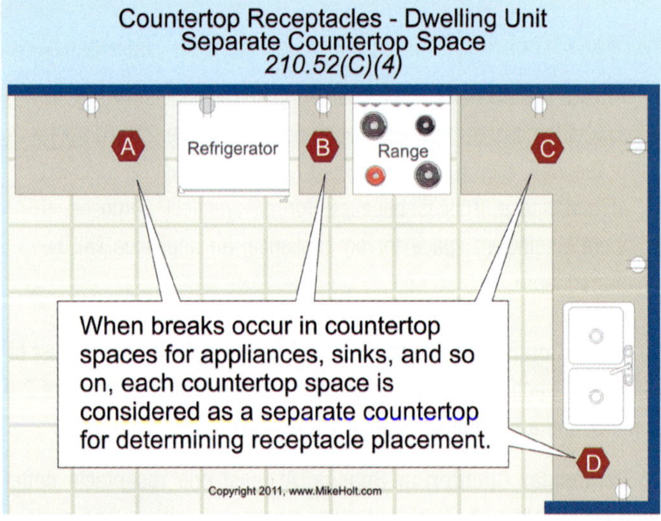

Figure 210–24

If a range, counter-mounted cooking unit, or sink is installed in an island or peninsular countertop, and the depth of the counter behind the range, counter-mounted cooking unit, or sink is less than 12 in., the countertop space is considered to be two separate countertop spaces. Figure 210–25

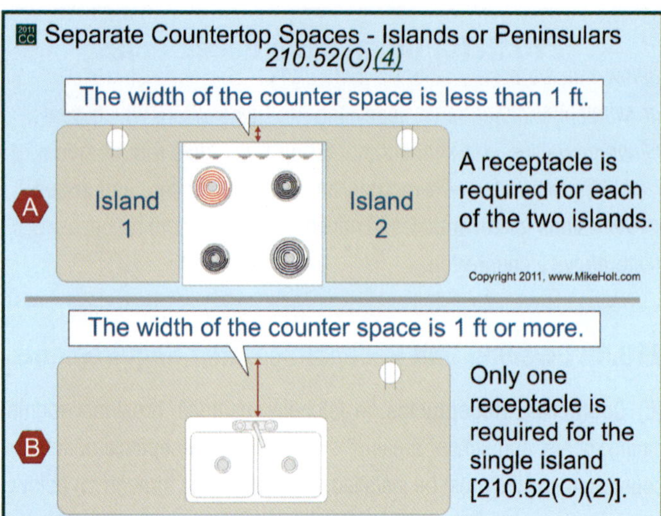

Figure 210–25

Author's Comment: GFCI protection is required for all 15A and 20A, 125V receptacles that supply kitchen countertop surfaces [210.8(A)(6)].

(5) Receptacle Location. Receptacle outlets required by 210.52(C)(1) for the countertop space must be located on or above, but not more than 20 in. above, the countertop surface.

Receptacle outlet assemblies listed for the application can be installed in countertops. Figure 210–26

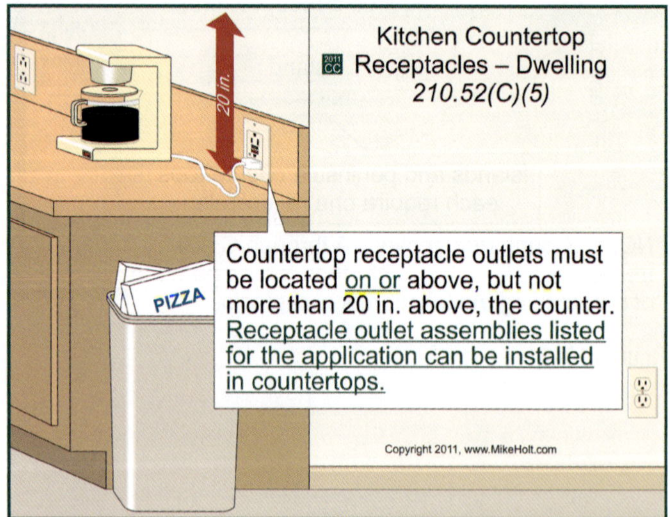

Figure 210–26

Note: Receptacles must not be installed in a face-up position in countertops or similar work surface areas in a dwelling unit [406.5(E)].

Ex: The receptacle outlet for the countertop space can be installed below the countertop only for construction for the physically impaired or when wall space or a backsplash isn't available, such as in an island or peninsular counter. Under these conditions, the required receptacle(s) must be located no more than 1 ft below the countertop surface and no more than 6 in. from the countertop edge, measured horizontally. Figure 210–27

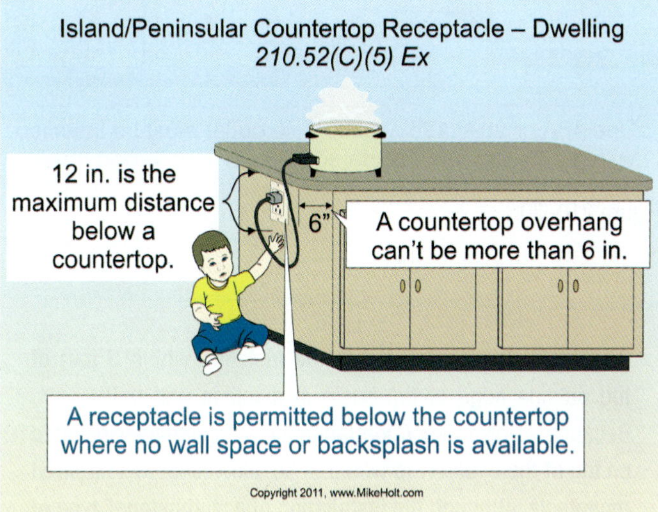

Figure 210–27

Receptacle outlets rendered not readily accessible by appliances fastened in place, located in an appliance garage, behind sinks, or rangetops [210.52(C)(1) Ex], or supplying appliances that occupy dedicated space don't count as the required countertop receptacles.

Author's Comment: An "appliance garage" is an enclosed area on the countertop where an appliance can be stored and hidden from view when not in use. If a receptacle is installed inside an appliance garage, it doesn't count as a required countertop receptacle outlet.

ANALYSIS: Section 210.52(C)(4) provides the *Code* user with the requirements for countertop spaces that are separated by sinks and cooking appliances. The opening statement of 210.52 also contained provisions for these countertops, forcing the *NEC* user to go back and forth between the two subsections to figure out what the rules were for these installations. This change takes all of the requirements from 210.52(C) and puts them into 210.52(C)(4), a more appropriate place. Previous editions of the *NEC* have stated that the required countertop receptacles must be above the countertop. Although subtle, this effectively prohibited receptacles from being installed in the countertop. This change recognizes this fact, and now allows for receptacle assemblies, if listed for the application, to be installed in the countertop.

A new product provides a "pop-up" receptacle for kitchen or bathroom countertops with a "tombstone" profile so it isn't face-up in the countertop, but will rotate down into the countertop surface to become concealed in a face-down position, leaving an exposed finished surface such as stainless steel or a finish to match the countertops.

A new Informational Note refers the *Code* user to 406.5(E), which prohibits such a receptacle from being installed in the face-up position.

210.52(D) Bathroom Receptacles

This subsection has been changed to allow a receptacle on top of the bathroom countertop surface. A new Informational Note has also been added in regard to such an installation.

210.52 Dwelling Unit Receptacle Outlet Requirements.

(D) Dwelling Unit Bathroom Receptacles. In dwelling units, not less than one 15A or 20A, 125V receptacle outlet must be installed within 3 ft from the outside edge of each bathroom basin, Figure 210–28. The receptacle outlet must be located on a wall or partition adjacent to the basin counter surface, or on the side or face of the basin cabinet not more than 12 in. below the countertop. Figure 210–29

Receptacle outlet assemblies listed for the application can be installed in countertops.

Note: Receptacles must not be installed in a face-up position in countertops or similar work surface areas in a dwelling unit [406.5(E)].

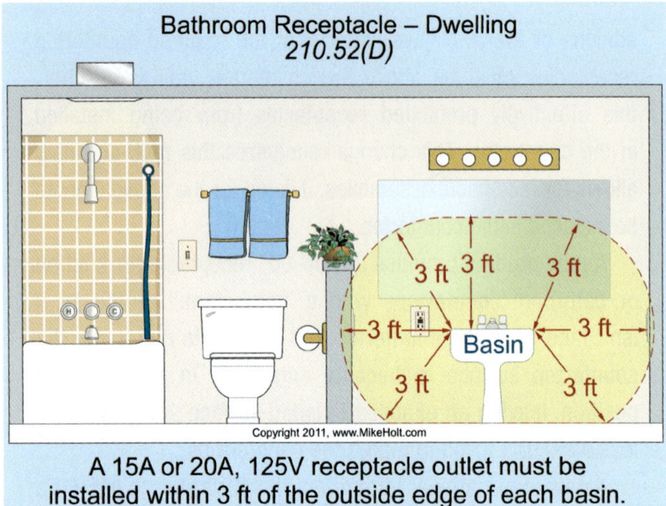

Figure 210–28

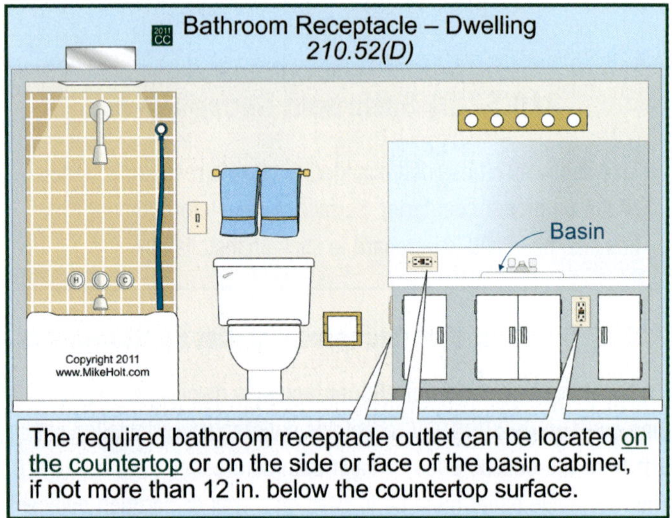

Figure 210–29

Author's Comments:

- One receptacle outlet can be located between two basins to meet this requirement, but only if it's located within 3 ft of the outside edge of each basin. **Figure 210–30**
- The bathroom receptacles must be GFCI protected [210.8(A)(1)].

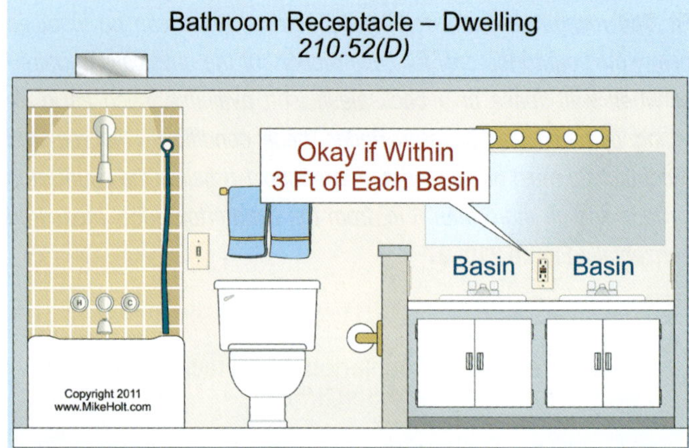

Figure 210–30

ANALYSIS: A receptacle must be installed within 3 feet of the outside edge of the basin in dwelling unit bathrooms. Because of previous *Code* language, a receptacle installed on top of the countertop wouldn't be allowed as this required receptacle. Although the installation of a "tombstone" type of outlet would be rather uncommon in a bathroom, it presents no real safety hazard and therefore should be allowed.

A new product provides a "pop-up" receptacle for kitchen or bathroom countertops with a "tombstone" profile so it isn't face-up in the countertop, but it will rotate down into the countertop surface to become concealed in a face-down position, leaving an exposed finished surface such as stainless steel or a finish to match the countertops.

A new Informational Note refers the *NEC* user to 406.5(E), which prohibits such a receptacle from being installed in the face-up position.

210.52(E)(3) Other Receptacles

The exception for receptacle placement at small decks and patios has been deleted.

210.52 Dwelling Unit Receptacle Outlet Requirements.

(E) Dwelling Unit Outdoor Receptacles.

(1) One- and Two-Family Dwellings. Two GFCI-protected 15A or 20A, 125V receptacle outlets that are accessible while standing at grade level must be installed outdoors for each dwelling unit, one at the front and one at the back, no more than 6½ ft above grade. Figure 210–31

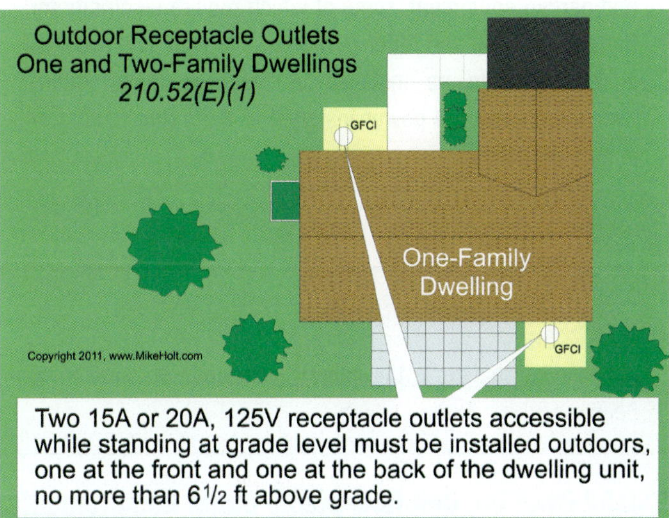

Figure 210–31

(2) Multifamily Dwelling. Each dwelling unit of a multifamily dwelling that has an individual entrance at grade level must have at least one GFCI-protected 15A or 20A, 125V receptacle outlet accessible from grade level located not more than 6½ ft above grade. Figure 210–32

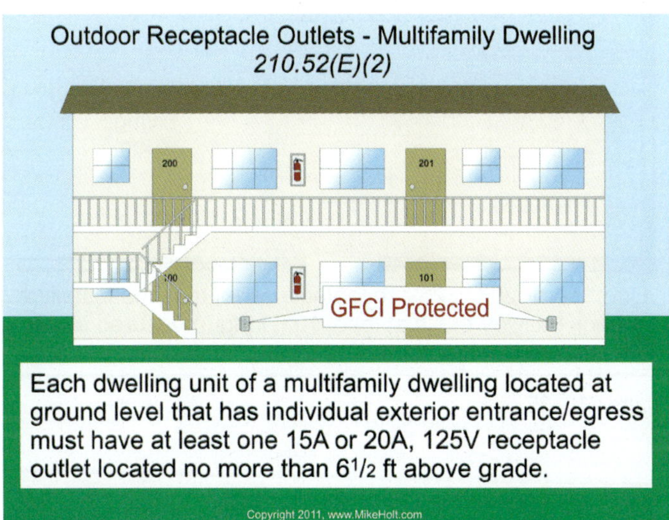

Figure 210–32

(3) Balconies, Decks, and Porches. At least one 15A or 20A, 125V receptacle must be installed within the perimeter and not more than 6½ ft above the balcony, deck, or porch surface that's accessible from the inside of a dwelling unit. Figure 210–33

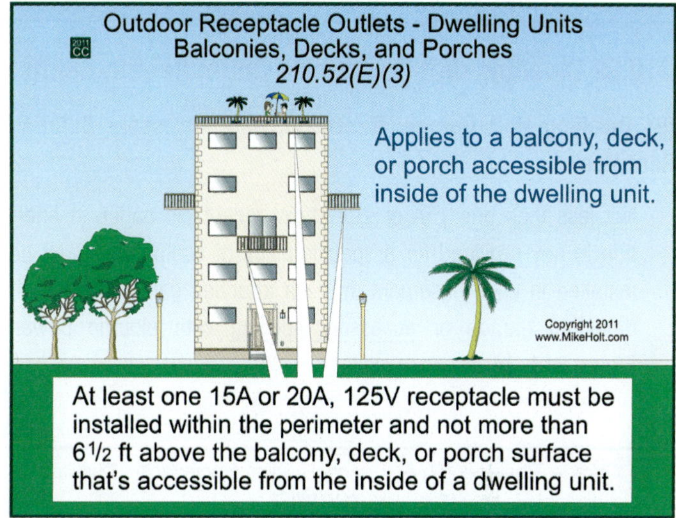

Figure 210–33

Author's Comment: These receptacles must be GFCI protected [210.8(A)(3)].

ANALYSIS: There are many small decks and patios that can accommodate only a single person engaged in no activity other than looking at something. The *Code* has recognized this in the past by omitting decks and patios smaller than 20 square feet from the outdoor receptacle requirement. Not all small decks and patios are used for leisure activity, however, and the *NEC* has recognized many home owners use receptacles in these small decks and patios for installing holiday lighting. The concern that many people have is that owners will use these small decks as nothing more than an accessible place to install holiday lighting, and stretch extension cords through doorways to provide power to them, resulting in an obvious violation of 400.8(3). It's also worth noting that using cords in such a manner will result in a lack of GFCI protection as well.

210.52(G) and (G)(1) Basement, Garage, and Accessory Building Receptacles

A 15A or 20A, 125V receptacle is now required in dwelling unit accessory buildings.

210.52 Dwelling Unit Receptacle Outlet Requirements.

(G) Dwelling Unit Garage, Basement, and Accessory Building Receptacles.

(1) Not less than one 15A or 20A, 125V receptacle outlet, in addition to any provided for a specific piece of equipment, must be installed in each basement, in each attached garage, and each detached garage or accessory building with electric power. Figure 210–34

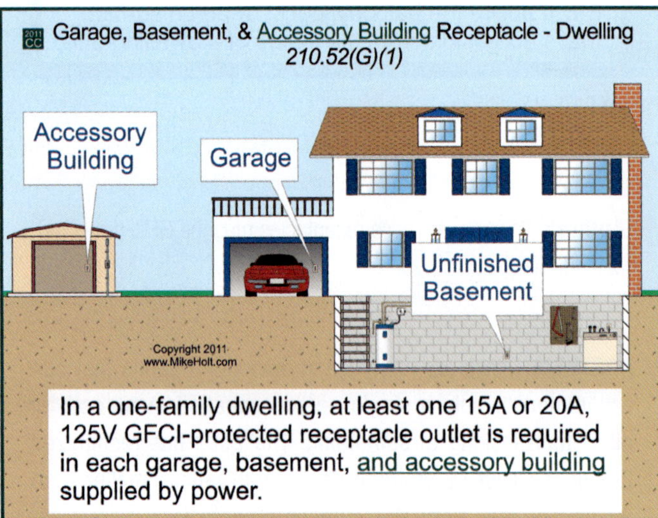

Figure 210–34

Author's Comment: GFCI protection is required for all 15 or 20A, 125V receptacles installed in unfinished basements [210.8(A)(5)], garages and accessory buildings [210.8(A)(2)] of dwelling units.

ANALYSIS: The *NEC* has long required a 15A or 20A, 125V receptacle for detached dwelling unit garages that are provided with electric power. This *Code* change recognizes the fact that many accessory buildings to dwellings aren't garages, but rather workshops, storage sheds, and similar buildings. Storage sheds are often used to house lawn and garden equipment, some of which require electricity for battery charging and other purposes. The *NEC* now requires a receptacle to be installed in these buildings whenever there's electric power installed in them (for lighting or similar purposes).

210.52(H) Hallway Receptacles

An editorial change to the hallway provisions of 210.52 has been made.

210.52 Dwelling Unit Receptacle Outlet Requirements.

(H) Dwelling Unit Hallway Receptacles. One 15A or 20A, 125V receptacle outlet must be installed in each hallway that's at least 10 ft long, measured along the centerline of the hallway without passing through a doorway. Figure 210–35

Figure 210–35

ANALYSIS: The term "hall" isn't defined in any known dictionary, whereas the term "hallway" is. This simple change is intended to use a more accurate word than "hall." No technical changes to the requirements have been made to this section.

210.52(I) Foyer Receptacles

A new requirement to provide receptacles in foyers was added.

210.52 Dwelling Unit Receptacle Outlet Requirements.

(I) Foyer Receptacles. Foyers that aren't part of a hallway [210.52(H)] having an area greater than 60 sq ft must have a receptacle located on any wall space 3 ft or more in width and unbroken by doorways, floor to ceiling windows, and similar openings. Figure 210–36

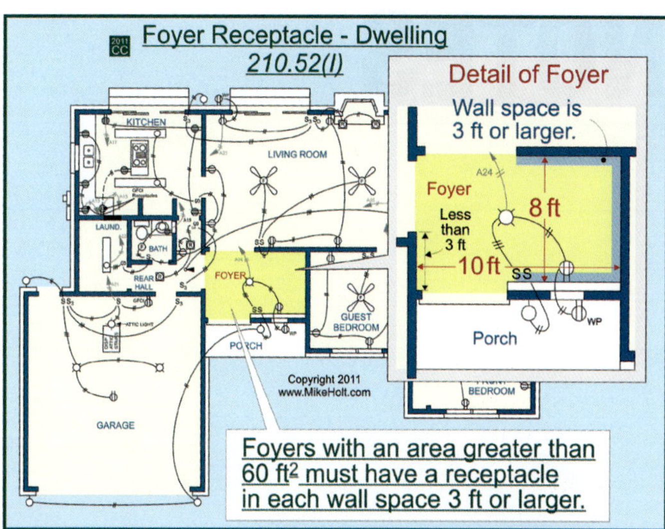

Figure 210–36

ANALYSIS: Newer homes are often built with substantial foyers, some of which can be larger than other rooms of the house. In previous editions of the *Code*, these areas were typically treated as hallways, with only one receptacle being required and only one being installed. This change will now require foyers to have the same receptacle requirements as a bedroom, family room, dining room or similar area. I guess the only question now is...what's a foyer?

NOTES

ARTICLE

215 FEEDERS

INTRODUCTION TO ARTICLE 215—FEEDERS

Article 215 covers the rules for the installation, minimum size, and ampacity of feeders. The requirements for feeders have some similarities to those for branch circuits, but in some ways, feeders bear a resemblance to service conductors. It's important to understand the distinct differences between these three types of circuits in order to correctly apply the *Code* requirements.

Feeders are the conductors between the service equipment, the separately derived system, or other supply source and the final branch-circuit overcurrent device. Conductors past the final overcurrent device protecting the circuit and the outlet are branch-circuit conductors and fall within the scope of Article 210 [Article 100 Definitions].

Service conductors are the conductors from the service point of the electric utility to the service disconnecting means [Article 100 Definition]. If there's no serving utility, and the electrical power is derived from a generator or other on-site power source, then the conductors from the supply source are defined as feeders and there are no service conductors.

It's easy to be confused between feeder, branch circuit, and service conductors, so it's important to evaluate each installation carefully using the Article 100 Definitions to be sure the correct *Code* rules are followed.

215.2(A)Feeder Conductor Size

The requirements on how to size neutral conductors in feeder circuits have been put into a new subsection.

215.2 Minimum Rating.

(A) Feeder Conductor Size.

(1) Continuous and Noncontinuous Loads. The minimum feeder conductor ampacity, before the application of ambient temperature correction [310.15(B)(2)(a)], conductor bundling adjustment [310.15(B)(3)(a)], or both, must be no less than 125 percent of the continuous load, plus 100 percent of the noncontinuous load, based on the terminal temperature rating ampacities as listed in Table 310.15(B)(16) [110.14(C)]. Figure 215–1

Author's Comment: See 215.3 for the feeder overcurrent device sizing requirements for continuous and noncontinuous loads.

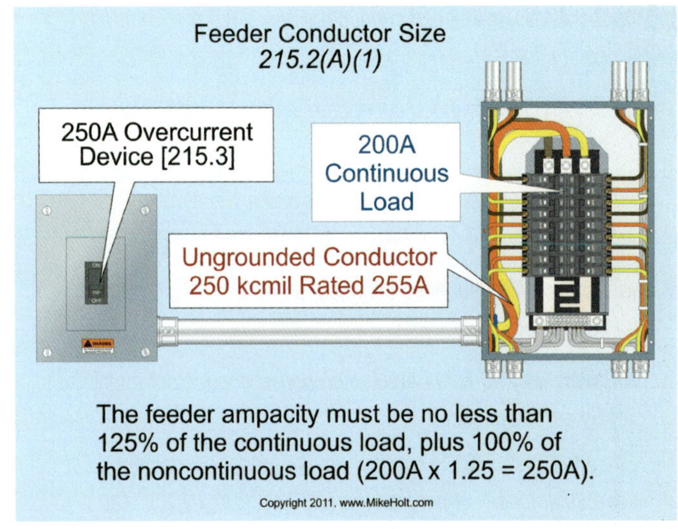

Figure 215–1

Ex 1: If the assembly and the overcurrent device are both listed for operation at 100 percent of its rating, the conductors can be sized at 100 percent of the continuous load.

Author's Comment: Equipment suitable for 100 percent continuous loading is rarely available in ratings under 400A.

Ex 2: Neutral conductors can be sized at 100 percent of the continuous and noncontinuous load. Figure 215–2

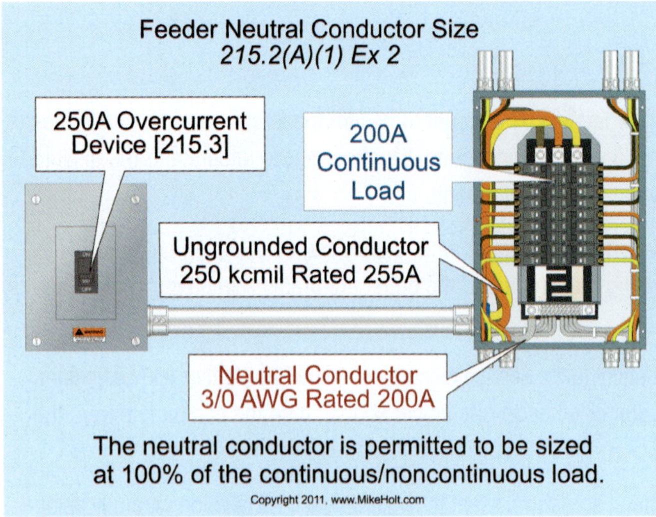

Figure 215–2

Question: *What size feeder conductors are required for a 200A continuous load if the terminals are rated 75°C?*

(a) 2/0 AWG ungrounded conductors and a 1/0 AWG neutral conductor

(b) 3/0 AWG ungrounded conductors and a 1/0 AWG neutral conductor

(c) 4/0 AWG ungrounded conductors and a 1/0 AWG neutral conductor

(d) 250 kcmil ungrounded conductors and a 3/0 AWG neutral conductor

Answer: *(d) 250 kcmil AWG ungrounded conductors and a 3/0 AWG neutral conductor*

Since the load is 200A continuous, the feeder conductors must have an ampacity of not less than 250A (200A x 1.25). The neutral conductor is sized to the 200A continuous load according to the 75°C column of Table 310.15(B)(16). According to the 75°C column of Table 310.15(B)(16), 250 kcmil has an ampacity of 255A, and 3/0 has an ampacity of 200A.

(2) Neutral Conductor Size. The feeder neutral conductor must be sized to carry the maximum unbalanced load, in accordance with 220.61, and must not be smaller than the size listed in 250.122, based on the rating of the feeder overcurrent device. The sizing requirements of 250.122(F) for parallel conductors don't apply.

Question: *What size neutral conductor is required for a feeder consisting of 250 kcmil ungrounded conductors and one neutral conductor protected by a 250A overcurrent device, where the unbalanced load is only 50A, with 75°C terminals?* Figure 215–3

(a) 6 AWG *(b) 4 AWG* *(c) 1/0 AWG* *(d) 3/0 AWG*

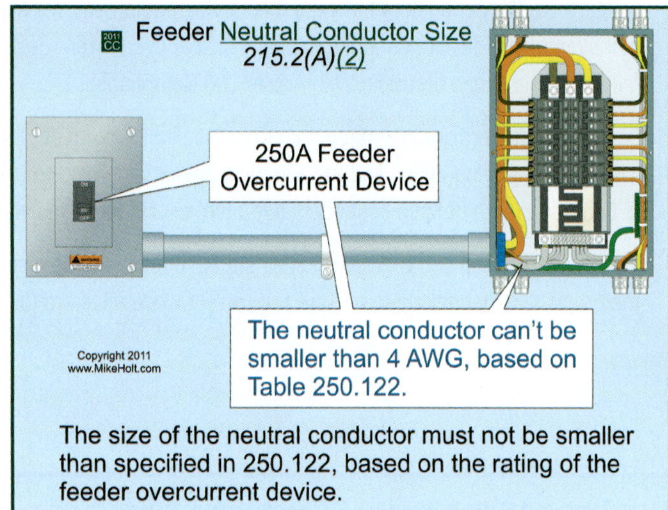

Figure 215–3

Answer: *(b) 4 AWG [based on Table 250.122]*

Table 310.15(B)(16) and 220.61 permit an 8 AWG neutral conductor, rated 50A at 75°C to carry the 50A unbalanced load, but the neutral conductor isn't permitted to be smaller than 4 AWG, as listed in Table 250.122, based on the 250A overcurrent device.

(3) Ampacity Relative to Service Conductors. The feeder conductor ampacity must not be less than that of the service conductors where the feeder conductors carry the total load supplied by service conductors with an ampacity of 55A or less.

(4) Dwelling Unit and Mobile Home Feeder Sizing. Feeder conductors for individual dwelling units or mobile homes need not be larger than service conductors sized to 310.15(B)(7).

Note 2: To provide reasonable efficiency of operation of electrical equipment, feeder conductors should be sized to prevent a voltage drop not to exceed 3 percent. In addition, the maximum total voltage drop on both feeders and branch circuits shouldn't exceed 5 percent.

Note 3: See 210.19(A), Note 4, for voltage drop for branch circuits.

ANALYSIS: Although not technical in nature, this relocation of text is a welcome change. Often when exceptions occur in the middle of a paragraph, *Code* users stop reading the rule. This change remedies that problem by creating a new subsection directly after the two exceptions in this section.

NOTES

Branch-Circuit, Feeder, and SERVICE CALCULATIONS

INTRODUCTION TO ARTICLE 220—BRANCH-CIRCUIT, FEEDER, AND SERVICE CALCULATIONS

This five-part article focuses on the requirements for calculating the minimum size of branch circuit, feeder, and service conductors.

Part I describes the layout of Article 220 and provides a table of where other types of load calculations can be found in the *NEC.* Part II provides requirements for branch-circuit calculations and for specific types of branch circuits. Part III covers the requirements for feeder and service calculations, using what's commonly called the standard method of calculation. Part IV provides optional calculations that can be used in place of the standard calculations provided in Parts II and III—if your installation meets certain requirements. Farm Load Calculations are discussed in Part V of the article.

In many cases, either the standard method (Part III) or the optional method (Part IV) can be used; however, these two methods don't yield identical results. In fact, sometimes these two answers may be diverse enough to call for different service sizes. There's nothing to say that either answer is right or wrong. If taking an exam, read the instructions carefully to be sure which method the test wants you to use. As you work through Article 220, be sure to study the illustrations to help you fully understand it. Also be sure to review the examples in Annex D of the *NEC* to provide more practice with these calculations.

PART I. GENERAL

220.5(B) Fractions of an Ampere

A subtle change to the mathematical rounding provisions has been made.

220.5 Calculations.

(B) Fractions of an Ampere (Rounding Amperes). Calculations can be rounded to the nearest whole number and fractions less than 0.50A can be dropped.

Author's Comment: When do you round—after each calculation, or at the final calculation? The *NEC* isn't specific on this issue, but rounding at each calculation can lead to accumulated errors that can be an issue with the authority having jurisdiction.

Question: *According to 424.3(B), the branch-circuit conductors and overcurrent device for electric space-heating equipment must be sized at no less than 125 percent of the total load. What size conductor is required to supply a 9 kW (37.50A), 240V, single-phase fixed space heater with a 3A blower motor, if the equipment terminals are rated 75°C?* **Figure 220–1**

(a) 10 AWG (b) 8 AWG (c) 6 AWG (d) 4 AWG

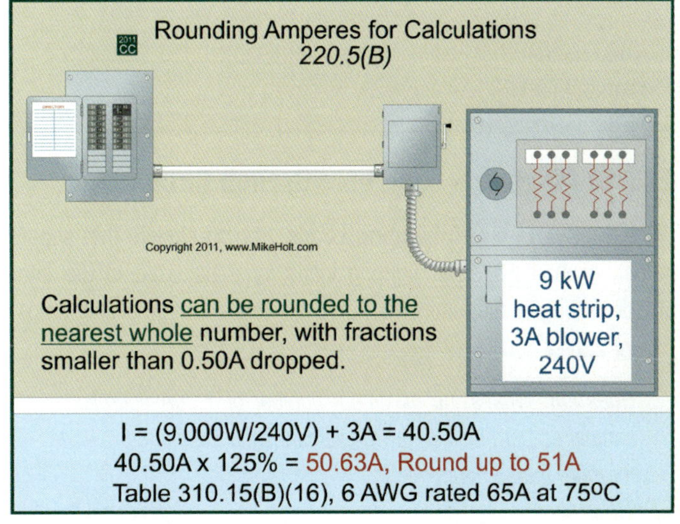

Figure 220–1

Answer: *(c) 6 AWG*

Step 1: Determine the load for the heater:

I = VA/E

I = 9,000 VA/240V

I = 37.50A

Step 2: Conductor size at 125% of the load:
Conductor Size = (37.50A + 3A) x 1.25
Conductor Size = 50.63A, round up to 51A

If we round down, then 8 AWG rated 50A at 75°C can be used, but since we must round up, 6 AWG rated 65A at 75°C is required.

ANALYSIS: Since the 1984 edition of the *NEC*, decimals smaller than 0.50 have been allowed to be rounded down to the nearest whole number. While this seems to be rather straight-forward, some *Code* users were confused by what to do when the decimal is 0.50 or greater. Is the decimal intended to be rounded up, or does the decimal remain in place? With this change it becomes clear that a decimal of 0.50 or more is to be rounded up to the next whole number.

PART II. BRANCH-CIRCUIT LOAD CALCULATIONS

220.18(B) Inductive and LED Lighting Load on Branch Circuit

This section has been revised to address the calculation required for LED luminaires.

220.18 Maximum Load on a Branch Circuit.

(B) Inductive and LED Lighting Loads. Branch circuits that supply inductive and LED driver lighting loads must be sized to the total ampere rating of the luminaire, not to the total wattage of the lamps. **Figure 220–2**

Question: *What's the maximum number of 1.34A fluorescent luminaires permitted on a 20A circuit if the luminaires operate for more than 3 hours?*

(a) 8 (b) 11 (c) 13 (d) 15

Answer: *(b) 11*

The maximum continuous load must not exceed 80 percent of the circuit rating [210.19(A)(1)].

Maximum Load = 20A x 0.80
Maximum Load = 16A

Luminaires on Circuit = 16A/1.34A
Luminaires on Circuit = 11.94 or 11 luminaires

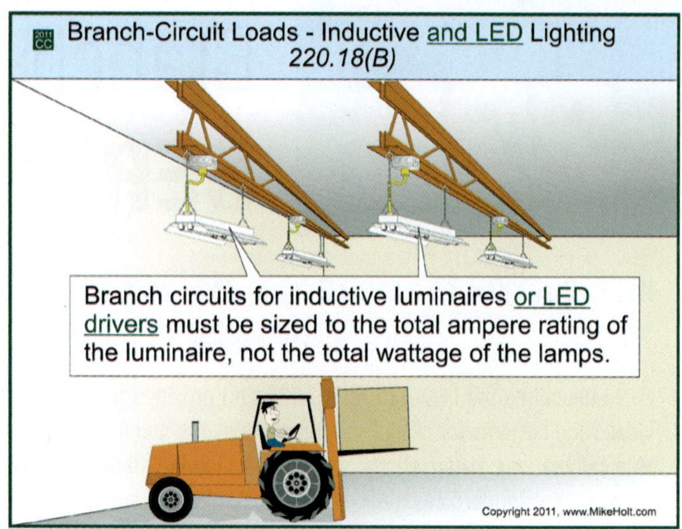

Figure 220–2

Author's Comment: Because of power factor (inductive luminaires), the input VA of each luminaire is 162 VA (120V x 1.34A), which is greater than the 136W (34W x 4 lamps) of the lamps. This may seem complicated, but just remember—size all circuits that supply lighting loads to the ampere rating of the luminaire, not to the wattage of the lamps.

ANALYSIS: Until this *Code* cycle, the *NEC* has never told the user how to address LED luminaires, as they relate to load calculations. The change to the title and text of this section make it clear that LED drivers are to be treated like the ballast of an inductive lighting load. As opposed to using the rating of the lamps, the rating of the LED driver is to be used when performing load calculations.

ARTICLE

225 Outside Branch Circuits AND FEEDERS

INTRODUCTION TO ARTICLE 225—OUTSIDE BRANCH CIRCUITS AND FEEDERS

This article covers the installation requirements for equipment, including conductors, located outdoors on or between buildings, poles, and other structures on the premises. Conductors installed outdoors can serve many purposes such as area lighting, power for outdoor equipment, or providing power to a separate building or structure. It's important to remember that the power supply for buildings or structures aren't always service conductors, but in many cases may be feeders or branch-circuit conductors originating in another building. Be careful not to assume that the conductors supplying power to a building are service conductors until you've identified where the utility service point is and reviewed the Article 100 Definitions for feeders, branch circuits, and service conductors. If they're service conductors, use Article 230. For outside branch circuit and feeder conductors, whatever they feed, use this article.

Section 225.2 provides a listing of other articles that may furnish additional requirements, then Part I of Article 225 goes on to address installation methods intended to provide a secure installation of outside conductors while providing sufficient conductor size, support, attachment means, and maintaining safe clearances.

Part II of the article limits the number of supplies (branch circuits or feeders) permitted to a building or structure and provides rules regarding disconnects for them. These rules include the disconnect rating, construction characteristics, labeling, and where to locate the disconnecting means and the grouping of multiple disconnects.

Outside branch circuits and feeders over 600V are the focus of Part III of Article 225.

PART I. GENERAL

225.18 Clearance for Overhead Conductors

Overhead conductor clearances above railroad tracks have been added.

225.18 Clearance for Overhead Conductors. Overhead conductor spans must maintain vertical clearances as follows:

(1) 10 ft above finished grade, sidewalks, platforms, or projections from which they might be accessible to pedestrians for 120V, 120/208V, 120/240V, or 240V circuits.

(2) 12 ft above residential property and driveways, and those commercial areas not subject to truck traffic for 120V, 120/208V, 120/240V, 240V, 277V, 277/480V, or 480V circuits. Figure 225–1

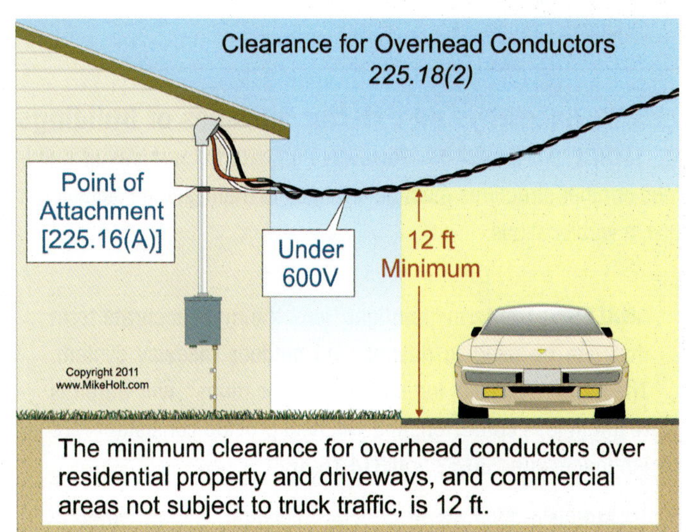

Figure 225–1

(4) 18 ft over public streets, alleys, roads, parking areas subject to truck traffic, driveways on other than residential property, and other areas traversed by vehicles (such as those used for cultivation, grazing, forestry, and orchards).

(5) 24½ ft over track rails of railroads.

Author's Comment: Overhead conductors located above pools, outdoor spas, outdoor hot tubs, diving structures, observation stands, towers, or platforms must be installed in accordance with the clearance requirements in 680.8.

ANALYSIS: The *Code* didn't previously provide any guidance on how to deal with overhead conductors and cables in the proximity of railroad tracks. Railroad tracks are often found in industrial facilities where overhead wiring is common. Standards other than the *NEC* address this issue, such as the *National Electrical Safety Code (NESC)*, which doesn't apply to premises wiring systems. It will be beneficial for industrial facilities to be able to use the *Code* as the governing document rather than having to refer to other standards.

225.22 Raceways on Exterior Surfaces of Buildings or Other Structures

A change in the *Code* language should clarify the requirements for outdoor raceways.

225.22 Raceways on Exterior Surfaces of Buildings or Other Structures. Raceways on exterior surfaces of buildings or other structures must be arranged to drain, and be suitable for use in wet locations.

ANALYSIS: The term "raintight" isn't the most accurate term that can be used to describe an outdoor raceway system. The term "suitable for use in wet locations" will perhaps result in less confusion, and will help provide consistent *NEC* language with 230.53 and 314.15(A).

Author's Comment: A "Wet Location" is an area subject to saturation with water and unprotected locations exposed to weather [Article 100].

225.27 Raceway Seal

A new requirement addresses the sealing of underground raceways.

225.27 Raceway Seal. Underground raceways (used or unused) entering buildings or structures must be sealed or plugged to prevent moisture from contacting energized live parts [300.5(G)].

ANALYSIS: Underground raceways can convey unwanted moisture from one location to another...oftentimes right into electrical panels and switchboards, resulting in obviously unsafe conditions. This change makes for safer underground wiring systems, and also puts the requirements for branch circuits and feeders in harmony with the rules for services found in 230.8.

Author's Comment: Sealing can be accomplished with the use of a putty-like material called duct seal, or a fitting identified for the purpose. A seal of the type required in Chapter 5 for hazardous (classified) locations isn't required.

PART II. BUILDINGS OR OTHER STRUCTURES SUPPLIED BY A FEEDER OR BRANCH CIRCUIT

Article 225, Part II and 225.30

The title of Part II has been revised to reduce confusion.

ANALYSIS: Part II of Article 225 was formerly titled "More than One Building or Other Structure." While this title was, in fact, accurate, it did lead to some unnecessary debate between *Code* users. Anytime a building is supplied by a feeder circuit, Part II of Article 225 applies. Buildings occasionally have a service disconnect that's remote from the building, which results in a building supplied by a feeder circuit. When these remote service disconnects consist of nothing more than a pedestal mounted meter and disconnect, the pedestal is considered a structure, as defined by Article 100. Many people have difficulty calling a pedestal a "structure" and want to argue that Article 225 doesn't apply. A simple solution to this argument has been presented here. By changing the title of Part II, the debate between "structure" and "building" goes away (for the most part), leaving the question only if the building or structure is served by service conductors (Article 230), a feeder circuit (Article 225, Part II), or a branch circuit (Article 225, Part II).

A change to the first sentence of 225.30 was also made to help clarify this concept.

Author's Comment: Article 100 defines a "Structure" as, "That which is built or constructed."

NOTES

ARTICLE

230 SERVICES

INTRODUCTION TO ARTICLE 230—SERVICES

This article covers the installation requirements for service conductors and service equipment. The requirements for service conductors differ from those for other conductors. For one thing, service conductors for one building/structure can't pass through the interior of another building or structure [230.3], and you apply different rules depending on whether a service conductor is inside or outside a building/structure. When are they "outside" as opposed to "inside?" The answer may seem obvious, but Section 230.6 should be consulted before making this decision.

Let's review the following definitions in Article 100 to understand when the requirements of Article 230 apply:

- Service Point—The point of connection between the serving utility and the premises wiring.
- Service Conductors—The conductors from the service point to the service disconnecting means. Service-entrance conductors can either be overhead or underground.
- Service Equipment—The necessary equipment, usually consisting of circuit breakers or switches and fuses and their accessories, connected to the load end of service conductors at a building or other structure, and intended to constitute the main control and cutoff of the electrical supply. Service equipment doesn't include individual meter socket enclosures [230.66].

After reviewing these definitions, you should understand that service conductors originate at the serving utility (service point) and terminate on the line side of the service disconnecting means. Conductors and equipment on the load side of service equipment are considered feeder conductors or branch circuits, and must be installed in accordance with Articles 210 and 215. They must also comply with Article 225 if they're outside branch circuits and feeders, such as the supply to a building/structure. Feeder conductors include: **Figure 230–1**

- Secondary conductors from customer-owned transformers,
- Conductors from generators, UPS systems, or photo-voltaic systems, and
- Conductors to remote buildings or structures

Article 230 consists of seven parts:

- PART I. GENERAL
- PART II. OVERHEAD SERVICE CONDUCTORS
- PART III. UNDERGROUND SERVICE CONDUCTORS
- PART IV. SERVICE-ENTRANCE CONDUCTORS
- PART V. SERVICE EQUIPMENT
- PART VI. DISCONNECTING MEANS
- PART VIII. OVERCURRENT PROTECTION

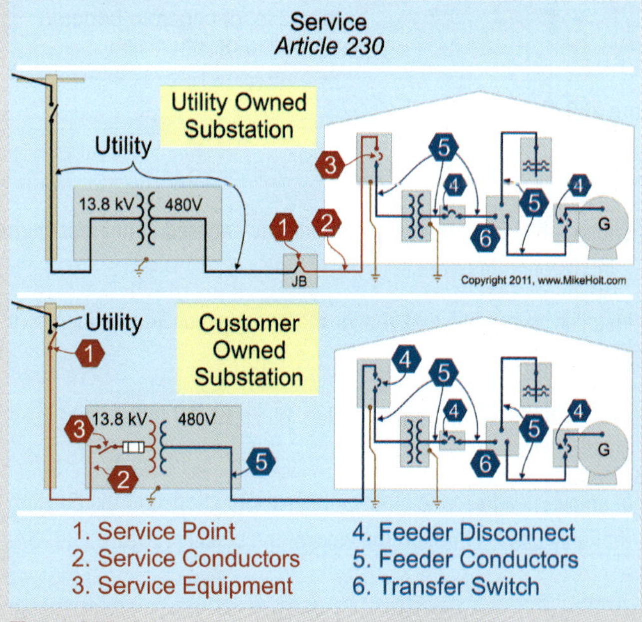

Figure 230–1

PART I. GENERAL

230.6 Conductors Considered Outside the Building

Service conductors in overhead masts that reenter a building have been addressed.

230.6 Conductors Considered Outside a Building. Conductors are considered outside of a building when they're installed:

(1) Under not less than 2 in. of concrete beneath a building/structure. Figure 230–2

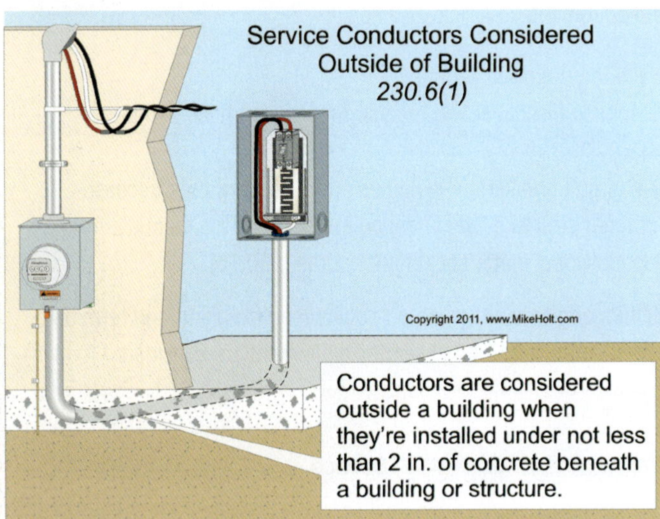

Figure 230–2

(2) Within a building/structure in a raceway encased in not less than 2 in. of concrete or brick.

(3) Installed in a vault that meets the construction requirements of Article 450, Part III.

(4) In a raceway under not less than 18 in. of the earth beneath a building/structure.

(5) In an overhead service mast on the outside surface of the building that only passes through the eave of the building. Figure 230–3

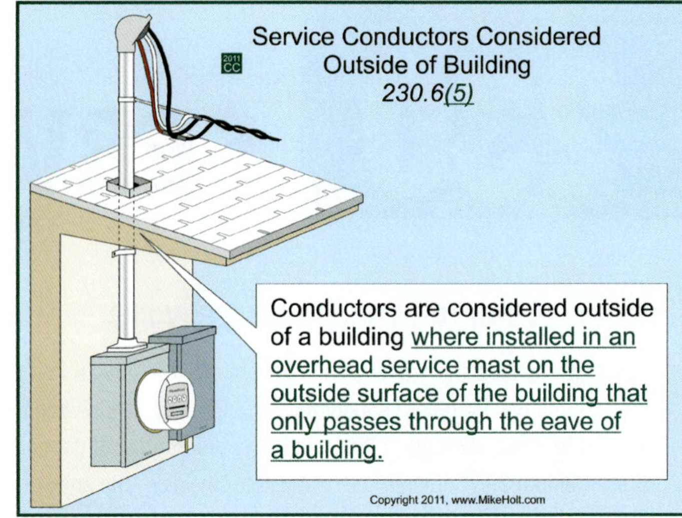

Figure 230–3

ANALYSIS: In overhead service installations, it's common for the mast to penetrate the eave of the building on its way through the roof. When this is the case, the conductors have reentered the building. Although few inspectors would ever prohibit such an installation, there's no denying that it violates the letter (but not the intent) of this section. In order to close this loophole, a new item (5) was added, clarifying that this practice is a permitted one.

PART II. OVERHEAD SERVICE CONDUCTORS

Article 230, Part II

The title of Part II has been revised to reflect changes made to service related terms in Article 100.

ANALYSIS: The terms "service drop," "service lateral," "service-entrance conductors (overhead)," "service-entrance conductors (underground)," "service conductors (overhead)," and "service conductors (underground)" have all been revised or created in Article 100 this *Code* cycle. These changes, and many changes in Article 230, are intended to help add clarity to the *NEC*, and to help the *Code* user more easily understand to what the *NEC* does and does not apply. The first of these changes is to the title of Article 230, Part II.

In previous editions of the *Code*, Part II of Article 230 applied to "overhead service-drop conductors" (a term no longer used). These conductors were seldom under the scope of the *NEC*, because they're typically on the supply side of the service point. Only in instances where the customer owned these overhead conductors did this Part of the Article apply. There's no technical change to this concept in this *Code* revision: these conductors typically still fall outside of the scope of the *NEC*. In the rare instance that these conductors do fall within the scope of the *Code*, they're now called "service conductors, overhead," a name that clearly states that these conductors are on the customer side of the service point. See Article 100 "Service Conductors, Overhead."

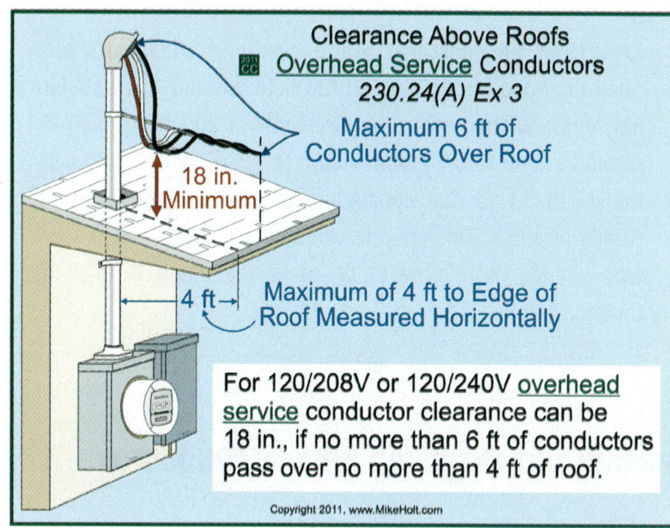

Figure 230–4

230.24(A) Exception 5, Vertical Clearance for Overhead Service Conductors

A new exception permits lower clearances for overhead service conductors.

230.24 Vertical Clearance for Overhead Service Conductors. Overhead service conductor spans must maintain the vertical clearances as follows:

(A) Above Roofs. A minimum of 8 ft above the surface of a roof for a minimum distance of 3 ft in all directions from the edge of the roof.

Ex 2: If the slope of the roof exceeds 4 in. of vertical rise for every 12 in. of horizontal run, 120/208V or 120/240V overhead service conductor clearances can be reduced to 3 ft over the roof.

Ex 3: If no more than 6 ft of conductors pass over no more than 4 ft of roof, 120/208V or 120/240V overhead service conductor clearances over the roof overhang can be reduced to 18 in. Figure 230–4

Ex 4: The 3 ft vertical clearance for overhead service conductors that extends from the roof doesn't apply when the point of attachment is on the side of the building below the roof.

Ex 5: If the voltage between conductors doesn't exceed 300V and the roof area is guarded or isolated, a reduction in clearance to 3 ft is permitted.

ANALYSIS: This new exception will allow a reduction in clearance from the standard 8 feet down to 3 feet under certain conditions. These conditions include a voltage limitation of no more than 300V between any two conductors, and a roof that's "guarded or isolated." Considering that the definition of "isolated" includes any area that isn't readily accessible without special means, it stands to reason that the exception will apply to nearly every roof. This new exception may become the standard to which overhead service conductors are installed.

230.24(E) Vertical Clearance—Communications Cables

A new subsection refers the user to the provisions of 800.44(A) for communications cable and clearances.

230.24 Vertical Clearance for Overhead Service Conductors.

(E) Clearance from Communications Cables. Where communications cables and electric light or power conductors are supported by the same pole, communications cables must have a minimum separation of 12 in. at any point in the span, including the point of attachment to the building [800.44(A)(4)].

ANALYSIS: Services that utilize overhead conductors are often changed or replaced in the field without the installer having knowledge of the requirements of 800.44(A)(4). That section requires a separation of at least 12 in. between the overhead service conductors and the communications cables or wires. This change will help the typical *Code* user who spends more time in Chapters 1 through 7, than in Chapter 8.

PART III. UNDERGROUND SERVICE CONDUCTORS

230.32 Protection Against Damage

A small clarification to the rule regarding physical protection of underground service conductors has been made.

230.32 Protection Against Damage. Underground service conductors must be installed in accordance with 300.5, and have minimum cover in accordance with Table 300.5. When entering a building or other structure, they must comply with 230.6 as it relates to conductors considered outdoors, and be a suitable wiring method as identified in 230.43.

ANALYSIS: The *NEC* has long required that service conductors installed under buildings must comply with the underground wiring provisions of 300.5. It's also required that they comply with 230.6 as it relates to conductors considered outdoors, and 230.43 regarding the wiring methods used for these underground conductors. These rules were specifically applied to conductors installed underneath buildings, but not underneath other structures. While all buildings are indeed structures, not all structures are buildings. This *Code* change corrects this oversight, affirming that the rules of the section apply to all underground service conductors installed under buildings or structures. The phrase "service-lateral conductors" has also been changed to "service conductors," in an effort to use defined terms in their correct context. This harmonizes with other similar changes to service conductor related terms.

PART IV. SERVICE-ENTRANCE CONDUCTORS

230.40 Number of Service-Entrance Conductor Sets

This section has been changed to promote the use of defined terms. Further changes address multiple accessory structures, and a dwelling unit with multiple accessory structures supplied by a single service.

230.40 Number of Service-Entrance Conductor Sets. Only one set of service conductors (drop, overhead, or underground) is permitted to supply a building/structure.

Ex 2: Service conductors can supply two to six service disconnecting means as permitted in 230.71(A).

Ex 3: A single-family dwelling unit and its accessory structure(s) can have one set of service conductors run to each structure.

Ex 4: Two-family dwellings, multifamily dwellings, and multiple occupancy buildings are permitted to have one set of service conductors to supply branch circuits for public or common areas.

Ex 5: One set of service-entrance conductors connected to the supply side of the normal service disconnecting means can supply standby power systems, fire pump equipment, and fire and sprinkler alarms [230.82(5)].

ANALYSIS: The opening paragraph of this section has been changed in an effort to correctly use defined terms. The *Code* user will recognize the new terms "overhead service conductors" and "underground service conductors" that have been added here.

The *NEC* recognizes the practice of having a single service supply power to a dwelling unit and its detached accessory structures. Because previous editions of the *Code*, in Ex 3, have used the word "structure" in the singular, some inspectors have viewed this allowance as only permitting a dwelling unit plus one accessory building from an individual service. By changing the word "structure" to "structure(s)," the *NEC* has made it quite clear that a single service is permitted to supply a dwelling unit and multiple accessory structures.

Exception 4 has also been revised. In multi-occupancy buildings, it's quite common to install a "house panel" to satisfy common use loads, such as parking lot lighting, alarm systems, and similar equipment. The house panels often require an additional set of service-entrance conductors to accommodate separate metering of the loads, and to comply with the requirements of 210.25(B), which prohibit such loads from being supplied by a panelboard that also serves an individual tenant space. The changes made to this section now address this very common installation.

230.43 Wiring Methods

The list of permitted wiring methods for service-entrance conductors has been expamded.

230.43 Wiring Methods. Service-entrance conductors must be installed with one of the following wiring methods:

(1) Open wiring on insulators

(3) Rigid metal conduit

(4) Intermediate metal conduit

(5) Electrical metallic tubing

(6) Electrical nonmetallic tubing

(7) Service-entrance cables

(8) Wireways

(9) Busways

(11) PVC conduit

(13) Type MC cable

(15) Flexible metal conduit or liquidtight flexible metal conduit not longer than 6 ft

(16) Liquidtight flexible nonmetallic conduit

(17) High-Density Polyethylene Conduit (HDPE)

(18) Nonmetallic Underground Conduit with Conductors (NUCC)

(19) Reinforced Thermosetting Resin Conduit (RTRC)

ANALYSIS: Several new wiring methods have been added to the *Code* over the last few cycles, but haven't previously been mentioned in the list contained in Section 230.43. The wiring methods which have been added include: High Density Polyethylene Conduit (HDPE), and Reinforced Thermosetting Resin Conduit (RTRC). Also added is the older Non-metallic Underground Conduit with Conductors (NUCC). Lastly, the term "Rigid Nonmetallic Conduit" has been replaced with "Rigid Polyvinyl Chloride Conduit (PVC), to address the renaming of this raceway in the 2008 *NEC*.

230.50(B)(1) Protection Against Physical Damage

Reinforced thermosetting resin conduit was added to the list of wiring methods permitted for aboveground service-entrance cables.

230.50 Protection Against Physical Damage.

(A) Underground Service-Entrance Conductors. Underground service-entrance conductors must be protected against physical damage in accordance with 300.5.

(B) All Other Service-Entrance Conductors. Service-entrance conductors that aren't installed underground must be protected against physical damage as follows:

(1) Service-Entrance Cables. Service-entrance cables that are subject to physical damage must be protected by one of the following: Figure 230–5

(1) Rigid metal conduit

(2) Intermediate metal conduit

(3) Schedule 80 PVC conduit

Author's Comment: If the authority having jurisdiction determines the raceway isn't subject to physical damage, Schedule 40 PVC conduit can be used. Figure 230–6

(4) Electrical metallic tubing

(5) Reinforced Thermosetting Resin Conduit (RTRC)

(6) Other means approved by the authority having jurisdiction

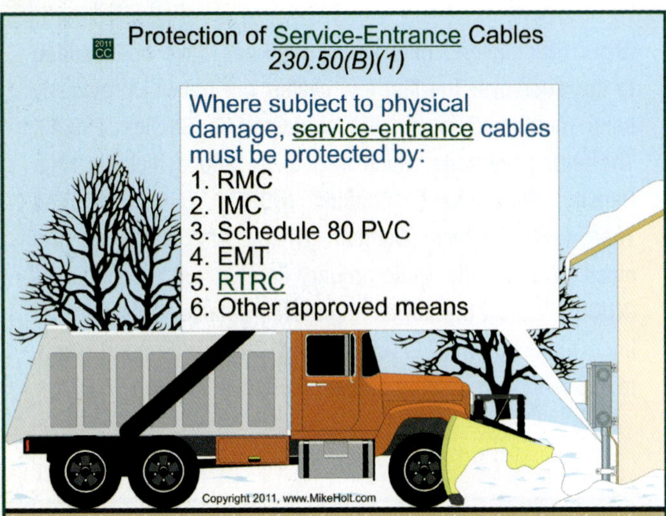

Figure 230–5

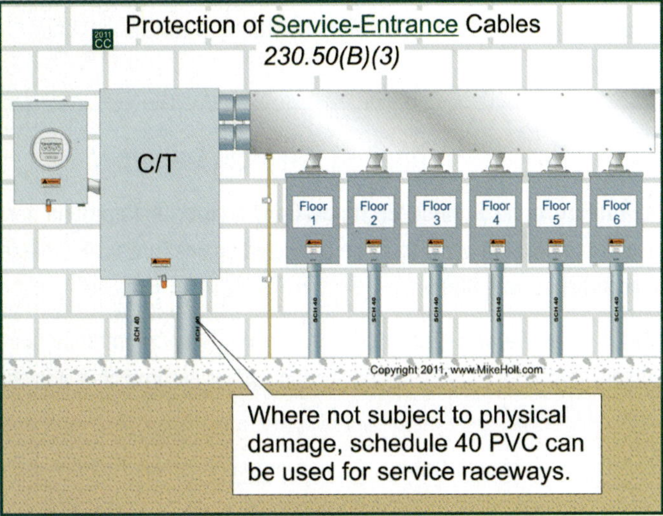

Figure 230–6

ANALYSIS: The 2008 *NEC* introduced a new raceway wiring method called "Reinforced Thermosetting Resin Conduit (RTRC)." Because of the physical properties of this raceway, it's deemed appropriate to provide physical protection to service-entrance cables that are subject to physical damage.

230.54 Overhead Services

The provisions for service heads have been editorially revised.

230.54 Overhead Service Locations.

(A) Service Head. Raceways for overhead service drops or overhead service conductors must have a weatherhead listed for wet locations.

(B) Service-Entrance Cable. Service-entrance cables must be equipped with a weatherhead listed for wet locations.

Ex: SE cable can be formed into a gooseneck and taped with self-sealing weather-resistant thermoplastic.

ANALYSIS: The 2008 *NEC* specified that service heads be installed in accordance with the provisions 314.15. Ultimately, this meant that service heads had to be listed for use in wet locations. This change simply borrows the language from 314.15 and places it in the rules 230.54(A) and (B), in an effort to avoid the inconvenience of the *Code* user having to flip back and forth through the *NEC* to figure out the requirements. This isn't a technical change in any way.

PART V. SERVICE EQUIPMENT—GENERAL

230.66 Marking

A new requirement for the listing of service equipment was added.

230.66 Listed as Suitable for Service Equipment. The service disconnecting means must be listed as suitable for use as service equipment.

Author's Comment: "Suitable for use as service equipment" means, among other things, that the service disconnecting means is supplied with a main bonding jumper so a neutral-to-case connection can be made, as required in 250.24(C) and 250.142(A). **Figure 230–7**

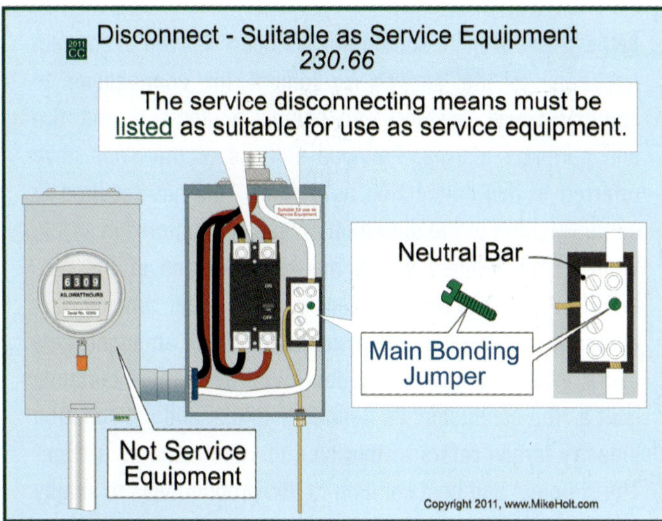

Figure 230–7

ANALYSIS: The *Code* has long required that service equipment be marked as being "suitable for use as service equipment." While most people agreed that this effectively requires the equipment to be listed, a literal reading of the *NEC* doesn't require it. For example, a person could use a magic marker and write the phrase "suitable for use as service equipment" to satisfy the requirement! With this change, that loophole is closed, and the requirement becomes both obvious and enforceable.

PART VI. SERVICE EQUIPMENT—DISCONNECTING MEANS

230.82(5) Equipment Connected to the Supply Side of Service Disconnect

Connecting ahead of the service for standby power systems, fire pump equipment, and fire and sprinkler alarms has been editorially revised.

230.82 Connected on Supply Side of the Service Disconnect. Electrical equipment must not be connected to the supply side of the service disconnect enclosure, except for the following:

(2) Meters and meter sockets.

(3) Meter disconnect switches. Figure 230–8

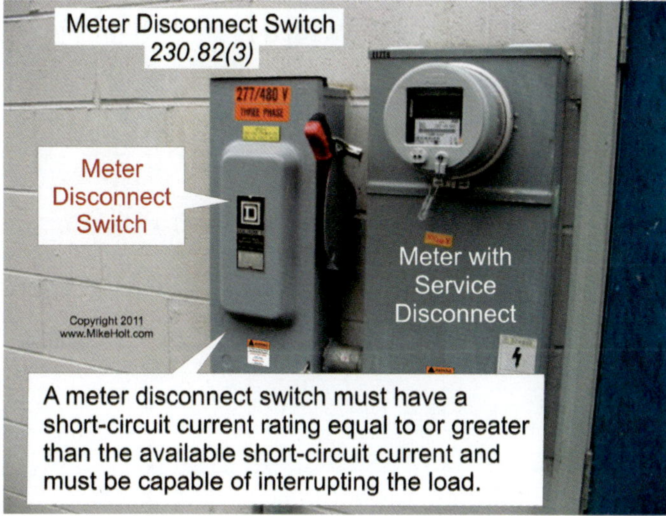

Figure 230–8

Author's Comment: Electric utilities often require a meter disconnect switch for 277/480V services to enhance safety for utility personnel when they install or remove a meter.

(4) Type 1 surge protective devices.

Author's Comment: A Type 1 surge protective device is listed to be permanently connected on the line side of service equipment [285.23].

(5) Connections used to supply legally required and optional standby power systems, fire pump equipment, fire and sprinkler alarms, and load (energy) management devices.

Author's Comment: Emergency standby power must not be supplied by a connection ahead of service equipment [700.12]. Figure 230–9

(6) Solar photovoltaic systems.

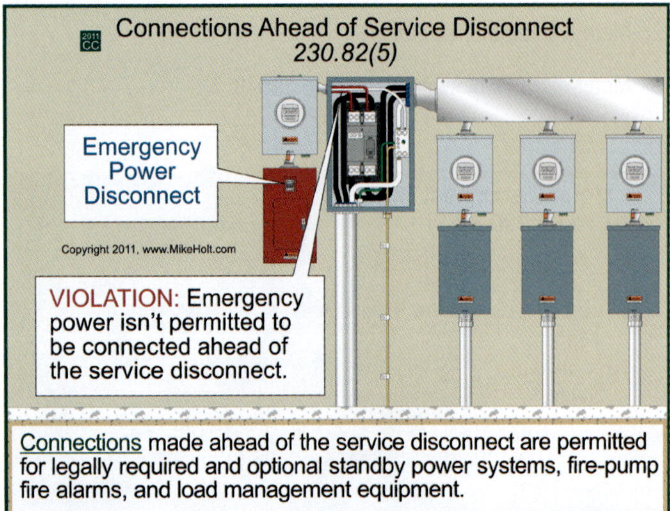

Figure 230–9

ANALYSIS: For quite some time, it's been allowed to connect upstream of the service equipment for connections to standby power systems, fire pump equipment, and fire and sprinkler alarms. Previous editions of the *Code* have referred to this connection as a "tap." This has resulted in confusion, due to the definition of "tap conductors" in 240.2. While terms defined within individual articles of the *NEC* aren't intended to apply to terms within other articles, this language has resulted in considerable debate amongst *Code* users. Whatever this connection might be, it most certainly isn't a "tap conductor" as defined in 240.2, and yet common industry jargon refers to this type of connection as a "tap." The simplest and best solution to this problem was to simply change the word "tap" to "connection," which is what the *NEC* now reads and really meant all along.

ARTICLE 240 Overcurrent PROTECTION

INTRODUCTION TO ARTICLE 240—OVERCURRENT PROTECTION

This article provides the requirements for selecting and installing overcurrent devices. Overcurrent exists when current exceeds the rating of equipment or the ampacity of a conductor. This can be due to an overload, short circuit, or ground fault [Article 100].

Overload. An overload is a condition where equipment or conductors carry current exceeding their current rating [Article 100]. A fault, such as a short circuit or ground fault, isn't an overload. An example of an overload is plugging two 12.50A (1,500W) hair dryers into a 20A branch circuit.

Ground Fault. A ground fault is an unintentional, electrically conducting connection between an ungrounded conductor of an electrical circuit and the normally noncurrent-carrying conductors, metallic enclosures, metallic raceways, metallic equipment, or the earth [Article 100]. During the period of a ground fault, dangerous voltages will be present on metal parts until the circuit overcurrent device opens.

Short Circuit. A short circuit is the unintentional electrical connection between any two normally current-carrying conductors of an electrical circuit, either line-to-line or line-to-neutral.

Overcurrent devices protect conductors and equipment. Selecting the proper overcurrent protection for a specific circuit can become more complicated than it sounds. The general rule for overcurrent protection is that conductors must be protected in accordance with their ampacities at the point where they receive their supply [240.4 and 240.21]. There are many special cases that deviate from this basic rule, such as the overcurrent protection limitations for small conductors [240.4(D)] and the rules for specific conductor applications found in other articles, as listed in Table 240.4(G). There are also a number of rules allowing tap conductors in specific situations [240.21(B)]. Article 240 even has limits on where overcurrent devices are allowed to be located [240.24].

An overcurrent protection device must be capable of opening a circuit when an overcurrent situation occurs, and must also have an interrupting rating sufficient to avoid damage in fault conditions [110.9]. Carefully study the provisions of this article to be sure you provide sufficient overcurrent protection in the correct location.

PART I. GENERAL

240.4(B)(1) Overcurrent Devices Rated 800 Amperes or Less

The allowance for the next higher standard overcurrent device has been revised for consistency.

240.4 Protection of Conductors.

(B) Overcurrent Devices Rated 800A or Less. The next higher standard rating of overcurrent device listed in 240.6 (above the ampacity of the ungrounded conductors being protected) is permitted, provided all of the following conditions are met:

(1) The conductors aren't part of a branch circuit supplying more than one receptacle for cord-and-plug-connected loads.

(2) The ampacity of a conductor, after the application of ambient temperature correction [310.15(B)(2)(a)], conductor bundling adjustment [310.15(B)(3)(a)], or both, doesn't correspond with the standard rating of a fuse or circuit breaker in 240.6(A).

(3) The overcurrent device rating doesn't exceed 800A.

Example: A 400A overcurrent device can protect 500 kcmil conductors, where each conductor has an ampacity of 380A at 75°C, in accordance with Table 310.15(B)(16). **Figure 240–1**

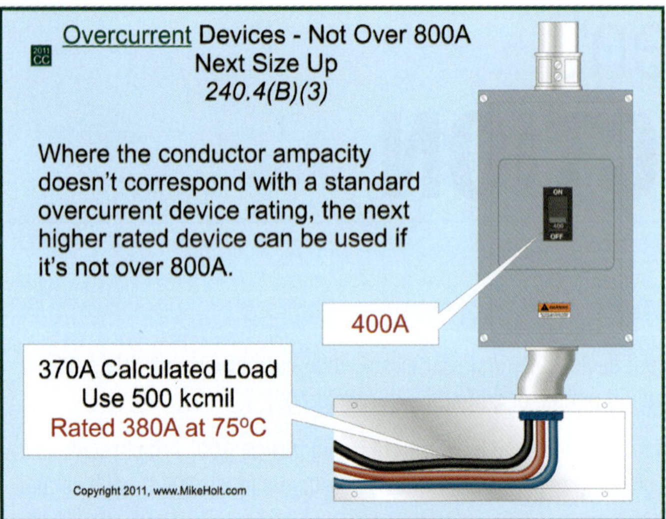

Figure 240–1

Author's Comment: This "next size up" rule doesn't apply to feeder tap conductors [240.21(B)] or transformer secondary conductors [240.21(C)].

ANALYSIS: This subsection was changed to provide consistency with 210.19(A)(2), which applies to conductors supplying more than one receptacle. This change more clearly establishes the intent of this section, and eliminates a subtle conflict between these two sections.

240.15(B) Circuit Breaker as Overcurrent Device

The text regarding single-pole circuit breakers for multiwire branch circuits has been revised.

240.15 Ungrounded Conductors.

(A) Overcurrent Device Required. A fuse or an overcurrent trip unit of a circuit breaker must be connected in series with each ungrounded conductor. A combination of a current transformer and overcurrent relay is considered equivalent to an overcurrent trip unit for the purpose of providing overcurrent protection of conductors.

(B) Circuit Breaker as an Overcurrent Device. Circuit breakers must automatically (and manually) open all ungrounded conductors of the circuit, except as follows:

(1) Multiwire Branch Circuits. Individual single-pole breakers with identified handle ties are permitted for a multiwire branch circuit that only supplies line-to-neutral loads.

Author's Comments:

- Multiwire branch circuits must be provided with a means to disconnect simultaneously all ungrounded conductors at the point where the branch circuit originates [210.4(B)]. This can be accomplished by individual single-pole circuit breakers with identified handle ties or a 2- or 3-pole breaker with a common internal trip. Figure 240–2

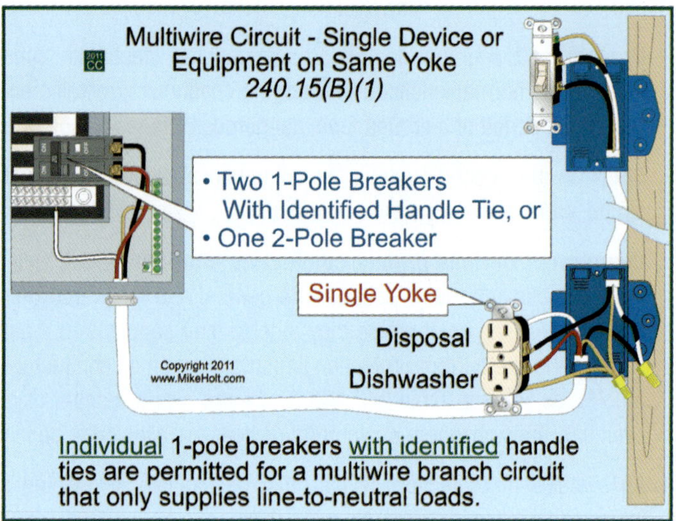

Figure 240–2

- Single-pole AFCI or GFCI circuit breakers aren't suitable for protecting multiwire branch circuits. AFCI or GFCI circuit breakers for multiwire branch circuits must be of the 2-pole type. Figure 240–3

(2) Single-Phase, Line-to-Line Loads. Individual single-pole circuit breakers rated 120/240V with handle ties identified for the purpose are permitted on each ungrounded conductor of a branch circuit that supplies single-phase, line-to-line loads. Figure 240–4

(3) Three-Phase, Line-to-Line Loads. Individual single-pole breakers rated 120/240V with handle ties identified for the purpose are permitted on each ungrounded conductor of a branch circuit that serves three-phase, line-to-line loads on systems not exceeding 120V to ground. Figure 240–5

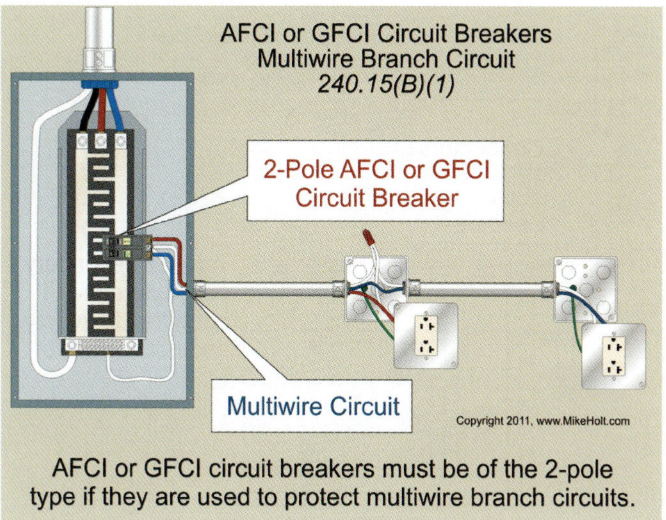

Figure 240–3

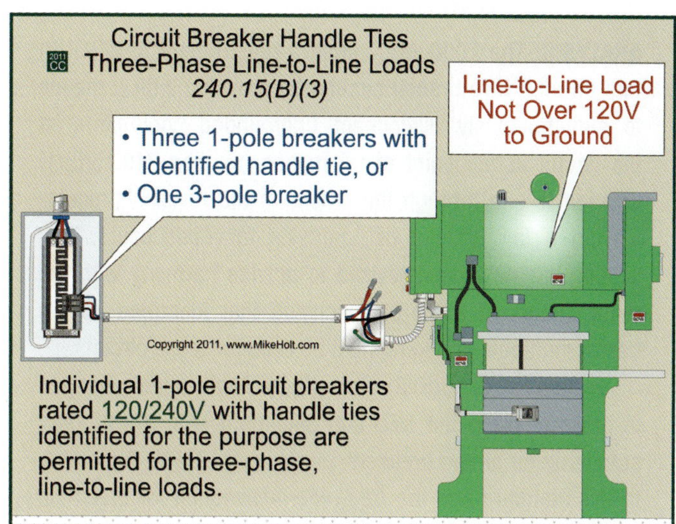

Figure 240–5

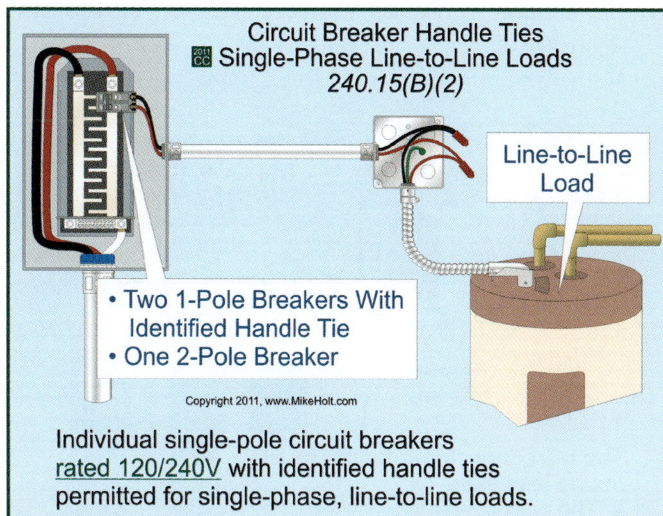

Figure 240–4

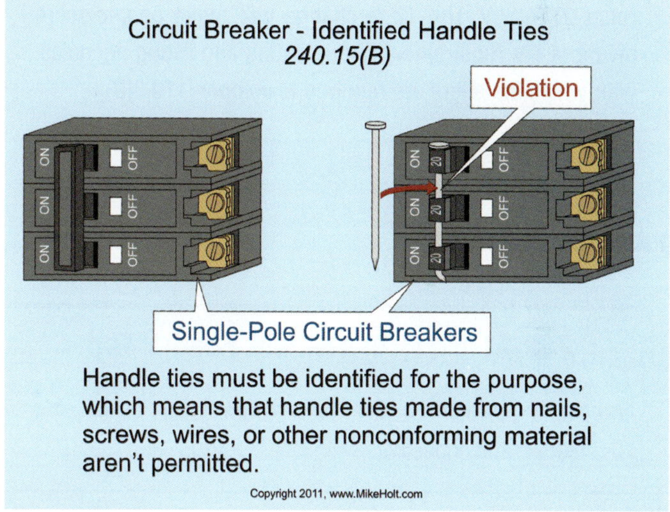

Figure 240–6

Author's Comment: According to Article 100, "Identified" means recognized as suitable for a specific purpose, function, or environment by listing, labeling, or other means approved by the authority having jurisdiction. This means handle ties made from nails, screws, wires, or other nonconforming materials aren't suitable. **Figure 240–6**

ANALYSIS: The 2008 *NEC* added a requirement in 210.4(B) that all multiwire branch circuits be provided with a means to simultaneously disconnect ungrounded conductors of the circuit at the point of origination. Section 240.15(B)(1) seemed to slip through the cracks in the revision process, leaving a fair amount of confusion for *Code* users. This section has now been revised to provide harmony with the requirements of 210.4(B) specifying that identified handle ties or multipole breakers must be used for these circuits.

Sections 240.15(B)(2) and (B)(3) have been changed in order to bring the *NEC* into alignment with the product standards for circuit breakers, particularly UL 489. According to this standard and the *UL Guide Information for Electrical Equipment* (White Book) category DIVQ, handle ties are only allowed to connect single-pole breakers together on a circuit rated no higher than 120V to ground. This change will effectively require 3-pole breakers for line-to-line loads rated 277/480V. The *Code* change will make people more aware of the requirements from testing and listing agencies, with which installers are required to comply [110.3(B)].

PART II. LOCATION

240.21(B)(1)(4) 10-Foot Feeder Tap

An editorial revision has been made to provisions for sizing a 10 ft feeder tap conductor.

240.21 Overcurrent Protection Location in Circuit.

Except as permitted by (A) through (G), overcurrent devices must be placed at the point where the branch circuit or feeder conductors receive their power. Taps and transformer secondary conductors aren't permitted to supply another conductor (tapping a tap isn't permitted). Figure 240–7

(B) Feeder Taps. Conductors can be tapped to a feeder as specified in 240.21(B)(1) through (B)(5).

(1) 10-Foot Feeder Tap. Feeder tap conductors up to 10 ft long are permitted without overcurrent protection at the tap location if the tap conductors comply with the following:

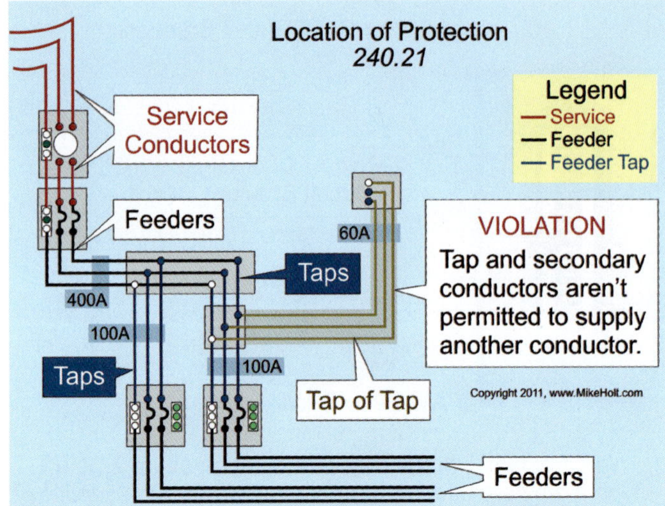

Figure 240–7

(1) The ampacity of the tap conductor must not be less than: Figure 240–8

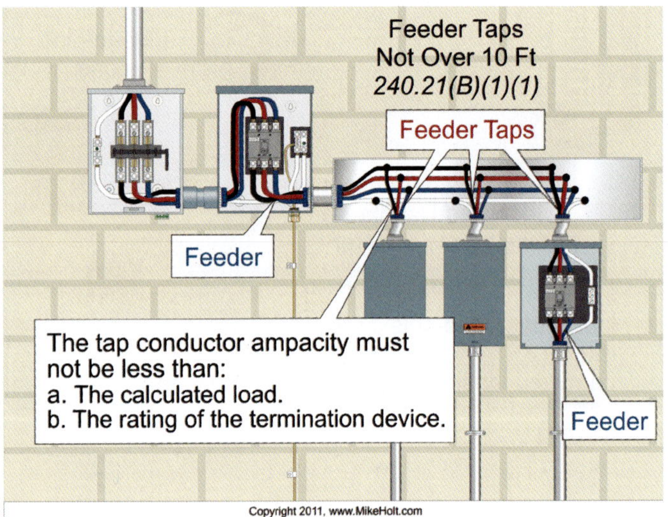

Figure 240–8

a. The calculated load in accordance with Article 220, and

b. The rating of the device or overcurrent device supplied by the tap conductors.

(2) The tap conductors must not extend beyond the equipment they supply.

(3) The tap conductors are installed in a raceway if they leave the enclosure.

(4) If the tap conductors leave the enclosure or vault in which the tap is made, the tap conductors must have an ampacity not less than 1/10th of the rating of the overcurrent device that protects the feeder.

Note: See 408.36 for the overcurrent protection requirements for panelboards.

Example: *A 400A breaker protects a set of 500 kcmil feeder conductors. There are three taps fed from the 500 kcmil feeders that supply disconnects with 200A, 150A, and 30A overcurrent devices. What are the minimum size conductors for these taps?* **Figure 240–9**

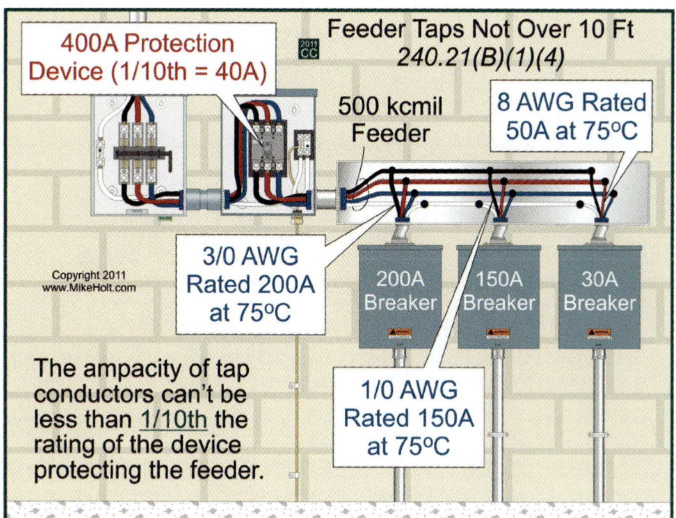

Figure 240–9

- *200A: 3/0 AWG is rated 200A at 75°, and is greater than 10 percent of the ampacity of 500 kcmil, which is rated 380A at 75°.*
- *150A: 1/0 AWG is rated 150A at 75°, and is greater than 10 percent of the ampacity of 500 kcmil, which is rated 380A at 75°.*
- *30A: 8 AWG is rated 50A at 75°, and is greater than 10 percent of the ampacity of 500 kcmil, which is rated 380A at 75°. Anything smaller than 8 AWG can't be used, as it will have an ampacity of less than 10 percent of 380A (38A) in the 75° column of 310.15(B)(16).*

ANALYSIS: Previous editions of the *Code* have required that the overcurrent device upstream of the feeder tap not exceed 10 times the ampacity of the conductor. This revision changes the wording to require that the conductor have an ampacity of not less than 1/10 the rating of the overcurrent device. This results in no technical change whatsoever, but provides a section that's easier to read. It also brings the *NEC* text into alignment with the existing text of 240.21(B)(2)(1).

240.24(E) Location of Overcurrent Devices

The prohibition of overcurrent devices in bathrooms has been added to dormitories.

240.24 Location of Overcurrent Devices.

(E) Not in Bathrooms. Overcurrent devices aren't permitted to be located in the bathrooms of dwelling units, dormitories, or guest rooms or guest suites of hotels or motels. **Figure 240–10**

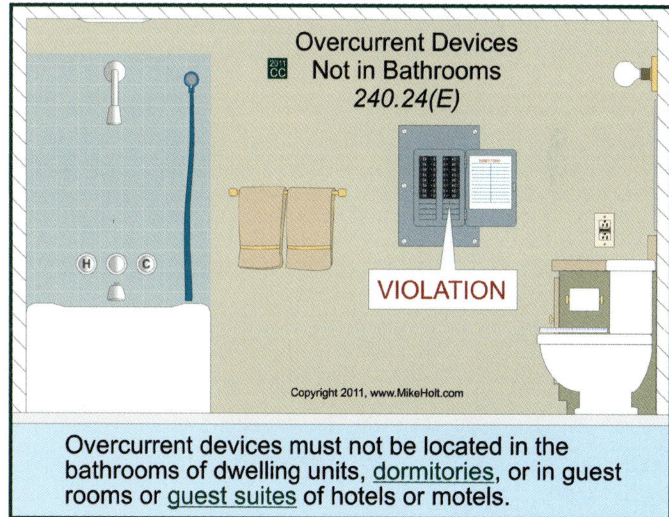

Figure 240–10

ANALYSIS: The *Code* has prohibited the installation of overcurrent devices in the bathrooms of dwelling units for some time. Since dormitories share similar usage characteristics with dwelling units, this requirement has been extended to include them. It's worth noting that many dormitories already meet the definition of a dwelling unit, so this change may not be as impactful as it appears.

Author's Comment: The service disconnecting means must not be located in a bathroom, even in commercial or industrial facilities [230.70(A)(2)].

ARTICLE

250 Grounding and BONDING

INTRODUCTION TO ARTICLE 250—GROUNDING AND BONDING

No other article can match Article 250 for misapplication, violation, and misinterpretation. The terminology used in this article has been a source for much confusion, but that has improved during the last few *NEC* revisions. It's very important to understand the difference between grounding and bonding in order to correctly apply the provisions of Article 250. Pay careful attention to the definitions that apply to grounding and bonding both here and in Article 100 as you begin the study of this important article. Article 250 covers the grounding requirements for providing a path to the earth to reduce overvoltage from lightning, and the bonding requirements for a low-impedance fault current path back to the source of the electrical supply to facilitate the operation of overcurrent devices in the event of a ground fault.

Over the past five *Code* cycles, this article was extensively revised to organize it better and make it easier to understand and implement. It's arranged in a logical manner, so it's a good idea to just read through Article 250 to get a big picture view—after you review the definitions. Next, study the article closely so you understand the details. The illustrations will help you understand the key points.

PART I. GENERAL

250.2 Bonding Jumper, Supply-Side

A new term "supply side bonding jumper" was added.

250.2 Definitions.

Bonding Jumper, Supply-Side. A conductor on the supply side or within a service or separately derived system to ensure the electrical conductivity between metal parts required to be electrically connected. Figure 250–1

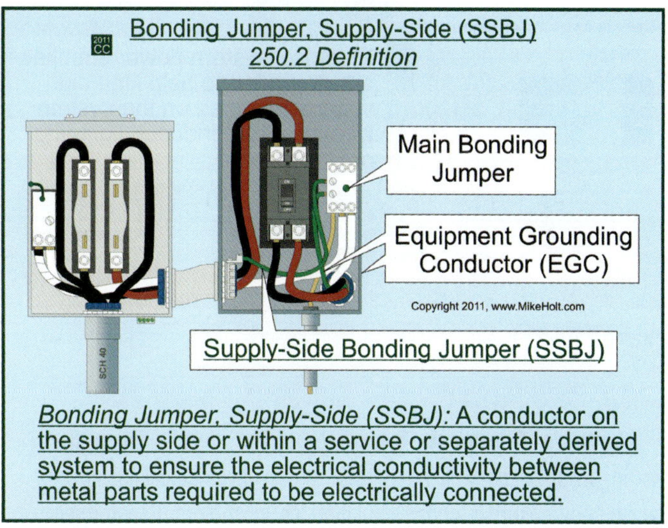

Figure 250–1

ANALYSIS: Equipment bonding jumpers are used often in the *NEC*, although the manner in which they're sized depends on the location (in the circuit) of the bonding jumper. Generally speaking, bonding conductors located downstream of an overcurrent device are sized in accordance with 250.122, based on the rating of the overcurrent device. Bonding conductors upstream of an overcurrent device, such as the supply side of a service or between a transformer and panelboard, are typically sized using Table 250.66 and the 12½ percent rule discussed in 250.102(C). This *Code* change not only provides a new term to more accurately describe an existing conductor, but also should help clear up the sizing confusion that many people have with bonding conductors.

250.4(A)(1) Solidly Grounded Systems

The Informational Note regarding the length of grounding electrode conductors has been revised.

250.4 General Requirements for Grounding and Bonding.

(A) Solidly Grounded Systems.

(1) Electrical System Grounding. Electrical power systems, such as the secondary winding of a transformer are grounded (connected to the earth) to limit the voltage induced by lightning, line surges, or unintentional contact by higher-voltage lines. **Figure 250–2**

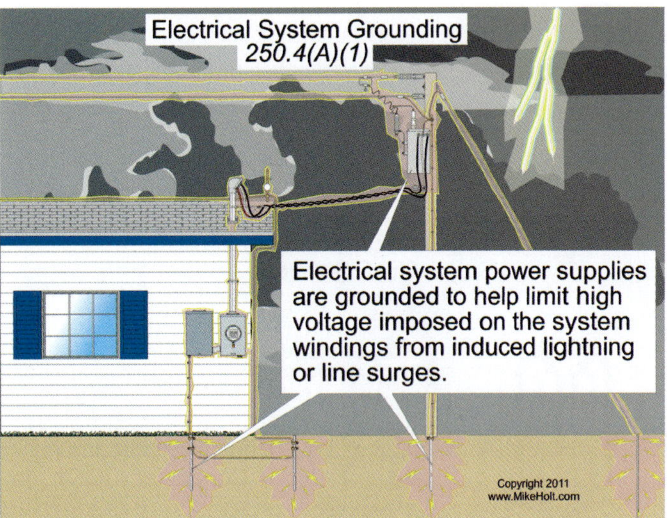

Figure 250–2

Author's Comment: System grounding helps reduce fires in buildings as well as voltage stress on electrical insulation, thereby ensuring longer insulation life for motors, transformers, and other system components. **Figure 250–3**

Note: An important consideration for limiting imposed voltage is to remember that grounding electrode conductors shouldn't be any longer than necessary and unnecessary bends and loops should be avoided. **Figure 250–4**

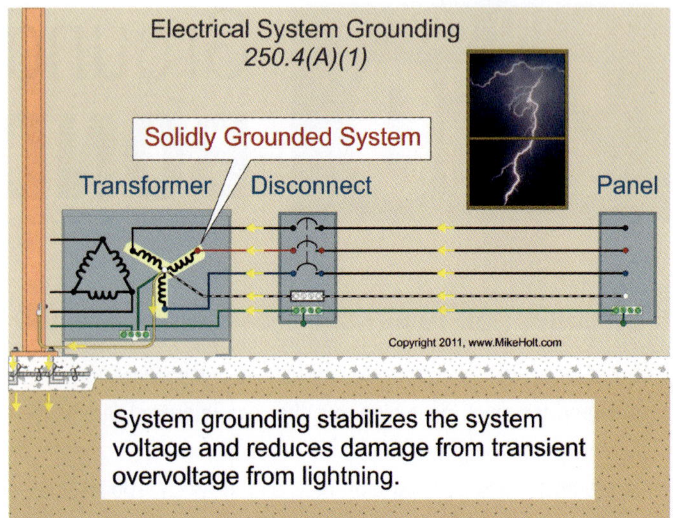

Figure 250–3

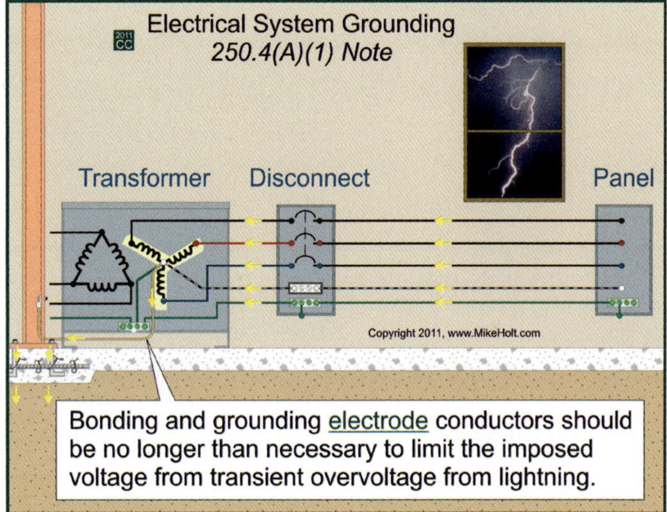

Figure 250–4

ANALYSIS: With the deletion of the term "grounding conductor" from Article 100, this rule was in need of revision. The *Code* now makes it quite clear that the length of grounding electrode conductors is of concern for the proper application of 250.4(A)(1). Because of the high frequency of lightning, the length of the grounding electrode conductor becomes critical in order to reduce inductive reactance.

250.6(C) Temporary Currents Not Classified as Objectionable Current

The description of currents that aren't considered objectionable has been revised.

250.6 Objectionable Current.

(C) Temporary Currents Not Classified as Objectionable Currents. Temporary currents from abnormal conditions, such as ground faults, aren't to be classified as objectionable current. **Figure 250–5**

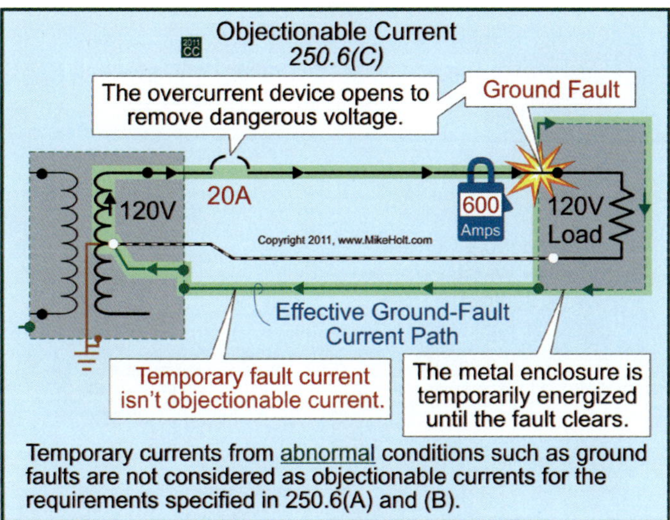

Figure 250–5

ANALYSIS: The term "accidental" was used in previous editions of the *NEC* to describe conditions that resulted in currents not deemed objectionable. Ground faults are listed in this section as an example of a condition that results in this current, but only under abnormal conditions. Because the term "abnormal" is used in the Article 100 definition of "circuit breaker," it was believed that it would be a better term for this *Code* section.

OBJECTIONABLE CURRENT

Objectionable neutral current occurs because of improper neutral-to-case connections or wiring errors that violate 250.142(B).

Improper Neutral-to-Case Connection [250.142]

Panelboards. Objectionable neutral current will flow when the neutral conductor is connected to the metal case of a panelboard that's not used as service equipment. **Figure 250–6**

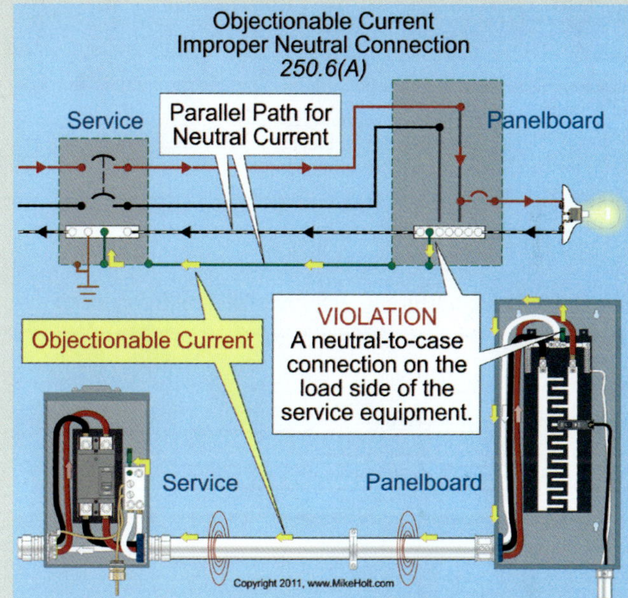

Figure Figure 250–6

Separately Derived Systems. Objectionable neutral current will flow on conductive metal parts and conductors if the neutral conductor is connected to the circuit equipment grounding conductor on the load side of the system bonding jumper for a separately derived system. **Figures 250–7 and 250–8**

Disconnects. Objectionable neutral current will flow when the neutral conductor is connected to the metal case of a disconnecting means that's not part of the service equipment. **Figure 250–9**

Wiring Errors. Objectionable neutral current will flow when the neutral conductor from one system is connected to a circuit of a different system. **Figure 250–10**

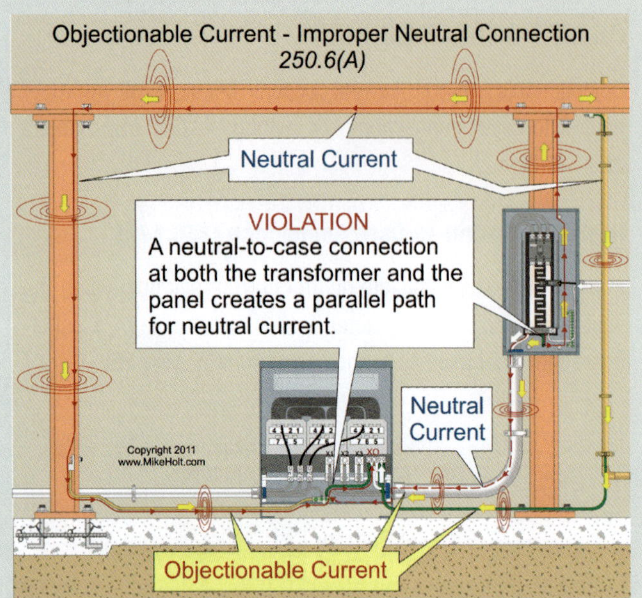

Figure 250–7

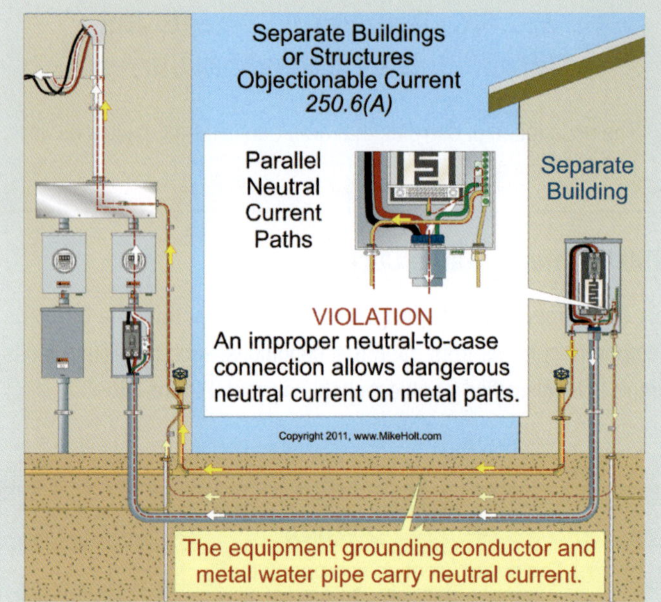

Figure 250–9

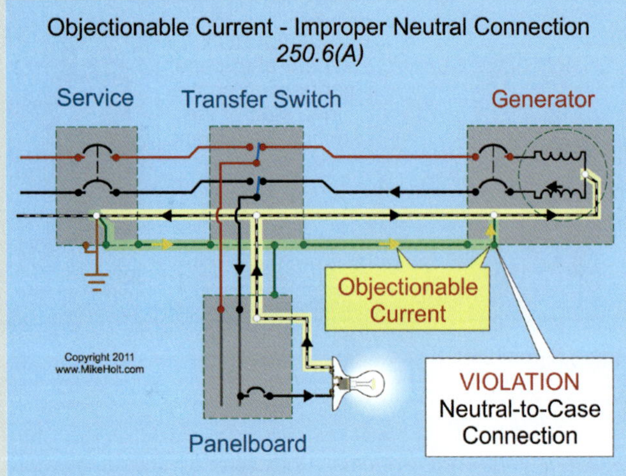

Figure 250–8

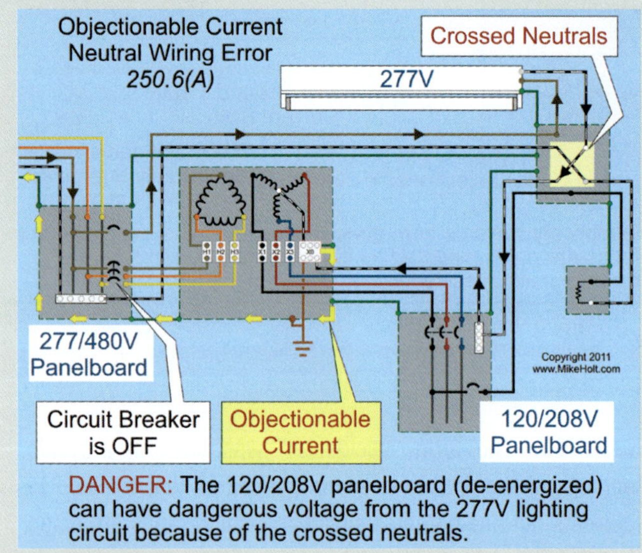

Figure 250–10

Objectionable neutral current will flow on metal parts when the circuit equipment grounding conductor is used as a neutral conductor such as where:

- A 230V time-clock motor is replaced with a 115V time-clock motor, and the circuit equipment grounding conductor is used for neutral return current.
- A 115V water filter is wired to a 240V well-pump motor circuit, and the circuit equipment grounding conductor is used for neutral return current. **Figure 250–11**
- The circuit equipment grounding conductor is used for neutral return current. **Figure 250–12**

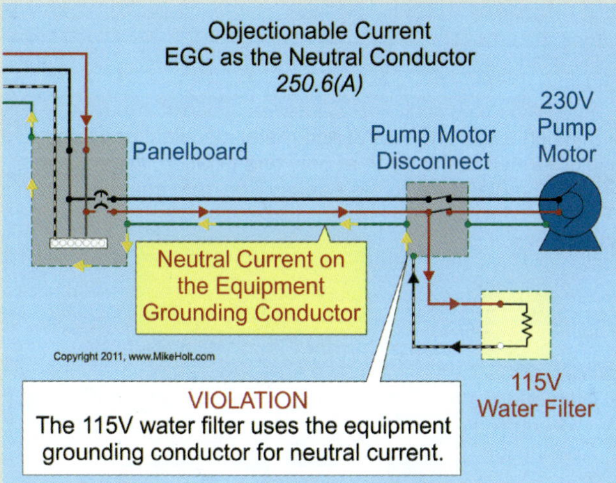

Figure 250–11

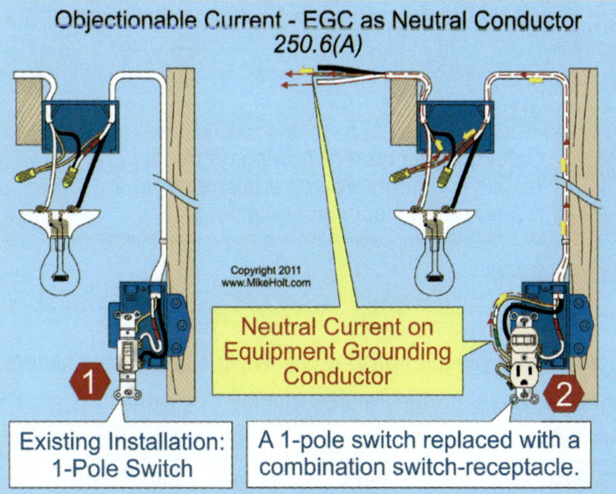

Figure 250–12

DANGERS OF OBJECTIONABLE CURRENT

Objectionable neutral current on metal parts can cause electric shock, fires, and improper operation of electronic equipment and overcurrent devices such as GFPs, GFCIs, and AFCIs.

Shock Hazard. When objectionable neutral current flows on metal parts, electric shock, and even death can occur from the elevated voltage on those metal parts. **Figures 250–13 and 250–14**

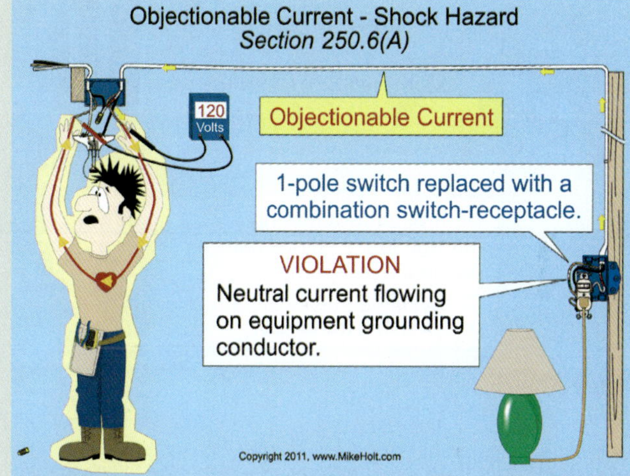

Figure 250–13

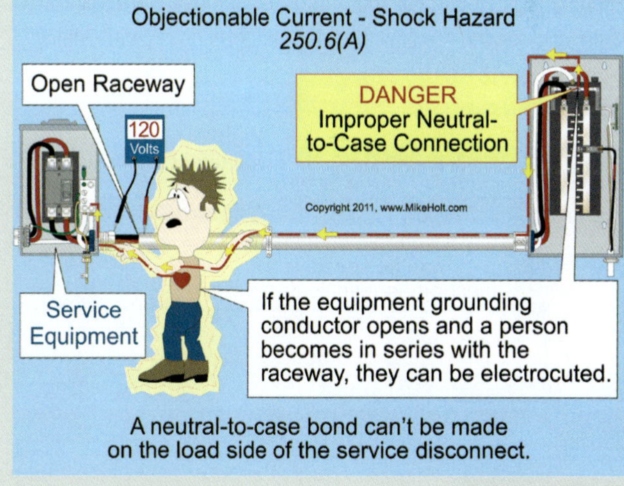

Figure 250–14

Fire Hazard. When objectionable neutral current flows on metal parts, a fire can ignite adjacent combustible material. Heat is generated whenever current flows, particularly over high-resistance parts. In addition, arcing at loose connections is especially dangerous in areas containing easily ignitible and explosive gases, vapors, or dust. Figure 250–15

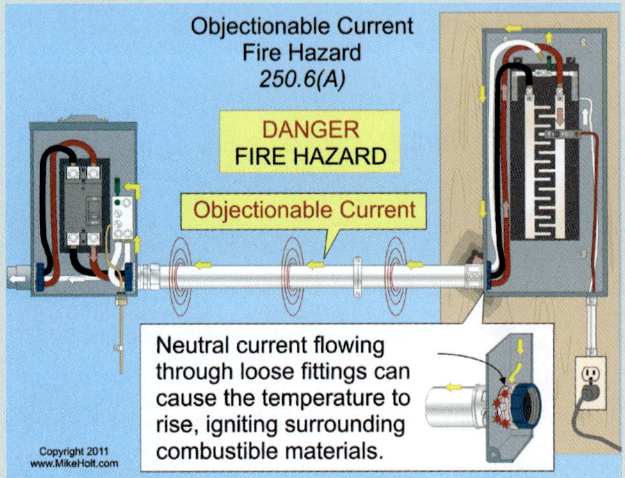

Figure 250–15

Improper Operation of Electronic Equipment. Objectionable neutral current flowing on metal parts of electrical equipment and building parts can cause electromagnetic fields which negatively affect the performance of electronic devices, particularly medical equipment. For more information, visit www.MikeHolt.com, click on the "Technical Link," and then on "Power Quality." Figure 250–16

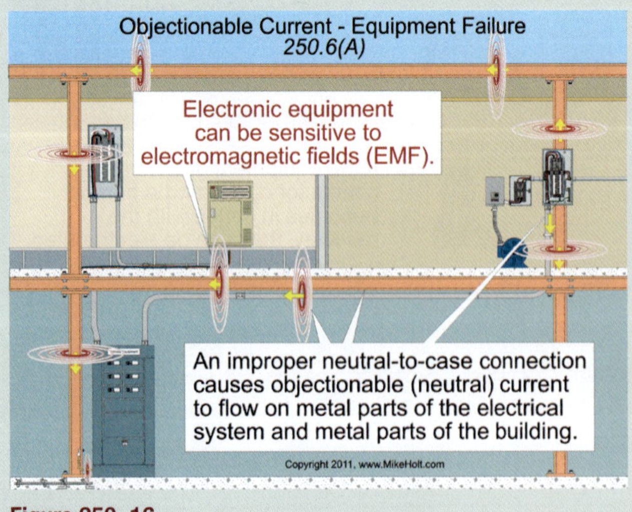

Figure 250–16

When a system is properly grounded and bonded, the voltage of all metal parts to the earth and to each other will be zero, Figure 250–17. When objectionable neutral current travels on metal parts because of the improper bonding of the neutral to metal parts in violation of the *NEC*, a difference of potential will exist between all metal parts. This situation can cause some electronic equipment to operate improperly. Figure 250–18

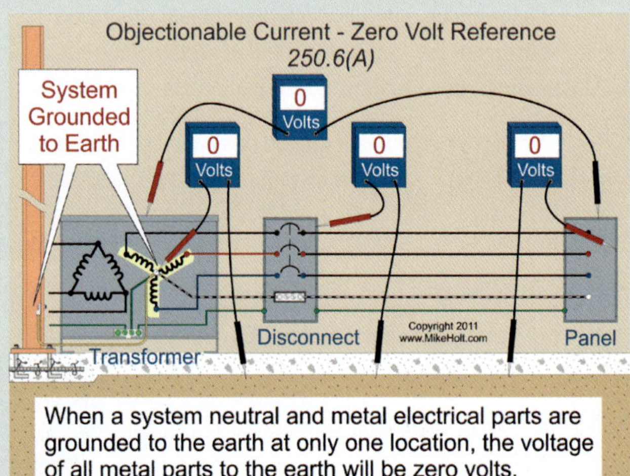

Figure 250–17

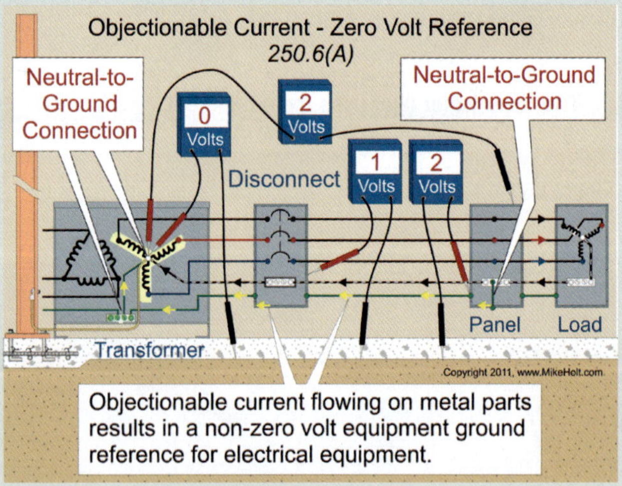

Figure 250–18

Operation of Overcurrent Devices. When objectionable neutral current travels on metal parts, tripping of electronic overcurrent devices equipped with ground-fault protection can occur because some neutral current flows on the circuit equipment grounding conductor instead of the neutral conductor.

250.8(A) Termination of Grounding and Bonding Conductors

Revisions to this section were made to clarify which conductors are covered by this rule.

250.8 Termination of Grounding and Bonding Conductors.

(A) Permitted Methods. Equipment grounding conductors, grounding electrode conductors, and bonding jumpers must terminate in one of the following methods:

(1) Listed pressure connectors

(2) Terminal bars

(3) Pressure connectors listed for direct burial or concrete encasement [250.70]

(4) Exothermic welding

(5) Machine screws that engage at least two threads or are secured with a nut, **Figure 250–19**

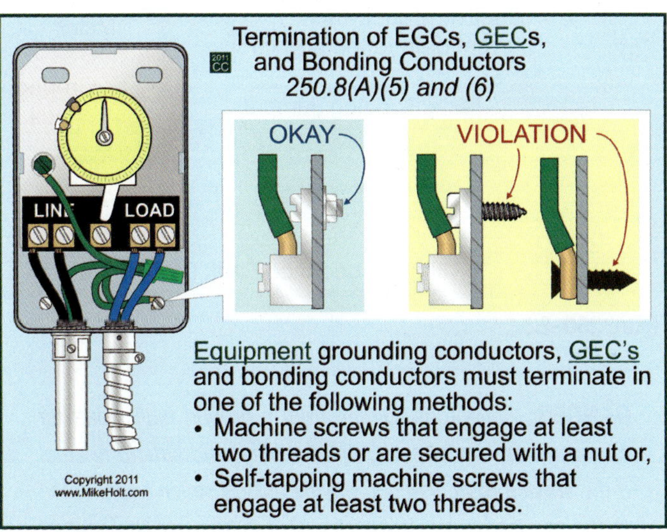

Figure 250–19

(6) Self-tapping machine screws that engage at least two threads

(7) Connections that are part of a listed assembly

(8) Other listed means

ANALYSIS: In order to correlate with the deletion of the term "grounding conductor" from Article 100, this section needed to be revised to clarify to which conductor(s) it applies. The *Code* is now very clear that the requirements of this section apply to bonding jumpers, equipment grounding conductors, and grounding electrode conductors.

PART II. SYSTEM GROUNDING AND BONDING

250.21 Alternating-Current Systems Not Required to be Grounded

The location of ground detection sensing equipment for ungrounded systems has been addressed, and marking requirements for ungrounded systems have been added.

250.21 Ungrounded Systems—50V to less than 100V.

(B) Ground Detectors.

(1) Systems that aren't required to be grounded in accordance with 250.20(B) [250.21(A)(4)] must have ground detectors installed.

(2) The ground detection sensing equipment must be connected as close as practicable to where the system receives its supply.

(C) Marking. Ungrounded systems must be legibly marked "Ungrounded System" at the source or first disconnecting means of the system, with sufficient durability to withstand the environment involved.

ANALYSIS: Ground detectors are required for ungrounded systems that operate between 120V and 1,000V. The location of the sensing equipment has never been spelled out in the *NEC* until now, leaving some people confused as to the intent of the requirement. With this revision, it's now required that these sensing devices be installed as close as practicable to the point where the system receives its supply. In previous editions of the *Code*, one could install this equipment at the branch circuit level, leaving all of the feeder circuits without the detection, and allowing them to operate under a ground fault without any indication.

250.24(C) Grounded Conductors Brought to Service Equipment

Several editorial revisions were made to this section.

250.24 Service Equipment—Grounding and Bonding.

(C) Grounded Conductor Brought to Service Equipment. A service neutral conductor from the electric utility must be routed with the ungrounded conductors and terminate to the service disconnecting means via a main bonding jumper [250.24(B)] that's installed between the service neutral conductor and the service disconnecting means enclosure [250.28]. **Figures 250–20 and 250–21**

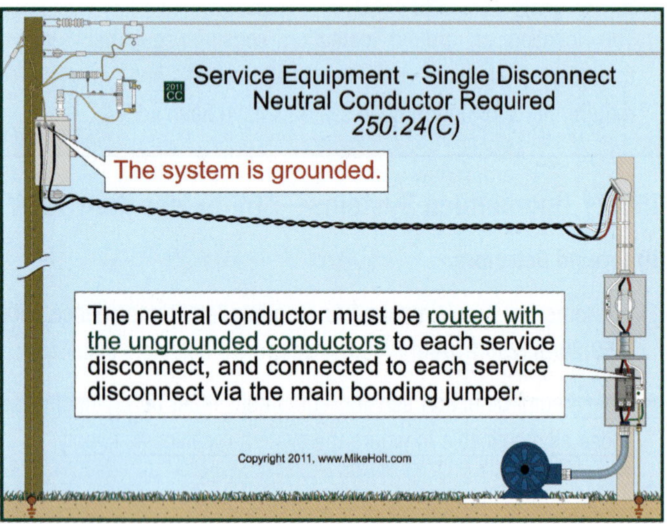

Figure 250–20

Author's Comment: The service neutral conductor provides the effective ground-fault current path to the power supply to ensure that dangerous voltage from a ground fault will be quickly removed by opening the overcurrent device [250.4(A)(3) and 250.4(A)(5)]. **Figure 250–22**

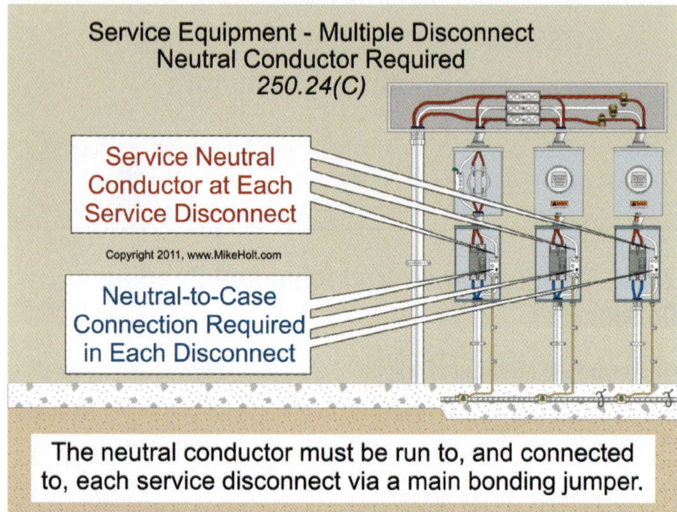

Figure 250–21

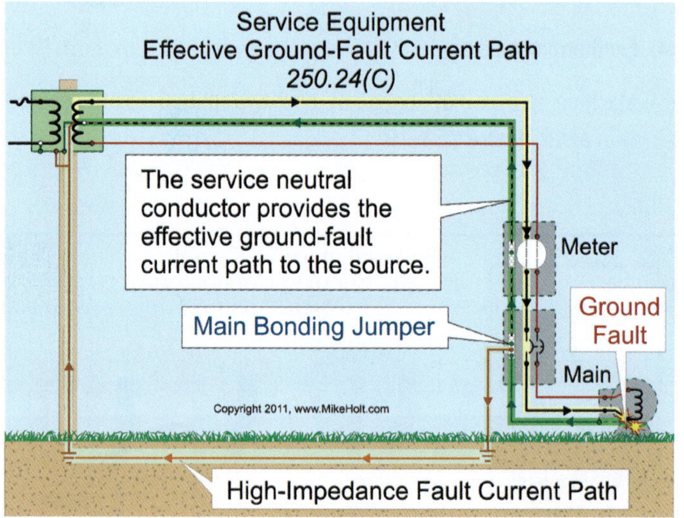

Figure 250–22

DANGER: *Dangerous voltage from a ground fault won't be removed from metal parts, metal piping, and structural steel if the service disconnecting means enclosure isn't connected to the service neutral conductor. This is because the contact resistance of a grounding electrode to the earth is so great that insufficient fault current returns to the power supply if the earth is the only fault current return path to open the circuit overcurrent device.* **Figure 250–23**

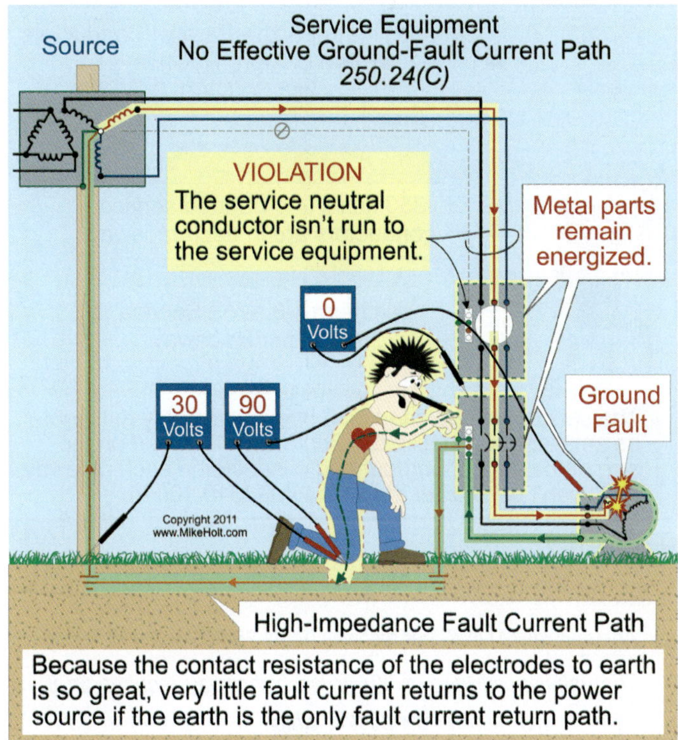

Figure 250–23

Author's Comment: For example, if the neutral conductor is opened, dangerous voltage will be present on metal parts under normal conditions, providing the potential for electric shock. If the earth's ground resistance is 25 ohms and the load's resistance is 25 ohms, the voltage drop across each of these resistors will be half of the voltage source. Since the neutral is connected to the service disconnect, all metal parts will be elevated to 60V above the earth's potential for a 120/240V system. **Figure 250–24**

To determine the actual voltage on the metal parts from an open service neutral conductor, you need to do some complex math calculations. Visit www.MikeHolt.com and go to the "Free Stuff" link to download a spreadsheet for this purpose.

(1) Single Raceway. Because the service neutral conductor serves as the effective ground-fault current path to the source for ground faults, the neutral conductor must be sized so it can safely carry the maximum fault current likely to be imposed on it [110.10 and 250.4(A)(5)]. This is accomplished by sizing the neutral conductor not smaller than specified in Table 250.66, based on the cross-sectional area of the largest ungrounded service conductor. **Figure 250–25**

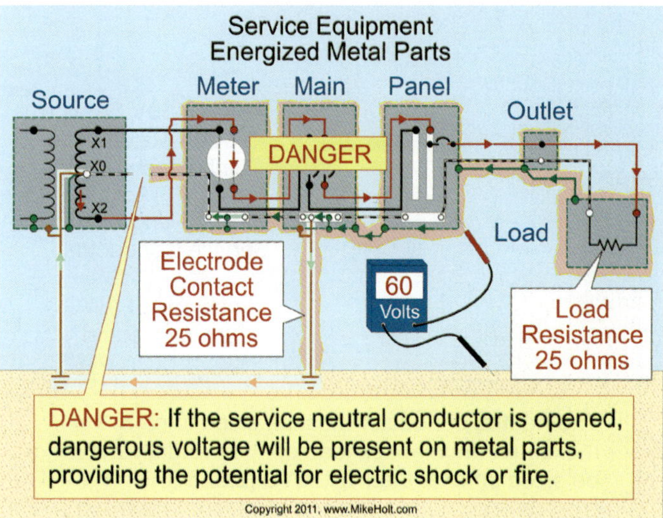

Figure 250–24

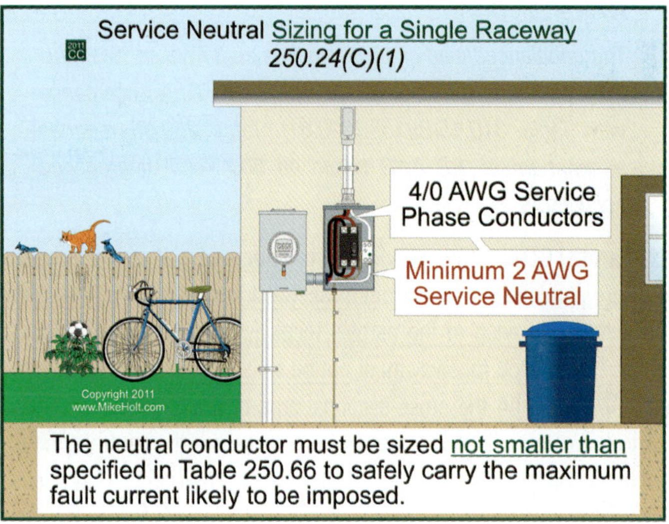

Figure 250–25

Author's Comment: In addition, the neutral conductors must have the capacity to carry the maximum unbalanced neutral current in accordance with 220.61.

Question: *What's the minimum size service neutral conductor required for a 480V, three-phase service installed in one raceway where the ungrounded service conductors are 500 kcmil and the maximum unbalanced load is 100A?* **Figure 250–26**

(a) 3 AWG *(b) 2 AWG* *(c) 1 AWG* *(d) 1/0 AWG*

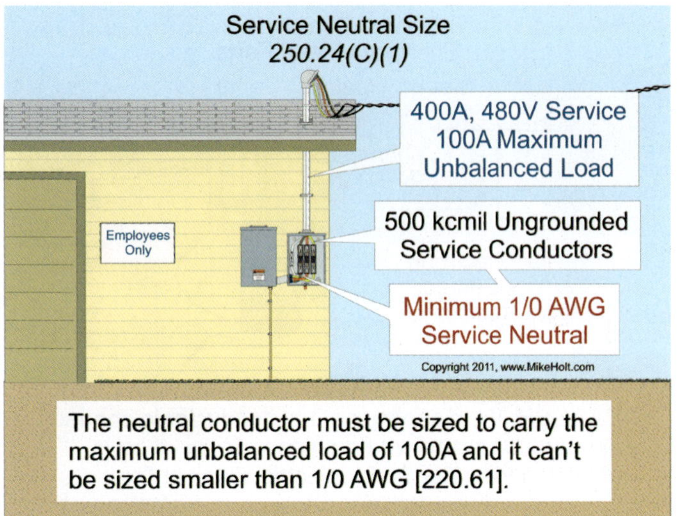

Figure 250–26

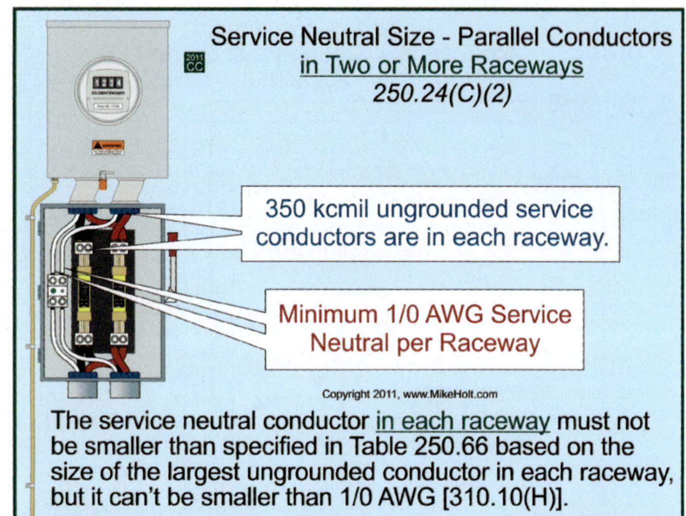

Figure 250–27

Answer: *(d) 1/0 AWG [Table 250.66]*

The unbalanced load of 100A requires an 3 AWG service neutral conductor, which is rated 10A at 75ºC in accordance with Table 310.15(B)(16) [220.61]. Table 250.66 requires a minimum of 1/0 AWG based on 500 kcmil ungrounded conductors.

(2) Parallel Conductors in Two or More Raceways. If service conductors are paralleled in two or more raceways, a neutral conductor must be installed in each of the parallel raceways. The size of the neutral conductor in each raceway must not be smaller than specified in Table 250.66, based on the cross-sectional area of the largest ungrounded service conductor in each raceway. In no case can the neutral conductor in each parallel set be sized smaller than 1/0 AWG [310.10(H)(1)].

Author's Comment: In addition, the neutral conductors must have the capacity to carry the maximum unbalanced neutral current in accordance with 220.61.

Question: *What's the minimum size service neutral conductor required for a 480V, three-phase service installed in two raceways where the ungrounded service conductors in each of the raceways are 350 kcmil and the maximum unbalanced load is 100A?* **Figure 250–27**

(a) 3 AWG (b) 2 AWG (c) 1 AWG (d) 1/0 AWG

Answer: *(d) 1/0 AWG per raceway [Table 250.66 and 310.10(H)]*

The unbalanced load of 50A in each raceway requires an 8 AWG service neutral conductor, which is rated 50A at 75ºC in accordance with Table 310.15(B)(16) [220.61]. Table 250.66 would require a minimum of 2 AWG, however, the smallest service neutral conductor permitted to be installed in parallel in each raceway must not be smaller than 1/0 AWG [310.10(H) and Table 310.15(B)(16)].

ANALYSIS: Several revisions were made to this section to make it an easier section to navigate. The *Code* now spells out what the rules are for sizing the grounded conductor when dealing with service conductors in a single raceway, as well as when parallel service conductors are installed in multiple raceways. A new subsection (3) was also added to clarify that the grounded conductor of a delta-connected, corner-grounded three-phase, 3-wire service must have an ampacity of no less than that of the ungrounded conductors.

250.30 Grounding Separately Derived Systems

This section has been reorganized and includes many revisions and Notes to clarify the grounding and bonding requirements of separately derived systems.

250.30 Separately Derived Systems—Grounding and Bonding.

Note 1: An alternate alternating-current power source such as an on-site generator isn't a separately derived system if the neutral conductor is solidly interconnected to a service-supplied system neutral conductor. An example would be a generator provided with a transfer switch that includes a neutral conductor that's not switched. **Figure 250–28**

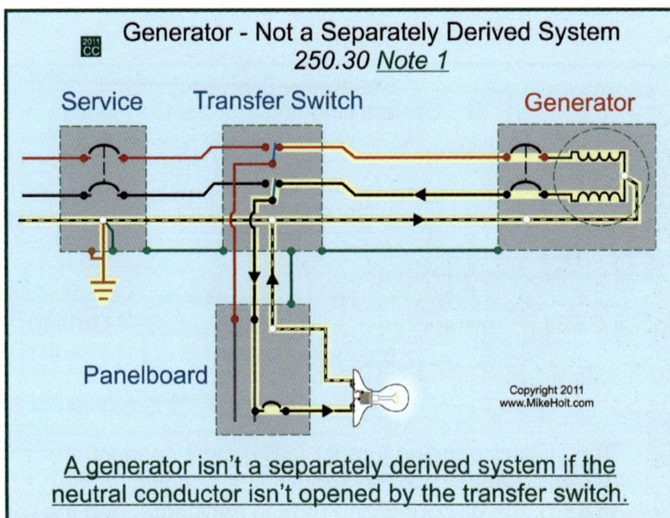

Figure 250–28

Author's Comments:

- According to Article 100, a separately derived system is a wiring system whose power is derived from a source where there's no direct electrical connection to the supply conductors of another system.
- Transformers are considered separately derived when the primary conductors have no direct electrical connection from circuit conductors of one system to circuit conductors of another system, other than connections through the earth, metal enclosures, metallic raceways, or equipment grounding conductors. **Figure 250–29**

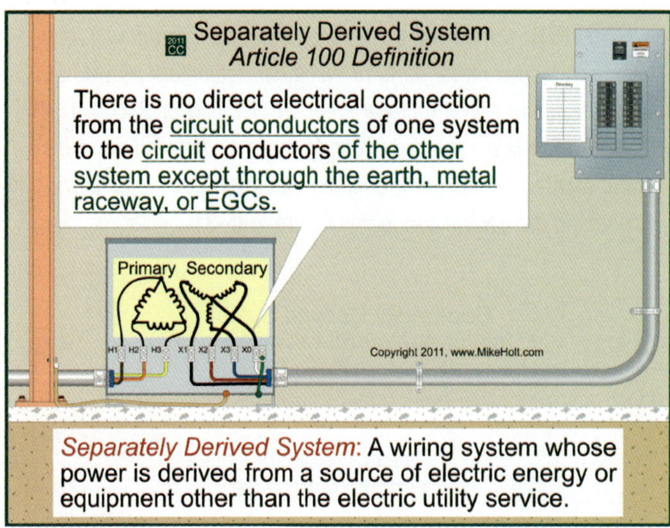

Figure 250–29

- A generator having transfer equipment that switches the neutral conductor, or one that has no neutral conductor at all, is a separately derived system and must be grounded and bonded in accordance with 250.30(A). **Figure 250–30**

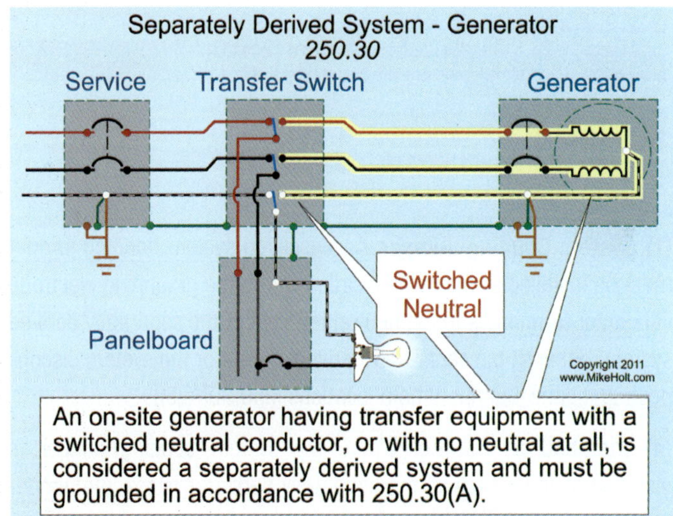

Figure 250–30

Note 2: See 445.13 for the minimum size neutral conductors necessary to carry fault current.

(A) Grounded Systems. Separately derived systems must be grounded and bonded in accordance with (A)(1) through (A)(8).

A neutral-to-case connection must not be made on the load side of the system bonding jumper, except as permitted by 250.142(B).

CAUTION: *Dangerous objectionable neutral current will flow on conductive metal parts of electrical equipment as well as metal piping and structural steel, in violation of 250.6(A), if more than one system bonding jumper is installed, or if it's not located where the grounding electrode conductor terminates to the neutral conductor.* **Figure 250–31**

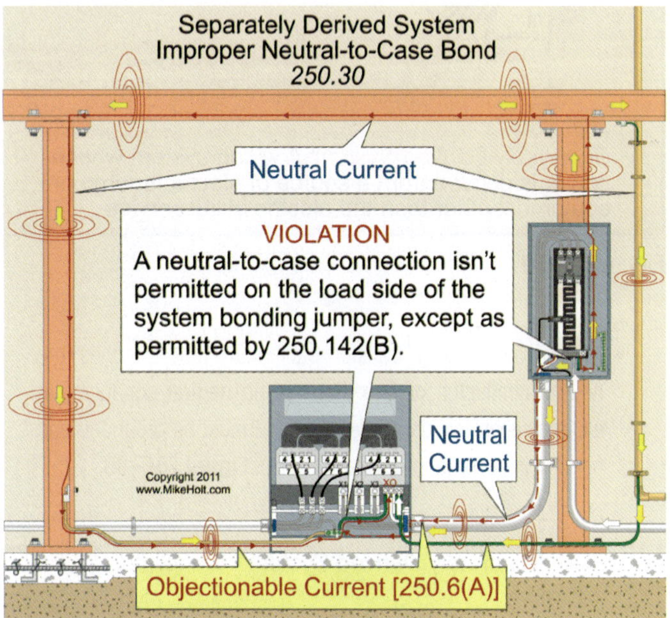

Figure 250–31

(1) System Bonding Jumper. An unspliced system bonding jumper must be installed at the same location where the grounding electrode conductor terminates to the neutral terminal of the separately derived system; either at the separately derived system or the system disconnecting means, but not at both locations [250.30(A)(5)].

(a) Installed at Source. Where the system bonding jumper is installed at the source of the separately derived system, the jumper must connect the neutral conductor of the derived system to the supply-side bonding jumper and the metal enclosure of the source (transformer case). **Figure 250–32**

(b) Installed at First Disconnecting Means. Where the system bonding jumper is installed at the first disconnecting means of a separately derived system, the jumper must connect the neutral conductor of the derived system to the supply-side bonding jumper and the metal disconnecting means enclosure. **Figure 250–33**

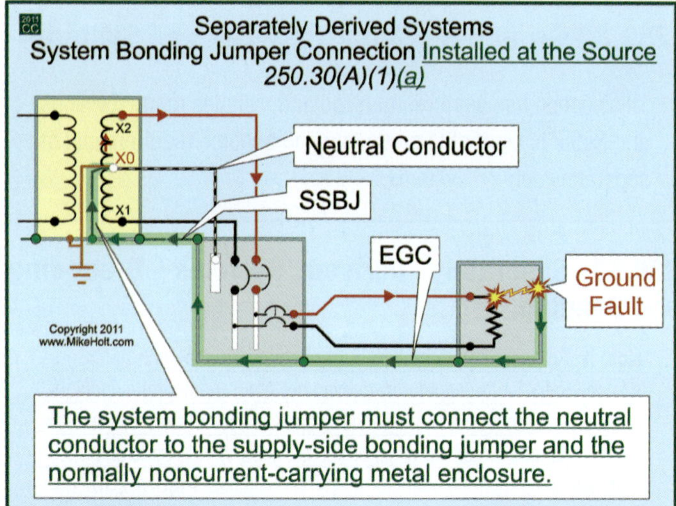

Figure 250–32

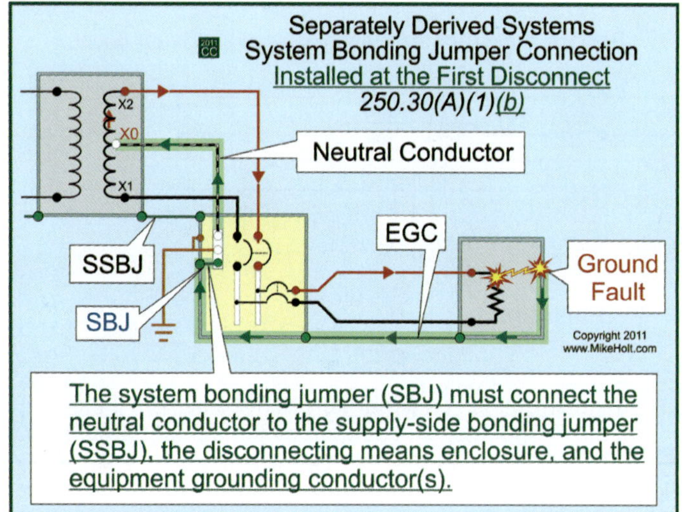

Figure 250–33

Author's Comment: A system bonding jumper is a conductor, screw, or strap that bonds the metal parts of a separately derived system to the system neutral point [Article 100 Bonding Jumper, System], and it's sized to Table 250.66 in accordance with 250.28(D).

DANGER: *During a ground fault, metal parts of electrical equipment, as well as metal piping and structural steel, will become and remain energized providing the potential for electric shock and fire if the system bonding jumper isn't installed.* **Figure 250–34**

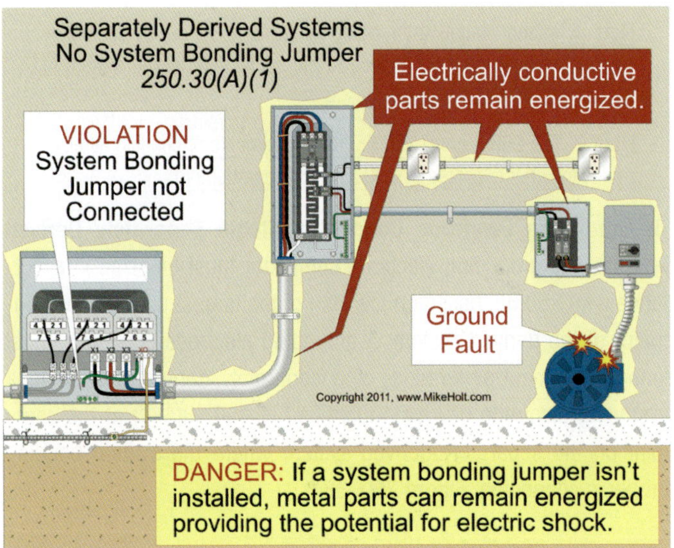

Figure 250–34

(2) Supply-Side Bonding Jumper. If the separately derived system and the first disconnecting means are located in separate enclosures, a supply-side bonding jumper must be run to the derived system disconnecting means. The supply-side bonding jumper can be a nonflexible metal raceway, a wire, or a bus.

(a) If the supply-side bonding jumper is of the wire type, it must be sized in accordance with Table 250.66, based on the area of the largest ungrounded derived system conductor in the raceway or cable.

Question: What size supply-side bonding jumper is required for flexible metal conduit containing 300 kcmil secondary conductors? **Figure 250–35**

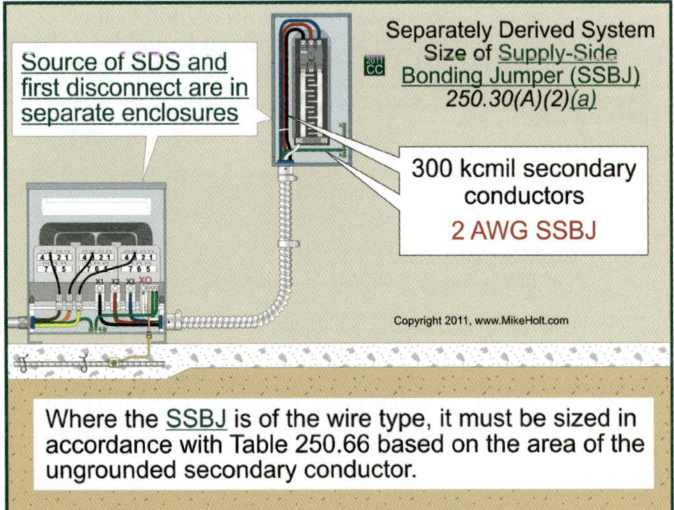

Figure 250–35

(a) 3 AWG (b) 2 AWG (c) 1 AWG (d) 1/0 AWG

Answer: *(b) 2 AWG [Table 250.66]*

(b) If the supply side bonding jumper is a bus, it must have a cross sectional area no smaller than required by Table 250.66.

(3) System Neutral Conductor Size. If the system bonding jumper is installed at the disconnecting means instead of at the source, the following requirements apply:

(a) Sizing for Single Raceway. Because the neutral conductor of a derived system serves as the effective ground-fault current path for ground-fault current, it must be routed with the ungrounded conductors of the derived system and be sized not smaller than specified in Table 250.66, based on the area of the ungrounded conductor of the derived system. **Figure 250–36**

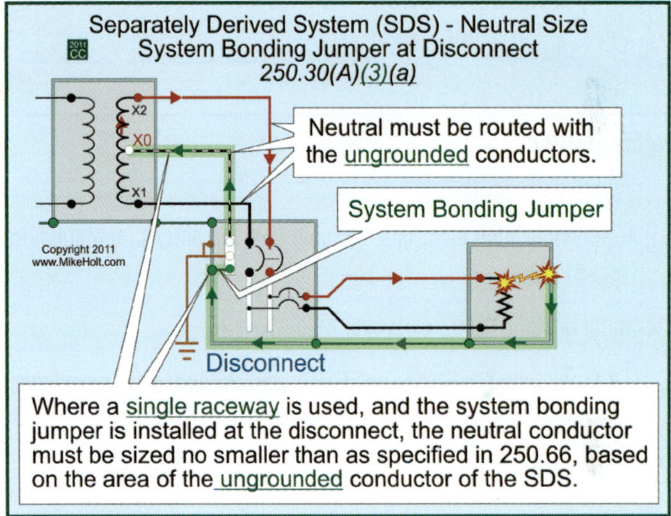

Figure 250–36

(b) Parallel Conductors in Two or More Raceways. If the conductors from the derived system are installed in parallel in two or more raceways, the neutral conductor of the derived system in each raceway or cable must be sized not smaller than specified in Table 250.66, based on the area of the largest ungrounded conductor of the derived system in the raceway or cable. In no case is the neutral conductor of the derived system permitted to be smaller than 1/0 AWG [310.10(H)].

Author's Comment: If the system bonding jumper is installed at the disconnecting means instead of at the source, an supply side system bonding conductor must connect the metal parts of the separately derived system to the neutral conductor at the disconnecting means in accordance with 250.30(A)(2).

(4) Grounding Electrode. The grounding electrode must be as near as practicable, and preferably in the same area where the system bonding jumper is installed and be one of the following: **Figure 250–37**

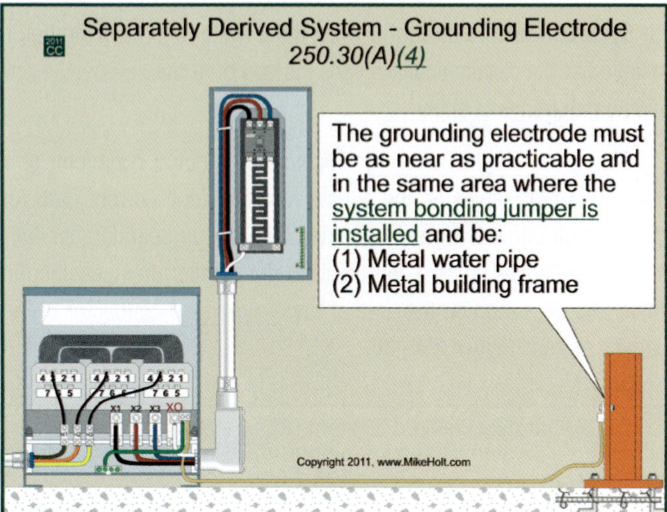

Figure 250–37

(1) Metal water pipe electrode, within 5 ft of the entry to the building [250.52(A)(1)].

(2) Metal building frame electrode [250.52(A)(2)].

Ex 1: If the electrodes listed specified in 250.30(A)(4) aren't available, one of the following electrodes can be used:

- *A concrete-encased electrode encased by not less than 2 in. of concrete, located horizontally near the bottom or vertically, and within that portion of concrete foundation or footing that's in direct contact with the earth [250.52(A)(3)].*
- *A ground ring electrode encircling the building/structure, buried not less than 30 in. below grade, consisting of at least 20 ft of bare copper conductor not smaller than 2 AWG [250.52(A)(4) and 250.53(F)].*
- *A ground rod electrode having not less than 8 ft of contact with the soil meeting the requirements of 250.52(A)(5) and 250.53(G)].*
- *Other metal underground systems, piping systems, or underground tanks [250.52(A)(8)].*

Note 1: Interior metal water piping in the area served by separately derived systems must be bonded to the separately derived system in accordance with 250.104(D).

Note 2: See 250.50 and 250.58 for requirements of bonding all electrodes together if located at the same building/structure.

(5) Grounding Electrode Conductor, Single Separately Derived System. The grounding electrode conductor must be sized in accordance with 250.66, based on the area of the largest ungrounded conductor of the derived system. A grounding electrode conductor must connect the neutral terminal of a separately derived system to a grounding electrode of a type identified in 250.30(A)(4) at the same point on the separately derived system where the system bonding jumper is connected. **Figure 250–38**

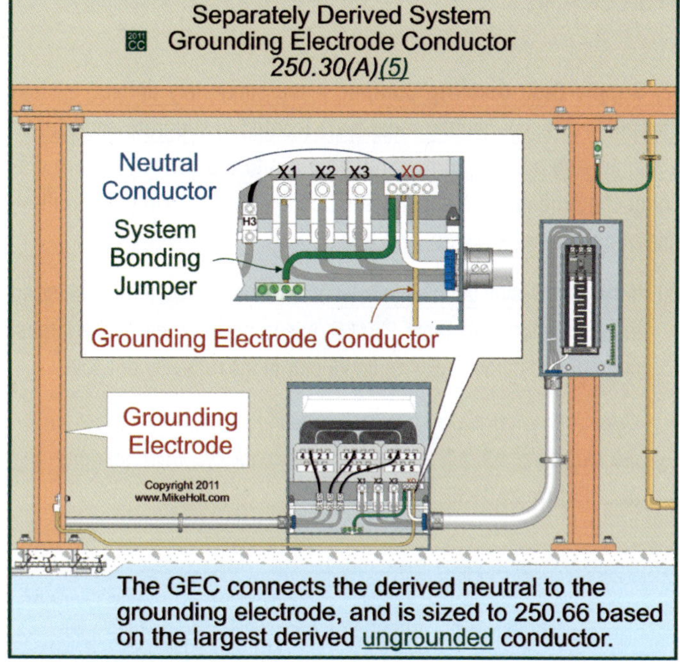

Figure 250–38

Author's Comments:

- System grounding is intended to reduce overvoltage caused by induction from indirect lightning, or restriking/intermittent ground faults. Induced voltage imposed from lightning can be reduced by short grounding conductors and eliminating unnecessary bends and loops [250.4(A)(1) Note]. **Figure 250–39**

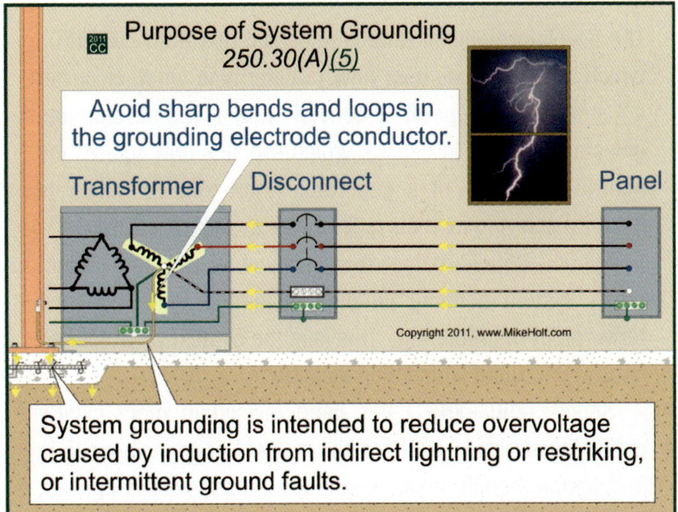

Figure 250–39

- System grounding also helps reduce fires in buildings as well as voltage stress on electrical insulation, thereby ensuring longer insulation life for motors, transformers, and other system components.

Ex 1: If the system bonding jumper is a wire or busbar, the grounding electrode conductor is permitted to terminate to either the neutral terminal or the equipment grounding terminal, bar, or bus in accordance with 250.30(A)(1). **Figure 250–40**

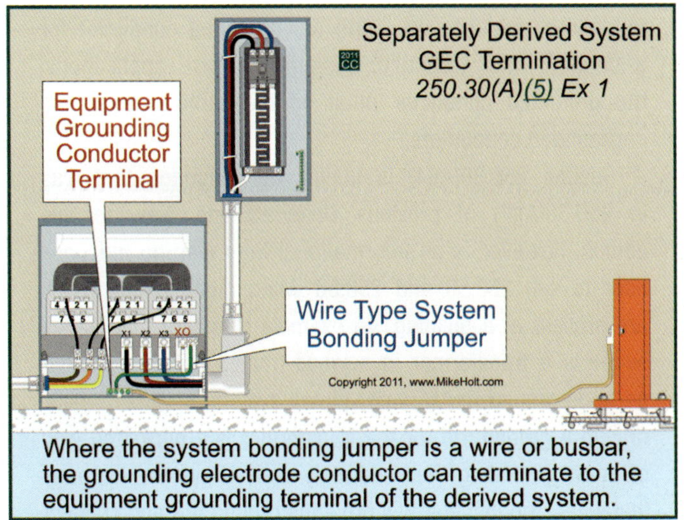

Figure 250–40

Ex 3: Separately derived systems rated 1 kVA or less aren't required to be grounded (connected to the earth).

(6) Grounding Electrode Conductor, Multiple Separately Derived Systems. Where there are multiple separately derived systems, a grounding electrode conductor tap from each separately derived system to a common grounding electrode conductor is permitted. This connection is to be made at the same point on the separately derived system where the system bonding jumper is connected [250.30(A)(1)]. **Figure 250–41**

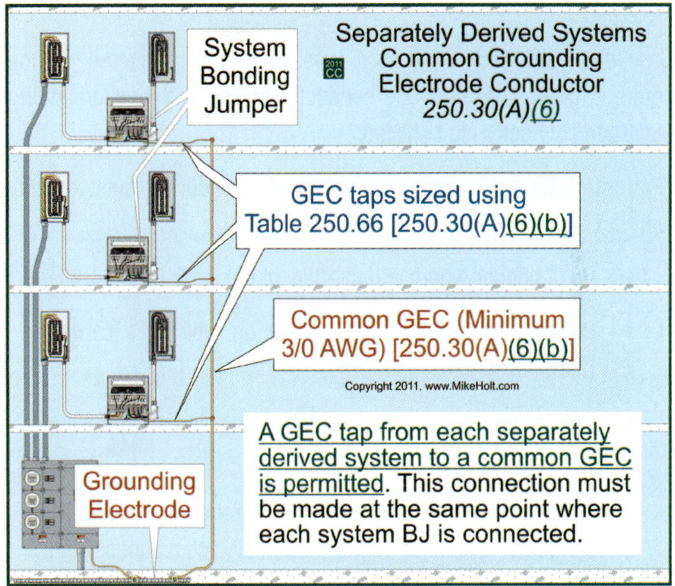

Figure 250–41

Ex 1: If the system bonding jumper is a wire or busbar, the grounding electrode conductor tap can terminate to either the neutral terminal or the equipment grounding terminal, bar, or bus in accordance with 250.30(A)(1).

Ex 2: Separately derived systems rated 1 kVA or less aren't required to be grounded (connected to the earth).

(a) Common Grounding Electrode Conductor. The common grounding electrode conductor can be one of the following:

(1) A conductor not smaller than 3/0 AWG copper or 250 kcmil aluminum.

(2) The metal frame of the building/structure that complies with 250.52(A)(2) or is connected to the grounding electrode system by a conductor not smaller than 3/0 AWG copper or 250 kcmil aluminum.

(b) Tap Conductor Size. Grounding electrode conductor taps must be sized in accordance with Table 250.66, based on the area of the largest ungrounded conductor of the given derived system.

(c) Connections. All tap connections to the common grounding electrode conductor must be made at an accessible location by one of the following methods:

(1) A connector listed as grounding and bonding equipment.

(2) Listed connections to aluminum or copper busbars not less than ¼ x 2 in.

(3) Exothermic welding.

Grounding electrode conductor taps must be connected to the common grounding electrode conductor so the common grounding electrode conductor isn't spliced.

(7) Installation. The grounding electrode conductor must comply with the following:

- Be of copper where within 18 in. of the earth [250.64(A)].
- Securely fastened to the surface on which it's carried [250.64(B)].
- Adequately protected if exposed to physical damage [250.64(B)].
- Metal enclosures enclosing a grounding electrode conductor must be made electrically continuous from the point of attachment to cabinets or equipment to the grounding electrode [250.64(E)].

(8) Structural Steel and Metal Piping. To ensure dangerous voltage from a ground fault is removed quickly, structural steel and metal piping in the area served by a separately derived system must be connected to the neutral conductor at the separately derived system in accordance with 250.104(D).

(C) Outdoor Source. If the separately derived system is located outside the building/structure, a connection to the grounding electrode must be made at the separately derived system location.

ANALYSIS: Considering the amount of changes that have occurred in this section, it wouldn't be entirely inaccurate to say that the whole section has been rewritten. Taking the changes one at a time, they're as follows:

A new opening paragraph and two Informational Notes have been added. These changes alert the *NEC* user to other sections in Part II of the article that must be complied with. The first Informational Note is relocated text from 250.20(D), which tells the *Code* user how to determine whether or not a generator is a separately derived system. The second note gives a reference to 445.13, which explains how to size the neutral conductor of a generator when that conductor is used for carrying fault current as well as neutral current.

Section 250.30(A) has been revised to use the correct term "system bonding jumper" instead of the undefined term "point of grounding." This is in the context of prohibited neutral to ground connection locations.

Section 250.30(A)(1) has been revised to more clearly detail the options of where the system bonding jumper is installed. Although previous editions gave the same options, this *NEC* edition more clearly spells them out.

Section 250.30(A)(2) introduces the new term "supply side bonding jumper" to this section. When the source of the separately derived system doesn't contain an overcurrent device, a supply side bonding jumper must be installed to the first overcurrent device (although the *Code* uses the term "disconnecting means" instead of overcurrent device). The ungrounded conductors in such an application don't have overcurrent protection, so the bonding jumper that's routed with these circuit conductors must be larger in size than a typical equipment grounding conductor. A supply side bonding jumper satisfies this requirement.

Section 250.30(A)(3) mainly borrows the text that was previously in 250.30(A)(8). It does, however, add new text to provide guidance on sizing the grounded conductor for a delta (corner grounded) system. In these applications, the grounded conductor must be the same size as the ungrounded conductors.

Section 250.30(A)(4) is mainly the language that was in 250.30(A)(7) of previous *Code* editions. New to this edition, however, is an Informational Note alerting the *Code* user to see 250.50 and 250.58 when multiple electrodes are present at a building. An example of where this makes sense is a transformer in a wood-framed building without an underground metal water piping system. In such a case, driving a ground rod for the transformer is a permitted way of earth grounding the separately derived system. In many instances, the installer will drive the ground rod and connect it to the transformer, without considering the fact that he or she has just created an electrode that isn't connected to the other electrodes in the building. In an installation such as this, the installer will be required to connect this "new" electrode to the "other" electrodes in the building, such as, perhaps, a ground rod located outside near the service equipment. By adding this new Informational Note, both installers and inspectors will be reminded of this requirement.

In 250.30(A)(6), the grounding electrode conductor(s) for multiple separately derived systems, has been changed to clarify that structural metal can be used to ground multiple separately derived systems, provided that the structural metal complies with 250.52(A)(2) or is connected to the grounding electrode system by a conductor not smaller than 3/0 AWG CU or 250 kcmil AL.

Section 250.30(C) is new to the *NEC*. This subsection addresses separately derived systems that are installed outside of a building or other structure. When this is the case, a grounding electrode connection to the transformer must be provided.

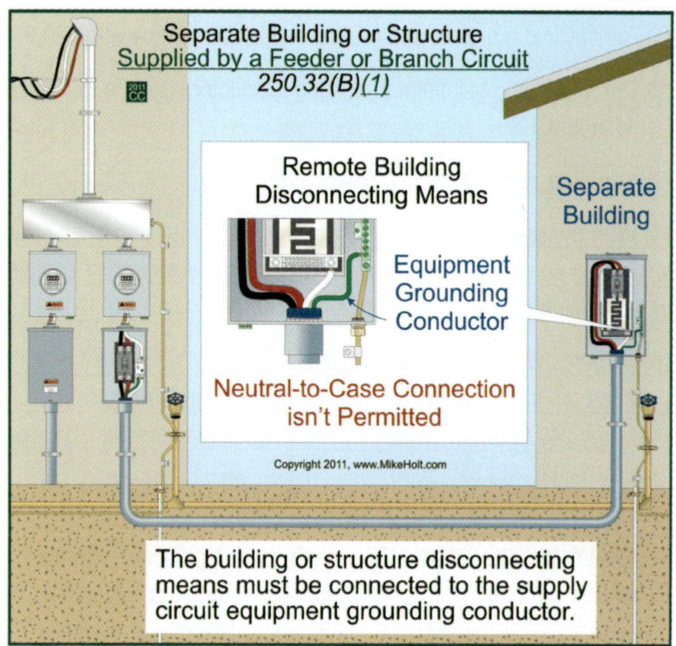

Figure 250–42

250.32 Buildings or Structures Supplied by a Feeder or Branch Circuit

The exception dealing with existing installations has been clarified, and a new subsection was added to address buildings supplied by a separately derived system.

250.32 Buildings or Structures Supplied by a Feeder or Branch Circuit.

(B) Equipment Grounding Conductor.

(1) Supplied by a Feeder or Branch Circuit. To quickly clear a ground fault and remove dangerous voltage from metal parts, the building/structure disconnecting means must be connected to the circuit equipment grounding conductor, which must be one of the types described in 250.118. If the supply circuit equipment grounding conductor is of the wire type, it must be sized in accordance with 250.122, based on the rating of the overcurrent device. **Figure 250–42**

CAUTION: *To prevent dangerous objectionable neutral current from flowing onto metal parts [250.6(A)], the supply circuit neutral conductor isn't permitted to be connected to the remote building/structure disconnecting means [250.142(B)].* **Figure 250–43**

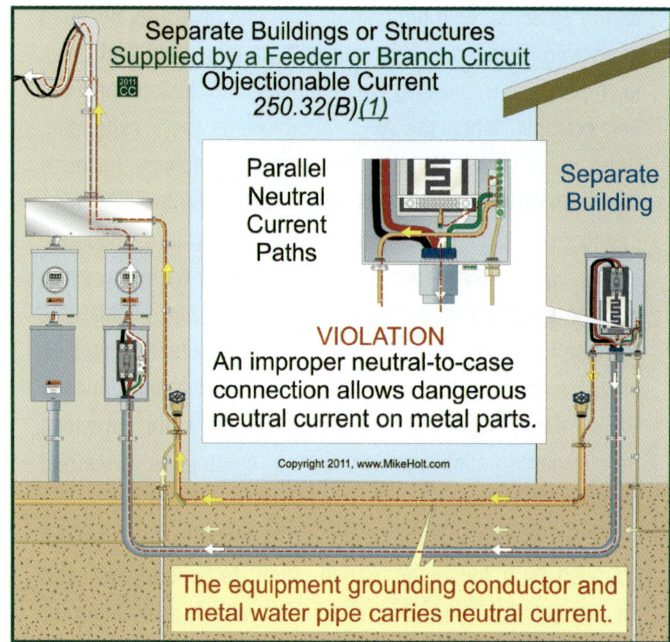

Figure 250–43

Ex: The neutral conductor can serve as the ground-fault return path for the building/structure disconnecting means for existing installations in compliance with previous editions of the Code where there are no continuous metallic paths between buildings and structures, ground-fault protection of equipment isn't installed on the supply side of the circuit, and the neutral conductor is sized no smaller than the larger of:

(1) The maximum unbalanced neutral load in accordance with 220.61.

(2) The minimum equipment grounding conductor size in accordance with 250.122.

(2) Supplied by Separately Derived System.

(a) With Overcurrent Protection. If overcurrent protection is provided where the conductors originate, the supply conductors must contain an equipment grounding conductor in accordance with 250.32(B)(1).

(b) Without Overcurrent Protection. If overcurrent protection isn't provided for the supply conductors to the building/structure as permitted by 240.21(C)(4), the installation must be grounded and bonded in accordance with 250.30(A).

ANALYSIS: The 2008 *NEC* contained a significant change to this section by requiring that an equipment grounding conductor be installed for buildings or structures supplied by feeders or branch circuits. With this change, an exception was added to the 2008 *Code*, clarifying that existing premises wiring systems need not comply with this new rule. Because most *NEC* changes don't come with an exception that gives exemption for existing installations, confusion ensued. For example, when the AFCI requirements were expanded, there wasn't an exception for existing buildings, because the *Code* isn't retroactive (90.2(A) tells us that the *NEC* is an installation standard, not a maintenance standard). Because of this, when the exception was added, many *Code* users had no idea what it really pertained to. The change in this *NEC* revision cycle, however, clarifies that this exception applies only to existing buildings or structures that met the previous *Code* requirements and continue to meet the previous requirements, such as not having continuous grounded metal paths between the two buildings or structures.

Previous *NEC* editions required a building or structure supplied by a feeder or branch circuit to be supplied with an equipment grounding conductor. When a building or structure is supplied by a separately derived system, with no overcurrent protection at the source, there's no equipment grounding conductor by definition. This revision clarifies that when this occurs, a supply side bonding jumper must be run to the building or structure, and it's to be installed in accordance with 250.30(A).

PART III. GROUNDING ELECTRODE SYSTEM AND GROUNDING ELECTRODE CONDUCTOR

250.35(B) Nonseparately Derived System

An editorial revision to this requirement was made to create consistency with other *Code* sections.

250.35 Permanently Installed Generators.

(B) Nonseparately Derived System. A generator without integral overcurrent protection that's not a separately derived system must have a supply-side bonding jumper installed between the generator equipment grounding terminal and the equipment grounding terminal, bar, or bus of the disconnecting mean(s). The supply-side bonding jumper is sized in accordance with 250.102(C), based on the size of the ungrounded circuit conductors of the generator.

ANALYSIS: This section was added in the 2008 *NEC* to clarify the rules for permanently installed generators when they're installed as nonseparately derived systems. The language of this section was somewhat inconsistent with similar *Code* rules. It's now been changed to add consistency and to clarify that the equipment grounding conductor for these systems can terminate to a grounding bar as well as a terminal or bus. Similar language can be found in 250.30 and 250.24.

Author's Comment: The frame of a nonseparately derived system generator isn't required to be connected to a grounding electrode.

250.52(A) Electrodes Permitted for Grounding

The rule explaining when a structural metal frame can serve as a grounding electrode has been changed...again, and the requirements for concrete encased electrodes, ground rods, and ground plates have been clarified.

250.52 Grounding Electrode Types.

(A) Electrodes Permitted for Grounding.

(1) Underground Metal Water Pipe Electrode. Underground metal water pipe in direct contact with the earth for 10 ft or more can serve as a grounding electrode. **Figure 250–44**

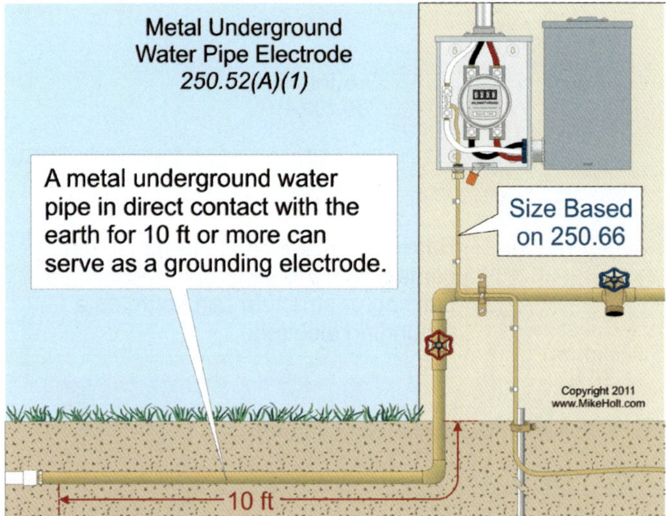

Figure 250–44

Author's Comment: Controversy about using metal underground water supply piping as a grounding electrode has existed since the early 1900s. The water industry believes that neutral current flowing on water piping corrodes the metal. For more information, contact the American Water Works Association about their report *Effects of Electrical Grounding on Pipe Integrity and Shock Hazard*, Catalog No. 90702, 1.800.926.7337. **Figure 250–45**

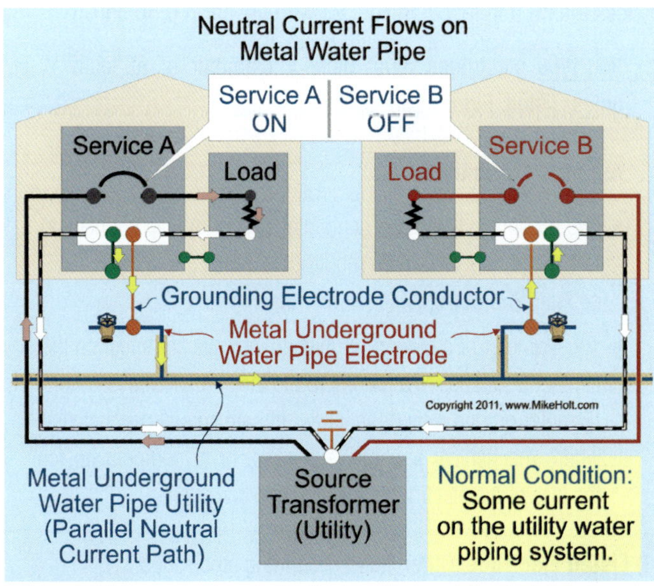

Figure 250–45

(2) Metal Frame Electrode. The metal frame of a building/structure can serve as a grounding electrode when it meets at least one of the following conditions:

(1) At least one structural metal member is in direct contact with the earth for 10 ft or more, with or without concrete encasement.

(2) The bolts securing the structural steel column are connected to a concrete encased electrode [250.52(A)(3)] by welding, exothermic welding, steel tie wires, or other approved means. **Figure 250–46**

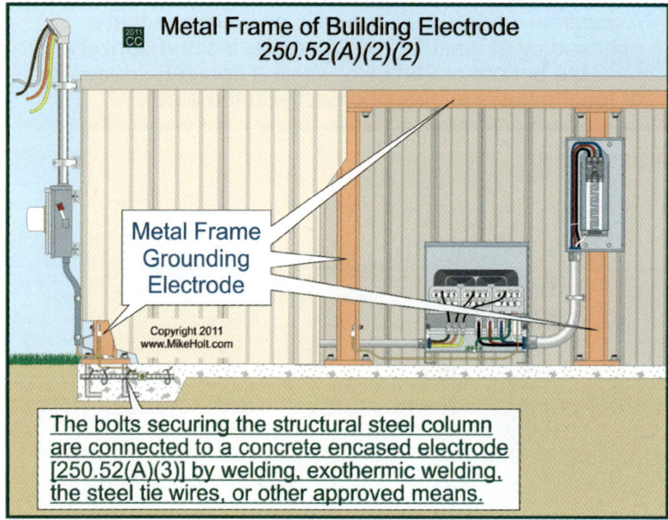

Figure 250–46

(3) Concrete-Encased Electrode. At least 20 ft of either (1) or (2): **Figure 250–47**

(1) One or more of bare, zinc-galvanized, or otherwise electrically conductive steel reinforcing bars of not less than ½ in. diameter, mechanically connected together by steel tie wires, welding, or other effective means, to create a 20 ft or greater length.

(2) Bare copper conductor not smaller than 4 AWG.

The reinforcing bars or bare copper conductor must be encased by at least 2 in. of concrete located horizontally near the bottom of a concrete footing or vertically within a concrete foundation that's in direct contact with the earth.

If multiple concrete-encased electrodes are present at a building/structure, only one is required to serve as a grounding electrode. **Figure 250–48**

Note: Concrete containing insulation, vapor barriers, films or similar items separating it from the earth isn't considered to be in "direct contact" with the earth.

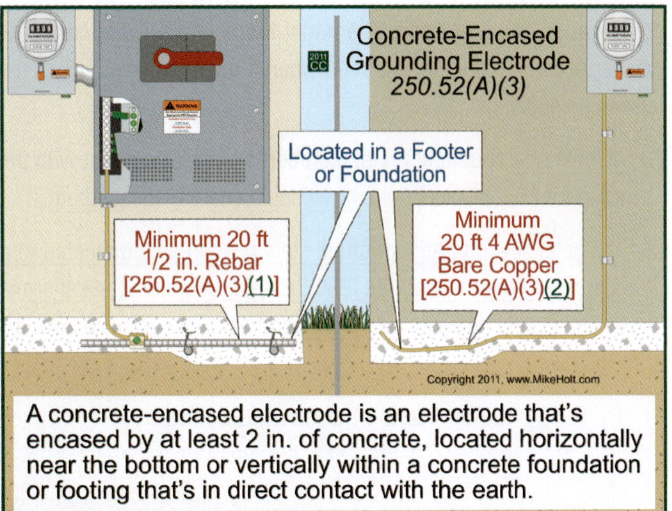

Figure 250–47

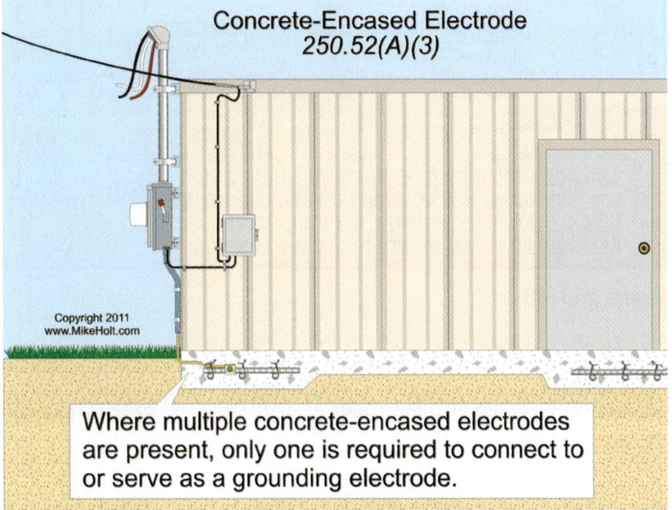

Figure 250–48

Author's Comments:

- The grounding electrode conductor to a concrete-encased grounding electrode isn't required to be larger than 4 AWG copper [250.66(B)].
- The concrete-encased grounding electrode is also called a "Ufer Ground," named after a consultant working for the U.S. Army during World War II. The technique Mr. Ufer came up with was necessary because the site needing grounding had no underground water table and little rainfall. The desert site was a series of bomb storage vaults in the area of Flagstaff, Arizona. This type of grounding electrode generally offers the lowest ground resistance for the cost.

(4) Ground Ring Electrode. A ground ring consisting of at least 20 ft of bare copper conductor not smaller than 2 AWG buried in the earth encircling a building/structure, can serve as a grounding electrode. **Figure 250–49**

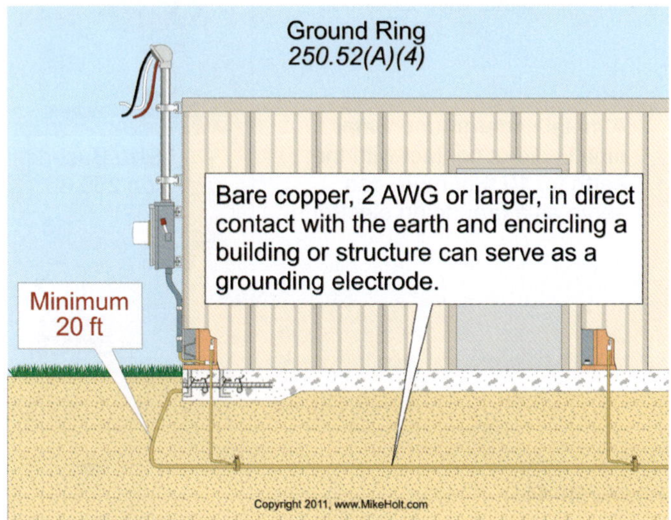

Figure 250–49

Author's Comment: The ground ring must be buried not less than 30 in. [250.53(F)], and the grounding electrode conductor to a ground ring isn't required to be larger than the ground ring conductor size [250.66(C)].

(5) Ground Rod and Pipe Electrode. Ground rod electrodes must not be less than 8 ft in length in contact with the earth [250.53(G)].

(b) Rod-type electrodes must have a diameter of at least ⅝ in., unless listed. **Figure 250–50**

Author's Comments:

- The grounding electrode conductor, if it's the sole connection to the ground rod, isn't required to be larger than 6 AWG copper [250.66(A)].
- The diameter of a ground rod has an insignificant effect on the contact resistance of a ground rod to the earth. However, larger diameter ground rods (¾ in. and 1 in.) are sometimes installed where mechanical strength is desired, or to compensate for the loss of the electrode's metal due to corrosion.

(6) Listed Electrode. Other listed grounding electrodes.

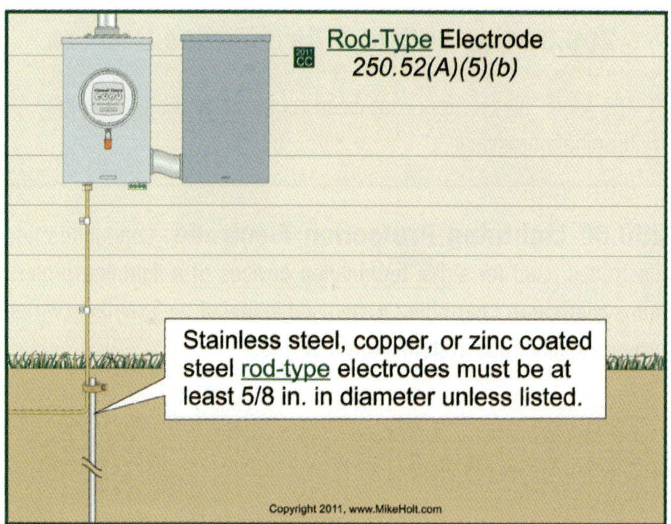

Figure 250–50

(7) Ground Plate Electrode. A bare or conductively coated iron or steel plate with not less than ¼ in. of thickness, or a solid uncoated copper metal plate not less than 0.06 in. of thickness, with an exposed surface area of not less than 2 sq ft.

(8) Metal Underground Systems Electrode. Metal underground piping systems, underground tanks, and underground metal well casings can serve as a grounding electrode.

> **Author's Comment:** The grounding electrode conductor to the metal underground system must be sized according to Table 250.66.

ANALYSIS: Over the last few *Code* cycles, the *NEC* has tried to make clear when the structural metal of a building or structure can be used as a grounding electrode. The first prescribed method will find the structural metal with direct earth contact for 10 ft or more. As an alternative, the hold-down bolts securing the structural metal column can be connected to a concrete-encased electrode. Previously, the *Code* allowed the structural metal to serve as an electrode if it was connected to a ground rod meeting the 25 ohm requirement of (formerly) 250.56. This option has now been removed, and is no longer a suitable method of bonding the structural metal to qualify it as a grounding electrode.

The ways of creating a concrete-encased electrode have been changed into an easy-to-use list format, and a clarification has been made regarding the use of vapor barriers. When a vapor barrier (typically a plastic sheet) is installed beneath the footing, *NEC* users have debated whether or not the concrete is still considered to be in direct contact with earth. A new Informational Note was added to clarify that such a footing isn't considered to be in direct contact with the earth, therefore the rebar or bare copper conductor can't be used as a grounding electrode.

Section 250.52(A)(5) has been changed to eliminate the minimum size for listed electrodes. Previous editions of the *Code* have stated that listed ground rods must be at least ½ in. in diameter. Because the *NEC* is typically not the place to find listing requirements, this text has been removed, which might open the door to smaller ground rods being listed.

Lastly, a change was made to 250.52(A)(7) which clarifies that plate electrodes must be conductive(!).

250.53(A) Rod, Pipe, and Plate Electrodes

The 25 ohm rule has been relocated and greatly clarified. Editorial changes to this section have also been made, and the Informational Note has been revised.

250.53 Grounding Electrode Installation Requirements.

(A) Rod, Pipe, or Plate Electrodes.

(1) Below Permanent Moisture Level. If practicable, rod, pipe, and plate electrodes must be embedded below the permanent moisture level and be free from nonconductive coatings such as paint or enamel.

(2) Supplemental Electrode. A single rod, pipe or plate electrode must be supplemented by an additional electrode that's bonded to one of the following:

(1) The single rod, pipe, or plate electrode

(2) The grounding electrode conductor of the single electrode

(3) The neutral service-entrance conductor

(4) The nonflexible grounded service raceway

(5) The service enclosure

Ex: If a single rod, pipe, or plate grounding electrode has an earth contact resistance of 25 ohms or less, the supplemental electrode isn't required.

(3) Spacing. The supplemental electrode for a single rod, pipe, or plate electrode must be installed not less than 6 ft from the single electrode. **Figure 250–51**

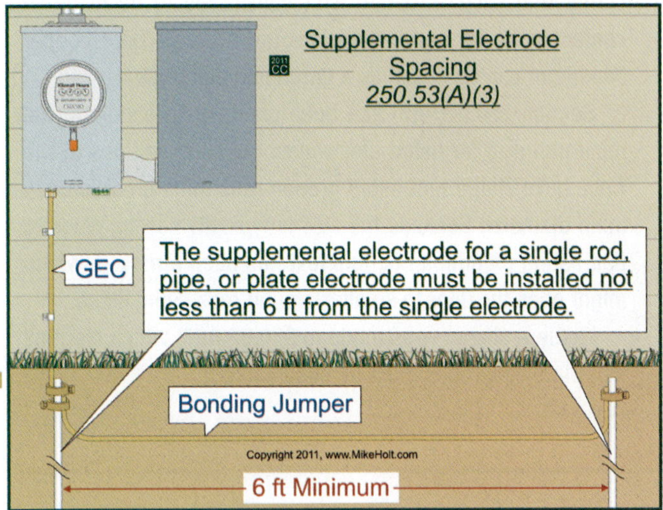

Figure 250–51

Note: The efficiency of paralleling electrodes is improved by spacing them at least twice the length of the longest rod.

ANALYSIS: The long standing rule that a ground rod, as well as a pipe or plate electrode, must have a resistance to earth of 25 ohms or less or be supplemented by an additional electrode was well understood until recent revisions to the *NEC* created confusion. These revisions left the *Code* user trying to figure out if a concrete-encased electrode required a supplement, and when a ground rod is actually required. Revisions to this section now match the standard industry practice of (when required) driving two ground rods instead of testing the resistance of a single driven rod. The 25 ohm language is now written as an exception, recognizing this practice. *Code* users will notice that 250.56 has been deleted as a result of this change, but the technical provisions contained therein haven't disappeared.

The Informational Note explaining the logic of spacing ground rods more than 6 ft apart, while technically true, didn't provide any guidance as to what the spacing should be. This change clarifies that the driven rods should be at least twice the length of the longer of the two rods. For example, two rods 8 ft in length should be driven at least 16 ft apart. It's worth remembering that this is an Informational Note, and not a *Code* requirement [90.5(C)].

250.60 Use of Strike Termination Devices

The term "air terminal" has been replaced by the term "strike termination device(s)."

250.60 Lightning Protection Electrode. Conductors and electrodes used for strike termination devices of a lightning protection system aren't permitted to be used in lieu of the premises wiring grounding electrode system. **Figure 250–52**

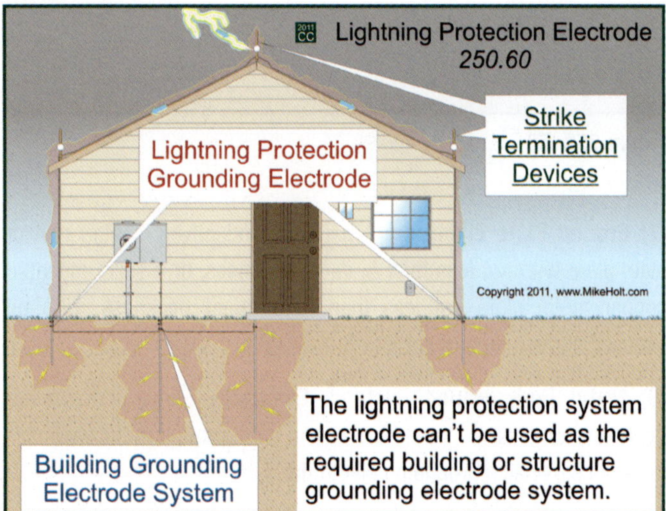

Figure 250–52

Note 2: If a lightning protection system is installed, the lightning protection system must be bonded to the building/structure grounding electrode system so as to limit potential difference between it and the electrical system wiring as per 250.106. **Figure 250–53**

ANALYSIS: The industry standard for lightning protection systems is NFPA 780. It uses the term "strike termination device(s)" when discussing the component of the lightning protection system that intercepts lightning flashes and connects them to a path to ground. In order to create consistency with that standard and this *Code*, the terms are now the same.

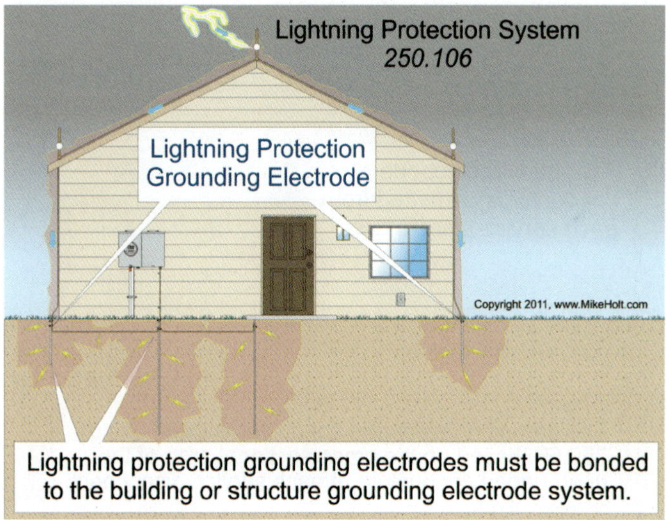

Figure 250–53

250.64 Grounding Electrode Conductor Installation

Several changes to this section have been made for clarity and technical accuracy.

250.64 Grounding Electrode Conductor Installation. Grounding electrode conductors must be installed as specified in (A) through (F).

(A) Aluminum Conductors. Aluminum grounding electrode conductors must not be in contact with masonry, subject to corrosive conditions, or within 18 in. of the earth.

(B) Conductor Protection. Where installed exposed, grounding electrode conductors must be protected where subject to physical damage and are permitted to be installed on or through framing members. Grounding electrode conductors 6 AWG copper and larger can be installed exposed along the surface of the building if securely fastened and not subject to physical damage.

Grounding electrode conductors sized 8 AWG must be protected by installing them in rigid metal conduit, intermediate metal conduit, PVC conduit, electrical metallic tubing, or reinforced thermosetting resin conduit.

> **Author's Comment:** A ferrous metal raceway containing a grounding electrode conductor must be made electrically continuous by bonding each end of that type of raceway to the grounding electrode conductor [250.64(E)], so it's best to use PVC conduit.

(C) Continuous. Grounding electrode conductor(s) must be installed without a splice or joint except:

(1) By irreversible compression-type connectors or exothermic welding.

(2) Sections of busbars connected together to form a grounding electrode conductor.

(3) Bolted, riveted, or welded connections of structural metal frames of buildings or structures.

(4) Threaded, welded, brazed, soldered or bolted-flange connections of metal water piping.

(D) Grounding Electrode Conductor for Multiple Service Disconnects. If a service consists of more than a single enclosure, grounding electrode connections must be made in one of the following methods:

(1) Common **Grounding Electrode Conductor and Taps.** A grounding electrode conductor tap must extend to the inside of each service disconnecting means enclosure.

The common grounding electrode conductor must be sized in accordance with 250.66, based on the sum of the circular mil area of the largest ungrounded service-entrance conductors. Figure 250–54

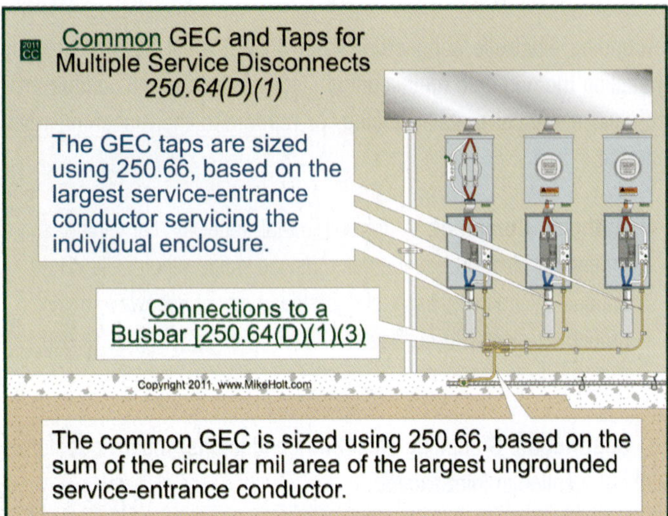

Figure 250–54

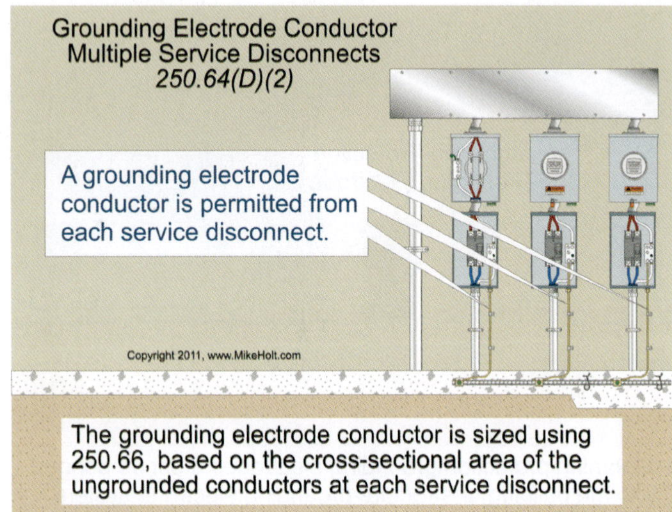

Figure 250–55

A grounding electrode conductor must extend from each service disconnecting means, sized not smaller than specified in Table 250.66, based on the area of the largest ungrounded conductor for each service disconnecting means.

The grounding electrode tap conductors must be connected to the common grounding electrode conductor, without splicing the common grounding electrode conductor, by one of the following methods:

(1) Exothermic welding

(2) Connectors listed as grounding and bonding equipment

(3) Connections to a busbar not less than ¼ in. × 2 in. that's securely fastened and installed in an accessible location.

(2) Individual Grounding Electrode Conductors. A grounding electrode conductor must be connected between the grounded conductor in each service equipment disconnecting means enclosure and the grounding electrode system, each sized in accordance with 250.66 based on the ungrounded service-entrance conductor(s) supplying the individual service disconnecting means. **Figure 250–55**

(3) Common Location. A single grounding electrode conductor is permitted from a common location, sized not smaller than specified in Table 250.66, based on the area of the ungrounded conductor at the location where the connection is made. **Figure 250–56**

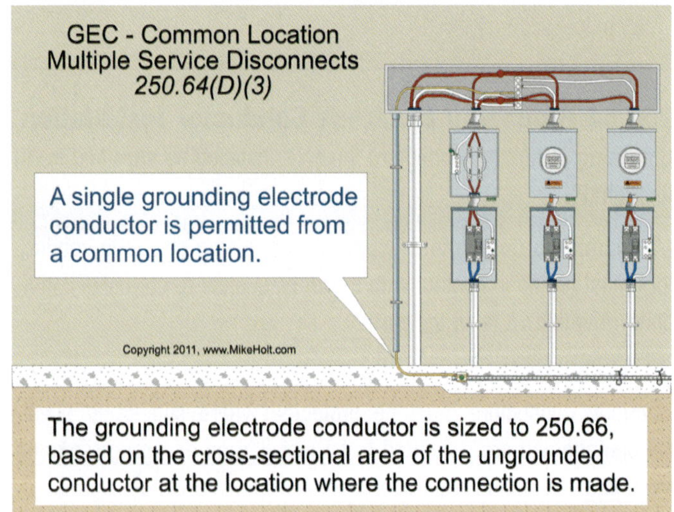

Figure 250–56

(E) Ferrous Metal Enclosures Containing Grounding Electrode Conductors. To prevent inductive choking of grounding electrode conductors, ferrous raceways and enclosures containing grounding electrode conductors must have each end of the raceway or enclosure bonded to the grounding electrode conductor in accordance with 250.92(B) for installations at service equipment. **Figure 250–57**

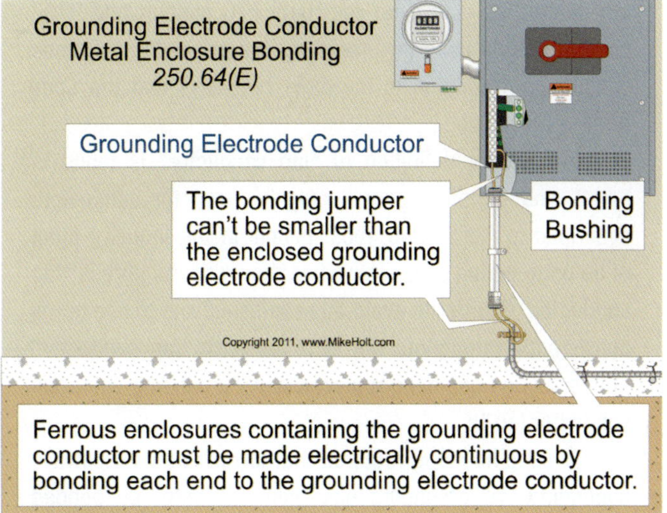

Figure 250–57

For other than service equipment locations, ferrous raceways and enclosures containing grounding electrode conductors must have each end of the raceway or enclosure bonded to the grounding electrode conductor in accordance with 250.92(B)(2) through (B)(4).

> **Author's Comment:** Nonferrous metal raceways, such as aluminum rigid metal conduit, enclosing the grounding electrode conductor aren't required to meet the "bonding each end of the raceway to the grounding electrode conductor" provisions of this section.

CAUTION: *The effectiveness of a grounding electrode is significantly reduced if a ferrous metal raceway containing a grounding electrode conductor isn't bonded to the ferrous metal raceway at both ends. This is because a single conductor carrying high-frequency induced lightning current in a ferrous raceway causes the raceway to act as an inductor, which severely limits (chokes) the current flow through the grounding electrode conductor. ANSI/IEEE 142, Recommended Practice for Grounding of Industrial and Commercial Power Systems (Green Book) states: "An inductive choke can reduce the current flow by 97 percent."*

> **Author's Comment:** To save a lot of time and effort, install the grounding electrode conductor exposed if it's not subject to physical damage [250.64(B)], or enclose it in PVC conduit suitable for the application [352.10(F)].

(F) Termination to Grounding Electrode.

(1) Single Grounding Electrode Conductor. A single grounding electrode conductor is permitted to terminate to any grounding electrode of the grounding electrode system. **Figure 250–58**

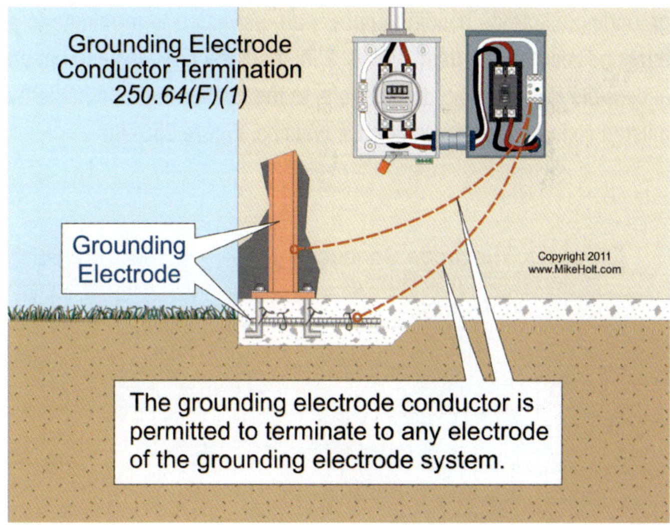

Figure 250–58

(2) Multiple Grounding Electrode Conductors. When multiple grounding electrode conductors are installed [250.64(D)(2)], each grounding electrode conductor is permitted to terminate to any grounding electrode of the grounding electrode system. **Figure 250–59**

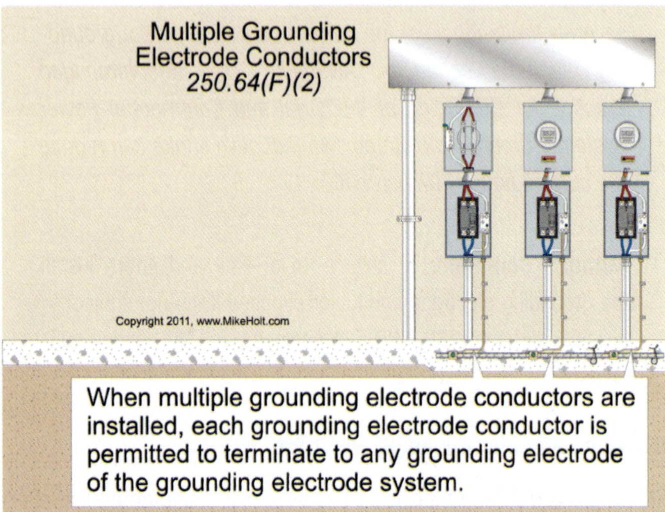

Figure 250–59

(3) Termination to Busbar. A grounding electrode conductor and grounding electrode bonding jumpers are permitted to terminate to a busbar sized not less than ¼ in. × 2 in. that's securely fastened at an accessible location. The terminations to the busbar must be made by a listed connector or by exothermic welding. **Figure 250–60**

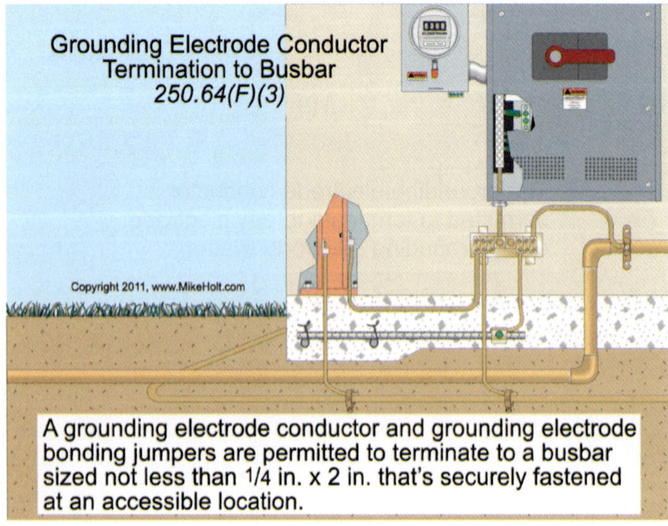

Figure 250–60

ANALYSIS: Previous editions of the *Code* used the now obsolete term "grounding conductors" in this subsection, although the title of 250.64 is "grounding electrode conductor installation." This change clarifies that the grounding electrode conductor is the topic.

With the new raceway systems that have been added to the *NEC* over the past few years, 250.64(B) was in need of an update. It's now clear that both PVC conduit and RTRC conduit can be used for protecting the grounding electrode conductor, in addition to the other raceways that the *Code* already recognized.

Although the definition of "tap conductor" is found in 240.2, and therefore should only be used for conductors described in Article 240, most people in the industry think of an ungrounded conductor when they read the phrase "tap conductor." In order to avoid this confusion, and to use terms consistently throughout the *NEC*, the term "tap conductor" in this section has been replaced with "grounding electrode conductor tap."

The *Code* has long required that ferrous metal raceways containing the grounding electrode conductor be bonded at each end, in an effort to reduce the effects of "inductive choke" on the conductors. The manner in which the bonding is to be performed, however, has never been addressed. Revisions to this section now clarify that the bonding method must be recognized by 250.92(B) (service bonding) in order to meet this requirement. Considering that most electricians use bonding bushings with a bonding jumper, this revision probably isn't that significant.

250.68(C) Termination to Grounding Electrode

The locations for the connection of grounding electrode conductors and bonding jumpers have been editorially revised.

250.68 Termination to the Grounding Electrode.

(C) Metal Water Pipe and Structural Metal. Grounding electrode conductors and grounding electrode bonding jumpers are permitted to terminate to:

(1) Interior metal water piping located not more than 5 ft from the point of entrance to the building/structure. **Figure 250–61**

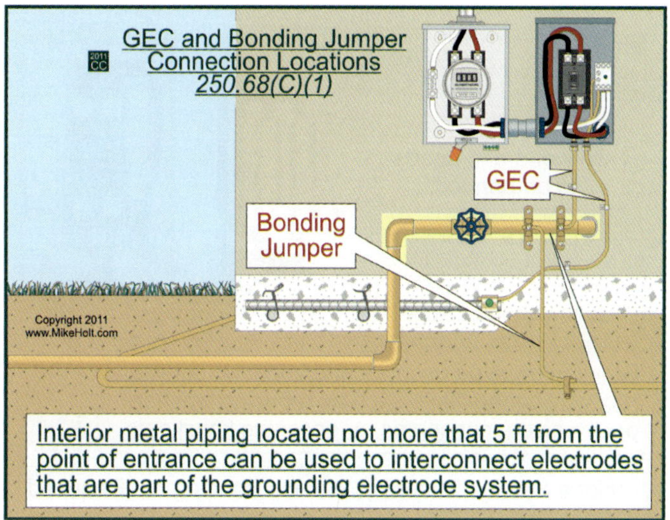

Figure 250–61

Ex: In industrial, institutional, and commercial buildings where conditions of maintenance and supervision ensure only qualified persons service the installation, the entire length of the metal water piping system can be used for grounding purposes, provided the entire length, other than short sections passing through walls, floors, or ceilings, is exposed.

(2) The metal frame of a building/structure that's in direct contact with the earth for 10 ft or more [250.52(A)(2)] or connected to one or more of the following:

(a) Concrete-encased electrode [250.52(A)(3)] or ground ring [250.52(A)(4)],

(b) Ground rod [250.52(A)(5)],

(c) Other approved earth connection.

ANALYSIS: If the *Code* user receives a sense of déjà vu when reading this section, it's because the language found in here is borrowed from 250.52. This section was revised to correlate with changes made to 250.53, as it relates to supplemental electrodes. No technical changes have been made to the requirements.

250.80 Exception, Metal Service Raceway Elbow Underground

The exception that allows a metal elbow in an underground raceway has been slightly revised.

250.80 Service Raceways and Enclosures. Metal enclosures and raceways containing service conductors must be connected to the neutral conductor at service equipment if the electrical system is grounded or to the grounding electrode conductor for electrical systems that aren't grounded.

Ex: Metal elbows having a minimum of 18 in. of cover installed in an underground nonmetallic raceway system aren't required to be connected to the service neutral or grounding electrode conductor.

ANALYSIS: Previous editions of the *NEC* have recognized that metal elbows in an underground system of PVC conduit don't need to be grounded. With recent changes in the *Code* allowing for more nonmetallic raceways, this rule was revised to clarify that metal elbows in an underground system of any nonmetallic raceway need not be grounded.

PART V. BONDING

250.92 Bonding Equipment for Services

The requirements for the bonding of service equipment were editorially revised, and the bonding of equipment containing service conductors has been revised for clarity and accuracy.

250.92 Bonding Equipment for Services.

(A) Bonding Requirements for Equipment for Services. The metal parts of equipment indicated below must be bonded together in accordance with 250.92(B). Figure 250–62

(1) Metal raceways containing, enclosing, or supporting service conductors.

(2) Metal enclosures containing service conductors.

Author's Comment: Metal raceways or metal enclosures containing feeder and branch-circuit conductors are required to be connected to the circuit equipment grounding conductor in accordance with 250.86. Figure 250–63

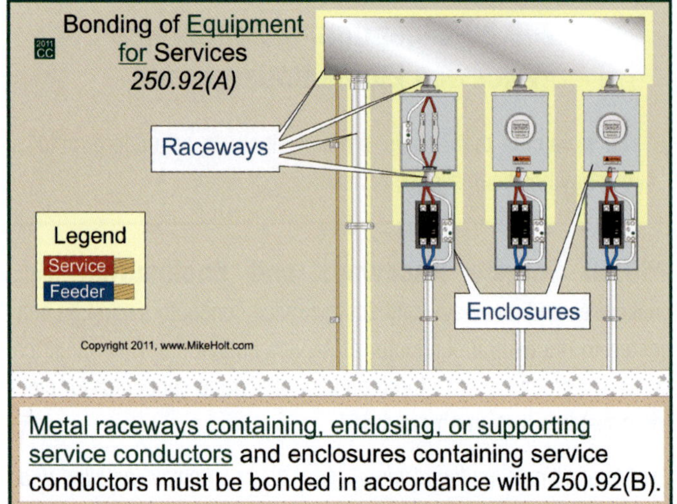

Figure 250–62

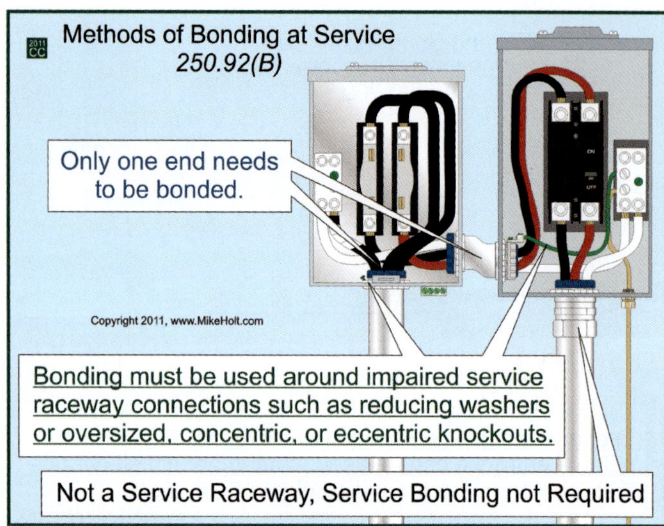

Figure 250–64

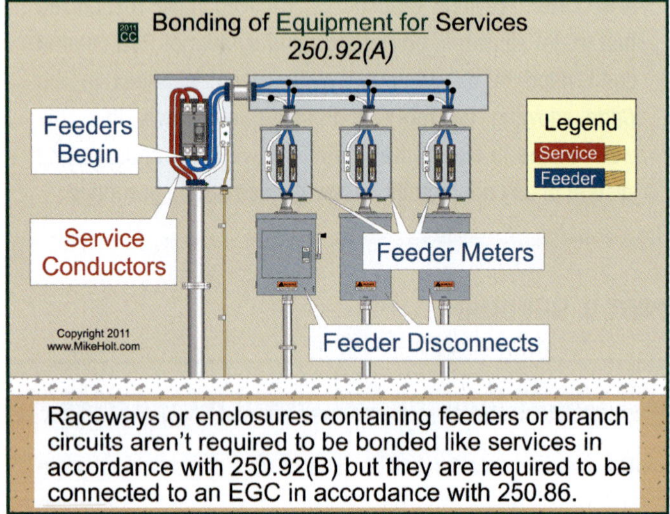

Figure 250–63

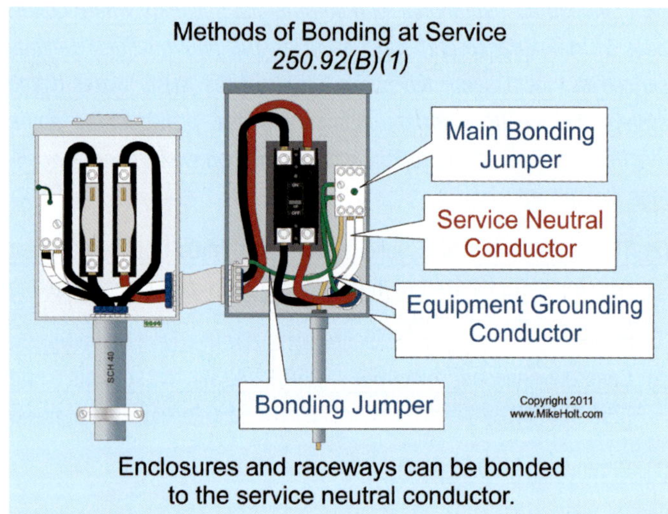

Figure 250–65

(B) Methods of Bonding. Bonding jumpers around reducing washers or oversized, concentric, or eccentric knockouts are required. Standard locknuts are permitted to make a mechanical connection of the raceway(s), but they can't serve as the bonding means required by this section. Figure 250–64

Electrical continuity at service equipment, service raceways, and service conductor enclosures must be ensured by one of the following methods:

(1) Neutral Conductor. By bonding the metal parts to the service neutral conductor. Figure 250–65

Author's Comments:

- A main bonding jumper is required to bond the service disconnect to the service neutral conductor [250.24(B) and 250.28].
- At service equipment, the service neutral conductor provides the effective ground-fault current path to the power supply [250.24(C)]; therefore, an equipment grounding conductor isn't required to be installed within PVC conduit containing service-entrance conductors [250.142(A)(1) and 352.60 Ex 2]. Figure 250–66

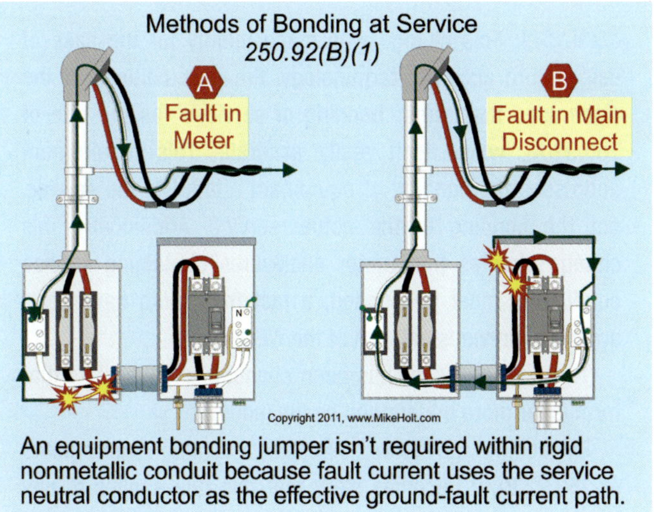

Figure 250–66

(2) Threaded Fittings. By terminating metal raceways to metal enclosures by threaded hubs on enclosures if made up wrenchtight. Figure 250–67

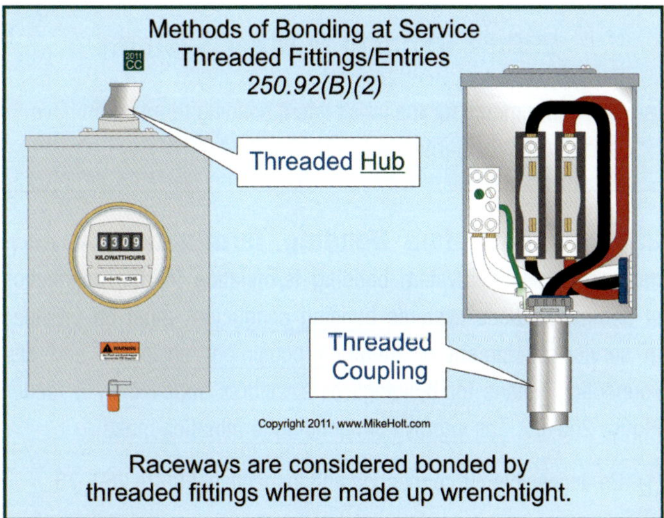

Figure 250–67

(3) Threadless Fittings. By terminating metal raceways to metal enclosures by threadless fittings if made up tight. Figure 250–68

(4) Other listed devices, such as bonding-type locknuts, bushings, wedges, or bushings with bonding jumpers.

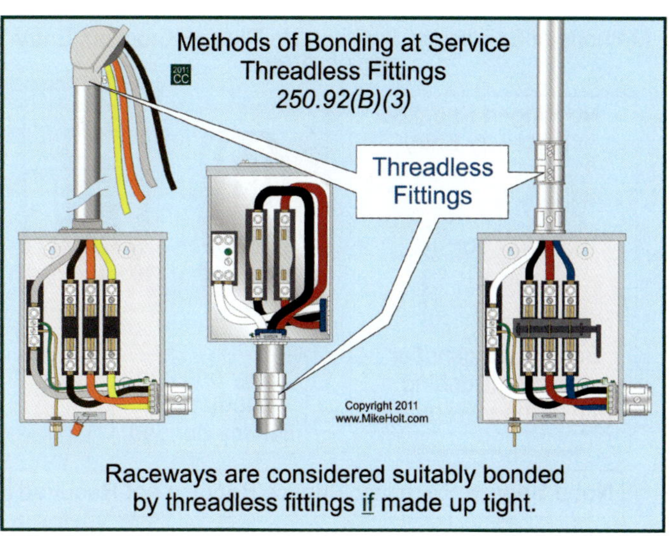

Figure 250–68

Author's Comments:

- A listed bonding wedge or bushing with a bonding jumper must be used to bond one end of the service raceway to the service neutral conductor. The bonding jumper used for this purpose must be sized in accordance with Table 250.66, based on the area of the largest ungrounded service conductors within the raceway [250.102(C)]. Figure 250–69

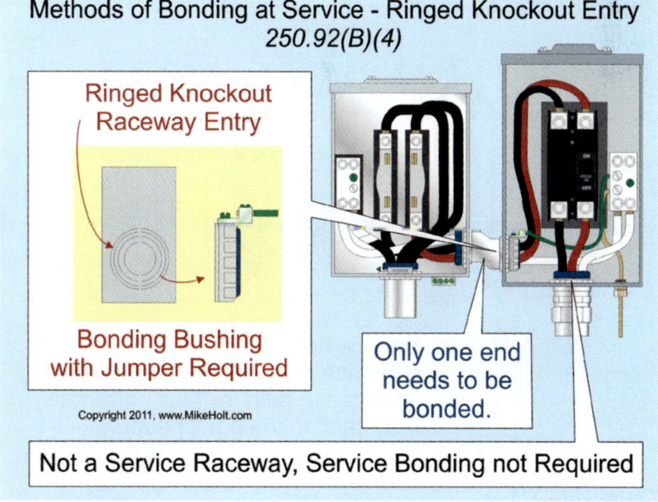

Figure 250–69

- When a metal raceway containing service conductors terminates to an enclosure without a ringed knockout, a bonding-type locknut can be used. Figure 250–70

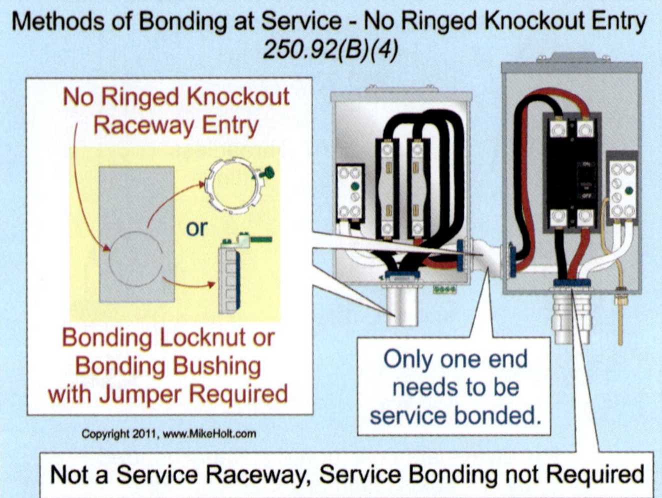

Figure 250–70

- A bonding locknut differs from a standard locknut in that it's a bonding screw with a sharp point that drives into the metal enclosure to ensure a solid connection.

- Bonding one end of a service raceway to the service neutral provides the low-impedance fault current path to the source. **Figure 250–71**

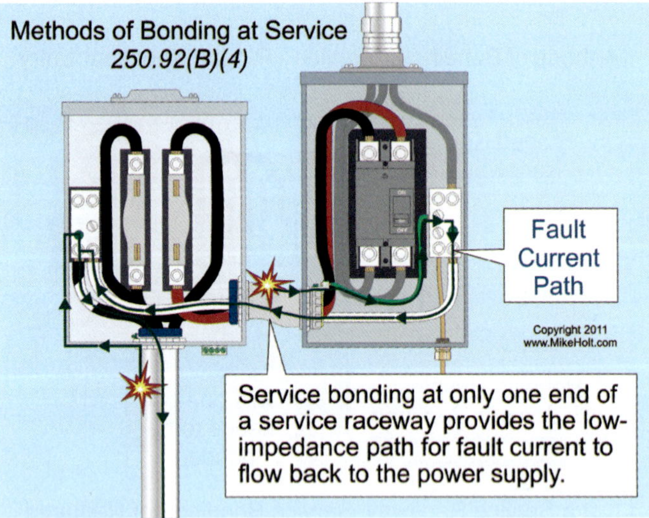

Figure 250–71

ANALYSIS: This change was made mainly for the sake of using more accurate terminology. Previous editions of the *Code* used the terms "bonding of services" as the title of 250.92(A), which isn't really accurate. This requirement addresses the bonding of equipment related to the service, not the bonding of the actual service. Additionally, this change clarifies that meter enclosures containing service conductors must be bonded, a fact that could have been argued in previous editions of the *NEC*.

The term "bosses" has been changed to "hubs," as that term is far more understood by the industry.

By adding the term "oversized" to the requirements of 250.92(B), it becomes clear that this rule applies to any knockout that isn't the correct size, whether it's the result of concentric or eccentric knockouts, or simply a mistake made in the field.

An additional change to the language in this section clarifies that while standard locknuts can't be used to satisfy this rule, they're allowed to be used *in addition to* the requirements of this subsection.

250.94 Bonding of Other Systems

The requirements for the intersystem bonding termination have been revised for clarity.

250.94 Intersystem Bonding Termination. An external accessible intersystem bonding termination for the connection of communications systems bonding conductors must be provided at service equipment or metering equipment enclosure and disconnecting means for buildings or structures supplied by a feeder, **Figure 250–72.** The intersystem bonding termination must:

(1) Be accessible for connection and inspection. **Figure 250–73**

(2) Consist of a set of terminals with the capacity for connection of not less than three intersystem bonding conductors.

(3) Not interfere with opening the enclosure for a service, building/structure disconnecting means, or metering equipment.

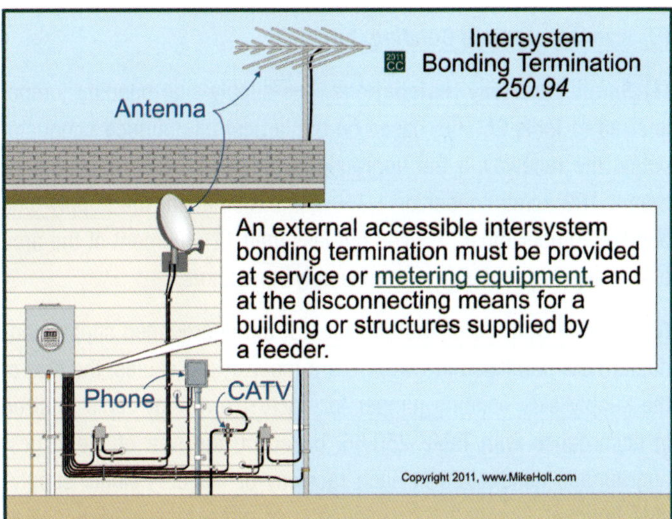

Figure 250–72

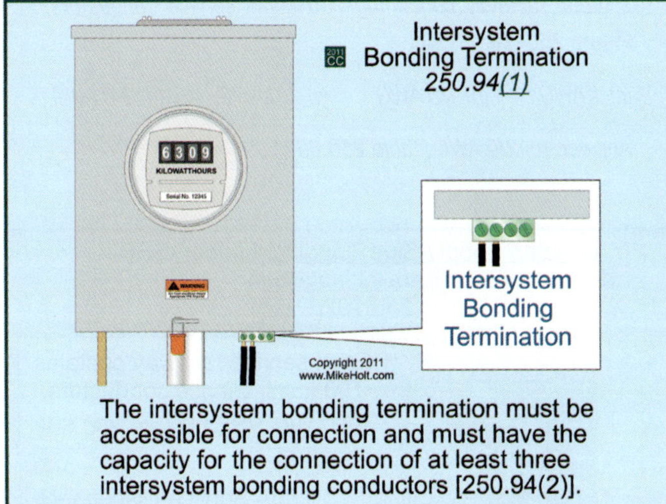

Figure 250–73

(4) Be securely mounted and electrically connected to service equipment, the meter enclosure, or exposed nonflexible metallic service raceway, or be mounted at one of these enclosures and be connected to the enclosure or grounding electrode conductor with a minimum 6 AWG copper conductor.

(5) Be securely mounted to the building/structure disconnecting means, or be mounted at the disconnecting means and be connected to the metallic enclosure or grounding electrode conductor with a minimum 6 AWG copper conductor. Figure 250–74

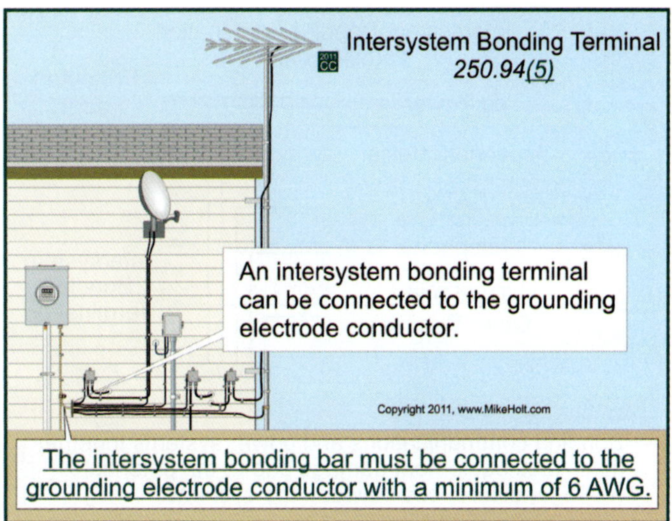

Figure 250–74

(6) The terminals must be listed as grounding and bonding equipment.

Author's Comment: According to Article 100, an intersystem bonding termination is a device that provides a means to connect communications systems grounding and bonding conductors to the building grounding electrode system.

Ex: At existing buildings or structures, an external accessible means for bonding communications systems together can be by the use of a:

(1) Nonflexible metallic raceway,

(2) Grounding electrode conductor, or

(3) Connection approved by the authority having jurisdiction.

Note 2: Communications systems must be bonded to the intersystem bonding termination in accordance with the following *Code* requirements: **Figure 250–75**

- Antennas/Satellite Dishes, 810.15 and 810.21
- CATV, 820.100
- Telephone Circuits, 800.100

Author's Comment: All external communications systems must be connected to the intersystem bonding terminal to minimize the damage to them from induced potential (voltage) differences between the systems from a lightning event.

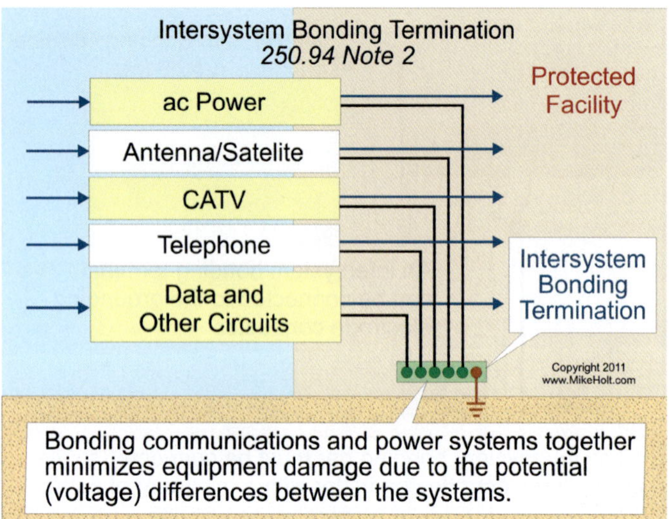

Figure 250–75

ANALYSIS: The requirements for the bonding of communications and other limited energy systems were greatly revised in the 2008 *NEC*. While these changes make for a better system, the language that was used resulted in a lot of confusion and misapplication. Many changes were made to this section, including:

- Changing the term "bonding and grounding conductors" to "bonding and grounding electrode conductors."
- Adding metering equipment enclosures as an allowable location for the intersystem bonding termination.
- Updating *Code* references in the exception.
- Adding optical fiber cables and network powered broadband systems into the Informational Note.

250.102 Bonding Conductors and Jumpers

This section has been revised extensively to incorporate the new term "supply-side bonding jumper." Several revisions were also made to enhance usability of the *NEC*.

250.102 Bonding Conductors and Jumpers.

(A) Material. Equipment bonding jumpers must be copper.

(B) Termination. Equipment bonding jumpers must terminate by listed pressure connectors, terminal bars, exothermic welding, or other listed means [250.8(A)].

(C) Size Supply-Side Bonding Jumper.

(1) Single Raceway Installations. The supply-side bonding jumper is sized to Table 250.66, based on the largest ungrounded conductor within the raceway. If the ungrounded supply conductors are larger than 1,100 kcmil copper or 1,750 kcmil aluminum, the supply-side bonding jumper must be sized not less than 12½ percent of the area of the largest set of ungrounded supply conductors.

(2) Parallel Conductor Installations. If the ungrounded supply conductors are paralleled in two or more raceways or cables, the size of the supply-side bonding jumper for each raceway or cable is sized in accordance with Table 250.66, based on the size of the largest ungrounded conductors in each raceway or cable. A single supply-side bonding jumper for bonding two or more raceways or cables must be sized in accordance with (C)(1).

Question: What size equipment bonding jumper is required for a metal raceway containing 700 kcmil service conductors? Figure 250–76

(a) 1 AWG (b) 1/0 AWG (c) 2/0 AWG (d) 3/0 AWG

Answer: (c) 2/0 AWG [Table 250.66]

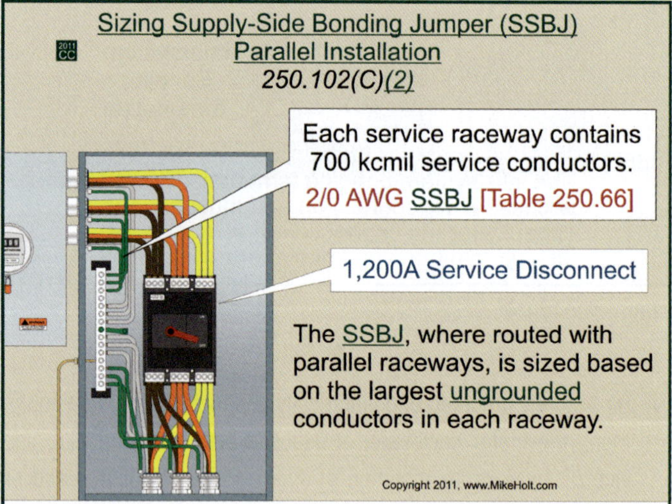

Figure 250–76

(3) Different Materials. If the ungrounded supply conductors and the supply-side bonding jumper are of different materials (copper or aluminum), the supply-side bonding jumper is sized on the assumed use of the same material.

(D) Load Side Equipment Bonding Jumper Sizing. Bonding jumpers on the load side of feeder and branch-circuit overcurrent devices are sized in accordance with 250.122, based on the rating of the circuit overcurrent device.

> **Author's Comment:** The equipment bonding jumper isn't required to be larger than the largest ungrounded circuit conductors [250.122(A)].

> ***Question:*** *What size equipment bonding jumper is required for a metal raceway where the circuit conductors are protected by a 1,200A overcurrent device?* **Figure 250–77**
>
> *(a) 1 AWG (b) 1/0 AWG (c) 2/0 AWG (d) 3/0 AWG*
>
> ***Answer:*** *(d) 3/0 AWG [Table 250.122]*

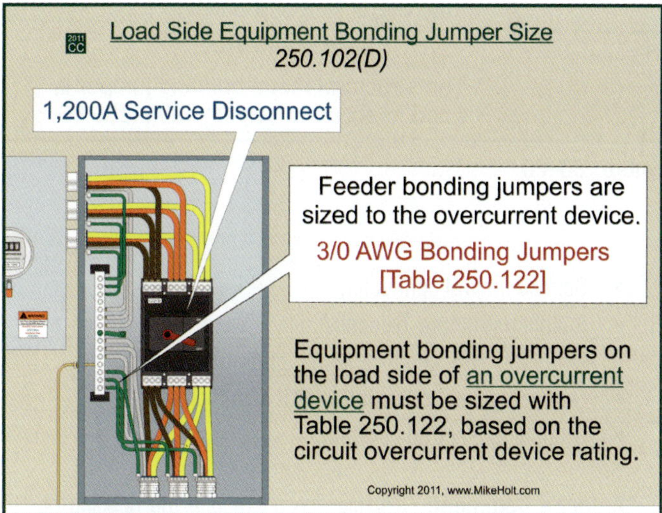

Figure 250–77

If a single equipment bonding jumper is used to bond two or more raceways, it must be sized according to 250.122, based on the rating of the largest circuit overcurrent device. **Figure 250–78**

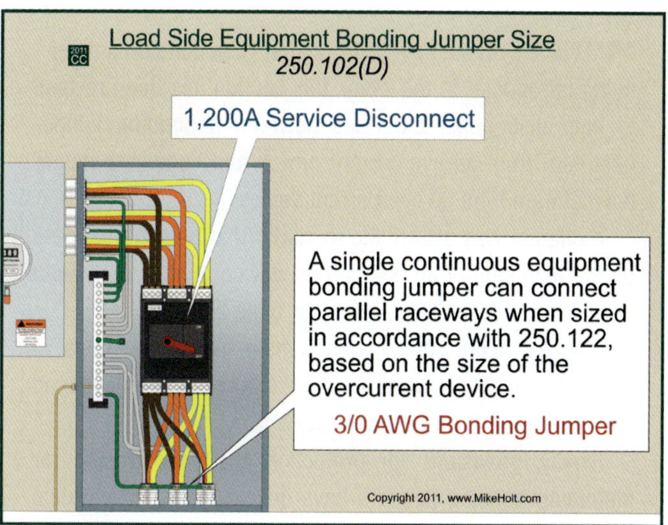

Figure 250–78

(E) Installation. Equipment bonding jumpers, as well as bonding jumpers or conductors can be installed inside or outside of a raceway.

(1) Inside a Raceway or Enclosure. If installed inside a raceway, the conductors must be identified in accordance with 250.119 and if circuit conductors are spliced or terminated on equipment within a metal box, the equipment grounding conductor associated with those circuits must be connected to the box in accordance with 250.148.

(2) Outside a Raceway. If the equipment bonding jumper is installed outside of a raceway, its length must not exceed 6 ft and it must be routed with the raceway. **Figure 250–79**

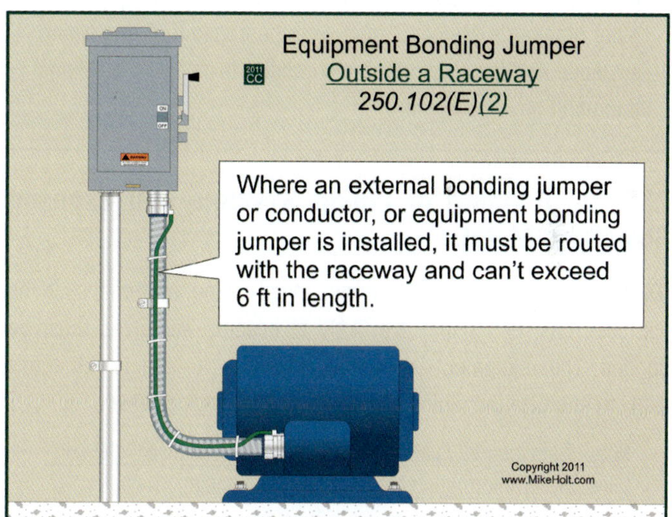

Figure 250–79

(3) Protection. Aluminum bonding jumpers or conductors and equipment bonding jumpers must not be in contact with masonry, subject to corrosive conditions, or within 18 in. of the earth [250.64(A)] and conductors must be protected where subject to physical damage in accordance with 250.64(B).

ANALYSIS: With the new term "supply-side bonding jumper" being introduced to the *Code*, this section has been revised to help distinguish the rules between a bonding jumper upstream from an overcurrent device and bonding jumpers downstream from an overcurrent device.

A change was also made to clarify that bonding jumpers on the load side of an overcurrent device must comply with all of Section 250.122, and not just Table 250.122.

Changes were also made to help clarify the rules in regard to bonding jumpers installed in a raceway as opposed to those installed outside of a raceway.

Finally, provisions for protection against corrosion for aluminum bonding jumpers have been added, and physical protection for all bonding jumpers have now been addressed.

250.104 Bonding of Piping Systems and Exposed Structural Metal

An Informational Note was added to alert the *Code* user that other standards are concerned with the bonding of gas piping systems. Additional text was also added to address buildings that don't have a service.

250.104 Bonding of Piping Systems and Exposed Structural Metal.

(B) Other Metal-Piping Systems. Metal-piping systems such as sprinkler, gas, or air that are likely to become energized must be bonded. The equipment grounding conductor for the circuit that's likely to energize the piping can serve as the bonding means.

Note*: The National Fuel Gas Code, NFPA* 54, Section 7.13 contains further information about bonding gas piping.

Author's Comment: Informational Notes in the *NEC* are for information purposes only and aren't enforceable as a requirement of the *Code* [90.5(C)].

(C) Structural Metal. Exposed structural metal that forms a metal building frame that's likely to become energized must be bonded to the: Figure 250–80

- Service equipment enclosure,

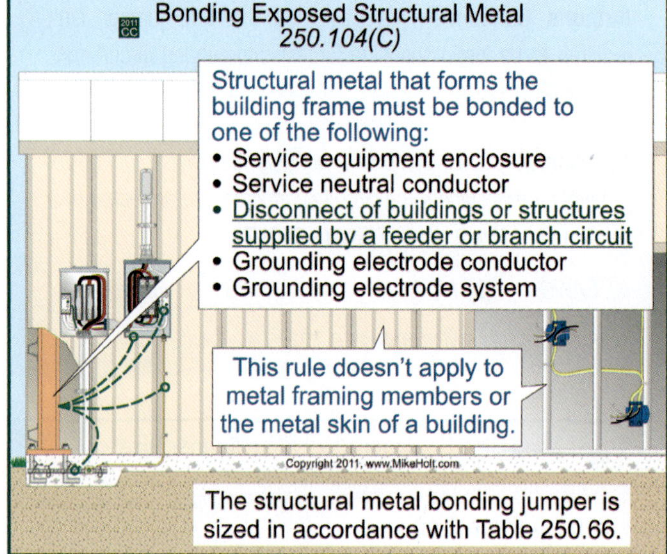

Figure 250–80

- Service neutral conductor,
- Building/structure disconnecting means for buildings or structures supplied by a feeder or branch circuit,
- Grounding electrode conductor if of sufficient size, or
- Grounding electrode system.

Author's Comment: This rule doesn't require the bonding of sheet metal framing members (studs) or the metal skin of a wood frame building.

The bonding jumper must be sized in accordance with Table 250.66, based on the area of the ungrounded supply conductors. The bonding jumper must be copper where within 18 in. of the earth [250.64(A)], securely fastened to the surface on which it's carried [250.64(B)], and adequately protected if exposed to physical damage [250.64(B)]. In addition, all points of attachment must be accessible, except as permitted in 250.68(A) Ex 2.

(D) Separately Derived Systems. Metal water piping systems and structural metal that forms a building frame must be bonded as required in (D)(1) through (D)(3).

(1) Metal Water Pipe. The nearest available point of the metal water piping system in the area served by a separately derived system must be bonded to the neutral point of the separately derived system where the grounding electrode conductor is connected. **Figure 250–81**

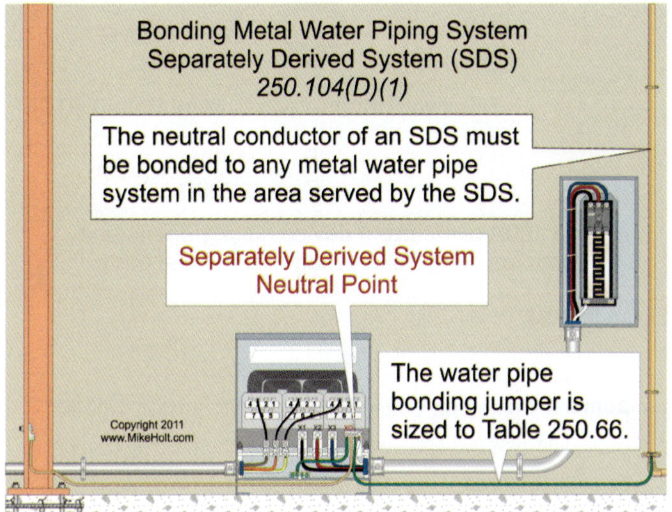

Figure 250–81

The bonding jumper must be sized in accordance with Table 250.66, based on the area of the largest ungrounded conductor of the derived system.

Ex 2: The metal water piping system is permitted to be bonded to the structural metal building frame if it serves as the grounding electrode [250.52(A)(1)] for the separately derived system. **Figure 250–82**

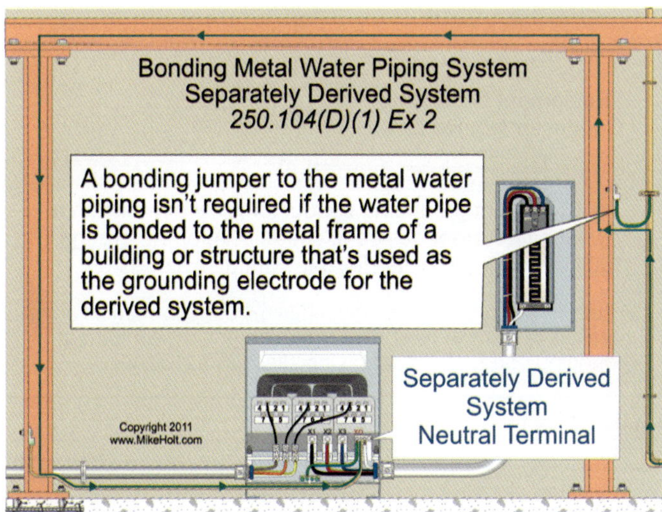

Figure 250–82

(2) Structural Metal. Exposed structural metal interconnected to form the building frame must be bonded to the neutral point of each separately derived system where the grounding electrode conductor is connected.

The bonding jumper must be sized in accordance with Table 250.66, based on the area of the largest ungrounded conductors of the derived system.

Ex 1: Bonding to the separately derived system isn't required if the metal structural frame serves as the grounding electrode [250.52(A)(2)] for the separately derived system.

ANALYSIS: Previous editions of the *Code* required that structural metal likely to become energized be bonded to the service equipment enclosure. This doesn't provide clear guidance in those cases when the building or structure is supplied by a feeder or branch circuit. This revision makes it clear that the structural metal (if likely to become energized) is to be bonded to the disconnecting means of the building or structure, regardless of the type of circuit feeding the premises.

An editorial change was also made to clarify that the point of bonding must be accessible except as permitted for fireproofed structural metal by 250.68(A) Ex 2.

PART VI. EQUIPMENT GROUNDING AND EQUIPMENT GROUNDING CONDUCTORS

250.118 Types of Equipment Grounding Conductors

Changes made to this section provide consistency with defined terms, and also address the vibration of equipment connected to flexible raceways.

250.118 Types of Equipment Grounding Conductors.

An equipment grounding conductor can be any one or a combination of the following: Figure 250–83

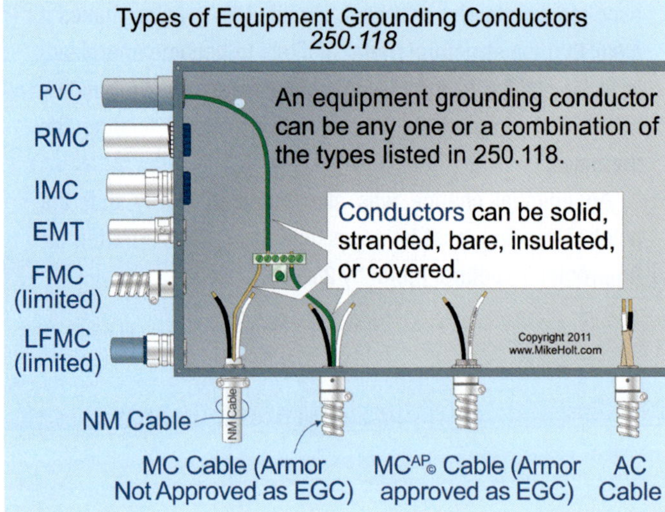

Figure 250–83

Note: The equipment grounding conductor is intended to serve as the effective ground-fault current path. See 250.2.

Author's Comment: The effective ground-fault path is an intentionally constructed low-impedance conductive path designed to carry fault current from the point of a ground fault on a wiring system to the electrical supply source. Its purpose is to quickly remove dangerous voltage from a ground fault by opening the circuit overcurrent device [250.2]. Figure 250–84

(1) A bare or insulated copper or aluminum conductor sized in accordance with 250.122.

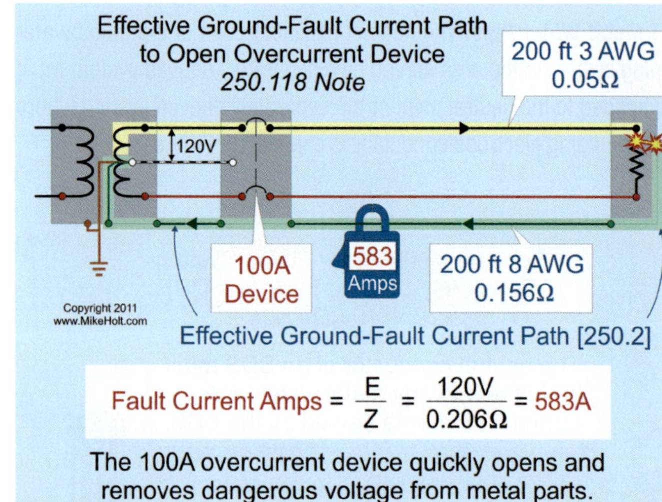

Figure 250–84

Author's Comment: Examples include PVC conduit, Type NM cable, and Type MC cable with an equipment grounding conductor of the wire type.

(2) Rigid metal conduit (RMC).

(3) Intermediate metal conduit (IMC).

(4) Electrical metallic tubing (EMT).

(5) Listed flexible metal conduit (FMC) where: Figure 250–85

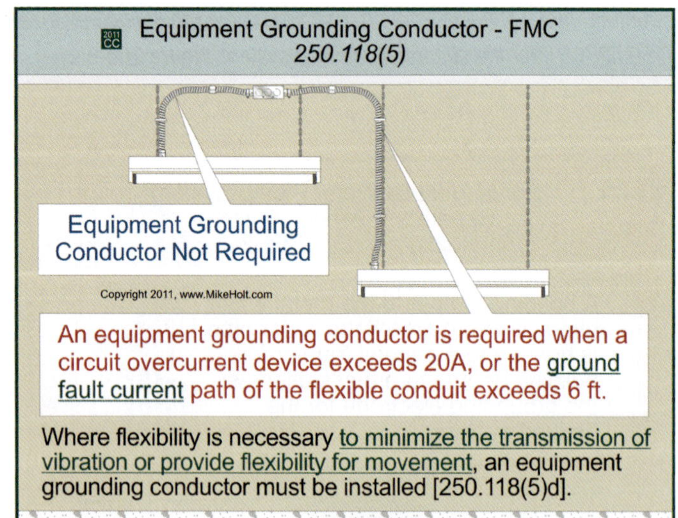

Figure 250–85

a. The raceway terminates in listed fittings.

b. The circuit conductors are protected by an overcurrent device rated 20A or less.

c. The combined length of the flexible conduit in the same ground-fault current path doesn't exceed 6 ft. **Figure 250–86**

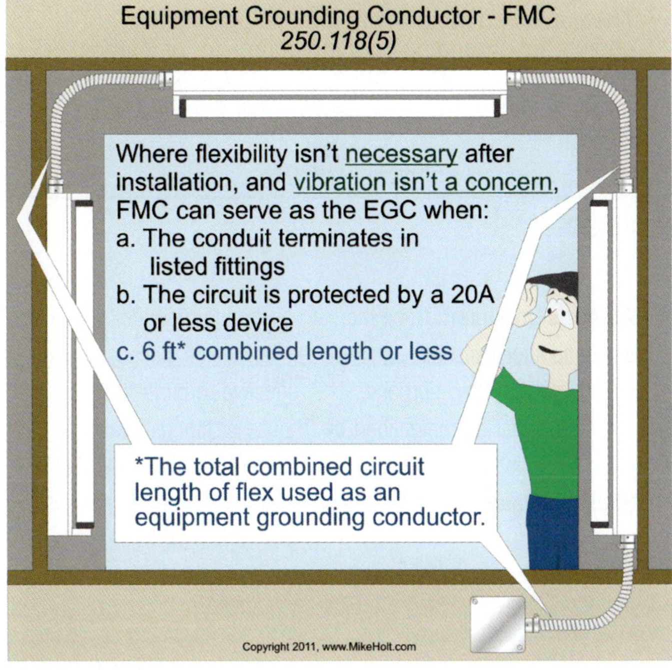

Figure 250–86

d. If flexibility is required to minimize the transmission of vibration from equipment or to provide flexibility for equipment that requires movement after installation, an equipment grounding conductor of the wire type must be installed with the circuit conductors in accordance with 250.102(E), and it must be sized according to 250.122, based on the rating of the circuit overcurrent device.

(6) Listed liquidtight flexible metal conduit (LFMC) where: **Figure 250–87**

a. The raceway terminates in listed fittings.

b. For ⅜ in. through ½ in., the circuit conductors are protected by an overcurrent device rated 20A or less.

c. For ¾ in. through 1¼ in., the circuit conductors are protected by an overcurrent device rated 60A or less.

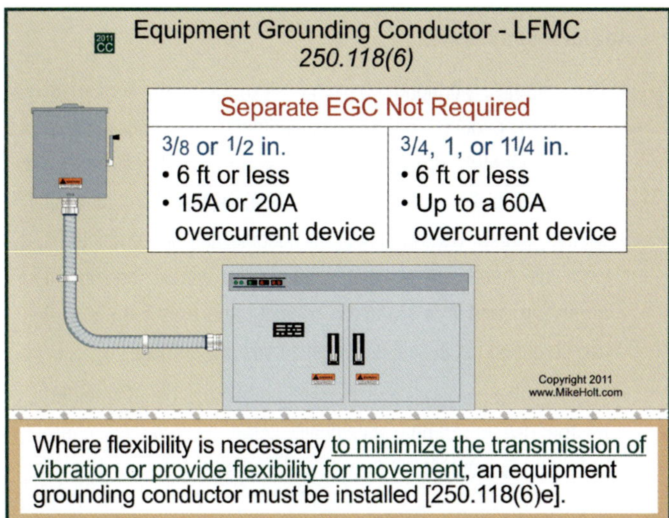

Figure 250–87

d. The combined length of the flexible conduit in the same ground-fault current path doesn't exceed 6 ft.

e. If flexibility is required to minimize the transmission of vibration from equipment or to provide flexibility for equipment that requires movement after installation, an equipment grounding conductor of the wire type must be installed with the circuit conductors in accordance with 250.102(E), and it must be sized in accordance with 250.122, based on the rating of the circuit overcurrent device.

(8) The sheath of Type AC cable containing an aluminum bonding strip. **Figure 250–88**

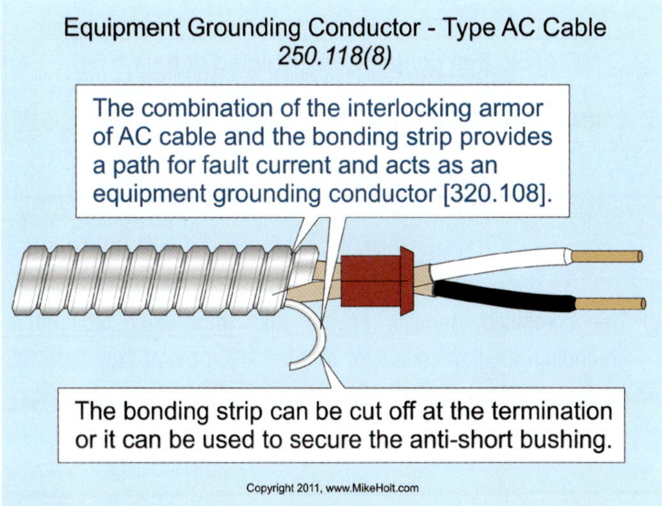

Figure 250–88

Author's Comments:

- The internal aluminum bonding strip isn't an equipment grounding conductor, but it allows the interlocked armor to serve as an equipment grounding conductor because it reduces the impedance of the armored spirals to ensure that a ground fault will be cleared. It's the aluminum bonding strip in combination with the cable armor that creates the circuit equipment grounding conductor. Once the bonding strip exits the cable, it can be cut off because it no longer serves any purpose.
- The effective ground-fault current path must be maintained by the use of fittings specifically listed for Type AC cable [320.40]. See 300.12, 300.15, and 320.100.

(9) The copper sheath of Type MI cable.

(10) Type MC cable that provides an effective ground-fault current path in accordance with one or more of the following:

(a) It contains an insulated or uninsulated equipment grounding conductor in compliance with 250.118(1). **Figure 250–89**

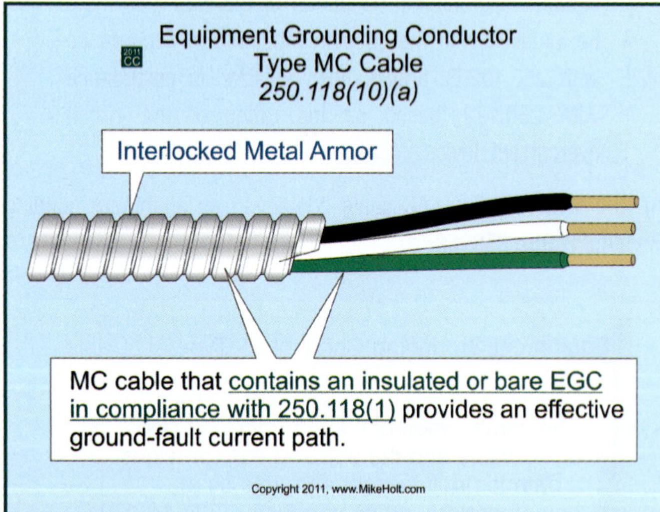

Figure 250–89

(b) The combined metallic sheath and uninsulated equipment grounding/bonding conductor of interlocked metal tape-type MC cable that's listed and identified as an equipment grounding conductor. **Figure 250–90**

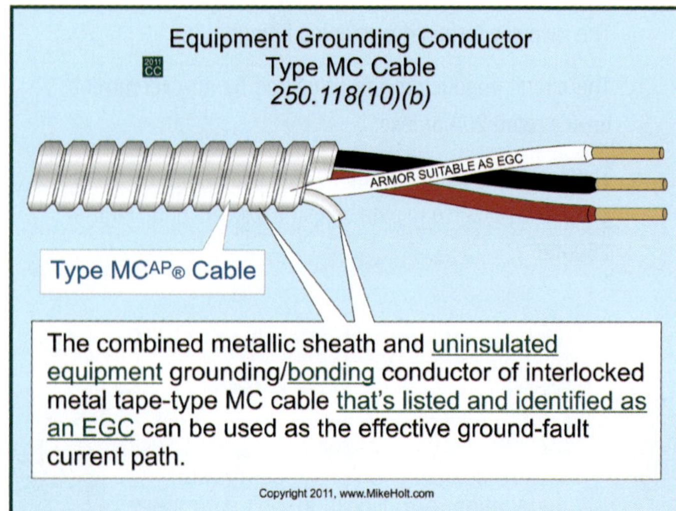

Figure 250–90

Author's Comment: Once the bare aluminum grounding/bonding conductor exits the cable, it can be cut off because it no longer serves any purpose. The effective ground-fault current path must be maintained by the use of fittings specifically listed for Type MCAP® cable [330.40]. See 300.12, 300.15, and 330.100. **Figure 250–91**

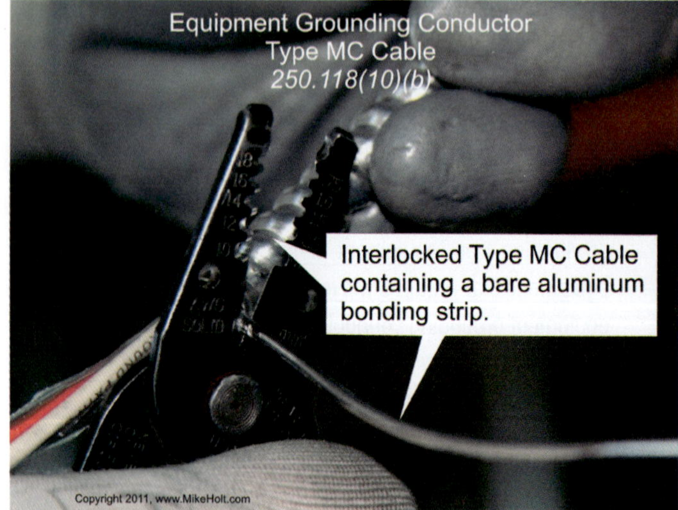

Figure 250–91

(c) The metallic sheath or the combined metallic sheath and equipment grounding conductors of the smooth or corrugated tube-type MC cable that's listed and identified as an equipment grounding conductor.

ANALYSIS: While the *Code* has recognized that equipment needing flexibility after installation requires an equipment grounding conductor of the wire type, it's been silent on the issue of vibration. It can be argued that an unusually high amount of vibration can compromise the integrity of the flexible metal conduit's ability to act as an equipment grounding conductor, so this change will require an EGC of the wire type in those instances. A similar change to the requirements for liquidtight flexible metal conduit has been made as well.

Previous editions of the *NEC* used the term "ground return path," instead of the term used throughout most of the *Code*, "ground-fault current path." This change replaces the undefined term with a defined one.

Changes made to 250.118(10) should help *NEC* users better understand the requirements for MC cable, and lastly, the term "grounding conductor" has been removed from the *Code* in this 2011 edition; therefore, this section has been revised to use the term "equipment grounding conductor" instead.

250.121 Use of Equipment Grounding Conductors

A new section was added to prohibit the use of the equipment grounding conductor as a grounding electrode conductor.

250.121 Use of Equipment Grounding Conductors.

An equipment grounding conductor isn't permitted to be used as a grounding electrode conductor.

ANALYSIS: The grounding electrode conductor (GEC) is intended to help direct lightning induced energy to the earth, while an equipment grounding conductor (EGC) is intended to provide a low-impedance ground-fault current path to the source to operate overcurrent devices in the event of a ground fault. The requirements for sizing are also different. An EGC is sized in accordance with 250.122, while a GEC is sized using 250.66. Because these conductors have different rules, different sizing requirements, and different installation requirements, this section was added to clarify that one conductor can't fill the roles of both an EGC and a GEC.

250.122(F) Equipment Grounding Conductors in Parallel

The provisions for equipment grounding conductors in parallel have been cleared up.

250.122 Sizing Equipment Grounding Conductor.

(F) Parallel Runs. If circuit conductors are installed in parallel in separate raceways as permitted by 310.10(H), an equipment grounding conductor must be installed for each parallel conductor set, **Figure 250–92**. Where conductors are installed in parallel in the same raceway or cable tray, a single equipment grounding conductor is permitted. **Figure 250–93**

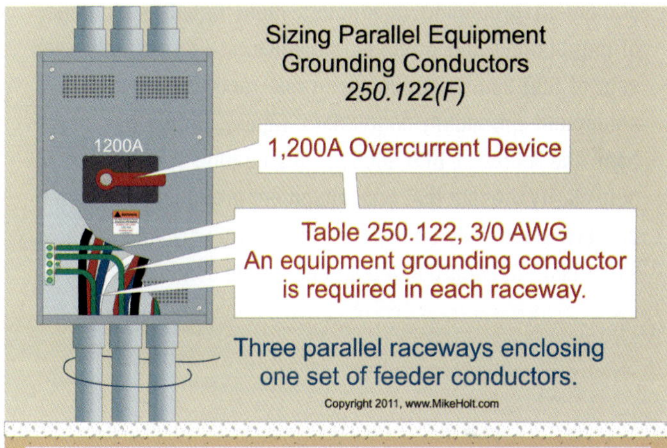

Figure 250–92

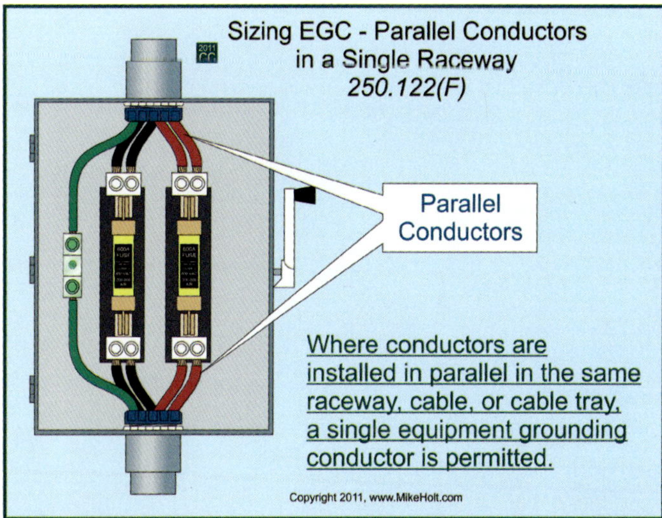

Figure 250–93

Each equipment grounding conductor must be sized in accordance with Table 250.122, based on the rating of the circuit overcurrent device, but it's not required to be larger than the circuit conductors [250.122(A)].

Author's Comment: In cable trays, single conductor equipment grounding conductors can be insulated, covered, or bare, but must be sized 4 AWG and larger [392.10(B)(1)(c)].

ANALYSIS: Some users of the *Code* have had a difficult time understanding the rules for equipment grounding when conductors in parallel sets were installed in the same raceway or cable tray. Although it's never been the intent of this section, some users believed that the number of equipment grounding conductors must equal the number of ungrounded and grounded conductors. For example, two sets of 500 kcmil conductors in one raceway required two equipment grounding conductors. Again, as this has never been the intent of this section, this change was passed to help clarify the fact that one equipment grounding conductor, properly sized, may be installed in the raceway with multiple sets of parallel ungrounded and grounded conductors.

Surge Protective DEVICES (SPDs)

INTRODUCTION TO ARTICLE 285—SURGE PROTECTIVE DEVICES (SPDS)

This article covers the general requirements, installation requirements, and connection requirements for surge protective devices rated 1kV or less that are permanently installed on premises wiring systems. The *NEC* doesn't require surge protective devices to be installed, but if they're, they must comply with this article.

Surge protective devices are designed to reduce transient voltages present on premises power distribution wiring and load-side equipment, particularly electronic equipment such as computers, telecommunications equipment, security systems, and electronic appliances. These transient voltages can originate from a number of sources, including anything from lightning to a laser printer. The best line of defense for all types of electronic equipment may be the installation of surge protective devices at the electrical service as well as at the location of the utilization equipment.

285.25 Type 3 Surge Protective Devices

The requirement for 30 ft of conductor length on Type 3 SPDs has been revised.

285.25 Type 3 SPDs—Branch Circuits. Type 3 surge protective devices can be installed on the load side of a branch-circuit overcurrent device up to the equipment served. If included in the manufacturer's instructions, the Type 3 SPD connection must be a minimum 30 ft of conductor distance from the service or separately derived system disconnect. Figure 285–1

ANALYSIS: Many Type 3 SPDs require 30 ft of conductor length between the branch-circuit overcurrent device and the SPD, but this isn't a requirement for many other SPDs. This *Code* reference in the 2008 edition included the 30 ft minimum for all SPDs regardless of the manufacturer's requirements. This section now requires the minimum conductor length only for SPDs that call for it in the manufacturer's instructions.

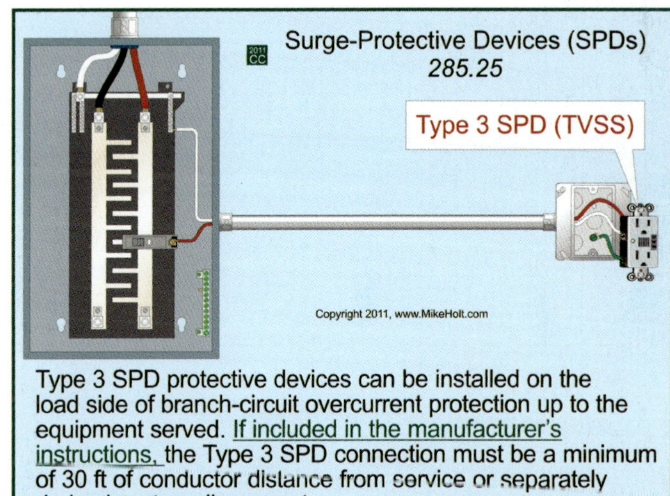

Type 3 SPD protective devices can be installed on the load side of branch-circuit overcurrent protection up to the equipment served. If included in the manufacturer's instructions, the Type 3 SPD connection must be a minimum of 30 ft of conductor distance from service or separately derived system disconnect.

Figure 285–1

NOTES

WIRING METHODS AND MATERIALS

INTRODUCTION TO CHAPTER 3—WIRING METHODS AND MATERIALS

Chapter 3 covers wiring methods and materials, and provides some very specific installation requirements for conductors, cables, boxes, raceways, and fittings. This chapter includes detailed information about the installation and restrictions involved with wiring methods.

It may be because of that detail that many people incorrectly apply the rules from this chapter. Be sure to pay careful attention to the details, and be sure that you make your installation in compliance with the rules in the *Code*, not just in the manner that's faster or easier to install. This is especially true when it comes to applying the Tables.

Violations of the rules for wiring methods found in Chapter 3 can result in problems with power quality and can lead to fire, shock, and other hazards.

The type of wiring method you'll use depends on several factors: Job specifications, *Code* requirements, the environment, need, and cost are among them.

Chapter 3 begins with rules that are common to most wiring methods [Article 300], it then covers conductors [Article 310], and enclosures [Articles 312 and 314]. The articles that follow become more specific and deal more in-depth with individual wiring methods such as specific types of cables [Articles 320 through 340] and various raceways [Articles 342 through 390]. The chapter winds up with Article 392, a support system, and the final articles [Articles 394 through 398] for open wiring.

Notice as you read through the various wiring methods that the *Code* attempts to use similar subsection numbering for similar topics from one article to the next, using the same digits after the decimal point in the section number for the same topic. This makes it easier to locate specific requirements in a particular article. For example, the rules for securing and supporting can be found in the section that ends with .30 of each article. In addition to this, you'll find a "uses permitted" and "uses not permitted" section in nearly every article.

Wiring Method Articles

- **Article 300—Wiring Methods.** Article 300 contains the general requirements for all wiring methods included in the *NEC*, except for signaling and communications systems, which are covered in Chapters 7 and 8.
- **Article 310—Conductors for General Wiring.** This article contains the general requirements for conductors, such as insulation markings, ampacity ratings, and conductor use. Article 310 doesn't apply to conductors that are part of flexible cords, fixture wires, or conductors that are an integral part of equipment [90.6 and 300.1(B)].
- **Article 312—Cabinets, Cutout Boxes, and Meter Socket Enclosures.** Article 312 covers the installation and construction specifications for cabinets, cutout boxes, and meter socket enclosures.

- **Article 314—Outlet, Device, Pull and Junction Boxes, Conduit Bodies, Fittings, and Handhole Enclosures.** Installation requirements for outlet boxes, pull and junction boxes, as well as conduit bodies, and handhole enclosures are contained in this article.

Cable Articles

Articles 320 through 340 address specific types of cables. If you take the time to become familiar with the various types of cables, you'll:

- Understand what's available for doing the work.
- Recognize cable types that have special *NEC* requirements.
- Avoid buying cable that you can't install due to *Code* requirements you can't meet with that particular wiring method.

Here's a brief overview of each one:

- **Article 320—Armored Cable (Type AC).** Armored cable is an assembly of insulated conductors, 14 AWG through 1 AWG, individually wrapped with waxed paper. The conductors are contained within a flexible spiral metal (steel or aluminum) sheath that interlocks at the edges. Armored cable looks like flexible metal conduit. Many electricians call this metal cable "BX®."
- **Article 330—Metal-Clad Cable (Type MC).** Metal-clad cable encloses insulated conductors in a metal sheath of either corrugated or smooth copper or aluminum tubing, or spiral interlocked steel or aluminum. The physical characteristics of Type MC cable make it a versatile wiring method permitted in almost any location and for almost any application. The most commonly used Type MC cable is the interlocking kind, which looks similar to armored cable or flexible metal conduit.
- **Article 334—Nonmetallic-Sheathed Cable (Type NM).** Nonmetallic-sheathed cable encloses two, three, or four insulated conductors, 14 AWG through 2 AWG, within a nonmetallic outer jacket. Because this cable is nonmetallic, it contains a separate equipment grounding conductor. Nonmetallic-sheathed cable is a common wiring method used for residential and commercial branch circuits. Many electricians call this plastic-sheathed cable "Romex®."
- **Article 336—Power and Control Tray Cable (Type TC).** Power and control tray cable is a factory assembly of two or more insulated conductors under a nonmetallic sheath for installation in cable trays, in raceways, or supported by a messenger wire.
- **Article 338—Service-Entrance Cable (Types SE and USE).** Service-entrance cable can be a single-conductor or a multiconductor assembly within an overall nonmetallic covering. This cable is used primarily for services not over 600V, but is also permitted for feeders and branch circuits.
- **Article 340—Underground Feeder and Branch-Circuit Cable (Type UF).** Underground feeder cable is a moisture-, fungus-, and corrosion-resistant cable suitable for direct burial in the earth, and it comes in sizes 14 AWG through 4/0 AWG [340.104]. Multiconductor UF cable is covered in molded plastic that surrounds the insulated conductors.

Raceway Articles

Articles 342 through 390 address specific types of raceways. Refer to Article 100 for the definition of a raceway. If you take the time to become familiar with the various types of raceways, you'll:

- Understand what's available for doing the work.
- Recognize raceway types that have special *Code* requirements.
- Avoid buying a raceway that you can't install due to *NEC* requirements you can't meet with that particular wiring method.

Here's a brief overview of each one:

- **Article 342—Intermediate Metal Conduit (Type IMC).** Intermediate metal conduit is a circular metal raceway with the same outside diameter as rigid metal conduit. The wall thickness of intermediate metal conduit is less than that of rigid metal conduit, so it's a greater interior cross-sectional area for holding conductors. Intermediate metal conduit is lighter and less expensive than rigid metal conduit, but it's permitted in all the same locations as rigid metal conduit. Intermediate metal conduit also uses a different steel alloy, which makes it stronger than rigid metal conduit, even though the walls are thinner.
- **Article 344—Rigid Metal Conduit (Type RMC).** Rigid metal conduit is similar to intermediate metal conduit, except the wall thickness is greater, so it's a smaller interior cross-sectional area. Rigid metal conduit is heavier than intermediate metal conduit and it's permitted to be installed in any location, just like intermediate metal conduit.

- **Article 348—Flexible Metal Conduit (Type FMC).** Flexible metal conduit is a raceway of circular cross section made of a helically wound, interlocked metal strip of either steel or aluminum. It's commonly called "Greenfield" or "Flex."

- **Article 350—Liquidtight Flexible Metal Conduit (Type LFMC).** Liquidtight flexible metal conduit is a raceway of circular cross section with an outer liquidtight, nonmetallic, sunlight-resistant jacket over an inner flexible metal core, with associated couplings, connectors, and fittings. It's listed for the installation of electric conductors. Liquidtight flexible metal conduit is commonly called "Sealtite®" or simply "liquidtight." Liquidtight flexible metal conduit is of similar construction to flexible metal conduit, but it's an outer thermoplastic covering.

- **Article 352—Rigid Polyvinyl Chloride Conduit (Type PVC).** Rigid polyvinyl chloride conduit is a nonmetallic raceway of circular cross section with integral or associated couplings, connectors, and fittings. It's listed for the installation of electrical conductors.

- **Article 353—High-Density Polyethylene Conduit (Type HDPE).** HDPE is a nonmetallic conduit that's light and durable. It resists decomposition, oxidation, and hostile elements that cause damage to other materials. HDPE is mechanically and chemically resistant to a host of environmental conditions. Uses include communication, data, cable television, and general-purpose raceways.

- **Article 354—Nonmetallic Underground Conduit with Conductors (Type NUCC).** Nonmetallic underground conduit with conductors is a factory assembly of conductors or cables inside a nonmetallic, smooth wall conduit with a circular cross section. It can be supplied on reels without damage or distortion and is of sufficient strength to withstand abuse, such as impact, when handled and installed, without damage to the conduit or conductors.

- **Article 356—Liquidtight Flexible Nonmetallic Conduit (Type LFNC).** Liquidtight flexible nonmetallic conduit is a raceway of circular cross section with an outer liquidtight, nonmetallic, sunlight-resistant jacket over an inner flexible core, with associated couplings, connectors, and fittings. It's listed for the installation of electrical conductors. LFNC is available in three types:
  - Type LFNC-A (orange). A smooth seamless inner core and cover bonded together with reinforcement layers inserted between the core and covers.
  - Type LFNC-B (gray). A smooth inner surface with integral reinforcement within the conduit wall.
  - Type LFNC-C (black). A corrugated internal and external surface without integral reinforcement within the conduit wall.

- **Article 358—Electrical Metallic Tubing (EMT).** Electrical metallic tubing is a nonthreaded thinwall raceway of circular cross section designed for the physical protection and routing of conductors and cables. Compared to rigid metal conduit and intermediate metal conduit, electrical metallic tubing is relatively easy to bend, cut, and ream. EMT isn't threaded, so all connectors and couplings are of the threadless type. Today, it's is available in a range of colors, such as red and blue.

- **Article 362—Electrical Nonmetallic Tubing (ENT).** Electrical nonmetallic tubing is a pliable, corrugated, circular raceway made of PVC. It's often called "Smurf Pipe" or "Smurf Tube," because it was available only in blue when it came out and at the time the children's cartoon characters "The Smurfs," were popular. It's now available in multiple colors such as red and yellow as well as blue.

- **Article 376—Metal Wireways.** A metal wireway is a sheet metal trough with hinged or removable covers for housing and protecting electrical conductors and cable, in which conductors are placed after the wireway has been installed as a complete system.

- **Article 380—Multioutlet Assemblies.** A multioutlet assembly is a surface, flush, or freestanding raceway designed to hold conductors and receptacles. It's assembled in the field or at the factory.

- **Article 384—Strut-Type Channel Raceway.** Strut-type channel raceway is a metallic raceway intended to be mounted to the surface or suspended with associated accessories, in which conductors are placed after the raceway has been installed as a complete system.

- **Article 386—Surface Metal Raceways.** A surface metal raceway is a metallic raceway intended to be mounted to the surface with associated accessories, in which conductors are placed after the raceway has been installed as a complete system.

- **Article 388—Surface Nonmetallic Raceways.** A surface nonmetallic raceway is intended to be surface mounted with associated accessories. Conductors are placed inside after the raceway has been installed as a complete system.

Cable Tray

- **Article 392—Cable Trays.** A cable tray system is a unit or assembly of units or sections with associated fittings that form a structural system used to securely fasten or support cables and raceways. A cable tray isn't a raceway; it's a support system for raceways, cables, and enclosures.

Wiring METHODS

INTRODUCTION TO ARTICLE 300—WIRING METHODS

Article 300 contains the general requirements for all wiring methods included in the *NEC*. However, it article doesn't apply to communications systems, which are covered in Chapter 8, except when Article 300 is specifically referenced in Chapter 8.

This article is primarily concerned with how to install, route, splice, protect, and secure conductors and raceways. How well you conform to the requirements of Article 300 will generally be evident in the finished work, because many of the requirements tend to determine the appearance of the installation. Because of this, it's often easy to spot Article 300 problems if you're looking for *Code* violations. For example, you can easily see when someone runs an equipment grounding conductor outside a raceway instead of grouping all conductors of a circuit together, as required by 300.3(B).

A good understanding of Article 300 will start you on the path to correctly installing the wiring methods included in Chapter 3. Be sure to carefully consider the accompanying illustrations, and refer to the definitions in Article 100 as needed.

PART I. GENERAL

300.3(C) Conductors of Different Systems

A new Informational Note was added addressing solar photovoltaic systems.

300.3 Conductors.

(C) Conductors of Different Systems.

(1) Mixing. Power conductors of alternating current and direct-current systems rated 600V or less can occupy the same raceway, cable, or enclosure if all conductors have an insulation voltage rating not less than the maximum circuit voltage. **Figure 300–1**

Note 1: See 725.136(A) on the limitations of mixing Class 2 and Class 3 circuit conductors with other circuits. **Figure 300–2**

Mixing Conductors of Different Systems
300.3(C)(1)

480V Circuit
600V Insulation

120V Circuit
600V Insulation

Copyright 2011, www.MikeHolt.com

Conductors of different systems can occupy the same raceway, cable, or enclosure if the insulation voltage rating isn't less than the maximum circuit voltage.

Figure 300–1

Author's Comments:

- Control, signal, and communications wiring must be separated from power and lighting circuits so the higher-voltage conductors don't accidentally energize the control, signal, or communications wiring:
  - CATV Coaxial Cable, 820.133(A).
  - Class 1, Class 2, and Class 3 Control Circuits, 725.48 and 725.136(A).
  - Communications Circuits, 800.133(A)(1)(c).
  - Fire Alarm Circuits, 760.136(A).
  - Instrumentation Tray Cable, 727.5.
  - Sound Circuits, 640.9(C).

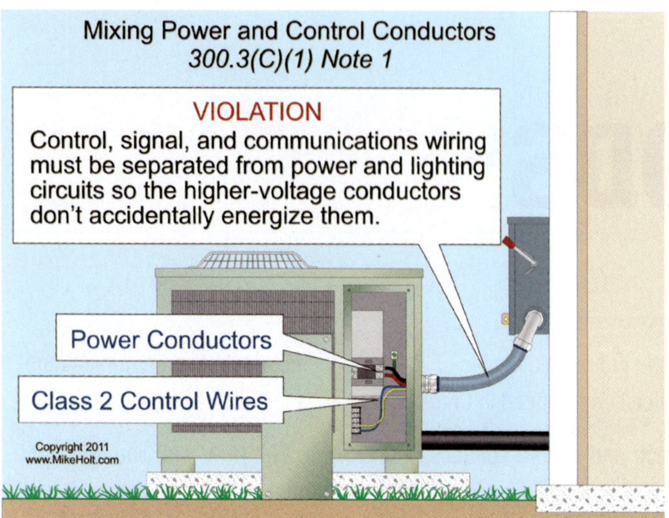

Figure 300–2

- A Class 2 circuit that's been reclassified as a Class 1 circuit [725.130(A) Ex 2] can be installed with associated power conductors [725.48(B)(1)] if all conductors have an insulation voltage rating not less than the maximum circuit voltage [300.3(C)(1)].

Note 2: PV system conductors, both direct current and alternating current, are permitted to be installed in the same raceways, outlet and junction boxes, or similar fittings with each other, but they must be kept entirely independent of all other non-PV system wiring [690.4(B)]. **Figure 300–3**

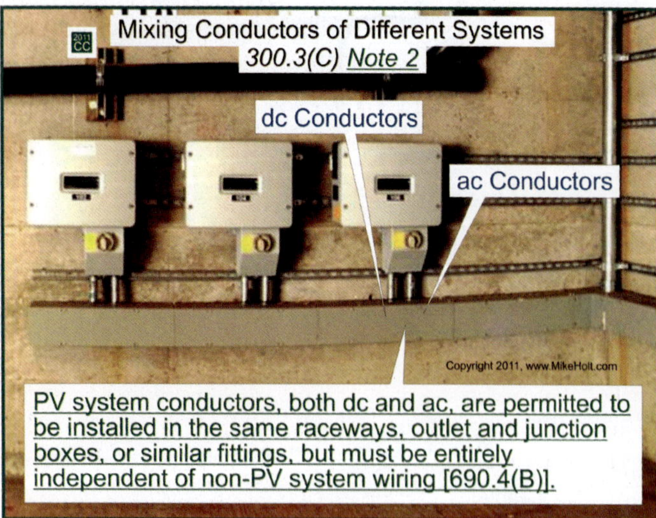

Figure 300–3

ANALYSIS: Installers of power and lighting conductors, such as the typical residential or commercial electrician, may not know of the requirements found in Article 690. With the addition of this Informational Note, electricians that don't spend time there can be made aware of the requirements of 690.4(B) should the need present itself.

Author's Comment: PV system conductors, both direct current and alternating current, are permitted to be installed in the same raceways, outlet and junction boxes, or similar fittings with each other, but they must be kept entirely independent of all other non-PV system wiring [690.4(B)].

300.4 Protection Against Physical Damage

This rule has been revised to be more technically accurate.

300.4 Protection Against Physical Damage. Conductors, raceways, and cables must be protected against physical damage [110.27(B)].

ANALYSIS: Previous editions of the *NEC* have required protection of conductors where subject to physical damage. While most *Code* users understand that this rule is intended to apply to all conductors in all wiring methods, it didn't clearly state that. This revision makes it clear that all conductors in all wiring methods must be protected from physical damage.

300.4(E) Wiring Under Roof Decking

The rule on protecting wiring methods under metal-corrugated sheet roof decking has been expanded.

300.4 Protection Against Physical Damage.

(E) Wiring Under Roof Decking. Cables, raceways, and enclosures under metal-corrugated sheet roof decking must not be located within 1½ in. of the roof decking, measured from the lowest surface of the roof decking to the top of the cable, raceway, or box. In addition, cables, raceways, and enclosures aren't permitted in concealed locations of metal-corrugated sheet decking type roofing.

Note: Roof decking material will be installed or replaced after the initial raceway or cabling which may be penetrated by the screws or other mechanical devices designed to provide "hold down" strength of the waterproof membrane or roof insulating material.

Ex: Spacing from roof decking doesn't apply to rigid metal conduit and intermediate metal conduit.

ANALYSIS: New to the 2008 *NEC* was a requirement for the protection of most raceways when installed within 1½ in. of the roof deck. Although this 2008 rule change went a long way toward protecting wiring systems from damaging roofing screws that can penetrate the raceways, it left out one critical part of the installation—boxes. With this change it's clear that the *Code* is concerned not only with protecting the raceways, but the boxes as well.

This rule was also changed to prohibit wiring methods from being installed in concealed locations above the roof decking. In some instances installers place raceways above the roof deck prior to the insulation being installed, which results in the same potential for damage from roofing screws.

300.4(G) Insulated Fittings

The requirement for protection of conductors 4 AWG and larger has been changed to add clarity.

300.4 Protection Against Physical Damage.

(G) Insulating Fittings. If raceways contain insulated circuit conductors 4 AWG and larger that enter an enclosure, the conductors must be protected from abrasion during and after installation by a fitting identified to provide a smooth, rounded insulating surface, such as an insulating bushing. Figure 300–4

Author's Comments:

- If IMC or RMC conduit enters an enclosure without a connector, a bushing must be provided, regardless of the conductor size [342.46 and 344.46].
- An insulated fitting isn't required for a grounding electrode. Figure 300–5

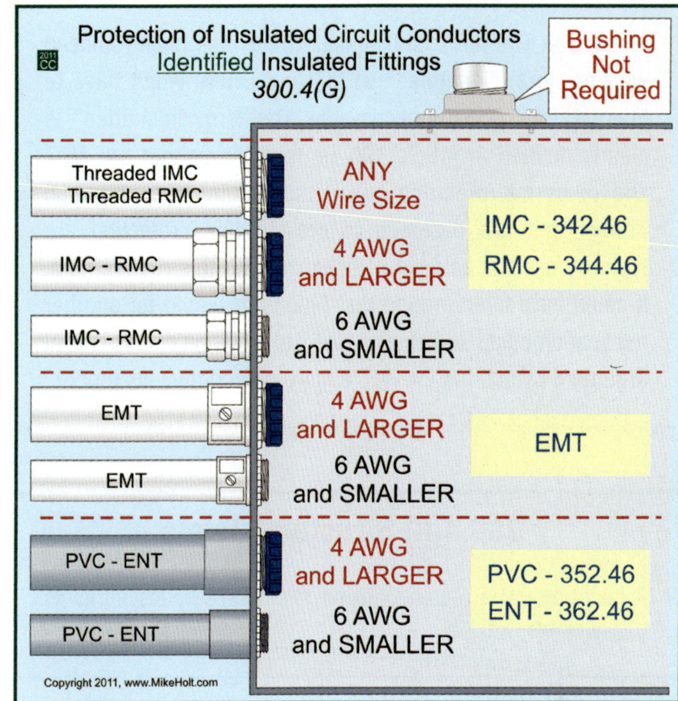

Figure 300–4

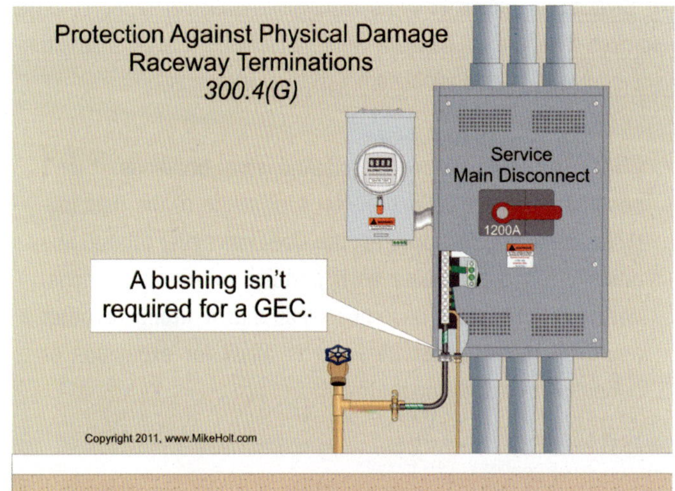

Figure 300–5

Ex: Insulating bushings aren't required if a raceway terminates in a threaded raceway entry that provides a smooth, rounded, or flared surface for the conductors. An example would be a meter hub fitting or a Meyer's hub-type fitting.

ANALYSIS: The term "substantial fitting" has been replaced with the term "identified" so that inspectors won't have to interpret the *Code* unnecessarily. The term "identified" is clearly defined in Article 100, is used throughout the *NEC*, and takes interpretation out of the requirement. Although fittings that are designed to provide this protection are typically used to achieve compliance with this requirement, it could have been argued that fittings designed for another application could satisfy this rule. This change removes that argument by making the *NEC* a more prescriptive document.

300.4(H) Structural Joints

A new protection requirement for structural (expansion) joints was added.

300.4 Protection Against Physical Damage.

(H) Structural Joints. A listed expansion/deflection fitting or other approved means must be used where a raceway crosses a structural joint intended for expansion, contraction or deflection.

ANALYSIS: In larger commercial/industrial buildings, it isn't uncommon to see an expansion joint inside of the building. When these are encountered, the *Code* has never offered any guidance to the installer as it pertains to wiring methods. With this change, it becomes clear that a fitting or other approved means must be used to allow for expansion or deflection of the wiring method.

300.5(C) Cables Under Buildings

Type MI and Type MC Cables are now allowed to be installed under buildings without a raceway.

300.5 Underground Installations.

(C) Cables Under Buildings. Cables installed under a building must be installed in a raceway that extends past the outside walls of the building.

Ex 2: Type MC Cable listed for direct burial is permitted under a building without installation in a raceway [330.10(A)(5)]. Figure 300–6

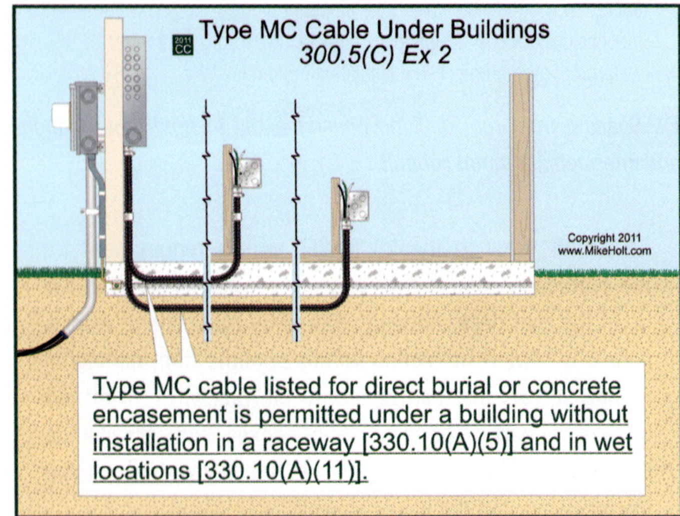

Figure 300–6

ANALYSIS: Although certain types of MC Cable are listed for direct burial and concrete encasement, this rule has prohibited them from being installed underneath buildings. This change now allows cables to be installed under the floor slab of a building, which has been accepted by many inspectors for some time. Interestingly, other cables that are listed for this application, such as UF Cable, aren't recognized by this change.

300.5(I) Exception 1 Conductors of the Same Circuit Grouped Together

This change clarifies the use of single conductor cables installed in parallel.

300.5 Underground Installations.

(I) Conductors Grouped Together. All conductors of the same circuit, including the equipment grounding conductor, must be inside the same raceway, or in close proximity to each other. See 300.3(B). Figure 300–7

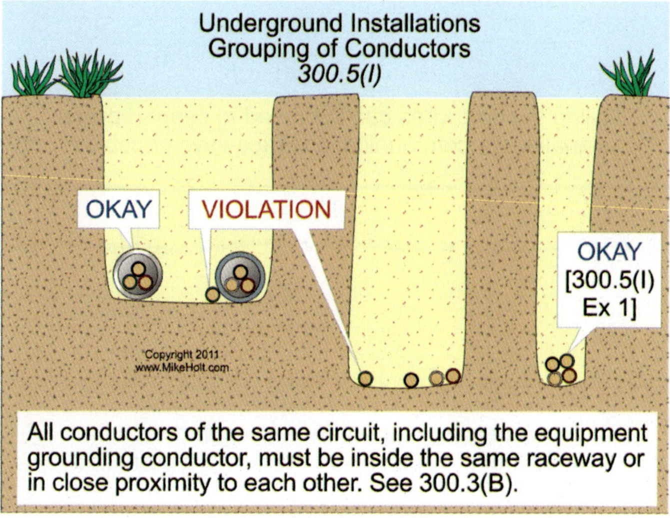

Figure 300–7

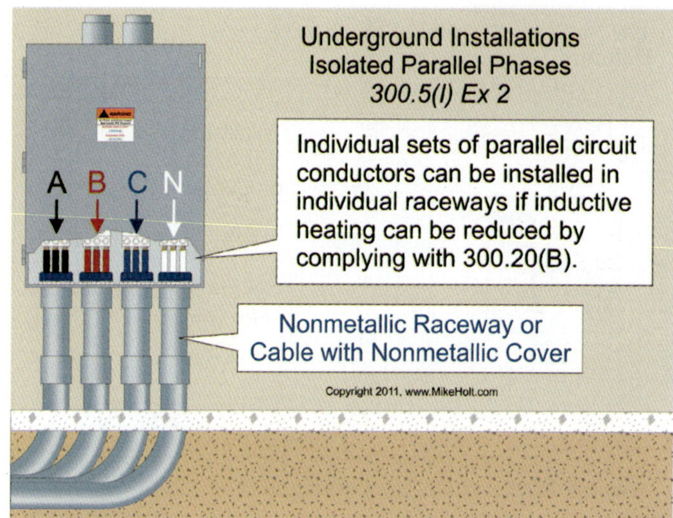

Figure 300–8

Ex 1: Conductors can be installed in parallel in raceways, multiconductor cables, or direct-buried single-conductor cables. Each raceway or multiconductor cable must contain all conductors of the same circuit including the equipment grounding conductor. Each direct buried single-conductor cable must be located in close proximity in the trench to the other single-conductor cables in the same parallel set of conductors, including equipment grounding conductors.

Ex 2: Parallel circuit conductors installed in accordance with 310.10(H) of the same phase or neutral can be installed in underground PVC conduits, if inductive heating at raceway terminations is reduced by the use of aluminum locknuts and cutting a slot between the individual holes through which the conductors pass as required by 300.20(B). Figure 300–8

Author's Comment: Installing ungrounded and neutral conductors in different PVC conduits makes it easier to terminate larger parallel sets of conductors, but it will result in higher levels of electromagnetic fields (EMF).

ANALYSIS: Conductors of the same circuit are required to be grouped in the same raceway or cable to help reduce the inductive reactance of the conductors. A very literal reading of previous *Code* editions didn't address the use of single-conductor cables, such as many USE Cables, in parallel installations. The *NEC* now recognizes this practice, while giving guidance on how to install these cables. The issues of inductive reactance are addressed by requiring these single-conductor cables to be installed within close proximity of each other.

300.7 Raceways Exposed to Different Temperatures

The provisions for condensation have been revised to remove the word "cable."

300.7 Raceways Exposed to Different Temperatures.

(A) Sealing. If a raceway is subjected to different temperatures, and where condensation is known to be a problem, the raceway must be filled with a material approved by the authority having jurisdiction that will prevent the circulation of warm air to a colder section of the raceway. An explosionproof seal isn't required for this purpose. Figure 300–9

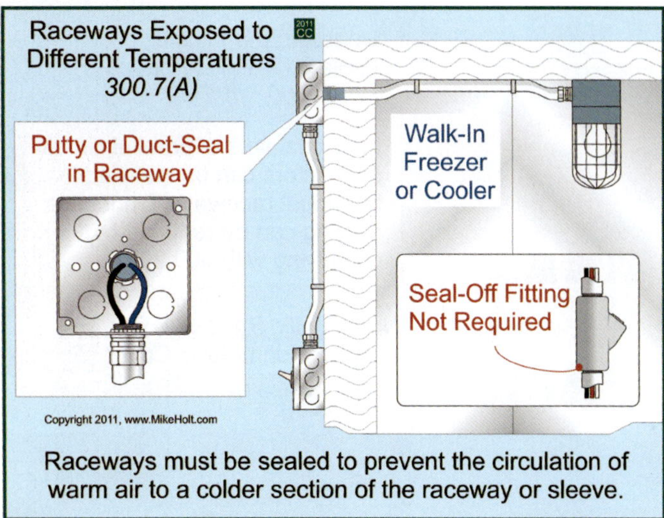

Figure 300–9

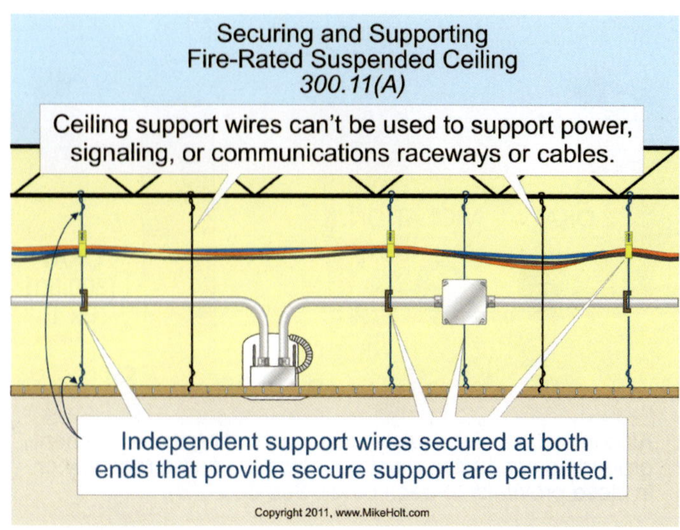

Figure 300–10

ANALYSIS: The phrase "cable raceway" has been in this section for a few *Code* cycles now, although it was never intended to be. There's no such thing as a "cable raceway," and introducing a comma between the two words would have resulted in requiring condensation protection for cables. Such protection has no technical merit, so this change is as much an editorial fix as it's a technical change.

300.11(A)(2) Nonfire-Rated Ceiling Assemblies

The rule requiring identification of electrical ceiling support wires has been expanded.

300.11 Securing and Supporting.

(A) Secured in Place. Raceways, cable assemblies, boxes, cabinets, and fittings must be securely fastened in place. The ceiling-support wires or ceiling grid must not be used to support raceways and cables (power, signaling, or communications). However, independent support wires that are secured at both ends and provide secure support are permitted. Figure 300–10

Author's Comment: Outlet boxes [314.23(D)] and luminaires can be secured to the suspended-ceiling grid if securely fastened to the ceiling-framing members by mechanical means such as bolts, screws, or rivets, or by the use of clips or other securing means identified for use with the type of ceiling-framing member(s) used [410.36(B)].

(1) Fire-Rated Ceiling Assembly. Electrical wiring within the cavity of a fire-rated floor-ceiling or roof-ceiling assembly can be supported by independent support wires attached to the ceiling assembly. The independent support wires must be distinguishable from the suspended-ceiling support wires by color, tagging, or other effective means.

(2) Nonfire-Rated Ceiling Assembly. Wiring in a nonfire-rated floor-ceiling or roof-ceiling assembly can be supported by independent support wires attached to the ceiling assembly. The independent support wires must be distinguishable from the suspended-ceiling support wires by color, tagging, or other effective means. Figure 300–11

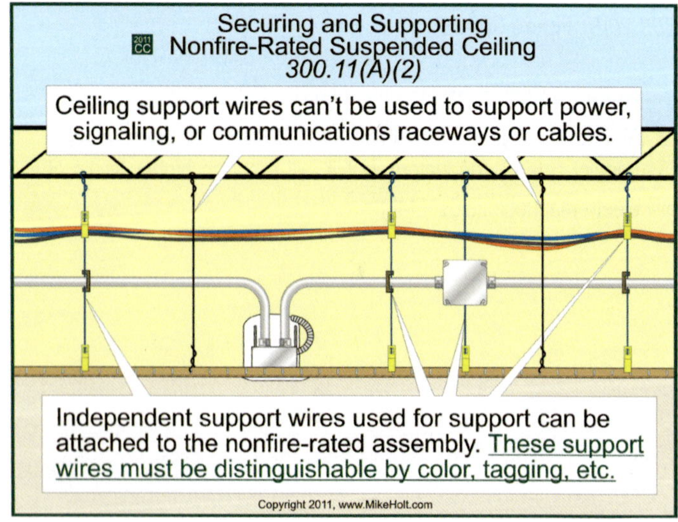

Figure 300–11

ANALYSIS: Identification of ceiling-support wires that are used for electrical equipment was previously limited to those wires that are in fire-resistance-rated ceiling assemblies. In order to distinguish which wires are installed by the electrician and which are installed by the ceiling contractor, this change requires identification of the independent support wires for all ceiling systems, whether the ceiling assembly is fire-resistance rated or not.

300.21 Spread of Fire or Products of Combustion

The rule on protecting the integrity of fire-resistance rated assemblies was clarified.

300.21 Spread of Fire or Products of Combustion. Electrical circuits and equipment must be installed in such a way that the spread of fire or products of combustion won't be substantially increased. Openings into or through fire-rated walls, floors, and ceilings for electrical equipment must be fire-stopped using methods approved by the authority having jurisdiction to maintain the fire-resistance rating of the fire-rated assembly. Figure 300–12

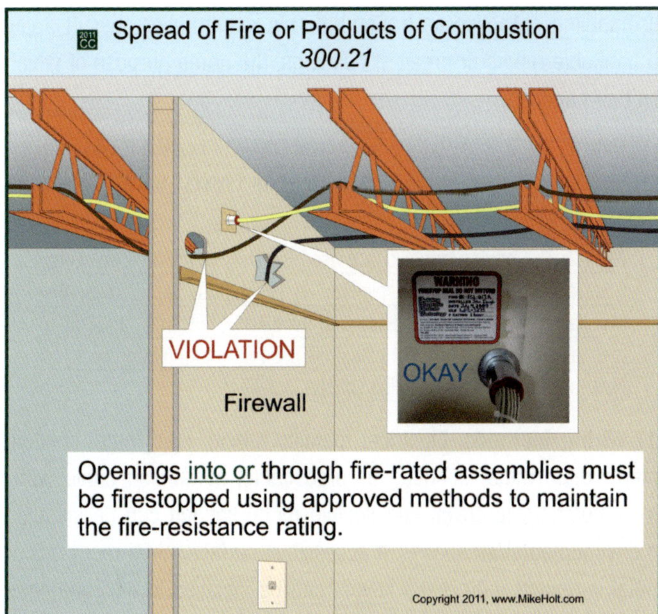

Figure 300–12

Author's Comment: Fire-stopping materials are listed for the specific types of wiring methods and the construction of the assembly that they penetrate.

Note: Directories of electrical construction materials published by qualified testing laboratories contain listing and installation restrictions necessary to maintain the fire-resistive rating of assemblies. Outlet boxes must have a horizontal separation not less than 24 in. when installed in a fire-rated assembly, unless an outlet box is listed for closer spacing or protected by fire-resistant "putty pads" in accordance with manufacturer's instructions.

Author's Comments:

- Boxes installed in fire-resistance rated assemblies must be listed for the purpose. If steel boxes are used, they must be secured to the framing member, so cut-in type boxes aren't permitted (UL White Book, *Guide Information for Electrical Equipment,* www.ul.com/regulators/2008_WhiteBook.pdf).
- This rule also applies to control, signaling, and communications cables or raceways.

  - CATV, 820.26
  - Communications, 800.26
  - Control and Signaling, 725.25
  - Fire Alarm, 760.3(A)
  - Optical Fiber, 770.26
  - Sound Systems, 640.3(A)

ANALYSIS: Because the 2008 *NEC* referred to protecting penetrations *through* fire-resistance rated assemblies, it was argued that it didn't address openings *into* these assemblies. The *Code* now clarifies that it intends to protect these assemblies for both through penetrations and membrane penetrations. Considering that this has long been required in the building codes, it really doesn't change any installation requirements in areas where those codes are enforced.

300.22 Wiring in Ducts and Other Spaces for Environmental Air (Plenums)

Extensive revisions have been made to the language of this section, and a new subsection was added addressing cable trays.

300.22 Wiring in Ducts Not for Air Handling, Fabricated Ducts for Environmental Air, and Other Spaces For Environmental Air (Plenums). The provisions of this section apply to the installation and uses of electrical wiring and equipment in ducts used for dust, loose stock, or vapor removal; ducts specifically fabricated for environmental air, and spaces used for environmental air (plenums).

(A) Ducts Used for Dust, Loose Stock, or Vapor. Ducts that transport dust, loose stock, or vapors must not have any wiring method installed within them. **Figure 300–13**

Figure 300–13

(B) Ducts Specifically Fabricated for Environmental Air. If necessary for direct action upon, or sensing of, the contained air, Type MC cable that has a smooth or corrugated impervious metal sheath without an overall nonmetallic covering, electrical metallic tubing, flexible metallic tubing, intermediate metal conduit, or rigid metal conduit without an overall nonmetallic covering can be installed in ducts specifically fabricated to transport environmental air. Flexible metal conduit in lengths not exceeding 4 ft can be used to connect physically adjustable equipment and devices within the fabricated duct.

Equipment is only permitted within the duct specifically fabricated to transport environmental air if necessary for the direct action upon, or sensing of, the contained air. Equipment, devices, and/or illumination are only permitted to be installed in the duct if necessary to facilitate maintenance and repair. **Figure 300–14**

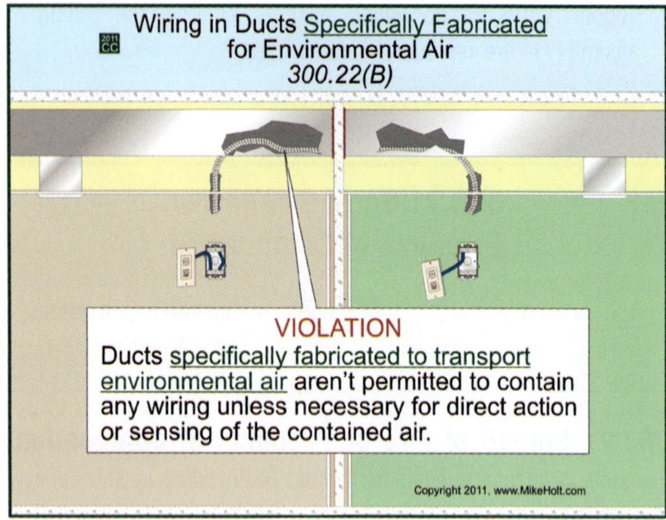

Figure 300–14

(C) Other Spaces Used for Environmental Air (Plenums). This section applies to wiring and equipment in spaces not specifically fabricated for environmental air-handling purposes (plenums) but used for air-handling purposes as a plenum. This requirement doesn't apply to habitable rooms or areas of buildings, the prime purpose of which isn't air handling.

> **Note 1:** The spaces above a suspended ceiling or below a raised floor used for environmental air are examples of the type of space to which this section applies. **Figure 300–15**
>
> **Note 2:** The phrase "other space used for environmental air (plenum) " correlates with the term "plenum" in NFPA 90A, Standard for the Installation of Air-Conditioning and Ventilating Systems, and other mechanical codes where the plenum is used for return air purposes, as well as some other air-handling spaces.

(1) Wiring Methods. Electrical metallic tubing, rigid metal conduit, intermediate metal conduit, armored cable, metal-clad cable without a nonmetallic cover, and flexible metal conduit can be installed in environmental air spaces. If accessible, surface metal raceways or metal wireways with metal covers can be installed in environmental air spaces. **Figure 300–16**

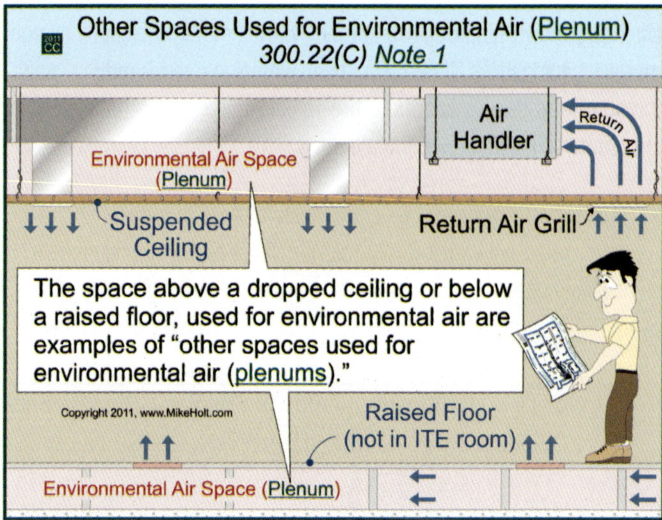

Figure 300–15

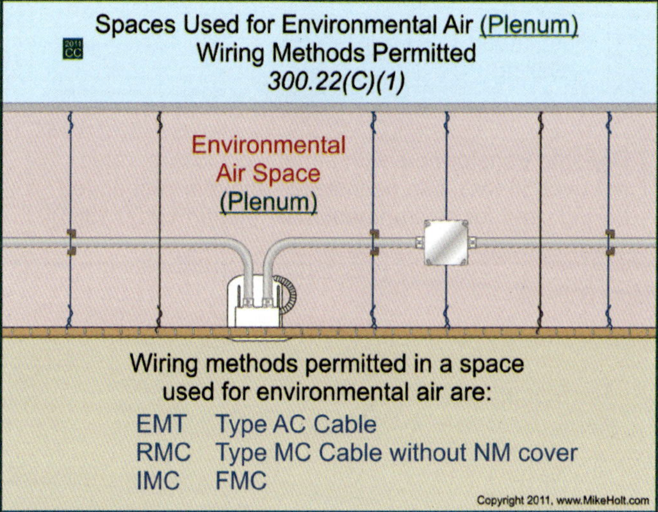

Figure 300–16

Author's Comments:

- PVC conduit [Article 352], electrical nonmetallic tubing [Article 362], liquidtight flexible conduit, and nonmetallic cables aren't permitted to be installed in spaces used for environmental air because they give off deadly toxic fumes when burned or superheated.

- Control, signaling, and communications cables installed in spaces used for environmental air must be suitable for plenum use. **Figure 300–17**

  - CATV, 820.179(A)
  - Communications, 800.21
  - Control and Signaling, 725.154(A)
  - Fire Alarm, 760.7
  - Optical Fiber Cables and Raceways, 770.113(C)
  - Sound Systems, 640.9(C) and 725.154(A)

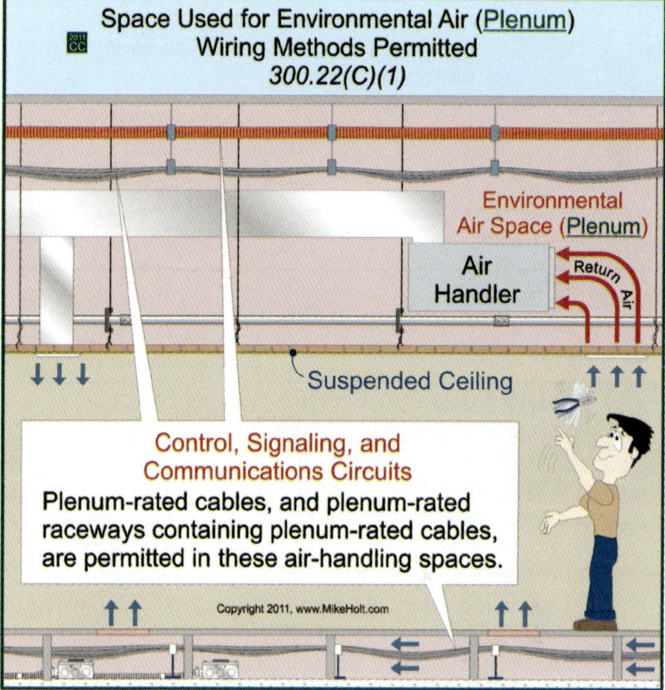

Figure 300–17

- Any wiring method suitable for the condition can be used in a space not used for environmental air-handling purposes. **Figure 300–18**

(2) Cable Tray Systems.

(a) Metal Cable Tray Systems. Metal cable tray systems can be installed to support the wiring methods and equipment permitted by this section. **Figure 300–19**

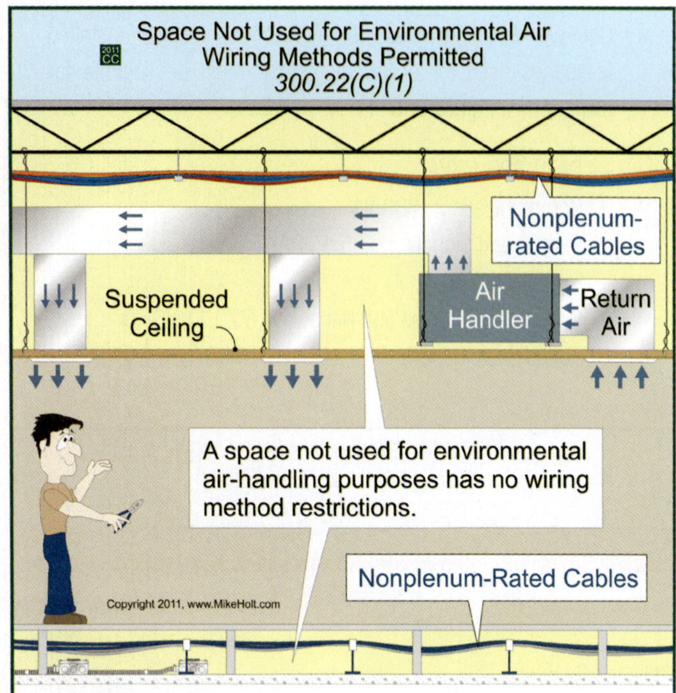

Figure 300–18

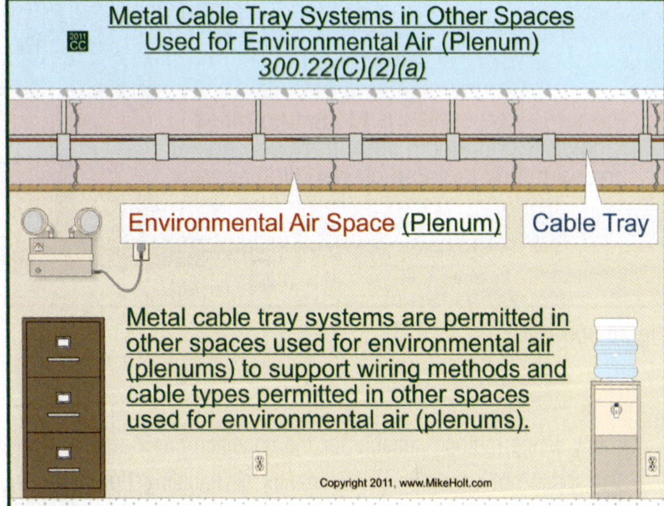

Figure 300–19

(3) **Equipment.** Electrical equipment with a metal enclosure or nonmetallic enclosures listed for use within an air-handling space (plenum) and having adequate fire-resistant and low-smoke-producing characteristics can be installed.

Author's Comment: Dry-type transformers with a metal enclosure, rated not over 50 kVA, can be installed above suspended ceilings used for environmental air [450.13(B)]. **Figure 300–20**

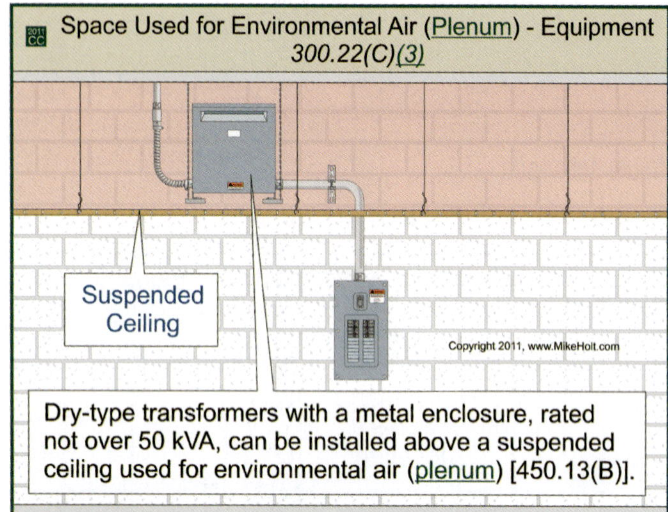

Figure 300–20

ANALYSIS: There's long, long been confusion about the terms "plenum" and "other space(s) used for environmental air." While nearly all mechanical codes (NFPA 90A *Standard for the Installation of Air-Conditioning and Ventilating Systems*, *International Mechanical Code* (IMC), and *Uniform Mechanical Code* (UMC)) use the term "plenum" for anything that moves environmental air, the *NEC* only referred to a physically constructed duct as a "plenum." The space beneath a raised floor and the space above a suspended ceiling (when used for air handling) were referred to as "other spaces used for environmental air." Obviously the *Code* shouldn't be the document that defines air system components, yet manufacturers were forced to have their product literature include provision for these "other spaces," which created massive confusion for people installing, designing and inspecting mechanical systems. The confusion was rampant enough to require an Informational Note in the *NEC* trying to explain what these spaces really were! With change, a component of an air-handling system that's created for the sole purpose of moving air (such as a duct made of tin or drywall) is now called a "duct specifically fabricated for environmental air." The space above a ceiling or below a floor that's used for air moving isn't fabricated for that sole purpose and therefore isn't a "duct," according to mechanical codes. These spaces are now referred to as "other spaces used for environmental air (plenums)," which correlates with other codes and also has the desired effect of using commonly accepted trade language—most people refer to the space above a suspended ceiling as a "plenum ceiling," not an "other space used for environmental air ceiling."

Additional changes to this section include a new provision dealing with cable trays in other spaces used for environmental air (plenums), which requires these cable trays to be metallic. Solid metal cable trays with metal covers can be used to support and enclose wiring methods that traditionally weren't allowed in these locations.

NOTES

Conductors for GENERAL WIRING

INTRODUCTION TO ARTICLE 310—CONDUCTORS FOR GENERAL WIRING

This article contains the general requirements for conductors, such as insulation markings, ampacity ratings, and conditions of use. Article 310 doesn't apply to conductors that are part of flexible cords, fixture wires, or to conductors that are an integral part of equipment [90.7 and 300.1(B)].

People often make errors in applying the ampacity tables contained in Article 310. If you study the explanations carefully, you'll avoid common errors such as applying Table 310.15(B)(17) when you should be applying Table 310.15(B)(16).

Why so many tables? Why does Table 310.15(B)(17) list the ampacity of 6 THHN as 105 amperes, yet Table 310.15(B)(16) lists the same conductor as having an ampacity of only 75 amperes? To answer that, go back to Article 100 and review the definition of ampacity. Notice the phrase "conditions of use." These tables set a maximum current value at which premature failure of the conductor insulation shouldn't occur during normal use, under the conditions described in the tables.

The designations THHN, THHW, RHH, and so on, are insulation types. Every type of insulation has a limit to how much heat it can withstand. When current flows through a conductor, it creates heat. How well the insulation around a conductor can dissipate that heat depends on factors such as whether that conductor is in free air or not. Think about what happens when you put on a sweater, a jacket, and then a coat—all at the same time. You heat up. Your skin can't dissipate heat with all that clothing on nearly as well as it dissipates heat in free air. The same principal applies to conductors.

Conductor insulation also fails with age. That's why we conduct cable testing and take other measures to predict failure and replace certain conductors (for example, feeders or critical equipment conductors) while they're still within design specifications. But conductor insulation failure takes decades under normal use—and it's a maintenance issue. However, if a conductor is forced to exceed the ampacity listed in the appropriate table, and as a result its design temperature is exceeded, insulation failure happens much more rapidly—often catastrophically. Consequently, exceeding the allowable ampacity of a conductor is a serious safety issue.

Article 310 Conductors for General Wiring

Many of the sections in Article 310 have been renumbered.

ANALYSIS: Many changes in the numbering of Article 310 have occurred in this edition of the *Code.* While some of these are welcome changes, such as creating a new "uses permitted" section in 310.10, many of the changes seem to be "change only for the sake of change," like renaming Table 310.16 to "310.15(B)(16) (formerly Table 310.16)."

310.10(H) Conductors in Parallel

Revisions to this section resolve a long standing issue of enforceability.

310.10 Uses Permitted.

(H) Conductors in Parallel.

(1) General. Ungrounded and neutral conductors can be connected in parallel, only in sizes 1/0 AWG and larger.

(2) **Conductor Characteristics.** When circuit conductors are installed in parallel, the conductors must be connected so that the current will be evenly distributed between the individual parallel conductors by requiring all circuit conductors within each parallel set to: **Figure 310–1**

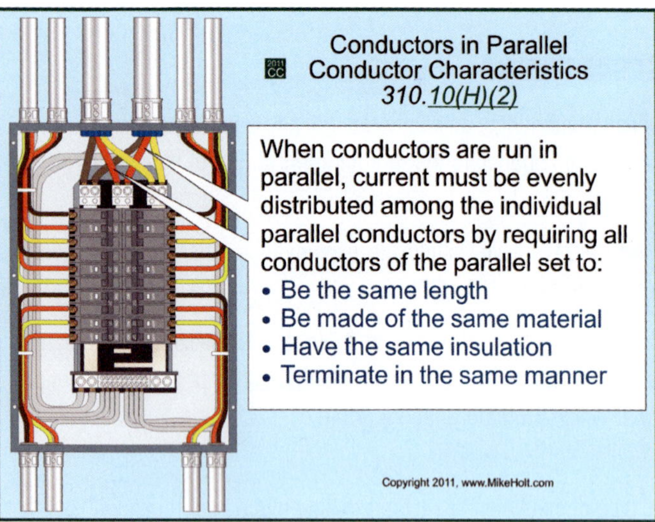

Figure 310–1

(1) Be the same length.

(2) Consist of the same conductor material (copper/aluminum).

(3) Be the same size in circular mil area (minimum 1/0 AWG).

(4) Have the same type of insulation (like THHN).

(5) Terminate in the same method (set screw versus compression).

> **Author's Comment:** Conductors aren't required to have the same physical characteristics as those of another ungrounded or neutral conductor to achieve balance.

(3) **Separate Raceways or Cables.** Raceways or cables containing parallel conductors must have the same electrical characteristics and the same number of conductors. **Figure 310–2**

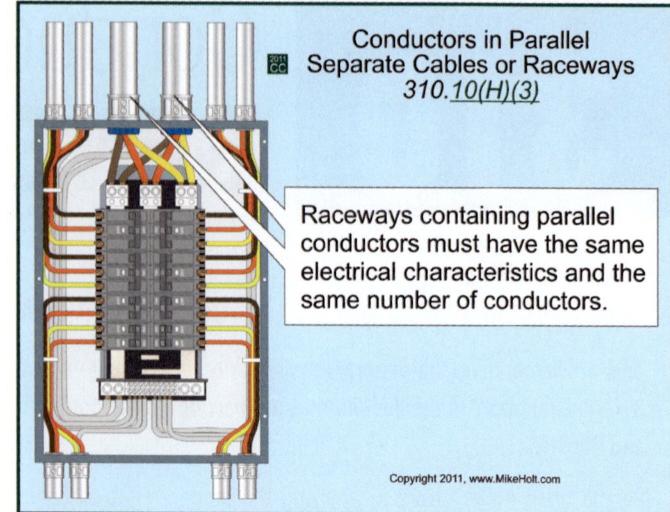

Figure 310–2

> **Author's Comment:** If one set of parallel conductors is installed in a metallic raceway and the other conductors are installed in PVC conduit, the conductors in the metallic raceway will have an increased opposition to current flow (impedance) as compared to the conductors in the nonmetallic raceway. This results in an unbalanced distribution of current between the parallel conductors.

Parallel sets of conductors aren't required to have the same physical characteristics as those of another set to achieve balance.

> **Author's Comment:** For example, a 400A feeder with a neutral load of 240A can be paralleled as follows: **Figure 310–3**

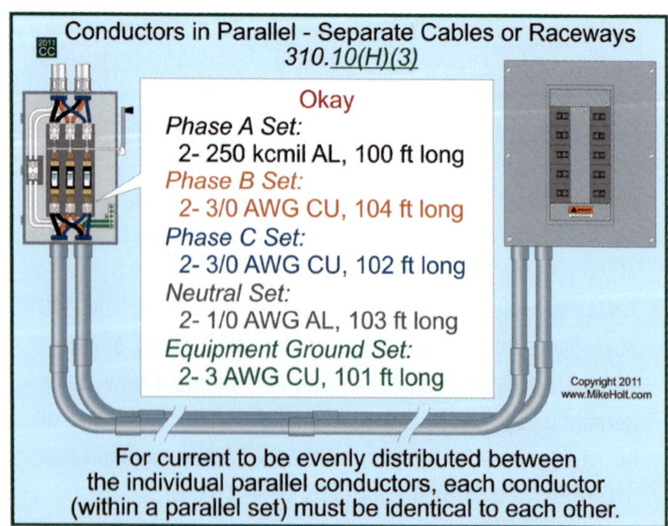

Figure 310–3

- Phase A, Two—250 kcmil THHN aluminum, 100 ft
- Phase B, Two—3/0 THHN copper, 104 ft
- Phase C, Two—3/0 THHN copper, 102 ft
- Neutral, Two—1/0 THHN aluminum, 103 ft
- Equipment Grounding Conductor, Two—3 AWG copper, 101 ft*

**The minimum 1/0 AWG requirement doesn't apply to equipment grounding conductors [310.10(H)(5)].*

(4) Conductor Ampacity Adjustment. Each current-carrying conductor of a paralleled set of conductors must be counted as a current-carrying conductor for the purpose of conductor ampacity adjustment, in accordance with Table 310.15(B)(3)(a). **Figure 310–4**

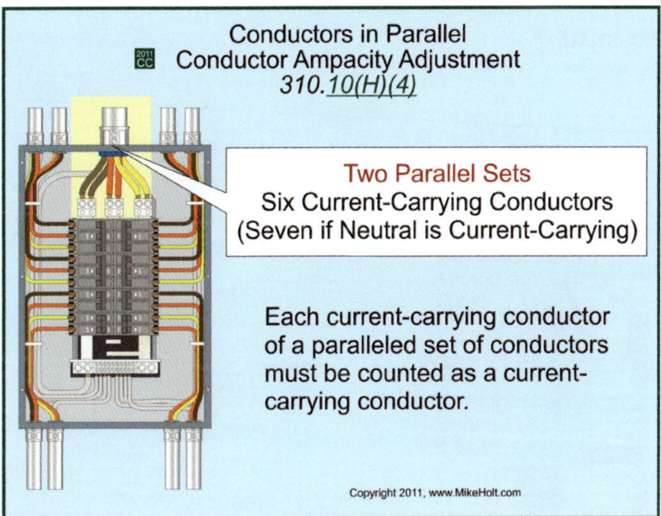

Figure 310–4

(5) Equipment Grounding Conductors. The equipment grounding conductors for circuits in parallel must be sized in accordance with 250.122(F). **Figure 310–5**

Author's Comment: The minimum 1/0 AWG parallel conductor size rule of 310.10(H) doesn't apply to equipment grounding conductors.

(6) Equipment Bonding Jumpers. Equipment bonding jumpers are sized in accordance with 250.102.

Author's Comment: The equipment bonding jumper isn't required to be larger than the largest ungrounded circuit conductors supplying the equipment.

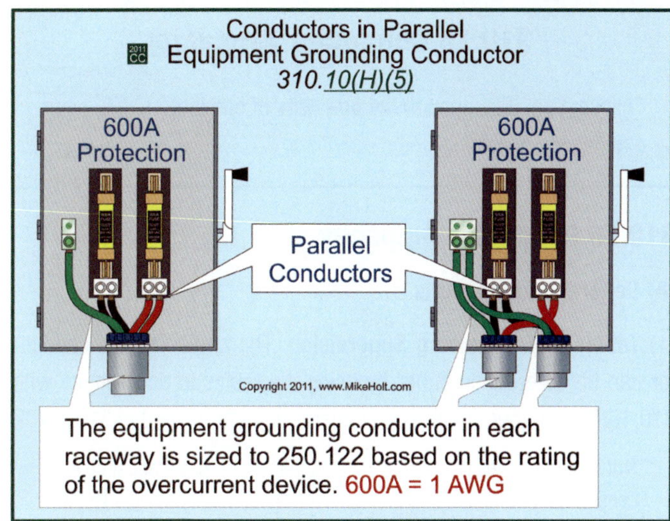

Figure 310–5

ANALYSIS: A careful reading of this section in previous editions of the *Code* showed that there was no prohibition of installing conductors 1 AWG and smaller in parallel. This was due to the fact that the language of the section, by using the word "shall be permitted" instead of "shall not" or just "shall," only gave an allowance to connect large (1/0 AWG and larger) conductors in parallel without placing a prohibition on smaller conductors (smaller than 1/0) AWG) from being installed in parallel. With the change to this language, it's clear that connecting these smaller conductors in parallel, although popular in many parts of the world, isn't permitted by the *NEC*.

Another change to this section deals with equipment bonding jumpers. Many times, such as with a transformer secondary, an equipment bonding jumper (not an equipment grounding conductor) is installed alongside ungrounded and grounded conductors in parallel. Although it seems rather obvious that these bonding jumpers don't need to meet the minimum size requirements of 310.10(H) (1/0 AWG or larger), the *NEC* really didn't address the issue. The *Code* now refers to 250.102 for conductor sizing, making this principle much clearer.

310.15 Conductor Ampacity

This section, dealing with the ampacity of conductors, has been extensively revised.

310.15 Conductor Ampacity.

(A) General Requirements.

(1) Tables or Engineering Supervision. The ampacity of a conductor can be determined either by using the tables in accordance with 310.15(B), or under engineering supervision as provided in 310.15(C).

Note 1: Ampacities provided by this section don't take voltage drop into consideration. See 210.19(A) Note 4, for branch circuits and 215.2(D) Note 2, for feeders.

(2) Conductor Ampacity—Lower Rating. Where more than one ampacity applies for a given circuit length, the lowest value must be used. Figure 310–6

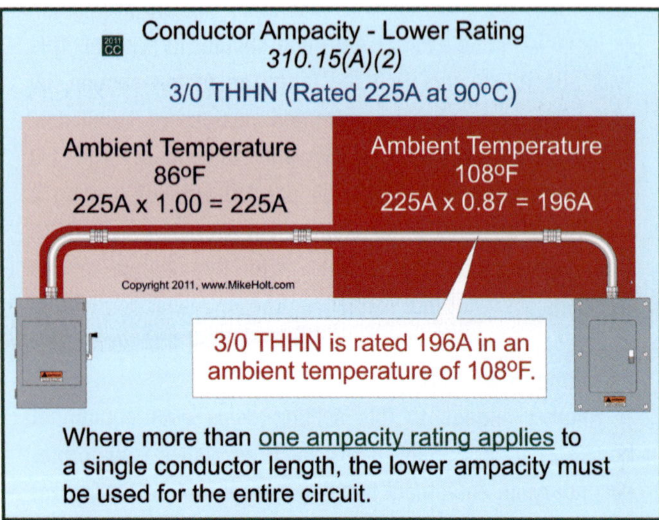

Figure 310–6

Ex: When different ampacities apply to a length of conductor, the higher ampacity is permitted for the entire circuit if the reduced ampacity length doesn't exceed 10 ft and its length doesn't exceed 10 percent of the length of the higher ampacity. Figures 310–7 and 310–8

(3) Insulation Temperature Limitation. Conductors must not be used if the operating temperature exceeds that designated for the type of insulated conductor involved.

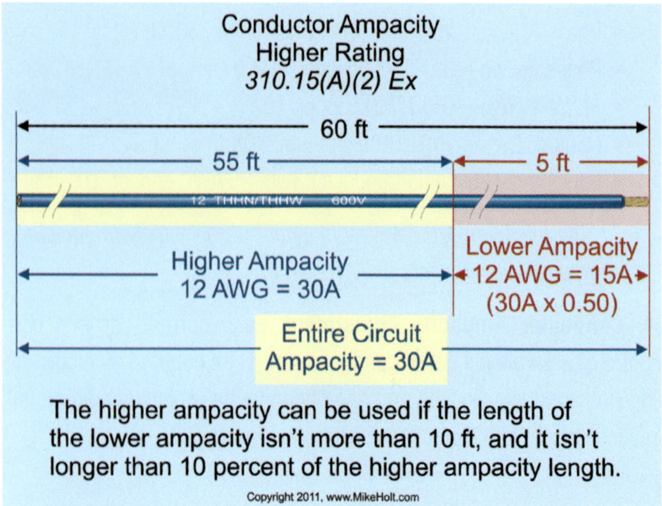

Figure 310-7

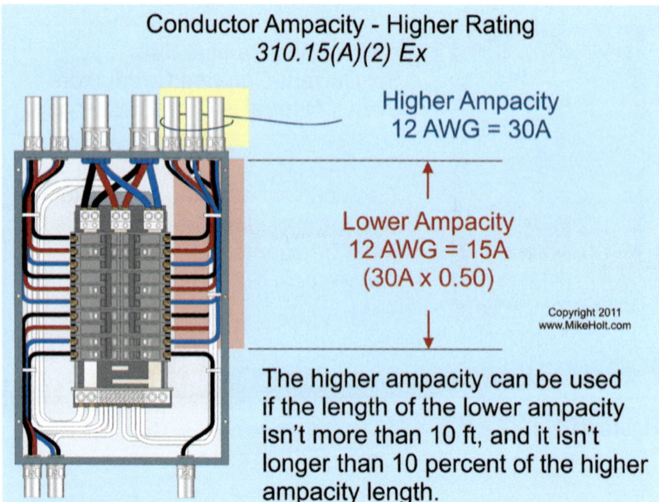

Figure 310-8

Note 1: The insulation temperature rating of a conductor is the maximum temperature a conductor [310.104(A)] can withstand over a prolonged time period without serious degradation. The main factors to consider for conductor operating temperature include:

(1) Ambient temperature may vary along the conductor length as well as from time to time [Table 310.15(B)(2)(a)].

(2) Heat generated internally in the conductor—load current flow.

(3) The rate at which generated heat dissipates into the ambient medium.

(4) Adjacent load-carrying conductors have the effect of raising the ambient temperature and impeding heat dissipation [Table 310.15(B)(3)(a)].

Note 2: See 110.14(C) for the temperature limitation of terminations.

(B) Ampacity Table. The allowable conductor ampacities listed in Table 310.15(B)(16) are based on conditions where the ambient temperature isn't over 86°F, and no more than three current-carrying conductors are bundled together. **Figure 310–9**

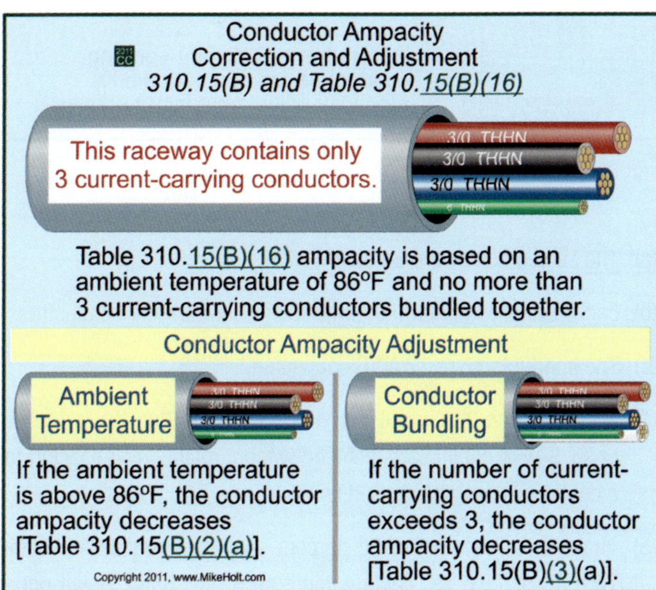

Figure 310–9

The temperature correction and adjustment factors apply to the ampacity for the temperature rating of the conductor, provided the corrected and adjusted ampacity doesn't exceed the ampacity for the temperature rating of the termination in accordance with the provisions of 110.14(C).

(2) Ambient Temperature Correction Factors. When conductors are installed in an ambient temperature other than 78°F to 86°F, the ampacities listed in Table 310.15(B)(16) must be corrected in accordance with the multipliers listed in Table 310.15(B)(2)(a). **Figure 310–10**

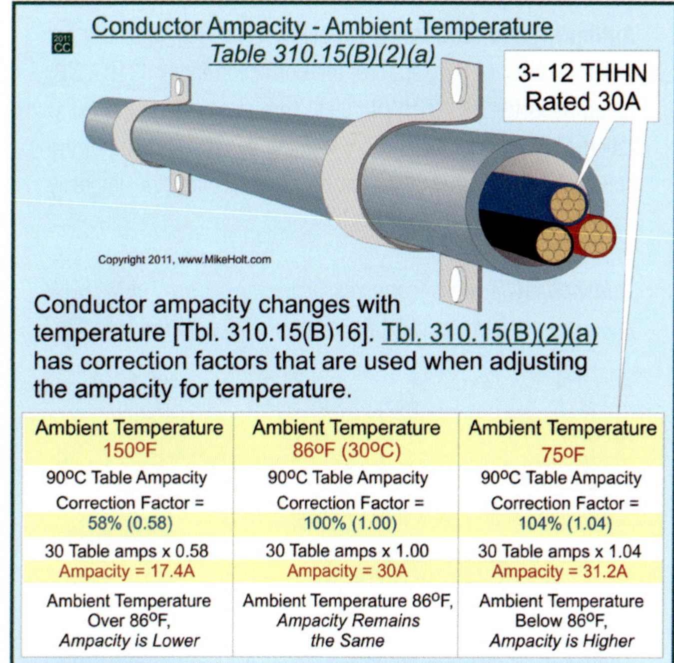

Figure 310–10

Table 310.15(B)(2)(a) Ambient Temperature Correction

Ambient Temperature °F	Ambient Temperature °C	Correction Factor 75°C Conductors	Correction Factor 90°C Conductors
50 or less	10 or less	1.20	1.15
51–59°F	11–15°C	1.15	1.12
60–68°F	16–20°C	1.11	1.08
69–77°F	21–25°C	1.05	1.04
78–86°F	26–30°C	1.00	1.00
87–95°F	31–35°C	0.94	0.96
96–104°F	36–40°C	0.88	0.91
105–113°F	41–45°C	0.82	0.87
114–122°F	46–50°C	0.75	0.82
123–131°F	51–55°C	0.67	0.76
132–140°F	56–60°C	0.58	0.71
141–149°F	61–65°C	0.47	0.65
150–158°F	66–70°C	0.33	0.58
159–167°F	71–75°C	0.00	0.50
168–176°F	76–80°C	0.00	0.41
177–185°F	81–85°C	0.00	0.29

Author's Comment: When correcting conductor ampacity for elevated ambient temperature, the correction factor [310.15(B)(2)(a)] used for THHN/THWN conductors is based on the 90°C rating of the conductor in a dry location and 75°C rating of the conductor in a wet location, based on the conductor ampacity listed in Table 310.15(B)(16) [110.14(C)].

Question: *What's the corrected ampacity of 3/0 THHN/THWN conductors in a dry location if the ambient temperature is 108°F?*

(a) 173A *(b) 196A* *(c) 213A* *(d) 241A*

Answer: *(b) 196A*

Conductor Ampacity [90°C] = 225A
Correction Factor [Table 310.(B)(2)(a)] = 0.87
Corrected Ampacity = 225A x 0.87
Corrected Ampacity = 196A

Question: *What's the corrected ampacity of 3/0 THHN/THWN conductors in a wet location if the ambient temperature is 108°F?*

(a) 164A *(b) 196A* *(c) 213A* *(d) 241A*

Answer: *(a) 164A*

Conductor Ampacity [75°C] = 200A
Correction Factor [Table 310.(B)(2)(a)] = 0.82
Corrected Ampacity = 200A x 0.82
Corrected Ampacity = 164A

Author's Comment: When adjusting conductor ampacity, the ampacity is based on the temperature insulation rating of the conductor as listed in Table 310.15(B)(16), not the temperature rating of the terminal [110.14(C)].

(B) Ampacity Table.

(3) Adjustment Factors.

(a) Conductor Bundle.

(4) Ampacity adjustment factors don't apply to conductors within Type AC or Type MC cable under the following conditions: **Figure 310–11**

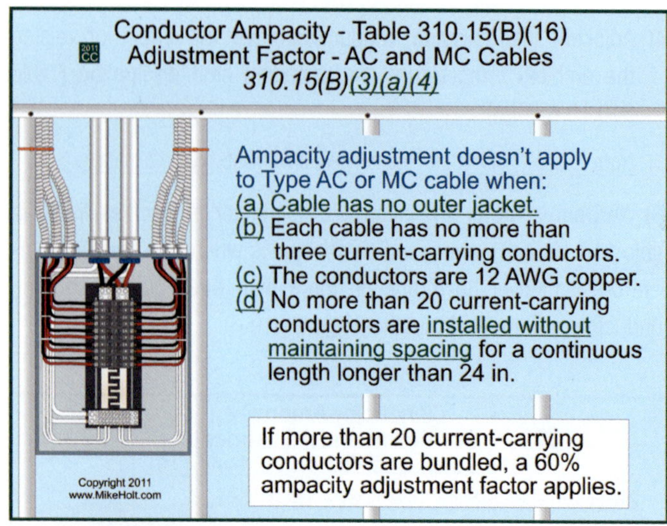

Figure 310–11

(a) The cables don't have an outer jacket,

(b) Each cable has no more than three current-carrying conductors,

(c) The conductors are 12 AWG copper, and

(d) No more than 20 current-carrying conductors (ten 2-wire cables or six 3-wire cables) are installed without maintaining spacing for a continuous length longer than 24 in.

(5) Ampacity adjustment of 60 percent applies to conductors within Type AC or Type MC cable without an overall outer jacket under the following conditions:

(b) The number of current-carrying conductors exceeds 20.

(c) The cables are stacked or bundled longer than 24 in. without spacing being maintained.

(c) Circular Raceways Exposed to Sunlight on Rooftops. When applying ampacity adjustment correction factors, the ambient temperature adjustment contained in Table 310.15(B)(3)(c) is added to the outdoor ambient temperature for conductors installed in circular raceways exposed to direct sunlight on or above rooftops to determine the applicable ambient temperature for ampacity correction factors in Table 310.15(B)(2)(a) or Table 310.15(B)(2)(b).

Note 1: See the ASHRAE *Handbook—Fundamentals* (www.ashrae.org) as a source for the average ambient temperatures in various locations.

Note 2: The temperature adders in Table 310.15(B)(3)(c) are based on the results of averaging the ambient temperatures.

Table 310.15(B)(3)(c) Ambient Temperature Adder for Raceways On or Above Rooftops		
Distance of Raceway Above Roof	C°	F°
0 to ½ in.	33	60
Above ½ in. to 3½ in.	22	40
Above 3½ in. to 12 in.	17	30
Above 12 in. to 36 in.	14	25

Author's Comment: This rule requires the ambient temperature used for ampacity correction to be adjusted where conductors or cables are installed in a circular raceway on or above a rooftop and the raceway is exposed to direct sunlight. The reasoning is that the air inside circular raceways in direct sunlight is significantly hotter than the surrounding air, and appropriate ampacity corrections must be made in order to comply with 310.10.

For example, a conduit with three 6 THWN-2 conductors with direct sunlight exposure that's ¾ in. above the roof will require 40°F to be added to the correction factors on Table 310.15(B)(2)(a). Assuming an ambient temperature of 90°F, the temperature to use for conductor ampacity correction will be 130°F (90°F + 40°F), the 6 THWN-2 conductor ampacity after correction will be 57A (75A x 0.76). **Figure 310–12**

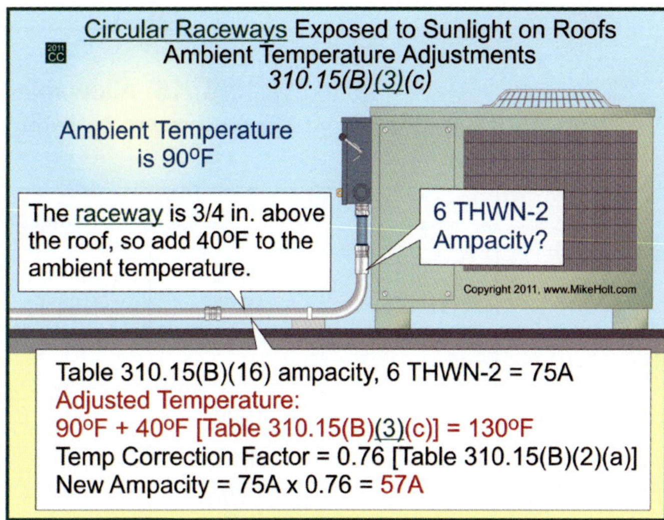

Figure 310–12

When adjusting conductor ampacity, use the conductor ampacity as listed in Table 310.15(B)(16) based on the conductors' insulation rating; in this case, it's 75A at 90°F. Conductor ampacity adjustment isn't based on the temperature terminal rating in accordance with 110.14(C).

Table 310.15(B)(16) Allowable Ampacities of Insulated Conductors Based on Not More Than Three Current-Carrying Conductors and Ambient Temperature of 30°C (86°F)*

Size	Temperature Rating of Conductor, See Table 310.13						Size
	60°C (140°F)	75°C (167°F)	90°C (194°F)	60°C (140°F)	75°C (167°F)	90°C (194°F)	
AWG kcmil	TW UF	THHW THW THWN XHHW Wet Location	THHN THW-2 THWN-2 THHW XHHW XHHW-2 Dry Location	TW UF	THHN THW THWN XHHW Wet Location	THHN THW-2 THWN-2 THHW XHHW XHHW-2 Dry Location	AWG kcmil
	Copper			Aluminum/Copper-Clad Aluminum			
14*	15	20	25				14*
12*	20	25	30	15	20	25	12*
10*	30	35	40	25	30	35	10*
8	40	50	55	35	40	45	8
6	55	65	75	40	50	55	6
4	70	85	95	55	65	75	4
3	85	100	115	65	75	85	3
2	95	115	130	75	90	100	2
1	110	130	145	85	100	115	1
1/0	125	150	170	100	120	135	1/0
2/0	145	175	195	115	135	150	2/0
3/0	165	200	225	130	155	175	3/0
4/0	195	230	260	150	180	205	4/0
250	215	255	290	170	205	230	250
300	240	285	320	195	230	260	300
350	260	310	350	210	250	280	350
400	280	335	380	225	270	305	400
500	320	380	430	260	310	350	500

*See 240.4(D)

ANALYSIS: Although many *Code* users still use the term "derating," it's a term that's been mostly phased out over the last several *NEC* cycles. In this edition of the *Code*, the term "derate(ing)" isn't used at all, save for in a very few instances. The term "ampacity adjustment" is used throughout the *NEC* when referring to conductors that are bundled or used on rooftops, and the term "correction" is used when conductors are subjected to temperatures other than 86°F.

Properly sizing conductors is one of the most difficult things *Code* users have to deal with. It takes a thorough knowledge of Articles 240 and 310, as well as knowledge of individual sections and subsections. Section 110.14(C) is one of these subsections. It contains the guidelines on how to size conductors based on the temperature ratings of the terminals of various electrical equipment. While experienced users of the *NEC* may know of its existence, those people who are new to the *Code* will benefit greatly by having this new Informational Note, which reminds them that there's much more to conductor sizing than just putting a 12 AWG conductor on a 20A breaker.

Conductors with insulation temperature ratings higher than the termination's temperature rating can be used for conductor ampacity adjustment, correction, or both [110.14(C)]. This means conductor ampacity must be based on the conductor's insulation temperature rating listed in Table 310.15(B)(16), as adjusted for ambient temperature correction factors, conductor bundling adjustment factors, or both. This change clarifies that, after applying these adjustments and corrections, the resulting ampacity still can't exceed the temperature limitations of the equipment termination.

The temperature correction factors formerly found at the bottom of (then) Table 310.16 in the 2008 *NEC*, were some of the least user friendly in the *Code*. The fact that they were buried beneath the ampacity table, and the fact that it was broken up into copper, aluminum, Fahrenheit, and Celsius certainly didn't help. This new table provides a remarkably easier format, with less confusion and proper application being the end result. An interesting addition to this table is borrowed from the *Canadian Electrical Code*, and that's the allowance of smaller conductors when installed in an ambient temperature of less than 70°F. With this allowance, the *NEC* user can use up to 115 percent of the conductor's ampacity in certain conditions, which can result in a smaller conductor. While previous editions of the *Code* recognized colder environments, it allowed only for an increase to 104 percent of the conductor's ampacity, a value that never really made the math worthwhile.

Previous editions of the *NEC* used the term "nipple" to describe a raceway that's 24 in. or less in length. This resulted in *Code* users debating about the physical characteristics of the raceways, such as whether or not the raceway could contain bends. This change takes away that argument by removing the term "nipple(s)" and replacing it with "raceway(s)." One no longer needs to guess at the intent of this section, and needs now only to measure the length and determine the appropriate rules.

The term "bundled" has been used for several *Code* cycles to describe when ampacity adjustment is required. Because the term isn't defined in Article 100, many people struggle in their attempts to determine when to apply the adjustment provisions of this section. While the phrase "installed without maintaining spacing" is also not defined, some *NEC* users may find it an easier phrase to understand and apply. This change isn't intended to be a technical one, but rather an editorial one.

New to the 2008 *Code* came a rule requiring that all conductors installed in conduits on rooftops have their ampacities adjusted dramatically. The term "conduit," while not defined in the *NEC*, doesn't include raceways such as EMT, ENT, and FMT. With this change, conductors installed in these raceways will now have to have their ampacities adjusted as well.

The ampacity of some conductors in Table 310.15(B)(16) (formerly 310.16) didn't match those found in the *Canadian Electrical Code* and were therefore changed. While no technical evidence was submitted showing insulation failure of the conductors, this proposal was passed. The end result was a change to the ampacities of:

Copper conductors: 14, 12, 3, and 1 AWG, and 600 kcmil, 1,500 kcmil and 2,000 kcmil.

Aluminum conductors: 12, 8, and 6 AWG, and 300 kcmil, 700 kcmil, and 800 kcmil.

NOTES

ARTICLE 312 Cabinets, Cutout Boxes, and Meter SOCKET ENCLOSURES

INTRODUCTION TO ARTICLE 312—CABINETS, CUTOUT BOXES, AND METER SOCKET ENCLOSURES

This article addresses the installation and construction specifications for the items mentioned in its title. In Article 310, we observed that the conditions of use have an effect on the ampacity of a conductor. Likewise, the conditions of use have an effect on the selection and application of cabinets, cutout boxes, and meter socket enclosures. For example, you can't use just any enclosure in a wet location or in a hazardous (classified) location. The conditions of use impose special requirements for these situations.

For all such enclosures, certain requirements apply—regardless of the use. For example, you must cover any openings, protect conductors from abrasion, and allow sufficient bending room for conductors.

Notice that Article 408 covers switchboards and panelboards, with primary emphasis on the interior, or "guts" while the cabinet that would be used to enclose a panelboard is covered here in Article 312. Therefore you'll find that some important considerations such as wire-bending space at terminals of panelboards are included in this article.

Article 312 covers the installation and construction specifications for cabinets, cutout boxes, and meter socket enclosures. [312.1]. Figure 312–1

Author's Comment: A cabinet is an enclosure for either surface mounting or flush mounting and provided with a frame in which a door may be hung. A cutout box is designed for surface mounting with a swinging door [Article 100]. The industry name for a meter socket enclosure is "meter can."

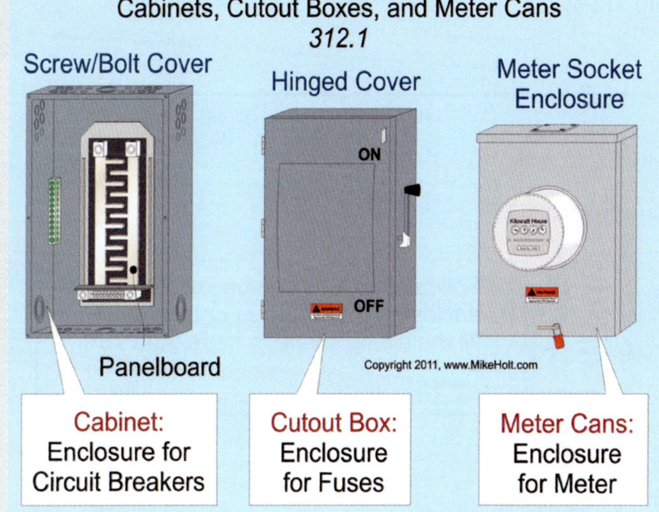

Figure 312–1

312.8 Enclosures With Splices, Taps, and Feed-Through Conductors

The title and text of this section have been changed to more accurately describe the rule and make it easier to read.

312.8 Enclosures With Splices, Taps, and Feed-Through Conductors. Cabinets, cutout boxes, and meter socket enclosures can be used for conductors as feeding through, spliced, or tapping off to other enclosures, switches, or overcurrent devices where all of the following conditions are met:

(1) The total area of the conductors at any cross section doesn't exceed 40 percent of the cross-sectional area of the space. Figure 312–2

(2) The total area of conductors, splices, and taps installed at any cross section doesn't exceed 75 percent of the cross-sectional area of that space. Figure 312–3

(3) A warning label on the enclosure identifies the disconnecting means for feed-through conductors.

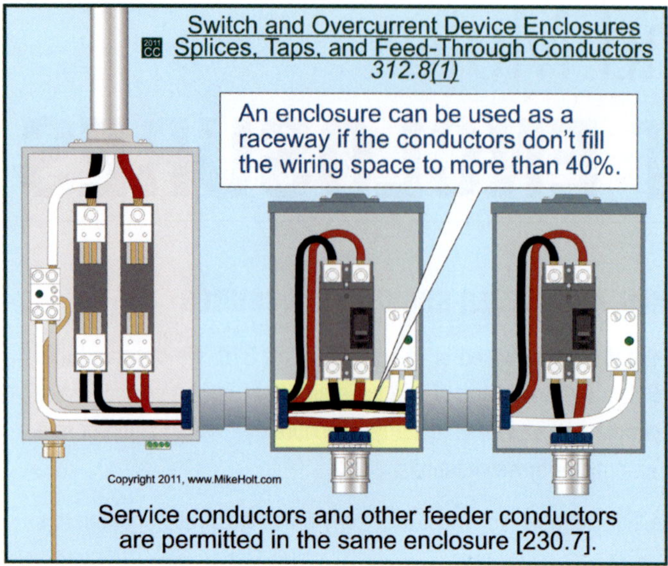

Figure 312–2

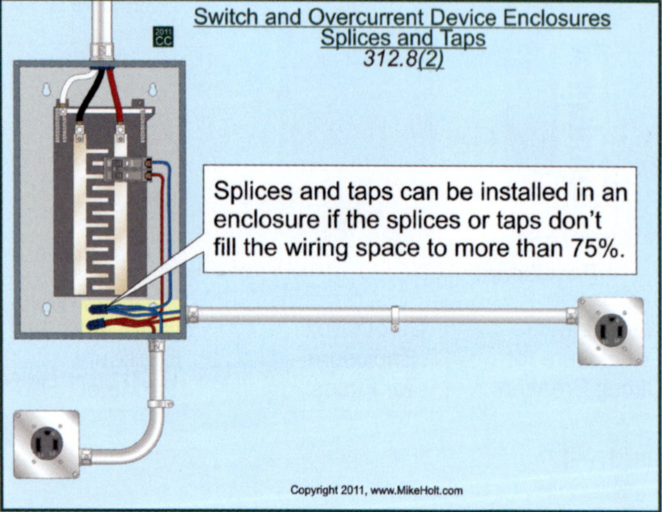

Figure 312–3

ANALYSIS: The allowance for splicing conductors in a cabinet containing a panelboard has always been one of the more difficult rules for *Code* users to find. The title of this section previously referred to "enclosures for switches or overcurrent devices," which was accurate, but didn't alert the *NEC* user to everything covered in this section. The title has been revised to provide for a more user-friendly document.

With the previous language and format of this rule, there may have been a tendency to read only the first portion of the text, and incorrectly assume that splicing wasn't allowed in such a cabinet. With the new list format, the likelihood of the user reading all of the requirements is increased.

New to this section is a requirement addressing conductors that "feed through" these enclosures, such as circuits that don't originate or terminate in the cabinet. Industry experience has shown that there are times when a panelboard is de-energized for maintenance or troubleshooting, only to surprise the electrician with energized conductors in the cabinet. Due to these types of hazards, a warning must now be placed on the enclosure alerting qualified persons to the fact that there are feed-through conductors in the enclosure, and identifying the closest disconnecting means for them.

ARTICLE 314 Outlet, Device, Pull and Junction Boxes; Conduit Bodies; and HANDHOLE ENCLOSURES

INTRODUCTION TO ARTICLE 314—OUTLET, DEVICE, PULL AND JUNCTION BOXES; CONDUIT BODIES; AND HANDHOLE ENCLOSURES

Article 314 contains installation requirements for outlet boxes, pull and junction boxes, conduit bodies, and handhole enclosures. As with Article 312, the conditions of use have a bearing on the type of material and equipment selected for a particular installation. If a raceway is installed in a wet location, for example, the correct fittings and the proper installation methods must be used.

Article 314 provides guidance for selecting and installing outlet, device, and junction boxes. Information in this article will help you size an outlet box using the proper cubic inch capacity as well as calculating the minimum dimensions for larger pull boxes. There are limits on the amount of weight that can be supported by an outlet box and rules on how to support a device or outlet box to various surfaces. This article will help you understand these type of rules so that your installation will be compliant with the *NEC*. As always, the clear illustrations in this unit will help you visualize the finished installation.

PART II. INSTALLATION

314.21 Repairing Noncombustible Surfaces

The rule for repairing the surfaces of walls and floors around electrical boxes has been revised.

314.21 Repairing Noncombustible Surfaces. Gaps around boxes with flush-type covers that are recessed in noncombustible surfaces (such as plaster, drywall, or plasterboard) must be repaired so there will be no gap more than ⅛ in. at the edge of the box. Figure 314–1

ANALYSIS: The 2008 *NEC* brought about a change to 312.4 requiring that noncombustible wall surfaces must be repaired if there are gaps or open spaces greater than ⅛ in. at the edge of a cabinet, cutout box, or meter socket enclosure. This differed from previous *Code* language that required only drywall, plasterboard and plaster surfaces to be repaired.

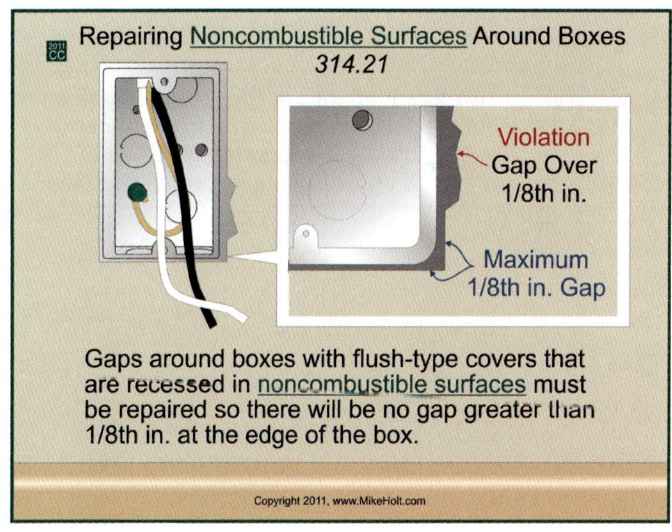

Figure 314–1

In this *NEC* cycle, 314.21 has been changed to mirror the language found in 312.4. Now in addition to drywall, plaster, and plasterboard surfaces, any noncombustible surface must be repaired so there are no gaps or open spaces greater than ⅛ in. at the edge of outlet, device, pull and junction bodies.

314.23(E) Raceway Supported Enclosure, Without Devices, Luminaires, or Lampholders

The rule addressing raceway supported boxes (without other equipment) has been slightly revised.

314.23 Support of Boxes and Conduit Bodies. Boxes must be securely supported by one of the following methods:

(E) Raceway—Boxes and Conduit Bodies Without Devices or Luminaires. Two intermediate metal or rigid metal conduits, threaded wrenchtight into the enclosure, can be used to support an outlet box that doesn't contain a device or luminaire, if each raceway is supported within 36 in. of the box or within 18 in. of the box if all conduit entries are on the same side. **Figure 314–2**

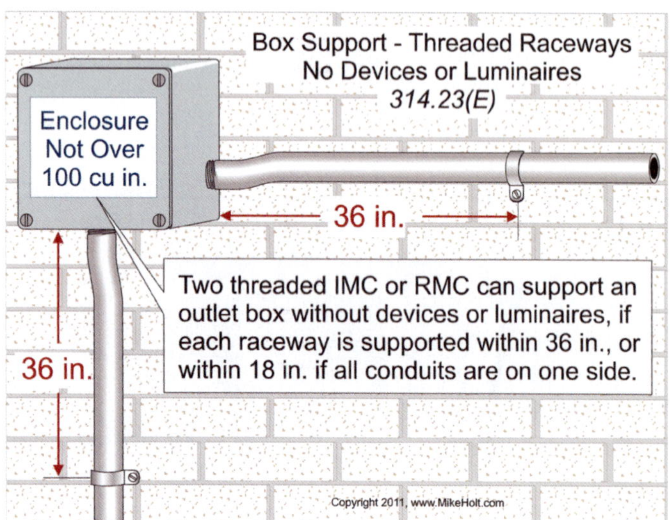

Figure 314–2

Ex: Conduit bodies are permitted to be supported by any of the following wiring methods:

(1) Intermediate metal conduit, Type IMC

(2) Rigid metal conduit, Type RMC

(3) Rigid polyvinyl chloride conduit, Type PVC

(4) Reinforced thermosetting resin conduit, Type RTRC

(5) Electrical metallic tubing, Type EMT

ANALYSIS: The allowance for a raceway supported box or conduit body has been one of the more difficult rules for a *Code* user to read, due to the length of the rule and the number of technical requirements found in it. The exception for the support of conduit bodies has been equally difficult to navigate through. With this change, the exception is written in an easier to understand list format, and the types of raceways that can use this exception has been expanded. Type RTRC conduit has been added to the raceway types that can use this exception.

314.27 Outlet Boxes

Luminaire box ratings have been revised for clarity and ease of reading, and provisions for lampholders have been added.

314.27 Outlet Box.

(A) Boxes at Luminaire and Lampholder Outlets.

(1) Outlets in the Wall. Boxes and fittings for luminaires and lampholders in a wall must be marked on the interior of the box to indicate the maximum weight of the luminaire if other than 50 lb. **Figure 314–3**

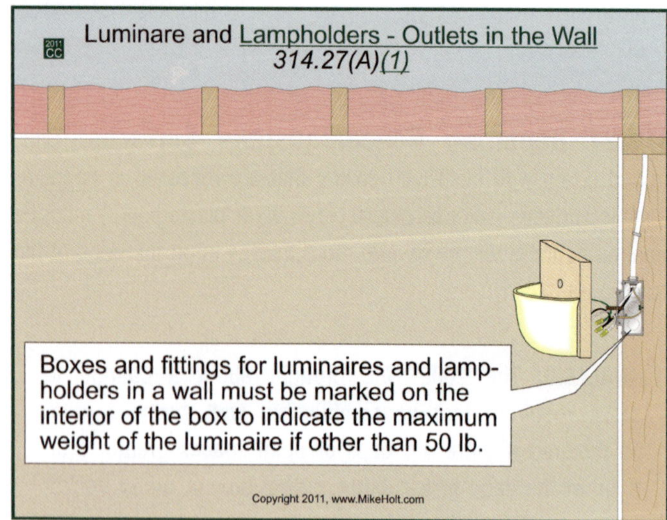

Figure 314–3

Ex: A wall-mounted luminaire or lampholder weighing no more than 6 lb can be supported to a device box or plaster ring secured to a device box. Figure 314–4

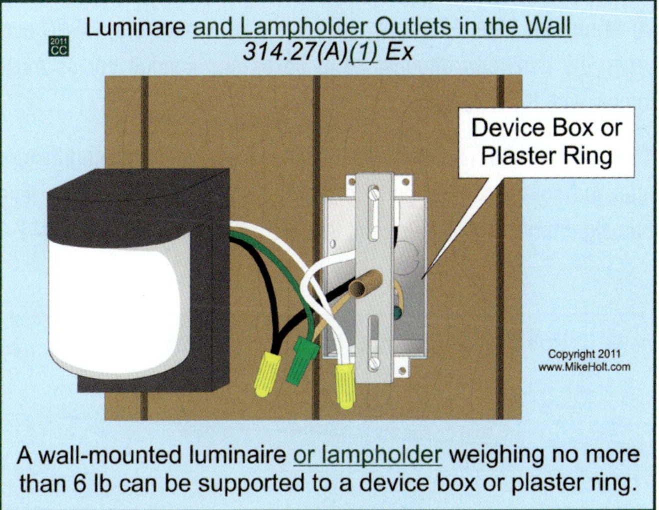

Figure 314–4

(2) Outlets in the Ceiling. Boxes for a luminaire or lampholder in a ceiling must be designed to support a luminaire weighing a minimum of 50 lb. Luminaires weighing more than 50 lb must be supported independently of the outlet box unless the outlet box is listed and marked for the maximum weight to be supported. Figure 314–5

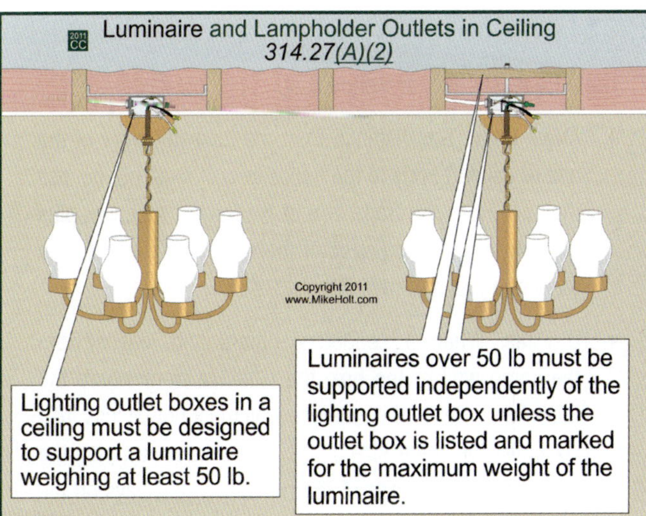

Figure 314–5

ANALYSIS: Significant revisions were made to this section in the 2008 *Code* cycle. When several changes are made to a section mistakes will often result. This revision corrects an error in the previous *NEC* by requiring that boxes installed in a wall for luminaire support must be marked on the interior of the box to indicate the weight ratings of the box. This error only occurred in the first printing of the 2008 *Code.*

The requirements have also been broken up into a list format for easier reading, and provisions for lampholders have been incorporated into the title of the rule.

314.27(C) Boxes at Ceiling-Suspended (Paddle) Fan Outlets

A new requirement was added addressing the probability of ceiling fan installations.

314.27 Outlet Box.

(C) Ceiling Paddle Fan Box. Outlet boxes for a ceiling paddle fan must be listed and marked as suitable for the purpose, and must not support a fan weighing more than 70 lb. Outlet boxes for a ceiling paddle fan that weighs more than 35 lb must include the maximum weight to be supported in the required marking. Figure 314–6

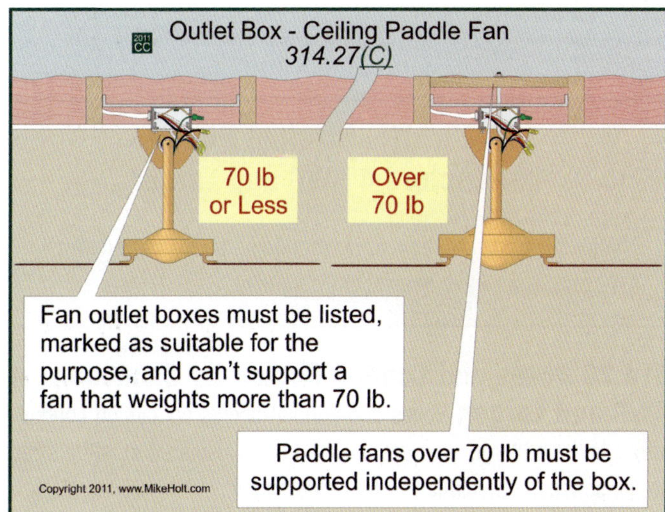

Figure 314–6

Author's Comment: If the maximum weight isn't marked on the box, and the fan weighs over 35 lb, the fan must be supported independently of the outlet box. Ceiling paddle fans over 70 lb must be supported independently of the outlet box.

Where spare, separately switched, ungrounded conductors are provided to a ceiling-mounted outlet box in a location acceptable for a ceiling-suspended (paddle) fan in a dwelling unit, the outlet box must be listed for the support of a ceiling-suspended (paddle) fan.

ANALYSIS: In new construction, it isn't uncommon to see an unused conductor in a luminaire outlet box installed in the ceiling. It's also not uncommon to see this unused conductor independently switched, in the same box as the luminaire. Many builders advertise this to potential home buyers as a provision for a future ceiling fan. While this may be a nice feature, it's also often a *Code* violation when the ceiling fan is finally installed, because the box may not be rated to support one. This change was accepted after initial reluctance, because the *NEC* isn't in the habit of dealing with future violations, no matter how probable they might be.

The result of this change is that such an installation must incorporate a box that's suitable for ceiling fan support, despite the fact that a ceiling fan isn't installed. Considering the effort required to install the separate, independently switched conductor, this change doesn't add too much of a burden to the electrical community, and adds an enforceable requirement for AHJs who didn't have one before.

314.28(A)(1) Straight Pulls—Conductors 4 AWG and Larger

The junction and pull box sizing requirements for conductors 4 AWG and larger have been slightly clarified.

314.28 Boxes and Conduit Bodies for Conductors 4 AWG and Larger. Boxes and conduit bodies containing conductors 4 AWG and larger that are required to be insulated must be sized so the conductor insulation won't be damaged.

Author's Comments:

- The requirements for sizing boxes and conduit bodies containing conductors 6 AWG and smaller are contained in 314.16.
- If conductors 4 AWG and larger enter a box or other enclosure, a fitting that provides a smooth, rounded, insulating surface, such as a bushing or adapter, is required to protect the conductors from abrasion during and after installation [300.4(G)].

(A) Minimum Size. For raceways containing conductors 4 AWG and larger, the minimum dimensions of boxes and conduit bodies must comply with the following:

(1) Straight Pulls. The minimum distance from where the conductors enter the box or conduit body to the opposite wall must not be less than eight times the trade size of the largest raceway. Figure 314–7

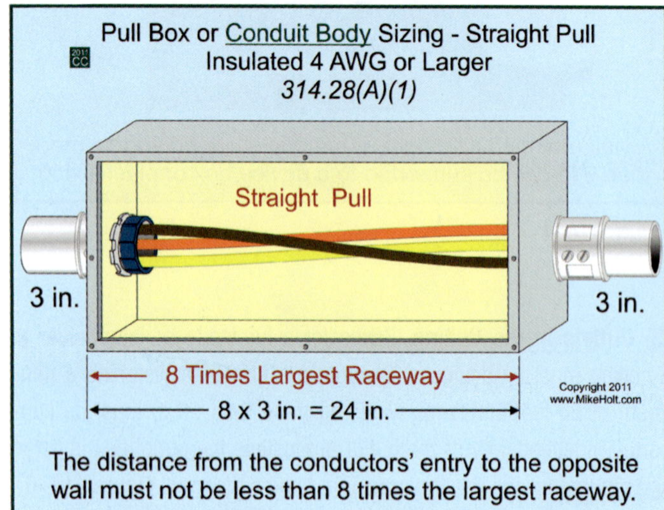

Figure 314–7

(2) Angle Pulls, U Pulls, or Splices.

- **Angle Pulls.** The distance from the raceway entry of the box or conduit body to the opposite wall must not be less than six times the trade size of the largest raceway, plus the sum of the trade sizes of the remaining raceways on the same wall and row. Figure 314–8
- **U Pulls.** When a conductor enters and leaves from the same wall of the box, the distance from where the raceways enter to the opposite wall must not be less than six times the trade size of the largest raceway, plus the sum of the trade sizes of the remaining raceways on the same wall and row. Figure 314–9

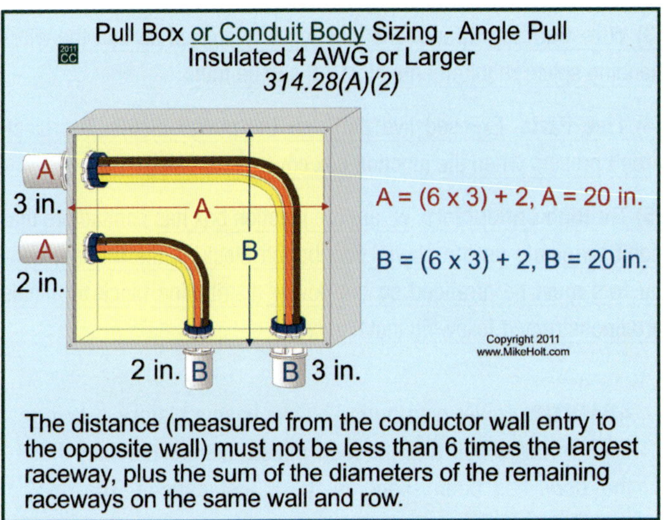

Figure 314–8

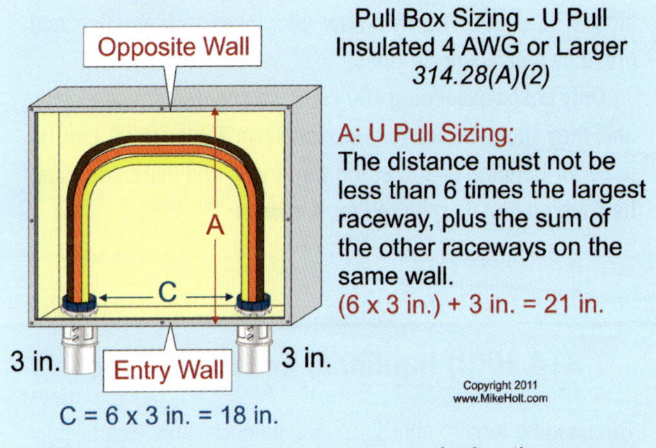

Figure 314–9

- **Splices.** When conductors are spliced, the distance from where the raceways enter to the opposite wall must not be less than six times the trade size of the largest raceway, plus the sum of the trade sizes of the remaining raceways on the same wall and row. **Figure 314–10**

- **Rows.** If there are multiple rows of raceway entries, each row is calculated individually and the row with the largest distance must be used.

- **Distance Between Raceways.** The distance between raceways enclosing the same conductor must not be less than six times the trade size of the largest raceway, measured from the raceways' nearest edge-to-nearest edge.

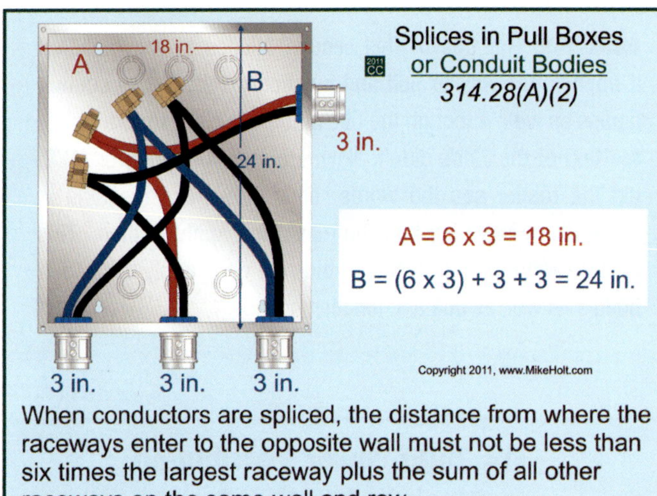

Figure 314–10

Ex: When conductors enter an enclosure with a removable cover, the distance from where the conductors enter to the removable cover must not be less than the bending distance as listed in Table 312.6(A) for one conductor per terminal. **Figure 314–11**

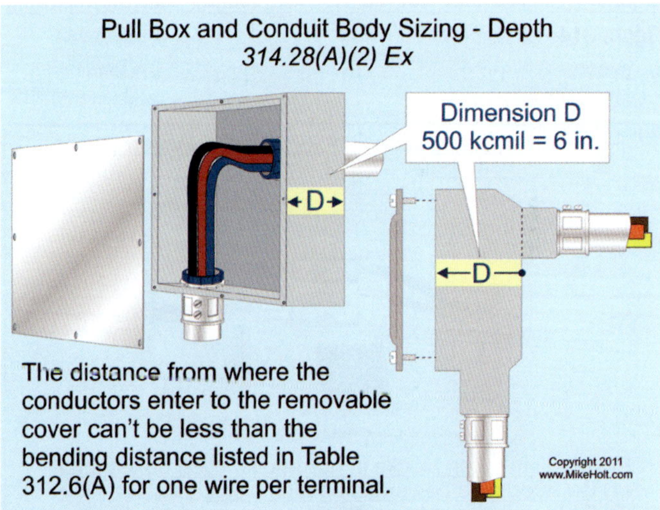

Figure 314–11

(3) Smaller Dimensions. Boxes or conduit bodies smaller than those required in 314.28(A)(1) and 314.28(A)(2) are permitted, if the enclosure is permanently marked with the maximum number and maximum size of conductors.

ANALYSIS: The title of this section alludes to the fact that it applies not only to pull and junction boxes, but to conduit bodies as well. Although the title made this clear, unfortunately the text of the *Code* didn't. Nowhere in 314.28(A)(1) or (A)(2) did the reader see the words "conduit bodies," resulting in some users believing that the rule didn't apply to them. This change will make it clear that the rule does apply to conduit bodies as well as pull and junction boxes.

314.28(E) Power Distribution Block in Junction Box

New provisions for power distribution blocks in pull and junction boxes have been added.

314.28 Boxes and Conduit Bodies for Conductors 4 AWG and Larger.

(E) Power Distribution Block. Power distribution blocks installed in junction boxes over 100 cu in. must comply with the following: Figure 314–12

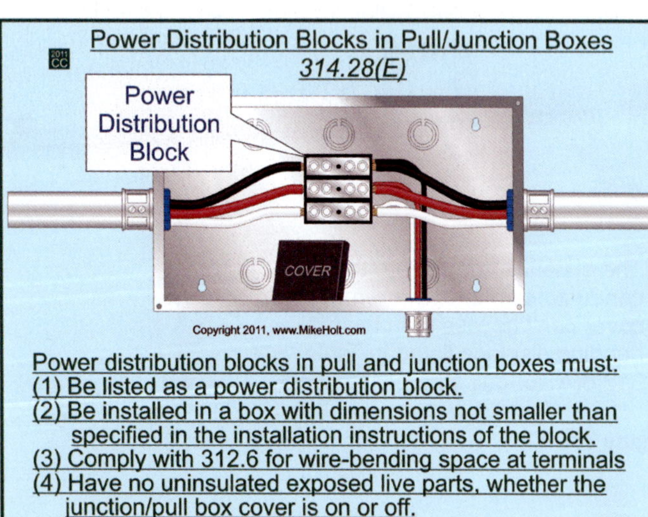

Figure 314–12

(1) Installation. Be listed as a power distribution block.

(2) Size. Be installed in a box not smaller than required by the installation instructions of the power distribution block.

(3) Wire-Bending Space. The junction box is sized so that the wire-bending space requirements of 312.6 can be met.

(4) Live Parts. Exposed live parts on the power distribution block aren't present when the junction box cover is removed.

(5) Through Conductors. Where the junction box has conductors that don't terminate on the power distribution block(s), the through conductors must be arranged so the power distribution block terminals are unobstructed following installation.

ANALYSIS: Power distribution blocks have a history of being used in large pull and junction boxes despite the fact that the *Code* has been silent on these installations. The only requirements for power distribution blocks were found in Article 376, which applies only to metal wireways. This left uncertainty regarding the installation requirements for these blocks in boxes. The *NEC* now addresses this practice and provides clear, concise rules.

Only boxes exceeding 100 cu in. can contain these blocks, and they must be listed. The values in Table 312.6 can be used for bending space at the terminals, and live parts must be covered just as required for wireways.

314.30(D) Handhole Enclosure Cover

The bonding requirement for handhole enclosures was slightly revised.

314.30 Handhole Enclosures. Handhole enclosures must be identified for underground use, and be designed and installed to withstand all loads likely to be imposed on them. Figure 314–13

(D) Covers. Handhole enclosure covers must have an identifying mark or logo that prominently identifies the function of the enclosure, such as "electric." Handhole enclosure covers must require the use of tools to open, or they must weigh over 100 lb.

Metal covers and other exposed conductive surfaces of handhole enclosures must be connected to an equipment grounding conductor sized to the overcurrent device in accordance with 250.122. Metal covers of handhole enclosures containing service conductors must be connected to an equipment bonding jumper sized in accordance with Table 250.66 [250.92 and 250.102(C)]. Figure 314–14

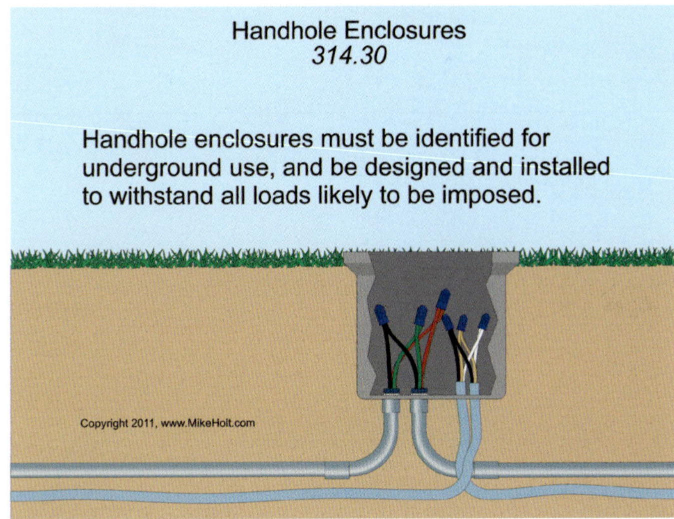

Figure 314–13

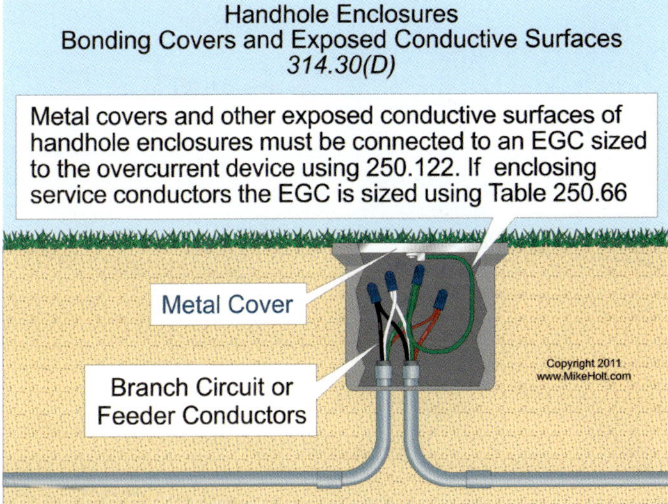

Figure 314–14

ANALYSIS: This change is more clerical than technical. The previous *Code* rule required that covers of handhole enclosures containing service conductors be bonded in accordance with 250.92(A). While the bonding requirements for metallic equipment containing service conductors are indeed found in 250.92, they're found in Subsection (B), not (A). This error has been removed by referring to 250.92.

NOTES

ARTICLE 320 Armored Cable (TYPE AC)

INTRODUCTION TO ARTICLE 320—ARMORED CABLE (TYPE AC)

Armored cable is an assembly of insulated conductors, 14 AWG through 1 AWG, individually wrapped within waxed paper and contained within a flexible spiral metal sheath. The outside appearance of armored cable looks like flexible metal conduit as well as metal-clad cable to the casual observer.

320.2 Definitions

A slight change to the definition has been made for accuracy.

320.2 Definitions.

Armored Cable (Type AC). A fabricated assembly of conductors in a flexible interlocked metal armor with an internal bonding strip in intimate contact with the armor for its entire length. See 320.100. Figure 320–1

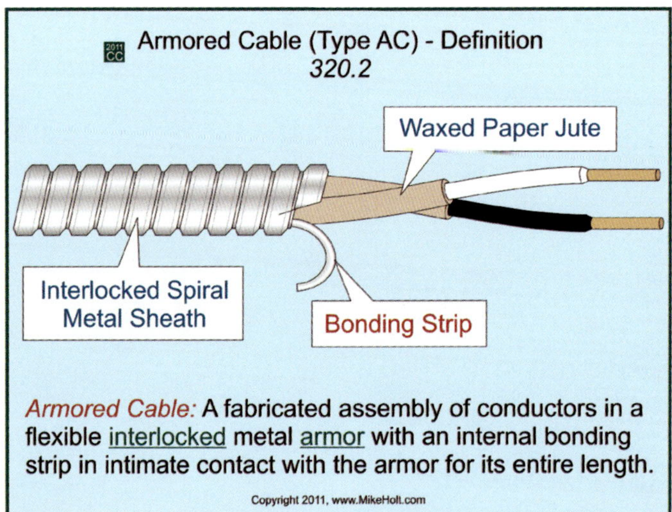

Figure 320–1

Author's Comment: The conductors are contained within a flexible metal sheath that interlocks at the edges, with an internal aluminum bonding strip, giving the cable an outside appearance similar to that of flexible metal conduit. Many electricians call this metal cable "BX®" The advantages of any flexible cables, as compared to raceway wiring methods, are that there's no limit to the number of bends between terminations and the cable can be quickly installed.

ANALYSIS: Previous editions of the *NEC* used the word "enclosure" to describe the jacket of this type of cable. The word "enclosure" is defined in Article 100 as "recognizable as suitable for the specific purpose, function, use, environment, application, and so forth, where described in a particular *Code* requirement," and therefore isn't the correct term to describe the jacket of the cable. The term "armor" is used in several sections of the *NEC* (such as 200.2, 250.64(B) and (E), 250.84, and others) to describe the jacket of a metallic cable. Additionally, the word "interlocked" was added to accurately describe the physical make up of the cable armor.

320.12 Uses Not Permitted

The prohibition of AC cable subject to corrosive elements has been expanded.

320.12 Uses Not Permitted. Type AC cable must not be installed in any of the following locations:

(1) If subject to physical damage.

(2) In damp or wet locations.

(3) In air voids of masonry block or tile walls where such walls are exposed or subject to excessive moisture or dampness.

(4) Where exposed to corrosive conditions.

ANALYSIS: Exposure of AC Cable to corrosive fumes and vapors has previously been a violation; however protection against corrosive solids and liquids wasn't included in this section. While 300.6 contains a general rule regarding this type of protection, it was absent from 320.12(4). This change isn't a technical one, since 300.6 provided the missing requirement, but this will contribute to a more user friendly *Code*.

320.23 In Accessible Attics or Roof Spaces

This change expands the requirements for protection of cables in accessible attics.

320.23 In Accessible Attics or Roof Spaces.

(A) Cables Run Across the Top of Floor Joists. Where run across the top of floor joists, or across the face of rafters or studding within 7 ft of floor or floor joists, the cable must be protected by substantial guard strips that are at least as high as the cable. If this space isn't accessible by permanent stairs or ladders, protection is required only within 6 ft of the nearest edge of the scuttle hole or attic entrance.

(B) Cable Installed Parallel to Framing Members. Where Type AC cable is installed on the side of rafters, studs, ceiling joists, or floor joists, no protection is required if the cable is installed and supported so the nearest outside surface of the cable or raceway is at least 1¼ in. from the nearest edge of the framing member [300.4(D)].

ANALYSIS: Previous editions of the *NEC* have required that cables across the face of rafters, studs and floor joists be protected by substantial guard strips. Notably missing from this list of framing elements was ceiling joists. This change adds that previously absent framing member.

Nonmetallic-Sheathed Cable (TYPES NM AND NMC)

INTRODUCTION TO ARTICLE 334—NONMETALLIC-SHEATHED CABLE (TYPES NM AND NMC)

Nonmetallic-sheathed cable is flexible, inexpensive, and easily installed. It provides very limited physical protection for the conductors, so the installation restrictions are strict. Its low cost and relative ease of installation make it a common wiring method for residential and commercial branch circuits. In the field, Type NM cable is typically referred to as "Romex®."

334.10 Uses Permitted

The question on the use of NM Cable in dwelling unit accessory structures has been answered, and a provision for cables inside of raceways has been added.

334.10 Uses Permitted.

Type NM and Type NMC cables can be used in the following:

(1) One- and two-family dwellings and their attached/detached garages or storage buildings. Figure 334–1

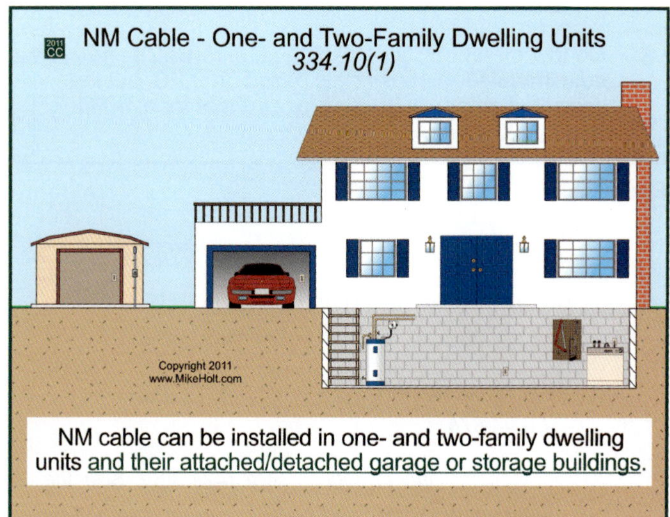

Figure 334–1

(2) Multifamily dwellings permitted to be of Types III, IV, and V construction. Figure 334–2

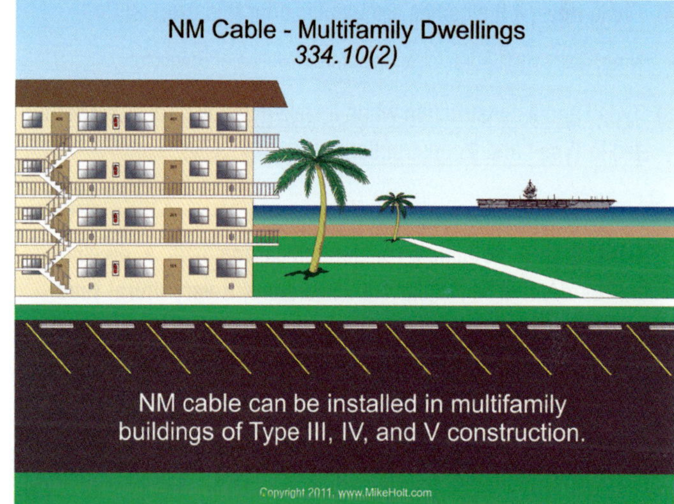

Figure 334–2

(3) Other structures permitted to be of Types III, IV, and V construction, except as prohibited in 334.12. Cables must be concealed within walls, floors, or ceilings that provide a thermal barrier of material with at least a 15-minute finish rating, as identified in listings of fire-rated assemblies. Figure 334–3

Author's Comment: See the definition of "Concealed" in Article 100.

Note 1: Building constructions are defined in NFPA 220-2006, Standard on Types of Building Construction, the applicable building code, or both.

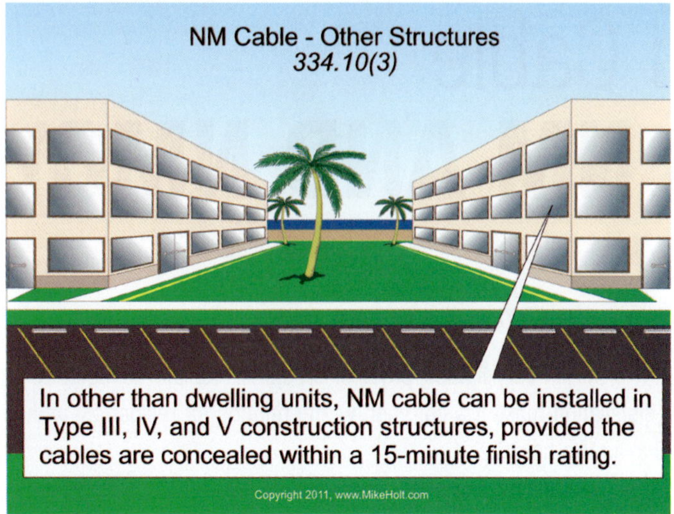

Figure 334–3

Note 2: See Annex E for the determination of building types [NFPA 220, Table 3-1].

(4) Cable trays, if the cables are identified for this use.

Note: See 310.15(A)(3) for temperature limitation of conductors.

(5) Type I and II construction when installed within a raceway permitted in Type I and II construction.

ANALYSIS: A detached residential garage isn't a dwelling unit as defined in Article 100. Therefore, a very literal reading of 334.10(3) of the *Code* would require types NM, NMC, and NMS cables to be concealed within walls, floors, or ceilings using a material with a 15-minute finish rating, such as drywall. This change to the *NEC* allows the use of NM Cables in all dwelling unit garages and accessory storage buildings without the 15-minute finish rating, provided the cables aren't subject to physical damage [334.15(B)].

The exception from 334.12(A) for raceways in buildings permitted to be of Types III, IV, or V construction has been changed into positive text and moved to 334.10(5).

While there are still a great many exceptions in the *Code*, there's been a real effort made to convert existing exceptions into positive *NEC* text. This change takes the exception from 334.12(A)(1) that allowed for NM cables installed in raceways to be permitted in buildings that could be built of Type I and II construction and puts it into positive text into a new 334.10(A)(5).

334.80 Conductor Ampacity

The requirements for ampacity adjustment for NM Cables in bored holes have been clarified.

334.80 Conductor Ampacity. Conductor ampacity used for ambient temperature correction [310.15(B)(2)(a)], conductor bundling adjustment [310.15(B)(3)(a)], or both, based on the 90°C conductor insulation rating [310.15(B)(2)], provided the adjusted or corrected ampacity doesn't exceed that for a 60°C rated conductor.

Question: *What size Type NM cable is required to supply a 10 kW, 240V, single-phase fixed space heater with a 3A blower motor? The terminals are rated 75°C.* **Figure 334–4**

(a) 2 AWG *(b) 4 AWG* *(c) 6 AWG* *(d) 8 AWG*

Answer: *(b) 4 AWG*

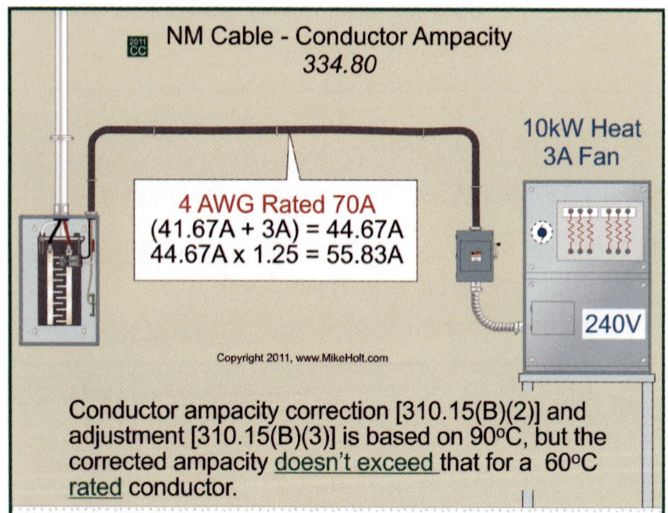

Figure 334-4

Step 1: Determine the total load in amperes:

I = VA/E
I = 10,000W/240V + 3A
I = 44.67A

Step 2: Conductor and Protection Size [424.3(B)]. Size the ungrounded conductors and overcurrent device at no less than 125 percent of the total heating load.

Conductor/Protection Size = Load x 1.25
Conductor/Protection Size = 44.67A x 1.25
Conductor/Protection Size = 56A

According to Table 310.15(B)(16), a 4 AWG conductor rated 70A at 60°C will be required to be protected with a 60A overcurrent device [240.6(A)].

If multiple Type NM cables pass through the same wood framing opening that's to be sealed with thermal insulation, caulking, or sealing foam, the allowable ampacity of each conductor must be adjusted in accordance with Table 310.15(B)(3)(a). **Figure 334–5**

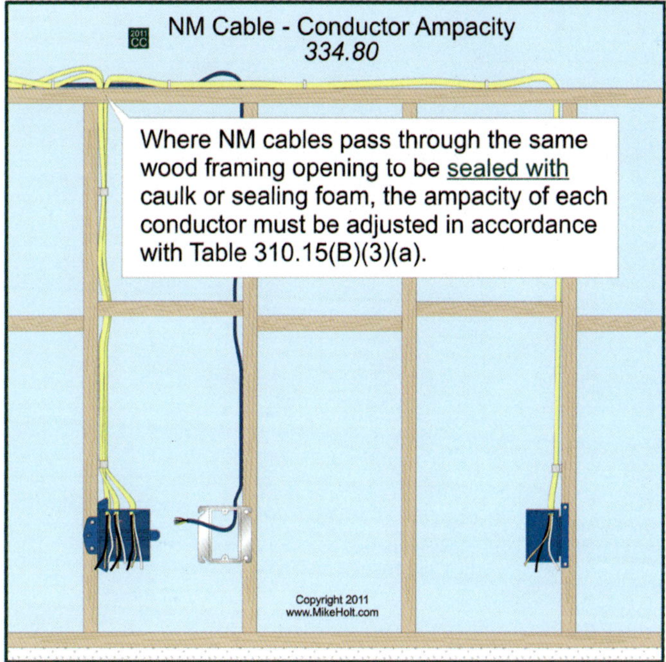

Figure 334–5

> **Author's Comment:** This requirement has no effect on conductor sizing if you bundle no more than nine current-carrying 14 or 12 AWG conductors together. For example, three 14/2 cables and one 14/3 cable (nine current-carrying 14 THHN conductors) are bundled together in a dry location, the ampacity for each conductor (25A at 90°C, Table 310.15(B)(16)) is adjusted by a 70 percent adjustment factor [Table 310.15(B)(3)(a)].
>
> Adjusted Conductor Ampacity = 25A x 0.70
> Adjusted Conductor Ampacity = 17.50A

If multiple Type NM cables are installed in contact with thermal insulation without maintaining spacing between cables, the allowable ampacity of each conductor must be adjusted in accordance with Table 310.15(B)(3)(a). **Figure 334–6**

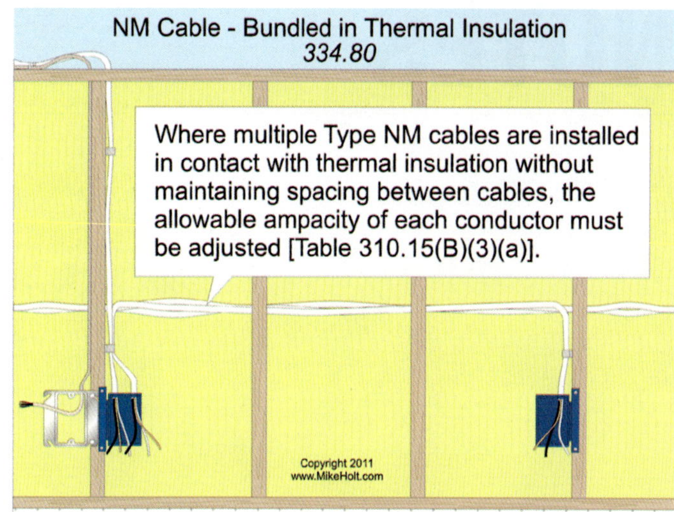

Figure 334–6

> **Author's Comment:** This requirement has no effect on conductor sizing if you bundle fewer than nine current-carrying 14 or 12 AWG conductors together. For example, if three 12/2 cables and one 12/3 cable (nine current-carrying 12 THHN conductors) are bundled together, the ampacity for each conductor (30A at 90°C, Table 310.15(B)(16)) is adjusted by a 70 percent adjustment factor [Table 310.15(B)(3)(a)].
>
> Adjusted Conductor Ampacity = 30A x 0.70
> Adjusted Conductor Ampacity = 21A

ANALYSIS: Bored holes containing NM cables are often filled with sealing foam (or caulk, or similar agents), but the foam doesn't always serve the purpose of fire-blocking or draft-stopping. When this occurred the ampacity adjustments of this section weren't required because the wording of the 2008 *NEC* unintentionally limited the requirements to fire-blocking or draft-stopping functions. Even when the foam wasn't used for fire-blocking or draft-stopping, the problems associated with this section still arose. This change removes the reference to fire- or draft- stopping to clarify that, regardless of the purpose of the thermal insulation, caulk, or sealing foam, the ampacity of the conductor must be adjusted.

***Code* users will no longer have to determine the role of the sealing foam with this change, as it's now required that any bored hole with foam in it will have to comply with this section.**

NOTES

ARTICLE 338

Service-Entrance Cable (TYPES SE AND USE)

INTRODUCTION TO ARTICLE 338—SERVICE-ENTRANCE CABLE (TYPES SE AND USE)

Service-entrance cable is a single conductor or multiconductor assembly with or without an overall moisture-resistant covering. This cable is used primarily for services not over 600V, but can also be used for feeders and branch circuits when the limitations of this article are observed.

338.10(B) Uses Permitted

Changes to the title clarify the use of this section, the ampacity calculations that were changed, and a new requirement that was added addressing cables in thermal insulation.

338.10 Uses Permitted.

(B) Branch Circuits or Feeders.

(1) Insulated Conductor. Type SE service-entrance cable is permitted for branch circuits and feeders where the circuit conductors are insulated.

(2) Uninsulated Conductor. SE cable is permitted for branch circuits and feeders if the insulated conductors are used for circuit wiring, and the uninsulated conductor is only used for equipment grounding purposes. **Figure 338–1**

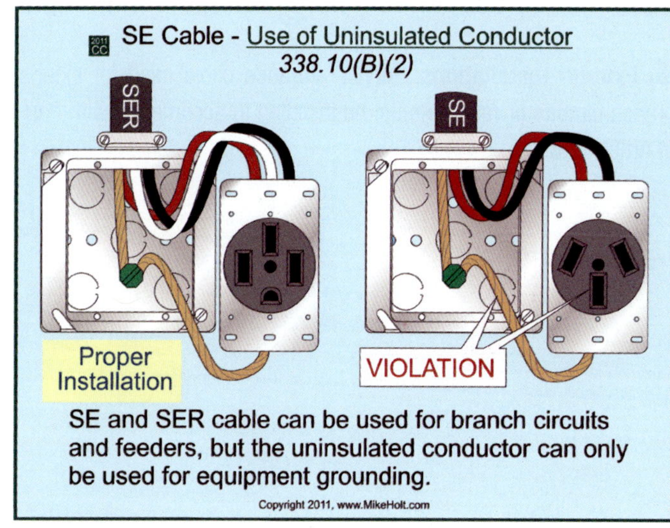

Figure 338–1

Ex: In existing installations, uninsulated conductors may be used for the neutral conductor if the uninsulated neutral conductor of the cable originates in service equipment.

(3) Temperature Limitations. SE cable must not be subjected to conductor temperatures exceeding its insulation rating.

(4) Installation Methods for Branch Circuits and Feeders. SE cable used for branch circuits or feeders must comply with (a) and (b).

(a) Interior Installations. SE cable used for interior branch circuit or feeder wiring must be installed in accordance with the same requirements as Type NM Cable—Article 334, excluding 334.80 **Figure 338–2**

The maximum conductor temperature rating can be used [310.15(B)(2)] for ampacity adjustment and correction purposes, but when installed in thermal insulation the final corrected ampacity must not exceed that for a 60°C rated conductor.

CAUTION: *Underground service-entrance cable (USE) must not be used for interior wiring because it doesn't have flame-retardant insulation.*

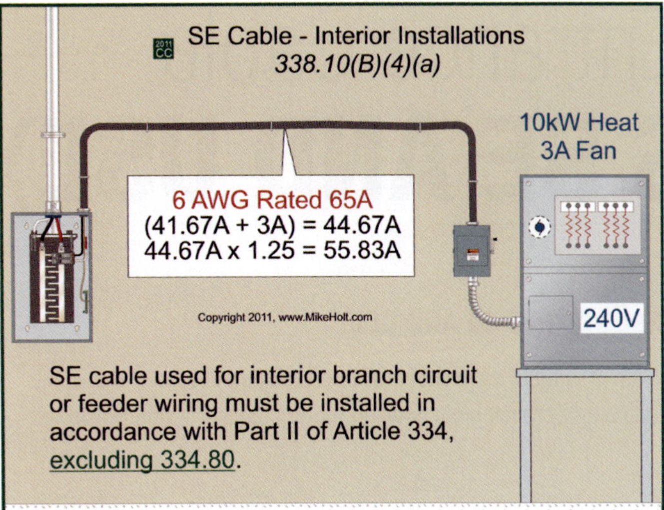

Figure 338–2

(b) Exterior Installations. Service-entrance cable used for exterior branch circuits or feeders must be installed in accordance with Part I of Article 225.

ANALYSIS: The uninsulated conductor of SE cable (when used as a feeder or branch circuit) is typically used as an equipment grounding conductor, but in very limited applications it can be used as a neutral conductor. The change to the title of this section reflects that fact. The exception allowing this practice has also been revised to only allow the bare conductor to be used as a neutral in certain existing applications.

Although the 2008 *NEC* created a new requirement for adjusting the ampacity of these cables when used indoors, there was no real technical substantiation for this change. No fires or incidents were reported to warrant this change, yet it still passed. This *Code* change removes a requirement that probably shouldn't have been there in the first place.

A new paragraph added to this section requires that SE cable installed in thermal insulation have its ampacity determined in accordance with the 60°C column of 310.15(B)(16). The 90°C (or 75°C) column is permitted to be used for ampacity adjustment and correction purposes for conductors having those insulation ratings.

A new Informational Note alerts *Code* users to Table 310.15(B)(7) for SE cables used as a main power feeder, which is a very common application in residential installations.

ARTICLE 342 Intermediate Metal CONDUIT (TYPE IMC)

INTRODUCTION TO ARTICLE 342—INTERMEDIATE METAL CONDUIT (TYPE IMC)

Intermediate metal conduit (IMC) is a circular metal raceway with an outside diameter equal to that of rigid metal conduit. The wall thickness of intermediate metal conduit is less than that of rigid metal conduit (RMC), so it's a greater interior cross-sectional area for containing conductors. Intermediate metal conduit is lighter and less expensive than rigid metal conduit, but it can be used in all of the same locations as rigid metal conduit. Intermediate metal conduit also uses a different steel alloy that makes it stronger than rigid metal conduit, even though the walls are thinner. Intermediate metal conduit is manufactured in both galvanized steel and aluminum; the steel type is much more common.

342.30(A) Securing and Supporting

The requirements for the securing of IMC have been formatted as a list.

342.30 Securing and Supporting. Intermediate metal conduit must be installed as a complete system in accordance with 300.18 [300.10 and 300.12], and it must be securely fastened in place and supported in accordance with (A) and (B).

(A) Securely Fastened. IMC must be secured in accordance with one of the following:

(1) Fastened within 3 ft of each outlet box, junction box, device box, cabinet, conduit body, or other conduit termination. Figure 342–1

Author's Comment: Fastening is required within 3 ft of terminations, not within 3 ft of each coupling.

(2) When structural members don't permit the raceway to be secured within 3 ft of a box or termination fitting, the raceway must be secured within 5 ft of the termination. Figure 342–2

(3) Conduits aren't required to be securely fastened within 3 ft of the service head for an above-the-roof termination of a mast.

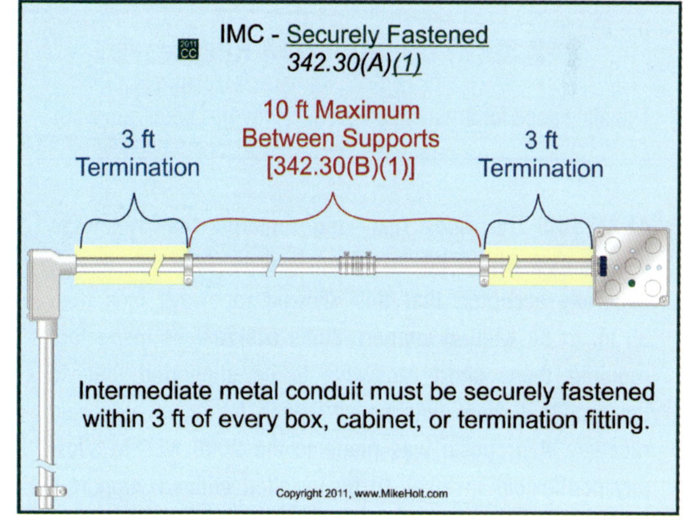

Figure 342–1

ANALYSIS: Whenever the *Code* has several requirements in the same section, it's generally preferred to include them in a "list" format." Not only does this add to the readability of the requirements, it also makes it easier to cite the exact requirements for an installation. Inspectors enjoy the list format because it allows them to cite the exact violation, without the installer having to read through the entire section, and then try to figure out exactly which part of the requirement the inspector was referring to.

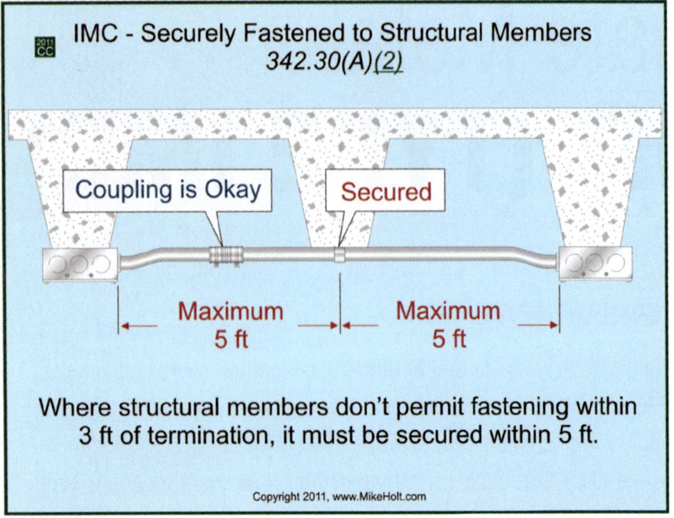

Figure 342–2

342.30(C) Unsupported Raceways

The allowance for an unsupported raceway has been removed.

ANALYSIS: The *Code* has long required that raceways be secured within 36 in. of enclosures. Although it was generally accepted that this allowed raceways less than 36 in. to be without support, some overzealous inspectors required these short raceways to be supported, due to the fact that there was no allowance for an unsupported raceway. A proposal was made to the 2008 *NEC* to allow any nonflexible raceway to be installed without support if the raceway was less than 36 in. to address this problem. The *Code*-Making Panel responsible for raceways decided to change it to require support for any length of raceway that's coupled or terminates in a ringed knockout. It also decreased the length to 18 in., without substantiation. In the 2011 *Code* the allowance has been removed altogether, resulting in language that matches the 2005 *NEC*. Hopefully those same overzealous inspectors won't begin enforcing 3 in. lengths of raceway to be supported again…

342.46 Bushings

The rule requiring a bushing for IMC has been editorially revised.

342.46 Bushings. To protect conductors from abrasion, a metal or plastic bushing must be installed on conduit termination threads, regardless of conductor size, unless the box, fitting, or enclosure is designed to provide this protection.

Note: Conductors 4 AWG and larger that enter an enclosure must be protected from abrasion, during and after installation, by a fitting that provides a smooth, rounded, insulating surface, such as an insulating bushing, unless the design of the box, fitting, or enclosure provides equivalent protection, in accordance with 300.4(G). **Figure 342–3**

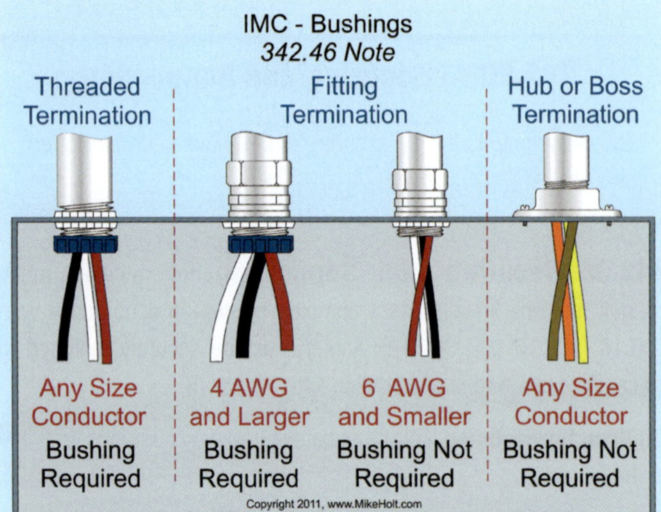

Conductors 4 AWG and larger must be protected by a fitting that provides a smooth, rounded, insulating surface, such as an insulating bushing [300.4(G)].

Figure 342–3

ANALYSIS: IMC requires a bushing wherever the conduit enters a box, fitting, or other enclosure, unless the design of the box ,fitting, or enclosure provides some sort of protection. The protection afforded has long been required to be "equivalent" to that of a bushing, but some *Code* users had a hard time understanding what "equivalent" meant. With this change the *NEC* now requires that these boxes, fittings, or enclosures be designed to provide this protection.

Rigid Metal Conduit (TYPE RMC)

INTRODUCTION TO ARTICLE 344—RIGID METAL CONDUIT (TYPE RMC)

Rigid metal conduit, commonly called "rigid," has long been the standard raceway for providing protection from physical impact and from difficult environments. The outside diameter of rigid metal conduit is the same as intermediate metal conduit. However, the wall thickness of rigid metal conduit is greater than intermediate metal conduit; therefore it's a smaller interior cross-sectional area. Rigid metal conduit is heavier and more expensive than intermediate metal conduit, and it can be used in any location. Rigid metal conduit is manufactured in both galvanized steel and aluminum; the steel type is much more common.

344.30(C) Unsupported Raceways

The allowance for an unsupported raceway has been removed.

ANALYSIS: The *Code* has long required that raceways be secured within 36 in. of enclosures. Although it was generally accepted that this allowed raceways less than 36 in. to be without support, some overzealous inspectors required these short raceways to be supported, due to the fact that there was no allowance for an unsupported raceway. A proposal was made to the 2008 *NEC* to allow any nonflexible raceway to be installed without support if the raceway was less than 36 in. to address this problem. The *Code*-Making Panel responsible for raceways decided to change it to require support for any length of raceway that's coupled or terminates in a ringed knockout. It also decreased the length to 18 in., without substantiation. In the 2011 *Code* the allowance has been removed altogether, resulting in language that matches the 2005 *NEC*. Hopefully those same overzealous inspectors won't begin enforcing 3 in. lengths of raceway to be supported again…

344.46 Bushings

The rule requiring a bushing for RMC has been editorially revised.

344.46 Bushings. To protect conductors from abrasion, a metal or plastic bushing must be installed on conduit threads at terminations, regardless of conductor size, unless the box, fitting, or enclosure is designed to provide this protection.

Note: Conductors 4 AWG and larger that enter an enclosure must be protected from abrasion, during and after installation, by a fitting that provides a smooth, rounded, insulating surface, such as an insulating bushing, unless the design of the box, fitting, or enclosure provides equivalent protection, in accordance with 300.4(G). **Figure 344–1**

ANALYSIS: RMC requires a bushing wherever the conduit enters a box, fitting, or other enclosure, unless the design of the box, fitting, or enclosure provides some sort of protection. The protection afforded has long been required to be "equivalent" to that of a bushing, but some *Code* users had a hard time understanding what "equivalent" meant. With this change the *NEC* now requires that these boxes, fittings or enclosures be designed to provide this protection.

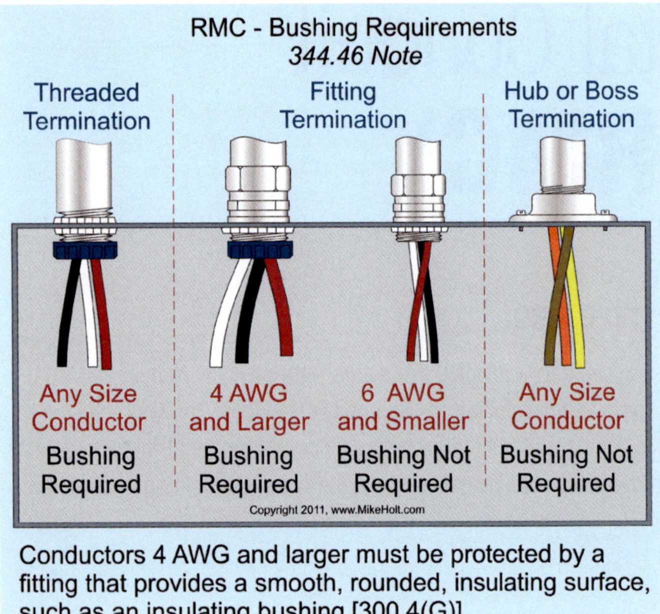

Conductors 4 AWG and larger must be protected by a fitting that provides a smooth, rounded, insulating surface, such as an insulating bushing [300.4(G)].

Figure 344–1

ARTICLE 348 Flexible Metal Conduit (TYPE FMC)

INTRODUCTION TO ARTICLE 348—FLEXIBLE METAL CONDUIT (TYPE FMC)

Flexible metal conduit (FMC), commonly called "Greenfield" or "flex," is a raceway of an interlocked metal strip of either steel or aluminum. It's primarily used for the final 6 ft or less of raceways between a more rigid raceway system and equipment that moves, shakes, or vibrates. Examples of such equipment include pump motors and industrial machinery.

348.30(A) Securing and Supporting

The exception allowing for unsupported lengths of FMC, as well as the exception for flexible installations, has been revised.

348.30 Securing and Supporting.

(A) Securely Fastened. Flexible metal conduit must be securely fastened by a means approved by the authority having jurisdiction within 1 ft of termination, and it must be secured and supported at intervals not exceeding 4½ ft. Figure 348–1

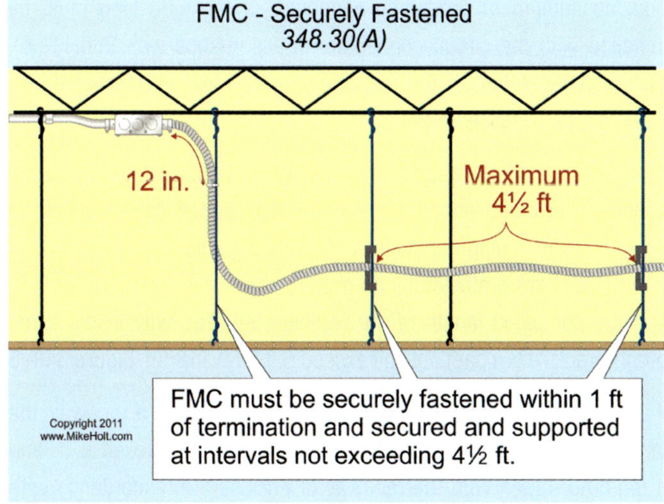

Figure 348–1

Ex 1: Flexible metal conduit isn't required to be securely fastened or supported where fished between access points through concealed spaces and supporting is impracticable.

Ex 2: If flexibility is necessary after installation, unsecured lengths from the last point the raceway is securely fastened must not exceed: Figure 348–2

(1) 3 ft for trade sizes ½ through 1¼

(2) 4 ft for trade sizes 1½ through 2

(3) 5 ft for trade sizes 2½ and larger

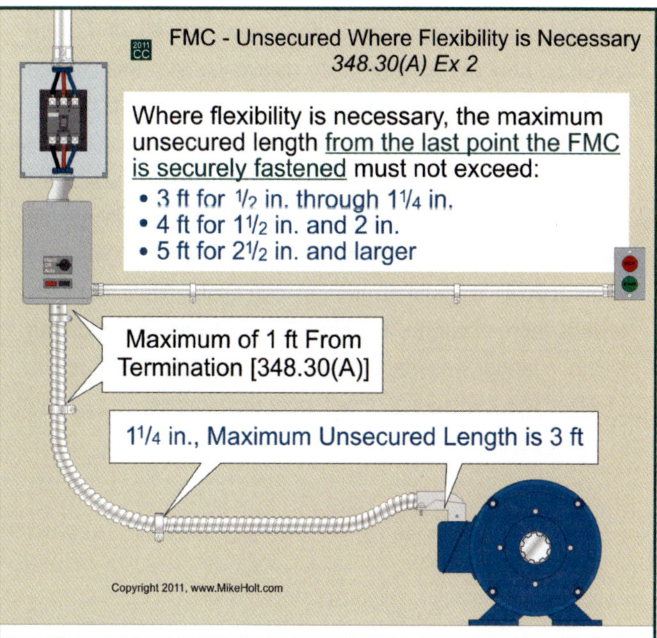

Figure 348–2

Ex 4: FMC to a luminaire or electrical equipment within an accessible ceiling is permitted to be unsupported for not more than 6 ft from the last point where the raceway is securely fastened. Figure 348–3

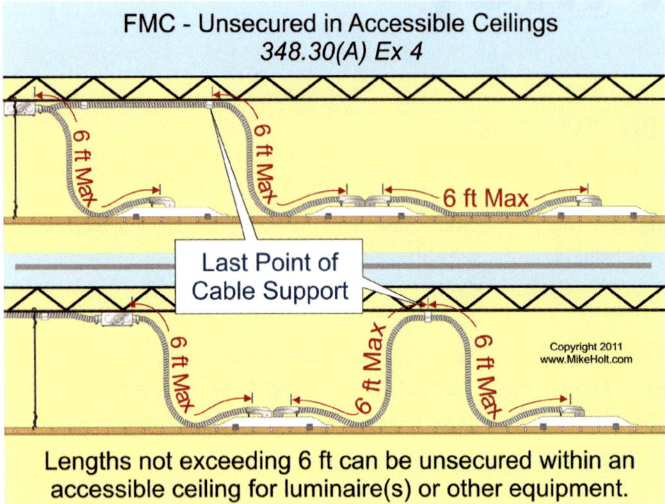

Figure 348–3

ANALYSIS: Over the last few *Code* cycles, revisions have been made to allow for greater lengths of unsupported Flexible Metal Conduit in installations where flexibility is a concern. While these changes have gone a long way toward uniform understanding and enforcement, not all *NEC* users agree on how to measure these raceways. With this change it becomes clear that measurement begins at the last point of support for these systems.

Additionally, a change was made to replace "impractical" with "impracticable." Impracticable is defined as "incapable of being put into practice with the available means," whereas "impractical" is defined as "not practical." While the new term is more accurate, this change leaves people wondering if the change was necessary, or if perhaps the *Code* is involved in a conspiracy to sell more dictionaries.

348.42 Couplings and Connectors

A small change to the rule regarding the concealment of angled connectors has been made.

348.42 Fittings. Angle connectors must not be concealed.

ANALYSIS: Previous editions of the *NEC* required that concealed raceway installations not contain angled connectors. While the intent of this section was quite obvious, some *Code* users were led to believe that if any portion of the raceway was concealed, an angled connector couldn't be used—even in the exposed portion. This change clarifies that the concern only exists when the angled connector itself is concealed.

348.60 Grounding and Bonding

The issue of flexibility as it relates to equipment grounding has been revised, again.

348.60 Grounding and Bonding. If flexibility is necessary to minimize the transmission of vibration from equipment or to provide flexibility for equipment that requires movement after installation, an equipment grounding conductor of the wire type must be installed with the circuit conductors in accordance with 250.118(5), based on the rating of the circuit overcurrent device in accordance with 250.122. Figure 348–4

If flexibility isn't necessary after installation, and vibration isn't a concern, the metal armor of flexible metal conduit can serve as an equipment grounding conductor if the circuit conductors contained in the raceway are protected by an overcurrent device rated 20A or less, and the combined length of the flexible metal raceway in the same ground-fault return path doesn't exceed 6 ft [250.118(5)]. Figure 348–5

If an equipment bonding jumper is installed outside of a raceway, the length of the equipment bonding jumper must not exceed 6 ft, and it must be routed with the raceway or enclosure in accordance with 250.102(E)(2).

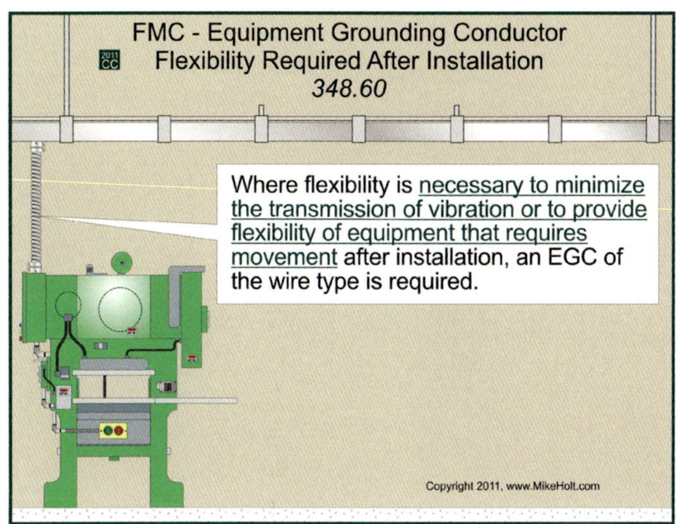

Figure 348–4

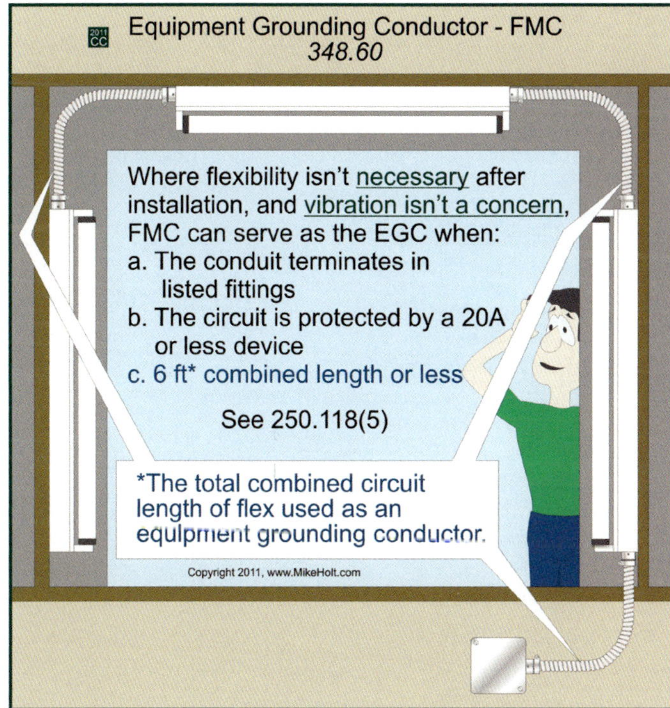

Figure 348–5

ANALYSIS: This section has been changed to provide consistency with the requirements contained in 250.118(5).

While the *Code* has recognized that equipment needing flexibility after installation requires an equipment grounding conductor of the wire type, it's been silent on the issue of vibration. It can be argued that an unusually high amount of vibration can compromise the integrity of the flexible metal conduit's ability to act as an equipment grounding conductor, so this change will require an EGC of the wire type in those instances.

NOTES

Liquidtight Flexible Metal **CONDUIT (TYPE LFMC)**

INTRODUCTION TO ARTICLE 350—LIQUIDTIGHT FLEXIBLE METAL CONDUIT (TYPE LFMC)

Liquidtight flexible metal conduit (LFMC), with its associated connectors and fittings, is a flexible raceway commonly used for connections to equipment that vibrate or are required to move occasionally. Liquidtight flexible metal conduit is commonly called "Sealtight®" or "liquidtight." Liquidtight flexible metal conduit is of similar construction to flexible metal conduit, but it also has an outer liquidtight thermoplastic covering. it's the same primary purpose as flexible metal conduit, but it also provides protection from moisture and some corrosive effects.

350.30(A) Securing and Supporting

The exception allowing for unsupported lengths of LFMC has been revised.

350.30 Securing and Supporting.

(A) Securely Fastened. Liquidtight flexible metal conduit must be securely fastened by a means approved by the authority having jurisdiction within 1 ft of termination, and must be secured and supported at intervals not exceeding 4½ ft. Figure 350–1

Figure 350–1

Ex 1: Liquidtight flexible metal conduit isn't required to be securely fastened or supported where fished between access points through concealed spaces and supporting is impracticable.

Ex 2: If flexibility is necessary after installation, unsecured lengths from the last point where the raceway is securely fastened must not exceed: Figure 350–2

(1) 3 ft for trade sizes ½ through 1¼
(2) 4 ft for trade sizes 1½ through 2
(3) 5 ft for trade sizes 2½ and larger

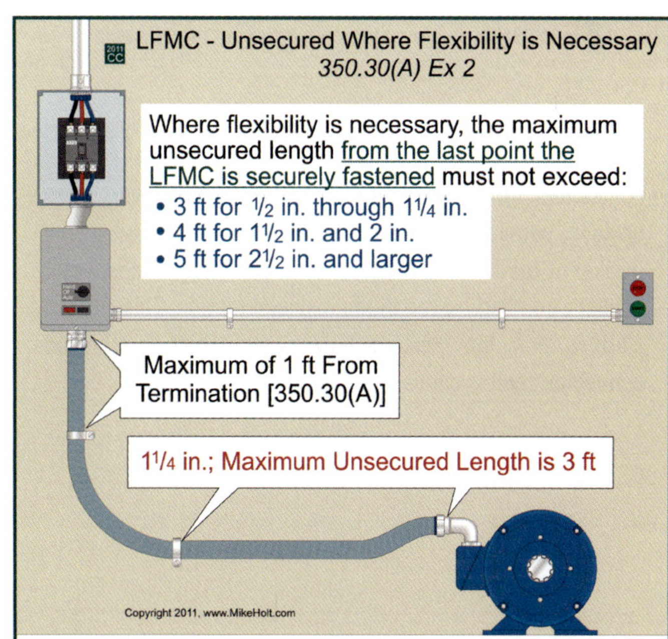

Figure 350–2

Ex 4: Lengths not exceeding 6 ft from the last point where the raceway is securely fastened can be unsecured within an accessible ceiling for luminaire(s) or other equipment.

ANALYSIS: Over the last few *Code* cycles, revisions have been made to allow for greater lengths of unsupported Liquidtight Flexible Metal Conduit in installations where flexibility is a concern. While these changes have gone a long way toward uniform understanding and enforcement, not all *NEC* users agree on how to measure these raceways. With this change it becomes clear that measurement begins at the last point of support for these systems.

Additionally, a change was made to replace "impractical" with "impracticable." Impracticable is defined as "incapable of being put into practice with the available means," whereas "impractical" is defined as "not practical." While the new term is more accurate, this change leaves people wondering if the change was necessary, or if perhaps the *Code* is involved in a conspiracy to sell more dictionaries.

350.42 Couplings and Connectors

A small change to the rule regarding the concealment of angled connectors has been made.

350.42 Fittings. Angle connectors must not be concealed.

ANALYSIS: Previous editions of the *NEC* required that concealed raceway installations not contain angled connectors. While the intent of this section was quite obvious, some *Code* users were led to believe that if any portion of the raceway was concealed, an angled connector couldn't be used—even in the exposed portion. This change clarifies that the concern only exists when the angled connector itself is concealed.

350.60 Grounding and Bonding

The issue of flexibility as it relates to equipment grounding has been revised, again.

350.60 Grounding and Bonding. If flexibility is necessary to minimize the transmission of vibration from equipment or to provide flexibility for equipment that requires movement after installation, an equipment grounding conductor of the wire type must be installed with the circuit conductors in accordance with 250.118(6), based on the rating of the circuit overcurrent device in accordance with 250.122. Figure 350–3

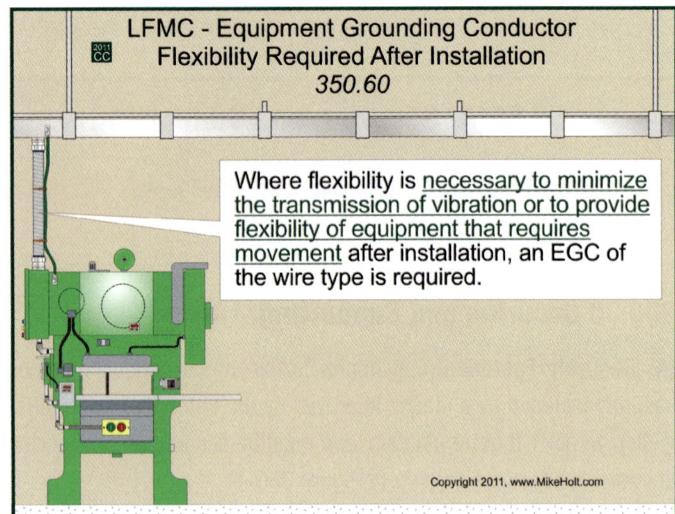

Figure Figure 350–3

If flexibility isn't necessary after installation, and vibration isn't a concern, the metal armor of flexible metal conduit can serve as an equipment grounding conductor if the circuit conductors contained in the raceway are protected by an overcurrent device rated 20A or less, and the combined length of the flexible metal raceway in the same ground-fault return path doesn't exceed 6 ft [250.118(6)].

If an equipment bonding jumper is installed outside of a raceway, the length of the equipment bonding jumper must not exceed 6 ft, and it must be routed with the raceway or enclosure in accordance with 250.102(E)(2).

ANALYSIS: This section has been changed to provide consistency with the requirements contained in 250.118(6).

While the *Code* has recognized that equipment needing flexibility after installation requires an equipment grounding conductor of the wire type, it's been silent on the issue of vibration. It can be argued that an unusually high amount of vibration can compromise the integrity of the liquidtight flexible metal conduit's ability to act as an equipment grounding conductor, so this change will require an EGC of the wire type in those instances.

NOTES

ARTICLE 352 Rigid Polyvinyl Chloride CONDUIT (TYPE PVC)

INTRODUCTION TO ARTICLE 352—RIGID POLYVINYL CHLORIDE CONDUIT (TYPE PVC)

Rigid polyvinyl chloride conduit (PVC) is a rigid nonmetallic conduit that provides many of the advantages of rigid metal conduit, while allowing installation in areas that are wet or corrosive. It's an inexpensive raceway, and easily installed. It's lightweight, easily cut, glued together, and relatively strong. However, conduits manufactured from polyvinyl chloride (PVC) are brittle when cold, and they sag when hot. This type of conduit is commonly used as an underground raceway because of its low cost, ease of installation, and resistance to corrosion and decay.

352.10(I) Insulation Temperature Limitations

The provision regarding the temperature of conductors in PVC Conduit has been changed to positive text.

352.10 Uses Permitted.

(I) Insulation Temperature Limitations. Conductors rated at a temperature higher than the listed temperature rating of PVC conduit must not be operated at a temperature above the raceway's listed temperature rating. Figure 352–1

ANALYSIS: While there are still a great many exceptions in the *NEC*, there's been a real effort made to convert existing exceptions into positive *Code* text. The result has been, for the most part, a very successful endeavor. This change takes the exception from 352.12(E) that addressed conductors rated with higher temperatures than the raceway and puts it into positive text in a new 352.10(I).

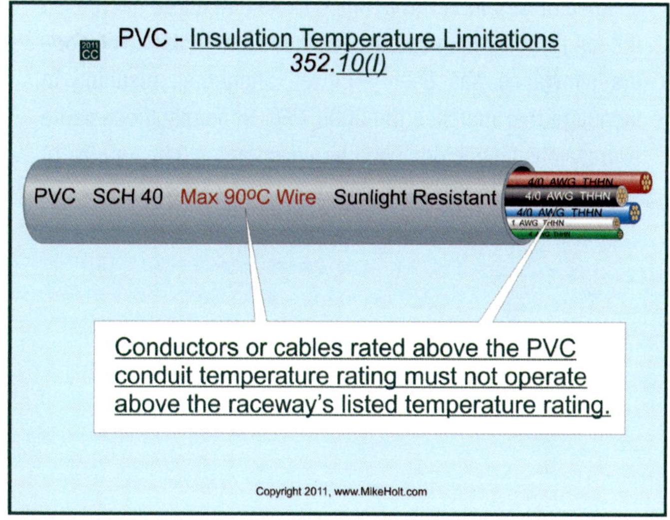

Figure 352–1

352.30(C) Unsupported Raceways

The allowance for an unsupported raceway has been removed.

ANALYSIS: The *Code* has long required that raceways be secured within 36 in. of enclosures. Although it was generally accepted that this allowed raceways less than 36 in. to be without support, some overzealous inspectors required these short raceways to be supported, due to the fact that there was no allowance for an unsupported raceway. A proposal was made to the 2008 *NEC* to allow any nonflexible raceway to be installed without support if the raceway was less than 36 in. to address this problem. The *Code*-Making Panel responsible for raceways decided to change it to require support for any length of raceway that's coupled or terminates in a ringed knockout. It also decreased the length to 18 in., without substantiation. In the 2011 *Code* the allowance has been removed altogether, resulting in language that matches the 2005 *NEC*. Hopefully those same overzealous inspectors won't begin enforcing 3 in. lengths of raceway to be supported again…

Electrical Metallic TUBING (TYPE EMT)

INTRODUCTION TO ARTICLE 358—ELECTRICAL METALLIC TUBING (TYPE EMT)

Electrical metallic tubing (EMT) is a lightweight raceway that's relatively easy to bend, cut, and ream. Because it isn't threaded, all connectors and couplings are of the threadless type and provide quick, easy, and inexpensive installation when compared to other metallic conduit systems, which makes it very popular. Electrical metallic tubing is manufactured in both galvanized steel and aluminum; the steel type is the most common type used.

358.10(B) Corrosion Protection

This subsection has been editorially revised to include defined terms.

358.10 Uses Permitted.

(B) Corrosion Protection. Electrical metallic tubing, elbows, couplings, and fittings can be installed in concrete, in direct contact with the earth, or in areas subject to severe corrosive influences if protected by corrosion protection and approved as suitable for the condition. Figure 358–1

EMT - Uses Permitted
Installed in Concrete or Earth
358.10(B)

Galvanized EMT installed in concrete on grade or above generally doesn't require supplemental corrosion protection.

Galvanized EMT in a below grade slab, in soil, or emerging from concrete to soil may require supplemental corrosion protection.

Copyright 2011, www.MikeHolt.com

Figure 358–1

CAUTION: *Supplementary coatings for corrosion protection (asphalted paint) haven't been investigated by a product testing and listing agency, and these coatings are known to cause cancer in laboratory animals.*

ANALYSIS: This subsection requires EMT to be protected against corrosion in areas that corrosion protection is required. Previous editions of the *Code* mandated that the corrosion resistance be "judged" as suitable. Obviously this isn't an issue that a Supreme Court Justice needs to rule on, so the word "judged" has been changed to "approved," allowing for the AHJ to make such a decision. I'm sure the 10th Circuit Court of Appeals will be glad for this change!

358.30(C) Unsupported Raceways

The allowance for an unsupported raceway has been removed.

ANALYSIS: The *Code* has long required that raceways be secured within 36 in. of enclosures. Although it was generally accepted that this allowed raceways less than 36 in. to be without support, some overzealous inspectors required these short raceways to be supported, due to the fact that there was no allowance for an unsupported raceway. A proposal was made to the 2008 *NEC* to allow any nonflexible raceway to be installed without support if the raceway was less than 36 in. to address this problem. The *Code*-Making Panel responsible for raceways decided to change it to require support for any length of raceway that's coupled or terminates in a ringed knockout. It also decreased the length to 18 in., without substantiation. In the 2011 *Code* the allowance has been removed altogether, resulting in language that matches the 2005 *NEC*. Hopefully those same overzealous inspectors won't begin enforcing 3 in. lengths of raceway to be supported again...

ARTICLE 376

Metal WIREWAYS

INTRODUCTION TO ARTICLE 376—METAL WIREWAYS

Metal wireways are commonly used where access to the conductors within the raceway is required to make terminations, splices, or taps to several devices at a single location. High cost precludes their use for other than short distances, except in some commercial or industrial occupancies where the wiring is frequently revised.

Author's Comment: Both metal wireways and nonmetallic wireways are often called "troughs" or "gutters" in the field.

376.10 Uses Permitted

This section was revised to recognize wet location use.

376.10 Uses Permitted.

(1) Exposed.

(2) In any hazardous (classified) locations, as permitted by other articles in the *Code*.

(3) Wet locations where listed for the purpose.

(4) Unbroken through walls, partitions, and floors.

Author's Comment: See 501.10(B), 502.10(B), and 504.20 for metal wireways used in hazardous locations.

ANALYSIS: This *Code* section was in desperate need of cleaning up. Previously, Item 3 included both hazardous (classified) locations and wet locations, causing confusion as to the relationship between these locations. This change eliminates the wet location confusion, and greatly enhances the readability of the *NEC*.

NOTES

ARTICLE 392

Cable TRAYS

INTRODUCTION TO ARTICLE 392—CABLE TRAYS

A cable tray system is a unit or an assembly of units or sections with associated fittings that forms a structural system used to securely fasten or support cables and raceways. Cable tray systems include ladder, ventilated trough, ventilated channel, solid bottom, and other similar structures. Cable trays are manufactured in many forms, from a simple hanger or wire mesh to a substantial, rigid, steel support system. Cable trays are designed and manufactured to support specific wiring methods, as identified in 392.10(A).

Article 392 Cable Trays

This article has been reconfigured to enhance usability and consistency with other *Code* articles.

ANALYSIS: Nearly all of the Chapter 3 articles have a 3xx.2 section for definitions, a 3xx.10 and 3xx.12 uses permitted/not permitted, and a Part II installation. This change adds all of these to this article, creating consistency. It also adds Part numbers and breaks up some of the requirements to enhance usability.

Author's Comment: Cable tray isn't a type of raceway. It's a support system for cables and raceways.

392.12 Uses Not Permitted

The provisions for cable trays in air-handling spaces have been removed from Article 392.

ANALYSIS: Previous editions of the *NEC* contained requirements for cable trays installed in air-handling spaces in 392.4 (uses not permitted). With the revisions that were made to 300.22 this *Code* cycle, it was decided to remove everything associated with air-handling from this article and let 300.22 deal with this topic.

392.60 Grounding and Bonding

A new requirement was added for cable trays containing only limited energy circuits.

392.60 Equipment Grounding Conductor.

(A) Metallic Cable Trays. Metallic cable trays can be used as equipment grounding conductors where continuous maintenance and supervision ensure that qualified persons service the installed cable tray system, Figure 392–1. The metallic cable trays that support conductors must be bonded together to ensure that they have the capacity to conduct safely any fault current likely to be imposed in accordance with 250.96(A).

Metal cable trays containing communications, data, and signaling, conductors and cables must be electrically continuous, through listed connections or the use of an insulated stranded bonding jumper not smaller than 10 AWG. Figure 392–2

Author's Comment: Nonconductive coatings such as paint, lacquer, and enamel on equipment must be removed to ensure an effective ground-fault current path, or the termination fittings must be designed so as to make such removal unnecessary [250.12].

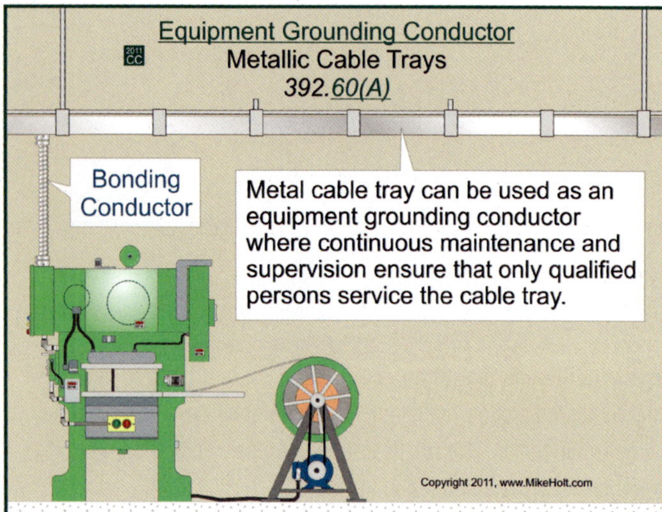

Figure Figure 392–1

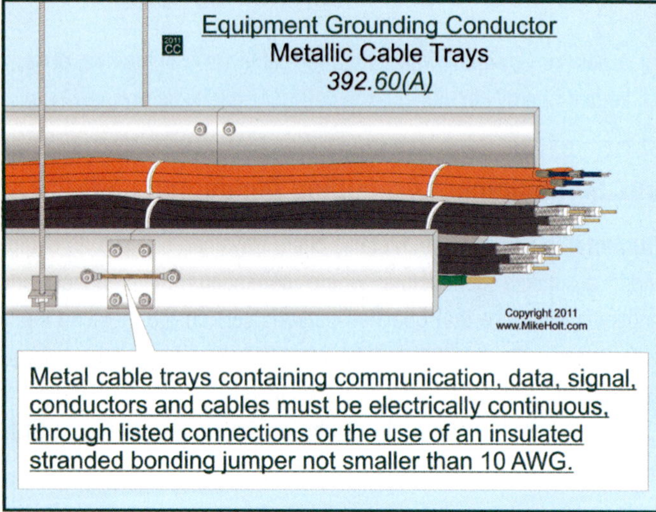

Figure 392–2

(B) Serve as Equipment Grounding Conductor. Metal cable trays can serve as equipment grounding conductors where maintenance and supervision ensure that qualified persons service the installed cable tray system, and the following requirements have been met [392.10(C)]:

(1) Cable tray sections and fittings are identified for grounding. Figure 392–3

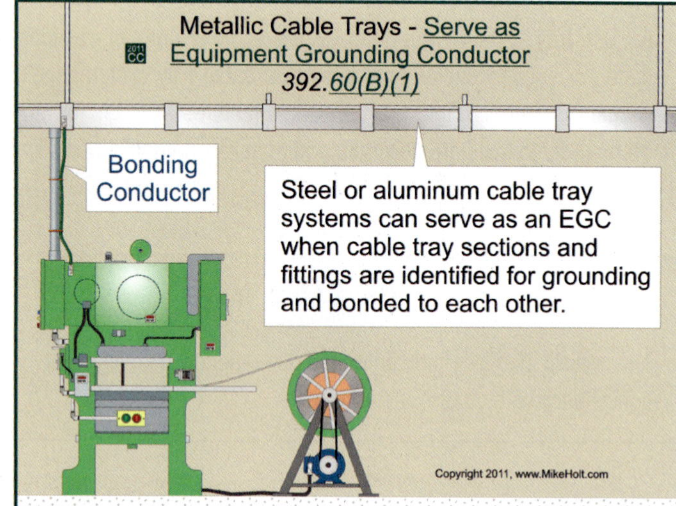

Figure 392–3

Author's Comment: Identification will be marked on each cable tray section.

(4) Cable tray sections, fittings, and connected raceways are effectively bonded to each other to ensure electrical continuity and the capacity to conduct safely any fault current likely to be imposed on them [250.96(A)]. This is accomplished by using bolted mechanical connectors or bonding jumpers sized in accordance with 250.102.

ANALYSIS: Although most limited energy systems aren't required to be grounded systems [250.20], this requirement will require sections of metal cable trays to be bonded together when they contain only conductors and cables of such systems. NECA/NEMA 105 *Standard for Installing Metal Cable Tray Systems* makes this recommendation, which was the basis for the argument of this change.

EQUIPMENT FOR GENERAL USE

INTRODUCTION TO CHAPTER 4—EQUIPMENT FOR GENERAL USE

With the first three chapters behind you, the final chapter in the NEC for building a solid foundation in general work is Chapter 4. This chapter helps you apply the first three chapters to installations involving general equipment. These first four chapters follow a natural sequential progression. Each of the next four *NEC* Chapters—5, 6, 7, and 8—build upon the first four, but in no particular order. You need to understand all of the first four chapters to properly apply any of the next four.

As in the preceding chapters, Chapter 4 is also arranged logically. Here are the groupings:

- Flexible cords and cables, fixture wires, switches, and receptacles.
- Switchboards and panelboards.
- Lamps, luminaires, appliances, and space heaters.
- Motors, refrigeration equipment, generators, and transformers.
- Capacitors and other components.

These groupings make sense. For example, motors, refrigeration equipment, generators, and transformers are all inductive equipment. This logical arrangement of the *NEC* is something to keep in mind when you're searching for a particular item. You know, for example, that transformers are general equipment. So you'll find the *Code* requirements for them in Chapter 4. You know they're wound devices, so you'll find transformer requirements located somewhere near motor requirements.

- **Article 400—Flexible Cords and Flexible Cables.** Article 400 covers the general requirements, applications, and construction specifications for flexible cords and flexible cables.
- **Article 402—Fixture Wires.** This article covers the general requirements and construction specifications for fixture wires.
- **Article 404—Switches.** The requirements of Article 404 apply to switches of all types. These include snap (toggle) switches, dimmer switches, fan switches, knife switches, circuit breakers used as switches, and automatic switches such as time clocks, timers, and switches and circuit breakers used for disconnecting means.
- **Article 406—Receptacles, Cord Connectors, and Attachment Plugs (Caps).** This article covers the rating, type, and installation of receptacles, cord connectors, and attachment plugs (cord caps). It also covers flanged surface inlets.
- **Article 408—Switchboards and Panelboards.** Article 408 covers specific requirements for switchboards, panelboards, and distribution boards that supply lighting and power circuits.
- **Article 410—Luminaires, Lampholders, and Lamps.** This article contains the requirements for luminaires, lampholders, and lamps. Because of the many types and applications of luminaires, manufacturer's instructions are very important and helpful for proper installation. Underwriters Laboratories produces a pamphlet called the *Luminaire Marking Guide*, which provides information for properly installing common types of incandescent, fluorescent, and high-intensity discharge (HID) luminaires.

- **Article 411—Lighting Systems Operating at 30V or Less.** Article 411 covers lighting systems, and their associated components, that operate at 30V or less.
- **Article 422—Appliances.** This article covers electric appliances used in any occupancy.
- **Article 424—Fixed Electric Space-Heating Equipment.** Article 424 covers fixed electric equipment used for space heating. For the purpose of this article, heating equipment includes heating cable, unit heaters, boilers, central systems, and other fixed electric space-heating equipment. Article 424 doesn't apply to process heating and room air-conditioning.
- **Article 430—Motors, Motor Circuits, and Controllers.** This article contains the specific requirements for conductor sizing, overcurrent protection, control circuit conductors, motor controllers, and disconnecting means. The installation requirements for motor control centers are covered in Article 430, Part VIII.
- **Article 440—Air-Conditioning and Refrigeration Equipment.** Article 440 applies to electrically driven air-conditioning and refrigeration equipment with a motorized hermetic refrigerant compressor. The requirements in this article are in addition to, or amend, the requirements in Article 430 and other articles.
- **Article 445—Generators.** Article 445 contains the electrical installation requirements for generators and other requirements, such as where they can be installed, nameplate markings, conductor ampacity, and disconnecting means.
- **Article 450—Transformers.** This article covers the installation of transformers.
- **Article 480—Batteries.** Article 480 covers stationary installations of storage batteries.

Flexible Cords and FLEXIBLE CABLES

INTRODUCTION TO ARTICLE 400—FLEXIBLE CORDS AND FLEXIBLE CABLES

This article covers the general requirements, applications, and construction specifications for flexible cords and flexible cables. The *NEC* doesn't consider flexible cords to be wiring methods like those defined in Chapter 3.

Always use a cord (and fittings) identified for the application. Table 400.4 will help you in that regard. For example, use cords listed for a wet location if you're using them outdoors. The jacket material of any cord is tested to maintain its insulation properties and other characteristics in the environments for which it's been listed. Tables 400.5(A)(1) and 400.5(A)(2) are also important tables to turn to when looking for the ampacity of flexible cords and cables.

Table 400.4 Types of Flexible Cords and Flexible Cables

The question of sunlight resistance for cords has been answered.

ANALYSIS: The suffix "W" at the end of a cord type designates that the cord is water resistant. Often when a cord is required to be resistant to the weather, it also needs to be resistant to the damaging rays of the sun. Previous *Code* editions didn't help identify which cord types were sunlight resistant, but this change remedies that problem. The notes to Table 400.4 now indicate that the suffix "W" not only means that a cord is weather resistant, but that it's also sunlight resistant.

400.5(A) Ampacity of Flexible Cords and Flexible Cables

An editorial change to the ampacity correction requirement has been made.

400.5 Ampacity of Flexible Cords and Flexible Cables.

(A) Ampacity Tables. Table 400.5(A)(1) lists the allowable ampacity for copper conductors in flexible cords and flexible cables and 400.5(A)(2) lists the allowable ampacity for copper conductors in flexible cords and flexible cables with not more than three current-carrying conductors at an ambient temperature of 86°F.

If the ambient temperature is other than 86°F, the flexible cord or flexible cable ampacity, as listed in Table 400.5(A)(1) or 400.5(A)(2), must be adjusted by using the ambient temperature correction factors listed in Table 310.15(B)(2)(a). Figure 400–1

Author's Comments:

- Temperature ratings for flexible cords and flexible cables aren't contained in the *NEC*, but UL listing standards state that flexible cords and flexible cables are rated for 60°C unless marked otherwise.
- See 400.13 for overcurrent protection requirements for flexible cords and flexible cables.

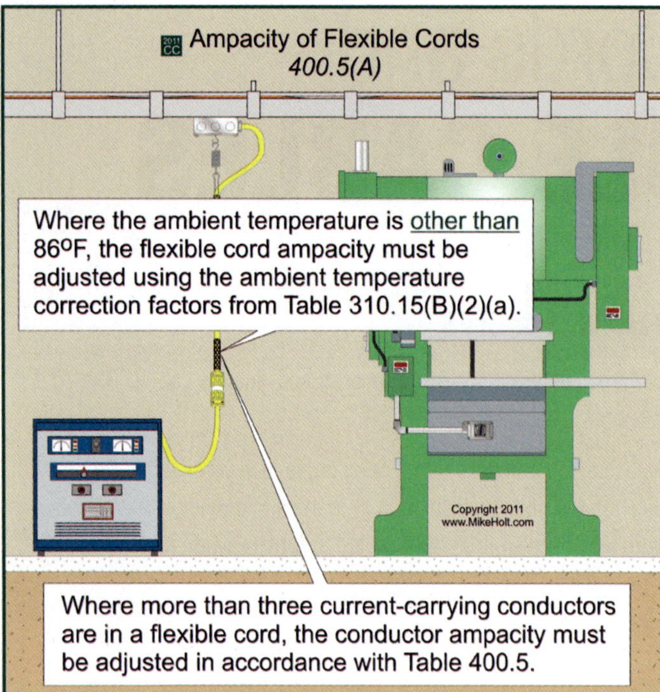

Figure 400–1

ANALYSIS: The *Code* has long required ampacity correction for cords that are used in ambient temperatures exceeding 86°F. The new version of this requirement allows correction for cords used in other than 86°F ambient temperatures. While it's subtle, no allowance was previously made for cords used in an ambient temperature of less than 86°F.

400.13 Overcurrent Protection

The requirement for overcurrent protection of cords was editorially revised.

400.13 Overcurrent Protection.

Flexible cords and flexible cables must be protected against overcurrent in accordance with 240.5.

Author's Comment: Section 240.5 contains the following requirements:

- Overcurrent devices must not be rated higher than the cord's ampacity as specified in Table 400.5(A)(1) and Table 400.5(A)(2) [240.5(A)].
- Flexible cord for listed utilization equipment is considered protected when used in accordance with the equipment listing requirements [240.5(B)(1)].
- Extension cord sets are considered protected when used in accordance with the extension cord listing requirements [240.5(B)(3)].
- Flexible cord used in field-installed extension cords, made with separately listed and installed components, can be supplied by a 20A branch circuit for 16 AWG and larger conductors [240.5(B)(4)].

ANALYSIS: Previous editions of the *NEC* required that cords be protected against overcurrent by the overcurrent devices described in 240.5. The mistake in the text was simply that overcurrent devices aren't "described" in 240.5. This change clarifies that the focus of this section isn't the types of overcurrent devices used to protect cords, but rather the ratings of the overcurrent devices.

SWITCHES

INTRODUCTION TO ARTICLE 404—SWITCHES

The requirements of Article 404 apply to switches of all types, including snap (toggle) switches, dimmer switches, fan switches, knife switches, circuit breakers used as switches, and automatic switches, such as time clocks and timers.

404.2(C) Switches Controlling Lighting

A new rule will require a neutral conductor at nearly every switch point.

404.2 Switch Connections.

(C) Switches Controlling Lighting. Switches controlling line-to-neutral lighting loads must have a neutral provided at the switch location.

Ex: The neutral conductor isn't required at the switch location if:

(1) The conductors for switches enter the device box through a raceway that has sufficient cross-sectional area to accommodate a neutral conductor. Figure 404–1

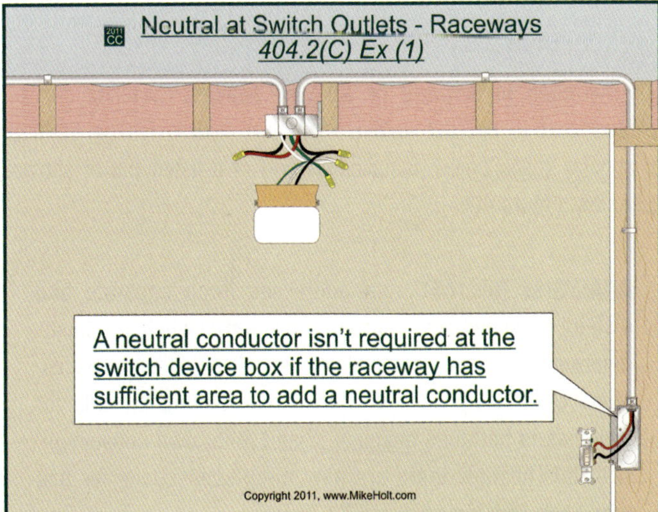

Figure 404–1

(2) Cable assemblies for switches enter the box through a framing cavity that's open at the top or bottom on the same floor level, or through a wall, floor, or ceiling that's unfinished on one side. Figure 404–2

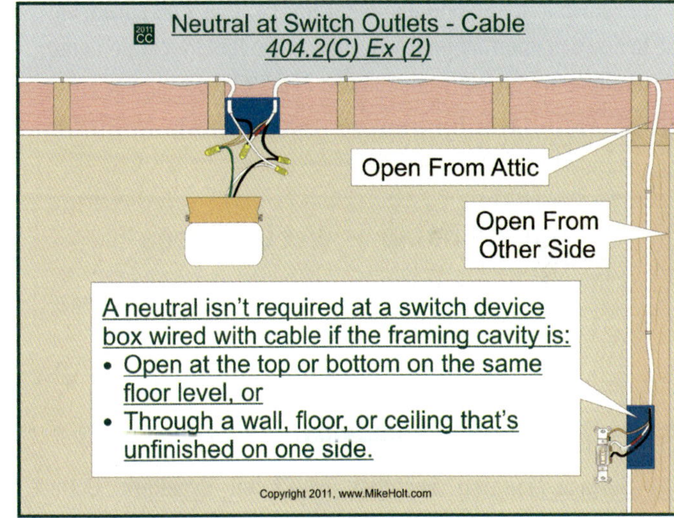

Figure 404–2

Note: The purpose of the neutral conductor is to complete a circuit path for electronic lighting control devices.

ANALYSIS: Many lighting control devices (such as occupancy sensors) require that the switch be provided with standby voltage and current at the switch in order to operate. Many electricians don't include a neutral conductor at switch locations, and the unfortunate result is the equipment grounding conductor being used as the neutral conductor. While the current on the equipment grounding conductor is typically less than 0.50 mA, the accumulation of many switches in a building can result in an unacceptable amount of current on the equipment grounding conductors. With this change, gone are the days of using dead end 3-way switches and two conductor switch loops.

The two exceptions address switch locations that use raceways, and locations that are at or near unfinished/accessible areas. The use of a raceway obviously allows the installer to pull in a neutral conductor should the need arise (provided the raceway is of adequate size), and the other exception allows for changing the wiring of the switch without resorting to removing drywall and other finish materials.

An Informational Note emphasizes the fact that this provision is for adding a dimmer switch. It is a bit surprising to see this Informational Note, due to the fact that statements of intent are typically not allowed in the *Code*.

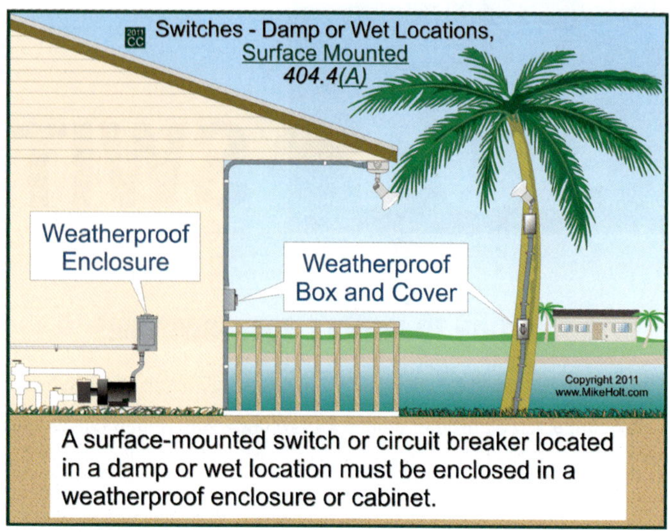

Figure 404–3

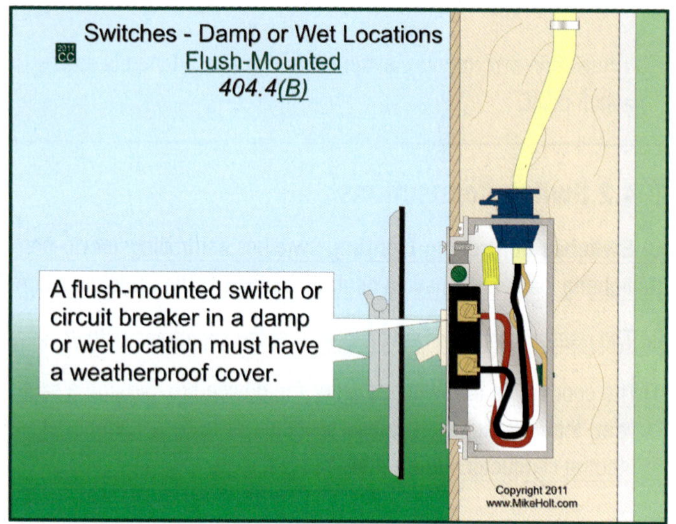

Figure 404–4

404.4 Damp or Wet Locations

The requirements for switches in damp or wet locations have been formatted into a list.

404.4 Damp or Wet Locations.

(A) Surface-Mounted Switches or Circuit Breakers. Surface-mounted switches and circuit breakers in a damp or wet location must be installed in a weatherproof enclosure. The enclosure must be installed so not less than ¼ in. of airspace is provided between the enclosure and the wall or other supporting surface [312.2]. Figure 404–3

(B) Flush-Mounted Switches or Circuit Breakers. A flush-mounted switch or circuit breaker in a damp or wet location must have a weatherproof cover. Figure 404–4

(C) Switches in Bathtub or Shower Spaces. Switches can be located next to but not within a bathtub, hydromassage bathtub, or shower space unless installed as part of a listed tub or shower assembly. Figure 404–5

ANALYSIS: This *NEC* rule addresses three separate and distinct installations: surface-mounted switches, flush-mounted switches, and switches in tub or shower spaces. Many *Code* users have a difficult time finding the rule for switches in bathtubs because it isn't in its own subsection. With this change, there are now three subsections for this rule, each addressing a specific issue.

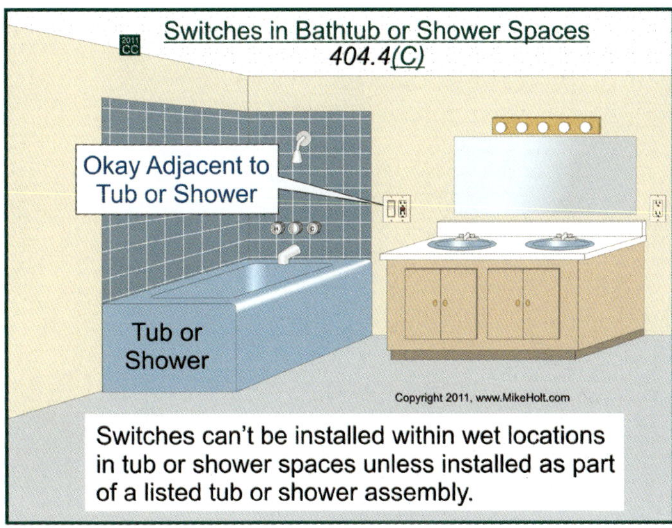

Figure 404–5

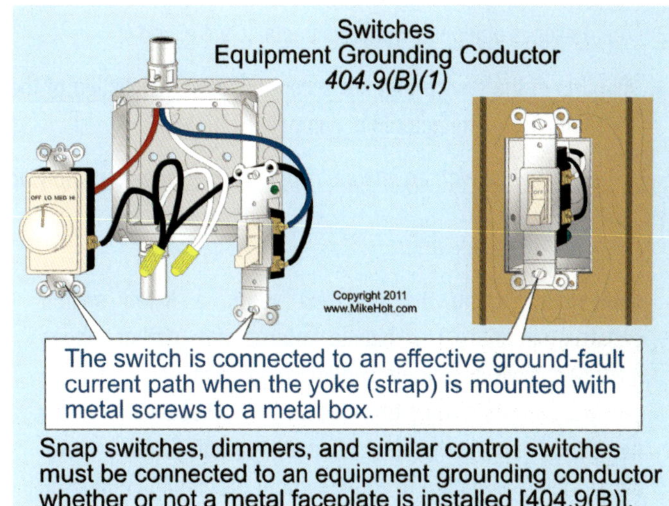

Figure 404–6

404.9(B) Grounding Switch Plates

Two new exceptions for connecting switches to an equipment grounding conductor have been added.

404.9 Switch Faceplates.

(A) Mounting. Faceplates for switches must be installed so they completely cover the outlet box opening and, where flush mounted, the faceplate must seat against the wall surface.

(B) Grounding. The metal mounting yokes for switches, dimmers, and similar control switches must be connected to an equipment grounding conductor of a type recognized in 250.118, whether or not a metal faceplate is installed. The metal mounting yoke is considered part of the effective ground-fault current path [250.2] by the use of one of the following means:

(1) Mounting Screw. The switch is mounted with metal screws to a metal box or a metal cover that's connected to an equipment grounding conductor of a type recognized in 250.118. Figure 404–6

Author's Comment: Direct metal-to-metal contact between the device yoke of a switch and the box isn't required.

(2) Equipment Grounding Conductor. An equipment grounding conductor or equipment bonding jumper is connected to the grounding terminal of the metal mounting yoke. Figure 404–7

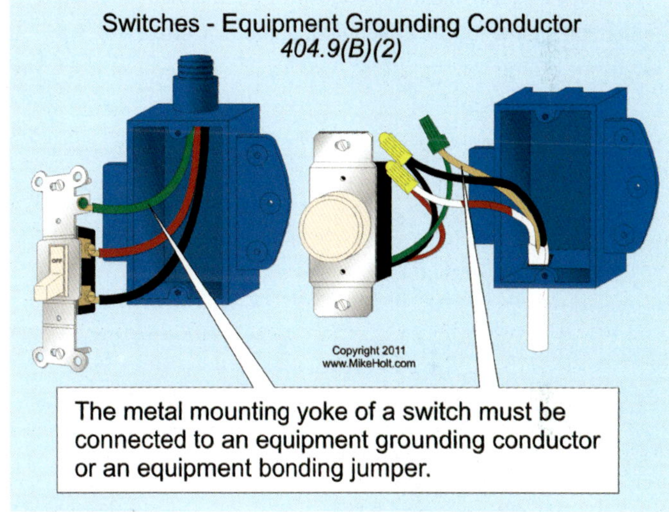

Figure 404–7

Ex 1: The metal mounting yoke of a replacement switch isn't required to be connected to an equipment grounding conductor if the wiring at the existing switch doesn't contain an equipment grounding conductor, and the switch faceplate is nonmetallic with nonmetallic screws, or the replacement switch is GFCI protected.

Ex 2: Listed assemblies aren't required to be connected to an equipment grounding conductor if all of the following conditions are met:

(1) The device is provided with a nonmetallic faceplate that can't be installed on any other type of device,

(2) The device doesn't have mounting means to accept other configurations of faceplates,

(3) The device is equipped with a nonmetallic yoke, and

(4) All parts of the device that are accessible after installation of the faceplate are manufactured of nonmetallic material.

Ex 3: A snap switch with an integral nonmetallic enclosure complying with 300.15(E).

ANALYSIS: During the last few years, a listed switch constructed entirely of plastic entered the market. These switches have a unique configuration, and don't allow a metallic faceplate to be installed on them. Because a plastic (nonconductive) component is inherently safer than a metal component connected to an equipment grounding conductor, a new exception was added to allow for this product.

Another exception was added to address the use of wiring devices with integral enclosures. Similar to the switches discussed above, these switches have nonmetallic faceplates and don't allow for the attachment of metallic ones.

Receptacles, Cord Connectors, and ATTACHMENT PLUGS (CAPS)

INTRODUCTION TO ARTICLE 406—RECEPTACLES, CORD CONNECTORS, AND ATTACHMENT PLUGS (CAPS)

This article covers the rating, type, and installation of receptacles, cord connectors, and attachment plugs (cord caps). It also addresses their grounding requirements. Some key points to remember include:

- Follow the grounding requirements of the specific type of device you're using.
- Provide GFCI protection where specified by 406.4(D)(3).
- Mount receptacles according to the requirements of 406.5 which are highly detailed.

406.2 Definitions

A new definition for "child care facility" was added.

406.2 Definitions.

Child Care Facility. A building/structure used for educational, supervision, or personal care services for more than four children seven years in age or less.

ANALYSIS: With new requirements being added to this edition of the *NEC* for child care facilities, this term has been defined and placed in a new Section 406.2, definitions. Some *Code* users are a bit concerned about the term "personal care services," as it's undefined and highly subject to interpretation.

406.4(D) Receptacle Replacements

A new requirement addresses the replacement of receptacles in areas requiring AFCI protection, tamper-resistant receptacles, or weather-resistant receptacles.

406.4 General Installation Requirements.

(D) Receptacle Replacement.

(4) Arc-Fault Circuit Interrupters. Effective January 1, 2014, where a receptacle outlet is supplied by a branch circuit that requires arc-fault circuit-interrupter protection [210.12(A)], a replacement receptacle at this outlet must be one of the following.

(1) A listed (receptacle) outlet branch-circuit type arc-fault circuit-interrupter receptacle.

(2) A receptacle protected by a listed (receptacle) outlet branch-circuit type arc-fault circuit-interrupter type receptacle.

(3) A receptacle protected by a listed combination type arc-fault circuit interrupter type circuit breaker.

(5) Tamper-Resistant Receptacles. Listed tamper-resistant receptacles must be provided where replacements are made at receptacle outlets that are required to be tamper resistant elsewhere in this *Code*.

(6) Weather-Resistant Receptacles. Weather-resistant receptacles must be provided where replacements are made at receptacle outlets that are required to be so protected elsewhere in the *Code*.

ANALYSIS: As aging wiring systems become more and more of a concern in the electrical industry, the *Code* is taking a proactive approach to providing protection of these systems. Many areas of a dwelling require the use of AFCI protection, in an effort to help avoid electrical fires. When AFCIs were first introduced into the *NEC*, the substantiation for their inclusion was based largely on electrical fires in older homes. With the inception of these devices the *Code* began protecting new and future wiring systems, but didn't address the older ones that contained many of the fires discussed in the AFCI arguments. This change expands the AFCI requirements to older homes. These older homes often don't contain an equipment grounding conductor, so installation of an AFCI circuit breaker does very, very little in the way of protecting the branch circuits. The receptacle type AFCIs also provide a significantly lower level of protection, but they will be required nonetheless.

This requirement has an effective date of Jan. 1, 2014.

The 2008 *NEC* introduced the concept of tamper-resistant receptacles in dwelling units. The requirements of that section (406.11, now 406.12) apply to new installations. It could have been argued that one could install tamper-resistant receptacles in the locations required by 406.11, then remove them and replace them with traditional receptacles. While most people will agree that this argument is a huge stretch of the imagination, this change eliminates it before it can come up. It also requires that on existing dwelling units, any receptacles that are replaced will need to be replaced using tamper-resistant receptacles.

A similar change was made for weather-resistant receptacles, using the same logic as tamper-resistant receptacles.

406.9(B)(1) Receptacles in a Wet Location

A new requirement for "extra-duty outlet box hoods" was added.

406.9 Receptacles in Damp or Wet Locations.

(B) Wet Locations.

(1) 15A and 20A Receptacles. All 15A and 20A receptacles installed in a wet location must be within an enclosure that's weatherproof when an attachment plug is inserted, Figure 406–1. For other than one- or two-family dwellings, the outlet box hood must be listed for "extra-duty" use if supported from grade. Figure 406–2

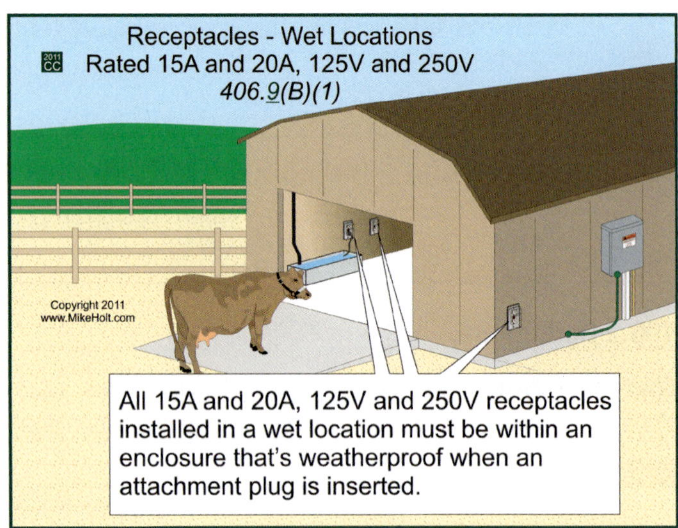

Figure 406–1

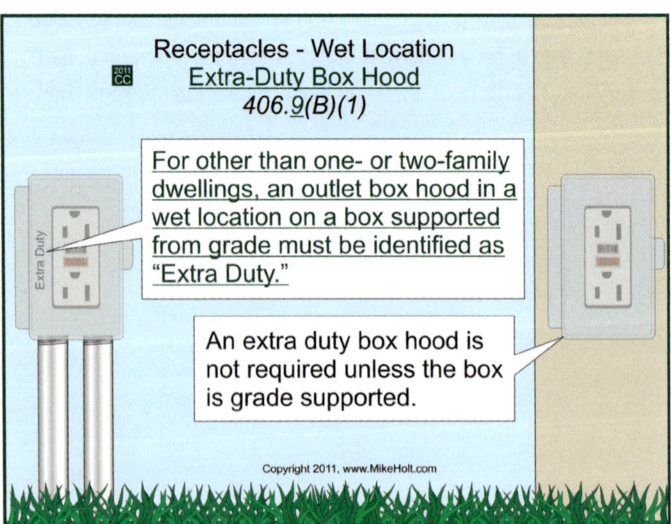

Figure 406–2

All nonlocking type 15A and 20A, 125V and 250V receptacles in a wet location must be listed as weather resistant. Figure 406–3

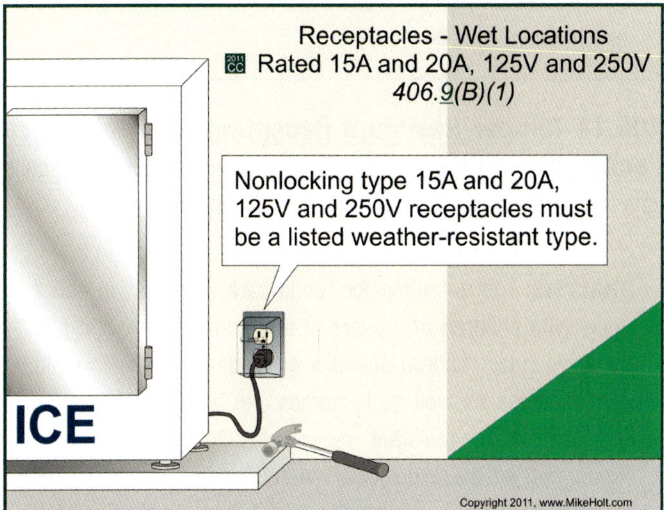

Figure 406–3

Author's Comment: Exposed plastic surface material of weather-resistant receptacles must have UV resistance to ensure that deterioration from sunlight doesn't take place, or that it's minimal. In testing, receptacles are subjected to temperature cycling from very cold to very warm conditions, and then subjected to additional dielectric testing. The rapid transition from the cold to warm temperatures will change the relative humidity and moisture content on the device, and the dielectric test ensures that this won't create a breakdown of the insulation properties.

Ex: Receptacles rated 15A and 20A that are subjected to routine high-pressure washing spray may have an enclosure that's weatherproof when the attachment plug is removed.

Author's Comment: A wet location is an area subject to saturation with water, as well as unprotected locations that are exposed to weather [Article 100].

ANALYSIS: Most people agree that "in-use" receptacle covers are an abomination when it comes to durability and protection against damage. This is particularly true when the receptacle box is supported by raceways, or where the receptacle is supported by grade. In these instances the *Code* will now require a heavier duty cover, when installed at other than one- or two-family dwellings.

406.12 Tamper-Resistant Receptacles in Dwelling Units

The required locations for tamper-resistant receptacles in dwellings have been lessened, and a clarification has been made.

406.12 Tamper-Resistant Receptacles in Dwelling Units. All nonlocking type 15A and 20A, 125V receptacles in the following areas of a dwelling unit [210.52] must be listed as tamper resistant.

- Wall Space—210.52(A)
- Small-Appliance Circuit—210.52(B)
- Countertop Space—210.52(C)
- Bathroom Area—210.52(D)
- Outdoors—210.52(E)
- Laundry Area—210.52(F)
- Garage and Outbuildings—210.52(G)
- Hallways—210.52(H)

Ex: Receptacles in the following locations aren't required to be tamper-resistant:

(1) Receptacles located more than 5½ ft above the floor.
(2) Receptacles that are part of a luminaire or appliance.
(3) A receptacle located within dedicated space for an appliance that in normal use isn't easily moved from one place to another.
(4) Nongrounding receptacles used for replacements as permitted in 406.4(D)(2)(a).

ANALYSIS: Receptacles installed above 5½ ft obviously don't pose the same risk to small children as those receptacles below that elevation. Likewise, receptacles that are rendered inaccessible by equipment, and those that are part of luminaires don't pose the same risk. The *Code* has recognized these facts and included an exception for them in this edition of the *NEC*.

An allowance has also been made to address the replacement of nongrounding receptacles, since, currently, there are no nongrounding tamper-resistant receptacles.

Additionally, the term "nonlocking" was added to describe the types of receptacles to which this rule is intended to apply. Only those receptacles that are of the straight blade configuration will be required to comply with this section.

406.13 Tamper-Resistant Receptacles in Guest Rooms and Guest Suites

A new requirement for tamper-resistant receptacles in guest rooms and guest suites was added.

406.13 Tamper-Resistant Receptacles in Guest Rooms and Guest Suites. Nonlocking type 15A and 20A, 125V receptacles in guest rooms and guest suites must be listed as tamper resistant.

ANALYSIS: Guest rooms and guest suites often have children staying in them, so tamper-resistant receptacles have been added as a requirement for these locations. Guest suites that provide complete facilities for living, sleeping, cooking and sanitation are considered to be dwelling units by the *NEC*, and as such were already required to provide tamper-resistant receptacles. This change will now require tamper-resistant receptacles in all guest rooms and guest suites.

406.14 Tamper-Resistant Receptacles in Child Care Facilities

A new requirement for tamper-resistant receptacles in "child care facilities" was added.

406.14 Tamper-Resistant Receptacles in Child Care Facilities. Nonlocking type 15A and 20A, 125V receptacles in child care facilities must be listed as tamper resistant.

ANALYSIS: The definition for "child care facilities" in 406.2 deals with children of 7 years of age and younger. Many of these younger children spend a great deal of time in child care facilities as well as in homes, yet the 2008 *NEC* only required tamper-resistant receptacles in dwelling units. Proponents of these devices immediately began hoping for expansion of these receptacles to other areas that are full of children. With this change, areas such as schools and day care facilities will be forced to use them. Other areas that aren't quite as clear, however, include hospitals and other medical centers.

ARTICLE

408 Switchboards and PANELBOARDS

INTRODUCTION TO ARTICLE 408—SWITCHBOARDS AND PANELBOARDS

Article 408 covers the specific requirements for switchboards and panelboards that control power and lighting circuits. Some key points to remember:

- One objective of Article 408 is that the installation prevents contact between current-carrying conductors and people or equipment.
- The circuit directory of a panelboard must clearly identify the purpose or use of each circuit that originates in the panelboard.
- You must understand the detailed grounding and overcurrent protection requirements for panelboards.

408.3(F) Switchboard or Panelboard Identification

A new requirement for labeling panelboards in ungrounded systems was added.

408.3 Arrangement of Busbars and Conductors.

(F) Switchboard or Panelboard Identification.

(1) **High-Leg Identification.** Switchboards and panelboards containing a 4-wire, delta-connected system where the midpoint of one phase winding is grounded (high-leg system), must be legibly and permanently field-marked with the following. Figure 408–1

"CAUTION B PHASE HAS 208V TO GROUND"

(2) Ungrounded Systems. A switchboard or panelboard containing an ungrounded electrical system is required to be legibly and permanently field-marked as follows:

"CAUTION UNGROUNDED SYSTEM OPERATING _____ VOLTS BETWEEN CONDUCTORS"

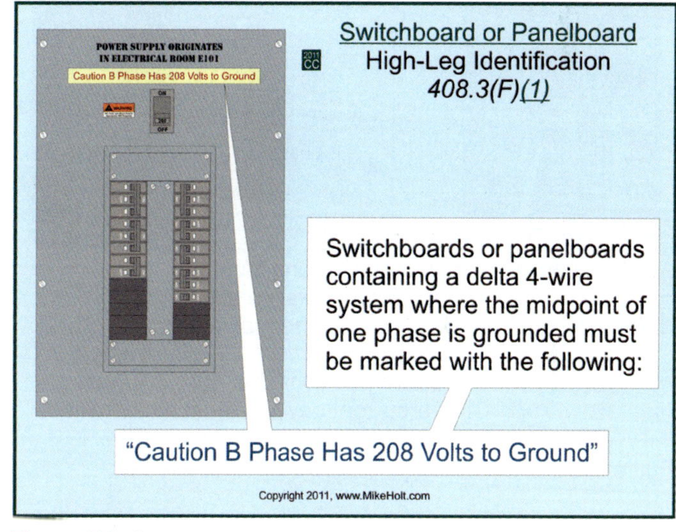

Figure 408–1

ANALYSIS: The 2008 *Code* added a requirement in this section for high-leg systems, requiring that panelboards installed in these systems be marked accordingly. While a high-leg system does present some challenges for electricians, particularly those who have never worked on one, the challenges encountered working on an ungrounded system are even greater. Due to the unusual characteristics of an ungrounded system, panelboards must now be marked to warn qualified persons that the panelboard they're about to work on is installed as part of an ungrounded system.

408.4 Field Identification

A new subsection was added with marking requirements for panelboards, and an editorial revision has been made.

408.4 Field Identification.

(A) Circuit Directory or Circuit Identification. All circuits, and circuit modifications, must be legibly identified as to their clear, evident, and specific purpose. Spare positions that contain unused overcurrent devices must also be identified. Identification must include sufficient detail to allow each circuit to be distinguished from all others, and the identification must be on a circuit directory located on the face or inside of the door of the panelboard. See 110.22. **Figure 408–2**

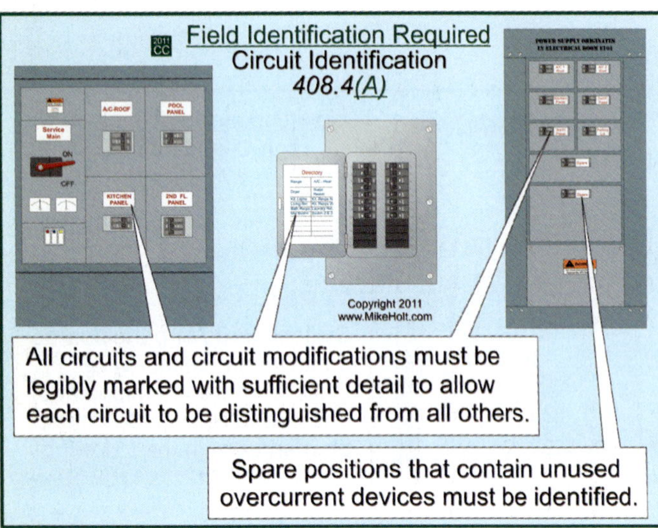

Figure 408–2

Author's Comment: Circuit identification must not be based on transient conditions of occupancy, such as Steven's, or Brittney's bedroom. **Figure 408–3**

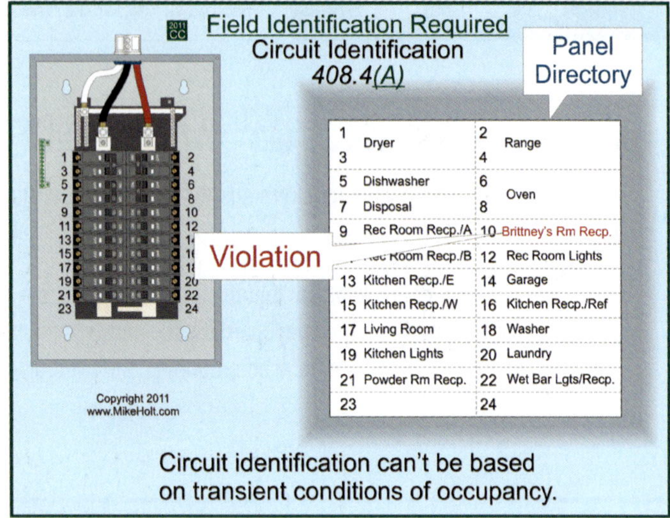

Figure 408–3

(B) Source of Supply. All switchboards and panelboards supplied by a feeder in other than one- or two-family dwellings must be marked as to the device or equipment where the power supply originates.

ANALYSIS: In large commercial and industrial applications it isn't unheard of to have over 100 panelboards in a building or at a facility. When this is the case, it becomes very difficult to determine where these panelboards receive their electrical supply. Unfortunately, this may result in electricians working on energized panelboards, simply because they can't locate the disconnecting means needed to de-energize the equipment. This new rule will require that all panelboards (other than one- and two-family dwellings) be marked to indicate where their source of supply is located. This change should greatly reduce the risk encountered on service calls and maintenance work.

Article 410 Luminaires, Lampholders, AND LAMPS

INTRODUCTION TO ARTICLE 410—LUMINAIRES, LAMPHOLDERS, AND LAMPS

This article covers luminaires, lampholders, lamps, decorative lighting products, lighting accessories for temporary seasonal and holiday use, including portable flexible lighting products, and the wiring and equipment of such products and lighting installations. Even though Article 410 is highly detailed, it's broken down into 16 parts. The first five are sequential, and apply to all luminaires, lampholders, and lamps:

- GENERAL, PART I
- LOCATION, PART II
- BOXES AND COVERS, PART III
- SUPPORTS, PART IV
- EQUIPMENT GROUNDING CONDUCTORS, PART V

This is mostly mechanical information, and it's not hard to follow or absorb. Part VI, Wiring, ends the sequence. The seventh, ninth, and tenth parts provide requirements for manufacturers to follow—use only equipment that conforms to these requirements. Part VIII provides requirements for installing lampholders. The rest of Article 410 addresses specific types of lighting.

Author's Comment: Article 411 addresses "Lighting Systems Operating at 30 Volts or Less."

PART II. LUMINAIRE LOCATIONS

410.16 Luminaires in Clothes Closets

Clarifications have been made to the allowances of LED luminaires in clothes closets, and a small grammatical revision makes this section more enforceable.

410.16 Luminaires in Clothes Closets.

(A) Luminaire Types Permitted. Only the following types of luminaires are permitted to be installed in a clothes closet:

(1) Surface or recessed incandescent or LED luminaires with an enclosed light source.

(2) Surface or recessed fluorescent luminaires.

(3) Surface-mounted or recessed LED luminaires identified for use within the closet storage space.

(B) Luminaire Types Not Permitted. Incandescent luminaires with open or partially open lamps and pendant-type luminaires must not be installed in a clothes closet. Figure 410–1

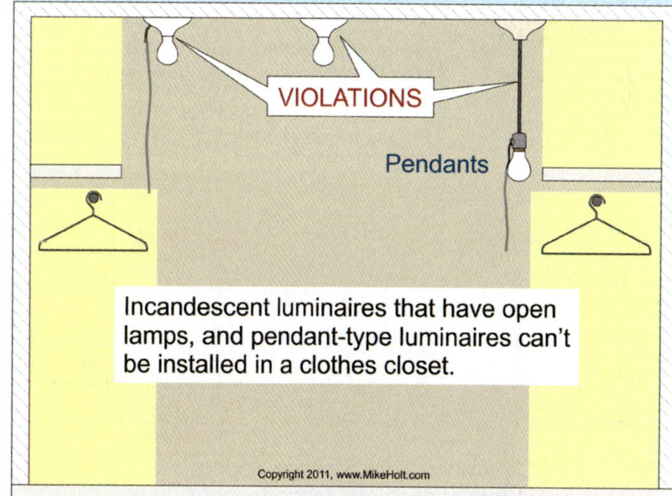

Figure 410–1

(C) Installation of Luminaires. Luminaires must maintain a minimum clearance from the closet storage space as follows:

(1) 12 in. for surface-mounted incandescent or LED luminaires with an enclosed light source. **Figure 410–2**

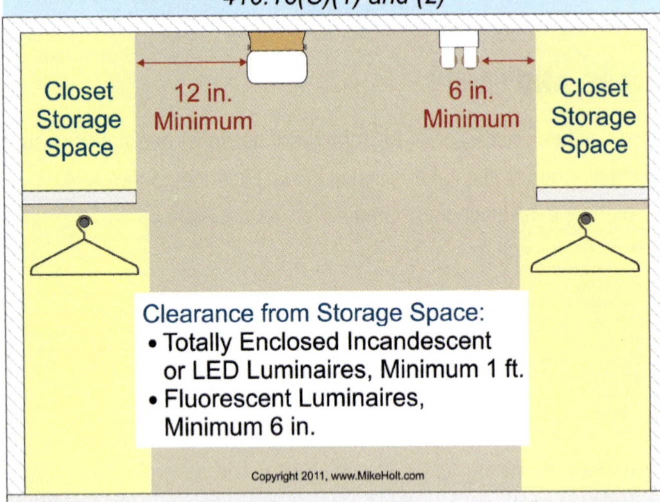

Figure 410–2

(2) 6 in. for surface-mounted fluorescent luminaires.

(3) 6 in. for recessed incandescent or LED luminaires with an enclosed light source. **Figure 410–3**

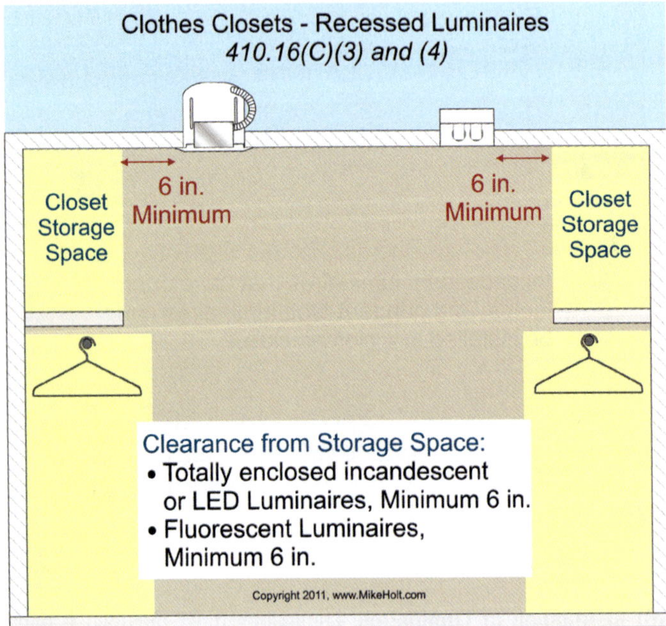

Figure 410–3

(4) 6 in. for recessed fluorescent luminaires.

(5) Surface-mounted fluorescent or LED luminaires are permitted within the closet storage space if identified for this use. **Figure 410–4**

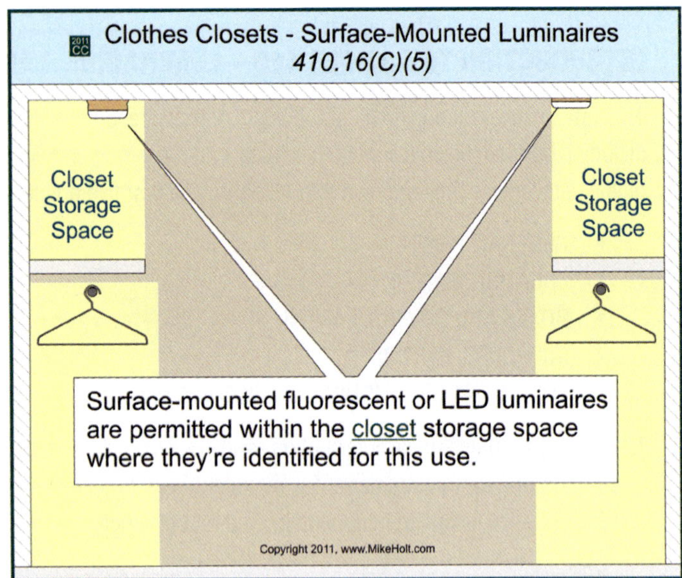

Figure 410–4

ANALYSIS: The 2008 *NEC* added allowances for LED luminaires in clothes closets. Small oversights are often made when a new requirement is added to the *Code*. In this case, the *NEC* inadvertently allowed an LED luminaire to be installed in a *clothes closet* only if it was identified for that application. The true intent is to allow an LED luminaire to be installed directly within the *closet storage space* when it's identified for that application. Due to the remarkably low amount of heat created by LED luminaires, they're acceptable anywhere in the closet without any special identification for the application, except in the actual storage area. The *Code* is now clear on the requirements for installing an LED luminaire in a clothes closet.

The word "only" was added to the opening statement of 410.16(A), clarifying that only the luminaire types in this section are permitted in a clothes closet.

PART III. LUMINAIRE OUTLET BOXES AND COVERS

410.24 Connection of Electric-Discharge and LED Luminaires

The requirements for boxes and wiring methods for electric-discharge luminaires have been revised to include LED luminaires.

410.24 Connection of Electric-Discharge and LED Luminaires.

(A) Luminaires Supported Independently of the Outlet Box. Electric-discharge and LED luminaires supported independently of the outlet box must be connected to the branch circuit with a raceway, or with Types MC, AC, or NM cable. Figure 410–5

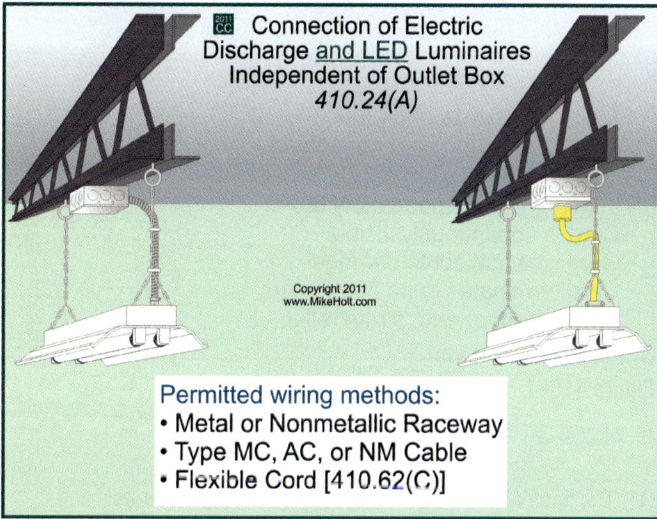

Figure 410–5

Electric-discharge luminaires can be cord-connected if the luminaires are provided with internal adjustments to position the lamp [410.62(B)].

Electric-discharge luminaires can be cord-connected if the cord is visible for its entire length and is plugged into a receptacle, and the installation complies with 410.62(C).

(B) Access to Outlet Box. When an electric-discharge luminaire or LED luminaire is surface mounted over a concealed outlet box, and not supported by the outlet box, the luminaire must be provided with suitable openings that permit access to the branch-circuit wiring within the outlet box. Figure 410–6

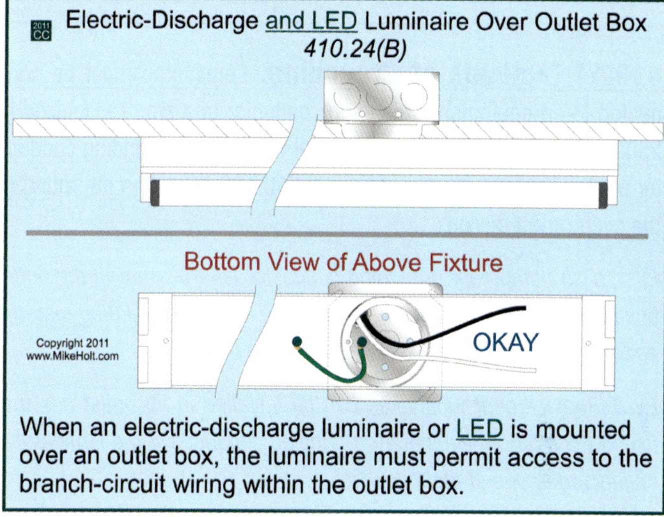

Figure 410–6

ANALYSIS: According to the submitter of this proposal, "luminaires employing LED lamp technology will be replacing similar shaped products that have employed fluorescent lamp technology." Only time will tell if his prediction into the future is accurate. LED lamp technology provides an energy saving, long-lasting alternative to more traditional light sources. A cost hurdle may need to be overcome for wider acceptance, but the use of LED lamps is growing.

PART IV. GROUNDING (BONDING)

410.44 Methods of Grounding

Revisions to this section, as well as 410.42 and 410.146, provide for a more logical *Code* arrangement.

410.44 Methods of Grounding. Luminaires must be connected to an equipment grounding conductor of a type recognized in 250.118. If of the wire type, the circuit equipment grounding conductor must be sized in accordance with 250.122, based on the rating of the overcurrent device.

Ex 1: If an equipment grounding conductor isn't present in the outlet box for a luminaire, the luminaire must be made of insulating material and must not have any exposed conductive parts.

Ex 2: Replacement luminaires can be installed in an outlet box that doesn't contain an equipment grounding conductor if the luminaire is connected to one of the following:

(1) Grounding electrode system [250.50].

(2) Grounding electrode conductor.

(3) Panelboard equipment grounding terminal.

(4) Service neutral conductor within the service equipment enclosure.

Ex 3: GFCI-protected replacement luminaires aren't required to be connected to an equipment grounding conductor of a type recognized in 250.118 if no equipment grounding conductor exists at the outlet box.

Author's Comment: This is similar to the rule for receptacle replacements in locations where an equipment grounding conductor isn't present in the outlet box [406.4(D)(3)].

ANALYSIS: In previous editions of the *NEC*, the rules addressing the grounding and bonding of luminaires have been a hodge-podge of requirements in an illogical arrangement. Changes to these sections have been made to make for a more user friendly *Code*, with no technical changes being made.

PART VI. WIRING OF LUMINAIRES

410.62(C) Electric-Discharge and LED Luminaires

The rules governing cord-and-plug-connected electric-discharge luminaires have been updated to include LED luminaires.

410.62 Cord-Connected Luminaires.

(C) Electric-Discharge and LED Luminaires. A luminaire can be cord connected if: Figure 410–7

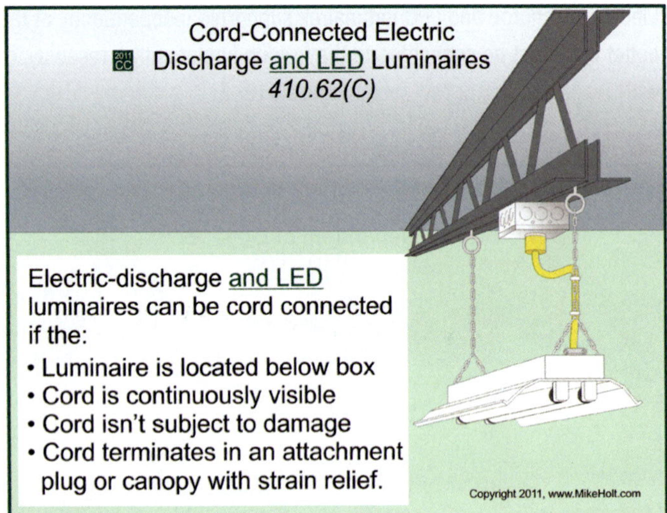

Figure 410–7

(1) The luminaire is mounted directly below the outlet box, and

(2) The flexible cord:

a. Is visible for its entire length,

b. Isn't subject to strain or physical damage [400.10], and

c. Terminates in an attachment plug, canopy with strain relief, or manufactured wiring system connector in accordance with 604.6(C).

Author's Comment: The *Code* doesn't require twist-lock receptacles for this application.

ANALYSIS: With the increasing popularity of LED luminaires, the *NEC* is including them in installation requirements. Because LED drivers and electric-discharge luminaires are quite similar, the logical place to include LED requirements is alongside electric-discharge luminaires. Where LED luminaires are supplied via a cord-and-plug-connection, they must now comply with the provisions of this section.

410.64 Luminaires as Raceways

The provisions for luminaires used as raceways have been revised for *Code* usability.

410.64 Luminaires as Raceways.

(A) Listed. Luminaires aren't permitted to be used as a raceway for circuit conductors unless listed and marked for use as a raceway. Figure 410–8

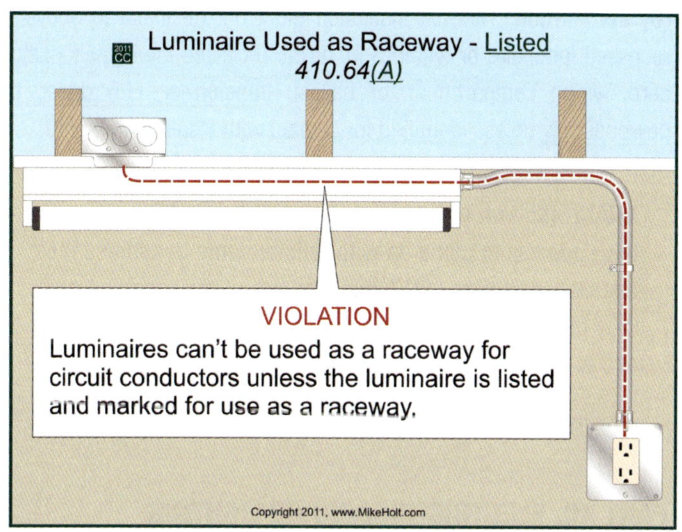

Figure 410–8

(B) Through-Wiring. Luminaires with an outlet box that's an integral part of a luminaire can be used as a conductor raceway.

(C) Luminaires Connected Together. Luminaires designed for end-to-end assembly, or luminaires connected together by recognized wiring methods, can contain a 2-wire branch circuit, or one multiwire branch circuit, supplying the connected luminaires. One additional 2-wire branch circuit supplying a night light is permitted. Figure 410–9

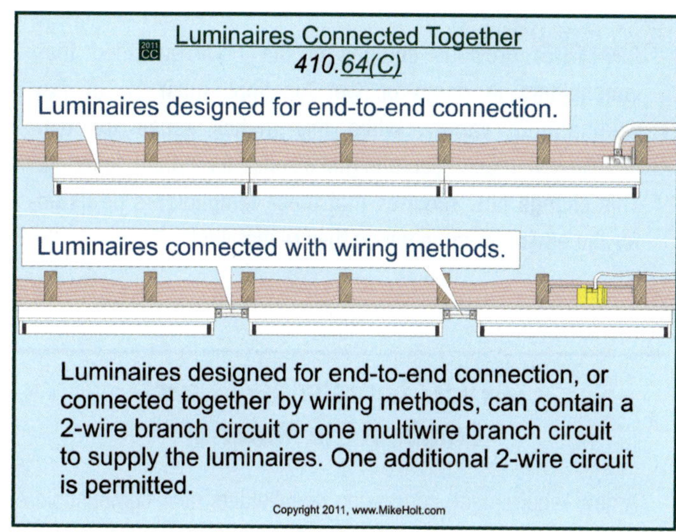

Figure 410–9

ANALYSIS: In previous editions of the *NEC*, if the *Code* user wanted to find out whether or not he or she could use a luminaire as a raceway, they would find their answer in 410.64. The answer was a resounding "no," it isn't permitted. Section 410.65, however, acted as an exception to this rule. The problem with that concept is that the *NEC* user probably had stopped looking for allowances to the rule of 410.64, because there were no exceptions to that section. By deleting (2008) 410.65 and incorporating its text into 410.64, the *Code* becomes a much easier document to navigate and understand. While this change isn't a technical one, it will likely help all users of the *NEC*.

PART VIII. INSTALLATION OF LAMPHOLDERS

410.96 Lampholders in Wet or Damp Locations

This section has been revised to more accurately specify the requirements for damp and wet locations.

410.96 Lampholders in Wet or Damp Locations. Lampholders installed in wet locations must be listed for use in wet locations and lampholders installed in damp locations must be listed for damp or wet locations.

ANALYSIS: Previous editions of the *Code* specified that lampholders in damp or wet locations must be of the weatherproof variety. While this makes sense for wet locations, it doesn't seem to make sense for a damp location. This change now requires that these lampholders be listed for the environment in which they're installed.

410.97 Lampholders Near Combustible Material

A new requirement, addressing lampholders near combustible materials, was added.

410.97 Lampholders Near Combustible Material. Lampholders must be constructed, installed, or equipped with shades or guards so that combustible material isn't subjected to temperatures in excess of 90°C (194°F).

ANALYSIS: 410.11 has long required that luminaires installed near combustible material contain shades or guards to prevent the ignition of surrounding products. While that requirement certainly makes sense, there's a gaping hole in the rule—it doesn't address lampholders. Lampholders often contain lamps that produce more heat than a standard luminaire, and very seldom has an apparatus been designed to contain that heat. Because lampholders aren't included in the definition of luminaires, this new section was added. The location of this new requirement in Part VIII also seems to be quite logical.

PART X. RECESSED LUMINAIRES

410.110 General

The applicability of this section has been clarified.

410.110 General. Luminaires installed in recessed cavities in walls or ceilings, including suspended ceilings, must comply with this part.

ANALYSIS: The provisions of Part X of this article apply to luminaires installed in the recessed cavities of walls and ceilings. Many users of the *NEC* have questioned whether or not these rules are intended to apply to luminaires in suspended ceilings. Because of this, there's been a long standing formal interpretation provided by the technical committee clarifying that these rules do, in fact, apply to suspended ceilings. This *Code* change takes that formal interpretation and puts it right in the *NEC* text, alerting *Code* users to this fact.

410.116(B) Installation

Revisions to this subsection have been made to include LED luminaires.

410.116 Recessed Luminaire Clearances.

(B) Installation. Thermal insulation must not be installed above a recessed luminaire or within 3 in. of the recessed luminarie's enclosure, wiring compartment, or ballast, transformer, LED driver, or power supply unless identified for contact with insulation, Type IC.

ANALYSIS: With the increasing popularity of LED luminaires, the *Code* has to come up with requirements to address their installation. Where LED luminaires are of the recessed type, they must be marked as "Type IC," or must have a clearance of 3 in. from thermal insulation.

PART XII. ELECTRIC-DISCHARGE LIGHTING

410.130(G) Disconnecting Means

The requirements for a disconnecting means in fluorescent luminaires have been revised to address changing of ballasts.

410.130 General.

(G) Disconnecting Means.

(1) General. In indoor locations, other than dwellings and associated accessory structures, fluorescent luminaires that utilize double-ended lamps (typical fluorescent lamps) and contain ballasts that can be serviced in place must have a disconnecting means.

For existing installed luminaires, a disconnecting means must be added at the time a ballast is replaced.

Author's Comment: Changing the ballast while the circuit feeding the luminaire is energized has become a regular practice because a local disconnect isn't available.

Ex 2: A disconnecting means isn't required for the emergency illumination required in 700.16.

Ex 3: For cord-and-plug-connected luminaires, an accessible separable connector, or an accessible plug and receptacle, is permitted to serve as the disconnecting means.

Ex 4: A disconnecting means isn't required in industrial establishments with restricted public access where written procedures and conditions of maintenance and supervision ensure that only qualified persons will service the installation.

Ex 5: If more than one luminaire is installed and is supplied by a branch circuit that isn't of the multiwire type, a disconnecting means isn't required for every luminaire; but, only when the light switch for the space ensures that some of the luminaires in the space will still provide illumination.

(2) Multiwire Branch Circuits. When connected to multiwire branch circuits, the fluorescent luminaire disconnect must simultaneously break all circuit conductors of the ballast, including the neutral conductor.

Author's Comment: This rule requires the disconnecting means to open "all circuit conductors of a multiwire branch circuit," including the neutral conductor. If the neutral conductor in a multiwire circuit isn't disconnected at the same time as the ungrounded conductors, a false sense of security can result in an unexpected shock from the neutral conductor.

(3) Location. The fluorescent luminaire disconnecting means must be accessible to qualified persons, and if the disconnecting means is external to the luminaire, it must be a single device and must be located in sight from the luminaire.

ANALYSIS: Since its inception in the 2005 *NEC*, few people would argue that the ballast disconnect in fluorescent luminaires has resulted in increased safety to electricians and maintenance workers. New to the *Code* this year is a requirement that when a ballast is changed on an existing luminaire, a disconnecting means must also be added. Considering the low cost of these disconnects and the level of increased safety, few people seem to be bothered by this.

NOTES

ARTICLE 422 APPLIANCES

INTRODUCTION TO ARTICLE 422—APPLIANCES

Article 422 covers electric appliances used in any occupancy. The meat of this article is contained in Parts II and III. Parts IV and V are primarily for manufacturers, but you should examine appliances for compliance before installing them. If the appliance has a label from a recognized labeling authority (for example, UL), it complies [90.7].

422.2 Definitions

A new definition for "vending machine" was added.

422.2 Definitions.

Vending Machine. A self-service device that dispenses products or merchandise, designed to require insertion of coin, paper currency, token, card, key, or receipt of payment by other means. Figure 422–1

Figure 422–1

ANALYSIS: Most articles of the *Code* include an xxx.2 section to include definitions that are unique to their specific article. Article 422 hasn't had such a section until now, and the first definition in it's for vending machine, a term previously defined in 422.51. The existing definition of "vending machine" has been relocated into this new section in order to be consistent with other articles.

422.30 General

The requirements for the disconnecting means of appliances have been clarified.

422.30 General. Each appliance must have a means that disconnects simultaneously all ungrounded circuit conductors.

ANALYSIS: The *NEC* has required appliances to have a means to disconnect the ungrounded conductors supplying them for a long time. Although it's a subtle point, this section has never required that the disconnecting means open the ungrounded conductors simultaneously. This change helps to correlate this requirement with the provisions that are already found in 240.15.

422.31(C) Motor-Operated Appliances Rated Over ⅛ Horsepower

The requirements for a disconnecting means of motor-driven appliances have been revised to enhance usability.

422.31 Permanently Connected Appliance Disconnects.

(B) Appliances Rated Over 300 VA. A switch or circuit breaker can serve as the disconnect if located within sight of the appliance, or the switch or circuit breaker is capable of being locked in the open position. The provision for locking or adding a lock to the disconnecting means must be on the switch or circuit breaker and remain in place with or without the lock installed. Figure 422–2

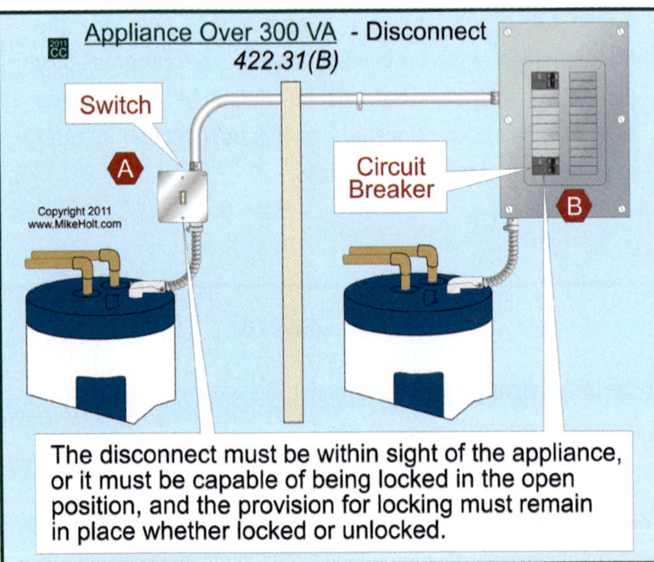

Figure 422–2

Author's Comment: "Within Sight" is visible and not more than 50 ft from one to the other [Article 100].

(C) Motor-Operated Appliances Rated Over ⅛ Horsepower. A switch or circuit breaker located within sight from the motor-operated appliance can serve as the appliance disconnect.

Ex: An appliance containing a unit switch that complies with 422.34.

ANALYSIS: There's been confusion regarding the allowance of a lockable disconnect that isn't within sight of an appliance. The requirements of this section hinge on both the VA rating of the appliance, as well as the horsepower rating of the appliance. Rules that discuss horsepower ratings are typically in regard to motors (or in this case, motor-driven appliances). Confusion has arisen because the requirements of 422.32 pertained only to motor-driven appliances, and these requirements differed from those found in 422.31. With this change, 422.32 is deleted altogether, and a new Subsection (C) is created for appliances rated over ⅛ horsepower (motor driven). In this new edition of 422.31, Subsection (A) applies to nonmotor-operated appliances not over 300VA and motor-operated appliances of less than ⅛ horsepower. Subsection (B) applies to nonmotor-operated appliances of greater than 300VA. Subsection (C) applies to motor-operated appliances greater than ⅛ horsepower. The exception formerly found in 422.32 now applies to 422.31(C).

Fixed Electric Space-Heating EQUIPMENT

INTRODUCTION TO ARTICLE 424—FIXED ELECTRIC SPACE-HEATING EQUIPMENT

Many people are surprised to see how many pages Article 424 has. This is a nine-part article on fixed electric space heaters. Why so much text for what seems to be a simple application? The answer is that Article 424 covers a variety of applications—heaters come in various configurations for various uses. Not all of these parts are for the electrician in the field—the requirements in Part IV are for manufacturers.

Fixed space heaters (wall-mounted, ceiling-mounted, or free-standing) are common in many utility buildings and other small structures, as well as in some larger structures. When used to heat floors, space-heating cables address the thermal layering problem typical of forced-air systems—so it's likely you'll encounter them. Duct heaters are very common in large office and educational buildings. These provide a distributed heating scheme. Locating the heater in the ductwork, but close to the occupied space, eliminates the waste of transporting heated air through sheet metal routed in unheated spaces, so it's likely you'll encounter those as well.

424.3(B) Branch-Circuit Sizing

Fixed electric space-heating motors are now considered a continuous load.

424.3 Branch Circuits.

(B) Branch-Circuit Sizing. For the purpose of sizing branch-circuit conductors, fixed electric space-heating equipment and motor(s) are to be considered a continuous load.

Author's Comment: The branch-circuit conductors and overcurrent devices for fixed electric space-heating equipment must have an ampacity not less than 125 percent of the total heating load [210.19(A)(1) and 210.20(A)].

Question: *What size conductor and overcurrent device (are required for a 10 kW, 240V fixed electric space heater that has a 3A blower motor with 75°C terminals?* **Figure 424–1**

(a) 10 AWG, 30A *(b) 8 AWG, 40A*
(c) 6 AWG, 60A *(d) 4 AWG, 80A*

Answer: *(c) 6 AWG, 60A*

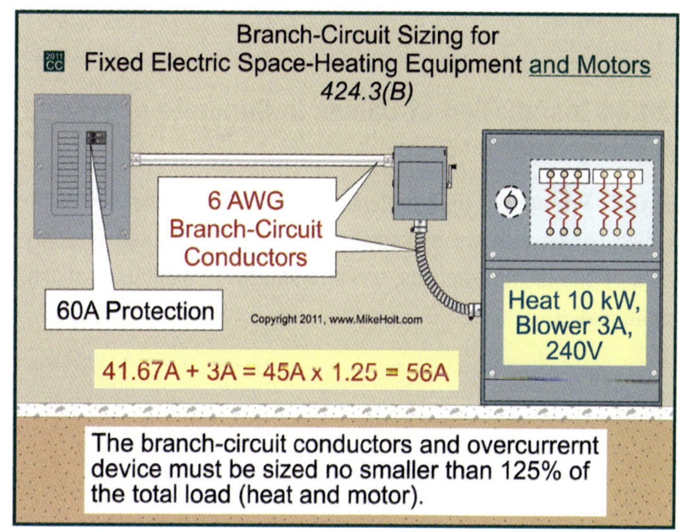

Figure 424–1

Step 1: *Determine the total load:*

I = VA/E

I = 10,000 VA/240V

I = 41.67A + 3A = 44.67A, round to 45A [220.5(B)]

Step 2: *Size the conductors at 125 percent of the total current load [110.14(C), 210.19(A)(1), and Table 310.15(B)(16)]:*

Conductor = 45A x 1.25
Conductor = 56A, 6 AWG, rated 65A at 75°C

Step 3: *Size the overcurrent device at 125 percent of the total current load [210.20(A), 240.4(B), and 240.6(A)]:*

Overcurrent Protection = 45A x 1.25
Overcurrent Protection = 56A, next size up is 60A

ANALYSIS: Electric space-heating equipment is considered to be a continuous load for calculating branch-circuit sizing requirements, but the 2008 *NEC* didn't address motors associated with the electric heating equipment. This change includes motors in the calculation as a continuous load, meaning the branch circuit should be sized at 125 percent.

424.44(G) GFCI Protection of Heating Cables

The GFCI requirements for electric space-heating cables have been expanded.

424.44 Installation of Cables in Concrete or Poured Masonry Floors.

(G) GFCI Protection. GFCI protection is required for electric space-heating cables that are embedded in concrete or poured masonry floors of bathrooms, kitchens, and hydromassage bathtub locations. Figure 424–2

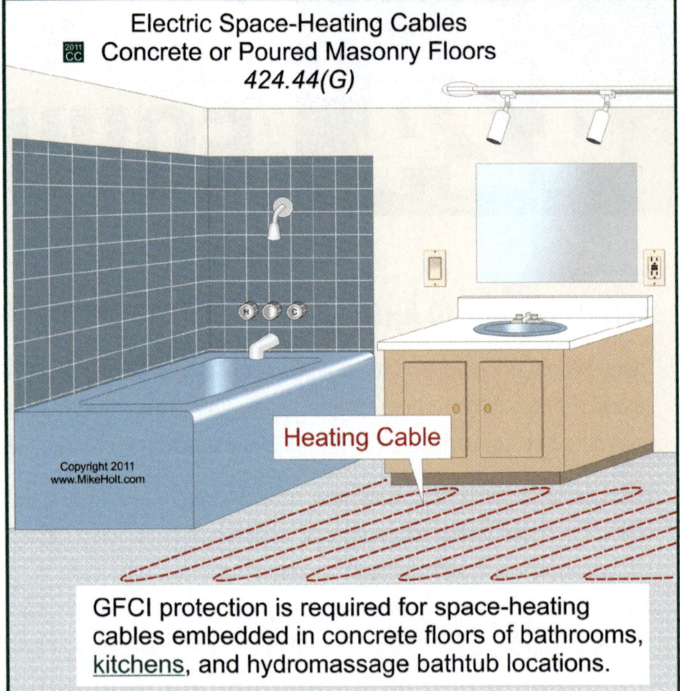

Figure 424–2

ANALYSIS: When the floor is heated with electric space heating cables in bathrooms and hydromassage locations, the *NEC* has long required GFCI protection of those heating cables. In this edition of the *Code*, these cables must also be GFCI protected when they serve a kitchen floor. According to the submitter of the change, it's intended to provide protection "for personnel while washing dishes or while in the vicinity of a wet floor in the instance of a plumbing leak at the dishwasher."

Author's Comment: See 680.28(C)(3) for restrictions on the installation of radiant-heating cables for spas and hot tubs installed outdoors.

ARTICLE

430 Motors, Motor Circuits, AND CONTROLLERS

INTRODUCTION TO ARTICLE 430—MOTORS, MOTOR CIRCUITS, AND CONTROLLERS

Article 430 contains the specific rules for conductor sizing, overcurrent protection, control circuit conductors, controllers, and disconnecting means for electric motors. The installation requirements for motor control centers are covered in Part VIII, and air-conditioning and refrigeration equipment are covered in Article 440.

Article 430 is one of the longest articles in the *NEC.* It's also one of the most complex, but motors are also complex equipment. They're electrical and mechanical devices, but what makes motor applications complex is the fact that they're inductive loads with a high-current demand at start-up that's typically six, or more, times the running current. This makes overcurrent protection for motor applications necessarily different from the protection employed for other types of equipment. So don't confuse general overcurrent protection with motor protection—you must calculate and apply them differently using the rules in Article 430.

You might be uncomfortable with the allowances for overcurrent protection found in this article, such as protecting a 10 AWG conductor with a 60A overcurrent protection device, but as you learn to understand how motor protection works, you'll understand why these allowances aren't only safe, but necessary.

430.109(F) Cord-and-Plug-Connected Motors

A change to this section addresses cord-connected motors.

430.109 Disconnecting Means Rating.

(F) Cord-and-Plug-Connected Motors. A horsepower-rated attachment plug or flanged surface inlet or cord connector and receptacle having a horsepower rating not less than the motor rating can be used as the motor disconnecting means.

ANALYSIS: While portable motors are connected to receptacles most of the time, often they're connected to the cord connector of a pendant cord or a flanged surface inlet. While 210.50(A) clearly addresses cord connectors attached to a pendant cord, this section has been revised to address it as well.

NOTES

Air-Conditioning and REFRIGERATION EQUIPMENT

INTRODUCTION TO ARTICLE 440—AIR-CONDITIONING AND REFRIGERATION EQUIPMENT

This article applies to electrically driven air-conditioning and refrigeration equipment. The rules in this article add to, or amend, the rules in Article 430 and other articles.

Each equipment manufacturer has the motor for a given air-conditioning unit built to its own specifications. Cooling and other characteristics are different from those of nonhermetic motors. For each motor, the manufacturer has worked out all of the details and supplied the correct protection, conductor sizing, and other information on the nameplate. So when wiring an air conditioner, trust the information on the nameplate and don't try to over-complicate the situation. The math for sizing the overcurrent protection and conductor minimum ampacity has already been done for you.

440.63 Disconnecting Means

A change to this section addresses cord-connected room air conditioners.

440.63 Disconnecting Means. An attachment plug and receptacle or cord connector can serve as the disconnecting means for a room air conditioner, provided: **Figure 440–1**

Figure 440–1

(1) The manual controls on the room air conditioner are readily accessible and within 6 ft of the floor, or

(2) A readily accessible disconnecting means is within sight from the room air conditioner.

Author's Comment: "Within Sight" is visible and not more than 50 ft from each other [Article 100].

ANALYSIS: While cord-and-plug-connected room air conditioners are connected to receptacles most of the time, oftentimes they're connected to the cord connector of a pendant cord. While 210.50(A) clearly addresses this fact, this section has been revised to address it as well.

NOTES

GENERATORS

INTRODUCTION TO ARTICLE 445—GENERATORS

This article contains the electrical installation, and other requirements, for generators. These requirements include such things as where generators can be installed, nameplate markings, conductor ampacity, and disconnecting means.

Generators are basically motors that operate in reverse—they produce electricity when rotated, instead of rotating when supplied with electricity. Article 430, which covers motors, is the longest article in the *NEC*. Article 445, which covers generators, is one of the shortest. At first, this might not seem to make sense. But you don't need to size and protect conductors to a generator. You do need to size and protect them to a motor.

Generators need overload protection, and it's necessary to size the conductors that come from the generator. But these considerations are much more straightforward than the equivalent considerations for motors. Before you study Article 445, take a moment to read the definition of "Separately Derived System" in Article 100.

445.1 Scope

The Scope of this article has been revised to become more accurate.

445.1 Scope. Article 445 contains the installation and other requirements for generators.

Author's Comment: Generators, associated wiring, and equipment must be installed in accordance with the following requirements depending on their use:

- Article 695, Fire Pumps
- Article 700, Emergency Systems
- Article 701, Legally Required Standby Systems
- Article 702, Optional Standby Systems

ANALYSIS: While this article does in fact cover the installation of generators, it also covers the location, marking, overcurrent protection, internal bushing requirements, terminal housings and disconnecting means for generators and the ampacity of conductors from the generator terminal to the first disconnecting means with overcurrent protection. Instead of including this long list of items, the *Code*-Making Panel decided to shorten it by stating that this article covers "installation and other requirements" for generators.

NOTES

ARTICLE 450 TRANSFORMERS

INTRODUCTION TO ARTICLE 450—TRANSFORMERS

Article 450 opens by saying, "This article covers the installation of all transformers." Then it lists eight exceptions. So what does Article 450 really cover? Essentially, it covers power transformers and most kinds of lighting transformers.

A major concern with transformers is preventing overheating. The *Code* doesn't completely address this issue. Article 90 explains that the *NEC* isn't a design manual, and it assumes that the person using the *Code* has a certain level of expertise. Proper transformer selection is an important part of preventing transformer overheating.

The *NEC* assumes you've already selected a transformer suitable to the load characteristics. For the *Code* to tell you how to do that would push it into the realm of a design manual. Article 450 then takes you to the next logical step—providing overcurrent protection and the proper connections. But this article doesn't stop there; 450.9 provides ventilation requirements, and 450.13 contains accessibility requirements.

Part I of Article 450 contains the general requirements such as guarding, marking, and accessibility, Part II contains the requirements for different types of transformers, and Part III covers transformer vaults.

450.14 Disconnecting Means

A new section will require a disconnecting means for most transformers.

450.14 Disconnecting Means. For transformers, other than Class 2 and Class 3, a means is required to disconnect all transformer ungrounded primary conductors. The disconnecting means must be located within sight of the transformer unless the location of the disconnect is field-marked on the transformer and the disconnect is lockable. Figure 450–1

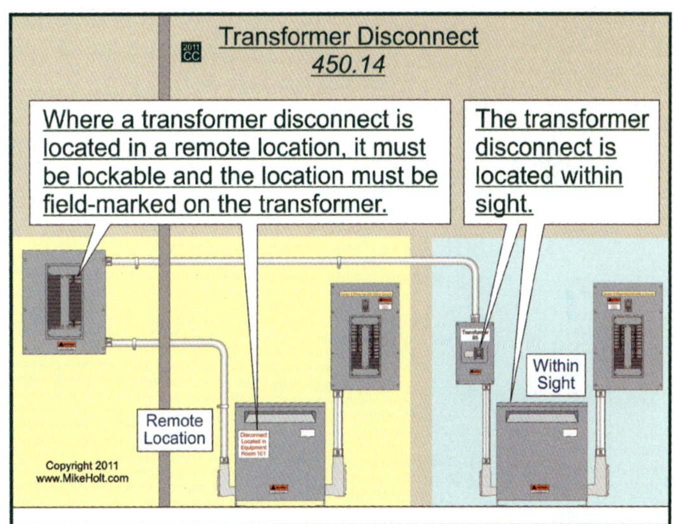

Figure 450–1

Author's Comment: "Within Sight" is visible and not more than 50 ft from each other [Article 100].

ANALYSIS: Although many *Code* users have believed that this requirement already existed, in previous *NEC* editions transformers were one of the only pieces of equipment that didn't require a disconnecting means. Although there were no documented injuries to warrant this change, it's hard to argue that this requirement doesn't enhance safety.

NOTES

Storage BATTERIES

INTRODUCTION TO ARTICLE 480—STORAGE BATTERIES

The stationary battery is the heart of any uninterruptible power supply. Article 480 addresses stationary batteries for commercial and industrial grade power supplies, not the small, "point of use" UPS boxes.

Stationary batteries are also used in other applications, such as emergency power systems. Regardless of what the application is, if it uses stationary batteries then Article 480 applies.

Lead-acid stationary batteries fall into two general categories: flooded, and valve regulated (VRLA). These differ markedly in such ways as maintainability, total cost of ownership, and scalability. The *NEC* doesn't address these differences, as they're engineering issues and not fire safety or electrical safety issues [90.1].

The *Code* doesn't address such design issues as optimum tier height, distance between tiers, determination of charging voltage, or string configuration. Nor does it address battery testing, monitoring, or maintenance. All of these involve highly specialized areas of knowledge, and are required for optimizing operational efficiency. Standards other than the *NEC* address these issues.

What the *Code* does address, in Article 480, are issues related to preventing electrocution and the ignition of the gases that all stationary batteries (even "sealed" ones) emit.

480.2 Definitions

A new definition for "battery system" was added, and the terms "nominal battery voltage" and "sealed cell or sealed battery" have been revised.

480.2 Definitions.

Battery System. Storage batteries, battery chargers, inverters, converters, and associated electrical equipment.

Nominal Battery Voltage. The voltage of a battery based on 2V per cell for lead-acid type, 1.50V per cell for alkali type, and 4V per cell for lithium-ion types.

Sealed Cell or Battery. A cell or battery with no provision for the routine addition of water or electrolyte.

Storage Battery. Battery consisting of one or more rechargeable cells.

ANALYSIS: Although the term "battery system" is used throughout Article 480, it's never been defined. This change remedies this obvious oversight, and addresses the fact that a battery system can include batteries, chargers, inverters, converters, and other associated equipment.

The previous definition of "nominal battery voltage" contained the calculation used to determine the voltage of a battery. This has been moved into a new Informational Note. The new Note also provides guidance for lithium-ion batteries, whereas previous *Code* editions provided none.

Previous editions of the definition of "sealed cell or battery" were riddled with *NEC* Manual of Style violations. The definition provided requirements, repeated the term being defined, and contained references to other *Code* sections. Revisions to this definition not only satisfy the Style Manual, but also make for a more clear and concise definition.

480.5 Disconnecting Means

The voltage limit for systems requiring a disconnecting means has been increased, and a new Informational Note was added.

480.5 Disconnecting Means. A readily accessible disconnecting means is required within sight of the storage battery for all ungrounded battery system conductors operating at over 50V nominal.

Note: Overcurrent protection for ungrounded battery conductors must be located as close as practical to the storage battery terminals [240.21(H)].

ANALYSIS: The voltage of 30V was added to the 2008 *NEC* without any technical data to substantiate the change. According to IEEE, the industry standard has always been 50V, so this change was accepted without any real resistance. It's also worth pointing out that the future edition of NFPA 70E is being revised to 50V, so this change promotes harmony with that document.

A new Informational Note has also been added to this section, reminding the *Code* user of the provision found in 240.21(H). These provisions contain the overcurrent protection requirements for battery conductors.

SPECIAL OCCUPANCIES

INTRODUCTION TO CHAPTER 5—SPECIAL OCCUPANCIES

Chapter 5, which covers special occupancies, is the first of three *NEC* chapters that deals with special topics.

Chapters 6, and 7 cover special equipment, and special conditions, respectively. Remember, the first four chapters of the *Code* are sequential and form a foundation for each of the subsequent three chapters. Chapter 8 covers communications systems and isn't subject to the requirements of Chapters 1 through 7 except where the requirements are specifically referenced in Chapter 8.

What exactly is a "Special Occupancy?" It's a location where the facility or use of the physical facility creates specific conditions that require additional measures to ensure the "practical safeguarding of people and property" purpose of the *NEC*, as put forth in Article 90.

The *Code* groups these logically, as you might expect. Here are the general groupings:

- Environments that pose additional hazards. Articles 500 through 510—Examples include hazardous locations.
- Specific types of facilities that pose additional hazards. Articles 511 through 516—Examples include motor fuel dispensing facilities, aircraft hangars, and bulk storage plants.
- Facilities that pose evacuation difficulties. Articles 517 through 525—Examples include hospitals, theaters, and carnivals.
- Motion picture related facilities. Articles 530 and 540.
- Specific types of buildings. Articles 545 through 553—Examples include park trailers and floating buildings.
- Marinas and boatyards. Article 555.
- Temporary installations. Article 590.

Many people struggle to understand the requirements for special occupancies, mostly because of the narrowness of application. However, if you study the illustrations and explanations here, you'll clearly understand them.

- **Article 500—Hazardous Locations.** A hazardous location is an area where the possibility of fire or explosion exists due to the presence of flammable or combustible gases or vapors, combustible dusts, or ignitible fibers/flyings.
- **Article 501—Class I Hazardous Locations.** A Class I hazardous location is an area where flammable or combustible gases or vapors of flammable liquids may present the hazard of a fire or explosion.
- **Article 502—Class II Hazardous Locations.** A Class II hazardous location is an area where the possibility of fire or explosion may exist due to combustible dust.
- **Article 503—Class III Hazardous Locations.** Class III locations are hazardous because fire or explosion risks may exist due to ignitible fibers/flyings. This includes materials such as cotton and rayon, which are found in textile mills and clothing manufacturing plants. It can also include establishments and industries such as sawmills and woodworking plants. There are no "Group" classifications for Class III locations as there are for Class I and Class II locations.

- **Article 511—Commercial Garages, Repair, and Storage.** These occupancies include locations used for service and repair operations in connection with self-propelled vehicles (including, but not limited to, passenger automobiles, buses, trucks, and tractors) in which petroleum-based chemicals (volatile organic compounds) are used for fuel or power.
- **Article 514—Motor Fuel Dispensing Facilities.** Article 514 covers gasoline dispensing and service stations where gasoline or other volatile liquid-produced vapors or gases are transferred to the fuel tanks of self-propelled vehicles. Wiring and equipment in the area of service and repair rooms of service stations must comply with the installation requirements in Article 511.
- **Article 517—Health Care Facilities.** This article applies to electrical wiring in human health care facilities such as hospitals, nursing homes, limited-care facilities, clinics, medical and dental offices, and ambulatory care, whether permanent or movable. It doesn't apply to animal veterinary facilities.
- **Article 518—Assembly Occupancies.** Article 518 covers buildings or portions of buildings or structures specifically designed or intended for the assembly of 100 or more persons.
- **Article 525—Carnivals, Circuses, Fairs, and Similar Events.** This article covers the installation of portable wiring and equipment for temporary carnivals, circuses, exhibitions, fairs, traveling attractions, and similar functions, including wiring in or on structures.
- **Article 547—Agricultural Buildings.** Article 547 covers agricultural buildings or those parts of buildings or adjacent areas where excessive dust or dust with water may accumulate, or where a corrosive atmosphere exists.
- **Article 550—Mobile and Manufactured Homes.** The provisions of Article 550 cover electrical conductors and equipment within or on mobile and manufactured homes, conductors that connect mobile and manufactured homes to the electrical supply, and the installation of electrical wiring, luminaires, and electrical equipment within or on mobile and manufactured homes.
- **Article 555—Marinas and Boatyards.** This article covers the installation of wiring and equipment in the areas that comprise fixed or floating piers, wharves, docks, and other areas in marinas, boatyards, boat basins, boathouses, and similar locations used, or intended to be used, for the purpose of repair, berthing, launching, storing, or fueling of small craft and the mooring of floating buildings. It doesn't apply to docks or boathouses for single-family dwelling units.
- **Article 590—Temporary Installations.** Article 590 covers temporary power and lighting for construction, remodeling, maintenance, repair, demolitions, and decorative lighting.

Hazardous LOCATIONS

INTRODUCTION TO ARTICLE 500—HAZARDOUS LOCATIONS

A hazardous location is an area where the possibility of fire or explosion can be created by the presence of flammable or combustible gases or vapors, combustible dusts, or ignitible fibers/flyings. Electric arcs, sparks, and/or heated surfaces can serve as a source of ignition in such environments. Article 500 provides a foundation for applying Article 501 (Class I Locations), Article 502 (Class II Locations), Article 503 (Class III Locations), and Article 504 (Intrinsically Safe Systems)—all of which immediately follow Article 500. This article also provides a foundation for applying Articles 510 through 516.

Before you apply any of the articles just mentioned, you must understand and apply Article 500. It's a fairly long and detailed article. You'll notice when studying Article 500 that there are many Informational Notes that you should review. Although Informational Notes aren't *NEC* requirements [90.5(C)], they contain information that should help the *Code* user to better understand the related *NEC* requirement.

A Fire Triangle (fuel, oxygen, and ignition) helps to illustrate the concept of how combustion occurs. Figure 500–1

- Fuel—Flammable gases or vapors, combustible dusts, and ignitible fibers/flyings.
- Oxygen—Air and oxidizing atmospheres.
- Ignition—Electric arcs or sparks, heat-producing equipment such as luminaires and motors, conductor insulation, failure of transformers, coils, or solenoids, as well as sparks caused by metal tools dropping on metal surfaces.

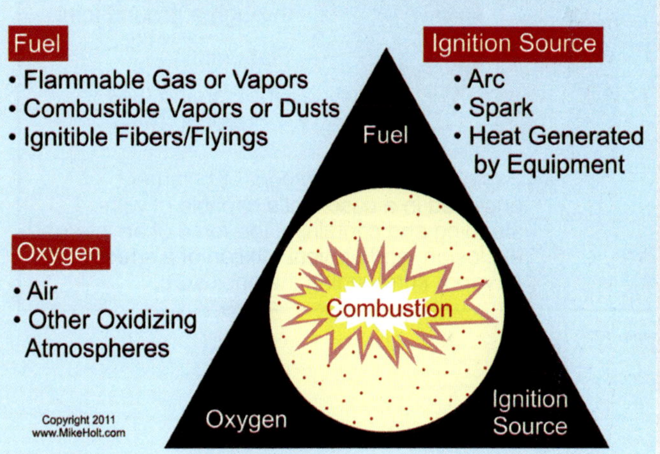

Figure 500–1

500.2 Definitions

A new definition for "combustible dust" was added.

Combustible Dust. Finely divided solid material that's 420 microns or smaller in diameter and presents a fire or explosion hazard when dispersed and ignited in air.

Author's Comment: In some cases, the size of the material may be a significant factor in distinguishing dust (Class II) from fibers and flyings (Class III).

ANALYSIS: Article 502 covers areas that are hazardous due to the presence of combustible dusts, yet there's never been a definition of that term. Like many other definitions in this article, the typical *Code* user won't reap any benefit, due to its complex definition. This reinforces the fact that area classification is best left to those that are extremely knowledgeable in the topic.

500.2 Definitions

A small change to the definition of explosionproof related items has been made.

Explosionproof Equipment. Equipment enclosed in a case capable of withstanding an internal explosion of a specified gas or vapor and of preventing the ignition of a specified gas or vapor surrounding the enclosure. It operates so that the external temperature won't ignite the surrounding atmosphere. **Figure 500–2**

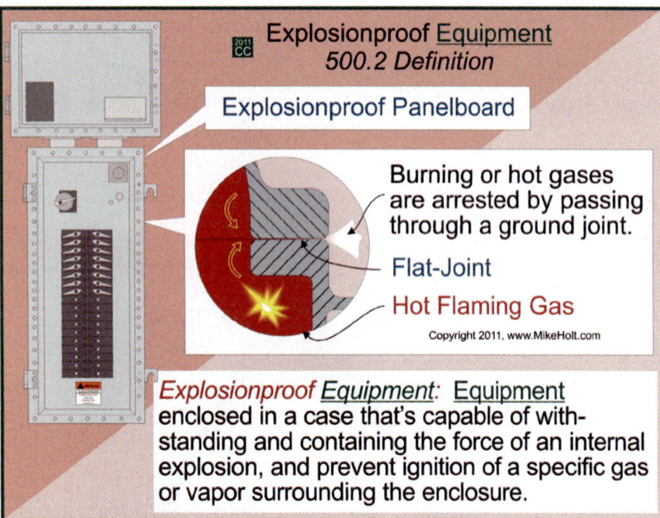

Figure 500–2

ANALYSIS: Previous editions of the *Code* used the term "explosionproof apparatus" when discussing electrical items that are commonly used in a Class I area. While this term is an accurate one, it isn't often used by tradespeople or other professionals in the electrical industry. The term "explosionproof equipment" isn't only the term more commonly used, but also includes a term (equipment) that's defined in Article 100. This change, while not a technical one, does make the *NEC* a more accurate and consistent document.

Similar changes have been made throughout the *Code* to provide consistency with this change.

500.8(C)(5) Equipment Ambient Temperature Range

A new sentence regarding the marking of hazardous location equipment was added.

500.8 Equipment.

(C) Equipment Markings. In addition to the class and division, heat-producing equipment, such as luminaires, motors, and so forth, installed in a hazardous location must be marked to indicate its operation temperature or temperature range (T-rating).

Author's Comment: The T-ratings of explosionproof luminaires (Class I, Division 1) are based on the hottest exposed surface area of the luminaire, and the T-ratings of luminaires installed in Class I, Division 2 locations are based on the hottest surface temperature of the lamp. **Figure 500–3**

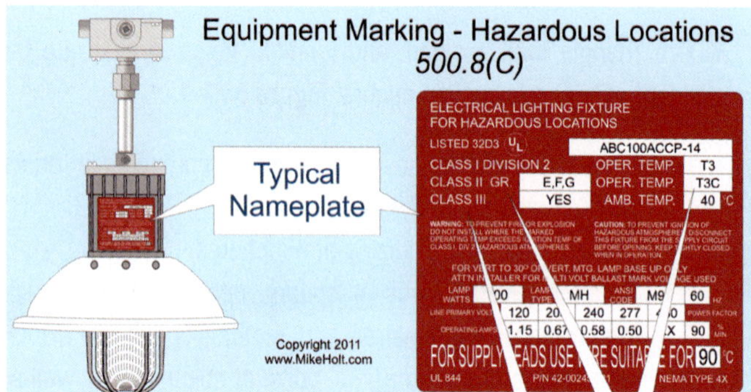

Figure 500–3

(5) Ambient Temperature Range. Electrical equipment designed for use in the ambient temperature range between -25°C and +40°C require no ambient temperature marking. For equipment rated for a temperature range other than –25°C to +40°C, the marking must specify the range of ambient temperatures in degrees Celsius.

ANALYSIS: This subsection requires manufacturers to mark their hazardous location equipment if the temperature range of the equipment is less than –25°C or greater than +40°C. While this language led one to believe that equipment operating within that temperature boundary need not be marked, the *Code* didn't come right out and say it. With this change it now does.

500.8(E) Threaded Conduit

The provisions addressing conduit threads and fitting have been extensively revised.

500.8 Equipment.

(E) Threaded Conduit. All threaded conduits must be made wrenchtight to prevent arcing when ground-fault current flows through the raceway system and to ensure the explosionproof or dust-ignitionproof integrity of the raceway system.

(1) Equipment with NPT Threaded Entries. Threaded entries into explosionproof equipment must be made up with at least five threads fully engaged.

Ex: For listed explosionproof equipment, factory threaded entries must be made up with at least 4½ threads fully engaged.

Author's Comments:

- This requirement ensures that if an explosion occurs within a raceway or enclosure, the expanding gas will sufficiently cool as it dissipates through the threads. This prevents hot flaming gases from igniting the surrounding atmosphere of a hazardous location.
- Keep in mind—it's assumed that the flammable atmosphere outside the raceway will seep into the raceway system over time. The goal of the *Code* is to contain any explosion that occurs inside the raceway so the event won't ignite the flammable mixture outside the raceway system.

(2) Equipment with Metric Threaded Entries. Equipment with metric threaded entries must be installed using listed fittings.

(3) Unused Openings. All unused openings must be closed with listed metal close-up plugs [110.12(A)]. Figure 500–4

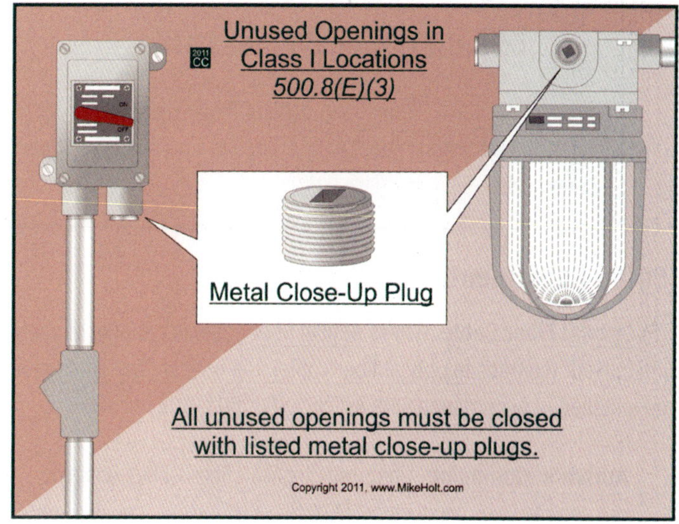

Figure 500–4

ANALYSIS: The 2008 *NEC* did a lackluster job of dealing with metric threaded conduits and fittings. Manufacturers had little guidance as to what the requirements were for metric threads in the *Code*, unlike NPT (National Pipe Taper, American Standard) threads that had more information in this subsection.

Of particular interest is a requirement for metric threads to have eight threads fully engaged for Class I, groups A and B. This requirement doesn't apply to NPT threaded raceways.

Lastly, a new subsection was added to address unused openings. While it's repetition of 110.12(A), it was added here to emphasize that these fittings must have five threads fully engaged (unless metric in a group A or B).

500.8(F) Optical Fiber Cable

Changes to the term "fiber optic cables" have been made for consistency, and a parenthetical reference to composite cables has been added.

500.8 Equipment.

(F) Optical Fiber Cable. Where optical fiber cable is capable of carrying current (composite optical fiber cable), the optical fiber cable must be installed in accordance with Articles 500, 501, 502, or 503.

Author's Comment: Composite optical fiber cable contains current-carrying conductors [770.2] and they're capable of causing a dangerous spark that can ignite flammable atmospheres, so they must be installed just like other conductors in a hazardous location. On the other hand, nonconductive optical fiber cable [770.2] has no current-carrying conductors or metallic strength members so it need not be installed in accordance with Articles 500, 501, 502. or 503. This is because optical fiber cable without current-carrying conductors or strength members can't ignite flammable atmospheres. Figure 500–5

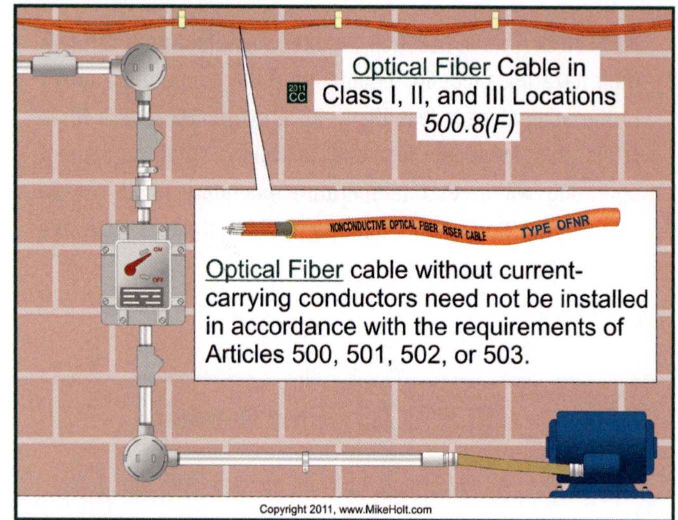

Figure 500–5

ANALYSIS: Previous editions of the *NEC* used the term "fiber optic" cables in this subsection, instead of the more accurate term "optical fiber cable." This change corrects that error.

Additionally, the term "composite optical fiber cable" was added to help the *Code* user understand which types of optical fiber cable are required to comply with this section. While this change isn't a technical one, it does add usability of the *NEC* for those users that struggle with the differences between conductive, composite, and nonconductive optical fiber cables.

Class I HAZARDOUS LOCATIONS

INTRODUCTION TO ARTICLE 501—CLASS I HAZARDOUS LOCATIONS

If sufficient flammable or combustible gases, vapors, or liquids are or may be present to produce an explosive or ignitible mixture, you have a Class I location. Examples of such locations include fuel storage areas, certain solvent storage areas, grain processing (where hexane is used), plastic extrusion where oil removal is part of the process, refineries, and paint storage areas.

Article 500 contained a general background on hazardous locations as well as describing the differences between Class I, II, and III locations and the differences between Division 1 and Division 2 in each of the three classifications.

Article 501 contains the actual Class I, Division 1 and Division 2 installation requirements, including wiring methods, seals, and specific equipment requirements.

501.10(A) Wiring Methods Class I, Division 1

Cross references for types MC cable and ITC cable have been added to this section, and a new listing requirement for flexible cords was added.

501.10 Wiring Methods.

(A) Class I, Division 1. Figure 501–1

(1) General. Only the following wiring methods are permitted within a Class I, Division 1 location.

(a) Threaded rigid metal conduit or intermediate metal conduit with explosionproof fittings.

(b) MI cable terminated with fittings listed for the location.

(c) In industrial establishments with restricted public access where only qualified persons will service the installation, MC-HL cable listed for use in Class I, Zone 1, or Division 1 locations, with a gas/vaportight continuous corrugated metallic sheath, an overall jacket of suitable polymeric material, a separate equipment grounding conductor(s) in accordance with 250.122, and terminated with fittings listed for the application. Such cable must comply with Part II of Article 330. Figure 501–2

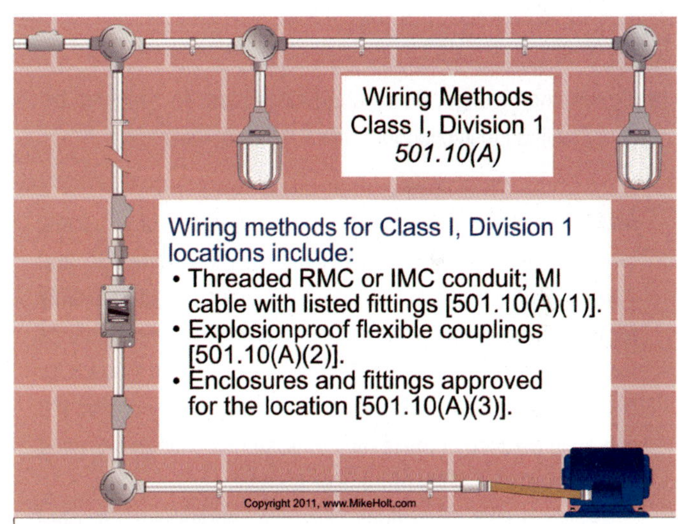

Figure 501–1

Author's Comment: Article 100 defines a "Qualified Person" as one who has skills and knowledge related to the construction and operation of the equipment and has received safety training on the hazards involved.

(d) In industrial establishments with restricted public access where only qualified persons will service the installation, ITC-HL cable terminated with fittings listed for the location.

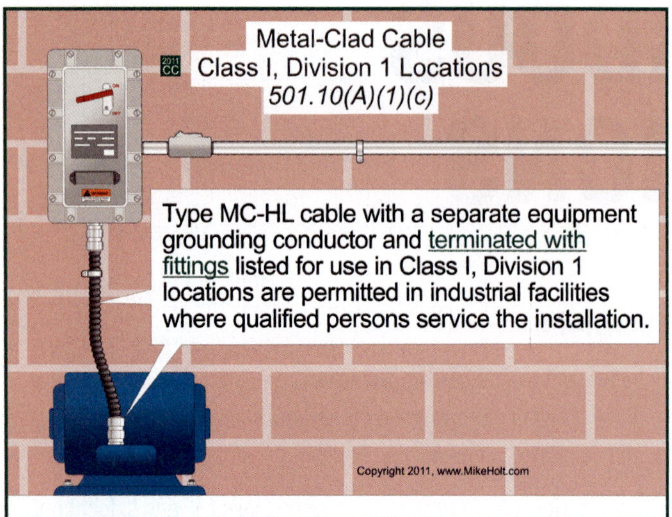

Figure 501–2

(2) Flexible Wiring. Explosionproof flexible metal couplings listed for the location are permitted in a Class I, Division 1 location when necessary for vibration, movement, or for difficult bends or flexible cord in accordance with 501.140 if terminated with cord connectors listed for the location.

(3) Boxes and Fittings. Boxes and fittings must be approved by the authority having jurisdiction for Class I, Division 1 locations.

ANALYSIS: Installations consisting of Types MC or ITC cable in a hazardous location must comply with Article 330 and 727, respectively. While 90.3 already tells us this quite plainly for MC cable (Article 330), it doesn't give the same guidance for a wiring method that's described in Chapter 7, such as ITC cable (Article 727). Section 727.4 specifically allows ITC cables to be used in these locations, so this change is a good way to make the *Code* more user friendly.

Unlike most hazardous location equipment, flexible fittings haven't required listing in years past. This revision will now require listing for these products.

501.10(B) Wiring Methods Class I, Division 2

The provisions addressing ITC Cable in hazardous locations have been moved to this section from 725.154(D), and the provisions for flexible cords now contain listing requirements.

501.10 Wiring Methods.

(B) Class I, Division 2.

(1) General. Only the following wiring methods are permitted within a Class I, Division 2 location. Figure 501–3

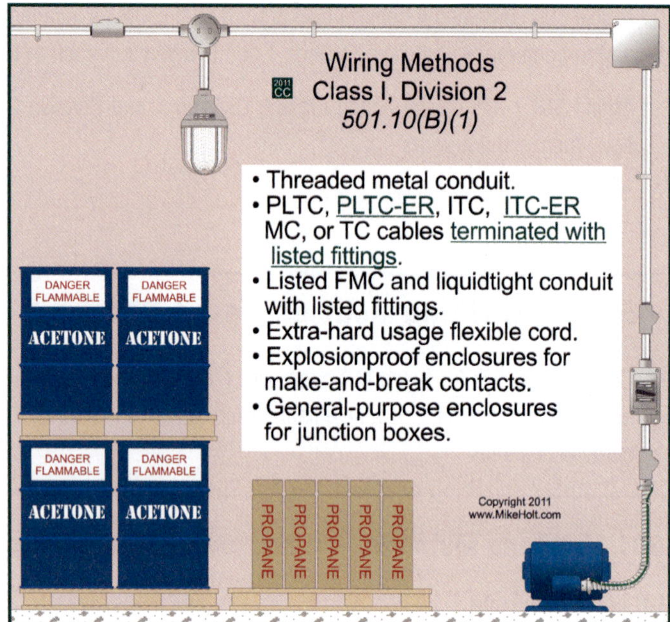

Figure 501–3

(1) Wiring methods permitted in Class I, Division 1 locations [501.10(A)].

(2) Enclosed gasketed busways and enclosed gasketed wireways.

(3) PLTC and Type PLTC-ER cable terminated with listed fittings in accordance with Article 725.

(4) ITC and ITC-ER cable terminated with listed fittings as permitted in 727.4.

(5) Types MC, MV, or TC cables including installation in cable tray systems and terminated with listed fittings.

(6) Where metallic conduit doesn't provide sufficient corrosion resistance, reinforced thermosetting resin conduit and Schedule 80 PVC conduit can be used, but only in industrial establishments where maintenance and supervision ensure that only qualified persons service the installation.

(2) Flexible Wiring. If flexibility is necessary, the following wiring methods are permitted:

(1) Listed flexible metal fittings.

(2) Flexible metal conduit with listed fittings.

(3) Liquidtight flexible metal conduit with listed fittings.

(4) Liquidtight flexible nonmetallic conduit with listed fittings.

(5) Flexible cords listed for extra-hard usage, containing an equipment grounding conductor, and terminated with listed fittings.

Author's Comments:

- See the definition of "Grounding Conductor, Equipment" in Article 100.
- If flexible cords are used, they must comply with 501.140.

Note: See 501.30(B) for equipment grounding requirements where flexible conduit is used.

(4) Boxes and Fittings. General-purpose enclosures and fittings are permitted unless the enclosure contains make-and-break contacts for meters, instruments, and relays [501.105(B)(1)], switches, circuit breakers, or motor controllers [501.115(B)(1)], signaling, alarm, remote-control, and communications systems [501.150(B)].

Author's Comment: See the definition of "Controller" in Article 100.

ANALYSIS: Installations consisting of Types MC or ITC cable in a hazardous location must comply with Article 330 and 727, respectively. While 90.3 already tells us this quite plainly for MC cable (Article 330), it doesn't give the same guidance for a wiring method that's described in Chapter 7, such as ITC cable (Article 727). Section 727.4 specifically allows ITC cables to be used in these locations, so this change is a good way to make the *NEC* more user friendly.

Article 725 deals with Class 1, Class 2, and Class 3 Remote-Control, Signaling, and Power-Limited Circuits. When the *Code* user needs to figure out what the rules are for these types of circuits, Article 725 is the one they turn to. When *they* need to figure out what the rules are for these cables when they're installed in a hazardous location, Chapter 5 is the part of the *NEC* they will probably turn to...only to find out that they're in the wrong place. The change to 501.10(B)(1)(c) fixes that problem, with the result being a more user friendly *Code*.

Listing requirements were also added for flexible fittings installed in Class I, Division 2 locations. Much of the equipment used in hazardous locations require listing, and this is no longer an exception.

501.30(B) Types of Equipment Grounding Conductors

This section has been revised to add clarity to the requirement.

501.30 Grounding and Bonding. Because of the explosive conditions associated with electrical installations in hazardous locations [500.5], electrical continuity of metal parts of equipment and raceways must be ensured by one of the following methods whether or not an equipment grounding conductor of the wire type is installed within the metal raceway [250.100]:

- Threaded couplings or threaded entries on enclosures [250.92(B)(2)].
- Threadless raceway couplings and connectors [250.92(B)(3)].
- Bonding the raceway to an enclosure with listed devices such as a bonding-type locknut, bonding wedge, or bushing with a bonding jumper [250.92(B)(4)].

Standard locknuts alone aren't suitable for this purpose.

(B) Bonding—Flexible Raceway. Flexible metal conduit and liquidtight flexible metal conduit must have an equipment bonding jumper of the wire type installed in accordance with 250.102. **Figure 501–4**

Author's Comment: Bonding jumpers are sized in accordance with Table 250.122, based on the rating of the overcurrent device [250.102(D)], and where installed outside of a raceway, the length of bonding jumpers must not exceed 6 ft and they must be routed with the raceway [250.102(E)(2)]. **Figure 501–5**

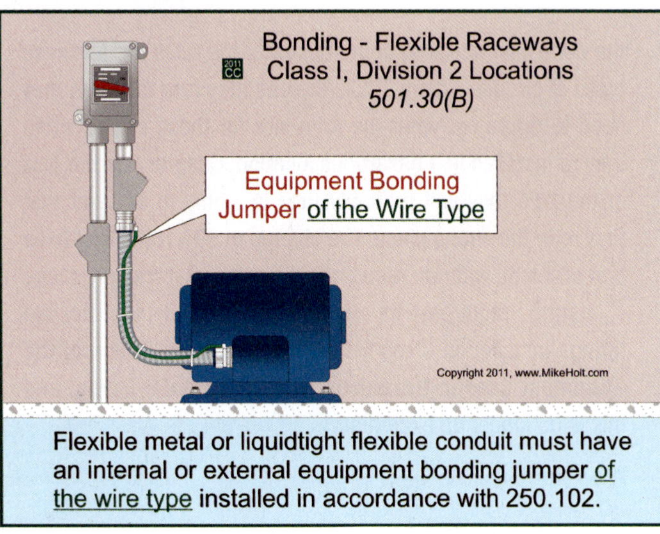

Figure 501–4

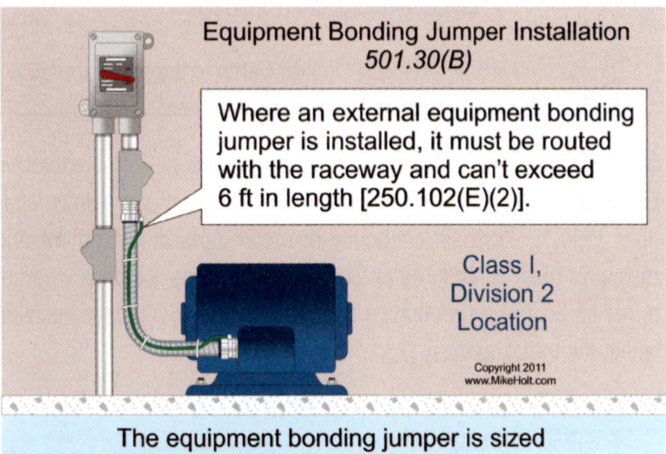

Figure 501–5

ANALYSIS: Previous editions of the *NEC* stated that, in a hazardous location, "flexible metal conduit and liquidtight flexible metal conduit shall not be used as the sole ground-fault current path." While this sounds like a great *Code* rule, it really doesn't work, due to the definition of "ground-fault current path" in 250.2. Many things are "ground-fault current paths," including the earth itself, although paths such as the earth certainly don't achieve the goal of this requirement. While the term "effective ground-fault current path" is better than the previous *NEC* language, this change makes it even simpler than that. It now tells the *Code* user exactly what to do: use a green or bare wire in or next to these flexible wiring methods.

501.140 Flexible Cord Permitted Uses

A new subsection now allows temporary portable assemblies to utilize flexible cords in Class I locations.

501.140 Flexible Cords.

(A) Permitted Uses. Flexible cord is permitted for:

(1) Portable lighting or portable utilization equipment. Figure 501–6

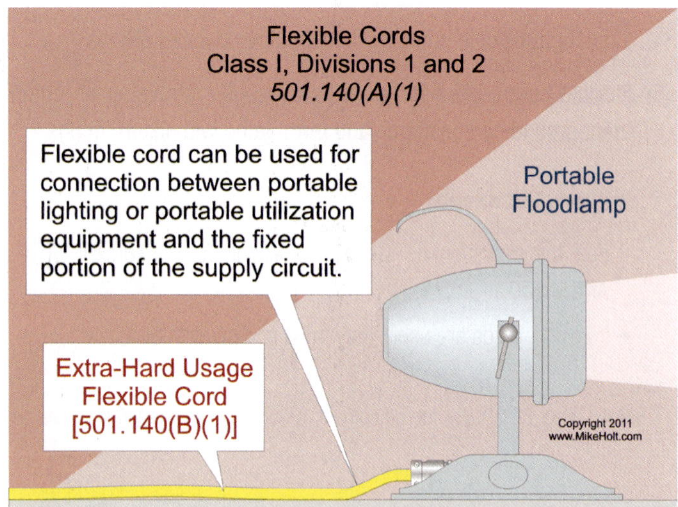

Figure 501–6

(2) In an industrial establishment where conditions of maintenance and engineering supervision ensure that only qualified persons install and service the installation where the fixed wiring methods of 501.10(A) can't provide the flexibility necessary or where necessary for mobile electrical equipment, and the flexible cord is protected by location or suitable guard.

(3) The extension within a suitable raceway between the submersible pump in a wet-pit and the power source.

(4) Electric mixers intended for travel into and out of open-type mixing tanks or vats.

(5) Temporary portable assemblies consisting of receptacles, switches, and other devices listed for the location.

ANALYSIS: Manufacturers are often asked to provide portable power carts, consisting of such items as receptacles, switches, and similar devices, for Class I locations. These carts are used during maintenance activities in areas such as refineries. The previous *Code* language didn't include a provision for this type of equipment to be supplied by a cord-and-plug-connection, due to the limitations placed on flexible cord usage. Equipment such as this will now be allowed, provided the individual components of the cart (or similar equipment) are listed for the application.

501.140(B) Flexible Cord Installation

Clarifications to the requirements of flexible cord in Class I locations have been made, and a correlating change to the new 501.140(B)(5) has been made.

501.140 Flexible Cords.

(B) Installation. If flexible cords are used, the cords must:

(1) Be listed for extra-hard usage.

(2) Contain an equipment grounding conductor.

(3) Be supported so that no tension will be transmitted to the terminal connections.

(4) In Division 1 or Division 2 locations where the boxes, fittings, or enclosures are required to be explosionproof, the cord must terminate with a cord connector or attachment plug listed for the location, or a cord connector or attachment plug with a seal that's listed for the location. In Division 2 locations where explosionproof equipment isn't required, the cord can terminate with a listed cord connector or attachment plug.

(5) Where 501.140(A)(5) is applied, cords must be of continuous length from the power source to the temporary portable assembly and from the temporary portable assembly to the utilization equipment.

Author's Comment: 400.8 specifies that flexible cords must not be used for any of the following:

- As a substitute for fixed wiring.
- Run through holes in walls, structural, suspended or dropped ceilings, or floors.
- Run through doorways, windows, or similar openings.
- Attached to the building surface except as allowed by 368.8 for extensions from busways.
- Concealed behind building walls, floors, ceilings, or located above suspended or dropped ceilings.
- Within a raceway.

ANALYSIS: While the *NEC* was clear on the topic of requiring seals on flexible cords in Class I locations, it didn't address cord connectors and attachment plugs. Even though it seems obvious that a cord connector/attachment plug in a Class I location would have to be listed for the application, the *Code* didn't clearly state this requirement. This change makes it clear that such a cord connector or attachment plug must be listed for the location in which it's installed.

The change to (B)(5) is a correlating change to the one that occurred in 501.140(A)(5). When the temporary portable assemblies discussed in that section are used, the cord must be a single, continuous length.

NOTES

Class II HAZARDOUS LOCATIONS

INTRODUCTION TO ARTICLE 502—CLASS II HAZARDOUS LOCATIONS

If an area has combustible dust present, it may be classified as a Class II location.

Examples of such locations include flour mills, grain silos, coal bins, wood pulp storage areas, and munitions plants.

Article 502 follows a logical arrangement similar to that of Article 501. Article 502 provides guidance in selecting equipment and wiring methods for Class II locations, including distinctions between Class II Division 1 and Class II Division 2 requirements.

502.10 Wiring Methods

Some editorial changes have been made to this section, and listing requirements have been added for cables and cords.

502.10 Wiring Methods.

(A) Class II, Division 1.

(1) General. The following wiring methods can be installed in a Class II, Division 1 location: Figure 502–1

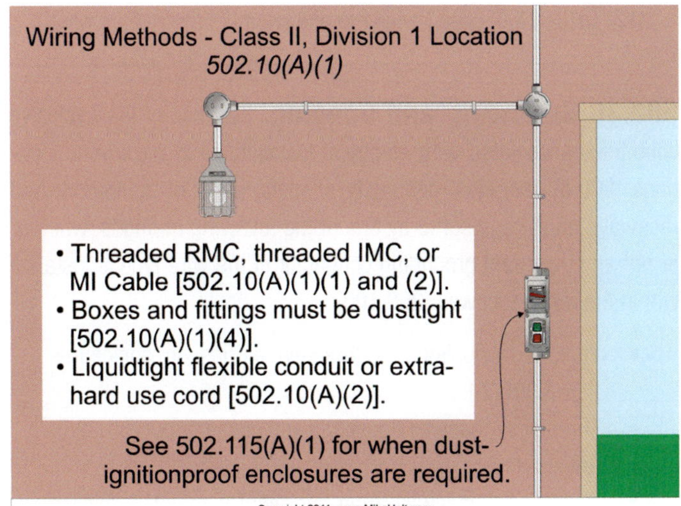

Figure 502–1

(1) Threaded rigid metal conduit or threaded intermediate metal conduit.

(2) MI cable terminated with fittings listed for the location.

(3) In industrial establishments with restricted public access where only qualified persons will service the installation, MC-HL cable listed for use in Class II, Division 1 locations, with a gas/vapor-tight continuous corrugated metallic sheath, an overall jacket of suitable polymeric material, a separate equipment grounding conductor(s) in accordance with 250.122, and terminated with fittings listed for the application.

(4) Boxes and fittings in which taps, joints, or terminal connections are made, or used in locations where dusts are of a combustible, electrically conductive nature, must be dust-ignitionproof (identified for Class II locations). Boxes and fittings that don't contain taps, joints, or terminal connections must be dusttight and must have threaded entries for raceway or cable terminations.

(2) Flexible Wiring. If flexibility is necessary, any of the following wiring methods are permitted in a Class II, Division 2 location:

(1) Dusttight flexible connectors.

(2) Liquidtight flexible metal conduit with listed dusttight fittings.

(3) Liquidtight flexible nonmetallic conduit with listed fittings.

(4) Type MC cable with an impervious jacket and termination fittings listed for Class II, Division 1 locations.

(5) Flexible cords listed for extra-hard usage, containing an equipment grounding conductor and terminated with listed dusttight fittings. The flexible cord must be installed in accordance with 502.140.

Note: See 502.30(B) for the equipment grounding requirements where flexible conduit is used.

(B) Class II, Division 2. Figure 502–2

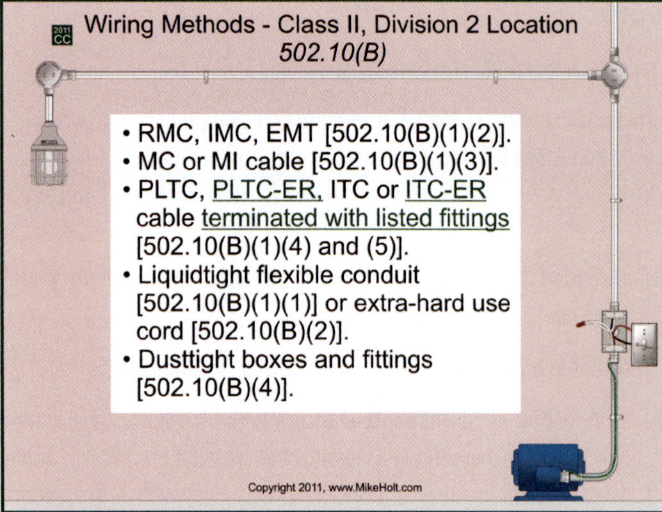

Figure 502–2

(1) General. In Class II, Division 2 locations, the following wiring methods are permitted:

(1) Any of the wiring methods in 502.10(A).

(2) Rigid metal conduit, intermediate metal conduit (either threaded or with compression fittings), electrical metallic tubing with compression fittings, and dusttight wireways.

(3) Type MC or MI cable with listed termination fittings.

(4) Type PLTC and PLTC-ER cable terminated with listed fittings in accordance with Article 725.

(5) Type ITC and ITC-ER cable terminated with listed fittings as permitted in 727.4.

(2) Flexible Wiring. If flexibility is required, the following wiring methods are permitted in a Class II, Division 2 location [502.10(A)(2)]:

(1) Dusttight flexible connectors.

(2) Liquidtight flexible metal conduit with listed fittings.

(3) Liquidtight flexible nonmetallic conduit with listed fittings.

(4) Interlocked armor Type MC cable having an overall jacket of suitable polymeric material and terminated with listed fittings.

(5) Flexible cord listed for extra-hard usage, containing an equipment grounding conductor and terminated with listed fittings.

(4) Boxes and Fittings. Boxes and fittings in Class II, Division 2 areas must be dusttight.

Author's Comment: A standard weatherproof box with a cover and gasket meets this requirement.

ANALYSIS: Article 725 deals with Class 1, Class 2, and Class 3 Remote-Control, Signaling, and Power-Limited Circuits. When the *Code* user needs to figure out what the rules are for these types of circuits, Article 725 is where they go. When they need to figure out what the rules are for these cables when they're installed in a hazardous location, Chapter 5 is the part of the *NEC* they would probably turn to...only to find out that they're in the wrong place. This change fixes that problem, with the result being a more user friendly *Code.*

Listing requirements have been added for several of the methods discussed in this section, providing consistency with the other hazardous location rules.

502.30(B) Bonding—Flexible Raceway

This section has been revised to add clarity to the requirement.

502.30 Grounding and Bonding. Because of the explosive conditions associated with electrical installations in hazardous locations [500.5], electrical continuity of metal parts of equipment and raceways must be ensured by one of the following methods, whether or not an equipment grounding conductor of the wire type is installed within the metal raceway [250.100]:

- Threaded couplings or threaded entries on enclosures [250.92(B)(2)].
- Threadless raceway couplings and connectors [250.92(B)(3)].
- Bonding the raceway to an enclosure with listed devices such as a bonding-type locknut, bonding wedge, or bushing with a bonding jumper [250.92(B)(4)].

Standard locknuts alone aren't suitable for this purpose.

(B) Bonding—Flexible Raceway. Liquidtight flexible metal conduit must have an equipment bonding jumper of the wire type in accordance with 250.102. **Figure 502–3**

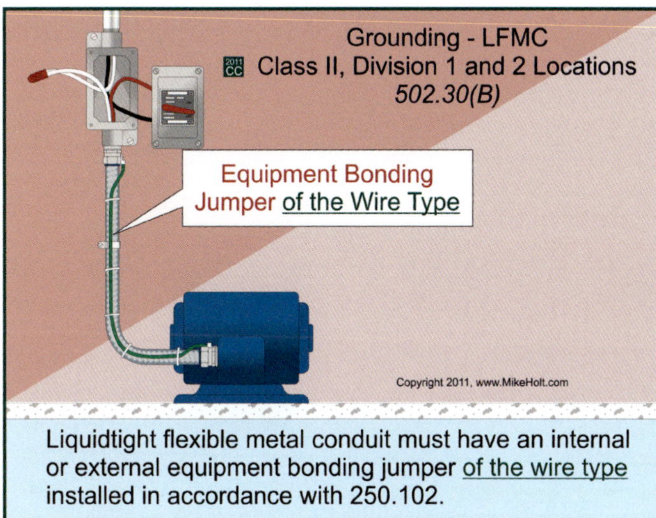

Figure 502–3

Author's Comment: Bonding jumpers are sized in accordance with Table 250.122, based on the rating of the overcurrent device [250.102(D)], and where installed outside of a raceway, the length of bonding jumpers must not exceed 6 ft and they must be routed with the raceway [250.102(E)(2)]. **Figure 502–4**

ANALYSIS: Previous editions of the *NEC* stated that, in a hazardous location, "liquidtight flexible metal conduit shall not be used as the sole ground-fault current path." While this sounds like a great *Code* rule, it really doesn't work, due to the definition of "ground-fault current path" in 250.2. Many things are "ground-fault current paths," including the earth itself, although paths such as the earth certainly don't achieve the goal of this requirement. While the term "effective ground-fault current path" is better than the previous *NEC* language, this change makes it even simpler than that. It now tells the *Code* user exactly what to do: use a green or bare wire in or next to these flexible wiring methods.

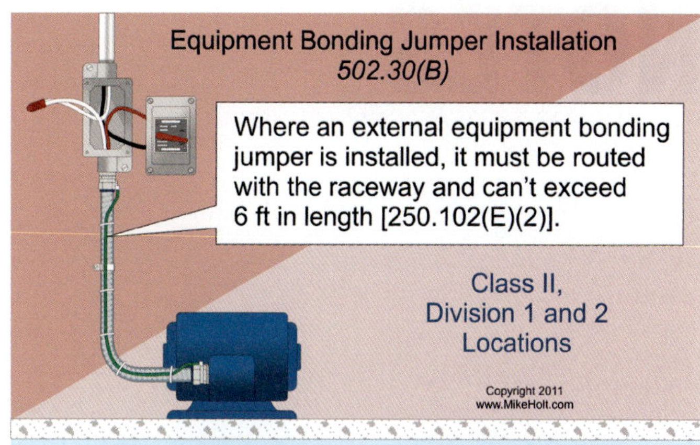

Figure 502–4

502.140 Flexible Cords

Clarifications to the requirements of flexible cords in Class II locations have been made.

502.140 Flexible Cords. Flexible cords used in Class II, Division 1 and 2 locations must:

(1) Be of a type listed for extra-hard usage,

(2) Contain an equipment grounding conductor,

(3) Be supported in such a manner that there will be no tension on the terminal connections, and

(4) In Division 1 locations, the cord must terminate with a cord connector listed for the location or a listed cord connector installed with a seal listed for the location. In Division 2 locations, the cord must be terminated with a listed dusttight cord connector.

ANALYSIS: While the *Code* was clear on the topic of requiring seals on flexible cords in Class II locations, it didn't address cord connectors and attachment plugs. Even though it seems obvious that a cord connector/attachment plug in a Class II location would have to be listed for the application, the *NEC* didn't clearly state this requirement. This change makes it clear that such a cord connector or attachment plug must be listed for the location in which it's installed.

NOTES

Class III HAZARDOUS LOCATIONS

INTRODUCTION TO ARTICLE 503—CLASS III HAZARDOUS LOCATIONS

The Class III location definition is cumbersome, and many people have a hard time grasping what it means. If you have easily ignitible fibers/flyings present, you may have a Class III location. Examples of such locations include sawmills, textile mills, and fiber processing plants. In many cases, the distinction between Class II and Class III locations may be simply the size of the particulate. A new definition added to Article 502 defines dust based on the size of the particles, so the same material (such as sawdust) may be subject to Article 503 if the predominant material is "larger" than the definition of dust which is covered by Article 502.

503.10(A) Wiring Class III, Division 1

Additional wiring methods have been added to the list of acceptable methods in Class III locations, and the section has been restructured. Listing requirements have also been added.

503.10 Wiring Methods. The wiring methods permitted in Class III locations include:

(A) Class III, Division 1 Location.

(1) General. Figure 503–1

Wiring Methods - Class III, Division 1 Location
503.10(A)

- RMC, PVC, IMC, EMT, and dusttight wireways [503.10(A)(1)(1)].
- Types MC, MI, PLTC and PLTC-ER, ITC, UTC-ER cables terminated with listed fittings [503.10(A)(1)(2)].
- Boxes and fittings must be dusttight [503.10(A)(2)].
- Dusttight flexible connectors, LFMC, LFNC, interlock MC cable with suitable overall jacket, and flexible cord [503.10(A)(3)].

Copyright 2011, www.MikeHolt.com

Figure 503–1

(1) Rigid metal conduit, PVC, XW-type RTRC conduit, intermediate metal conduit, electrical metallic tubing, dusttight wireways.

(2) Type MC or MI cable terminated with listed fittings.

(3) Type PLTC and PLTC-ER cable terminated with listed fittings in accordance with Article 725.

(4) Type ITC and ITC-ER cable terminated with listed fittings as permitted in 727.4.

(2) Boxes and Fittings. Boxes and fittings must be dusttight.

Author's Comment: A standard weatherproof box with a cover and gasket meets this requirement.

(3) Flexible Connections.

(1) Dusttight flexible connectors.

(2) Liquidtight flexible metal conduit with listed fittings.

(3) Liquidtight flexible nonmetallic conduit with listed fittings.

(4) Interlocked armor Type MC cable having an overall jacket of suitable polymeric material and installed with listed dusttight termination fittings.

(5) Flexible cord in accordance with 503.140.

ANALYSIS: As newer conduit types are added to the *NEC*, certain rules require updating to catch up to previous changes. PVC conduit has been allowed for quite some time, and with this change, type RTRC-XW is also permitted. New to this edition of the *Code*, type MC cable with an overall jacket meeting the requirements of this section is also permitted.

Article 725 deals with Class 1, Class 2, and Class 3 Remote-Control, Signaling, and Power-Limited Circuits. When the *NEC* user needs to figure out what the rules are for these types of circuits, Article 725 is where they go. When they need to figure out what the rules are for these cables when they're installed in a hazardous location, Chapter 5 is the part of the *Code* they will probably turn to...only to find out that they're in the wrong place. This change fixes that problem, with the result being a more user friendly *NEC*.

Lastly, listing requirements for fittings have been added, in order to be consistent with other similar provisions in the *Code*.

503.30(B) Bonding—Flexible Raceway

This section has been revised to add clarity to the requirement.

503.30 Grounding and Bonding. Because of the explosive conditions associated with electrical installations in hazardous locations [500.5], electrical continuity of metal parts of equipment and raceways must be ensured by one of the following methods, whether or not an equipment grounding conductor of the wire type is installed within the metal raceway [250.100]:

- Threaded couplings or threaded entries on enclosures [250.92(B)(2)].
- Threadless raceway couplings and connectors [250.92(B)(3)].
- Bonding the raceway to an enclosure with listed devices such as a bonding-type locknut, bonding wedge, or bushing with a bonding jumper [250.92(B)(4)].

Standard locknuts alone aren't suitable for this purpose.

(B) Bonding—Flexible Raceway. Liquidtight flexible metal conduit must have an equipment bonding jumper of the wire type in accordance with 250.102. **Figure 503–2**

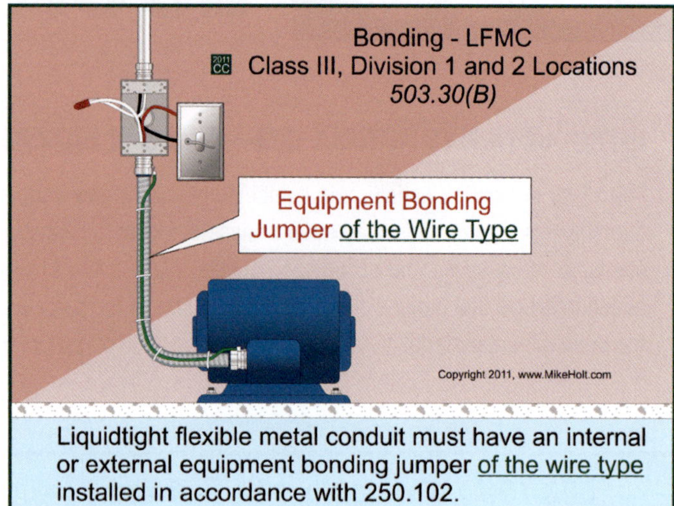

Figure 503-2

Author's Comment: Bonding jumpers are sized in accordance with Table 250.122, based on the rating of the overcurrent device [250.102(D)], and where installed outside of a raceway, the length of bonding jumpers must not exceed 6 ft and they must be routed with the raceway [250.102(E)(2)]. **Figure 503–3**

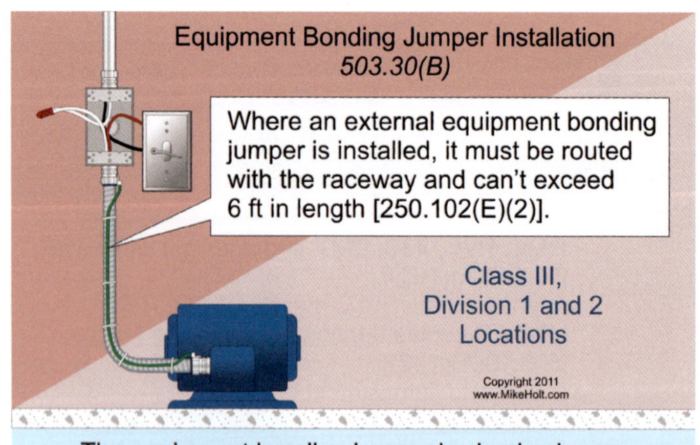

Figure 503–3

ANALYSIS: Previous editions of the *NEC* stated that, in a hazardous location, "liquidtight flexible metal conduit shall not be used as the sole ground-fault current path." While this sounds like a great *Code* rule, it really doesn't work, due to the definition of "ground-fault current path" in 250.2. Many things are "ground-fault current paths," including the earth itself, although paths such as the earth certainly don't achieve the goal of this requirement. While the term "effective ground-fault current path" is better than the previous *NEC* language, this change makes it even simpler than that. It now tells the *Code* user exactly what to do: use a green or bare wire in or next to these flexible wiring methods.

503.140 Flexible Cords

Clarifications to the requirements of flexible cords in Class III locations have been made.

503.140 Flexible Cords. Flexible cords must:

(1) Be of the extra-hard usage type.

(2) Contain an equipment grounding conductor.

(3) Be supported so there's no tension on the terminal connections.

(4) Be terminated with a listed dusttight connector.

ANALYSIS: While the *NEC* was clear on the topic of requiring suitable means of excluding fibers/flyings in flexible cords in Class III locations, it didn't address cord connectors and attachment plugs. Even though seems obvious that a cord connector/attachment plug in a Class III location would have to be listed for the application, the *Code* didn't clearly state this requirement. This change makes it clear that such a cord connector or attachment plug must be listed for the location in which it's installed.

NOTES

Motor Fuel DISPENSING FACILITIES

INTRODUCTION TO ARTICLE 514—MOTOR FUEL DISPENSING FACILITIES

Facilities where fuel is dispensed from storage tanks into the fuel tanks of vehicles must conform to Article 514.

What's most striking about Article 514 is the large table that makes up about half of it. This table doesn't provide any electrical requirements, list any electrical specifications, or address any electrical equipment. What it does tell you is how to classify a motor fuel dispensing area based on the equipment contained therein. The rest of this article contains specific provisions, and refers to other articles that must be applied.

Author's Comment: Diesel fuel isn't a flammable liquid. Therefore, diesel dispensing equipment and associated wiring aren't required to comply with the hazardous location requirements of Article 514.

514.11 Circuit Disconnects

Changes made to this section will require a disconnecting means for communications, data, and video circuits for dispensing equipment.

514.11 Circuit Disconnect.

(A) General. Each circuit that leads to or through a dispenser including power, communications, data, and video circuits and equipment must have a clearly identified and readily accessible switch or other approved means located remote from the dispenser to disconnect simultaneously all conductors of the circuit, including the neutral conductor. Single-pole breakers with handle ties must not be used for this purpose.

Author's Comment: See the definitions of "Accessible, Readily" and "Neutral Conductor" in Article 100.

ANALYSIS: Flammable and combustible liquid produced vapors will ignite when heated to the correct temperature (at the correct volatile mixture). This type of ignition can occur from circuits that most users of electricity consider "safe," such as a Class 2 power-limited circuit. While a Class 2 circuit is safe from an electrical shock and fire perspective, it's still capable of igniting the vapors present in the environment of a Class I location, such as those found in fuel dispensing areas.

This change now clarifies that all circuits to the dispensing equipment in fuel dispensing facilities, must be provided with a means to disconnect them from their power supply regardless of the voltage level.

514.13 Maintenance and Service of Dispensing Equipment

Changes made to this section will clarify that a disconnecting means for communications, data and video circuits for dispensing equipment is required.

514.13 Maintenance and Service of Dispensing Equipment. Each dispensing device must be provided with a means to remove all external voltage sources, including power, communications, data, and video circuits and equipment, during periods of maintenance and service of the dispensing equipment. The disconnecting means must be capable of being locked in the open position, and it's not required to be within sight from the dispenser. Remote pump control wiring for each dispenser must be kept isolated to prevent electrical feedback. Figure 514–1

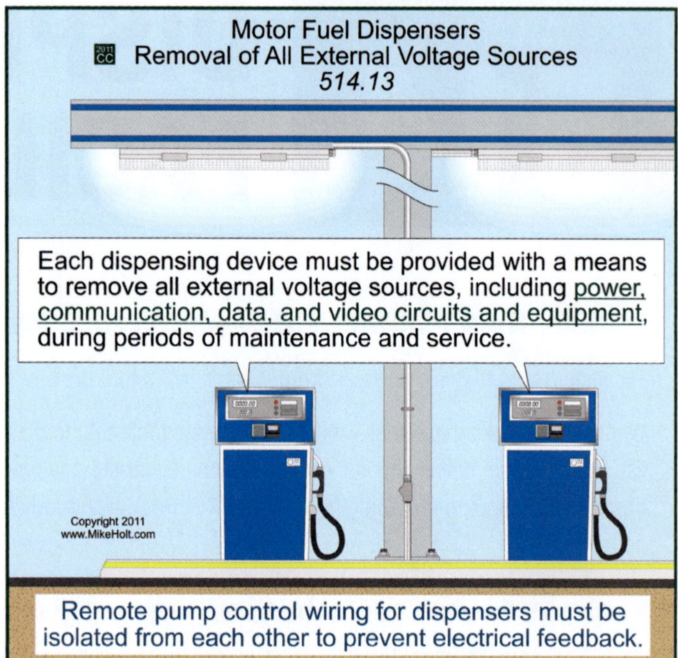

Figure 514–1

ANALYSIS: The *NEC* has long required that a disconnect be used in an effort to isolate the dispensing equipment from any voltage sources present. Although subtle, this includes low-voltage and limited-energy circuits, such as data and communications. With this change the requirement becomes quite clear, although (due to misunderstandings of previous text) many *Code* users will probably view this as a new requirement.

Health Care FACILITIES

INTRODUCTION TO ARTICLE 517—HEALTH CARE FACILITIES

Health care facilities differ from other types of buildings in many important ways. Article 517 is primarily concerned with those parts of health care facilities where patients are examined and treated. Whether those facilities are permanent or movable, they still fall under this article. However, Article 517 wiring and protection requirements don't apply to business offices, patient sleeping areas, or waiting rooms. It doesn't apply to animal veterinary facilities either.

Article 517 contains many specialized definitions that only apply to health care facilities. While you don't need to be able to quote these definitions, you should have a clear understanding of what the terms mean. As you study Parts II and III, keep in mind the special requirements of hospitals and why these requirements exist. The requirements in Parts II and III are highly detailed and not intuitively obvious. These are three of the main objectives of Article 517, Parts II and III:

- Maximize the physical and electromagnetic protection of wiring by requiring metal raceways.
- Minimize electrical hazards by keeping the voltage potential between patients' bodies and medical equipment low. This involves many specific steps, beginning with 517.11.
- Minimize the negative effects of power interruptions by establishing specific requirements for essential electrical systems.

Part IV addresses gas anesthesia stations. The main objective of Part IV is to prevent ignition. Part V addresses X-ray installations and really has two main objectives:

- Provide adequate ampacity and protection for the branch circuits.
- Address the safety issues inherent in high-voltage equipment installations.

Part VI provides requirements for low-voltage communications systems, such as fire alarms and intercoms. The main objective there's to prevent compromising those systems with inductive couplings or other sources of interference. Part VII provides requirements for isolated power systems; the main objective is to keep them actually isolated.

Be aware that the *NEC* is just one of the standards that apply to health care locations, and there may be additional requirements from other standards and special requirements for sophisticated equipment.

517.12 Wiring Methods

A change has been made to this section to fix a language error.

517.12 Wiring Methods. Wiring methods must comply with the Chapter 1 through 4 provisions, except as modified in this article [90.3].

ANALYSIS: This section, like many others in Chapters 5 through 7, reiterates the requirement of 90.3, which tells the *Code* user that they supplement or modify the general rules of Chapters 1 through 4. This section said (in previous editions) that the *requirements* of Chapters 1 through 4 applied to Article 517 except as modified by Article 517. Although it's a very subtle point, one could argue that only the requirements (not the allowances) of Chapters 1 through 4 pertained. This is certainly not the intent of this rule, nor has it ever been. This change closes a loophole that very, very few *NEC* users probably realized existed at all.

517.13(B) Insulated Equipment Grounding Conductor

This subsection has been changed into a list format, and changes have been made for clarity.

517.13 Grounding of Equipment in Patient Care Areas. Wiring in patient care areas must comply with (A) and (B):

Author's Comment: Patient care areas include patient rooms as well as examining rooms, therapy areas, treatment rooms, and some patient corridors. They don't include business offices, corridors, lounges, day rooms, dining rooms, or similar areas not classified as patient care areas [517.2].

(A) Wiring Methods. All branch circuits serving patient care areas must be provided with an effective ground-fault current path by installing circuits that serve patient care areas in a metal raceway or cable having a metallic armor or sheath that qualifies as an equipment grounding conductor in accordance with 250.118. Figure 517–1

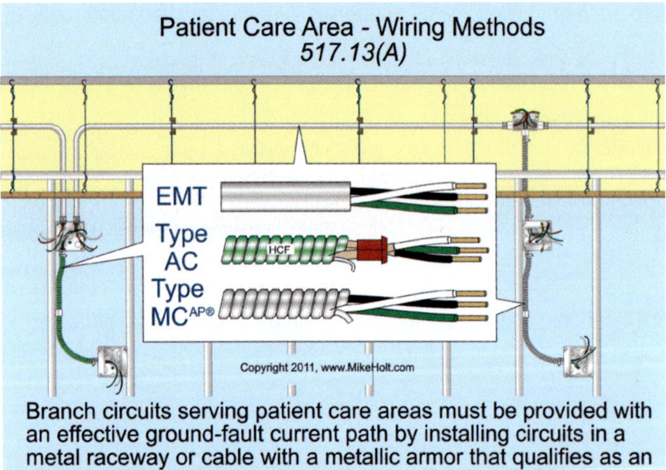

Figure 517–1

Author's Comments:

- The metal outer sheath of AC cable is listed as an equipment grounding conductor because it contains an internal bonding strip in direct contact with the metal sheath of the cable [250.118(8)]. Figure 517–2A

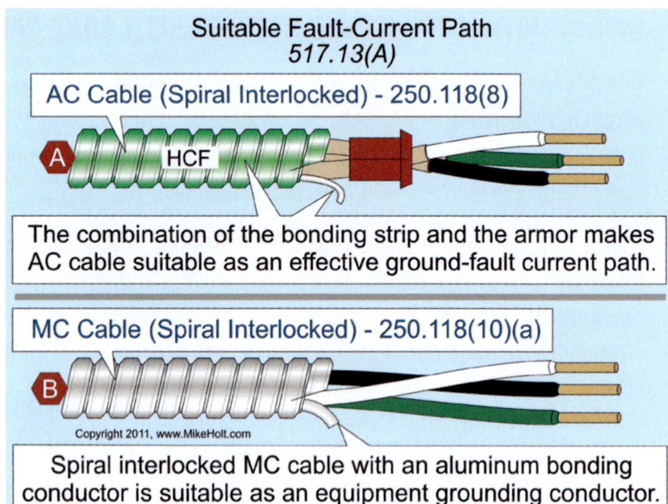

Figure 517–2

- The metal outer sheath of interlocked Type MC cable isn't listed as an equipment grounding conductor unless it contains an uninsulated equipment grounding/bonding conductor and it's listed and identified as an equipment grounding conductor. Once the bare aluminum grounding/bonding conductor exits the cable, it can be cut off because it no longer serves any purpose, Figure 517–2B. In addition, the effective ground-fault current path must be maintained by the use of fittings specifically listed for the cable [330.40]. See 300.12, 300.15, and 330.100.

(B) Insulated Equipment Grounding Conductor.

(1) General. The following must be directly connected to an insulated copper equipment grounding conductor that's installed with the branch-circuit conductors in wiring methods required in 517.13(A).

Ex: An insulated equipment bonding jumper from a receptacle that directly connects to the equipment grounding conductor is permitted.

(1) The grounding terminals of all receptacles. Figure 517–3

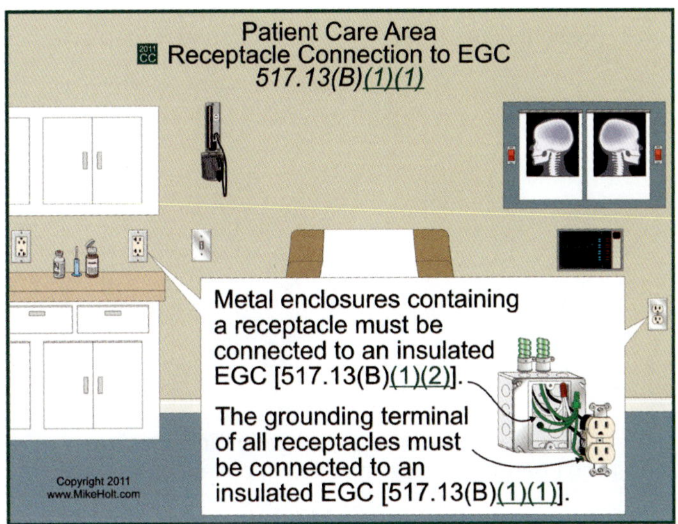

Figure 517–3

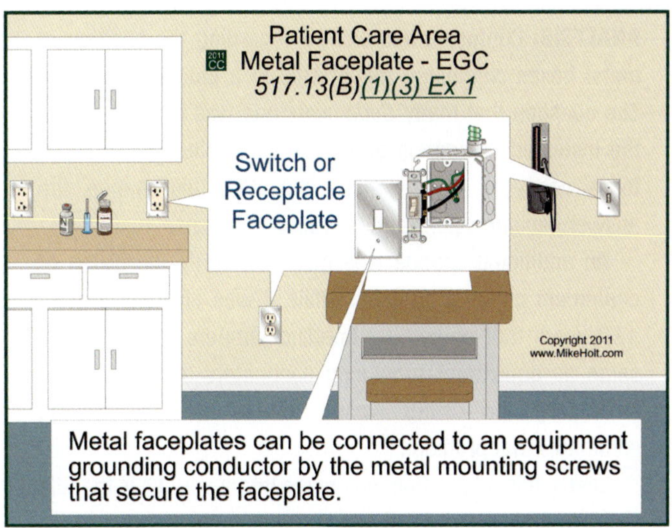

Figure 517–5

(2) Metal enclosures containing receptacles.

(3) Fixed electrical equipment operating at over 100V. Figure 517–4

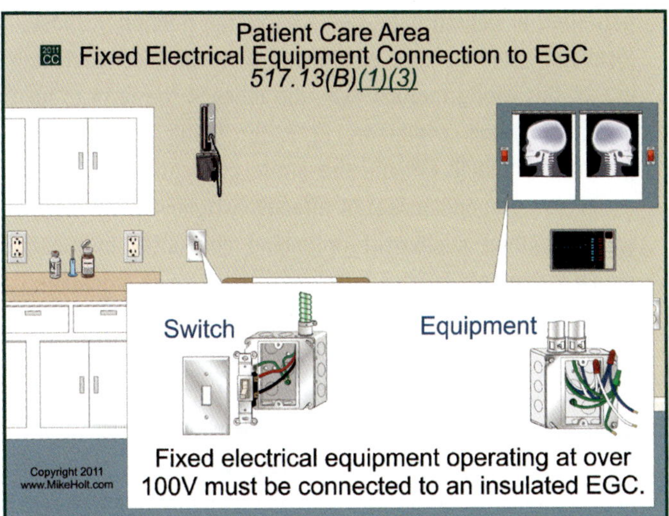

Figure 517-4

Ex 1: Metal faceplates for switches and receptacles can be connected to the equipment grounding conductor by the metal mounting screws that secure the faceplate to a metal outlet box or metal mounting yoke of switches [404.9(B)] and receptacles [406.4(C)]. Figure 517–5

Ex 2: Luminaires located more than 7½ ft above the floor can be connected to the equipment grounding return path complying with 517.13(A), without being connected to an insulated equipment grounding conductor.

(2) Sizing. Equipment grounding conductors and equipment bonding jumpers must be sized in accordance with 250.122. Figure 517–6

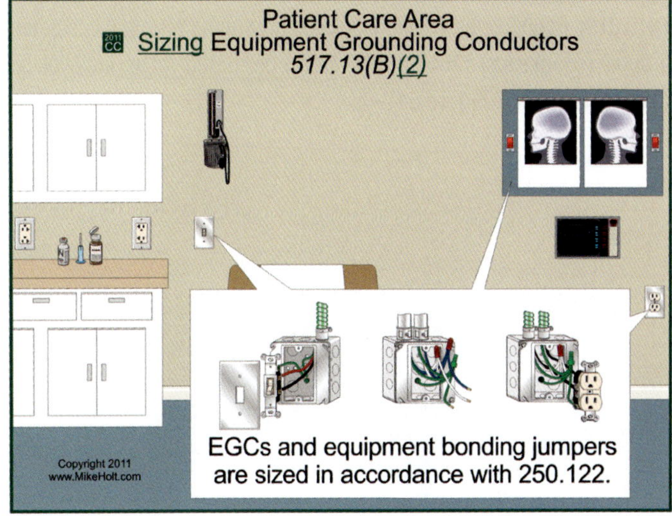

Figure 517–6

ANALYSIS: Confusion has existed regarding the bonding of metal boxes containing receptacles in a patient care area. The question that many *Code* users had was whether or not the insulated equipment grounding conductor was required to be connected to the metal box. With this change, the answer becomes clear, and that answer is "yes."

An additional change was made to clarify the sizing of equipment bonding jumpers. While it was obvious to most *NEC* users that equipment bonding jumpers are sized the same as equipment grounding conductors in these areas, technically the sizing wasn't addressed. This change eliminates that problem.

Lastly, this subsection was made into a very user friendly "list" format, for ease of reading and understanding. Few people disagree that lists are easier to read and comprehend than long sentences and paragraphs.

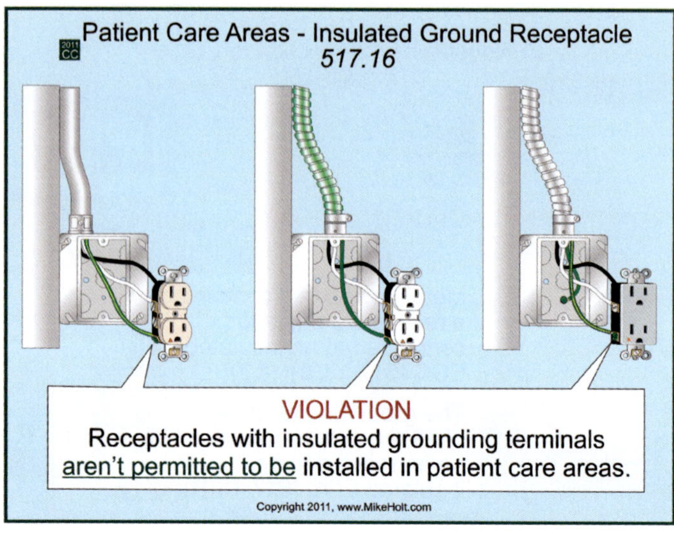

Figure 517–7

517.16 Receptacles with Insulated Grounding Terminal

Receptacles with insulated grounding terminals are no longer allowed in a patient care area.

517.16 Receptacles With Insulated Grounding Terminals. Receptacles having insulated grounding terminals (isolated ground receptacles) [250.146(D)] aren't permitted to be installed in patient care areas. Figure 517–7

ANALYSIS: In a rather substantial change to the health care provisions, isolated ground receptacles are no longer permitted in patient care area. The wiring method in these locations requires two equipment grounding conductors: one of the wiring method type, the other in the form of an insulated green conductor [517.13]. Using an isolated ground receptacle defeats the entire concept of this dual equipment ground concept by effectively removing the metal wiring method equipment grounding conductor. In these areas, the patient is often involved in an invasive procedure, meaning the human skin is broken, typically by an incision. When this is the case the patient is much more vulnerable to electric shock. In fact, current applied directly to the circulatory system of the patient can easily cause death at current levels lower than even a GFCI will protect against. Previous editions of the *NEC* included an Informational Note telling the *Code* user that the use of these receptacles was a bad idea in these areas. With this change the *Code* rule itself now recognizes that fact prohibits the practice altogether.

PART VI. COMMUNICATIONS AND SIGNALING SYSTEMS

517.80 Patient Care Areas

A change to this section clarifies that it applies to Class 2, Class 3, and power-limited fire alarm circuits only.

517.80 Patient Care Areas. Class 2 and 3 signaling, power-limited fire alarm, and communications systems aren't required to comply with the grounding requirements of 517.13, the mechanical protection requirements of 517.30(C)(3)(5), or be enclosed in raceways.

ANALYSIS: This change is intended to clarify that a Class 2 or Class 3 signaling or communications circuit, or a power limited fire alarm circuit, need not comply with some of the requirements of Article 517. These requirements include protection by a raceway system, utilizing an insulated equipment grounding conductor, and protection from physical damage like the circuits of the emergency system. However, the wording of this change leaves some confusion regarding the rules for communications circuits, since they aren't classified as Class 2 or Class 3—they're just "communications circuits."

Additionally, the Informational Note regarding nonelectrical equipment was deleted.

517.81 Other-Than-Patient-Care Areas

This section was changed to make it more complete.

517.81 Other-Than-Patient-Care Areas. In other-than-patient-care areas, installations of communications and signaling systems must be in accordance with Chapter 7 and Chapter 8 as applicable.

ANALYSIS: This section previously let the *Code* user know that circuits and equipment (in other than patient care areas) needed to comply with the provisions of Articles 640, 725, 760, and 800 for limited-energy systems and equipment. While this reference was certainly helpful, it was also incomplete in not addressing Articles 770, 810, 820, and 830. This change answers any question that the *NEC* user may have had in this regard.

NOTES

Assembly OCCUPANCIES

INTRODUCTION TO ARTICLE 518—ASSEMBLY OCCUPANCIES

If a building or portion of a building is specifically designed or intended for the assembly of 100 or more people, it falls under Article 518. This article goes out of its way to eliminate any confusion about the occupancies to which it's intended to apply. See 518.2 for a list of examples of what occupancies are covered. Article 518 recognizes that it's much harder to evacuate 100 or more people from a burning building than to evacuate just a few people. That concept underlies much of the reasoning behind the requirements of this article.

518.3(B) Temporary Installations

Changes to this section clarify the GFCI rules.

518.3 Other Articles.

(B) Temporary Installations. Wiring for display booths in exhibit halls can be installed in accordance with Article 590. Flexible hard or extra-hard usage cords and cables can be laid on the floor where protected from contact by the general public. GFCI protection must be provided for 15A or 20A, 125V receptacles where required by this *Code*, except for temporary wiring requirements of 590.6.

Where GFCI protection is supplied by plug-and-cord-connection, the GFCI-protection device must provide a level of protection equivalent to a portable GFCI, whether assembled in the field or at the factory.

ANALYSIS: This section allows for receptacles that aren't GFCI protected in exhibition halls, such as where trade shows typically occur. The GFCI provisions of this section have been misunderstood by *Code* users that have ignored 90.3. These people have read this as allowing the GFCI protection requirements of 210.8 (for example) to be waived by this section, despite the fact that 90.3 clearly mandates that 210.8 applies. An example of this might be a kitchen trade show. Assuming that the sinks are functional, the requirements of 210.8 will apply, requiring GFCI protection for some of the receptacles. Nothing in this section waives that requirement [90.3], yet people have been confused by the point.

An additional change will require the use of "portable GFCIs" for exhibition halls. Although there were no documented incidents of injury or death, one manufacturer was able to have this *NEC* change passed.

NOTES

Carnivals, Circuses, Fairs, and SIMILAR EVENTS

INTRODUCTION TO ARTICLE 525—CARNIVALS, CIRCUSES, FAIRS, AND SIMILAR EVENTS

Article 525 covers the installation of portable wiring and equipment for carnivals, circuses, exhibitions, fairs, traveling attractions, and similar functions [525.1]. At first glance, a couple of questions arise. "Aren't these just like assembly occupancies? Why do we need Article 525 if Article 518 covers the same thing?"

Yes, these locations are similar to assembly occupancies [Article 518], but they're not the same. In fact, there are two big differences:

- Article 525 applications are temporary, while Article 518 occupancies aren't.
- Article 518 doesn't cover amusement rides and attractions, while Article 525 does.

You may want to compare these two articles to see if you can spot other similarities and differences between them. Doing so will help you understand both articles better.

525.10(B) Service Equipment Mounting and Location

The mounting requirements for service equipment at carnivals, circuses, and fairs have been clarified.

525.10 Services. Services must comply with (A) and (B):

(A) Guarding. Service equipment must not be installed where accessible to unqualified persons, unless the equipment is lockable.

> **Author's Comment:** See the definition of "Accessible" as it relates to equipment including service equipment.

(B) Mounting and Location. Service equipment must be securely fastened to a solid backing and be protected from the weather, unless of weatherproof construction.

ANALYSIS: Evidently, the phrase "mounted on solid backing" was confusing to some *Code* users. Perhaps the term "securely fastened to a solid backing" will be easier to understand.

525.21(A) Disconnecting Means

Editorial revisions to the disconnecting means provisions have been made.

525.21 Rides, Tents, and Concessions.

(A) Disconnecting Means. Each portable structure must have a readily accessible means to disconnect each portable structure from all ungrounded conductors. The disconnecting means must be located within sight of, and within 6 ft of the operator's station, and be readily accessible to the operator. Where accessible to unqualified persons, the disconnect must be lockable.

(B) Inside Tent and Concessions. Electrical wiring for lighting inside tents and concession areas must be securely installed. If subject to physical damage, the wiring must be provided with mechanical protection and lamps for general illumination must be protected from accidental breakage by a suitable luminaire or lampholder with a guard.

ANALYSIS: The disconnecting means requirements discussed in this section were revised to correlate with the new term "lockable disconnect." The only problem is, the term "lockable disconnect" wasn't added to the *Code*! Although this change was intended to be accepted only if the new term was added to the *NEC*, the addition of the term somehow found its way into this section.

525.23 GFCI Protection Required

Changes to this section make the GFCI requirements enforceable, and the allowances for receptacles without GFCI protection have been further limited.

525.23 GFCI-Protected Receptacles and Equipment.

(A) GFCI Protection Required. GFCI protection is required for the following: Figure 525–1

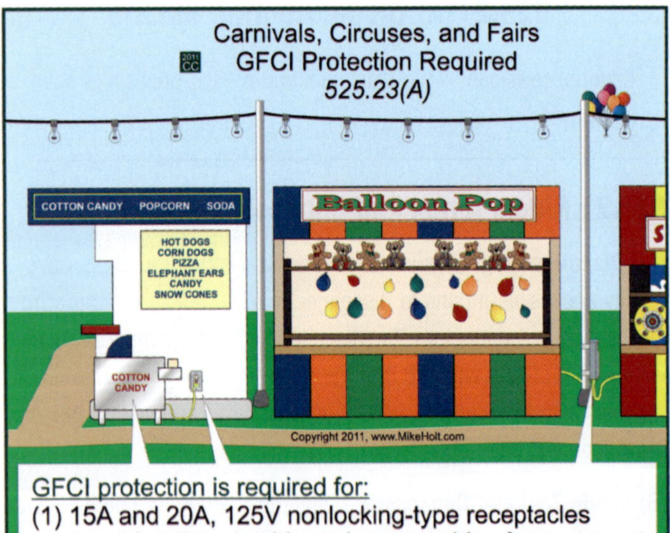

Figure 525–1

(1) All 15A and 20A, 125V, nonlocking-type receptacles used for disassembly and reassembly of amusement rides and attractions, or readily accessible to the general public.

Author's Comment: Circuits are rated 120V and receptacles are rated 125V.

(2) Equipment readily accessible to the general public if it's supplied from a 15A or 20A, 120V branch circuit.

GFCI protection can be integral with the attachment plug, power-supply cord within 12 in. of the attachment plug, or listed cord set incorporating GFCI protection.

(B) GFCI Protection Not Required. Locking-type receptacles not accessible from grade level.

(C) GFCI Protection Not Permitted. GFCI protection isn't permitted for egress lighting.

Author's Comment: The purpose of not permitting egress lighting to be GFCI protected is to ensure that exit lighting remains energized and stays illuminated.

ANALYSIS: This section was changed in a previous *Code* edition to help make the requirements for GFCI protection in carnivals, circuses, and fairs easier to understand. While these changes succeeded in making the requirements easier to read and understand, there was one glaring problem—the language used left this section without any enforceable requirements! The changes made to this section in the 2011 version create a rule in the opening statement of the section, requiring GFCI protection in the areas discussed. The requirement was also reorganized to make a more logical and consistent *NEC* rule.

GFCI protection is required for nearly all receptacles in carnivals, circuses, and fairs. One application that benefited from more relaxed use of GFCI protection is the use of receptacles for quick disconnecting and reconnecting of electrical equipment, provided that these receptacles are of the locking type. This *Code* edition now requires these receptacles to be high enough in elevation so that they aren't accessible from grade level. Considering that these receptacles are only for "quick" interchange, it leaves some people wondering if this allowance really serves any purpose. If a ladder is required to get to the receptacle, is that still a "quick" interchange?

Agricultural BUILDINGS

INTRODUCTION TO ARTICLE 547—AGRICULTURAL BUILDINGS

Two factors have a tremendous influence on the lifespan of agricultural equipment: dust and moisture.

Dust gets into mechanisms and causes premature wear. But with electricity on the scene, dust adds two other dangers: fire and explosion. Dust from hay, grain, and fertilizer is highly flammable. Litter materials, such as straw, are also highly flammable. Excrement from farm animals may cause corrosive vapors that eat at mechanical equipment and wiring methods and can cause electrical equipment to fail. For these reasons, Article 547 includes requirements for dealing with dust and corrosion.

Another factor to consider in agricultural buildings is moisture, which causes corrosion. Water is present for many reasons, including wash down. Thus, this article has requirements for dealing with wet and damp environments, and also includes other requirements. For example, it requires you to install equipotential planes in all concrete floor confinement areas of livestock buildings containing metallic equipment accessible to animals and likely to become energized.

Livestock animals have a low tolerance to small levels of stray electrical current, which can cause loss of milk production and, at times, livestock fatality. As a result, the *NEC* contains specific requirements for an equipotential plane in buildings that house livestock.

547.1 Scope

A change was made to the scope of this article to clarify when it applies.

547.1 Scope. Article 547 applies to agricultural buildings or to that part of a building or adjacent areas of similar nature as specified in (A) or (B).

(A) Excessive Dust and Dust with Water. Buildings or areas where excessive dust or dust with water may accumulate, such as areas of poultry, livestock, and fish confinement systems where litter or feed dust may accumulate.

(B) Corrosive Atmosphere. Buildings or areas where a corrosive atmosphere exists, and if the following conditions exist:

(1) Poultry and animal excrement.

(2) Areas where corrosive particles combine with water.

(3) Areas made damp or wet by periodic washing.

ANALYSIS: Previous editions of the *Code* stated that this article applied when the conditions of (A) and (B) are present. These conditions describe areas that have excessive dust and dust with water (A), and areas that contain a corrosive atmosphere (B). Either of these conditions warrants compliance with Article 547, yet the *NEC* seemed to imply that both conditions must be present before applying this article. This change removes the word "and" and replaces it with "or," which was probably the intent all along.

547.5(G) GFCI-Protected Receptacles

The allowance for non-GFCI protected receptacles was deleted.

547.5 Wiring Methods.

(G) GFCI-Protected Receptacles. GFCI protection is required for 15A and 20A, 125V, general-purpose receptacles located: **Figure 547–1**

(1) In areas having an equipotential plane in accordance with 547.10(A).

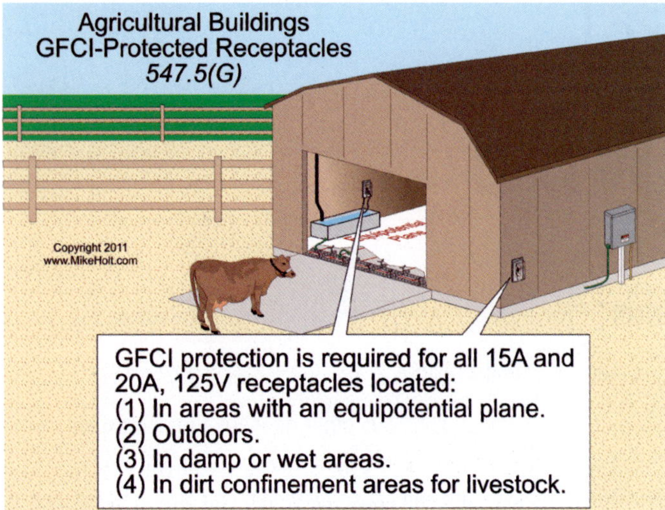

Figure 547–1

(2) Outdoors.

(3) In damp or wet locations.

(4) In dirt confinement areas for livestock.

ANALYSIS: The 2008 *NEC* added an allowance for receptacles for a dedicated load that aren't GFCI protected, provided that there was a GFCI-protected receptacle within 3 ft of the non-GFCI-protected receptacle. This baffled many users of the *Code*, as this change is exactly the opposite of the changes that were made in 210.8 in 2008. While exceptions and allowances were being removed from 210.8, this article seemed to be adding them—without any justification. GFCI devices open the circuit when there's more than 6 mA of leakage current. Because listed products should have no more than 0.50 mA of leakage (or 0.75 mA in certain instances), this exception isn't necessary.

547.8(C) Luminaires Exposed to Water

An editorial revision was made to the requirements for luminaires in locations that are subjected to water.

547.8 Luminaires.

(A) Minimize the Entrance of Dust. Luminaires must minimize the entrance of dust, foreign matter, moisture, and corrosive material.

(B) Exposed to Physical Damage. Luminaires must be protected against physical damage by a suitable guard.

(C) Exposed to Water. Luminaires exposed to water must be listed for use in wet locations.

ANALYSIS: In locations that are exposed to water from condensation or from building cleansing water and solution, luminaires must be of the appropriate type. Previous editions of the *Code* addressed this issue by requiring "watertight" luminaires. While the intent of this rule was obvious, the language could have been clearer. By changing the rule to require luminaires that are listed as suitable for use in wet locations, the rule is put into harmony with the general rules of Article 410.

547.10(B) Bonding of Equipotential Plane

The properties of the equipotential plane bonding conductor discussed in this section have been addressed.

547.10 Equipotential Planes and Bonding of Equipotential Planes.

The installation and bonding of equipotential planes must comply with (A) and (B).

(A) If an Equipotential Plane is Required. An equipotential plane must be installed in accordance with (A)(1) or (A)(2):

(1) Indoors. Indoor concrete floor confinement areas where metallic equipment is located that may become energized and is accessible to livestock. Figure 547–2

(2) Outdoors. Outdoor concrete confinement areas where metallic equipment is located that may become energized and is accessible to livestock. Figure 547–3

The equipotential plane must encompass the area around the equipment where the livestock stand.

(B) Bonding of Equipotential Planes. The equipotential plane must be connected to the building/structure's electrical grounding system. The bonding conductor used for this purpose must be solid, insulated, covered, or bare copper and not smaller than 8 AWG. The bonding conductor must terminate at pressure connectors or clamps of brass, copper, copper alloy, or an equally substantial means approved by the authority having jurisdiction [250.8].

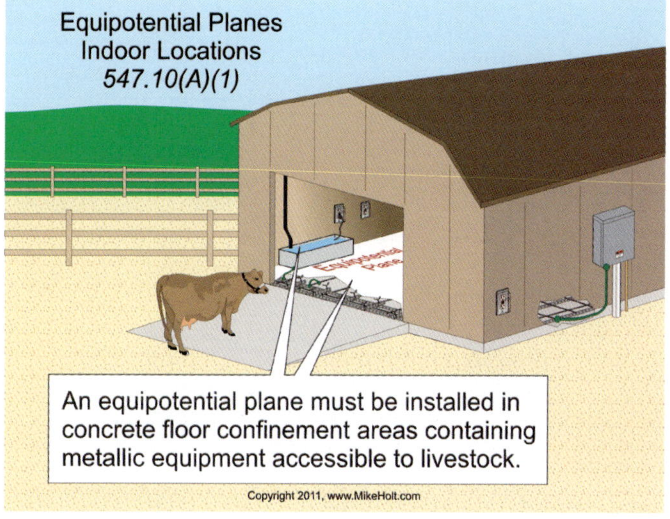

Figure 547–2

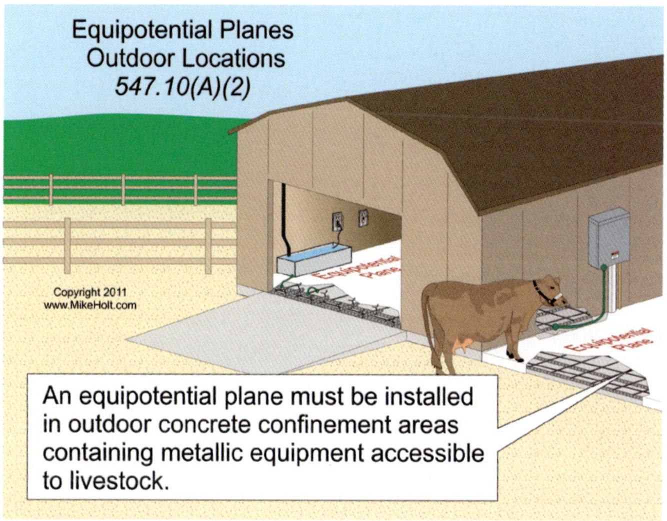

Figure 547–3

Author's Comment: See the definition of "Connector, Pressure" in Article 100.

Note 1: Methods to establish equipotential planes are described in the American Society of Agricultural and Biological Engineers Standard EP473, *Equipotential Planes in Animal Containment Areas.*

Author's Comment: This standard provides the recommendation of a voltage gradient ramp at the entrances of agricultural buildings. **Figure 547–4**

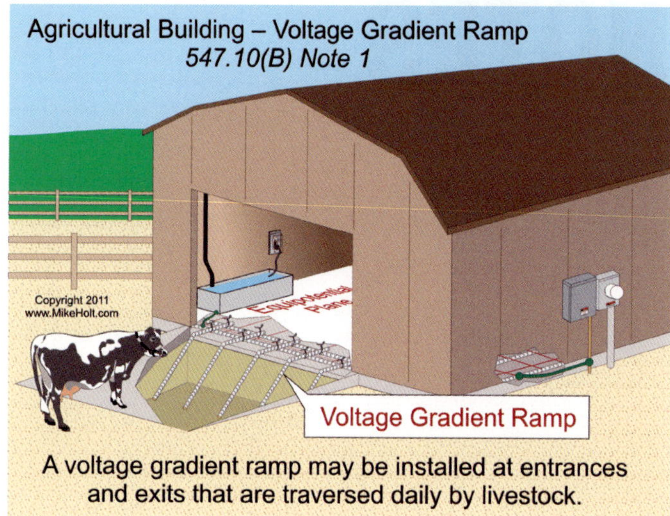

Figure 547–4

Note 2: See the American Society of Agricultural and Biological Engineers EP342.2, *Safety for Electrically Heated Livestock Waterers.*

Author's Comment: The bonding requirements contained in Article 547 are unique because of the sensitivity of livestock to stray voltage/current, especially in wet or damp concrete animal confinement areas.

In most instances the voltage difference between metal parts and the earth will be too low to present a shock hazard to persons. However, livestock might detect the voltage difference if they come in contact with the metal parts. Although potential differences may not be life threatening to the livestock, it's been reported that as little as 0.50V RMS can affect milk production.

The topic of stray voltage/current is beyond the scope of this textbook. For more information, visit www.MikeHolt.com. Click on the "Technical" link, then the "Stray Voltage" link for more details.

ANALYSIS: The equipotential bonding described in this section is quite similar to the requirements for bonding swimming pools in 680.26. Both of these rules require an 8 AWG or larger copper conductor, but only 680.26 required this conductor to be solid. This change brings these two rules into harmony on this issue by requiring that the bonding jumper used in the equipotential plane of an agricultural facility be solid.

NOTES

ARTICLE 550 Mobile Homes, Manufactured Homes, and Mobile HOME PARKS

INTRODUCTION TO ARTICLE 550—MOBILE HOMES, MANUFACTURED HOMES, AND MOBILE HOME PARKS

Among dwelling types, mobile homes have the highest rate of fire. Article 550 addresses some of the causes of those fires with the intent of reducing these statistics.

Article 550 recognizes that the same structures used for mobile or manufactured homes are also used for nondwelling purposes, such as construction offices or clinics [550.4(A)]. Thus, it excludes those structures from the 100A minimum service requirement.

According to the *National Electrical Code (NEC)* there's a difference between a mobile home and a manufactured home, and Article 550 has different requirements for each. For example, you can't locate service equipment on a mobile home. However, you can install service equipment on a manufactured home (provided you meet seven conditions). Pay close attention to the definitions in 550.2 to help you understand the *NEC* distinctions.

Mobile home and manufactured homes aren't covered by the same building codes as a site-built home, but are covered instead by HUD standards. According to HUD, both are referred to as manufactured homes and the term mobile home hasn't been used for many years. This disparity between the *NEC* and industry practices can cause confusion, so read the *NEC* carefully as you apply this article.

550.13(F) Receptacle Outlets Not Permitted

The requirements for receptacles in bathrooms of mobile and manufactured homes have been clarified.

550.13 Receptacle Outlets.

(F) Receptacle Outlets Not Permitted. Receptacle outlets aren't permitted in the following locations:

(1) Receptacle outlets must not be installed within or directly over a bathtub or shower space. Figure 550–1

(2) A receptacle must not be installed in a face-up position in any countertop.

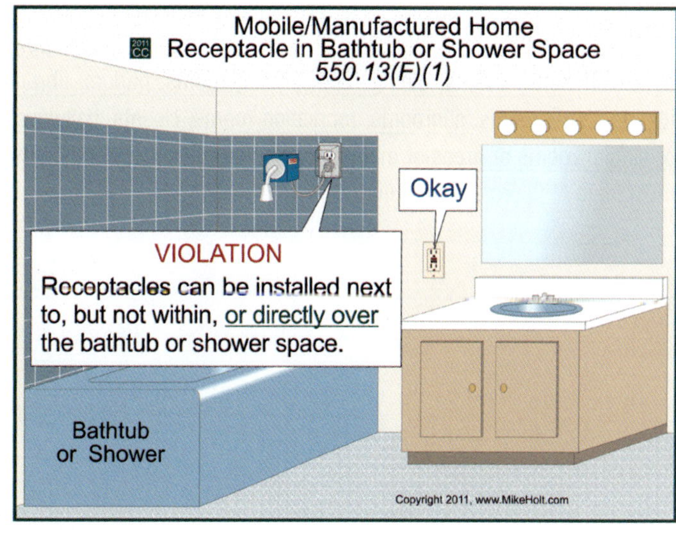

Figure 550–1

ANALYSIS: The requirements for bathroom receptacles are similar to those found In 406.9(C). Because this Article (550) doesn't receive a lot of *Code* change proposals, it's very common for requirements to become out of synch with similar requirements found elsewhere in the *NEC*. When somebody makes a proposal to the general rules in the rest of the *Code*, they typically forget to make a proposal to this article. This *NEC* change is yet another example of this phenomenon. Section 406.9(C) was recently changed to clarify that not only is a receptacle in a bathtub prohibited, but a receptacle above a bathtub is also prohibited. This change correlates these sections by adding the same text in this rule.

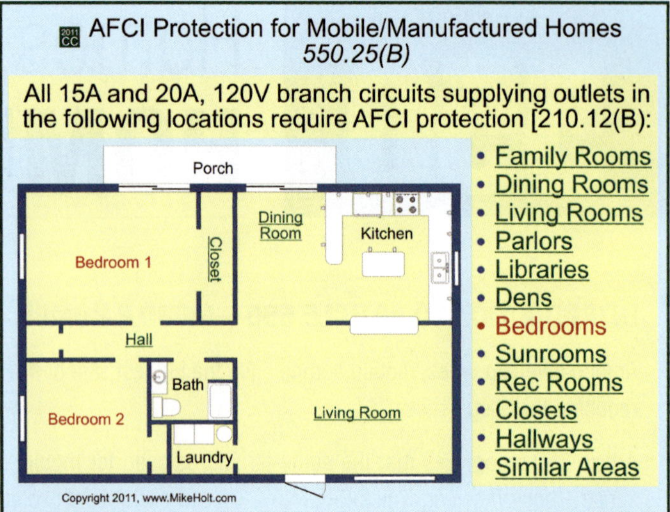

Figure 550–2

550.25 AFCI Protection

This section has been revised to "catch up" to changes made in 210.12.

550.25 AFCI Protection.

(A) Definition. Arc-fault circuit interrupters are defined in Article 100.

(B) Requirements. 15A or 20A, 120V branch circuits that supply outlets in family rooms, dining rooms, living rooms, parlors, libraries, dens, bedrooms, sunrooms, recreation rooms, closets, hallways, or similar rooms or areas of mobile homes and manufactured homes must have AFCI protection. Figure 550–2

ANALYSIS: This change is yet another example of the provisions for mobile and manufactured homes falling behind the rest of the *NEC* rules. Because this article doesn't receive a lot of *Code* change proposals, it's very common for requirements to become out of synch with similar requirements found elsewhere in the *NEC*. When somebody makes a proposal to the general rules in the rest of the *Code*, they typically forget to make a proposal to this article. In 550.25(A), a change was made to clarify that AFCIs are defined in Article 100, unlike previous editions that defined them in 210.12(A). Section 550.25(B) was changed to require AFCIs not only in bedrooms, but in all other areas required by 210.12(B). These areas include family rooms, dining rooms, living rooms, parlors, libraries, dens, bedrooms, sunrooms, recreation rooms, closets, hallways, or similar rooms.

Marinas and BOATYARDS

INTRODUCTION TO ARTICLE 555—MARINAS AND BOATYARDS

Water level isn't constant. Ocean tides rise and fall, while lakes and rivers vary in depth in response to rain. To provide power to a marina or boatyard, you must allow for these variations in water level between the point of use and the power source. Article 555 addresses this issue.

This article begins with the concept of the electrical datum plane. You might think of it as the border of a "demilitarized zone" for electrical equipment. Or, you can think of it as a line that marks the beginning of a "no man's land" where you simply don't place electrical equipment. Once you determine where this plane is, don't locate transformers, connections, or receptacles below that line.

555.2 Definitions

The types of equipment that can create a marine power outlet have been clarified.

555.2 Definitions.

Marine Power Outlet. An assembly that can include equipment such as receptacles, circuit breakers, fused switches, fuses, watt-hour meters, and distribution panelboards for marine use.

Author's Comment: This definition is necessary for the application of shore power receptacles [555.19(A)(1)] and disconnecting means [555.17(B)].

ANALYSIS: While the previous definition included most of the items that are often found in a marine power outlet, it didn't contain all of them. An example of equipment not included in the definition is a transformer. By changing the definition and adding the phrase "equipment such as," it addresses these items, without falling into the trap of creating a list of all the items—something that very seldom works as technologies change.

555.3 Ground-Fault Protection of Main Feeder

A new requirement for equipment ground-fault protection was added.

555.3 Ground-Fault Protection of Main Feeder.

The overcurrent protective device for the main marina feeder conductors must have ground-fault protection not exceeding 100 mA. If ground-fault protection is provided for each individual marina branch or feeder circuit, ground-fault protection isn't required for the main marina feeder conductors.

ANALYSIS: This new requirement was accepted after showing the technical committee evidence of over 50 deaths and 30 injuries from electrical incidents in marinas and boatyards. At first glance, it seems odd that "equipment" level protection instead of "personnel" protection is the requirement. A "Class A" GFCI device (for personnel) opens the circuit when the current to ground is between 4 mA and 6 mA, while a GFPE (for equipment) trips somewhere between 30 mA and 100 mA. While this value is too high to directly protect a human from a fatal electric shock, it will open the circuit under *most* fault conditions, which will ultimately protect humans against electric shock.

555.9 Electrical Connections

This section has been changed to create uniform language.

555.9 Electrical Connections.

Floating Piers. Electrical connections must be located not less than 12 in. above the deck of a floating pier, unless the conductor splices are contained within approved junction boxes utilizing sealed wire connector systems listed and identified for submersion located above the waterline but below the electrical datum plane for floating piers. Figures 555–1 and 555–2

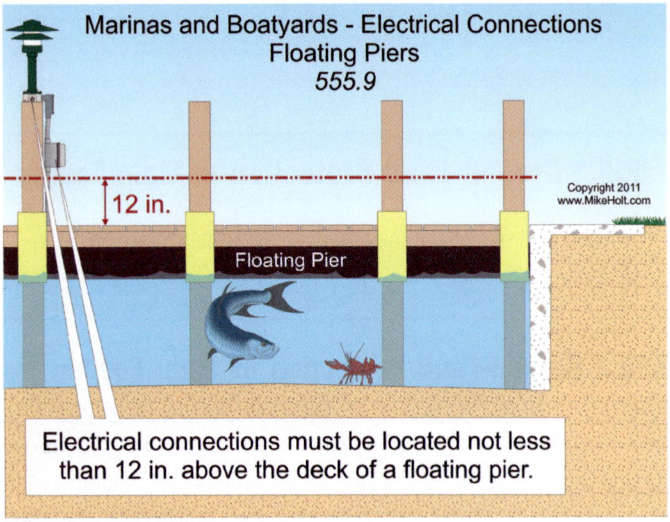

Figure 555–1

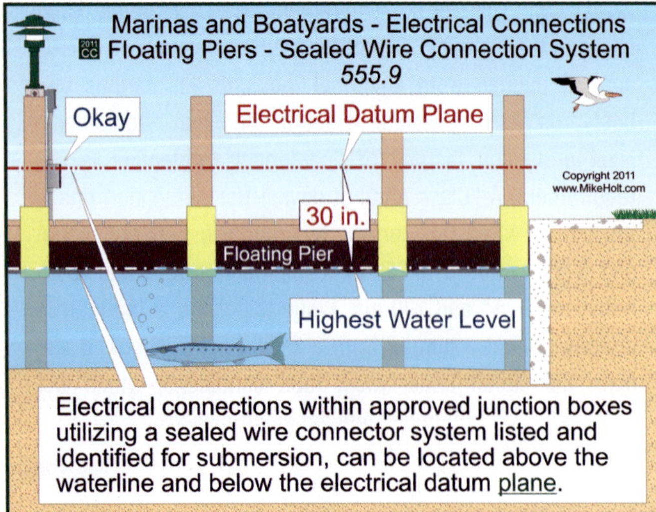

Figure 555–2

Fixed Piers. For a fixed pier, electrical connections must be located not less than 12 in. above the deck, and never below the electrical datum plane. Figure 555–3

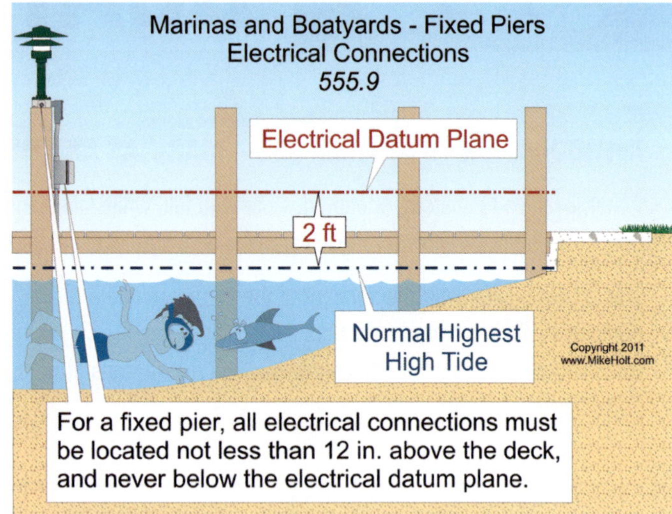

Figure 555–3

ANALYSIS: This section underwent drastic changes in the 2008 cycle. While many of them were beneficial to the *Code* user, there was a small error that needed to be addressed. The term "electrical datum plane" is used often in this article, yet the term "electrical datum field" was used here. By changing to the correct term (electrical datum plane), the *NEC* is more consistent and easier to understand.

555.19(B)(1) GFCI Protection of Receptacles

An editorial revision has been made to this requirement.

555.19 Receptacles. Receptacles must be mounted not less than 12 in. above the deck surface, and not below the electrical datum plane. Figure 555–4

(B) Other Than Shore Power.

(1) GFCI Protection of Receptacles. 15A and 20A, 125V receptacles installed outdoors, in boathouses, buildings/structures used for storage, maintenance, or repair for portable electric hand tools, electrical diagnostic equipment, or portable lighting equipment must be GFCI protected. Figure 555–5

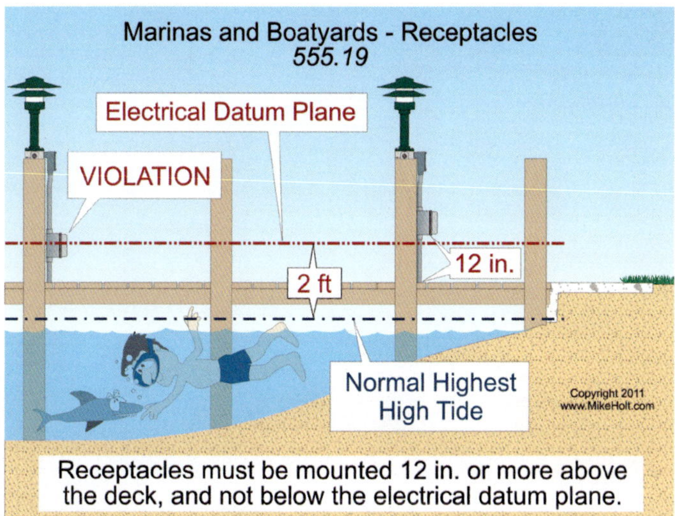

Figure 555–4

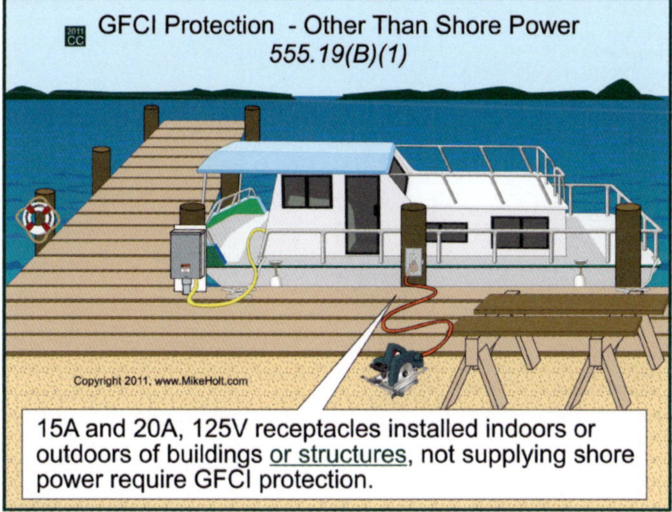

Figure 555–5

ANALYSIS: All buildings are structures, yet not all structures are buildings (see Article 100). By addressing only "buildings" in this section, there were no requirements for those structures that may not be classified as buildings. This change adds "or structures" to correct this omission.

NOTES

ARTICLE 590 Temporary INSTALLATIONS

INTRODUCTION TO ARTICLE 590—TEMPORARY INSTALLATIONS

It's a common misconception that temporary wiring represents a lower standard than that of other wiring. In truth, it merely meets a different standard. The same rules of workmanship, ampacity, and overcurrent protection apply to temporary installations as to other installations.

So, how is a temporary installation different? In one sense, it does represent a lower standard. For example, you can use Type NM cable rather than raceway-enclosed wiring without any height limitations based on the type of construction, and you don't have to put splices in boxes. You must remove a temporary installation upon completion of the purpose for which it was installed. If the temporary installation is for holiday displays, it can't last more than 90 days.

Article 590 addresses practicality and execution issues that are inherent in temporary installations, thereby making them less time consuming to install.

590.4(D)(2) Receptacles in Wet Locations

A change to this section clarifies the rules for receptacles in wet locations.

590.4 General.

(A) Services. Services must be installed in conformance with Article 230.

(B) Feeders. Open conductors aren't permitted for temporary installations; however, cable assemblies, and hard usage and extra-hard usage cords are permitted. Type NM cable, exposed or concealed, can be used in any building/structure, without any height limitations based on the type of construction. Figure 590–1

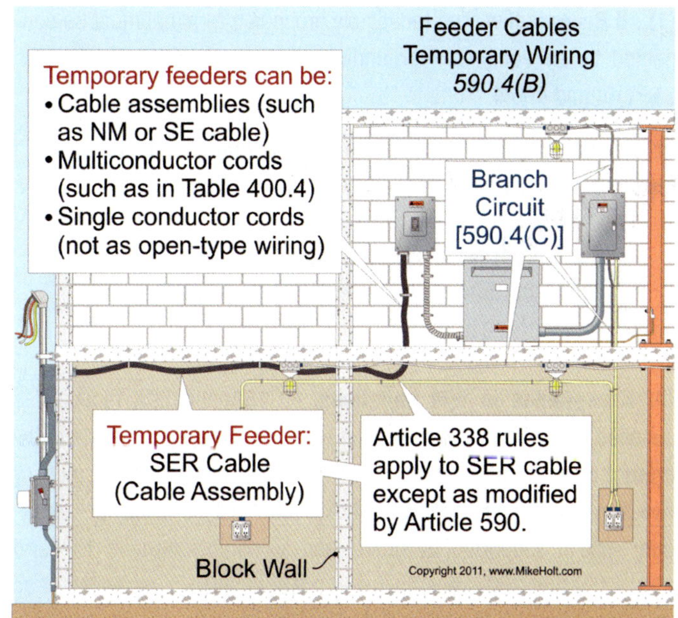

Figure 590–1

(C) Branch Circuits. Open conductors aren't permitted for temporary installations; however, cable assemblies, and hard usage and extra-hard usage cords are permitted. Type NM cable, exposed or concealed, can be used in any building/structure, without any height limitations based on the type of construction. Figure 590–2

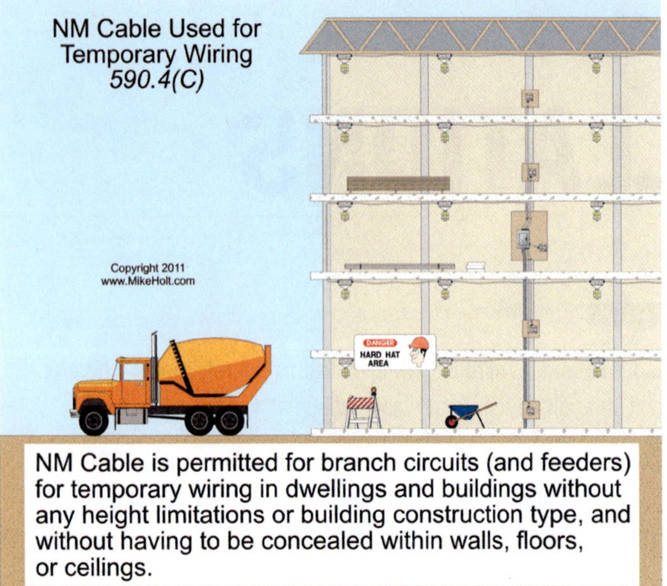

Figure 590–2

(D) Receptacles.

(1) All Receptacles. The receptacle grounding terminal must be connected to an equipment grounding conductor in accordance with 250.146 and 406.4.

On a construction site, receptacles aren't permitted to be placed on a branch circuit that supplies temporary lighting. Figure 590–3

> **Author's Comment:** This requirement is necessary so that illumination is maintained, even when the receptacle's GFCI-protection device opens.

(2) Receptacles in Wet Locations. All 15A and 20A receptacles installed in a wet location must be within an enclosure that's weatherproof when an attachment plug is inserted. For other than one- or two-family dwellings, the outlet box hood must be listed for "extra-duty" use if supported by grade, and all nonlocking-type 15A and 20A, 125V and 250V receptacles in a wet location must be listed as weather resistant [406.9(B)(1)]. Figure 590–4

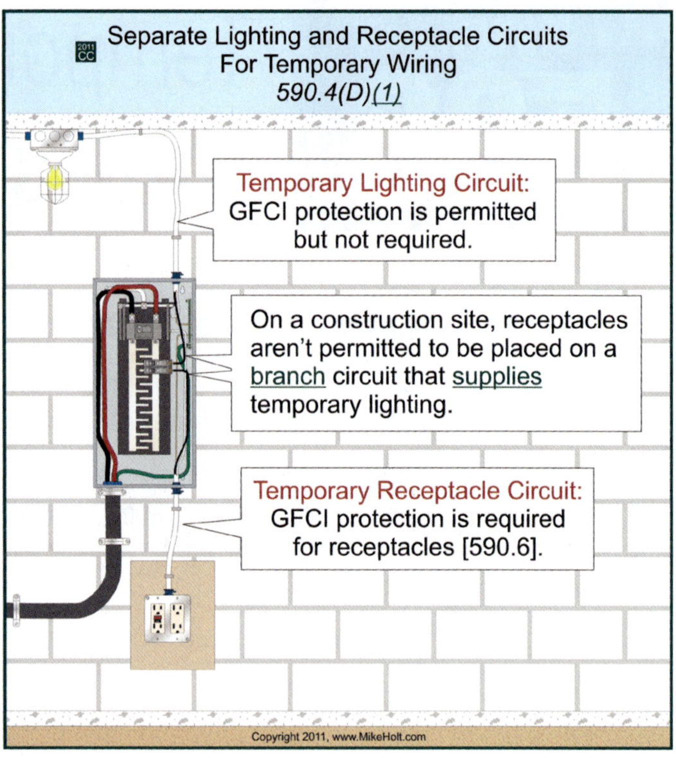

Figure 590-3

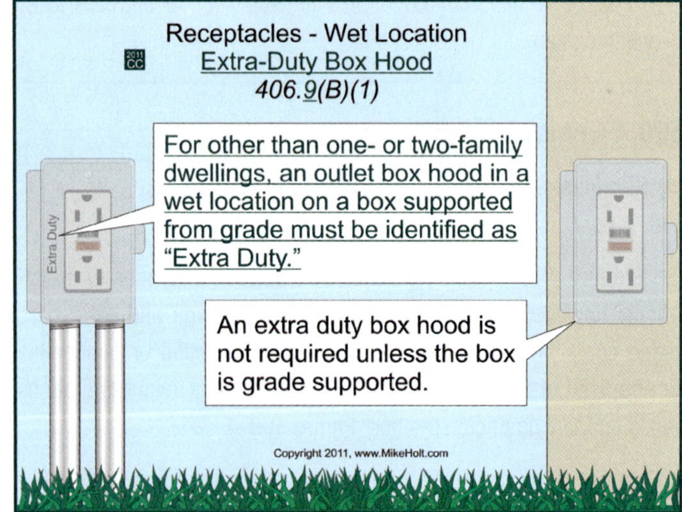

Figure 590–4

Author's Comment: Exposed plastic surface material of weather-resistant receptacles must have UV resistance to ensure that deterioration from sunlight doesn't take place, or that it's minimal. In testing, receptacles are subjected to temperature cycling from very cold to very warm conditions, and then subjected to additional dielectric testing. The rapid transition from the cold to warm temperatures will change the relative humidity and moisture content on the device, and the dielectric test ensures that this won't create a breakdown of the insulation properties.

ANALYSIS: Temporary wiring must comply with all provisions of the *NEC*, except where specifically addressed in Article 590 [590.2(A)]. Because there are no rules in Article 590 that address receptacles in wet locations, these receptacles must comply with 406.9. This change, while not a necessary one, does help to remind *Code* users of the requirements for wet locations.

590.6 Ground-Fault Protection for Personnel

The requirements for GFCI protection have been extensively revised.

590.6 Ground-Fault Protection for Personnel.

(A) Receptacle Outlets. Ground-fault protection for personnel is required for temporary wiring used for construction, remodeling, maintenance, repair, or demolition of buildings, structures, or equipment, from power derived from an electric utility company or from an on-site generated power source.

(1) Receptacles Not Part of Permanent Wiring. GFCI protection is required for 15A, 20A, and 30A, 125V receptacle outlets that aren't a part of the permanent wiring of the building/structure used by personnel. Figure 590–5

(2) Receptacle Outlets Existing or Installed as Permanent Wiring. GFCI protection is required for 15A, 20A, and 30A, 125V receptacle outlets that are installed or existing as part of the permanent wiring of the building/structure.

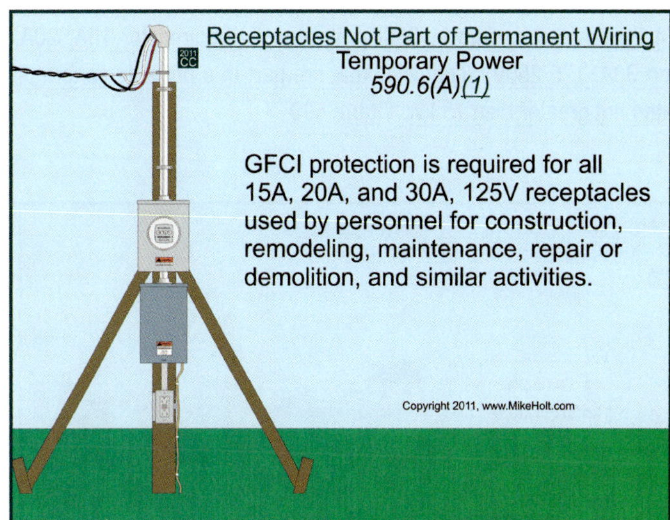

Figure 590-5

Listed cord sets or adapters that incorporate listed GFCI protection can be used to meet this requirement. Figure 590–6

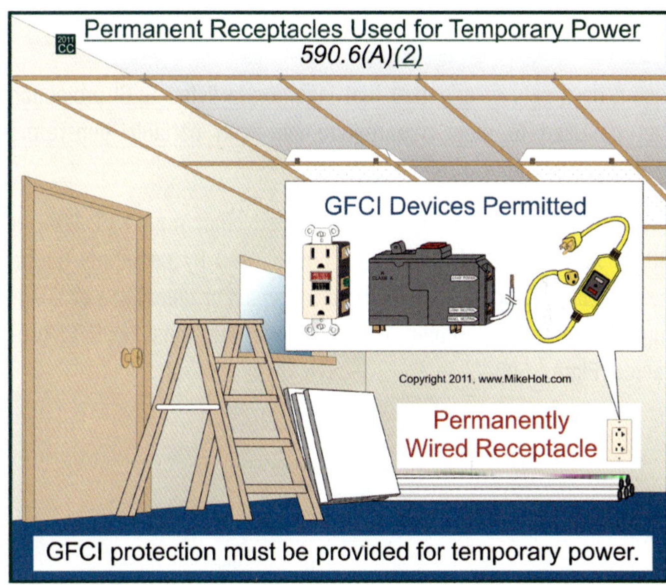

Figure 590-6

(3) Portable Generators. GFCI protection is required for 15A, 20A, and 30A, 125/250V receptacles that are part of a portable generator rated not greater than 15 kW. Figure 590–7

Figure 590-7

Listed cord sets or adapters that incorporate listed GFCI protection can be used to meet this requirement with portable generators manufactured prior to January 1, 2011.

(B) Other Receptacles. Receptacles rated other than 15A, 20A, or 30A, 125V that supply temporary power used by personnel during construction, remodeling, maintenance, repair, or demolition of buildings, structures, equipment, or similar activities must be GFCI protected. Figure 590–8

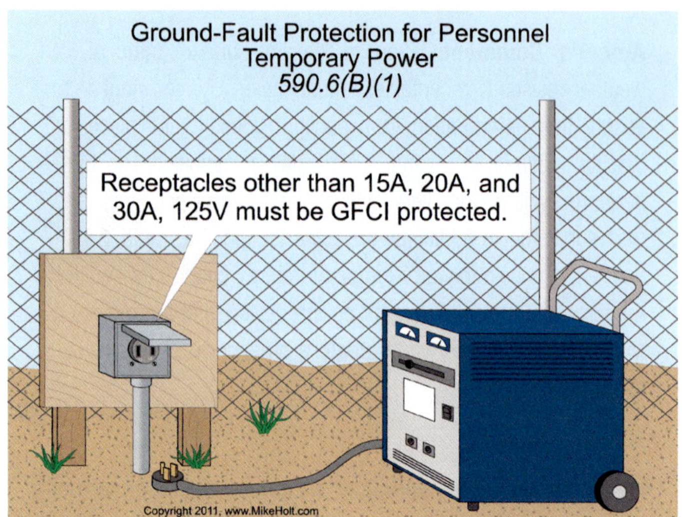

Figure 590–8

ANALYSIS: With this change, all 15 kW or smaller generators will be required to have GFCI protection for the 125V or 125/250V, single-phase, 15A, 20A, and 30A receptacles that are installed on them. For generators manufactured or remanufactured prior to January 1, 2011, cord sets or other devices that provide portable GFCI protection may be used.

This section was also rewritten using a list format for easier reading and understandability.

SPECIAL EQUIPMENT

INTRODUCTION TO CHAPTER 6—SPECIAL EQUIPMENT

Chapter 6, which covers special equipment, is the second of three *NEC* chapters that deal with special topics. Chapters 5 and 7 focus on special occupancies, and special conditions respectively. Remember, the first four chapters of the *Code* are sequential and form a foundation for each of the subsequent three. Chapter 8 covers communications systems and isn't subject to the requirements of Chapter 1 through 7 except where the requirements are specifically referenced in Chapter 8.

What exactly is "Special Equipment?" It's equipment that, by the nature of its use, construction, or by its unique nature creates a need for additional measures to ensure the "safeguarding of people and property" mission of the *NEC*, as stated in Article 90.

The *Code* groups the articles in this chapter logically, as you might expect. Here are the general groupings:

- Prefabricated items that are assembled in the field. Articles 600 through 605. These are signs, manufactured wiring systems, and office furnishings.
- Lifting equipment. Articles 610 and 620. These include cranes, hoists, elevators, dumbwaiters, wheelchair lifts, and escalators.
- Electric vehicle charging systems. Article 625.
- Electric welders. Article 630.
- Equipment for creating or processing information. Articles 640 through 650. These include amplifiers, computers (information technology), and pipe organs.
- X-ray equipment. Article 660.
- Process and production equipment. Articles 665 through 675. These include induction heaters, electrolytic cells, electroplating, and irrigation machines.
- Swimming Pools, Fountains, and Similar Installations. Article 680.
- "New energy" technologies. Article 690 covers solar photovoltaic systems, Article 692 covers fuel cells, and Article 694 covers small wind systems.
- Fire pumps. Article 695.

Author's Comment: The NFPA also produces a fire pump standard. It's NFPA 20, *Standard for the Installation of Stationary Pumps for Fire Protection.*

It's important to remember that Chapter 6 addresses only the minimum safety requirements for the special equipment it covers and that, in most cases, other standards also apply. The *NEC* isn't meant as a substitute for those other standards. So before you begin work on any of this special equipment, first obtain the standards written for that equipment. If you're not sure what standards apply, contact the manufacturer for assistance.

- **Article 600—Electric Signs and Outline Lighting.** This article covers the installation of conductors and equipment for electric signs and outline lighting as defined in Article 100. Electric signs and outline lighting include all products and installations that utilize neon tubing, such as signs, decorative elements, skeleton tubing, or art forms.
- **Article 604—Manufactured Wiring Systems.** Article 604 covers field-installed manufactured wiring systems used for branch circuits, remote-control circuits, signaling circuits, and communications circuits in accessible areas. The components of a listed manufactured wiring system can be assembled at the jobsite.
- **Article 605—Office Furnishings (Consisting of Lighting Accessories and Wired Partitions).** This article covers electrical equipment, lighting accessories, and wiring systems used to connect, or contained within or on, relocatable wired partitions.
- **Article 620—Elevators, Escalators, and Moving Walks.** This article covers electrical equipment and wiring used in connection with elevators, dumbwaiters, escalators, moving walks, wheelchair lifts, and stairway chair lifts.
- **Article 640—Audio Signal Processing, Amplification, and Reproduction Equipment.** Article 640 covers equipment and wiring for audio signal generation, recording, processing, amplification and reproduction, distribution of sound, public address, speech input systems, temporary audio system installations, and electronic musical instruments such as electric organs, electric guitars, and electronic drums/percussion.
- **Article 645—Information Technology Equipment.** This article applies to equipment, power-supply wiring, equipment interconnecting wiring and grounding of information technology equipment and systems, including terminal units in an information technology equipment room.
- **Article 680—Swimming Pools, Spas, Hot Tubs, Fountains, and Similar Installations.** Article 680 covers the installation of electric wiring and equipment that supplies swimming, wading, therapeutic and decorative pools, fountains, hot tubs, spas, and hydromassage bathtubs, whether permanently installed or storable.
- **Article 690—Photovoltaic Systems.** Article 690 focuses on reducing the electrical hazards that may arise from installing and operating a solar photovoltaic system, to the point where it can be considered safe for property and people. The requirements of the *NEC* Chapters 1 through 4 apply to these installations, except as specifically modified by Article 690.
- **Article 695—Fire Pumps.** This article covers the electric power sources and interconnecting circuits for electric motor-driven fire pumps. It also covers switching and control equipment dedicated to fire pump drivers. Article 695 doesn't apply to sprinkler system pumps in one- and two-family dwellings or to pressure maintenance (jockey) pumps.

Electric Signs and OUTLINE LIGHTING

INTRODUCTION TO ARTICLE 600—ELECTRIC SIGNS AND OUTLINE LIGHTING

One of the first things you notice when entering a strip mall is that there's a sign for every store. Every commercial occupancy needs a form of identification, and the standard method is the electric sign. Thus, 600.5 requires a sign outlet for the entrance of each tenant location. Article 600 requires a disconnecting means within sight of a sign unless the disconnecting means can be locked in the open position.

Author's Comment: Article 100 defines an electric sign as any "fixed, stationary, or portable self-contained, electrically illuminated utilization equipment with words or symbols designed to convey information or attract attention."

Another requirement is height. Freestanding signs, such as those that might be erected in a parking lot, must be located at least 14 ft above vehicle areas unless they're protected from physical damage.

Neon art forms or decorative elements are subsets of electric signs and outline lighting. If installed and not attached to an enclosure or sign body, they're considered skeleton tubing for the purpose of applying the requirements of Article 600. However, if that neon tubing is attached to an enclosure or sign body, which may be a simple support frame, it's considered a sign or outline lighting subject to all of the provisions that apply to signs and outline lighting, such as 600.3, which requires the product to be listed.

Author's Comment: Outline lighting is an arrangement of incandescent lamps or electric-discharge lighting to outline or call attention to certain features, such as the shape of a building or the decoration of a window [Article 100].

600.1 Scope

A change to the scope of this article has been made, and an Informational Note was added.

600.1 Scope. Article 600 covers the installation of conductors, equipment, and field wiring for electric signs and outline lighting, including neon tubing for signs, decorative elements, skeleton tubing, or art forms.

Author's Comment: See the definition of "Outline Lighting" in Article 100.

Note: Sign and outline lighting systems can include cold cathode neon tubing, high intensity discharge lamps (HID), fluorescent or incandescent lamps, light emitting diodes (LEDs), and electroluminescent and inductance lighting.

ANALYSIS: Article 600 not only applies to the installation of conductors and equipment for electric signs and outline lighting, it also applies to the associated field wiring of these products. A change to the scope of this article reinforces that concept.

An Informational Note has also been added to the scope, providing the *Code* user with a list of the various types of equipment that's contemplated in this article. Cold cathode neon tubing, high-intensity discharge lamps (HID), fluorescent or incandescent lamps, light emitting diodes (LEDs), and electroluminescent and inductance lighting are all covered here.

600.3 Listing

A clarification has made to clarify the applicability of listing

600.3 Listing. Electric signs, section signs, and outline lighting—fixed, mobile, or portable—regardless of voltage, must be listed and installed in accordance with the listing instructions, except as permitted in (A) or (B).

(A) Field-Installed Skeleton Tubing. Field-installed skeleton tubing isn't required to be listed.

(B) Outline Lighting. Field-installed outline lighting isn't required to be listed if wired in accordance with Chapter 3.

ANALYSIS: This section has long required that electric signs, section signs, and outline lighting be listed. Some users of the *Code* had a difficult time determining at what voltage level this requirement became effective. With this change, it's quite clear that the voltage isn't relevant—all electric signs, section signs, and outline lighting must be listed, regardless of voltage unless otherwise permitted in (A) or (B).

600.4 Marking

Additional requirements have been added for sign and outline lighting identification labels.

600.4 Markings.

(A) Signs and Outline Lighting Systems. Signs and outline lighting systems must be marked with the manufacturer's name, trademark, or other means of identification.

(C) Marking Visibility. The markings required in (A) and listing labels aren't required to be visible after installation, but must be visible during servicing.

(D) Durability. Marking must be permanent, durable, and weatherproof when in wet locations.

(E) Section Signs. Section signs must be marked to indicate that field-wiring and installation instructions are required.

ANALYSIS: While the *Code* has long required that signs and outline lighting systems be marked to indicate the manufacturer and input voltage and current ratings, there's been no direction from the *NEC* as to where this identification must occur, and there's been no direction as to the durability of the markings. This change clarifies both of those issues. The label need not be visible after the installation, but it does need to be visible during servicing. It must also be "weatherproof" when installed in a wet location.

600.5 Branch-Circuit Rating

A clarification has been made regarding sign calculations, and an editorial revision has also been made.

600.5 Branch Circuits.

(A) Required Branch Circuit. Each commercial building or occupancy accessible to pedestrians must be provided with an outlet at an accessible location for a sign. The sign outlet must be located at the entrance of each tenant space, and it must be supplied with an individual branch circuit rated not less than 20A. **Figure 600–1**

Figure 600–1

(B) Rating. Branch circuits that supply signs are to be considered a continuous load. **Figure 600–2**

Figure 600–2

(1) Neon Signs. Branch circuits that supply neon tubing installations must be rated 30A or less.

(2) Other Signs. Branch circuits that supply other signs and outline lighting systems must not be rated more than 20A

> **Authors Comment:** What this boils down to is that each commercial building and each commercial occupancy accessible to pedestrians requires a minimum of one 20A branch circuit for the sign outlet. If it's supplying a neon sign, that branch circuit is permitted to be rated up to 30A.

(C) Wiring Methods.

(1) Supply. The wiring for a sign must terminate at the sign or outline lighting enclosure, box, or conduit body.

(3) Poles. Poles used to support signs can contain the sign circuit conductors, provided the installation complies with 410.30(B).

> **ANALYSIS:** Because signs are almost always on for more than three continuous hours, they're a continuous load, by definition. While this change isn't a technical change (since signs are already a continuous load), it does serve as a reminder that they're a continuous load, and must be calculated as such.
>
> Additionally, this section was changed and reorganized to clarify that neon signs are allowed to be served by a branch circuit exceeding 20A, but not exceeding 30A. All other signs must not be on a branch circuit exceeding 20A.

600.6 Disconnecting Means

A revision has been made to clarify the disconnecting means requirements for signs and outline lighting systems. Skeleton tubing disconnects are also now required.

600.6 Disconnecting Means. Each circuit for a sign, outline lighting system, or skeleton tubing must be controlled by an externally operable switch or circuit breaker that will open all ungrounded conductors, Figure 600–3. Where the circuit is a multiwire branch circuit, the switch or circuit breaker must open all ungrounded conductors of the circuit simultaneously.

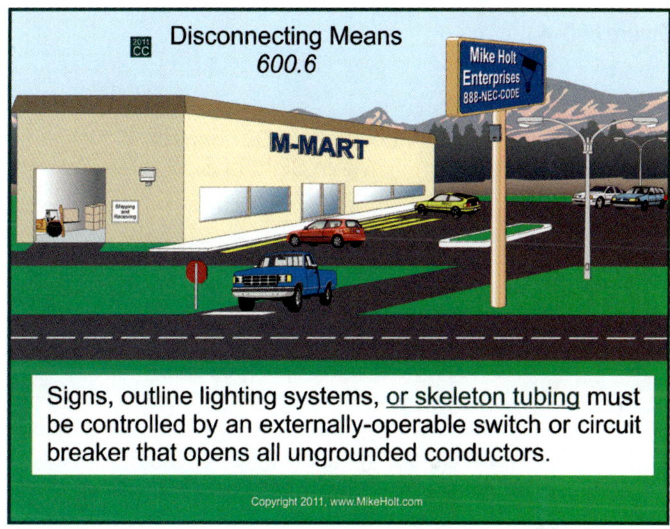

Figure 600–3

(A) Location.

(1) Within Sight of Sign. The disconnecting means must be within sight of the sign or outline lighting system. Figure 600–4

If the disconnecting means is out of the line of sight from any section of the sign or outline lighting able to be energized, the disconnecting means must be capable of being locked in the open position. The provision for locking or adding a lock to the disconnecting means must be on the switch or circuit breaker and remain in place with or without the lock installed. Figure 600–5

> **Author's Comment:** See the definition of "Within Sight" in Article 100.

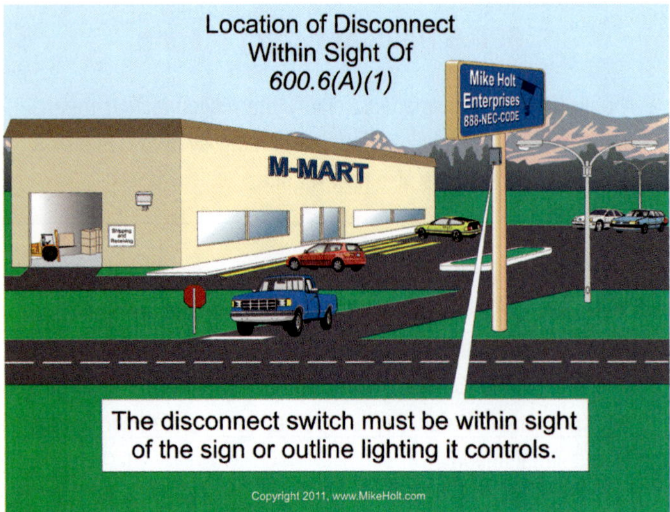

Figure 600–4

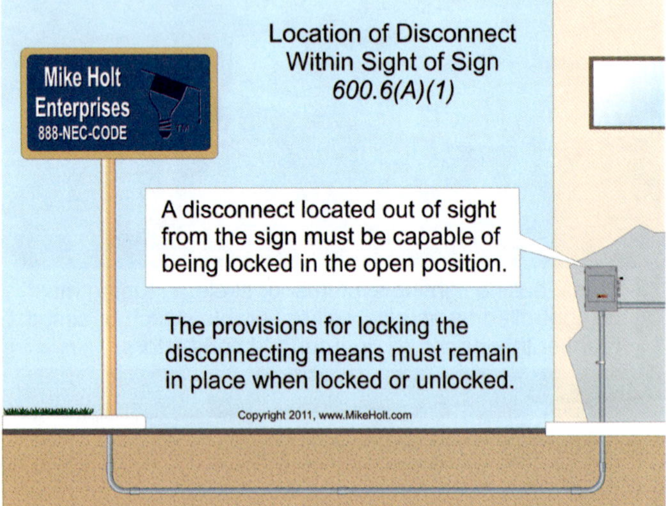

Figure 600–5

(2) Within Sight of the Controller. Signs or outline lighting systems operated by electronic or electromechanical controllers located external to the sign or outline lighting system must have the disconnecting means installed in accordance with (1) through (3):

(1) Located within sight of or in the same enclosure with the controller.

(2) Be capable of disconnecting the sign or outline lighting and the controller from all ungrounded supply conductors.

(3) Be capable of being locked in the open position. The provision for locking or adding a lock to the disconnecting means must be on the switch or circuit breaker and remain in place with or without the lock installed. A portable locking means doesn't meet the "locked in the open position" requirement. Figure 600–6

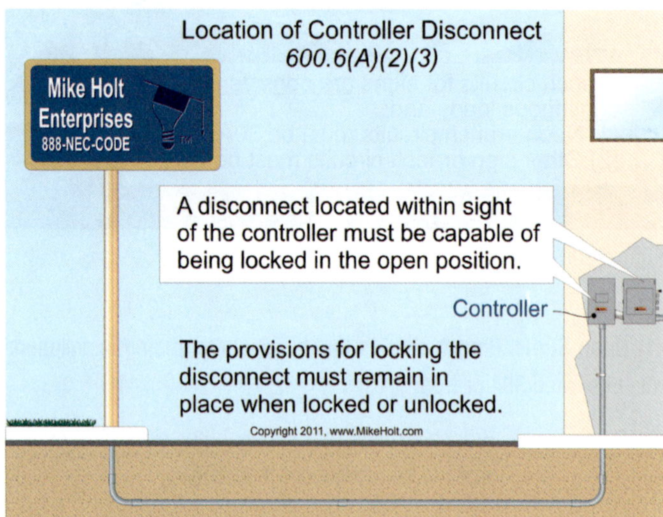

Figure 600–6

ANALYSIS: Each sign, skeleton tubing, and outline lighting system must have a disconnecting means that disconnects all ungrounded conductors of the circuit. When the circuit supplying the equipment is a multiwire branch circuit, the disconnect must open the ungrounded conductors simultaneously. Additionally, a disconnecting means for skeleton tubing is now required, adding to the safety of the workforce that deals with these systems.

600.7(B) Bonding of Metal Parts

A new exception for Class 2 power supplies was added.

600.7 Grounding and Bonding

(B) Bonding.

(1) Bonding of Metal Parts. Metal parts of signs and outline lighting systems must be bonded to the transformer or power-supply equipment grounding conductor of the branch circuit or feeder supplying the sign or outline lighting system.

Ex: Remote metal parts of a section sign or outline lighting system only supplied by a remote Class 2 power supply aren't required to be connected to an equipment grounding conductor.

(2) Bonding Connections. Bonding connections must be made in accordance with 250.8.

(4) Flexible Metal Conduit Length. Listed flexible metal conduit or listed liquidtight flexible metal conduit for secondary circuit conductors for neon tubing can be used as a bonding means if the total accumulative length of the conduit doesn't exceed 100 ft.

(7) Bonding Conductors.

(1) Bonding conductors must be copper and not smaller than 14 AWG.

(2) Bonding conductors installed externally of a sign or raceway must be protected from physical damage.

ANALYSIS: Because Class 2 power supplies aren't typically grounded systems [250.20(A)(1)], they don't contain an equipment grounding conductor. Without an equipment grounding conductor it's obviously not possible to bond metal parts, so this exception was added.

NOTES

Information Technology EQUIPMENT

INTRODUCTION TO ARTICLE 645—INFORMATION TECHNOLOGY EQUIPMENT

One of the unique things about Article 645 is the requirement for a shutoff switch readily accessible from the exit doors of information technology equipment rooms [645.10]. This requirement seems to be wrong on its face because it allows someone to shut off the IT room from a single point. So despite having a UPS and taking every precaution against a power outage, the IT system is still vulnerable to a shutdown from a readily accessible switch at the principal exit doors. What was the *Code*-Making Panel thinking of when they added this requirement?

They were thinking of fire and rescue teams. Having a means to shut down the power and disconnect the batteries before entering the IT room during a fire allows the rescue team to use fire hoses and other equipment without risking contact with energized equipment. Yes, there's loss of IT function during the shutdown, but if the room needs fire and rescue teams, loss of the IT function is the least of its problems at that time. The shutdown allows the rescue of people and property. A breakaway lock can protect the IT room from inadvertent shutdown via this switch.

What about the rest of Article 645? The major goal is to reduce the spread of fire and smoke. The raised floors common in IT rooms pose additional challenges to achieving this goal, so this article devotes a fair percentage of its text to raised floor requirements. Fire-resistant walls, separate HVAC systems, and other requirements further help to achieve this goal.

645.1 Scope

The Informational Note regarding NFPA 75 has been revised.

645.1 Scope. Article 645 covers equipment, power-supply wiring, and interconnecting wiring of information technology equipment and systems in an information technology equipment room that meets of the requirements of 645.4.

> **Note:** For information on the requirements for the protection of IT equipment and IT areas, see NFPA 75, Standard for the Protection of Information Technology Equipment.

ANALYSIS: The application of Article 645 is often difficult for *Code* users. Many of them don't understand how to apply this article, and, even worse, many don't know when to apply its provisions. In an effort to correct this problem, the Informational Note to the scope has been revised. Now it's clear that if the room isn't constructed in accordance with NFPA 75, *Standard for the Protection of Information Technology Equipment*, the provisions here don't apply. Does that mean you must follow that standard? No. You must comply with NFPA 75 only if you choose to reap the benefits allowed by Article 645.

645.2 Definitions

New definitions for "Information Technology Equipment," "Information Technology Equipment Room," and "Remote Disconnect Control" have been added.

645.2 Definitions.

Information Technology Equipment (ITE). Equipment used for creation and manipulation of data, voice, and video, but not communications equipment.

Information Technology Equipment Room. A room that contains the information technology equipment.

Remote Disconnect Control. An electrical device and circuit that controls the required disconnecting means through a relay or similar device.

> **Author's Comment:** A disconnecting means is required to disconnect power to electronic equipment in the information technology equipment room and dedicated HVAC systems that serve the room. See 645.10.

ANALYSIS: Confusion has occurred in the past when trying to determine the difference between "information technology equipment" and "communications equipment." IT equipment must comply with this article, whereas communications equipment is required to comply with Article 800. Because the provisions of Chapters 1 through 7 don't apply to communications systems [90.3], this becomes a very important distinction, especially considering the fact that IT equipment and communications equipment are very often installed in the same room. With this change it becomes clear that IT equipment doesn't process communications circuits, a difference that makes the distinction between the two different systems and equipment.

ITE room has now been defined...it's a room that contains IT equipment(!).

The term "remote disconnect control" was defined to help distinguish between the actual disconnecting means and the controls that operate it. It's a term used in 645.10, so a definition in this section should help the *Code* user better understand the requirements.

645.3 Other Articles

A new section was added to address the applicability of other articles and sections of the *Code*.

645.3 Other Articles.

(A) Spread of Fire or Products of Combustion. Electrical circuits and equipment must be installed in such a way that the spread of fire or products of combustion won't be substantially increased. Openings into or through fire-rated walls, floors, and ceilings for electrical equipment must be firestopped using methods approved by the authority having jurisdiction to maintain the fire-resistance rating of the fire-rated assembly [300.21].

(B) Plenums. Electrical metallic tubing, rigid metal conduit, intermediate metal conduit, armored cable, metal-clad cable without a nonmetallic cover, and flexible metal conduit can be installed in environmental air spaces. If accessible, surface metal raceways, or metal wireways with metal covers can be installed in environmental air spaces (plenums) [300.22(C)(1)]. **Figure 645–1**

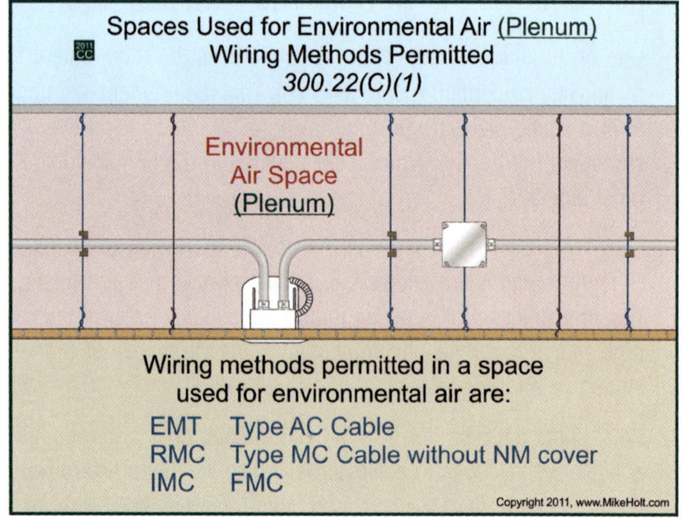

Figure 645–1

Author's Comments:

- PVC conduit [Article 352], electrical nonmetallic tubing [Article 362], liquidtight flexible conduits, and nonmetallic cables aren't permitted to be installed in spaces used for environmental air because they give off deadly toxic fumes when burned or superheated.
- Control, signaling, and communications cables installed in spaces used for environmental air (plenums) must be suitable for plenum use. **Figure 645–2**
  - CATV, 820.179(A)
  - Communications, 800.21
  - Control and Signaling, 725.154(A)
  - Fire Alarm, 760.7
  - Optical Fiber Cables and Raceways, 770.113(C)
  - Sound Systems, 640.9(C) and 725.154(A)
- Any wiring method suitable for the condition can be used in a space not used for environmental air-handling purposes. **Figure 645–3**

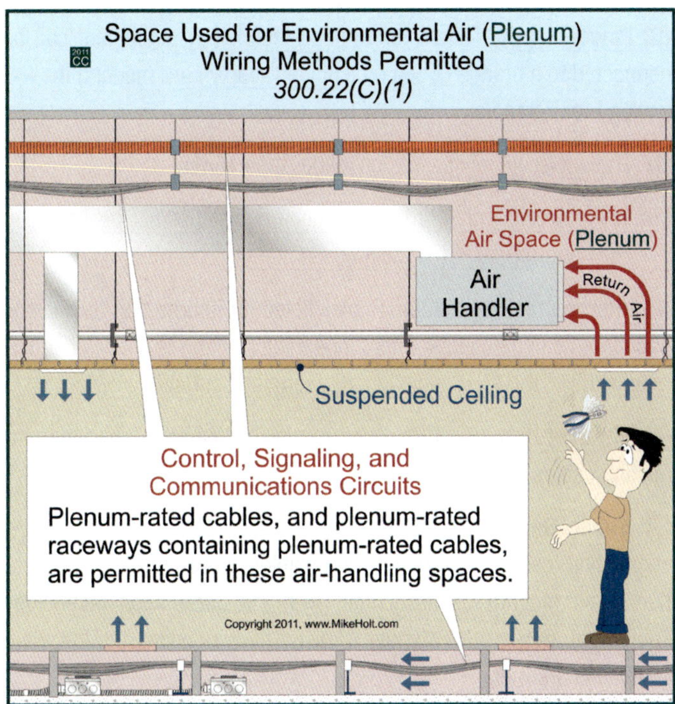

Figure 645–2

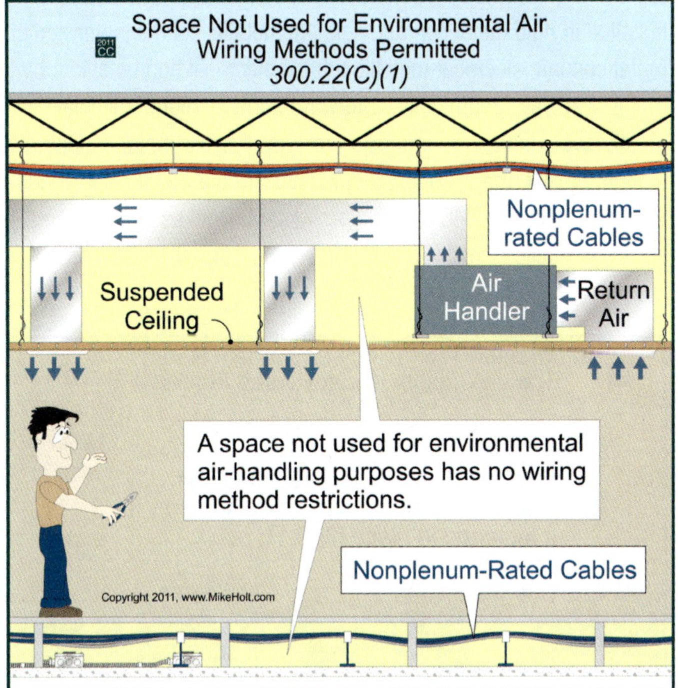

Figure 645–3

ANALYSIS: The requirements of Chapters 1 through 4 apply generally to all installations. Chapters 5 through 7 can supplement or modify these rules [90.3]. While this seems a simple enough concept, confusion often occurs when two different articles found in Chapters 5 through 7 address similar items, but have different provisions. For this reason, a new Section 645.3 was created to help the *Code* user. Among the "other articles" that this section references are 300.21, 770.26, 800.26, and 820.26 for penetrations through fire-resistance rated construction assemblies; Article 760 for fire alarm systems; Article 800 for communications systems; and others.

645.4 Information Technology Equipment Room

Clarifications have been made to address the applicability of this article, and a few technical changes have been made.

645.4 Information Technology Equipment Room. The provisions contained in this article are only permitted to apply if all of the following conditions are met:

(1) A disconnecting means that complies with 645.10 is provided.

(2) A dedicated heating/ventilating/air-conditioning (HVAC) system is provided for information technology equipment and is separated from other areas of the occupancy.

(3) All information technology and communications equipment in the information technology room is listed.

(4) The room is occupied and accessible only to persons needed for the maintenance and operation of information technology equipment.

(5) The information technology equipment room is separated from other occupancies by fire-resistant-rated walls, floors, and ceilings with protected openings.

Author's Comment: An information technology equipment room is an enclosed area specifically designed to comply with the construction and fire protection provisions of NFPA 75, *Standard for the Protection of Electronic Computer/Data Processing Equipment.*

(6) Only electrical equipment and wiring associated with the operation of the information technology room is installed in the room.

Note: This would include HVAC systems, communications systems, telephone, fire alarm systems, security systems, water detection systems, and other related protective equipment.

ANALYSIS: A real effort has been made in this *NEC* cycle to clarify when Article 645 applies and when it doesn't. While many *Code* users view this article to be beneficial, many don't. Oftentimes a room contains IT equipment, but the design professional, the installer, or the owner wish to not use these provisions. In the past, if the room met the provisions of 645.4 all of its requirements were thrust upon the *NEC* user. Because compliance with this article has always been intended to be optional, a change was made to clarify that these provisions are permitted to apply if 645.4 is met.

Additionally, list item (3) has been revised to clarify that all IT and communications equipment must be listed, and item (4) was changed to require that the ITE room be accessible only to qualified persons.

A new Informational Note has also been added to clarify the intent of Article 645, which is providing alternate practices from those found in other *Code* articles.

Lastly, a new item (6) was added to mandate that only electrical equipment and wiring that's associated with the IT room may be located in that room. A new Informational Note has also been added to clarify the types of equipment contemplated by this rule.

645.5 Supply Circuits and Interconnecting Cables

Clarifications have been made to the provisions for circuits and cables in the IT room.

645.5 Supply Circuits and Interconnecting Cables.

(A) Branch-Circuit Conductors. Branch-circuit conductors for information technology equipment must have an ampacity not less than 125 percent of the total connected load.

(B) Power-Supply Cords. Information technology equipment can be connected to a branch circuit by a power-supply cord meeting the following requirements:

(1) The power-supply cord is no longer than 15 ft.

(2) The power-supply cord and attachment plug must be listed for use on information technology equipment.

(C) Interconnecting Cables. Cables listed for information technology equipment can be used to interconnect information technology equipment without the 15 ft cable length limitation contained in 645.5(B).

(D) Physical Damage. If exposed to physical damage, the interconnecting cables must be protected.

(E) Under Raised Floors. Power cables, communications cables, connecting cables, interconnecting cables, cord-and-plug connections, and receptacles associated with the information technology equipment are permitted under a raised floor, provided the following conditions are met:

(1) Construction. The raised floor is of approved construction, and the area under the floor is accessible.

(2) Wiring Method. The branch-circuit supply conductors are installed in rigid metal conduit, rigid nonmetallic conduit, intermediate metal conduit, electrical metallic tubing, electrical nonmetallic tubing, metal wireway, nonmetallic wireway, surface metal raceway with metal cover, surface nonmetallic raceway, flexible metal conduit, liquidtight flexible metal conduit, liquidtight flexible nonmetallic conduit, Type MI cable, Type MC cable, Type AC cable, and associated metallic and nonmetallic boxes or enclosures. **Figure 645–4**

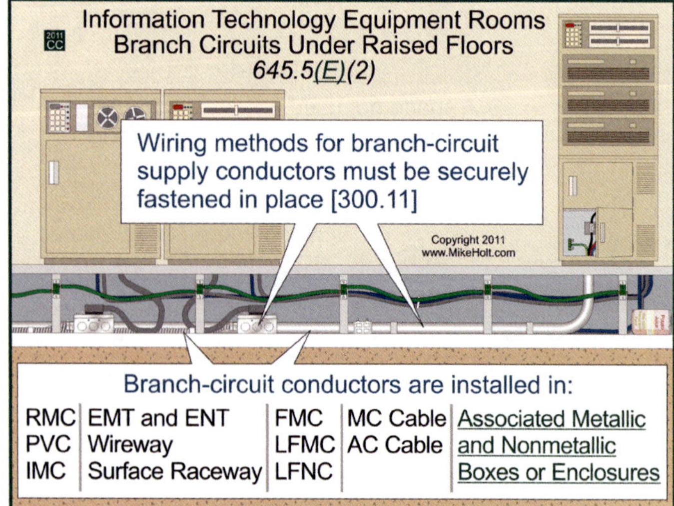

Figure 645–4

Author's Comment: Nonmetallic raceways are permitted within the raised floor area because this space is neither subject to physical damage, nor need it comply with the environmental air-space requirements of 300.22(A), (B), and (C) [300.22(D)].

Branch-circuit wiring methods must be securely fastened in place in accordance with 300.11.

(3) Supply Cords. Supply cords of listed information technology equipment no longer than 15 ft, with an attachment plug, and protected against physical damage are permitted [645.5(B)]. **Figure 645–5**

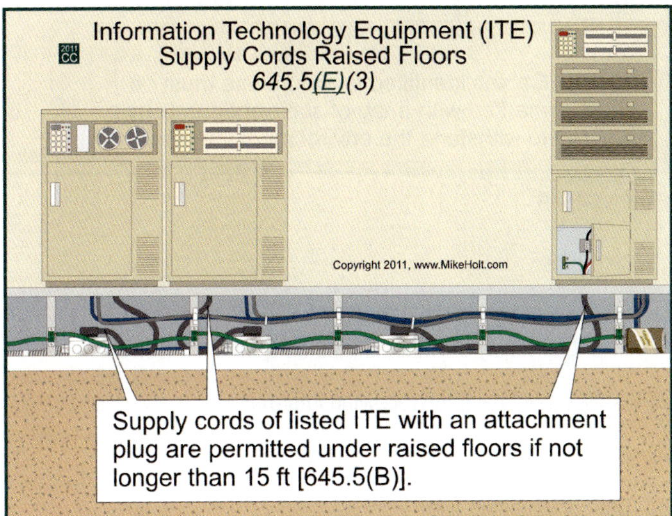

Figure 645–5

(4) Ventilation. Ventilation in the underfloor area is for the information equipment room only, and it's arranged so that air circulation will cease upon the detection of fire or products of combustion.

(5) Openings. Openings in raised floors protect the cables against abrasions.

(6) Cable Rating. Cables must be Type DP having adequate fire-resistant characteristics suitable for use under raised floors of an information technology equipment room, except for the power-supply cords discussed in 645.5(E)(3), and those listed in (a) through (c) below.

(a) Cables enclosed in a raceway.

(b) Signal or communications cable identified in Table 645.5.

Table 645.5 Cable Types Permitted Under Raised Floors

Article	Plenum	Riser	General Purpose
336			TC
725	CL2P & CL3P	CL2R & CL3R	CL2, CL3 & PLTC
727			ITC
760	NPLFP & FPLP	NPLFR & FPLR	NPLF & FPL
770	OFNP & OFCP	OFNR & OFCR	OFN & OFC
800	CMP	CMR	CM & CMG
820	CATVP	CATVR	CATV

Author's Comment: Table 645.5 demonstrates that any listed signal or communications cable is permitted within the raised floor area of an information technology equipment room. This includes plenum, riser, or general-purpose cables. **Figure 645–6**

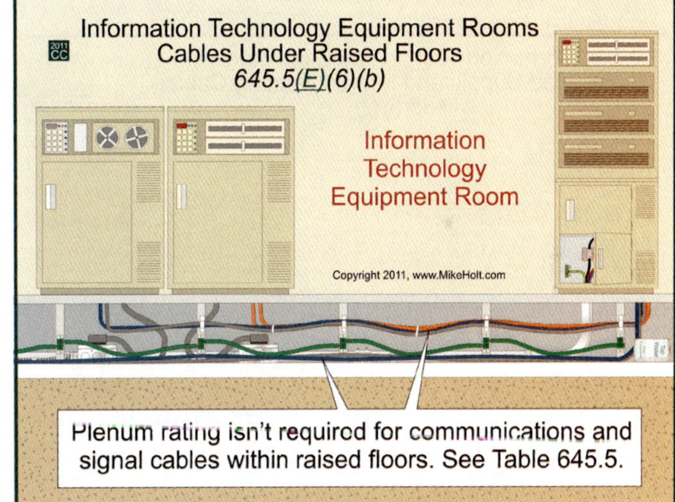

Figure 645–6

(F) Securing in Place. Power, communications, connecting, and interconnecting cables that are part of listed information technology equipment aren't required to be secured in place. **Figure 645–7**

Author's Comment: Branch-circuit supply conductors must be securely fastened in place in accordance with 300.11 [645.5(E)(2)].

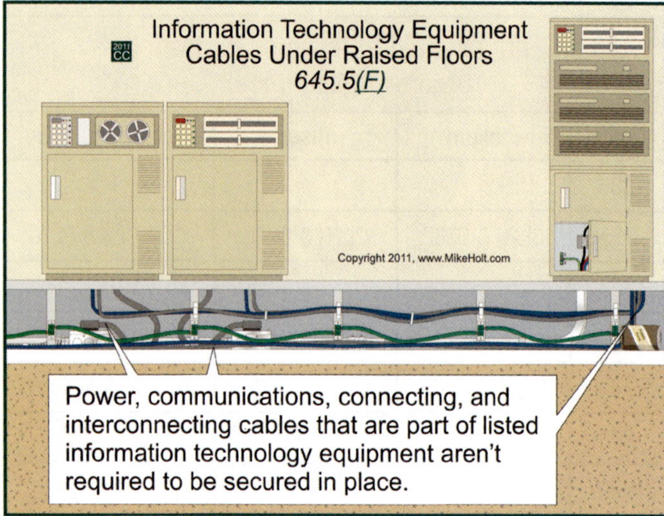

Figure 645–7

(G) Abandoned Supply Circuits and Interconnecting Cables. The accessible portion of abandoned cables must be removed unless contained in a raceway. Figure 645–8

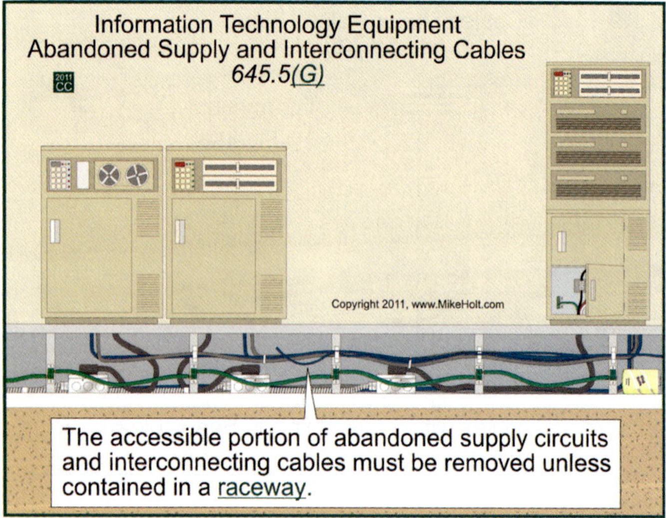

Figure 645–8

Author's Comment: An abandoned cable is one that isn't terminated to equipment and not identified for future use with a tag [645.2].

(H) Cables Identified for Future Use. Figure 645–9

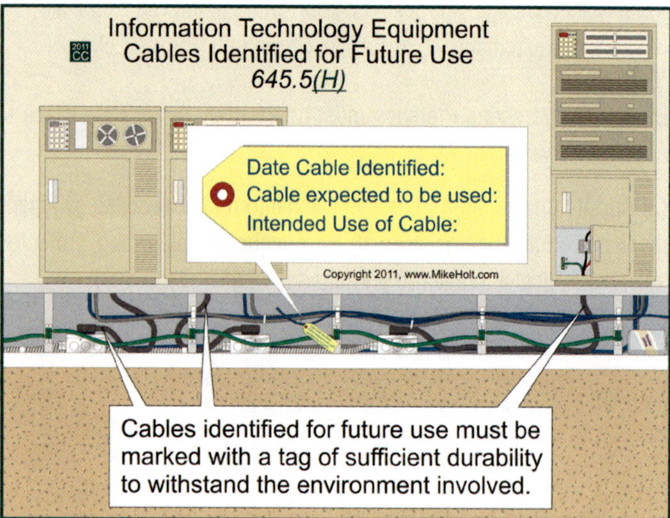

Figure 645–9

(1) Cables identified for future use must be marked with a tag of sufficient durability to withstand the environment involved.

(2) Cables must have the following information:

(a) Date cable was identified for future use

(b) Date of expected use

(c) Intended future use of the cable

ANALYSIS: Few *Code* users disagree that this section is a difficult one to understand. The phrase "data processing system" was used in the past without definition, and is now deleted and replaced with the defined term "information technology equipment."

The 15 ft. limitation of 645.5(B)(1) has been changed in order to clarify that only cord-and-plug-connected interconnecting cables, not all interconnecting cables, are limited in length. Listing requirements for power-supply cords and cord connectors have been also addressed.

The types of cords that may be "suitable" in these areas have been clarified as well. The term "suitable" isn't defined, and therefore has been replaced with "permitted," and a new Informational Note was added to help the *Code* user understand what types of cords are permitted.

The provisions for protection against physical damage have all been grouped together and put into the same location, Subsection (D).

Although it was implied, the *NEC* never addressed the use of boxes under raised floors of IT rooms. This problem is corrected in Subsection (E), and clarifies that both metallic and nonmetallic boxes are allowed.

Lastly, the baffling requirements for "DP" rated cables have been clarified in (E)(6).

645.10 Disconnecting Means

The requirements for the disconnecting means of the IT room have been changed to incorporate remote disconnect controls.

645.10 Disconnecting Means. An approved disconnecting means must disconnect power to electronic equipment in the information technology equipment room and dedicated HVAC systems that serve the room.

The controls for the disconnecting means must be identified and located so as to be readily accessible at the principal exit doors. A single means to control both the electronic equipment and HVAC systems is permitted. If a button is used as a means to disconnect power, pushing the button "in" must disconnect the power.

The disconnecting means must comply with 645.10(A), unless used for critical operations data systems.

Author's Comment: This is generally accomplished by using a normally open (NO) momentary-contact pushbutton at each principal exit door. When any one of these emergency buttons is pressed, it opens one or more shunt trip circuit breakers, thereby turning off power to the room.

(A) Remote Disconnect Controls.

(1) Remote disconnect controls must be at an approved readily accessible location.

(2) The remote disconnect controls for electronic equipment power and HVAC systems must be grouped and identified (a single means to control both is permitted).

(4) Additional means to prevent unintentional operations of remote disconnect controls are permitted.

ANALYSIS: One of the requirements of Article 645 that makes people hesitant to use it is the disconnecting means of this section. Because of the allowances in this article, a means to disconnect all power and air-handling equipment must be provided. While this provision sounds relatively harmless, a person accidentally using the disconnecting means can be catastrophic. Documented incidents have occurred where the IT room was shut off accidentally, resulting in thousands upon thousands of dollars being lost. To help address this, a new allowance has been created that provides for "additional means to prevent unintentional operations of remote disconnect controls." Other changes to this section are mainly editorial, other than the new allowances in (B), which apply only to Article 708 installations for critical operations data systems.

Correlating changes have been made to 645.10(B)(5) which point the *Code* user to particular sections in Articles 770, 800, and 820 as well.

NOTES

Swimming Pools, Spas, Hot Tubs, Fountains, and SIMILAR INSTALLATIONS

INTRODUCTION TO ARTICLE 680—SWIMMING POOLS, SPAS, HOT TUBS, FOUNTAINS, AND SIMILAR INSTALLATIONS

The requirements contained in Article 680 apply to the installation of electrical wiring and equipment for swimming pools, hot tubs, spas, fountains, and hydromassage bathtubs. The overriding concern of Article 680 is to keep people and electricity separated.

This article is divided into seven parts. The various parts apply to certain types of installations, so be careful to determine which parts of this article apply to what and where. For instance, Part I and Part II apply to spas and hot tubs installed outdoors, except as modified in Part IV. In contrast, hydromassage bathtubs are only covered by Part VII. Read the details of this article carefully so you'll be able to provide a safe installation.

- **Part I—General.**
- **Part II—Permanently Installed Pools.** Installations at permanently installed pools must comply with both Parts I and II of this article.
- **Part III—Storable Pools.** Installations of storable pools must comply with Parts I and III of Article 680.
- **Part IV—Spas and Hot Tubs.** Spas and hot tubs must comply with Parts I and IV of this article; outdoor spas and hot tubs must also comply with Part II in accordance with 680.42.
- **Part V—Fountains.** Parts I and II apply to permanently installed fountains. If they have water in common with a pool, Part II also applies. Self-contained, portable fountains are covered by Article 422, Parts II and III.
- **Part VI—Pools and Tubs for Therapeutic Use.** Parts I and VI apply to pools and tubs for therapeutic use in health care facilities, gymnasiums, athletic training rooms and similar installations. If they're portable appliances then Article 422, Parts II and III apply.
- **Part VII—Hydromassage Bathtubs.** Part VI applies to hydromassage bathtubs, but no other parts of Article 680 do.

PART I. GENERAL REQUIREMENTS FOR POOLS, SPAS, HOT TUBS, AND FOUNTAINS

Author's Comment: The requirements contained in Part I of Article 680 apply to permanently installed pools [680.20], storable pools [680.30], outdoor spas and hot tubs [680.42], and fountains [680.50].

680.2 Definitions

Revisions to the definition of "dry-niche luminaire" have been made.

Dry-Niche Luminaire. A luminaire intended for installation in the floor or wall of a pool, spa, or fountain in a niche that's sealed against the entry of water.

ANALYSIS: Dry-niche luminaires are typically installed in the wall of a swimming pool, and sometimes the wall of a fountain. Newer designs, however, accommodate floor mounting, and can also be found in spas. This definition has been revised to address these new designs.

680.2 Definitions

A new definition of "low-voltage contact limit" was added to clarify the use of voltages in this article.

Low-Voltage Contact Limit. A voltage not exceeding the following values:

(1) 15V (RMS) for sinusoidal ac

(2) 21.20V peak for nonsinusoidal ac

(3) 30V for continuous dc

(4) 12.40V peak for dc that's interrupted at a rate of 10 to 200 Hz.

ANALYSIS: The "safe" values of voltage are assumed to be in dry locations. When the human body is wet, his or her resistance is decreased, resulting in a lower voltage required to obtain the same amount of current flow (I=E/R). Because wet contact is quite probable when dealing with swimming pools and similar locations, this definition was added. Tables 11(A) and 11(B) of Chapter 9 discuss limited-energy power source limitations. These tables indicate the voltage and current ratings that a power source can have if it's to be a Class 2 or Class 3 power supply. For an inherently protected Class 2 ac power supply, for example, the voltage is limited to 20V and 8A. If this power supply is used in an area where wet contact is likely, it's limited to 15V, or else Class 3 wiring methods are required for the circuit (see Note 2 to Table 11(A)). This new definition contains the voltages discussed in these tables, resulting in the *Code* user not having to go to the back of the *NEC* book to find these values.

680.10 Underground Wiring

A new allowance for nonmetallic underground raceways with concrete cover was added to the table.

680.10 Underground Wiring. Underground wiring isn't permitted under permanently installed pools, storable pools, outdoor spas, outdoor hot tubs, or fountains or within 5 ft horizontally from the inside wall of the pool, spa, hot tub, or fountain, unless necessary to supply the permanently installed pool, storable pool, outdoor spa, outdoor hot tub, or fountain equipment. **Figure 680–1**

If space limitations prevent wiring from being at least 5 ft away, underground wiring must be installed in complete raceway systems of rigid metal conduit, intermediate metal conduit, or PVC conduit listed for direct burial, **Figure 680–2**. The minimum cover is 6 in. for rigid metal conduit, intermediate metal conduit and nonmetallic raceways with 4 in. of concrete cover and 18 in. of cover for nonmetallic raceways without concrete cover [Table 680.10].

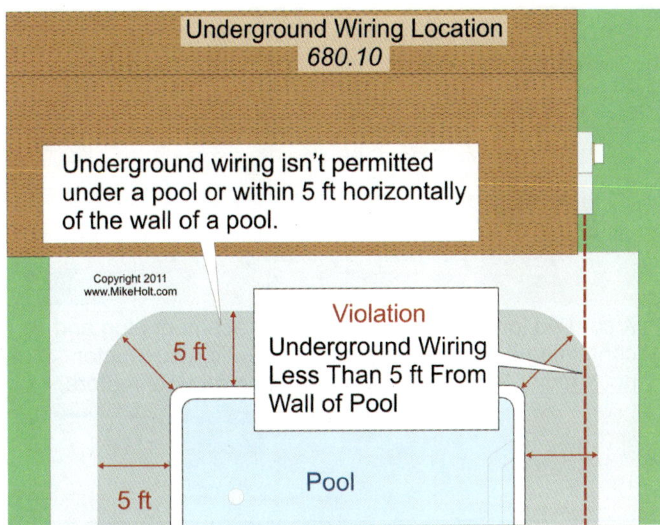

Figure 680–1

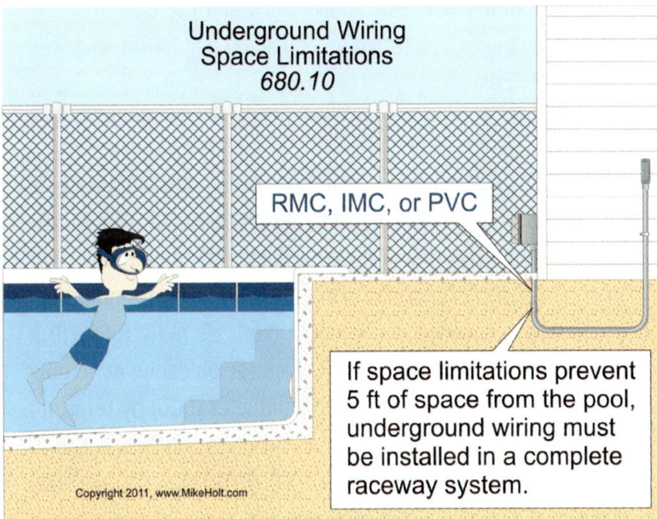

Figure 680–2

ANALYSIS: The 2008 edition of this table gave requirements for nonmetallic raceways near a pool that doesn't have concrete encasement. But it didn't give any guidance for such raceways that don't have concrete encasement but do have concrete cover. With this change it becomes clear that nonmetallic raceways with 4 in. of concrete cover may be installed near a pool without having to be buried 18 in. deep. An example of this might be raceways that are installed beneath a concrete pool deck.

PART II. PERMANENTLY INSTALLED POOLS, OUTDOOR SPAS, AND OUTDOOR HOT TUBS

680.21(A)(5) Cord-and-Plug Connection of Motors

This section has been changed to correlate with similar rules in 680.7(B).

680.21 Motors.

(A) Wiring Methods. The wiring to a motor must comply with (A)(1) unless modified by (A)(2), (A)(3), (A)(4), or (A)(5). **Figure 680–3**

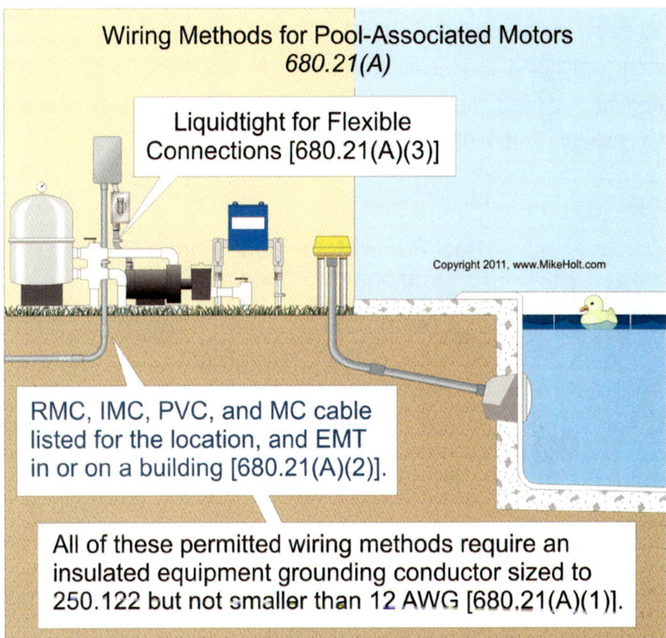

Figure 680–3

(1) General. Branch-circuit conductors for permanently installed pool, outdoor spa, and outdoor hot tub motors must be installed in rigid metal conduit, intermediate metal conduit, PVC conduit, or Type MC cable listed for the location (sunlight-resistant or for direct burial). The wiring methods must contain an insulated copper equipment grounding conductor sized in accordance with 250.122, but in no case can it be smaller than 12 AWG.

(2) On or Within Buildings. If installed on or within buildings, electrical metallic tubing is permitted to supply permanently installed pool, outdoor spa, and outdoor hot tub motors.

Author's Comment: If electrical metallic tubing is used, it must contain an insulated copper equipment grounding conductor as required by 680.21(A)(1).

(3) Flexible Connections. Liquidtight flexible metal or liquidtight flexible nonmetallic conduit is permitted for permanently installed pool, outdoor spa, and outdoor hot tub motors.

Author's Comment: If liquidtight flexible metal or liquidtight flexible nonmetallic conduit is used, it must contain an insulated copper equipment grounding conductor as required by 680.21(A)(1).

(4) One-Family Dwelling. In the interior of a dwelling unit or accessory building associated with a dwelling unit, any Chapter 3 wiring method is permitted. If branch-circuit conductors are installed in a raceway, the wiring method must contain an insulated copper equipment grounding conductor as required by 680.21(A)(1). If a cable assembly is used, the circuit equipment grounding conductor can be uninsulated. **Figure 680–4**

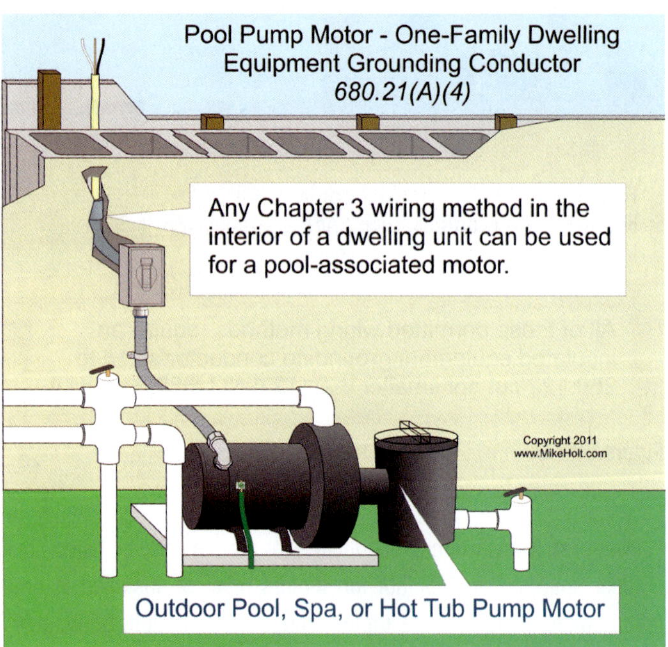

Figure 680–4

(5) Cord-and-Plug Connections. A cord no longer than 3 ft, with an attachment plug and containing a copper equipment grounding conductor, sized in accordance with 250.122, but not smaller than 12 AWG is permitted for pool associated motors. **Figure 680–5**

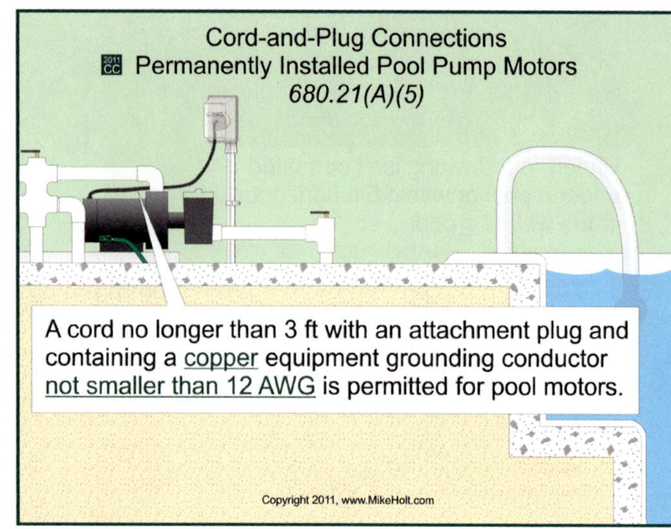

Figure 680–5

Author's Comment: For outdoor spas and hot tubs, the cord must be GFCI protected and it can be up to 15 ft long [680.42(A)(2)].

ANALYSIS: Permanently installed pools are required to comply with Parts I and II of this article [680.20]. Due to this requirement, any cord-and-plug-connected equipment, other than underwater luminaires, must have a copper equipment grounding conductor no smaller than 12 AWG [680.7(B)]. Section 680.21(A)(5) gives the *Code* user guidance as to how to size an equipment grounding conductor (EGC) by referring to 250.122, but it didn't include the provision that the EGC be copper and no smaller than 12 AWG. This change corrects that inconsistency for cord-and-plug-connected pool equipment.

680.21(C) GFCI Protection of Motors

208V circuits feeding pool motors are now required to have GFCI protection.

680.21 Motors.

(C) GFCI Protection. GFCI protection is required for outlets supplying pool pump motors connected to single-phase 120V through 240V branch circuits rated 15A or 20A, whether by receptacle or by direct connection. **Figure 680–6**

Figure 680–6

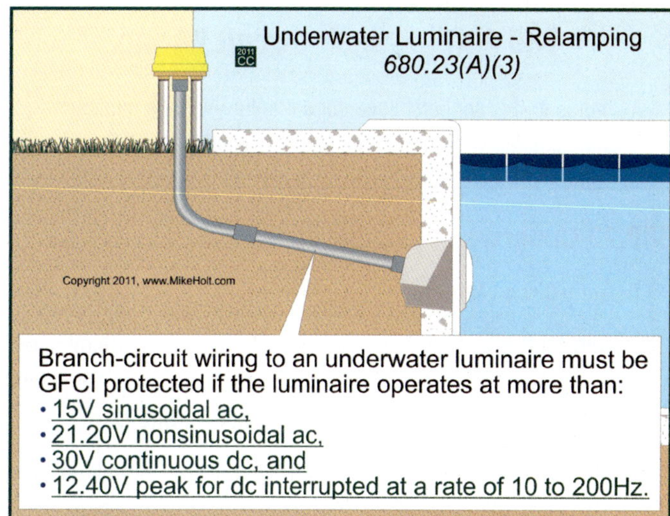

Figure 680–7

ANALYSIS: The 2008 *NEC* added a requirement for pool motors to have GFCI protection whenever they're rated 120V or 240V, 15A or 20A. It's believed the intent was to include 208V circuits as well. This change is intended to correct that mistake by replacing the "or" with "through."

The requirements have also been relocated to 680.21 from 680.22, with the subsections in 680.22 being renumbered accordingly.

680.23(A) Underwater Luminaires

This section has been revised to address LED technology. The voltage limitations of non-GFCI-protected luminaires have also been changed.

680.23 Underwater Luminaires.

(A) General.

(2) Transformers and Power Supplies. Transformers and power supplies for underwater luminaires must be listed.

(3) GFCI Protection of Underwater Luminaires, Relamping. Branch circuits that supply underwater luminaires operating at more than 15V for sinusoidal alternating current, 21.20V peak for nonsinusoidal alternating current, 30V for continuous direct-current, and 12.40V peak for direct current interrupted at a rate of 10 to 200 Hz or less [680.2 Low-Voltage Contact Limit] must be GFCI protected. Figure 680–7

(5) Wall-Mounted Luminaires. Underwater luminaires must be installed so that the top of the luminaire lens isn't less than 18 in. below the normal water level.

ANALYSIS: With the increasing popularity of LED luminaires, this section has been changed to accommodate the new technology. New LED luminaires use dc power supplies, not transformers, for their power source. LED luminaire power supplies are now required to be listed by this section.

Similar changes were made throughout this article to include the word "power supply" or "supplies" when references were made to transformers. This will allow the inclusion of new technologies that rely upon dc as well as ac power supplies.

The 15V threshold that has long been in this requirement was presumed to be a safe limit for ac when contact is possible. With the changing technologies of luminaires, this value no longer addresses all types of luminaires that are encountered. Many are supplied by dc voltage and many use nonsinusoidal voltage wave forms. This change reflects that by pointing the *Code* user to the definition of "low-voltage contact limit" in 680.2

Similar changes were made throughout Article 680.

680.23(F) Branch-Circuit Wiring

A change to this section allows for some low-voltage luminaires to be connected without an equipment grounding conductor.

680.23 Underwater Luminaires.

(F) Branch-Circuit Wiring.

(1) Wiring Methods. Branch-circuit wiring for underwater luminaires must be rigid metal conduit, intermediate metal conduit, liquidtight flexible nonmetallic conduit, or PVC conduit [680.23(B)(2)].

If installed on buildings, electrical metallic tubing is permitted, and where installed within buildings, electrical nonmetallic tubing, Type MC cable, electrical metallic tubing, or Type AC cable is permitted. The wiring methods must contain an insulated copper equipment grounding conductor sized in accordance with 250.122, but in no case can it be smaller than 12 AWG.

Ex: If connecting to transformers for pool lights, liquidtight flexible metal conduit is permitted in individual lengths not exceeding 6 ft.

(2) Equipment Grounding Conductor. For other than listed low-voltage luminaires not requiring grounding, branch-circuit conductors for an underwater luminaire must contain an insulated copper equipment grounding conductor sized in accordance with 250.122, but not smaller than 12 AWG, **Figure 680–8**. The circuit equipment grounding conductor for the underwater luminaire must not be spliced, except as permitted in (a) or (b).

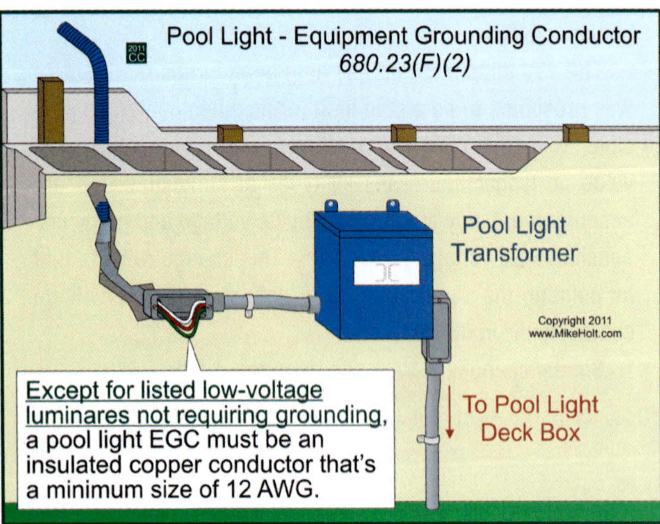

Figure 680–8

(a) If more than one underwater luminaire is supplied by the same branch circuit, the circuit equipment grounding conductor can terminate at a listed pool junction box that meets the requirements of 680.24(A).

(b) The circuit equipment grounding conductor can terminate at the grounding terminal of a listed pool transformer that meets the requirements of 680.23(A)(2).

(3) Conductors. The branch-circuit conductors on the load side of a GFCI or transformer for underwater luminaires must not occupy raceways or enclosures containing other conductors unless one of the following conditions applies:

(1) The other conductors are GFCI protected.

(2) The other conductors are equipment grounding conductors.

(3) The other conductors are the supply conductors to a feed-through type GFCI.

(4) The GFCI-protected conductors are within a panelboard.

ANALYSIS: Although there are listed low-voltage luminaires for swimming pools that don't include a grounding means, the *Code* hasn't provided for them. With this change, these luminaires (such as plastic LED luminaires) will become viable options for swimming pools.

680.25(A) Feeder Wiring Methods

A new allowance for MC cable feeder circuits was added, and the requirements have been changed into a "list" format.

680.25 Feeders.

(A) Wiring Methods.

(1) Feeder conductors to panelboards containing permanently installed pool, outdoor spa, or outdoor hot tub equipment circuits must be installed in rigid metal conduit or intermediate metal conduit. If not subject to physical damage, the following wiring methods are permitted: **Figure 680–9**

(a) Liquidtight flexible nonmetallic conduit

(b) PVC conduit

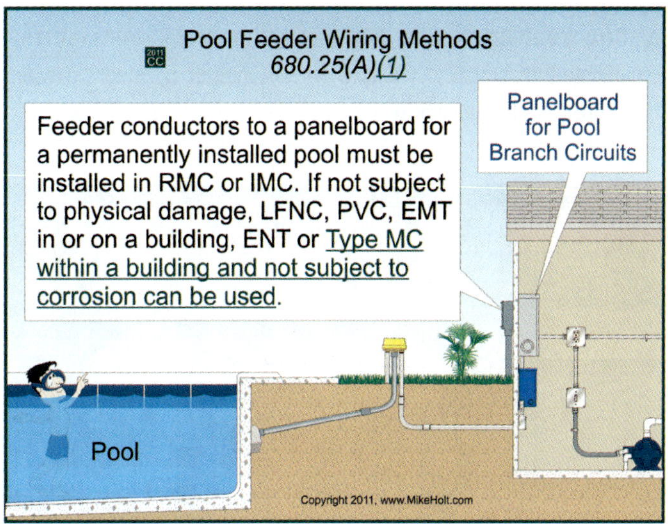

Figure 680–9

(d) Electrical metallic tubing is permitted where installed on or within a building

(e) Electrical nonmetallic tubing is permitted where installed within a building

(f) Type MC cable installed within a building and if not subject to a corrosive environment

Ex: Branch circuits for permanently installed pool, outdoor spa, or outdoor hot tub equipment can originate from an existing panelboard if the existing feeder contains an equipment grounding conductor within the outer sheath of a cable.

ANALYSIS: Previous editions of the *Code* didn't contain an allowance for Type MC cable to be used as a feeder circuit for permanently installed swimming pools. This change now allows for this wiring method, provided that the cable isn't subject to physical damage or corrosion.

The wiring methods allowed in this section have also been made into an easier to read list, which reduces the likelihood of misreading the requirements.

680.26 Equipotential Bonding

The requirements for swimming pool bonding were revised... again.

680.26 Equipotential Bonding.

(A) Performance. Equipotential bonding is intended to reduce voltage gradients in the area around a permanently installed pool, outdoor spa, or outdoor hot tub by the use of a common bonding grid in accordance with 680.26(B) and (C).

(B) Bonded Parts. The parts of a permanently installed pool, outdoor spa, or outdoor hot tub listed in (B)(1) through (B)(7) must be bonded together with a solid copper conductor not smaller than 8 AWG with listed pressure connectors, terminal bars, exothermic welding, or other listed means [250.8(A)]. Figure 680–10

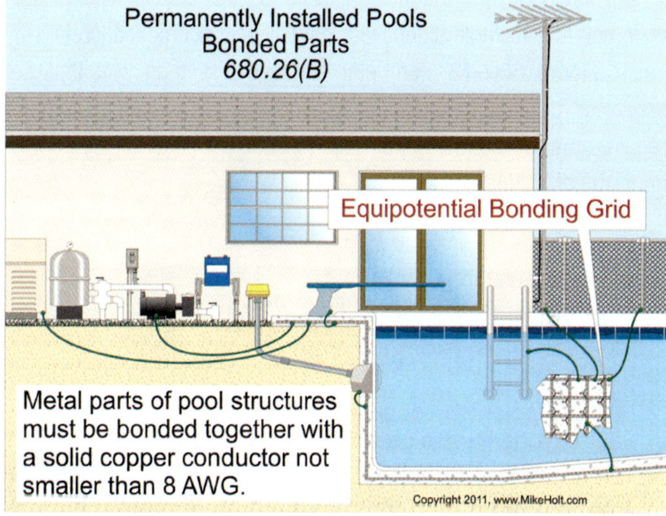

Figure 680–10

Equipotential bonding isn't required to extend to or be attached to any panelboard, service equipment, or grounding electrode.

(1) Concrete Pool, Outdoor Spa, and Outdoor Hot Tub Shells.

(a) Structural Reinforcing Steel. Unencapsulated structural reinforcing steel in concrete shells secured together by steel tie wires. Figure 680–11

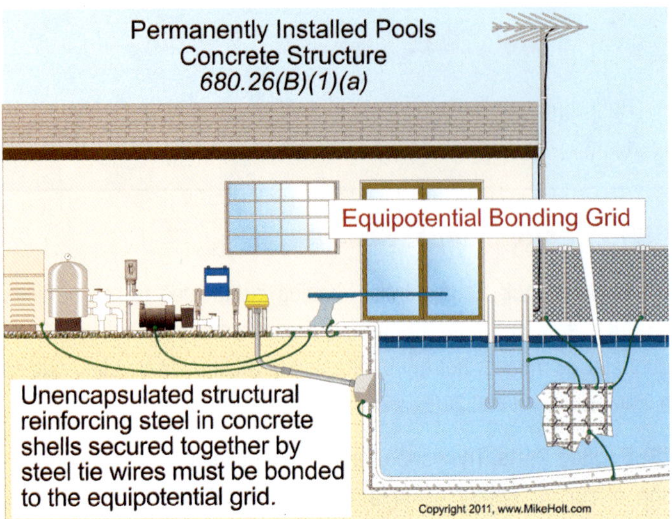

Figure 680–11

(2) Perimeter Surfaces. An equipotential bonding grid must extend 3 ft horizontally beyond the inside walls of a pool, outdoor spa, or outdoor hot tub, including unpaved, paved, and poured concrete surfaces, **Figure 680–12**. Perimeter surfaces less than 3 ft that are separated by a permanent wall or building 5 ft in height or more require an equipotential bonding grid on the pool side of the permanent wall or building.

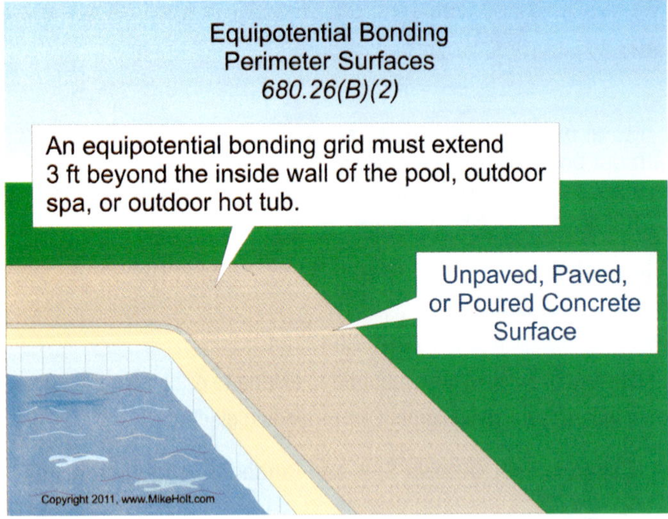

Figure 680–12

The bonding grid must comply with (a) or (b) and be attached to the conductive pool reinforcing steel at a minimum of four points uniformly spaced around the perimeter of the walls of a pool, outdoor spa, or outdoor hot tub.

(a) Structural Reinforcing Steel. Unencapsulated structural reinforcing steel in concrete shells secured together by steel tie wires [680.26(B)(1)(a)]. **Figure 680–13**

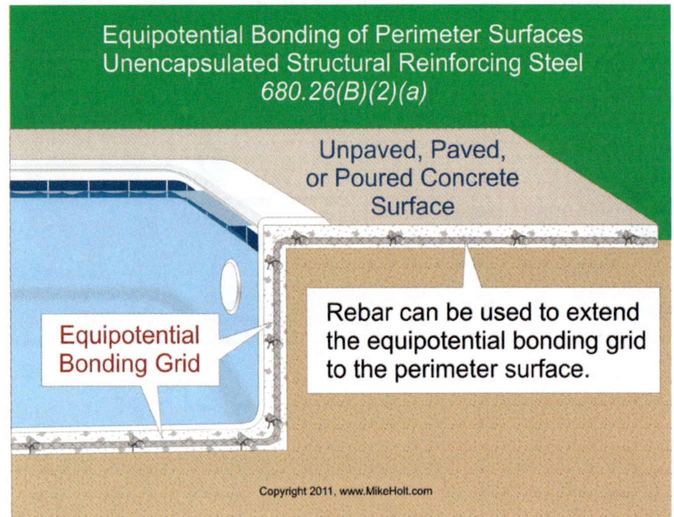

Figure 680–13

Author's Comment: The *NEC* doesn't provide any guidance on the installation requirements for structural reinforcing steel when used as a perimeter equipotential bonding grid.

(b) Alternative Means. Where the structural reinforcing steel isn't available (or is encapsulated in a nonconductive compound, such as epoxy), an equipotential bonding grid meeting all of the following requirements must be installed: **Figure 680-14**

(1) The bonding conductor must be 8 AWG solid copper.

(2) The bonding grid must follow the contour of the perimeter surface.

(3) Listed splicing devices must be used.

(4) Bonding conductor must be 18 to 24 in. from the inside walls of the pool.

(5) The bonding conductor must be secured in or under the deck or unpaved surface within 4 to 6 in. of the underside of the deck.

(3) Metallic Components. Metallic parts of the pool, outdoor spa, or outdoor hot tub structure must be bonded to the equipotential grid.

(4) Underwater Metal Forming Shells. Metal forming shells and mounting brackets for luminaires and speakers must be bonded to the equipotential grid.

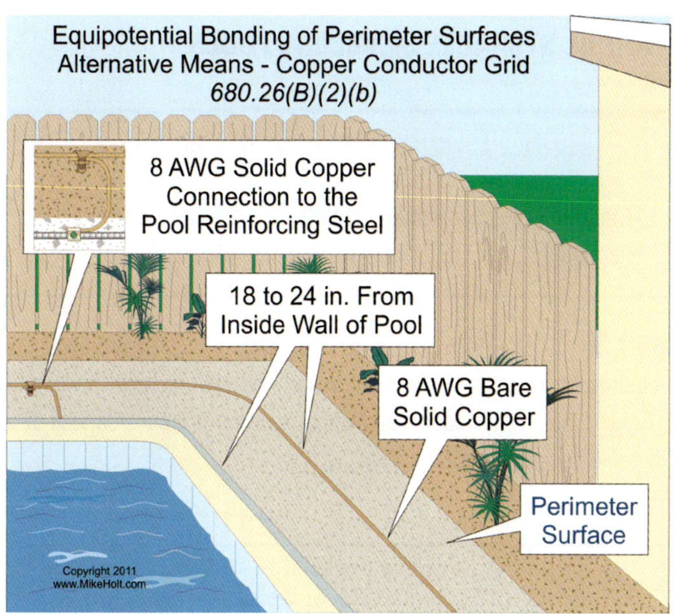

Figure 680–14

(5) Metal Fittings. Metal fittings sized 4 in. and larger that penetrate into the pool, outdoor spa, or outdoor hot tub structure, such as ladders and handrails must be bonded to the equipotential grid.

(6) Electrical Equipment. Metal parts of electrical equipment associated with the pool, outdoor spa, or outdoor hot tub water circulating system, such as water heaters and pump motors and metal parts of pool covers must be bonded to the equipotential grid. Figure 680–15

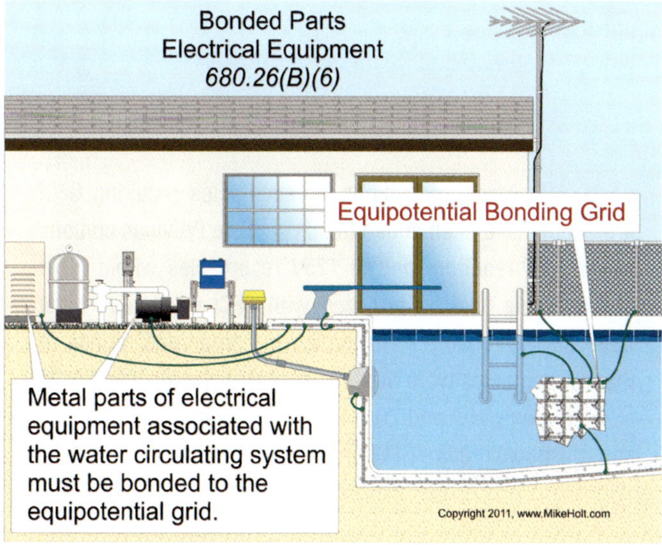

Figure 680–15

Ex: Metal parts of listed double insulation equipment isn't required to be bonded to the equipotential grid.

(a) Double-Insulated Water-Pump Motors. If a double-insulated water-pump motor is installed, a solid 8 AWG copper conductor from the bonding grid must be provided for a replacement motor.

(b) Pool Water Heaters. Pool water heaters must be grounded and bonded in accordance with equipment instructions.

(7) Fixed Metal Parts. All fixed metal parts must be bonded to the equipotential grid, including but not limited to, metal-sheathed cables and raceways, metal piping, metal awnings, metal fences, and metal door and window frames.

Ex 1: If separated from the pool, outdoor spa, or outdoor hot tub structure by a permanent barrier that prevents contact by a person.

Ex 2: If located more than 5 ft horizontally of the inside walls of the pool, outdoor spa, or outdoor hot tub structure.

Ex 3: If located more than 12 ft measured vertically above the maximum water level.

(C) Pool Water. Pool water must have an electrical connection to one or more of the bonded parts described in 680.26(B). If none of the bonded parts is in direct connection with the pool water, the pool water must be in direct contact with an approved corrosion-resistant conductive surface that exposes not less than 9 sq in. of surface area to the pool water at all times, and it must be bonded in accordance with 680.26(B). Figure 680–16

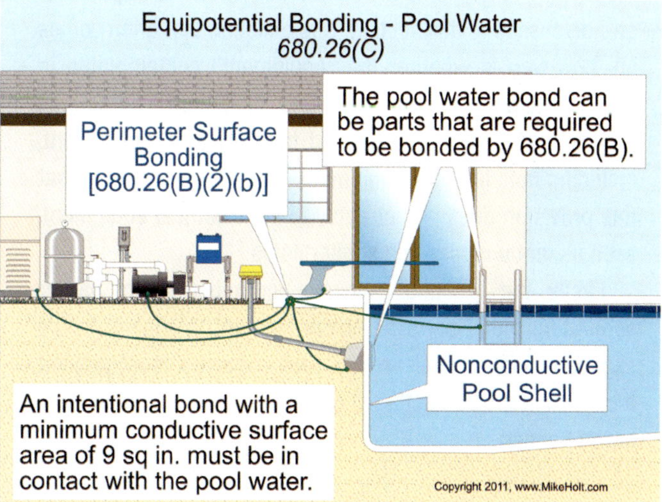

Figure 680–16

Author's Comment: The conductive surface should be located where it's not exposed to physical damage or dislodgement during usual pool activities.

ANALYSIS: This section has been revised extensively over the last few *Code* change cycles, and this one is no exception. Recent revisions have left gaping holes in the requirements, and plenty of room for misunderstanding, misinterpretation, and misapplication. The changes in the 2011 edition of the *NEC* seek to remedy these problems.

The connection of the copper bonding grid discussed in 680.26(B)(1)(b)(1) has been addressed. When nonconductive structural reinforcing steel is used in a pool, a bonding grid of 8 AWG copper conductors is required, but previous editions of the *Code* didn't address how to connect the grid to itself. This *NEC* cycle clarifies that the grid must be bonded together at all points of crossing in the grid, and the bonding means must comply with the connection provisions of 250.8.

A clarification was also made regarding the bonding of the pool deck. It isn't uncommon for a pool deck to be less than 3 ft when a wall, fence, or other structure is near the pool. Previous editions of the *Code* didn't tell the user how to handle the situations, but now it's clear that the bonding doesn't need to extend to the other side of the wall, provided the wall (or fence) is no less than 5 ft. in height.

The bonding of nonelectric metal parts has been clarified. Section 680.26(B)(7) has long required that "metal wiring methods and equipment" be bonded to the equipotential grid discussed in this section. One question that often comes up, however, is whether the "equipment" contemplated in this rule applies to only "electrical equipment," as defined in Article 100, or if it's intended to apply to all equipment, including nonelectrical equipment. This change clarifies that this provision does in fact apply to nonelectrical equipment, such as metal fences and similar items.

Lastly, the exception allowing for a permanent barrier separating metal parts has been clarified. A change to the exception makes it clear that such a barrier must prevent a person from contacting metal parts and equipment that aren't bonded.

PART III. STORABLE SWIMMING POOLS

680.32 GFCI-Protected Receptacles

The GFCI protection requirements for storable pools have been clarified.

680.32 GFCI-Protected Receptacles. GFCI protection is required for electrical equipment associated with storable pools and 15A and 20A, 125V receptacles within 20 ft from the inside wall of a storable pool. Figure 680–17

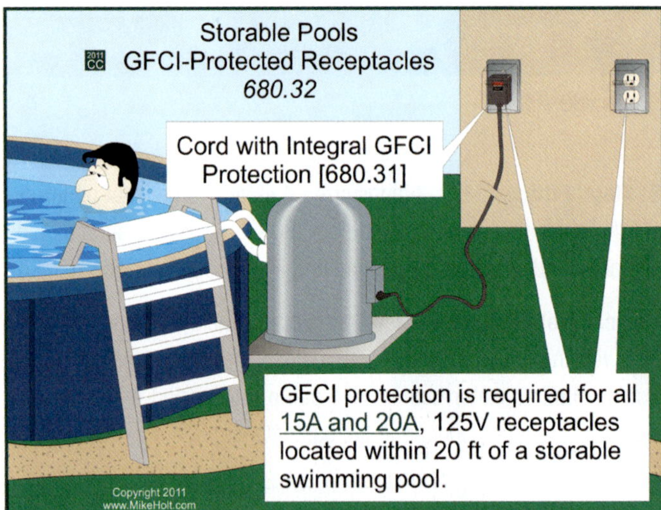

Figure 680–17

ANALYSIS: Amperage ratings of receptacles requiring GFCI protection have been added to this section. Previous editions of the *NEC* required that all 125V receptacles within 20 ft of a storable pool be provided with GFCI protection. Most *Code* users probably didn't notice the amperage ratings of these receptacles were missing. With this change, the *NEC* is clear that only 15A and 20A, 125V receptacles within 20 ft of storable pools require GFCI protection.

PART IV. SPAS AND HOT TUBS

680.43 Indoor Installations of Spas and Hot Tubs

The bonding of perimeter surfaces near spas and hot tubs has been addressed via a new exception.

680.43 Indoor Installations. Electrical installations for an indoor spa or hot tub must comply with Parts I and II of Article 680, except as modified by this section. Indoor installations of spas or hot tubs can be connected by any of the wiring methods contained in Chapter 3.

Ex 1: Listed packaged units rated 20A or less can be cord-and-plug-connected.

Ex 2: The equipotential bonding requirements for perimeter surfaces contained in 680.26(B)(2) don't apply to a listed self-contained spa or hot tub installed above a finished floor.

ANALYSIS: Sections 680.42 and 680.43 require that spas and hot tubs comply with Parts I and II of Article 680, including the bonding provisions of 680.26, except as modified by 680.42 for outdoor installations and 680.43 for indoor installations. Because of this, some inspectors have been requiring that a bonding grid (similar to the deck bonding for pools) be installed around indoor spas or hot tubs. While this was never the intent of the *Code*, there was a gaping hole in this section that didn't address that issue. With this new exception, it becomes clear that an equipotential bonding grid isn't required around the perimeter of an indoor spa or hot tub when installed above the finished floor.

680.43(C) Indoor Installation of Switches

The clearance requirements for switches near indoor spas and hot tubs have been clarified.

680.43 Indoor Installations.

(C) Switches. Switches must be located not less than 5 ft, measured horizontally, from the inside walls of the indoor spa or hot tub. Figure 680–18

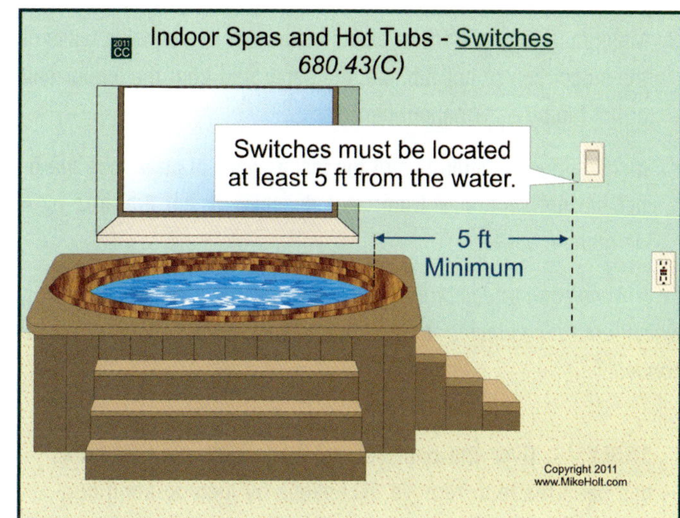

Figure 680–18

ANALYSIS: Switches have been prohibited within 5 ft of indoor spas and hot tubs. While this rule was probably intended to apply to all switches, the title of this subsection left room for argument. Previous editions of the *NEC* titled this rule "Wall Switches," which implied a general-use snap switch. While snap switches do require a 5 ft separation from a spa or hot tub, so do circuit breakers, disconnect switches, safety switches, and all other types of switches. This revision should help the *Code* user understand the scope of this rule.

680.43(D) Indoor Installation Bonding

Ex 2 has been deleted and incorporated into the text of 680.43(D)(2).

680.43 Indoor Installations.

(D) Bonding. The following parts of an indoor spa or hot tub must be bonded together:

(1) Metal fittings within or attached to the indoor spa or hot tub structure.

(2) Metal parts of electrical equipment associated with the indoor spa or hot tub water circulating system unless part of a listed self-contained spa or hot tub.

(3) Metal raceways and metal piping within 5 ft of the inside walls of the indoor spa or hot tub, and not separated from the indoor spa or hot tub by a permanent barrier.

(4) Metal surfaces within 5 ft of the inside walls of an indoor spa or hot tub not separated from the indoor spa or hot tub area by a permanent barrier.

Ex 1: Nonelectrical equipment, such as towel bars or mirror frames, which aren't connected to metallic piping, aren't required to be bonded.

ANALYSIS: Over the past several *Code* cycles a real effort has been made to remove exceptions by incorporating negative text in the form of exceptions into positive text that's included in the rule itself. This change is an example of that effort, removing (former) Exception 2 and adding a few words to 680.43(D)(2). While this change doesn't make any technical difference at first glance, it does help the *NEC* user to understand which portion of 680.43(D) the (former) exception applied to. Many *Code* users were unclear if the exception was a carte blanche exception to 680.43(D), or just to 680.43(D)(4).

PART VII. HYDROMASSAGE BATHTUBS

680.73 Accessibility

The accessibility of the receptacle supplying a hydromassage tub has been revised.

680.73 Accessibility. Electrical equipment for hydromassage bathtubs must be capable of being removed or exposed without damaging the building structure or finish. Where the hydromassage bathtub is cord-and plug-connected with the supply receptacle accessible only through an access opening, the receptacle must face toward the opening and be within 1 ft of the opening.

ANALYSIS: When a hydromassage tub is cord-and-plug-connected, it isn't uncommon to find the receptacle beneath the tub, arranged in a manner that makes it nearly impossible to see, much less use. Oftentimes these receptacles are several feet away from the access opening, facing away from the person trying to access the receptacle! This change now requires that such a receptacle be installed close to the access opening (within 1 ft.) and it must also be facing toward the opening.

680.74 Equipotential Bonding

Provisions for the replacement of a hydromassage tub motor have been made.

680.74 Equipotential Bonding. Metal piping systems and grounded metal parts in contact with the circulating water must be bonded to the hydromassage circulating pump motor that is not double insulated with an 8 AWG or larger bare copper conductor.

Where a metal piping systems or grounded metal part in contact with the circulating water is present with a double insulated motor, a 8 AWG or larger bare copper conductor must be provided at the hydromassage circulating motor with sufficient length to terminate on a replacement non-double insulated pump motor.

The metal piping to motor bonding jumper is not be required to be attached to any panelboard, service equipment, or electrode. **Figure 680–19**

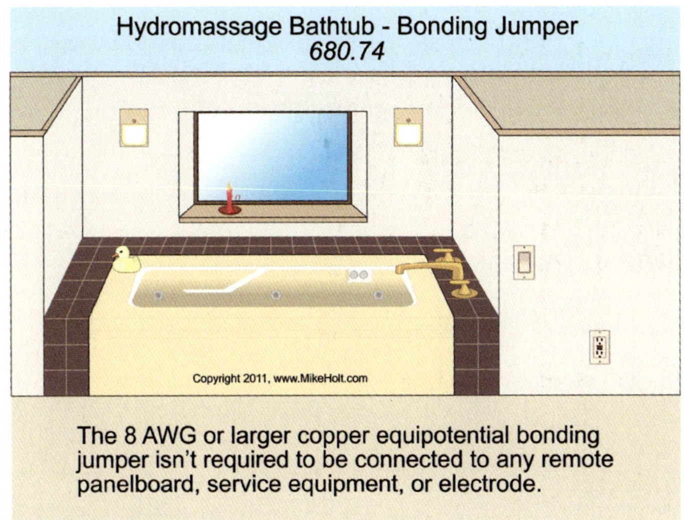

Figure 680–19

ANALYSIS: This section has required that the pump motor of a hydromassage tub (that isn't a double insulated motor) be bonded to a metal water piping system, if such a piping system is present, for a long time. There's some possibility that a double insulated motor (which didn't have a bonding jumper installed) might be replaced by a motor that isn't double insulated, resulting in a noncompliant installation. When such a replacement occurs, the installer must bond this new motor to the metal water piping system. It's conceivable that this can require extensive remodeling to access the metal water piping system. With this change, a bonding jumper must be routed to a double insulated motor for use should a replacement occur.

NOTES

Photovoltaic POWER SYSTEMS

INTRODUCTION TO ARTICLE 690—PHOTOVOLTAIC POWER SYSTEMS

You've seen, or maybe own, photocell-powered devices such as night lights, car coolers, and toys. These generally consist of a small solar panel and a small light or motor. Typically, these run on less than 10V dc and draw only a fraction of an ampere. These kinds of devices are very different from a system that can power a house or small commercial building.

Consider the sheer size and weight of solar panels for providing electrical power to a building. You're looking at mechanical and site selection issues that may require specialized expertise. The value of these panels also means there are security issues to consider, which may require more than just installing locks. There are also civil and architectural issues to address.

In summary, these installations are complicated and require expertise in several non-electrical areas, which the *NEC* doesn't address.

Article 690 focuses on reducing the electrical hazards that may arise from installing and operating a solar photovoltaic system, to the point where it can be considered safe for property and people.

This article consists of nine Parts, the last of which applies only to systems over 600V. The requirements of Chapters 1 through 4 apply to these installations, except as specifically modified by Article 690.

PART I. GENERAL

Article 690 Solar Photovoltaic (PV) Systems

The term "PV" was added throughout the article.

ANALYSIS: To those familiar with solar photovoltaic systems, the acronym "PV" is a familiar one. It's now been incorporated into the *NEC* text, which will allow *Code* users to perhaps avoid the somewhat laborious task of saying "photovoltaic" and replace it with "PV," which is already commonplace.

690.2 Definitions

A new definition for "subarray" was added.

Subarray. An electrical subset of an array.

ANALYSIS: Although subarrays are discussed in Article 690, they haven't been defined. This change adds a useful definition for the term, indicating that a subarray is nothing more than an electrical subset of an array.

690.4 Installation

Major changes were made to this section governing the installation of PV systems, including requiring the identification of conductors, circuit routing, and connections be made by qualified persons.

690.4 Installation.

(A) Photovoltaic System. A PV system is permitted to supply power to a building or other structure in addition to any other electricity supply system(s).

(B) Mixing Conductors of Different Systems. PV system conductors, both direct current and alternating current are permitted to be installed in the same raceways, outlet and junction boxes, or similar fittings with each other, but they must be kept entirely independent of all other non-PV system wiring. **Figure 690–1**

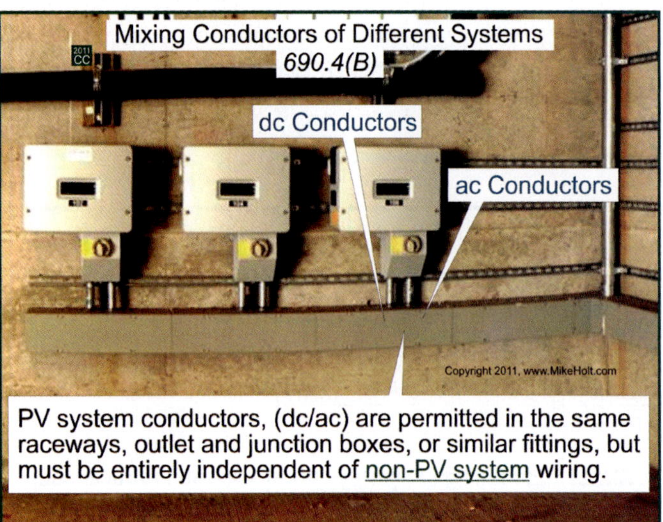

Figure 690–1

(1) Identification. PV system conductors must be identified by separate color coding, marking tape, tagging, or other approved means as follows:

(a) PV Source Circuits. Identified at points of termination, connection, and splices.

(b) PV Output and Inverter Circuits. Identified at points of termination, connection, and splices.

(c) Multiple Systems. Conductors of each system must be identified at termination, connection, and splice points.

Ex: Identification of different systems isn't required where the identification of the conductors is evident by spacing or arrangement.

(d) Grouping. Where the conductors of more than one PV system occupy the same junction box or raceway with removable cover, the ac and dc conductors of each system must be grouped by cable ties at least once and at intervals not to exceed 6 ft.

Ex: Grouping in the junction box or raceway with removable cover isn't required if the PV circuit enters from a cable or raceway unique to the circuit that makes the grouping obvious.

(C) Module Connection. Module connections must be arranged so that the removal of a module doesn't interrupt the grounded conductor to other PV source circuits.

(D) Equipment. Inverters, photovoltaic modules, source-circuit combiners, and charge controllers intended for use in photovoltaic power systems must be identified and listed for the application. **Figure 690–2**

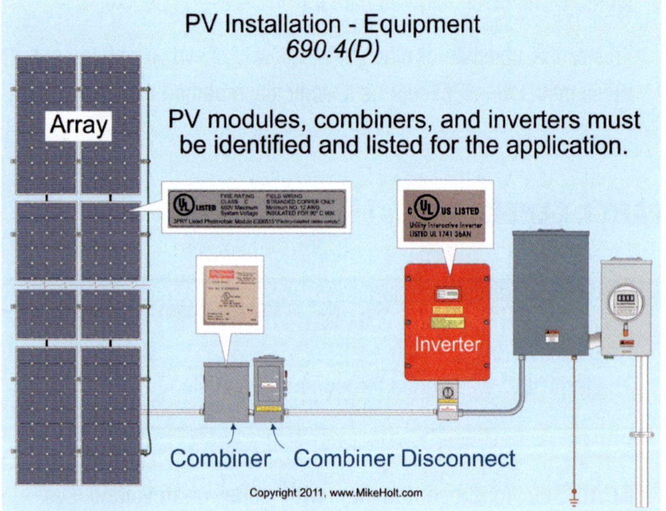

Figure 690–2

Author's Comments:

- Identified. Recognized as suitable for a specific purpose, function, or environment by listing [Article 100].
- Listed. Equipment or materials included in a list published by a testing laboratory acceptable to the authority having jurisdiction [Article 100].

(E) Wiring and Connections. The PV equipment, systems, associated wiring, and interconnections must only be installed by qualified persons.

Note: A qualified person has the knowledge related to construction and operation of PV equipment and installations; along with safety training to recognize and avoid hazards to persons and property [Article 100].

(F) Circuit Routing. PV source and output conductors must be routed along building structural members (beams, rafters, trusses, and columns) where the location of those structural members can be determined by observation.

The location of PV source and output conductors imbedded in built-up, laminate, or membrane roofing materials in areas not covered by PV modules and associated equipment must be clearly marked.

(H) Multiple Inverters. Where inverters are remotely located from each other, a permanent plaque or directory, denoting all electrical power sources on or in the premises, must be installed at each service equipment location and all interconnected electrical power production sources [705.10].

Ex: A directory isn't required where all inverters and PV dc disconnecting means are grouped at the main service disconnecting means.

ANALYSIS: Several changes to this section have been made to clarify and expand the requirements for PV systems. The term "solar" has been removed and replaced with "PV," as it's the more accepted term.

The separation requirements have been revised to require grouping of the conductors where conductors of more than one system occupy the same enclosure or raceway with a removable cover, unless grouping is obviously not necessary.

A new requirement for routing PV related conductors along structural members was added. Concern for firefighters was the driving force behind this change. When firefighters ventilate a roof where PV conductors are present, the danger of hitting these conductors is a very serious one. With this new rule, hopefully they'll either see the conductors, or see the markings this change requires.

In a very surprising change, PV systems must now be installed by qualified persons(!). Other (arguably more dangerous) areas of the *Code* have never required this, as it's typically covered by state or local agencies and their applicable licensing regulations. This change is considered by many as revolutionary, and may set an interesting precedent for future editions of the *NEC*.

Lastly, a new requirement for a plaque or directory was added. Such a plaque will be required when multiple inverters are used and are installed remote from each other.

PART II. CIRCUIT REQUIREMENTS

690.7 Maximum PV Voltage

A new Informational Note, dealing with ambient temperatures, has been added.

690.7 Maximum Voltage

(A) PV System Voltage. The maximum PV system voltage is equal to the sum of the rated open-circuit voltage (Voc) of the series-connected PV modules as corrected for the lowest-expected ambient temperature in accordance with the manufacturer's open-circuit voltage temperature coefficient for the PV modules used. Manufacturer temperature coefficient can be expressed as "%/°C" or "V/°C". Figure 690–3

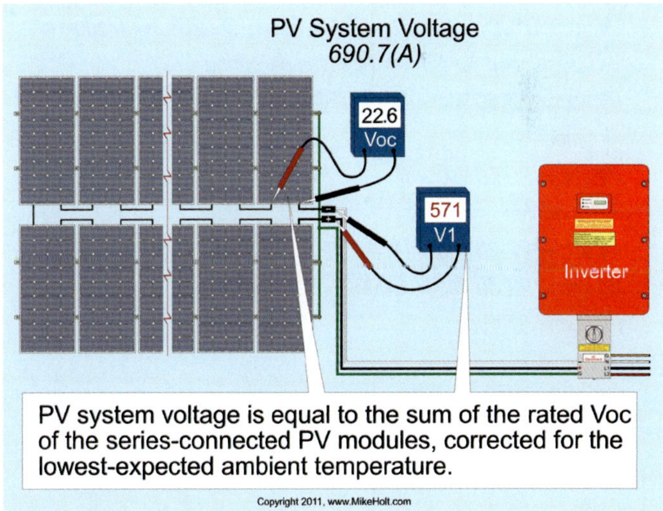

Figure 690–3

Note: One source for lowest-expected ambient temperature is the Extreme Annual Mean Minimum Design Dry Bulb Temperature found in the ASHRAE Handbook—Fundamentals.

PV System Voltage Based on Manufacturer Temperature Coefficient %/°C

Example: *The PV system voltage for an array of 23 modules each Voc 22.60, temperature coefficient -0.31%/°C, at an ambient temperature of -7°C/19°F will be 571V.* **Figure 690–4**

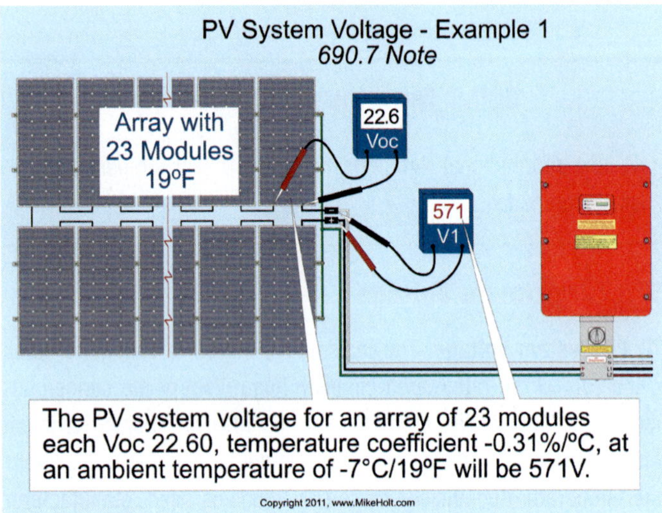

Figure 690–4

PV Voc (%/°C) = Voc × {1 + [(Min. Temp. °C - 25°C) × Module Coefficient %/°C]} × # Modules per String

PV Voc = 22.60 Voc × {1+ [(-7°C - 25°C) × -0.31%/°C]} × 23 modules

PV Voc = 22.60 Voc × {1 + [-32°C × -0.31%/°C]}) × 23 modules

PV Voc = 22.60 Voc × {1 + 9.92%} × 23 modules

PV Voc = 22.60 Voc × 1.0992 × 23 modules

PV Voc = 571 Voc

PV System Voltage Based on Manufacturer Temperature Coefficient V/°C

Example: *The PV system voltage for an array of 23 modules each Voc 22.60, temperature coefficient -0.075V/°C, at an ambient temperature of -7°C/19°F will be 575V.*

PV Voc (V/°C) = {Voc + [(Min. Temp. °C - 25°C) × Module Coefficient V/°C]} × # Modules per String

PV Voc = {22.60V + [(-7°C - 25°C) × -0.075V/°C]} × 23

PV Voc = {22.60V + [-32°C × -0.075V/°C]) × 23

PV Voc = (22.60V + 2.40V) × 23

PV Voc = 25V × 23

PV Voc = 575V

Table 690.7 Voltage Correction Factors

Lowest-Expected Ambient Temperature °C	°F	Temperature Correction Factor
0 to 4	32 to 40	1.10
-1 to -5	23 to 31	1.12
-6 to -10	14 to 22	1.14
-11 to -15	5 to 13	1.16
-16 to -20	4 to -4	1.18
-21 to -25	-5 to -13	1.20
-26 to -30	-14 to -22	1.21
-31 to -35	-23 to -31	1.23
-36 to -40	-32 to -40	1.25

Example (Table 690.7): *Using Table 690.7, the PV system voltage for an array of 23 modules each Voc 22.60, at an ambient temperature of -7°C/19°F will be 593V.* **Figure 690–5**

PV Voc Table 690.7 = Module Voc × Table 690.7 Correction Factor × # Modules per String

PV Voc = 22.60 Voc × 1.14 × 23 modules

PV Voc = 593 Voc

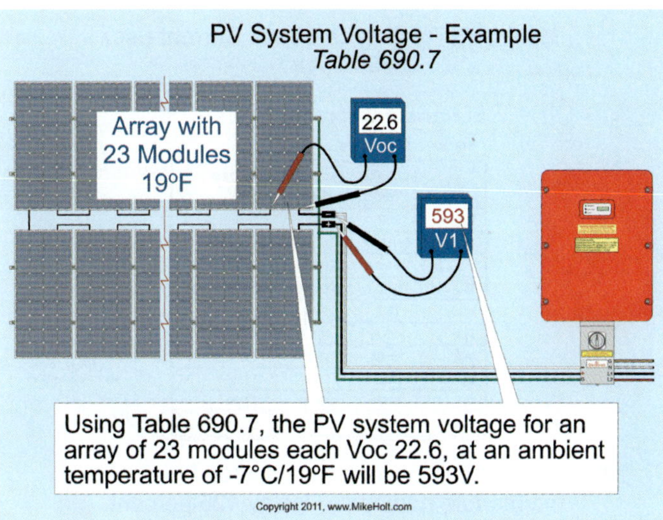

Figure 690–5

Author's Comment: All inverters require a minimum dc voltage to operate, which must be complied with [110.3(B)], and this information is marked on the inverter. Figure 690–6

Installation and Use
110.3(B)

	SB 5000US
Recommended Max. PV Power (Module STC)	6250 W
Max. DC Voltage	600 V
Peak Power Tracking Voltage	250 - 480 V
DC Max. Input Current	21 A
DC Voltage Ripple	< 5%
Number of Fused String Inputs	3 (inverter), 4 x 15 A (DC disconnect)
PV Start Voltage	300 V
AC Nominal Power	5000 W
AC Maximum Output Power	5000 W
AC Maximum Output Current (@ 208, 240, 277 V)	24 A, 21 A, 18 A
AC Nominal Voltage / Range	183 - 229 V @ 208 V 211 - 264 V @ 240 V 244 - 305 V @ 277 V

Inverters require a minimum dc voltage to operate in accordance with manufacturer's instructions.

Figure 690–6

CAUTION: *Illumination at dawn and dusk is sufficient to produce dangerous voltage, even when the sun isn't shining directly on the PV modules.* Figure 690–7

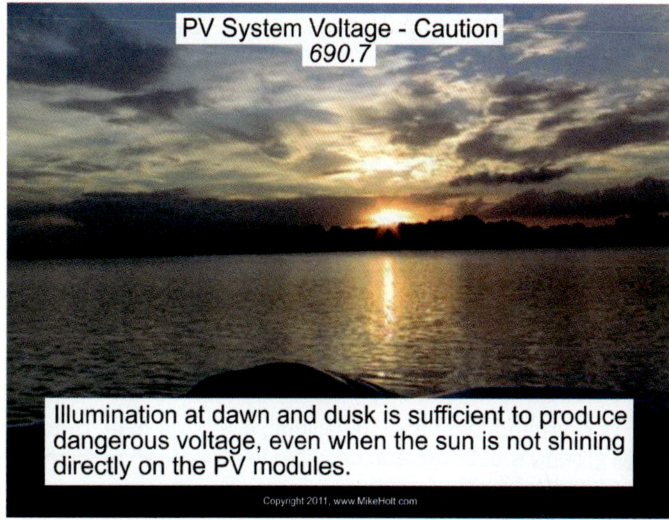

Figure 690–7

(C) Maximum PV System Voltage. For one- and two-family dwellings, the maximum PV system voltage is 600V. Figure 690–8

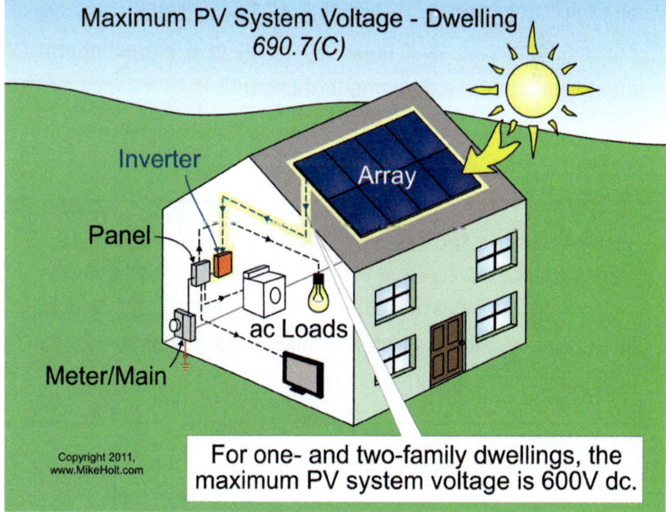

Figure 690–8

(D) Accessible. In one- and two-family dwellings, live parts over 150V to ground must not be accessible to other than qualified persons while energized. **Figure 690–9**

Maximum Voltage - Accessible
690.7(D)

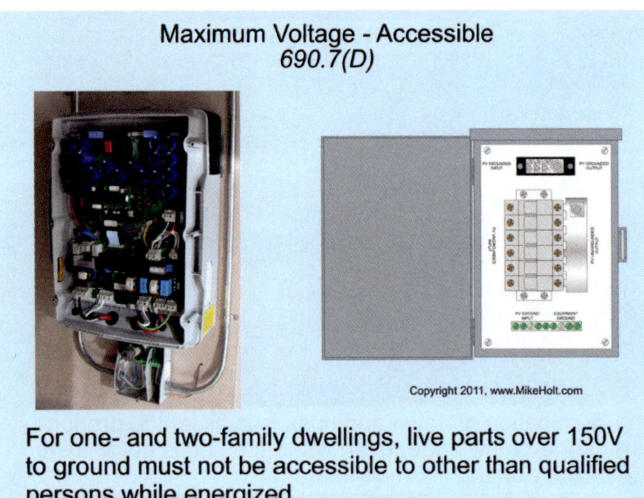

Copyright 2011, www.MikeHolt.com

For one- and two-family dwellings, live parts over 150V to ground must not be accessible to other than qualified persons while energized.

Figure 690–9

Maximum PV Source Circuit Current (Isc)
690.8(A)(1)

Electrical Characteristics

Standard Test Conditions (STC)[1]

	ES-A-200 -fa3*	ES-A-205 -fa3*	ES-A-210 -fa3*	
P_{mp}[2]	200	205	210	W
$P_{tolerance}$	-0/+4.99	-0/+4.99	-0/+4.99	W
$P_{mp, max}$	204.99	209.99	214.99	W
$P_{mp, min}$	200.00	205.00	210.00	W
η_{min}	12.7	13.1	13.4	%
P_{ptc}[3]	180.6	185.2	189.8	W
V_{mp}	18.10	18.20	18.30	V
I_{mp}	11.05	11.27	11.48	A
V_{oc}	22.60	22.70	22.80	V
I_{sc}	11.80	11.93	12.11	A

Copyright 2011, www.MikeHolt.com

PV source circuit current is calculated by multiplying the module nameplate Isc by 125 percent.

Figure 690–10

Author's Comment: The PV source circuit consists of the circuit conductors that run from the PV modules to the combiner, or if an inverter combiner isn't supplied, to the inverter [690.2].

Example: *What's the PV source circuit current for a string containing 23 PV modules having a nameplate Isc of 11.80A?* **Figure 690–11**

PV Source Circuit Current = Module Isc × 1.25

PV Source Circuit Current = 11.80A × 1.25

PV Source Circuit Current = 14.75A

PV Source Circuit Current - Example
690.8(A)(1)

Array
Module I_{SC} = 11.80A
Inverter

PV Source Circuit Current = Module I_{SC} x 1.25
PV Source Circuit Current = 11.80A x 1.25
PV Source Circuit Current = 14.75A

Copyright 2011, www.MikeHolt.com

Figure 690–11

ANALYSIS: This section discusses the "lowest-expected temperature, but provided no guidance on how it's to be determined. While personal experience may seem "good enough," it's terribly inconsistent. The addition of this Informational Note will hopefully result in a more uniform interpretation and enforcement of this rule.

690.8 Circuit Sizing and Protection

The sizing provisions for conductors and overcurrent devices have been revised to align with other *Code* requirements for conductors and overcurrent devices.

690.8 Circuit Sizing and Protection.

(A) Maximum Circuit Current.

(1) PV Source Circuit Current (Isc). The PV source circuit current is calculated by multiplying the module nameplate short-circuit current rating (Isc) by 125 percent. **Figure 690–10**

(2) PV Output Circuit Current (Isc). The PV output circuit current is equal to the sum of parallel PV source circuit current as calculated in 690.8(A)(1).

> **Author's Comment:** The PV output circuit consists of the circuit conductors that run from the combiner to the inverter [690.2].

> ***Example:*** *What's the PV output circuit current for two strings, each containing 12 PV modules having a nameplate Isc of 7.50A?* **Figure 690–12**

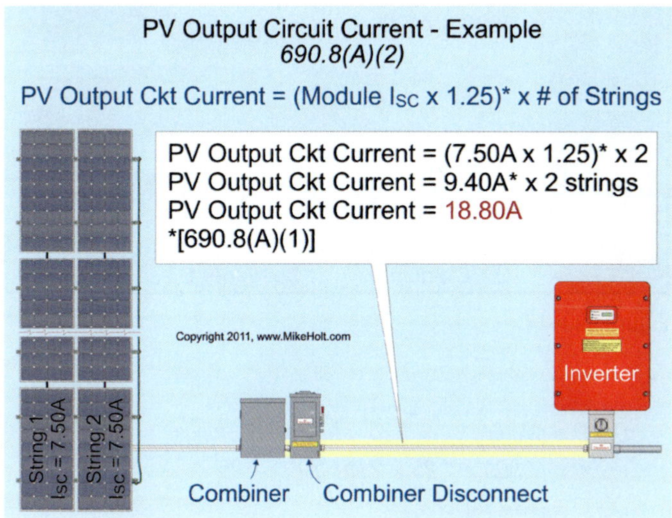

Figure 690–12

PV Output Circuit Current = (Module Isc × 1.25) × Number of Strings*

PV Output Circuit Current = (7.50A × 1.25) × 2*

PV Output Circuit Current = (9.40A) × 2*

PV Output Circuit Current = 18.80A

*[690.8(A)(1)]

(3) Inverter Output Circuit Current. The inverter output current is equal to the continuous output current marked on the inverter nameplate. **Figure 690–13**

> **Author's Comment:** The inverter output circuit consists of the circuit conductors that run from the alternating-current output terminals of the inverter to the alternating-current disconnect [690.2].

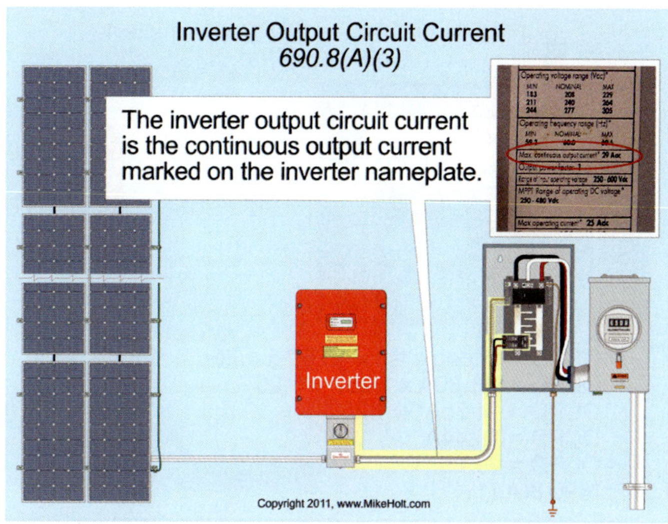

Figure 690–13

(B) Ampacity and Overcurrent Protection Device (OCPD) Ratings.

(1) Overcurrent Devices. Overcurrent devices, where required, must comply with the following:

(a) Be sized to carry not less than 125 percent of the current as calculated in 690.8(A). **Figure 690–14**

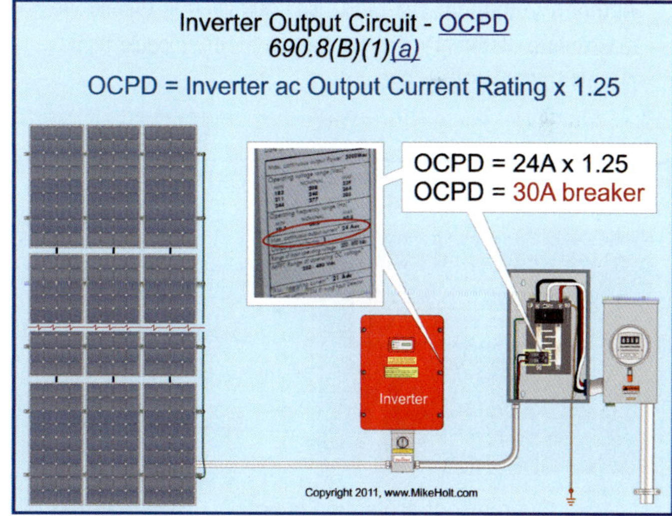

Figure 690–14

> ***Example 1—PV Source Circuit:*** *What size OCPD is required for a single PV string containing 12 PV modules, with a total nameplate Isc of 11.80A for the string?* **Figure 690–15**

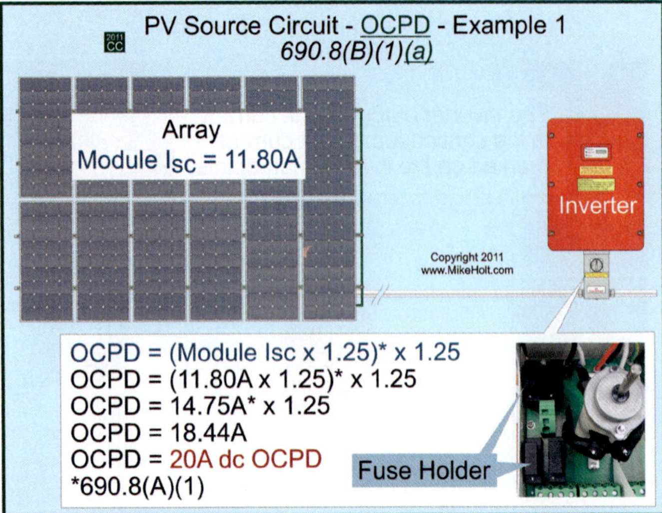

Figure 690–15

OCPD = (Module Isc × 1.25) × 1.25*

OCPD = (11.80A × 1.25) × 1.25*

OCPD = (14.75A) × 1.25*

OCPD = 18.44A

OCPD = 20A

**[690.8(A)(1)]*

Author's Comment: The OCPD isn't permitted to exceed the maximum overcurrent rating marked on the PV module nameplate [110.3(B)]. **Figure 690–16**

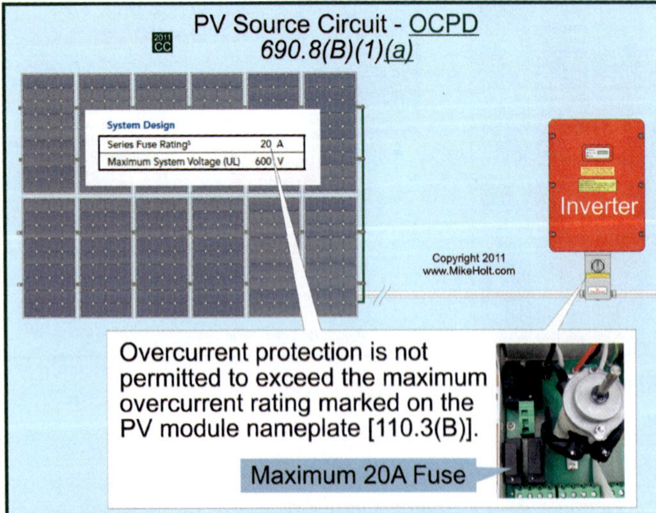

Figure 690–16

Example 2—PV Output Circuit: *What size OCPD is required for the PV output circuit supplying two PV strings, each string containing 12 PV modules, having a total nameplate Isc of 7.50A for the string?* **Figure 690–17**

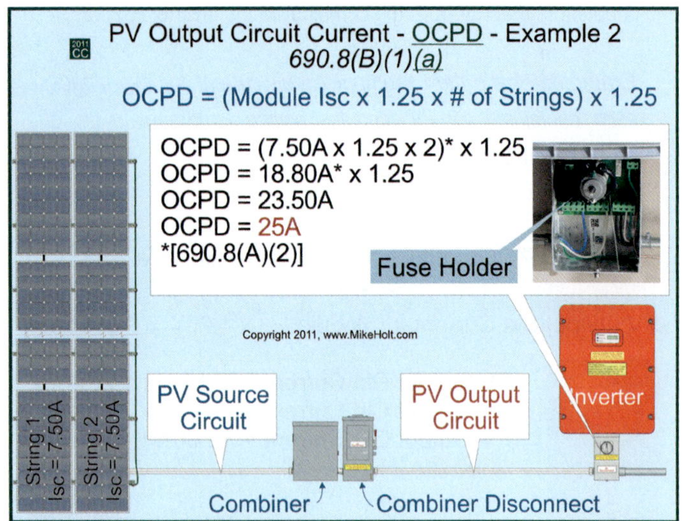

Figure 690–17

OCPD = (Module Isc × 1.25 × Number of Strings) × 1.25*

OCPD = (7.50A × 1.25 × 2 strings) × 1.25*

OCPD = (18.75A) × 1.25*

OCPD = 23.40A

OCPD = 25A direct-current fuse or direct-current circuit breaker [240.6(A) and 690.9(C)]

**[690.8(A)(2)]*

Example 3—Inverter Output Circuit: *What size OCPD is required for the inverter output circuit, if the maximum inverter continuous alternating-current output nameplate current rating is 24A?*

OCPD = Inverter ac Output Current Rating × 1.25*

OCPD = 24A × 1.25*

OCPD = 30A

OCPD = 30A circuit breaker [240.6(A)]

**[690.8(A)(3)]*

(b) When sizing conductors, the terminal temperature limits in 110.14(C) must be complied with.

(c) Where overcurrent devices operate at greater than 40°C, the ampacity rating of the OCPD must be adjusted in accordance with manufacturer's temperature correction factors.

(d) Overcurrent device ratings are permitted to comply with 240.4(B), 240.4(C), and 240.4(D).

Author's Comments:

- 240.4(B) Overcurrent Devices Rated 800A or Less. The next higher standard rating of an overcurrent device listed in 240.6 (above the ampacity of the ungrounded conductors being protected) is permitted, provided all of the following conditions are met:
  (1) The conductors don't supply multioutlet receptacle branch circuits.
  (2) The ampacity of a conductor, after the application of ambient temperature correction [310.15(B)(2)(a)], conductor bundling adjustment [310.15(B)(3)(a)], or both, doesn't correspond with the standard rating of a fuse or circuit breaker in 240.6(A).
  (3) The overcurrent device rating doesn't exceed 800A.
- **240.4(C) Overcurrent Devices Rated Over 800A.** If the circuit's overcurrent device exceeds 800A, the conductor ampacity (after the application of ambient temperature correction [310.15(B)(2)(a)], conductor bundling adjustment [310.15(B)(3)(a)], or both), must have an ampacity of not less than the rating of the overcurrent device listed in 240.6(A).

Example: *A 1,200A overcurrent device can protect three sets of 600 kcmil conductors per phase, where each conductor has an ampacity of 420A at75°C, in accordance with Table 310.15(B)(16).* **Figure 690–18**

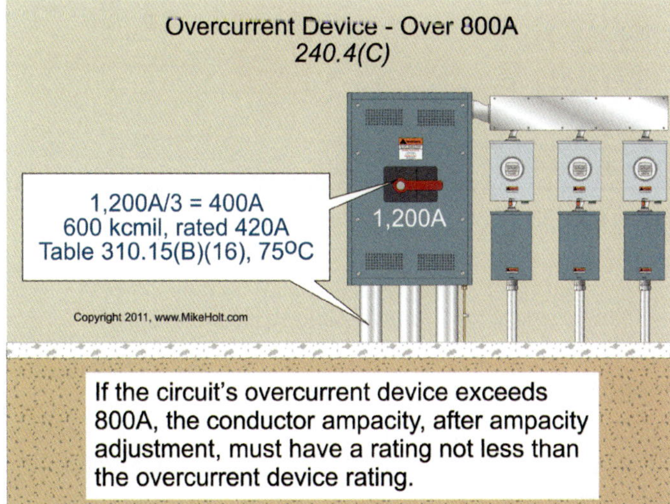

Figure 690–18

- **240.4(D) Small Conductors.** Overcurrent protection must not exceed the following: **Figure 690–19**
  (3) 14 AWG Copper—15A
  (5) 12 AWG Copper—20A
  (7) 10 AWG Copper—30A

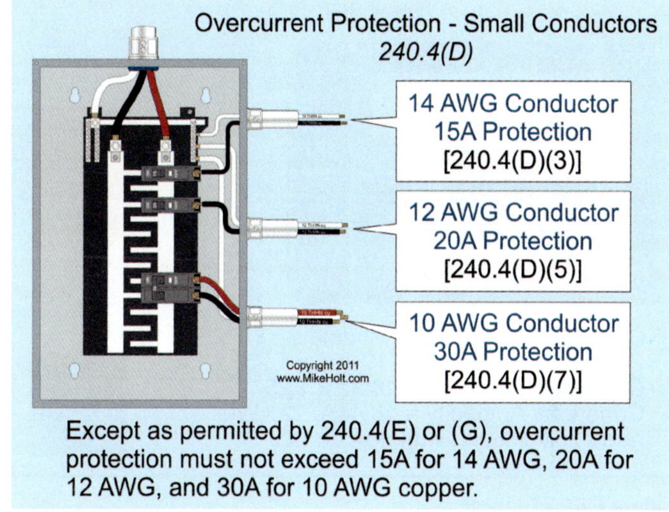

Figure 690–19

(2) Conductor Ampacity. Circuit conductors must be sized to carry the larger of 690.8(B)(2)(a) or 690.8(B)(2)(b).

(a) PV circuit conductors must be sized to carry not less than 125 percent of the currents as calculated in 690.8(A) before the application of conductor adjustment and correction of 310.15. **Figure 690–20**

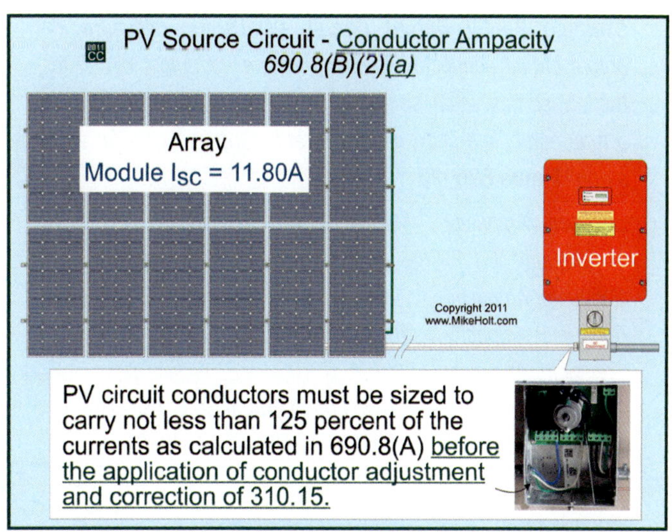

Figure 690–20

Example 1—PV Source Circuit: *What's the minimum PV source circuit conductor ampacity for a single PV string containing 23 PV modules having a total nameplate short-circuit current rating of 11.80A for the string?* **Figure 690–21**

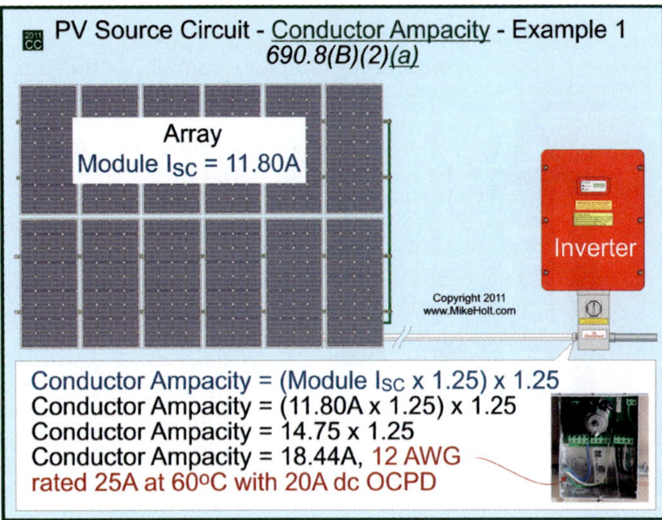

Figure 690–21

Conductor Ampacity = (Module Isc × 1.25) × 1.25*

Conductor Ampacity = (11.80A × 1.25) × 1.25*

Conductor Ampacity = (14.75A) × 1.25*

Conductor Ampacity = 18.44A

Conductor Ampacity = 12 AWG rated 25A at 60°C, with a 20A direct-current OCPD [110.14(C)(1) and Table 310.15(B)(16)]

**[690.8(A)(1)]*

Example 2—PV Output Circuit: *What's the minimum PV output circuit conductor ampacity for the PV output circuit for two PV strings, each string containing 12 PV modules having a total nameplate short-circuit current rating of 7.50A for each string?* **Figure 690–22**

Conductor Ampacity = (Module Isc × 1.25 × Number of Strings) × 1.25*

Conductor Ampacity = (7.50A × 1.25 × 2 strings) × 1.25*

Conductor Ampacity = (18.80A) × 1.25*

Conductor Ampacity = 23.50A

Conductor Ampacity = 10 AWG rated 30A at 60°C, with 25A of direct-current OCPD [110.14(C)(1), 240.4(D), 240.6(A), and Table 310.15(B)(16)]

**[690.8(A)(2)]*

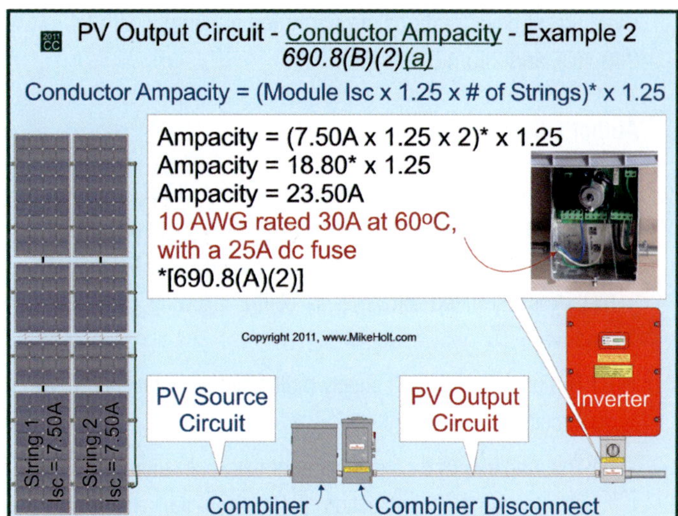

Figure 690–22

Example 3—Inverter Alternating-Current Output Circuit: *What's the minimum inverter alternating-current output circuit conductor ampacity if the maximum continuous nameplate current rating is 24A?* **Figure 690–23**

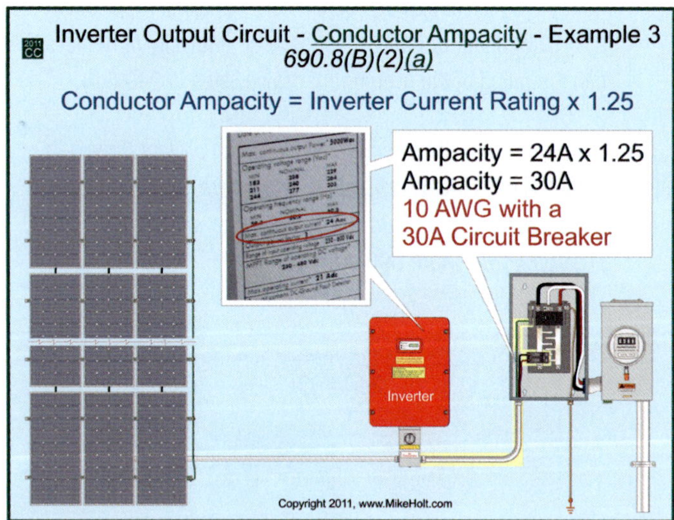

Figure 690–23

Conductor Ampacity = Inverter Nameplate Current Rating × 1.25*

Conductor Ampacity = 24A × 1.25*

Conductor Ampacity = 30A

Conductor Ampacity = 10 AWG rated 30A at 60°C with 30A OCPD [110.14(C)(1), 240.4(D) and Table 310.15(B)(16)]

**[690.8(A)(3)]*

(b) The maximum current calculated in 690.8(A) after the application of conductor adjustment and correction of 310.15.

(c) The conductor overcurrent protection must be sized to the conductor ampacity after the application of conductor adjustment and correction of 310.15 in accordance with 240.4(B), 240.4(C), and 240.4(D).

Example 1—PV Source Circuit: *What's the minimum PV source circuit conductor ampacity for a single PV string containing 12 PV modules having a total nameplate short-circuit current rating of 11.80A for the string? The conditions of use include an ambient temperature of 158°F with two current-carrying conductors in a raceway, and the conductors have an insulation rating of 90°C.*

Conductor Ampacity = (Module Isc × 1.25) × 1.25*
Conductor Ampacity = (11.80A × 1.25) × 1.25*
Conductor Ampacity = (14.75A) × 1.25*
Conductor Ampacity = 18.44A
Conductor Ampacity = 12 AWG rated 25A at 60°C, with 20A OCPD [110.14(C)(1) and Table 310.15(B)(16)]

Conductor Ampacity Conditions of Use = 12 AWG rated 30A at 90°C [Table 310.15(B)(16)]
Conductor Ampacity Conditions of Use = 30A × 0.58
Conductor Ampacity Conditions of Use = 17.40A, with 20A OCPD okay to supply 14.75A load*

**[690.8(A)(1)]*

Example 2—PV Output Circuit: *What's the minimum conductor ampacity for the PV output circuit for two PV strings, each string containing 12 PV modules, and each string having a total nameplate short-circuit current rating of 7.50A? The conditions of use include an ambient temperature of 158°F with four current-carrying conductors in a raceway, and the conductors have an insulation rating of 90°C.*

Conductor Ampacity = (Module Isc × 1.25 × Number of Strings) × 1.25*
Conductor Ampacity = (7.50A × 1.25 × 2 strings) × 1.25*
Conductor Ampacity = (18.80A) × 1.25*
Conductor Ampacity = 23.50A at 90°C with a 25A OCPD

Ampacity Conditions of Use = 10 AWG rated 40A, Table 310.15(B)(16) at 90°C
Ampacity Conditions of Use = 40A × 0.80 × 0.58 [310.15(B)(2)(a) and (B)(2)(c)]
Ampacity Conditions of Use = 18.60A, not sufficient for 18.80A load and not permitted to be protected by a 25A OCPD*
Ampacity Conditions of Use = 8 AWG rated 55A, Table 310.15(B)(16) at 90°C
Ampacity Conditions of Use = 55A × 0.80 × 0.58 [310.15(B)(2)(a) and (B)(2)(c)]
Ampacity Conditions of Use = 25.50A, sufficient for 18.80A load and permitted to be protected by 25A OCPD*

**[690.8(A)(2)]*

Example 3—Inverter Circuit: *What's the minimum circuit ampacity for the inverter output circuit conductors, if the maximum continuous nameplate current rating is 24A? The conditions of use include an ambient temperature of 93°F, two current-carrying conductors in a raceway, and the conductors have an insulation rating of 90°C.*

Conductor Ampacity = Inverter Nameplate Current Rating × 1.25*
Conductor Ampacity = 24A × 1.25*
Conductor Ampacity = 30A, with a 30A OCPD

Ampacity Conditions of Use = 10 AWG rated 40A, Table 310.15(B)(16) at 90°C
Ampacity Conditions of Use = 40A × 0.96 [310.15(B)(2)(a)]
Ampacity Conditions of Use = 38.40A, permitted to be protected by a 30A OCPD

**[690.8(A)(3)]*

ANALYSIS: Although the conductor and overcurrent device rules of Chapters 1 through 4 already apply [90.3], some installers of PV systems may not be that proficient with them. In order to make it easier for these people, the rules have been, more or less, copied and pasted into this section. Requirements for terminal temperature ratings, conductor ampacity correction and adjustment, and overcurrent devices are examples of these provisions.

690.9 Overcurrent Protection

Changes to this section clarify the overcurrent protection requirements for PV systems.

690.9 Overcurrent Protection.

(A) Circuits and Equipment. PV source circuits, PV output circuits, inverter output circuits, and equipment must be protected in accordance with the requirements of Article 240.

Ex: Overcurrent protection isn't required for PV direct-current circuits where the short-circuit currents (Isc) from all sources don't exceed the ampacity of the PV circuit conductors or the maximum overcurrent device size specified on the PV module nameplate. **Figure 690–24**

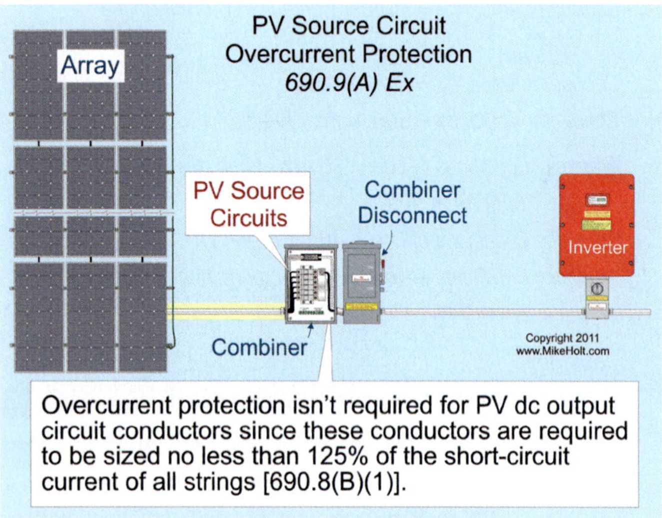

Figure 690–24

(C) PV Source Circuits. Overcurrent devices for PV source circuits aren't required to be readily accessible, but they must be accessible. Standard values of supplementary overcurrent devices come in one ampere size increments up to and including 15A; higher standard values are in accordance with 240.6(A). **Figure 690–25**

(D) Direct-Current Rating. Fuses or circuit breakers for PV direct-current circuits must be listed for direct-current circuits for the voltage and current necessary for the applied circuit. **Figure 690–26**

(E) Series Overcurrent Protection. A single OCPD can be used to protect PV modules and interconnecting PV source circuit conductors.

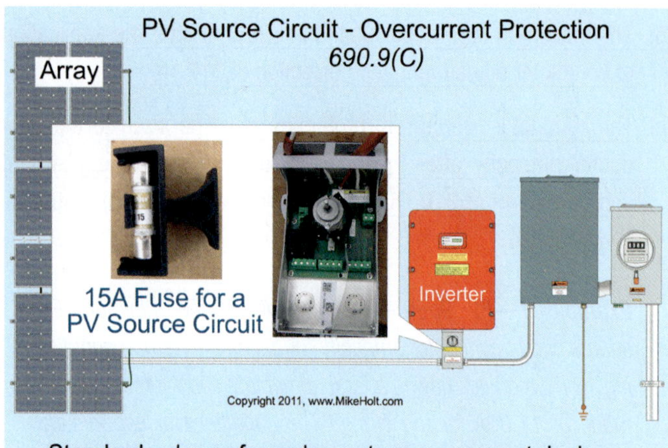

Figure 690–25

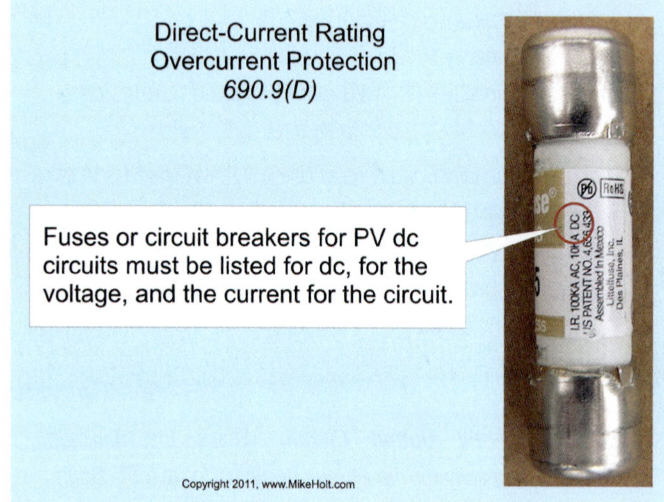

Figure 690–26

ANALYSIS: The exception to (A) has been revised to include language about the maximum overcurrent device of the PV module. Where the short-circuit current of the PV modules or PV source doesn't exceed the ampacity of the conductors or equipment, there's no hazard of overcurrent, and therefore no need to have overcurrent protection.

Clarification has also been made to (E), making it clear that the single overcurrent device being discussed can protect both the module and the source conductors.

690.10 Stand-Alone Systems

Provisions for backfed circuit breakers have been added to this section.

690.10 Stand-Alone Systems.

(A) Inverter Output. The alternating-current current output from a stand-alone inverter(s) can be less than the calculated load connected to the disconnect, but not less than the largest single utilization equipment connected to the system.

(B) Sizing and Protection. The alternating-current circuit conductors must have overcurrent protection at the output of the inverter sized in accordance with Article 240.

(C) Single 120V Supply. The inverter output is permitted to supply a 120V to single-phase, 3-wire, 120/240V distribution panel marked with the following words or equivalent:

WARNING
SINGLE 120-VOLT SUPPLY. DO NOT CONNECT MULTIWIRE BRANCH CIRCUITS

(D) Energy Storage or Backup Power System Requirements. Energy storage or backup power supplies aren't required.

(E) Backfed Circuit Breakers. Plug-in circuit breakers that are backfed from field-installed conductors must be secured in place by an additional fastener that requires other than a pull to release the breaker from the panelboard. Circuit breakers that are marked line and load must not be backfed.

Author's Comment: The purpose of the breaker fastener is to prevent the circuit breaker from being accidentally removed from the panelboard while energized, thereby exposing someone to dangerous voltage.

ANALYSIS: Although the requirements of Article 408 apply to PV installations [90.3], the powers that be decided to borrow language from 408.36(D). Because these rules were already in Article 408, this change wasn't a technical one.

PART III. DISCONNECTING MEANS

690.13 PV Conductors

A new exception for switching devices that open the direct-current grounded conductor was added.

690.13 PV Conductors. A disconnecting means is required to open ungrounded direct-current circuit conductors. A switch, circuit breaker, or other device isn't permitted to open the grounded direct-current conductor. Figure 690–27

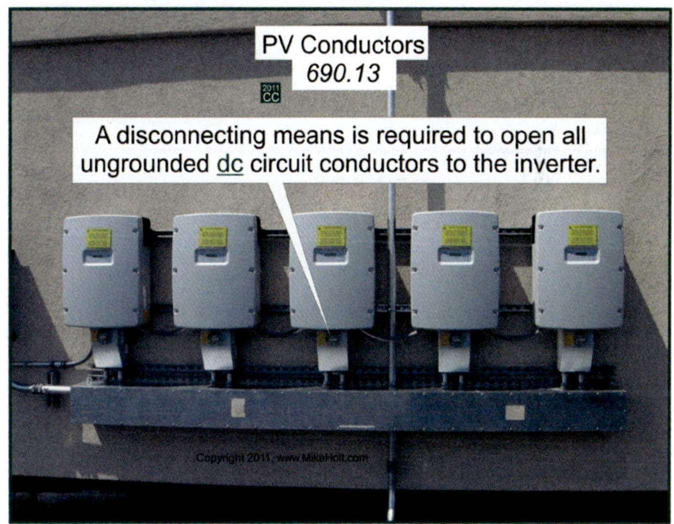

Figure 690–27

Ex 2: A switch is permitted to open the grounded direct-current conductor when all of the following conditions are met: Figure 690–28

(1) The switch is used only for PV array maintenance,

(2) The switch is accessible only by qualified persons, and

(3) The switch is rated for the maximum direct-current voltage and current, including ground-fault conditions.

ANALYSIS: This change permits a standard practice of switching all circuit conductors of dc PV systems, including the grounded conductor. Now we have specific requirements that must be met, to ensure a safe installation to qualified persons.

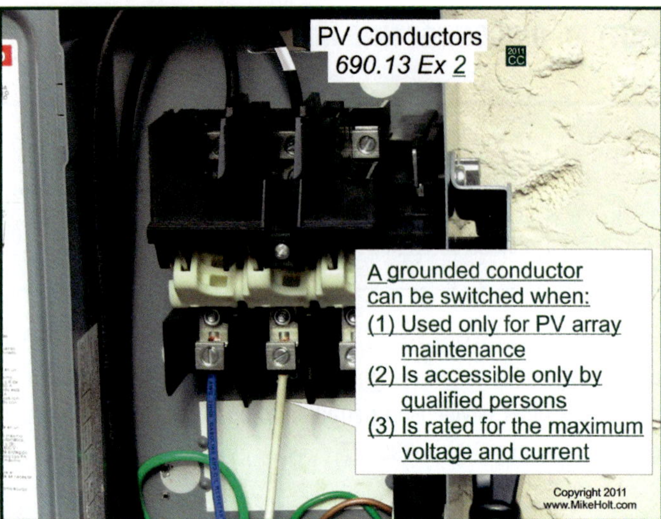

Figure 690–28

690.16 Fuses

A disconnecting means is now required for fuses on some PV output circuits.

690.16 Fuses

(A) Disconnecting Means. Disconnecting means must be provided to disconnect a fuse from all sources of supply if energized from both directions and be capable of being disconnected independently of fuses in other photovoltaic source circuits.

Author's Comment: Disconnects with pull-out fuses are one method to disconnect a fuse from all sources of energy.

(B) Fuse Servicing. Disconnecting means must be installed for PV output circuits where fuses that must be serviced can't be isolated from energized circuits. The disconnect must be within sight and accessible to the fuse or integral with the fuse holder, be externally operable without exposing the operator to contact with live parts, and plainly indicating whether in the open or closed position [690.17]. Where the disconnecting means is located more than 6 ft from the fuse, a directory showing the location of the fuse disconnect must be installed at the fuse location.

Non-load-break rated disconnecting means must be marked "Do not open under load."

ANALYSIS: Replacing a fuse under load is obviously an unsafe work practice, but unfortunately, this often occurs when the inverter has internal PV source and output circuit combining fuses on the input circuits connected directly to the inverter input terminals. When this is the case, an external disconnecting means must be installed to ensure worker safety.

PART IV. WIRING METHODS

690.31 Wiring Methods

The rules for PV system wiring methods have been extensively revised.

690.31 Wiring Methods.

(A) Wiring Systems. *NEC* Chapter 3 wiring methods and other wiring systems specifically intended and identified for use on PV systems can be used, Figure 690–29. PV system conductors (alternating-current and direct-current) run inside buildings or structures must be installed in a metal raceway, Type MC cable, or a metal enclosure [690.31(E)].

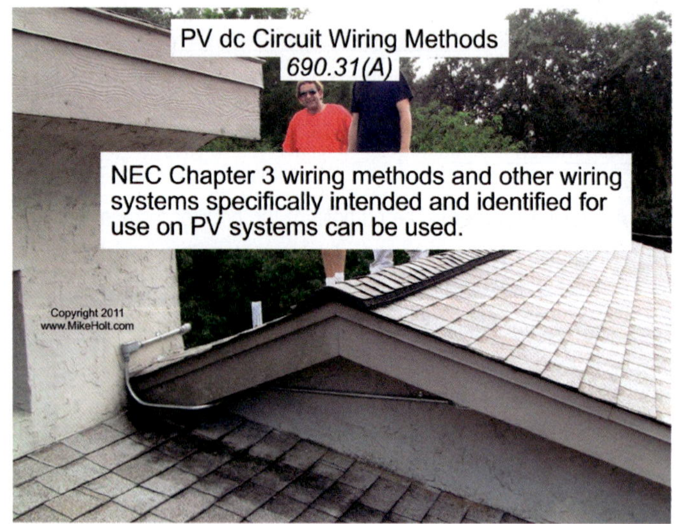

Figure 690–29

Exposed PV source and output circuits operating at greater than 30V must be installed in a Chapter 3 wiring method anytime the conductors are installed in a readily accessible location. Figure 690–30

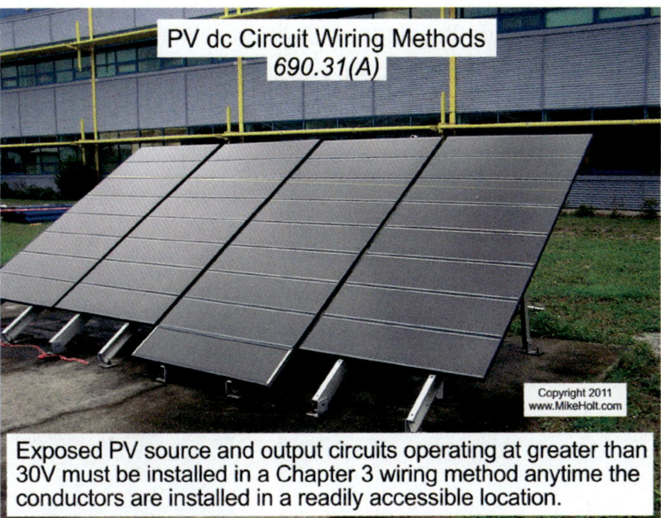

Figure 690–30

Note: PV modules operate at elevated temperature when exposed to high ambient temperatures and to bright sunlight (for example, on a rooftop). These temperatures can exceed 158°F. Module interconnection conductors are available with insulation rated for wet locations and temperature ratings of at least 90°F. **Figure 690–31**

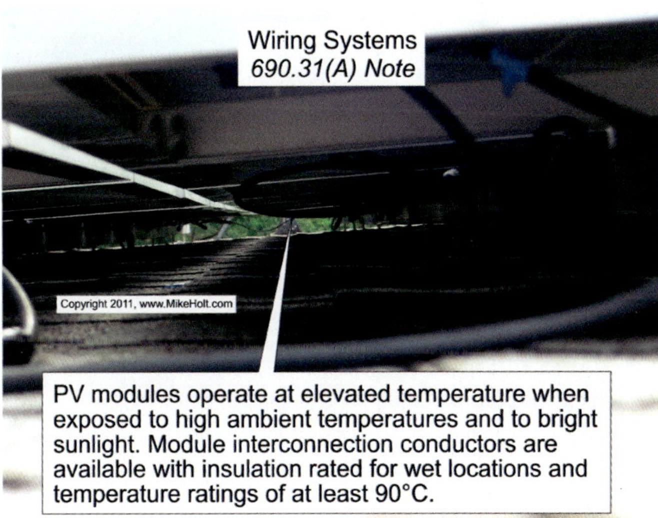

Figure 690–31

(B) Single-Conductor Cable. Single-conductor Type USE-2 or listed and labeled PV wire can be run exposed at outdoor locations for PV source circuits. **Figure 690–32**

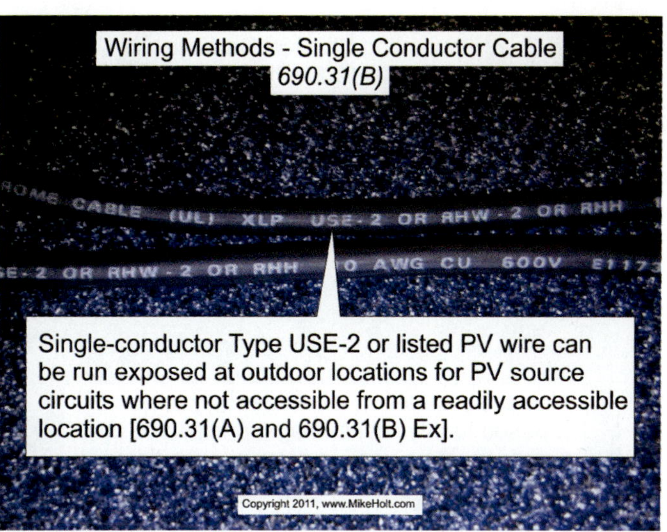

Figure 690–32

Ex: When required by 690.31(A), raceways must be used. **Figure 690–33**

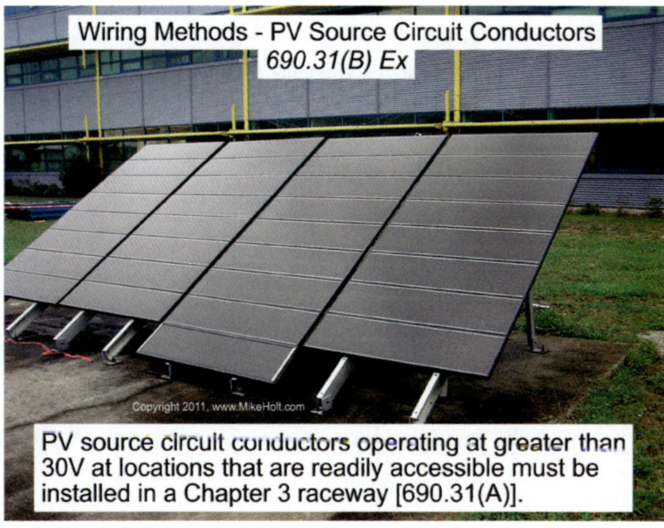

Figure 690–33

Author's Comment: Where single conductors are likely to be exposed to physical damage, enclosures or guards must be used to prevent such damage [110.27(B)]. **Figure 690–34**

Figure 690–34

Note: PV cable and wire raceway fill is based on the actual area of the cable/conductor (see manufacturer's specifications) in conjunction with Table 1 of Chapter 9. **Figure 690–35**

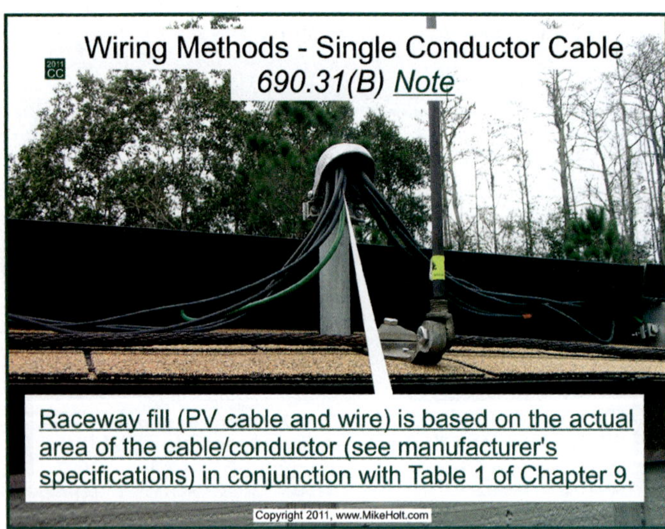

Figure 690–35

(E) Circuits Inside Buildings or Structures. Where direct-current input PV system conductors and alternating-current inverter output conductors are run inside a building/structure, they must be contained in a metal raceway, Type MC cable, or metal enclosure, **Figure 690–36.** In addition, the following installation requirements apply:

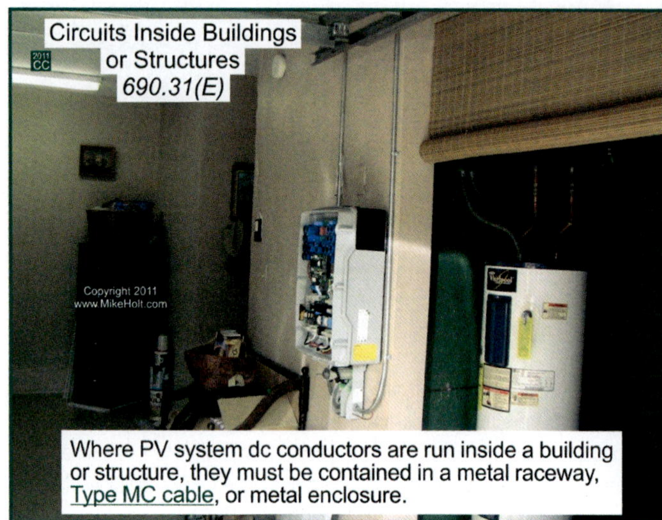

Figure 690–36

(1) Beneath Roofs. Wiring methods for PV system conductors aren't permitted within 10 in. of the roof decking or sheathing except where located directly below the roof surface that's covered by PV modules and associated equipment. Wiring methods for PV system conductors must be run perpendicular (90°) to the roof penetration point.

> **Note:** The 10 in. from the roof decking/sheathing requirement is to prevent accidental contact with energized conductors from saws used by firefighters for roof ventilation during a structure fire.

(2) Flexible Wiring Methods. FMC smaller than trade size ¾ or Type MC cable smaller than 1 in. in diameter installed across ceilings or floor joists must be protected by substantial guard strips that are at least as high as the wiring method.

Where run exposed, other than within 6 ft of their connection to equipment, wiring methods must closely follow the building surface or be protected from physical damage by an approved means.

(3) Marking or Labeling Required. Wiring methods and enclosures of (a) through (c) containing PV source conductors must be marked with the wording "Photovoltaic Power Source" by labels or other approved permanent marking means:

(a) Exposed wiring methods.

(b) Covers or enclosures of pull and junction boxes.

(c) Conduit bodies with unused openings.

(4) Marking and Labeling Methods. Markings of PV system raceways and enclosures must be suitable for the environment and be placed with a maximum of 10 ft of spacing.

(F) Flexible, Fine-Stranded Conductors. Flexible, fine-stranded conductors must terminate in terminals, lugs, devices, or connectors that are identified and listed for fine-stranded conductors [110.14(A)]. Figure 690–37

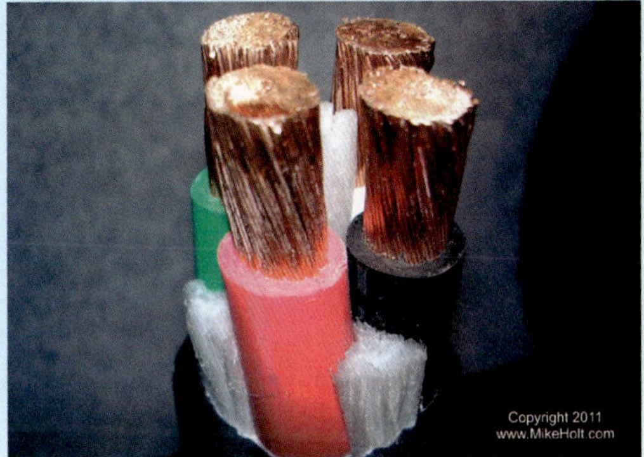

Figure 690–37

ANALYSIS: A new Informational Note was added to clarify how to perform raceway fill calculations when cables are used. This Note correlates with Note 5 in Chapter 9.

Perhaps long overdue, MC cable is now allowed as a permitted wiring method inside of buildings for PV systems.

New to this edition of the *Code* are requirements for separation of conductors from the underside of roofs. This change is intended, as the Informational Note clearly states, to protect firefighters from cutting through energized conductors while ventilating the roof of a structure.

Marking and labeling requirements have also been added to warn personnel, and to reduce the likelihood of improper connection to these conductors.

PART V. GROUNDING

690.43 Equipment Grounding

The equipment grounding provisions of this section have been formatted for ease of reading and understanding, and some technical changes have occurred.

690.43 Equipment Grounding.

(A) Equipment Grounding Required. Exposed metal parts of PV module frames, electrical equipment, raceways, and enclosures must be connected to an equipment grounding conductor of a type permitted in 250.118 [250.134]. Figure 690–38

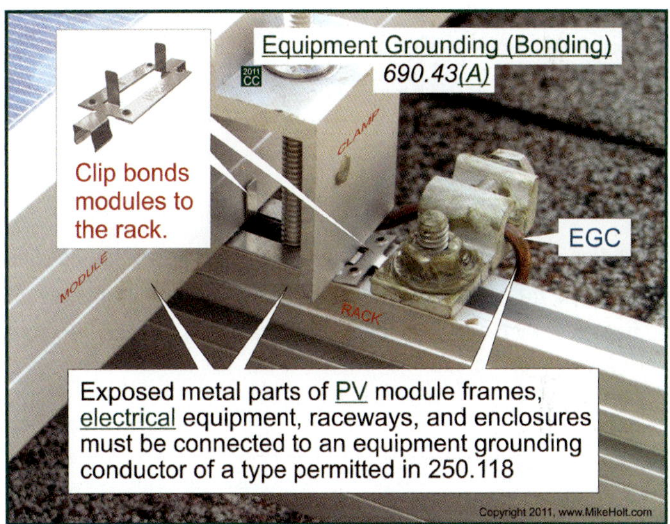

Figure 690–38

(B) Equipment Grounding Conductor Required. An equipment grounding conductor must be installed between the PV array and associated equipment.

(C) Structure as Equipment Grounding Conductor. Devices listed and identified for grounding the metallic frames of PV modules and associated equipment can be used to bond the exposed metal surfaces of the modules and equipment to the metal racks.

Metallic mounting racks used as an equipment grounding conductor must be identified as an equipment grounding conductor or have identified bonding jumpers/devices connected between the separate metallic racks and be connected to an equipment grounding conductor as required by 690.43(A).

(D) Securing Devices and Systems. Devices and systems used for securing PV modules to metal mounting racks that serve as an equipment grounding conductor must be identified for such purposes. **Figure 690–39**

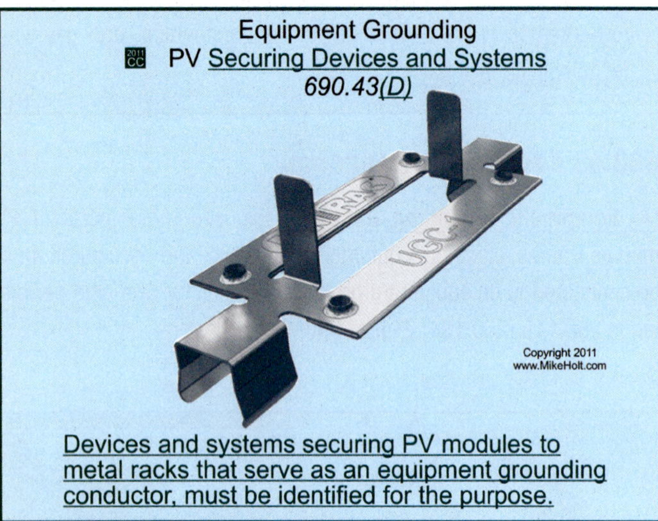

Figure 690–39

(E) Adjacent Modules. Devices identified and listed for bonding the metallic frames of PV modules can be used to bond the metallic frames of PV modules to the metallic frames of adjacent PV modules. **Figure 690–40**

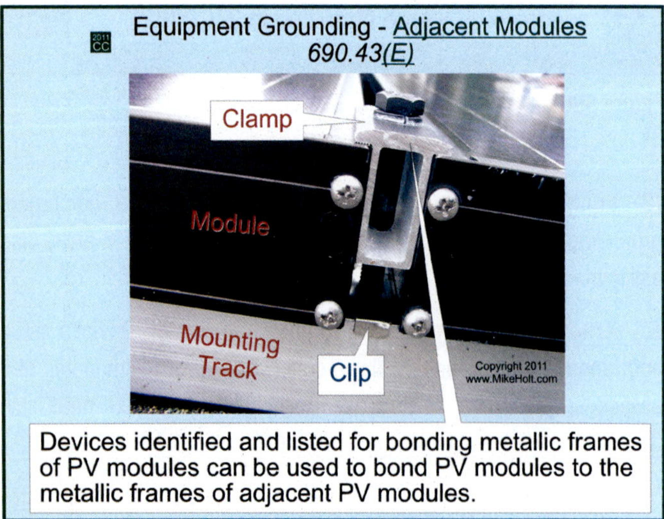

Figure 690–40

(F) Run Together. All conductors of a circuit, including the equipment grounding conductor, must be installed in the same raceway or cable, or otherwise run with the PV array circuit conductors when they leave the vicinity of the PV array [300.3(B)]. **Figure 690–41**

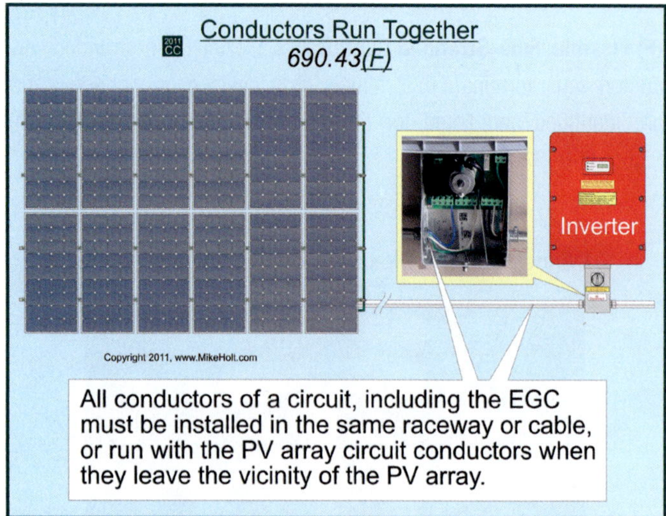

Figure 690–41

ANALYSIS: When multiple requirements or provisions are in a single section, a "list" format is often easier to read and understand. This section has been revised to reflect that fact, and many *Code* users will benefit from it.

Two new requirements have been added to this section as well. Subsection (C) now requires that metal mounting racks be identified as an equipment grounding conductors (EGC) or have a bonding jumper(s) and EGC installed.

Also new to the *NEC* is (D), which requires that devices for securing PV modules be identified for equipment grounding if they're in fact being used as an equipment grounding conductor. Considering the importance of the equipment grounding conductor, this change shouldn't upset anyone that's concerned with safety.

690.47 Grounding Electrode System

The requirements for PV grounding electrode systems have been greatly revised.

690.47 Grounding Electrode System.

(B) Direct-Current Systems. If installing a dc system, a grounding electrode system must be provided in accordance with 250.166 with a grounding electrode conductor in accordance with 250.64.

A common dc grounding-electrode conductor is permitted to serve multiple inverters with the size of the common grounding electrode and the tap conductors in accordance with 250.166. The tap conductors must be connected to the common grounding-electrode conductor in such a manner that the common grounding electrode conductor remains without a splice or joint.

(C) Alternating- and Direct-Current Grounding Requirements. PV systems with direct-current modules having no direct connection between the direct-current grounded conductor and alternating-current grounded conductor must be bonded to the alternating-current grounding system by one of the methods listed in (1), (2), or (3).

> **Note 1:** ANSI/UL 1741, *Standard for Inverters, Converters, and Controllers for Use in Independent Power Systems* have the grounding electrode conductor (GEC) connection point identified. In PV inverters, the terminals for the direct-current and alternating-current equipment grounding conductors common with each other are marked direct-current GEC terminal.

> **Note 2:** For utility-interactive systems, the existing premises grounding system serves as the alternating-current grounding system.

(1) Separate Direct-Current Grounding Electrode System Bonded to the Alternating-Current Grounding Electrode System. A separate direct-current grounding electrode bonded to the alternating-current grounding electrode system with a bonding jumper sized to the larger of the existing alternating-current grounding electrode conductor or direct-current grounding electrode conductor specified by 250.166. **Figure 690–42**

The direct-current grounding electrode conductor or bonding jumper to the alternating-current grounding electrode system can't be used as the required alternating-current equipment grounding conductor.

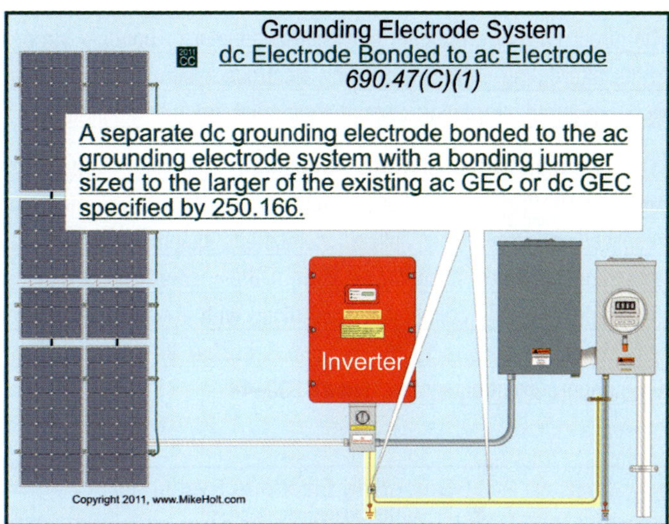

Figure 690–42

(2) Common Direct-Current and Alternating-Current Grounding Electrode. A direct-current grounding electrode conductor sized in accordance with 250.166 run from the marked direct-current grounding electrode connection point to the alternating-current grounding electrode. **Figure 690–43**

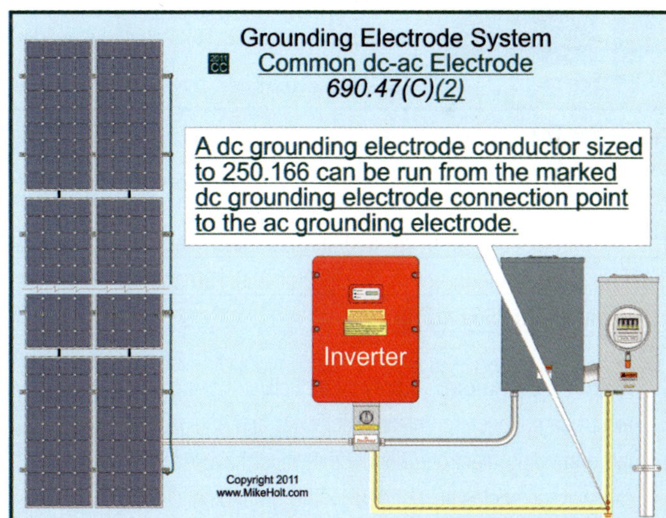

Figure 690–43

Where an alternating-current grounding electrode isn't accessible, the direct-current grounding electrode conductor is permitted to terminate to the alternating-current grounding electrode conductor by irreversible compression-type connectors listed as grounding and bonding equipment or by the exothermic welding process [250.64(C)(1)].

The direct-current grounding electrode conductor or bonding jumper to the alternating-current grounding electrode system can't be used as the required alternating-current equipment grounding conductor.

(3) Combined Direct-Current Grounding Electrode Conductor and Alternating-Current Equipment Grounding Conductor. An unspliced, or irreversibly spliced, combined equipment grounding/grounding electrode conductor run from the marked direct-current grounding electrode connection point along with the alternating-current circuit conductors to the grounding busbar in the associated alternating-current equipment. **Figure 690–44**

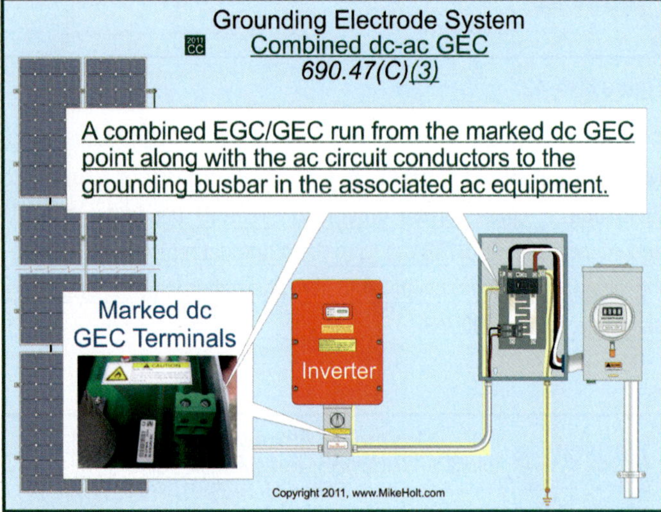

Figure 690–44

The combined equipment grounding/grounding electrode conductor must be sized to the larger of 250.122 or 250.166 and be installed in accordance with 250.64(E).

Author's Comment: To prevent inductive choking of grounding electrode conductors, ferrous raceways and enclosures containing grounding electrode conductors must have each end of the raceway or enclosure bonded to the grounding electrode conductor in accordance with 250.92(B) [250.64(E)]. Nonferrous metal raceways, such as aluminum rigid metal conduit, enclosing the grounding electrode conductor aren't required to meet the "bonding each end of the raceway to the grounding electrode conductor" provisions of this section.

CAUTION: *The effectiveness of a grounding electrode is significantly reduced if a ferrous metal raceway containing a grounding electrode conductor isn't bonded to the ferrous metal raceway at both ends. This is because a single conductor carrying high-frequency induced lightning current in a ferrous raceway causes the raceway to act as an inductor, which severely limits (chokes) the current flow through the grounding electrode conductor. ANSI/IEEE 142, Recommended Practice for Grounding of Industrial and Commercial Power Systems (Green Book) states: "An inductive choke can reduce the current flow by 97 percent."*

Author's Comment: To save a lot of time and effort, install the grounding electrode conductor in PVC conduit suitable for the application [352.10(F)].

ANALYSIS: Section 690.47(B) has been revised to clarify that a common grounding electrode conductor can be used to ground multiple inverters. This concept isn't new to the *Code*, as similar provisions can be found in 250.30 for separately derived systems.

As can be seen rather easily, (C) has been extensively revised, again. Changes to this edition of the *NEC* are intended to incorporate the concepts of the 2005 and 2008 editions into clear, easily understandable text.

In a somewhat surprising change, 690.47(D) was deleted. That section required that ground and pole-mounted PV arrays have a grounding electrode. This requirement was added in the 2008 edition and was intended to be optional. The *Code* language that was used, however, made it mandatory. By removing the rule altogether, it's still optional, but now isn't mandatory.

Small Wind ELECTRIC SYSTEMS

INTRODUCTION TO ARTICLE 694—SMALL WIND ELECTRIC SYSTEMS

Article 694 applies to small wind (turbine) electric systems that consist of one or more wind electric generators with individual systems up to and including 100 kW. These systems can include generators, alternators, inverters, and controllers.

Article 694 Small Wind Electric Systems

A new article addressing wind produced electrical systems was added.

ANALYSIS: The desire to use renewable resources isn't new. Sources of power such as solar photovoltaic systems have been increasing exponentially, and many people reading this book have probably seen the large "wind farms" that can now be found in many areas across the country. In response to the increasing popularity of these systems, the *NEC* added a new Article 694. This article is starting rather small, as is often the case with new articles, but it will certainly grow in future *Code* cycles.

It's worth noting that the systems covered here are limited to 100 kW, and can include inverters, alternators, generators, and controllers.

NOTES

ARTICLE 695

Fire PUMPS

INTRODUCTION TO ARTICLE 695—FIRE PUMPS

The general philosophy behind most *Code* requirements is to provide circuit protection that will shut down equipment before allowing the supply conductors to overheat and become damaged from overload. Article 695 departs from this philosophy. The idea is that the fire pump motor must run, no matter what; it supplies water to a facility's fire protection piping, which in turn supplies water to the sprinkler system and fire hoses. Article 695 contains many requirements to keep that supply of water uninterrupted.

Some of these requirements are obvious. For example, locating the pump where its exposure to fire is minimized. It's important to ensure that the fire pump and its jockey (pressure maintenance) pump have a reliable source of power. Also, fire pump wiring must remain independent of all other wiring.

Some of the requirements of Article 695 seem wrong at first glance, until you remember why that fire pump is there in the first place. For example, the disconnect must be lockable in the closed position. You would normally expect these to be lockable in the open position because other articles require that for the safety of maintenance personnel. But the fire pump runs to ensure the safety of an entire facility and everyone in it. For the same reason, fire pump power circuits can't have automatic protection against overloads.

Remember, the fire pump must be kept in service, even if doing so damages or destroys the pump. It's better to run the pump until its windings melt, than to save the fire pump and lose the facility. The intent of Article 695 is to save the facility.

695.3 Power Source(s)

The requirements relating to the power source for a fire pump have been extensively revised and clarified.

695.3 Power Source(s).

(A) Individual Source. Power to fire pump motors must be supplied by a reliable source of power that has the capacity to carry the locked-rotor current of the fire pump motor(s), pressure maintenance pump motors, and the full-load current of any associated fire pump equipment. Reliable sources of power include:

(1) Electric Utility Service. A separate service or a connection located ahead of but not within the service disconnecting means is allowed.

(2) On-Site Power. An on-site power supply, such as a generator, located and protected to minimize damage by fire is permitted to supply a fire pump.

Author's Comment: The determination of a reliable source of power is subject to the approval of the authority having jurisdiction.

(3) Dedicated Feeder. A dedicated feeder derived from a service connection in accordance with 695.3(A)(1).

(B) Multiple Sources. If reliable power can't be obtained from a source as described in 695.3(A), power must be supplied by one of the following:

(1) Individual Sources. A combination of two or more of the sources from 695.3(A).

(2) Individual Source and On-Site Standby Generator. A combination of one of the sources in 695.3(A) and an on-site standby generator.

Exception to 695.3(B)(1) and (B)(2): An alternate source of power isn't required where a back-up engine-driven or back-up steam turbine-driven fire pump is installed.

(F) Phase Converters. Phase converters are not permitted to be used for fire pump service.

ANALYSIS: With a quick glance at this section of the *Code* you can see the number of changes that have been made.

Feeders originating from a separate service (or a connection upstream of the service) are now addressed and are permitted as a power source.

The provisions for multiple sources have been expanded to address on-site standby generators and combinations of services and on-site generation. The use of a generator as an alternate source has also been addressed.

Lastly, phase converters are now specifically prohibited as a power source for fire pumps.

695.4 Continuity of Power

The provisions for continuity of power for fire pumps have been revised.

695.4 Continuity of Power. Circuits that supply electric motor-driven fire pumps must be supervised from inadvertent disconnection as covered in (A) or (B).

(A) Direct Connection. The supply conductors must directly connect the power source either to a listed fire pump controller or to a listed combination fire pump controller and power transfer switch.

(B) Connection Through Disconnecting Means and Overcurrent Device.

(1) Number of Disconnecting Means.

(a) General. A single disconnecting means and associated overcurrent protective device(s) is permitted between the fire pump power source and one of the following:

(1) A listed fire pump controller

(2) A listed fire pump power transfer switch

(3) A listed combination fire pump controller and power transfer switch

(2) Overcurrent Device Selection.

(a) Individual Sources. The overcurrent device(s) must be selected or set to carry indefinitely the sum of the locked-rotor current of the fire pump and pressure maintenance pump motor(s), and 100 percent of the ampere rating of the fire pump's accessory equipment. If the locked-rotor current value doesn't correspond to a standard overcurrent device size, the next standard overcurrent device size must be used in accordance with 240.6. The requirement to carry the locked-rotor currents indefinitely doesn't apply to fire pump motor conductors.

(2) When an on-site generator is used as the alternate power source, its disconnecting means must be installed in accordance with 700.9(B)(5) for emergency circuits. It must also be capable of being locked in the closed (on) position.

(3) Disconnecting Means. The disconnecting means must comply with all of the following:

(a) Features and Location.

(1) The disconnecting means for the normal power source must comply with all of the following:

(a) Be identified as suitable for use as service equipment

(b) Be lockable in the closed position

(c) Not be located within equipment that feeds loads other than the fire pump

(d) Be located sufficiently remote from other building or other fire pump source disconnecting means

(2) When an on-site generator is used as the alternate power source, its disconnecting means must be installed in accordance with 700.9(B)(5) for emergency circuits. It must also be capable of being locked in the closed (on) position.

(b) Disconnect Marking. The disconnecting means must be marked "Fire Pump Disconnecting Means." The letters must be at least 1 in. in height and be visible without opening enclosure doors or covers.

ANALYSIS: Like 695.3, much of this section has been revised to address the varying types of installations. Some technical changes were also made to add clarity and enhance safety.

Provisions for on-site standby generators have been added, with an allowance for additional disconnecting means when they're associated with the fire pump.

The requirement that the overcurrent devices carry the locked-rotor current indefinitely has also been clarified by stating that the "next size up" rule is required.

A new allowance has also been added, allowing for an on-site generator disconnecting means to not have to meet the requirements for normal power disconnecting means.

695.6 Power Wiring

Changes to this section have been made to incorporate the changes made in 695.3 and 695.4.

695.6 Power Wiring.

(A) Supply Conductors.

(1) **Services and** On-Site Power Production Facilities. Service conductors and conductors supplied by on-site power production facilities must be physically routed outside buildings and must be installed in accordance with Article 230. If supply conductors can't be routed outside of buildings, they must be encased in 2 in. of concrete or brick [230.6(1) or (2)].

(2) Feeder Conductors. Fire pump supply conductors must comply with all of the following:

(a) Independent Routing. Be kept entirely independent of all other wiring.

(b) Associated Fire Pump Loads. Conductors only supply loads directly associated with the fire pump system.

(c) Protection from Potential Damage. Conductors are protected from potential damage by fire, structural failure, or operational accident.

(d) Inside a Building. Fire pump conductors can be routed through a building using one of the following methods:

(1) Be encased in a minimum 2 in. of concrete

(2) Be within an enclosed construction dedicated to the fire pump circuit(s) and having a minimum of a 1-hour fire-resistive rating

(3) Be a listed electrical circuit protective system protected by a fire-rated assembly listed to achieve a minimum fire rating of 2 hours and dedicated to the fire pump circuit(s).

(D) **Pump Wiring.** Wiring from the fire pump controller to the fire pump motor [not installed through a building—695.6(B)] must be in rigid metal conduit, intermediate metal conduit, electrical metallic tubing, liquidtight flexible metal conduit, liquidtight flexible nonmetallic conduit Type B, listed Type MC cable with an impervious covering, or Type MI cable.

ANALYSIS: Changes to this section have been made to include provisions for on-site power production facilities, as well as the feeder circuits described in 695.3(A)(3) and 695.3(C).

Provisions for listed electrical circuit protective systems have also been added.

Lastly, EMT is now an allowed wiring method for fire pumps. Considering that liquidtight flexible nonmetallic conduit and MC cable were already allowed, this change certainly makes sense.

NOTES

SPECIAL CONDITIONS

INTRODUCTION TO CHAPTER 7—SPECIAL CONDITIONS

Chapter 7, which covers special conditions, is the third of the *NEC* chapters that deal with special topics. Chapters 5 and 6 cover special occupancies, and special equipment, respectively. Remember, the first four chapters of the *NEC* are sequential and form a foundation for each of the subsequent three chapters. Chapter 8 covers communications systems and isn't subject to the requirements of Chapters 1 through 7 except where the requirements are specifically referenced there.

What exactly is a "Special Condition?" It's a situation that doesn't fall under the category of special occupancies or special equipment, but creates a need for additional measures to ensure the "safeguarding of people and property" mission of the *NEC*, as stated in 90.1(A).

The *Code* groups these logically, as you might expect. Here are the general groupings:

- Emergency and standby power systems—Articles 700, 701, and 702. Article 700 addresses emergency systems, Article 701 addresses legally required standby systems, and Article 702 addresses optional standby systems.
- Interconnected power sources—Article 705. This primarily has to do with generators or photovoltaic systems used for on-site power generation.
- Low-voltage, low-power wiring—Articles 720 through 770. Examples include control, signaling, instrumentation, fire alarm systems, and optical fiber installations.

- **Article 700—Emergency Power Systems.** The requirements of Article 700 apply only to the wiring methods for "Emergency Power Systems" that are essential for safety to human life and required by federal, state, municipal, or other regulatory codes. When normal power is lost, emergency power systems must be capable of supplying emergency power in 10 seconds or less.

- **Article 701—Legally Required Standby Power Systems.** Legally required standby systems provide electrical power to aid in firefighting, rescue operations, control of health hazards, and similar operations, and are required by federal, state, municipal, or other regulatory codes. When normal power is lost, legally required systems must be capable of automatically supplying standby power in 60 seconds or less, instead of the 10 seconds or less required of emergency power systems.

- **Article 702—Optional Standby Power Systems.** Optional standby systems are intended to protect public or private facilities or property where life safety doesn't depend on the performance of the system. These systems are typically installed to provide an alternate source of electrical power for such facilities as industrial and commercial buildings, farms, and residences, and to serve loads that, when stopped during any power outage, can cause discomfort, serious interruption of a process, or damage to a product or process. Optional standby systems are intended to supply on-site generated power to loads selected by the customer, either automatically or manually.

- **Article 705—Interconnected Electric Power Production Sources.** Article 705 relates to power sources that operate in parallel with a primary source. Typically, a primary source is the utility supply, but it can be an on-site source, instead. For instance, in addition to the requirements of Article 690, provisions of this article apply to solar photovoltaic systems.
- **Article 720—Circuits and Equipment Operating at Less Than 50 Volts.** Because systems operation at 12V, 24V or 48V can melt conductors and cause a fire, the *NEC* has specific requirements for them.
- **Article 725—Remote-Control, Signaling, and Power-Limited Circuits.** Article 725 contains the requirements for remote-control, signaling, and power-limited circuits that aren't an integral part of a device or appliance.
    - Remote-Control Circuit—A circuit that controls other circuits through a relay or solid-state device. For example, a circuit that controls the coil of a motor starter or lighting contactor is one type of remote-control circuit.
    - Signaling Circuit—A circuit that supplies energy to an appliance or device that gives a visual and/or audible signal. Circuits for doorbells, buzzers, code-calling systems, signal lights, annunciators, burglar alarms, and other indication or alarm devices are examples of signaling circuits.
- **Article 760—Fire Alarm Systems.** This article covers the installation of wiring and equipment for fire alarm systems. Fire alarm systems include fire detection and alarm notification, voice communications, guard's tour, sprinkler waterflow, and sprinkler supervisory systems.
- **Article 770—Optical Fiber Cables and Raceways.** Article 770 covers the installation of optical fiber cables, which transmit signals using light for control, signaling, and communications. This article also contains the installation requirements for raceways that contain optical fiber cables, and requirements for composite cables (often called "hybrid" cables in the field) that combine optical fibers with current-carrying metallic conductors.

ARTICLE 700 Emergency POWER SYSTEMS

INTRODUCTION TO ARTICLE 700—EMERGENCY POWER SYSTEMS

Emergency power systems are legally required, often as a condition of an operating permit for a given facility. The authority having jurisdiction makes the determination as to whether such a system is necessary for a given facility and what it must entail. Sometimes, it simply provides power for exit lighting and exit signs upon loss of main power or in the case of fire. Its purpose isn't to provide power for normal business operations, but rather to provide lighting and controls essential for human life safety.

The general goal is to keep the emergency operation as reliable as possible. The emergency power system must be able to supply all emergency loads simultaneously. When the emergency power supply also supplies power for other nonemergency loads, the emergency loads take priority over the other loads, and those other loads must be subject to automatic load pickup and load shedding to support the emergency loads if the emergency system doesn't have adequate capacity and rating for all loads simultaneously.

As you study Article 700, keep in mind that emergency power systems are essentially lifelines for people. The entire article is based on keeping those lifelines from breaking.

700.2 Definitions

A new definition for "Emergency Systems" was added.

700.2 Definitions.

Emergency Systems. Emergency power systems are those systems legally required and classed as emergency by a governmental agency having jurisdiction. These systems are intended to automatically supply illumination and/or power essential for safety to human life. Figure 700–1

ANALYSIS: The scope of Article 700, in previous editions, stated that these systems were those classed as emergency by municipal jurisdictions or other codes, and further clarified the role that these systems played. What the scope was really doing was providing a definition for them. This change removes the text from 700.1 and places it in 700.2, with no technical changes resulting.

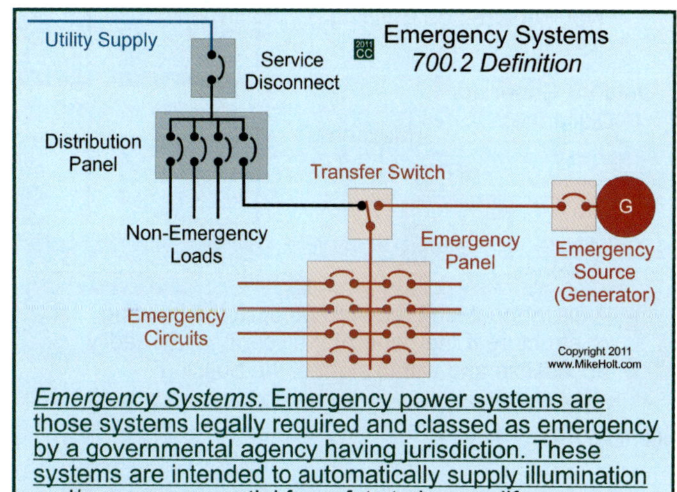

Figure 700–1

700.12(B)(6) Outdoor Generator Sets

A new exception for generator disconnects was added.

700.12 General Requirements. In the event of failure of the normal supply to the building/structure, emergency power must be available within 10 seconds. Emergency equipment must be designed and located so as to minimize the hazards that might cause complete failure due to flooding, fires, icing, and vandalism. The emergency power supply must be one of the following:

(B) Generator Set.

(6) Outdoor Generator Sets. If a generator located outdoors is equipped with a readily accessible disconnecting means located within sight (within 50 ft) of the building/structure, an additional disconnecting means isn't required on or at the building/structure for the generator feeder conductors that serve or pass through the building/structure. Figure 700–2

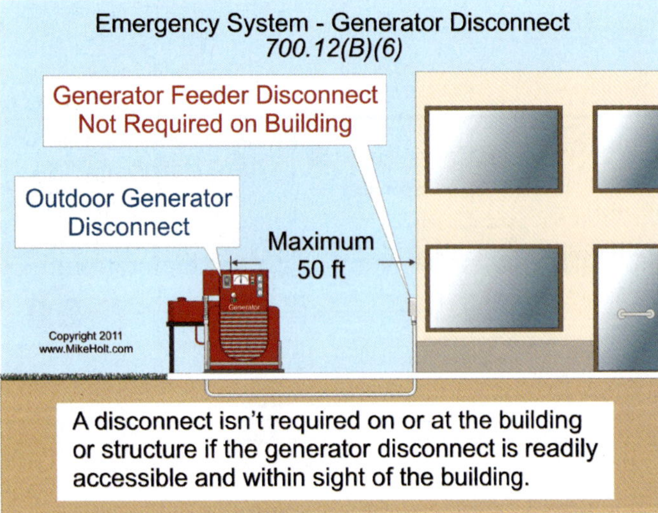

Figure 700–2

Ex: Where conditions of maintenance and supervision ensure that only qualified persons will monitor and service the installation and where documented safe switching procedures are established and maintained for disconnection, the generator disconnecting means isn't required to be located within sight of the building or structure served.

ANALYSIS: Section 225.32 has long had an exception for buildings under single management, with documented safe switching procedures, to have a disconnecting means for a building located remote from the building. The added exception to 700.12(B)(6) is meant only to correlate with this exception and remove an inconsistency that has existed between these two sections for some time.

700.12(F) Unit Equipment

An exception to the circuiting requirements for unit equipment was added.

700.12 General Requirements.

(F) Unit Equipment. Individual unit equipment (an emergency lighting battery pack) must consist of the following: Figure 700–3

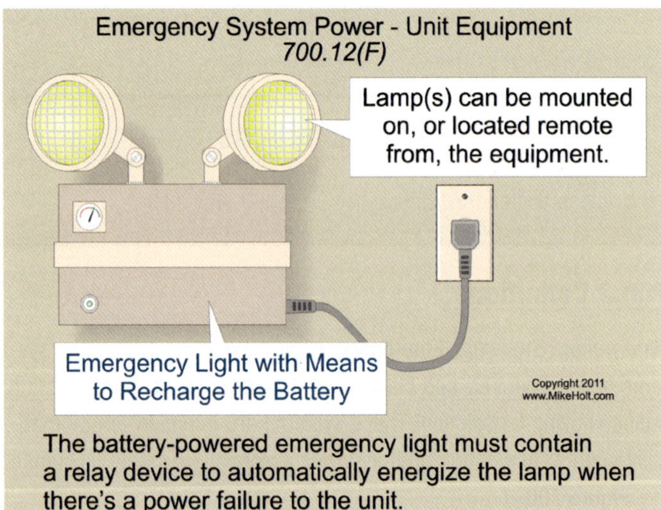

Figure 700–3

(1) A rechargeable battery,

(2) A battery charging means,

(3) Provisions for one or more lamps mounted on the equipment, or terminals for remote lamps (or both), and

(4) A relaying device arranged to energize the lamps automatically upon failure of the supply to the unit equipment. Emergency lighting battery pack equipment must be permanently fixed in place. Flexible cord-and-plug connection (a locking receptacle isn't required) is permitted for emergency lighting battery pack equipment designed for this purpose, provided the cord doesn't exceed 3 ft. Figure 700–4

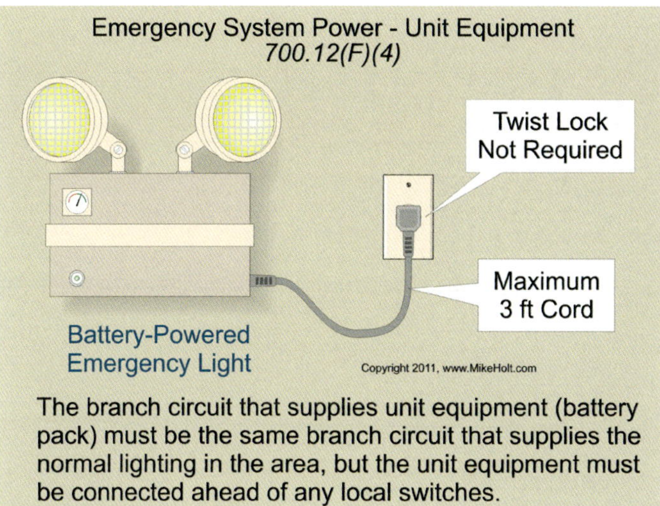

Figure 700–4

The branch-circuit wiring that supplies emergency lighting battery pack equipment must be the same branch-circuit wiring that supplies the normal lighting in the area, but the emergency lighting battery pack equipment must be connected ahead of any local switches. The branch circuit that feeds the emergency lighting battery pack equipment must be clearly identified at the distribution panel in accordance with 110.22(A) and 408.4.

Author's Comment: There are two reasons why the emergency lighting battery packs must be connected ahead of the switch controlling the normal area lighting: (1) in the event of a power loss to the lighting circuit, the emergency battery lighting packs will activate and provide emergency lighting for people to exit the building, and (2) the emergency lighting battery packs won't turn on when the switch controlling normal lighting is turned off.

CAUTION: *Individual unit equipment must not be connected to the emergency circuit, because it won't operate when normal power is lost, since the equipment is being supplied by the emergency power system*

Ex 2: Power for remote heads providing the exterior lighting of an exit door can be supplied by the unit equipment serving the area immediately inside the exit door.

ANALYSIS: Where unit equipment is used (such as "bug eyes" and typical exit signs), they must be on the same circuit as the general lighting that serves the area being served by the unit equipment. This results in a decreased likelihood of the unit equipment being shut off at the breaker, due to the fact that shutting it off also de-energizes the lighting in the area—an event that will be noticed by the building occupant. A new exception to this rule was added to allow for remote heads installed on the exterior of buildings. The general rule requires that these heads be on the circuit that provides exterior lighting. The new exception will allow for them to be on the circuit that serves the lighting inside of the exit door.

NOTES

Legally Required Standby POWER SYSTEMS

INTRODUCTION TO ARTICLE 701—LEGALLY REQUIRED STANDBY POWER SYSTEMS

In the hierarchy of electrical systems, Article 700 Emergency Power Systems receives first priority. Taking the number two spot are Legally Required Standby Power Systems, which fall under Article 701. Legally required standby systems must supply standby power in 60 seconds or less after a power loss, instead of the 10 seconds or less required for emergency power systems.

Article 700 basically applies to systems or equipment required to protect people who are in an emergency and trying to get out, while Article 701 basically applies to systems or equipment needed to aid the people responding to the emergency. For example, Article 700 lighting provides an exit path. But, Article 701 lighting might illuminate the fire hydrants and switchgear areas.

Article 701 Legally Required Standby Power Systems

Article 701 has been renumbered to provide consistency with Articles 700 and 702.

ANALYSIS: Over the last few *Code* cycles, efforts have been made to create parallel numbering between the sections of articles that are similar. For example, the Chapter 3 wiring methods, with 3xx.10 and 3xx.12 being uses permitted and uses not permitted, 3xx.30 reserved for securing and supporting, and so on. Articles 700, 701, and 702, while applying to different systems, are in fact quite similar in many requirements.

701.7(C) Automatic Transfer Switch

The listing requirement for transfer switches used on legally required standby systems has been revised.

701.7 Transfer Equipment.

(A) General. Transfer equipment must be listed for emergency use.

Author's Comment: Legally required standby systems and optional standby systems can be on the same transfer switch, but emergency power systems must have their own [700.6(D)].

(C) Automatic Transfer Switch. Automatic transfer switches must be electrically operated, mechanically held, and listed for emergency use. Figure 701–1

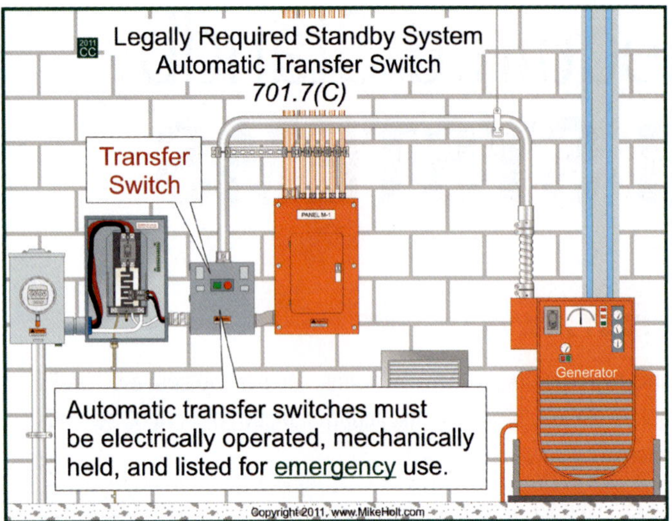

Figure 701–1

ANALYSIS: The 2008 *Code* added a new requirement to this section; that transfer switches used in a legally required standby system be listed for legally required standby system use. This resulted in a small problem, however, because there's no such piece of equipment. This rule has now been changed to clarify that these switches must be listed for use in emergency systems, which was the intent of this requirement all along.

Optional Standby POWER SYSTEMS

INTRODUCTION TO ARTICLE 702—OPTIONAL STANDBY POWER SYSTEMS

Taking third priority after Emergency and Legally Required Systems, Optional Standby Power Systems protect public or private facilities or property where life safety doesn't depend on the performance of the system. These systems aren't required for rescue operations.

Suppose a glass plant loses power. Once glass hardens in the equipment—which it will do when process heat is lost—the plant is going to suffer a great deal of downtime and expense before it can resume operations. An optional standby system can prevent this loss.

You'll see these systems in facilities where loss of power can cause economic loss or business interruptions. Data centers can lose millions of dollars from a single minute of lost power. A chemical or pharmaceutical plant can lose an entire batch from a single momentary power glitch. In many cases, the lost revenue can't be recouped.

This article also applies to the installation of optional standby generators in homes, farmsteads, small businesses and many other applications where standby power isn't legally required.

Article 702 Optional Standby Power Systems

Article 702 has been renumbered to provide consistency with Articles 700 and 701.

ANALYSIS: Over the last few *Code* cycles, efforts have been made to create parallel numbering between the sections of articles that are similar. For example, the Chapter 3 wiring methods, with 3xx.10 and 3xx.12 being uses permitted and uses not permitted, 3xx.30 reserved for securing and supporting, and so forth. Articles 700, 701, and 702, while applying to different systems, are in fact quite similar in many requirements. This change (and a similar change to Article 701) results in parallel numbering between these three articles.

NOTES

ARTICLE 705 Interconnected Electric Power PRODUCTION SOURCES

INTRODUCTION TO ARTICLE 705—INTERCONNECTED ELECTRIC POWER PRODUCTION SOURCES

Anytime there's more than one source of power production at the same building or structure, safety issues arise. In cases where a power production source such as a generator is used strictly for standby power, the *NEC* requires transfer switches and other safety considerations as covered in Articles 700, 701, or 702 depending on whether the standby power is legally required or optional. When interactive electrical power production sources such as wind powered generators, solar photovoltaic systems, or fuel cells are present, there usually isn't a transfer switch. In fact, it can be expected that there will be more than one source of electrical supply connected simultaneously. This can raise many questions in regard to how to maintain a satisfactory level of safety when more than one power source is present.

Article 705 answers these and other questions related to power sources that operate in parallel with a primary source. Typically, a primary source is the utility supply, but it can be an on-site source instead.

705.2 Definitions

A definition for "power production equipment" was added.

705.2 Definitions.

Power Production Equipment. The generating source, and all distribution equipment associated, that generates electricity from a source other than a utility supplied service. **Figure 705–1**

Author's Comment: Examples include generators, solar photovoltaic systems, and fuel cell systems.

ANALYSIS: Despite the fact that this article explicitly covers power production equipment, the term has never had a proper definition. This definition clarifies that such equipment includes a generating source that isn't a service, and includes any equipment that's associated with it.

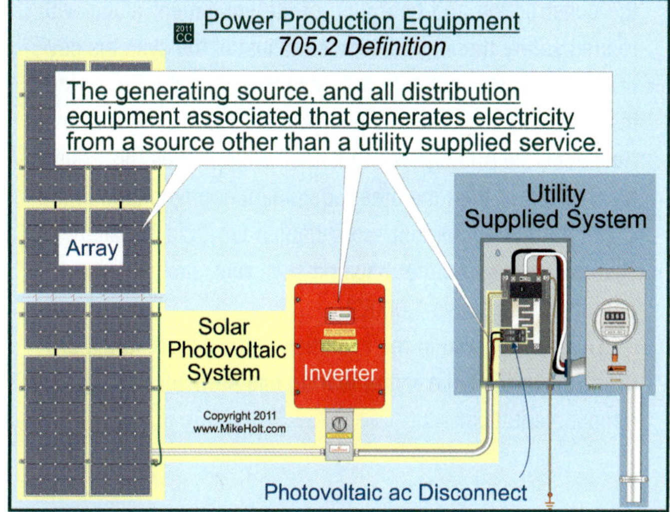

Figure 705–1

705.6 Qualified Persons

A new requirement mandates that only qualified persons install systems governed by this article.

705.6 System Installation. Installation of one or more electrical power production sources operating in parallel with a primary source(s) of electricity must be installed only by qualified persons.

> **Note:** A qualified person is one that has knowledge related to the construction and operation of equipment and installations along with the safety training to recognize and avoid hazards to persons and property [Article 100 Definition].

ANALYSIS: In a shocking and unprecedented turn of events, *Code*-Making Panel 13 has accepted a requirement that governs who installs the equipment covered in the *NEC*. Historically, the issues of individual qualification have been left with state or local municipalities and handled in the form of professional licensing or other mandates. This change now requires that only persons with knowledge related to the construction and operation of the equipment along with related safety training be allowed to install the systems covered by this article. While this may indeed make for a safer installation, it leaves many people asking difficult questions. How does the AHJ enforce this rule? What makes this equipment different than the other equipment contemplated in the *Code*? Is this equipment more dangerous than installations covered by the *NEC* that have no such rule, such as systems operating well above 1,000V?

Those interested in the evolution of the *Code* change process will certainly be remembering this particular change as a monumental one.

705.12(A) Supply Side Point of Connection

A new provision clarifies the installation of overcurrent devices on the supply side of the service.

705.12 Point of Connection.

(A) Supply Side. An electrical power production source is permitted to be connected to the supply side of the service disconnecting means, Figure 705–2. The sum of the ratings of all overcurrent devices connected to power production sources isn't permitted to exceed the rating of the service conductor ampacity.

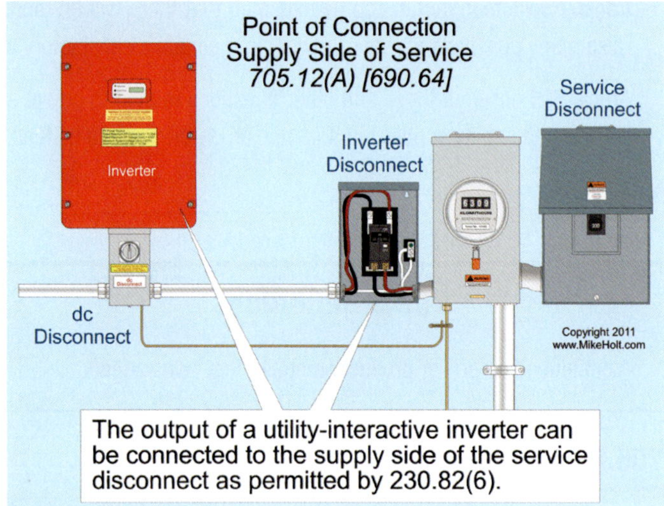

Figure 705–2

ANALYSIS: Previous editions of this Code rule gave a carte blanche allowance for power production equipment on the supply side of the service. Although common sense seems to indicate that the production equipment shouldn't exceed the rating of the service, there wasn't a rule that gave such guidance. This change clarifies that the combined ratings of overcurrent devices on the supply side of the service must not exceed the rating of the service itself.

705.12(D)(2) Load Side Point of Connection

A new exception for PV utility-interactive inverters was added.

705.12 Point of Connection.

(D) Load Side. The output of a utility-interactive inverter can be connected to the load side of the service disconnecting means at any distribution equipment on the premises.

(1) Dedicated Circuit. Each inverter circuit must terminate to a dedicated circuit breaker or fusible disconnect [690.64]. **Figure 705–3**

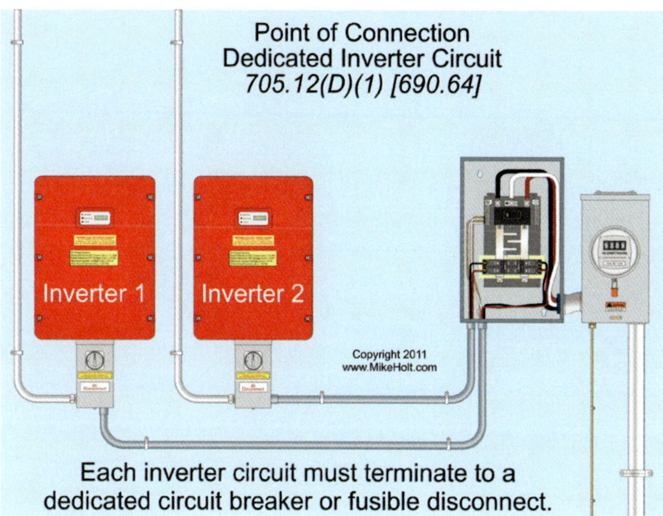

Figure 705–3

(2) Panelboard Bus Rating. The sum of the ampere rating of the inverter overcurrent devices and panelboard overcurrent device doesn't exceed 120 percent of the panelboard bus ampere rating [690.64]. **Figure 705–4**

> ***Example:*** *What's the maximum ampere rating of the dedicated inverter overcurrent device for a 200A bus panelboard where the overcurrent device of the panelboard is 150A, 175A, or 200A?*
>
> *Maximum Inverter OCPD = Panelboard Bus Ampere × 1.20, less Panelboard OCPD.*
>
> *Example 1:150A Panelboard OCPD*
>
> *Max. Inverter Device = 200A × 1.20 – 150A*
>
> *Max. Inverter Device = 240A – 150A*
>
> *Max. Inverter Device = 90A*
>
> *Example 2:175A Panelboard OCPD*

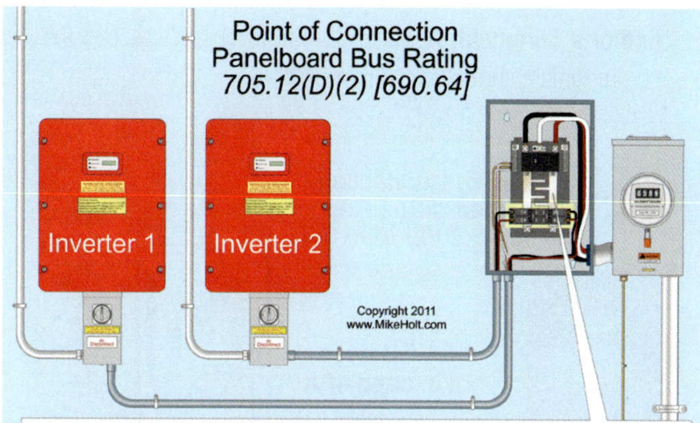

Figure 705–4

> *Max. Inverter Device = 200A × 1.20 – 175A*
>
> *Max. Inverter Device = 240A – 175A*
>
> *Max. Inverter Device = 65A*
>
> *Example 3: 200A Panelboard OCPD* **Figure 705–5**
>
> *Max. Inverter Device = 200A × 1.20 – 200A*
>
> *Max. Inverter Device = 240A – 200A*
>
> *Max. Inverter Device = 40A*

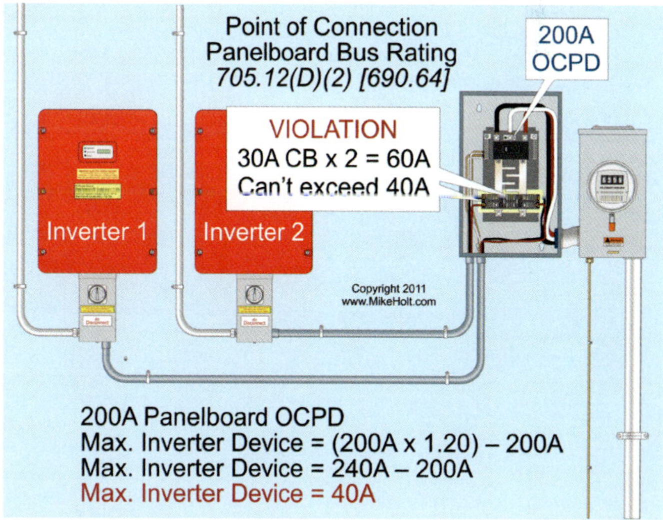

Figure 705–5

Author's Comment: A single 30A inverter won't exceed the 40A maximum current limit. **Figure 705–6**

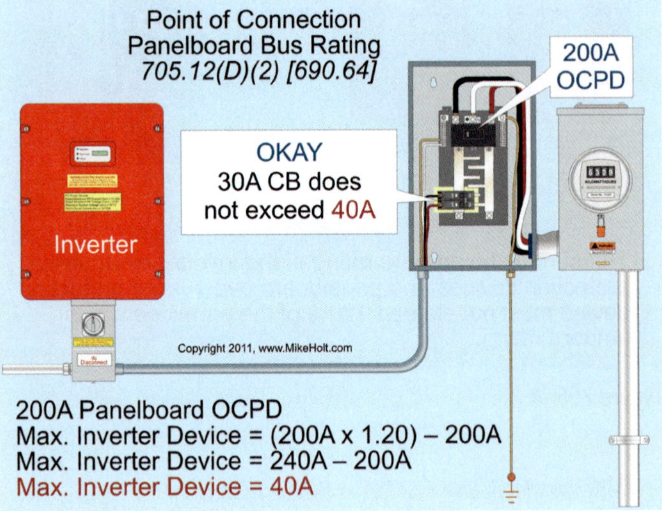

Figure 705–6

Ex: Where the PV system has energy storage for stand-alone operation, the value used in the calculation of bus or conductor loading is 125 percent of the output inverter current.

ANALYSIS: Some types of PV utility-interactive inverters can take up to 60A from the grid for the purposes of battery charging and supplying loads that are backed up by batteries. These same inverters, however, will only supply 30A in the utility-interactive mode of operation. Without this new exception, such a system would require a much larger panel than should be required, due to these inherent limitations of current.

ARTICLE 725 Remote-Control, Signaling, and Power-LIMITED CIRCUITS

INTRODUCTION TO ARTICLE 725—REMOTE-CONTROL, SIGNALING, AND POWER-LIMITED CIRCUITS

Circuits that fall under Article 725 are remote-control, signaling, and power-limited circuits that aren't an integral part of a device or appliance. This article includes circuits for burglar alarms, access control, sound, nurse call, intercoms, some computer networks, some lighting dimmer controls, and some low-voltage industrial controls.

Let's take a quick look at the types of circuits:

- A remote-control circuit controls other circuits through a relay or solid-state device, such as a motion-activated security lighting circuit.
- A signaling circuit provides output that's a signal or indicator, such as a buzzer, flashing light, or annunciator.
- A power-limited circuit is a circuit supplied by a transformer or other power source that limits the amount of power to provide safety from electrical shock and fire ignition.

The purpose of Article 725 is to allow for the fact that these circuits "are characterized by usage and power limitations that differentiate them from electrical power circuits." This article provides alternative requirements for minimum conductor sizes, overcurrent protection, insulation requirements, wiring methods, and materials.

Article 725 consists of four parts. Part I provides general information, Part II pertains to Class 1 circuits, and Part III pertains to Class 2 and Class 3 circuits while Part IV focuses on listing requirements. The key to understanding and applying each of these parts is in knowing the voltage and energy levels of the circuits, the wiring method involved, and the purposes of the circuit.

725.3(H) Raceways Exposed to Different Temperatures

A new subsection requires raceways that are subject to different temperatures to comply with 300.7(A).

725.3 Other Articles.

(H) Raceways Exposed to Different Temperatures. If a raceway is subjected to different temperatures, and where condensation is known to be a problem, the raceway must be filled with a material approved by the authority having jurisdiction that will prevent the circulation of warm air to a colder section of the raceway. An explosionproof seal isn't required for this purpose [300.7(A)]. **Figure 725–1**

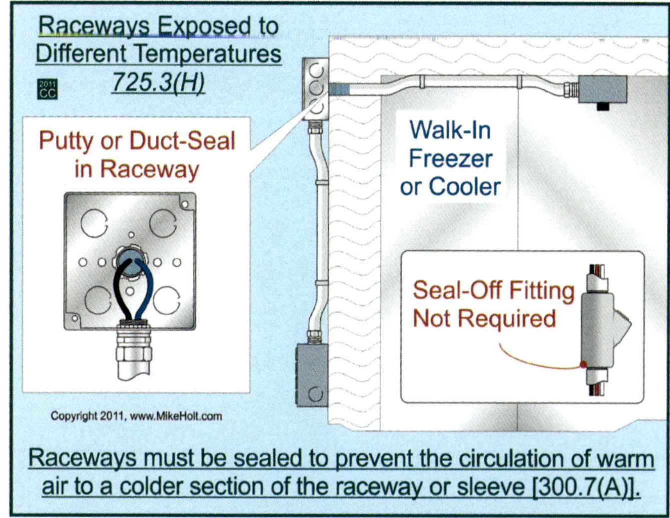

Figure 725–1

Author's Comment: Section 300.7(A) requires seals in raceways that are subject to different temperatures. This is a seal approved by the AHJ to prevent the circulation of warm air to a cooler section of the raceway, and isn't the same thing as an explosionproof seal.

ANALYSIS: Most of the rules found in Article 300 don't apply to installations that fall under the scope of Article 725. The rules in Article 300 that do apply are listed in 725.3. The list of rules here in Article 300 that apply to Article 725 installations are quite logical. Section 300.7(A) is an example of one that needs to be followed in an Article 725 installation.

When raceways are subjected to different temperatures, condensation is often the result. Such condensation can result in equipment and/or cable insulation failure.

725.3(J) Bushing

A new requirement for a bushing was added to this section.

725.3 Other Articles.

(J) Bushing. When a raceway is used for the support or protection of cables, a fitting to reduce the potential for abrasion must be placed at the location the cables enter the raceway [300.15(C)].

ANALYSIS: Section 90.3 of the *NEC* requires that all provisions found in Chapters 1 through 4 apply to Chapters 1 through 7. Section 725.3 removes compliance with Article 300, except as specifically listed here. Section 300.15(C) is an example of a requirement that hasn't applied to this article in previous *Code* editions. With this change a bushing will now be required where a remote-control, signaling, or power-limited cable emerges from a conduit or tubing that's used for protection from physical damage.

ARTICLE 760

Fire Alarm SYSTEMS

INTRODUCTION TO ARTICLE 760—FIRE ALARM SYSTEMS

Article 760 covers the installation of wiring and equipment for fire alarm systems, including circuits controlled and powered by the fire alarm system. These include fire detection and alarm notification, voice communications, guard's tour, sprinkler waterflow, and sprinkler supervisory systems. NFPA 72, *National Fire Alarm Code* provides other fire alarm system requirements.

PART I. GENERAL

760.3(H) Raceways or Sleeves Exposed to Different Temperatures

A new subsection requires raceways or sleeves that are subject to different temperatures to comply with 300.7(A).

760.3 Other Articles.

(H) Raceways or Sleeves Exposed to Different Temperatures. If a raceway or sleeve is subjected to different temperatures, and where condensation is known to be a problem, the raceway or sleeve must be filled with a material approved by the authority having jurisdiction that will prevent the circulation of warm air to a colder section of the raceway. An explosionproof seal isn't required for this purpose [300.7(A)]. Figure 760–1

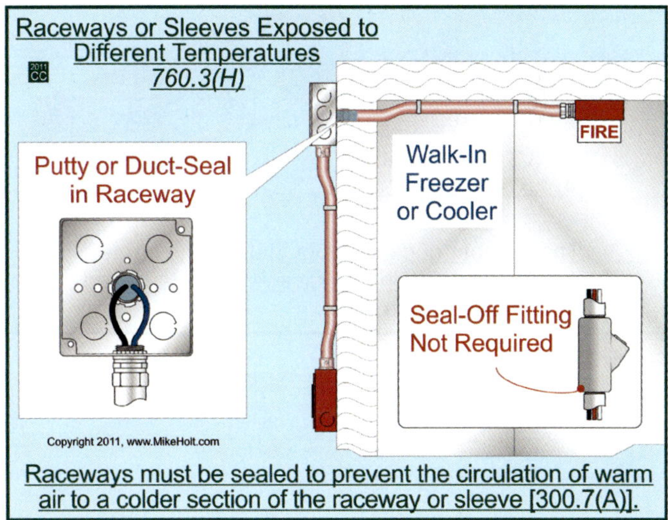

Raceways must be sealed to prevent the circulation of warm air to a colder section of the raceway or sleeve [300.7(A)].

Figure 760–1

ANALYSIS: Most of the rules found in Article 300 don't apply to installations that fall under the scope of Article 760. The rules in Article 300 that do apply are listed in 760.3 and are quite logical. Section 300.7(A) is an example of one that needs to be followed in an Article 760 fire alarm installation.

When raceways or sleeves are subjected to different temperatures, condensation is often the result. Such condensation can result in equipment and/or cable insulation failure.

760.3(J) Number and Size of Cables and Conductors in Raceway

Fire alarm system conductors and cables must now comply with the raceway fill provisions of 300.17.

760.3 Other Articles.

(J) Number and Size of Conductors in a Raceway. Raceways must be large enough to permit the installation and removal of conductors without damaging conductor insulation as limited by 300.17.

Author's Comment: When all conductors in a raceway are the same size and insulation, the number of conductors permitted can be found in Annex C for the raceway type.

Question: *How many 18 TFFN fixture wires can be installed in trade size ½ electrical metallic tubing?* Figure 760–2

(a) 22 (b) 26 (c) 30 (d) 40

Answer: *(a) 22 conductors [Annex C, Table C.1]*

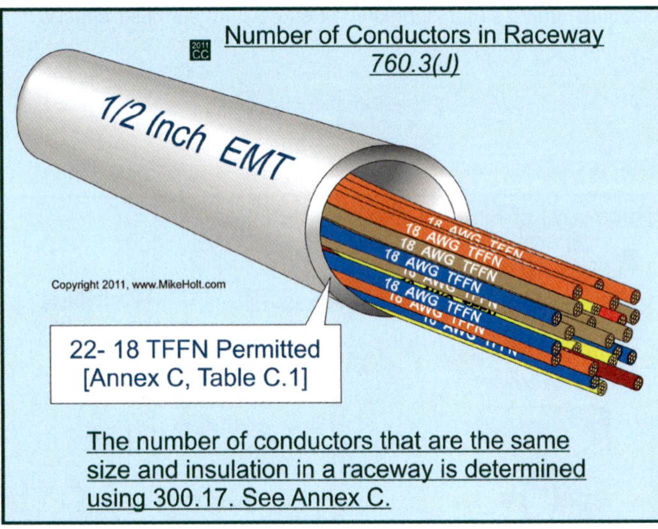

Figure 760–2

ANALYSIS: Most of the rules found in Article 300 don't apply to installations that fall under the scope of Article 760. The rules in Article 300 that do apply are listed in 760.3. The list of rules here in Article 300 that apply to Article 760 installations are quite logical. Section 300.17 is an example of a one that needs to be followed in an Article 760 fire alarm installation.

Overcrowded raceways can result in damaged conductor and cables during their installation. No one that has ever pulled wire into a raceway that's overfilled will argue this, so it makes good sense to extend these requirements to fire alarm systems.

760.3(K) Bushing

A new requirement for a bushing was added to this section.

760.3 Other Articles.

(K) Bushing. When a raceway is used for the support or protection of cables, a bushing to reduce the potential for abrasion must be placed at the location where the cables enter the raceway [300.15(C)].

ANALYSIS: Section 90.3 of the *NEC* requires that all provisions found in Chapters 1 through 4 apply to Chapters 1 through 7. Section 760.3 removes compliance with Article 300, except as specifically listed in this section. Section 300.15(C) is an example of a requirement that hasn't applied to this article in previous *Code* editions. With this change a bushing will now be required where fire alarm cable emerges from a conduit or tubing that's used for protection from physical damage.

PART III. POWER-LIMITED FIRE ALARM (PLFA) CIRCUITS

760.121(B) Branch Circuit

The circuiting requirements for power-limited fire alarm equipment has been revised, and marking requirements have been added.

760.121 Power Sources for Power-Limited Fire Alarm Circuits.

(B) Branch Circuit. Power-limited fire alarm equipment must be supplied by a branch circuit that supplies no other load and isn't GFCI or AFCI protected. The fire alarm circuit disconnecting means must have red identification, be accessible only to qualified personnel, and be identified as "FIRE ALARM CIRCUIT." The red identification isn't permitted to damage the overcurrent protective device or obscure the manufacturer's markings. Figure 760–3

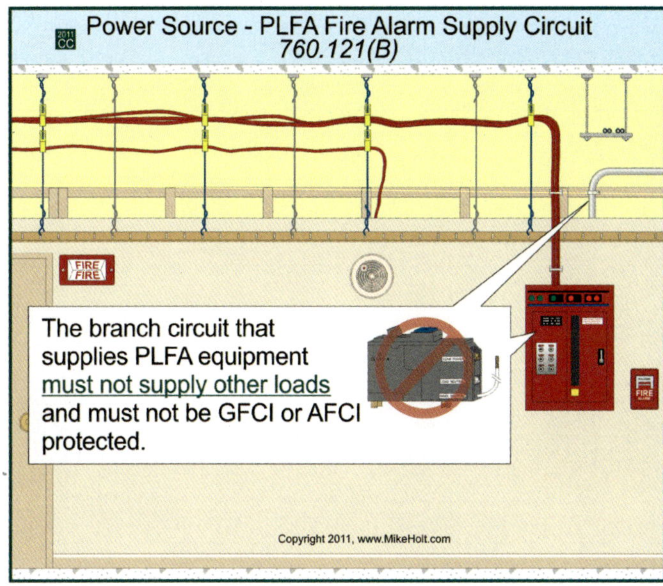

Figure 760–3

ANALYSIS: Previous editions of the Code have mandated that a power-limited fire alarm (PLFA) be supplied by an individual branch circuit. With this requirement, one branch circuit couldn't be used to supply multiple pieces of equipment that are all components of the same fire alarm system (for example, a fire alarm panel and a battery charger in separate enclosures). This change clarifies that the circuit need not be an "individual branch circuit," but rather, a circuit that supplies only fire alarm equipment.

A new provision will now require that a fire alarm control panel be marked to indicate the location of the branch circuit that supplies it. The disconnecting means identification must be red and also must be accessible to qualified persons only.

NOTES

Optical Fiber Cables AND RACEWAYS

INTRODUCTION TO ARTICLE 770—OPTICAL FIBER CABLES AND RACEWAYS

Article 770 provides the requirements for installing optical fiber cables and special raceways for optical fiber cables. It also contains the requirements for composite cables, often called "hybrid," that combine optical fibers with current-carrying conductors.

While we normally think of Article 300 in connection with wiring methods, you only need to use Article 770 methods for optical fiber cables, except where it makes specific references to Article 300 [770.3]. For instance, in 770.113, reference is made to 300.22, which applies when installing optical fiber cables and optical fiber raceways in ducts and other spaces used for environmental air-handling purposes (plenums).

This article doesn't refer to 300.15, so boxes aren't required for splices or terminations of optical fiber cable. Note 1 to 770.48 states that splice cases and terminal boxes are typically used as enclosures for splicing or terminating optical fiber cables.

Article 90 states that the *NEC* isn't a design guide or installation manual. Thus, Article 770 doesn't deal with the performance of optical fiber systems. For example, it doesn't mention cable bending radii. It doesn't tell how to install and test cable safely either, but that doesn't mean you should look into an optical fiber cable, even if you can't see any light coming through it. Light used in these circuits usually isn't visible, but it can still damage your eyes.

770.1 Scope

The scope has been changed to include "cable routing assemblies."

770.1 Scope. Article 770 covers the installation of optical fiber cables, which transmit light for control, signaling, and communications. This article also contains the installation requirements for optical fiber raceways and cable routing assemblies, as well as the requirements for composite cables that combine optical fibers with current-carrying conductors.

Author's Comment: The growth of high-tech applications and significant technological development of optical fibers and the equipment used to send and receive light pulses has increased the use of optical fibers. Since optical fiber cable isn't affected by electromagnetic interference, there's been a large growth in its uses in communications for voice, data transfer, data processing, and computer control of machines and processes.

ANALYSIS: Previously, the scope of this article included the installation of optical fiber cables and raceways. With this change, it now also includes "cable routing assemblies," which are typically a "U" shaped trough, with or without covers, designed to hold cables. These assemblies aren't raceways, by definition, so this change is necessary.

770.2 Definitions

Several revisions to the defined terms of Article 770 have been made, and some new ones have been added.

770.2 Definitions.

Cable Routing Assembly. Single/multiple channels as well as associated fittings, forming a structural system to support, route and protect communications wires and cables, optical fiber, and data (Class 2 and Class 3) cables.

Nonconductive Optical Fiber Cable. A factory assembly of one or more optical fibers containing no electrically conductive materials. **Figure 770–1**

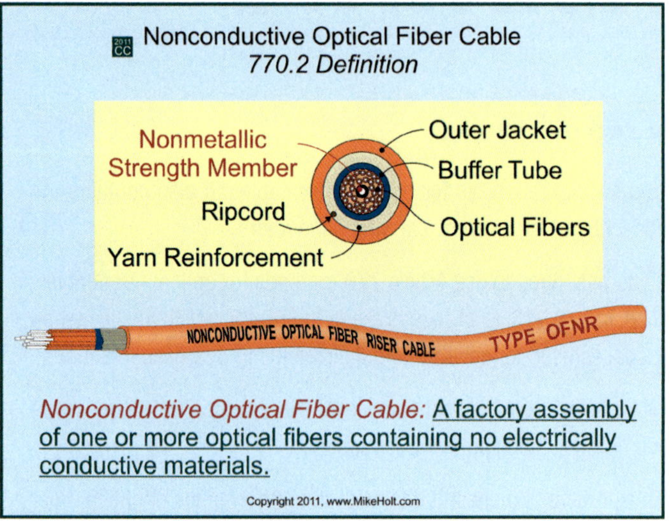

Figure 770–1

Optical Fiber Cable. A factory assembly of optical fibers having an overall covering which transmits light for control, signaling, and communications. **Figure 770–2**

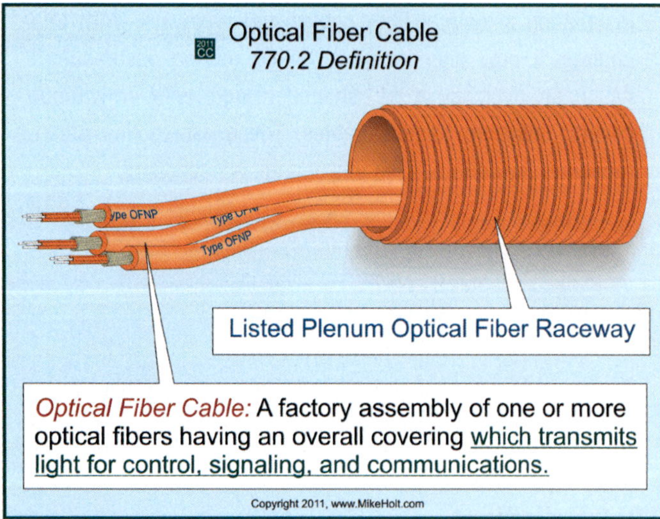

Figure 770–2

Optical Fiber Raceway. An enclosed channel of nonmetallic materials designed for holding optical fiber cables in plenum, riser, and general-purpose applications. **Figure 770–3**

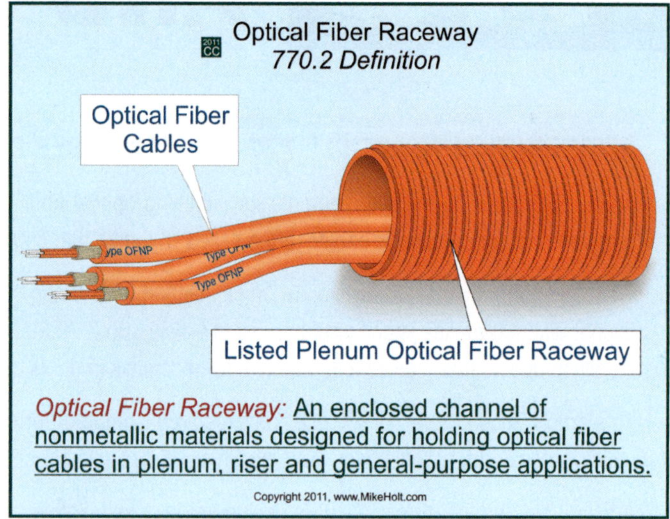

Figure 770–3

ANALYSIS: With the change to the scope of this article, a new definition for "cable routing assemblies" was added. These assemblies are typically a "U" shaped trough, with or without covers, designed to hold cables.

Previous definitions of the term "conductive optical fiber cable" included the phrase "these optical fiber cables." According to the NEC Manual of Style, a definition can't include the term being defined. This definition was primarily changed to comply with the Style Manual, and it also provided a more accurate definition. Similarly, "nonconductive optical fiber cable" was revised.

While the previous definition of "optical fiber cable" was accurate, it lacked any real substance. Changes to this defined term include language describing the function of the cable, which is to transmit light for control, signaling, and communications.

The existing definition of "optical fiber raceway" is a very broad one. By not specifying the type of raceway being discussed, it can easily be argued that any raceway containing optical fiber cables is an optical fiber raceway. This was never the intent of this definition and its subsequent provisions, so this change, clarifying that the raceway is designed for the application, was accepted rather easily.

770.48 Unlisted Cables Entering Buildings

The requirements for unlisted cables entering buildings have been revised.

770.48 Unlisted Cables Entering Buildings.

(A) Conductive and Nonconductive Cables. Unlisted optical fiber cables can be installed in building spaces, other than risers, ducts, or other spaces used for environmental air (plenums), if the length of the optical fiber cable measured from its point of entrance doesn't exceed 50 ft and the optical fiber cable terminates in an enclosure.

Note 2: The point of entrance is defined as the point within a building at which the optical fiber cable emerges from an external wall, from a concrete floor slab, or from a rigid metal conduit or an intermediate metal conduit connected by a grounding conductor to an electrode in accordance with 770.100 [770.2].

ANALYSIS: This subsection allows for an unlisted optical fiber cable in a building, provided the length doesn't exceed 50 ft. Although other sections of the *Code* already cover the requirements for cables installed in ducts used for environmental air and other spaces used for environmental air (plenums), they've been reiterated here. The unlisted cables entering buildings discussed in this section aren't allowed in these ducts, plenums, and air-handling spaces.

770.110 Raceways for Optical Fiber Cables

The provisions for raceways containing optical fiber cables have been revised, mainly for clarity and usability.

770.110 Raceways for Optical Fiber Cables.

(A) Types of Raceways.

(1) Chapter 3 Raceways. Optical fiber cables can be installed in any Chapter 3 raceways in accordance with the requirements of Chapter 3.

(2) Other Permitted Raceways. Optical fiber cables can be installed in a listed optical fiber raceway in accordance with 362.24 through 362.56. Figure 770–4

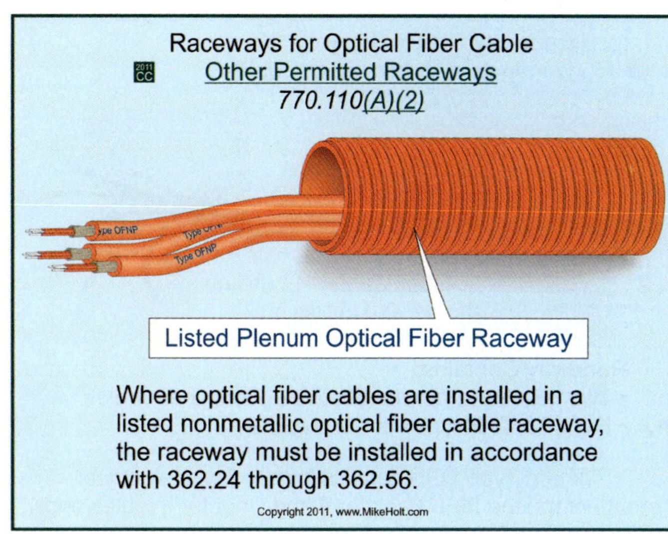

Figure 770–4

Author's Comment: In other words, listed optical fiber raceways must be installed according to the following ENT rules:

- 362.24 Bending radius
- 362.26 Maximum total bends between pull points, 360 degrees
- 362.28 Trimmed to remove rough edges
- 362.30 Support every 3 ft, within 3 ft of any enclosure
- 362.48 Joints between tubing, fittings, and boxes

(B) Raceway Fill for Optical Fiber Cables.

(1) Without Electric Light or Power Conductors. If optical fiber cables are installed in a raceway without current-carrying conductors, the raceway fill tables of Chapter 9 don't apply.

(2) Nonconductive Optical Fiber Cables With Electric Light or Power Conductors. If nonconductive optical fiber cables are installed with electrical conductors in a raceway, the raceway fill tables of Chapter 3 and Chapter 9 apply. Figure 770–5

ANALYSIS: Previous editions of this *Code* section contained many provisions in the form of a single paragraph, including one sentence with an incredible 71 words! By breaking the requirements up into a list format, the requirements and allowances are much easier to read and understand.

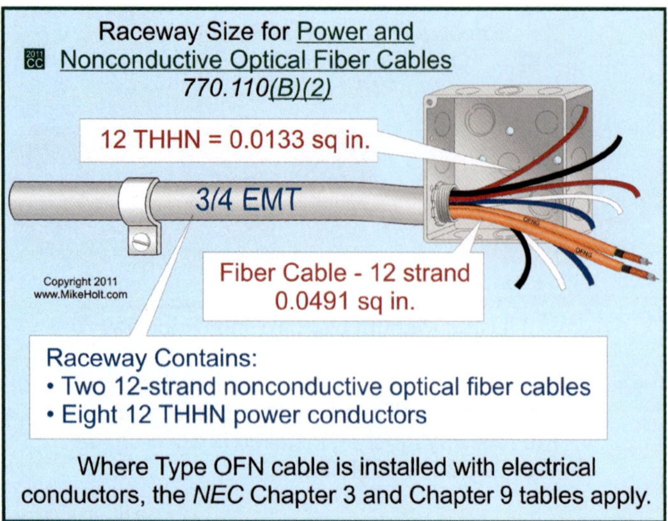

Figure 770–5

770.113 Installation of Cables, Raceways, and Cable Routing Assemblies

This section has been extensively revised to incorporate all of the requirements for the installation of optical fiber cables, optical fiber raceways, and cable routing assemblies.

770.113 Installation of Optical Fiber Cables, Optical Fiber Raceways, and Cable Routing Assemblies.

(A) Listing. Optical fiber cables and raceways installed within buildings must be listed.

Ex: Unless the length of the cable from its point of entrance, doesn't exceed 50 ft as permitted by 770.48.

Author's Comment: The *NEC* doesn't require outside or underground cable to be listed, but the cable must be approved by the authority having jurisdiction as suitable for the application in accordance with 90.4, 90.7, and 110.2.

(C) Other Spaces Used For Environmental Air (Plenums). The following cables and raceways are permitted in other spaces used for environmental air (plenums) as described in 300.22(C): Figure 770–6

(1) Types OFNP and OFCP cables

(2) Listed plenum optical fiber raceways

(3) Types OFNP and OFCP cables installed in listed plenum raceways

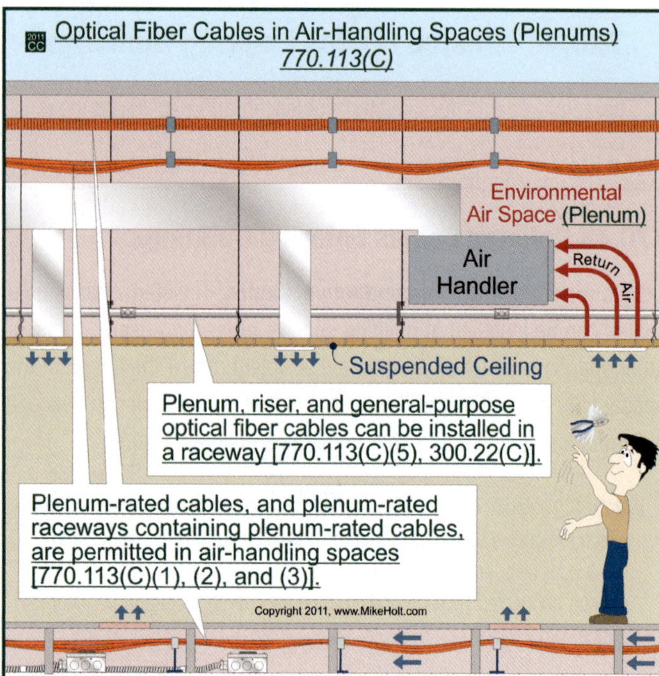

Figure 770–6

(4) Types OFNP and OFCP cables and optical fiber raceways supported by open metallic cable trays or cable tray systems

(5) Types OFNP, OFCP, OFNR, OFCR, OFNG, OFCG, OFN, and OFC cables installed in raceways in compliance with 300.22(C).

(H) Cable Trays. The following cables and raceways can be installed in cable trays:

(1) Types OFNP, OFCP, OFNR, OFCR, OFNG, OFCG, OFN, and OFC

(2) Optical fiber raceways

(3) Types OFNP, OFCP, OFNR, OFCR, OFNG, OFCG, OFN, and OFC installed in optical fiber raceways

(J) Other Building Locations. The following cables and raceways are permitted in the spaces not described in (B)(through (I):

(1) Types OFNP, OFCP, OFNR, OFCR, OFNG, OFCG, OFN, and OFC

(2) Optical fiber raceways

(3) Riser and general purpose cable routing assemblies

(4) Types OFNP, OFCP, OFNR, OFCR, OFNG, OFCG, OFN, and OFC installed in optical fiber raceways

(5) Types OFNP, OFCP, OFNR, OFCR, OFNG, OFCG, OFN, and OFC installed in a Chapter 3 type raceway

ANALYSIS: One need only glance at this section of the Code to understand the extent of the revisions to this section. While there seem to be many new requirements at first glance, a great deal of this change involved moving existing requirements out of another section and into this one. Section 770.154 has long provided the installation requirements for optical fiber cables and optical fiber raceways, but due to its location, the requirements were difficult to find.

The requirements for riser-rated cable have been clarified in 770.113(D) as well. Previous editions of the N*EC* required riser-rated cables whenever "more than one floor" was penetrated. This led to arguments about whether a cable extending from one level to another (penetrating one floor/ceiling assembly) was required to be riser-rated. A clarification has been made on this issue to show that such a cable does need to be riser-rated. The requirement for riser-rated cables comes into play once the cable penetrates a single floor.

770.133(B) Optical Fiber Cables With Communications Cables

Provisions for cable routing assemblies have been added to the separation requirements included in this section.

770.133 Installation of Optical Fiber Cables.

(B) With Communications Cables. Optical fiber cables can be in the same raceway, cable tray, cable routing assembly or enclosure with conductors of any of the following: **Figure 770–7**

(1) Communications circuits in compliance with Parts I and IV of Article 800.

(2) Coaxial cables in compliance with Parts I and IV of Article 820.

(C) With Other Circuits. Optical fiber cables can be in the same raceway, cable tray, cable routing assembly or enclosure with conductors of any of the following:

(1) Class 2 and Class 3 circuits in compliance with Parts I and III of Article 725.

(2) Power-limited fire alarm circuits in compliance with Parts I and III of Article 760.

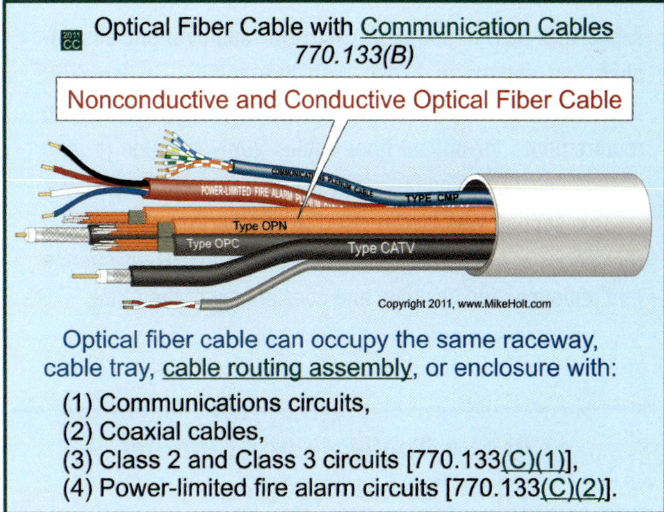

Figure 770–7

(D) Support of Cables. Optical fiber cables aren't permitted to be strapped, taped, or attached to the exterior of any raceway as a means of support. **Figure 770–8**

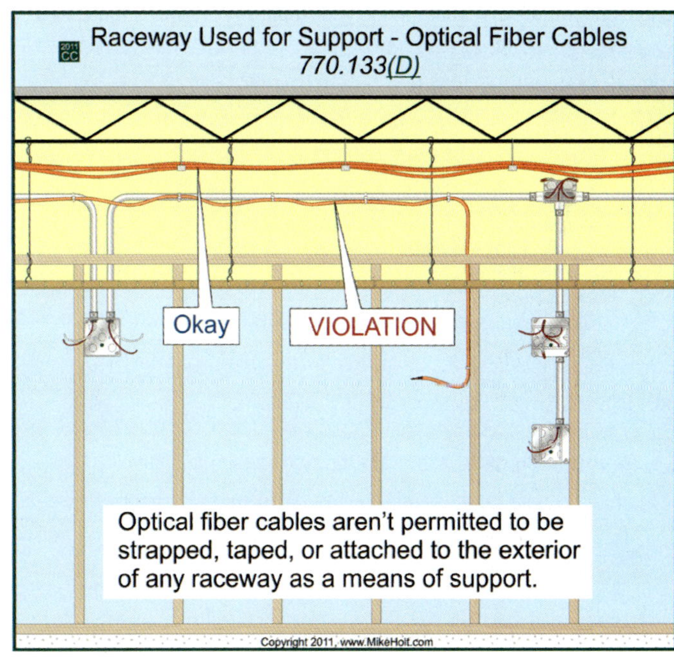

Figure 770–8

ANALYSIS: New to this *Code* cycle are "cable routing assemblies," as defined in 770.2. With this addition to the *NEC*, this section has been revised to clarify that the separation requirements for optical fiber cables apply to cable routing assemblies as well as raceways, cable trays, and enclosures.

This section was also revised to add Part numbers to the references of Articles 725, 760, 800, 820, and 830—a change that enhances the usability and consistency of the *Code*.

770.154 Applications of Optical Fiber Cables and Raceways

This section has been revised (and greatly reduced) due to other changes to this article.

770.154 Applications of Optical Fiber Cables and Raceways. Listed optical fiber cables and raceways can be installed as indicated in Table 770.154(A), as limited by 770.113, and cable substitutions in accordance with Table 770.154(B). **Figure 770–9**

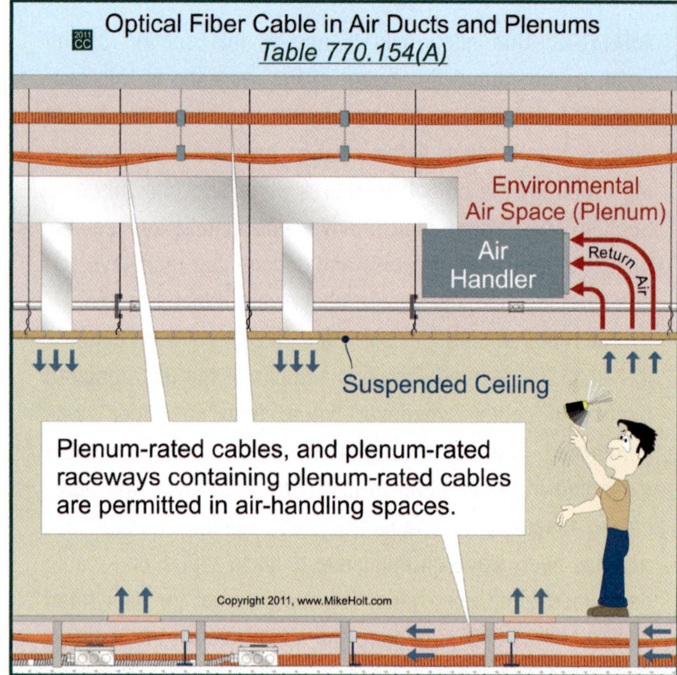

Figure 770–9

ANALYSIS: Most of the text that was found in this section in previous *NEC* editions has been relocated to 770.113. No technical changes have been made here, but editorial changes referring the *Code* user to 770.113 have been.

A new table has also been added, highlighting the permitted uses of the cable types discussed in this article.

CHAPTER 8

COMMUNICATIONS SYSTEMS

INTRODUCTION TO CHAPTER 8—COMMUNICATIONS SYSTEMS

Chapter 8 of the *National Electrical Code* covers the wiring requirements for communications systems such as telephones, radio and TV antennas, satellite dishes, closed-circuit television (CCTV), and cable TV (CATV) systems, as well as network-powered and broadband-powered communications systems. **Figure 1**

Communications systems aren't subject to the general requirements contained in Chapters 1 through 4 or the special requirements of Chapters 5 through 7, except where a Chapter 8 rule specifically refers to one of those chapters [90.3]. Also, installations of communications equipment under the exclusive control of communications utilities located outdoors, or in building spaces used exclusively for such installations, are exempt from the *NEC* [90.2(B)(4)]. **Figure 2**

- **Article 800—Communications Circuits.** Article 800 covers the installation requirements for telephone wiring and for other related telecommunications purposes such as computer local area networks (LANs), and outside wiring for fire and burglar alarm systems connected to central stations.
- **Article 810—Radio and Television Equipment.** This article covers antenna systems for radio and television receiving equipment, amateur radio transmitting and receiving equipment, and certain features of transmitter safety. It also includes antennas such as multi-element, vertical rod and dish, and the wiring and cabling that connects them to the equipment.

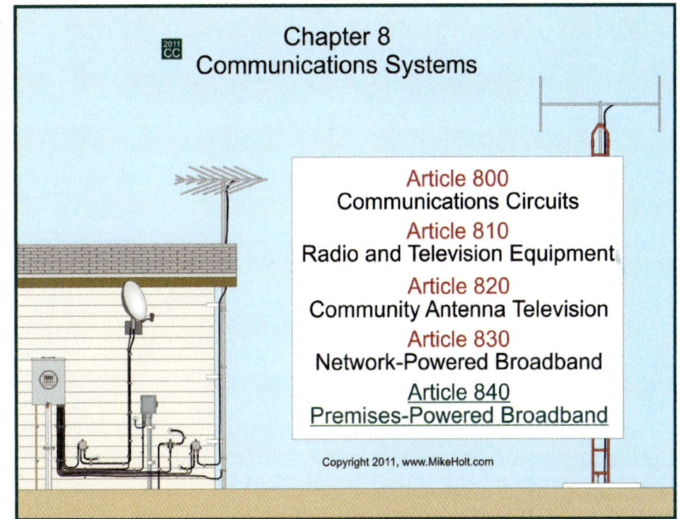

Figure 1

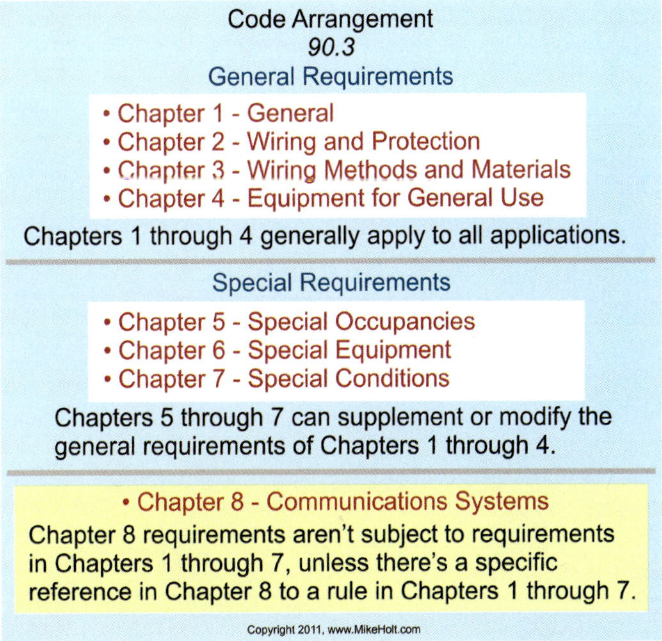

Code Arrangement
90.3

General Requirements

- Chapter 1 - General
- Chapter 2 - Wiring and Protection
- Chapter 3 - Wiring Methods and Materials
- Chapter 4 - Equipment for General Use

Chapters 1 through 4 generally apply to all applications.

Special Requirements

- Chapter 5 - Special Occupancies
- Chapter 6 - Special Equipment
- Chapter 7 - Special Conditions

Chapters 5 through 7 can supplement or modify the general requirements of Chapters 1 through 4.

- Chapter 8 - Communications Systems

Chapter 8 requirements aren't subject to requirements in Chapters 1 through 7, unless there's a specific reference in Chapter 8 to a rule in Chapters 1 through 7.

Figure 2

- **Article 820—Community Antenna Television (CATV) and Radio Distribution Systems.** Article 820 covers the installation of coaxial cables to distribute limited-energy high-frequency signals for television, cable TV, and closed-circuit television (CCTV), which is often used for security purposes. This article also covers the premises wiring of satellite TV systems where the dish antenna is outside and covered by Article 810.

- **Article 840—Premises-Powered Broadband Communications Systems.** Article 840 covers premises-powered optical fiber-based broadband communications systems. The systems use optical fiber cable to the premises supplying a broadband signal to an optical network terminal that converts the broadband signal into traditional telephone, video, high-speed internet, and interactive services.

ARTICLE 800 Communications CIRCUITS

INTRODUCTION TO ARTICLE 800—COMMUNICATIONS CIRCUITS

This article has its roots in telephone technology. Consequently, it addresses telephone and related systems that use twisted-pair wiring. Here are a few key points to remember about Article 800:

- Don't attach incoming communications cables to the service-entrance power mast.
- It's critical to determine the "point of entrance" for these circuits.
- Ground the primary protector as close as practicable to the point of entrance.
- Keep the grounding electrode conductor for the primary protector as straight and as short as possible.
- If you locate communications cables above a suspended ceiling, route and support them to allow access via ceiling panel removal.
- Keep these cables separated from lightning protection circuits.
- If you install communications cables in a Chapter 3 raceway, you must do so in conformance with the *NEC* requirements for the raceway system.
- Special labeling and marking provisions apply—follow them carefully.

Article 800 Scope

A new Informational Note and two new figures have been added.

800.1 Scope. This article covers circuits that extend voice, audio, video, interactive services, and outside wiring for fire alarms and burglar alarms from the communications utility to the customer's communications equipment up to and including equipment such as a telephone, fax machine, or answering machine [800.2] and communications equipment. **Figure 800-1**

> **Note:** The *NEC* installation requirements don't apply to communications utility equipment located outdoors or in building spaces where under the exclusive control of the communications utility [90.2(B)(4)]. **Figure 800-2**

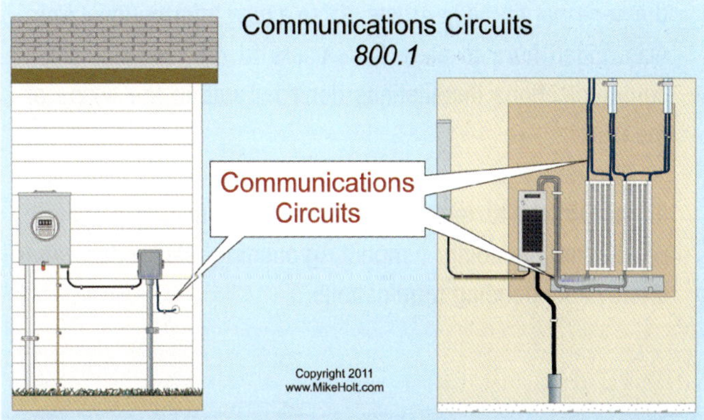

This article covers circuits that extend voice, audio, video, interactive services, and outside wiring for fire alarms and burglar alarms from the communications utility to the customer's communications equipment [800.2].

Figure 800-1

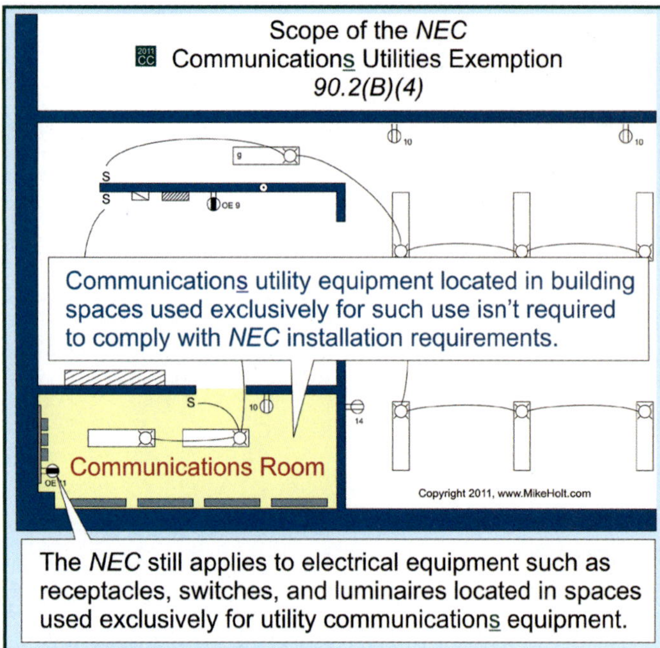

Figure 800-2

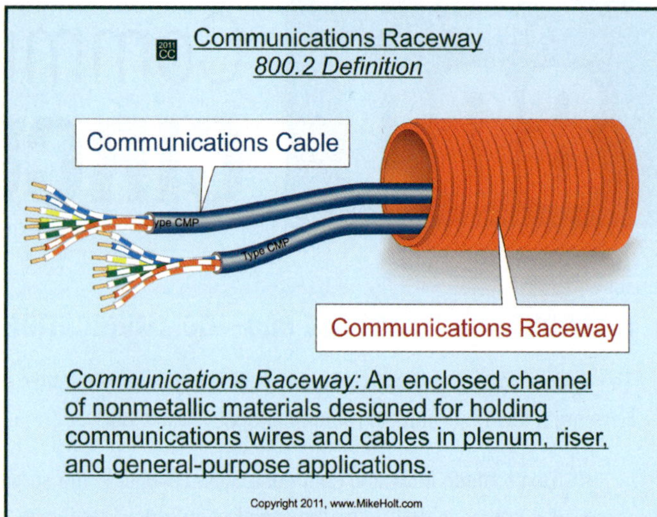

Figure 800-3

ANALYSIS: Section 90.2 discusses the items that are covered by the *NEC*, as well as the items that aren't. Although this information hasn't changed, some *Code* users fail to spend the necessary time in Article 90, so a new Informational Note was added here to alert *Code* users to the fact that some communications installations don't fall within the scope of the *NEC*.

Two new figures have also been added at the beginning of this article to graphically illustrate grounding electrode conductors, bonding jumpers, grounding electrodes, and intersystem bonding terminations.

800.2 Definitions

A new definition for "Communications Raceway" was added.

Communications Raceway. An enclosed channel of nonmetallic materials designed for holding communications wires and cables in plenum, riser and general-purpose applications. Figure 800-3

ANALYSIS: Although the term "communications raceway" is used throughout Article 800, it wasn't defined. New to this *Code* edition is a definition for the term, which indicates that these raceways are designed as plenum communications raceways, riser communications raceways, or general-purpose communications raceways.

800.3 Other Articles

Several new subsections have been added to this section, which relates to "other articles" of the *Code*.

800.3 Other Articles.

(C) Other Space Used for Environmental Air (Plenum). Communications cables and raceways identified as suitable for plenum use can be installed above a suspended ceiling or below a raised floor used for environmental air [300.22(C)]. Figure 800-4

(G) Cable Routing Assemblies. The definition in 770.2, the applications in 770.154, and installation rules in 770.113 apply.

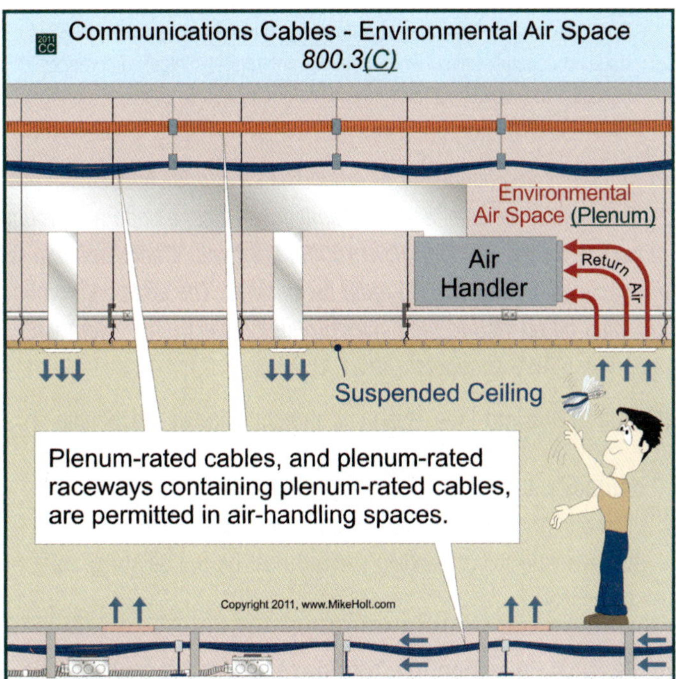

Figure 800-4

ANALYSIS: The provisions for communications cables and conductors in ducts, plenums, and similar environments have been in 800.133(C) for some time, although 800.3 is a much more appropriate and consistent location. A change to this section copies the text from 800.133(C) and places it here.

Also new to the *Code* in 2011 is the concept of "cable routing assemblies." The definition and provisions for these systems are all found in Article 770, so a new subsection was added here to recognize these assemblies.

800.48(A) Unlisted Cables Entering Buildings

The requirements for unlisted cables entering buildings have been revised.

800.48 Unlisted Cables Entering Buildings. Unlisted communications cables can be installed in building spaces other than risers, ducts, or other spaces used for environmental air (plenums) [300.22(C)], if the length of the cable within the building from its point of entrance doesn't exceed 50 ft and the cable terminates in an enclosure or primary protector. Figure 800-5

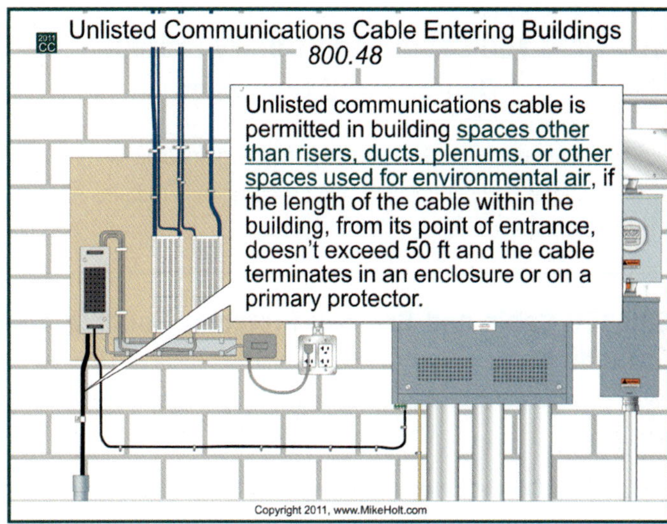

Figure 800-5

Note 2: The primary protector must be located as close as practicable to the point at which the cable enters the building [800.90(B)]. Therefore, unlisted outside plant communications cables may not be permitted to enter the building if it's practicable to place the primary protector closer than 50 ft to the point of entrance.

Author's Comment: The "point of entrance" is defined as the point within the building where the cable emerges from an external wall, from a concrete floor slab, or from rigid metal conduit or intermediate metal conduit connected to an electrode by a grounding conductor in accordance with 800.100 [800.2].

ANALYSIS: This subsection allows for an unlisted communications cable in a building, provided that the length doesn't exceed 50 ft. Although other sections of the *Code* already cover the requirements for cables installed in ducts used for environmental air, plenums used for environmental air, and other spaces used for environmental air (plenums), they've been reiterated here. The unlisted cables entering buildings discussed in this section aren't allowed in these ducts, plenums, and air-handling spaces.

800.100 Cable and Primary Protector Bonding and Grounding

The requirements for the insulation of the grounding electrode conductor have been relaxed, and the sizing requirements have been increased. A new Informational Note has also been added.

800.100 Cable and Primary Protector Bonding and Grounding. The primary protector and the metallic member of cable sheaths must be bonded or grounded in accordance with (A) through (D).

(A) Bonding Conductor or Grounding Electrode Conductor.

(1) Insulation. Listed and be insulated, covered, or bare.

(2) Material. Copper or other corrosion-resistant conductive material, stranded or solid.

(3) Size. Not be smaller than 14 AWG with a current-carrying capacity of not less than the grounded metallic sheath member or protected conductor of the communications cable, but not required to be larger than 6 AWG.

(4) Length. As short as practicable and for one- and two-family dwellings, the bonding conductor or grounding electrode conductor must not exceed 20 ft in length. Figure 800-6

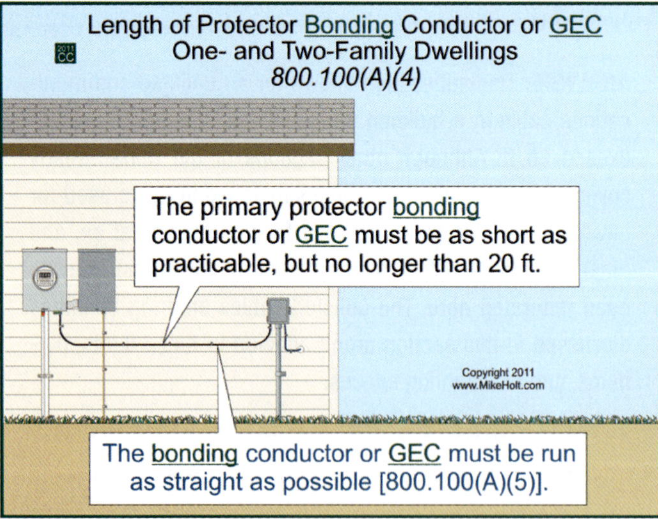

Figure 800-6

Note: Limiting the length of the bonding conductor or grounding electrode conductor helps limit induced potential (voltage) differences between the building's power and communications systems during lightning events.

Ex: If the bonding conductor or grounding electrode conductor is over 20 ft in length for one- and two-family dwellings, a separate ground rod not less than 5 ft long [800.100(B)(3)(2)] with fittings suitable for the application [800.100(C)] must be installed. The additional ground rod must be bonded to the power grounding electrode system with a minimum 6 AWG conductor [800.100(D)].

(5) Run in Straight Line. Run in as straight a line as practicable.

Author's Comment: Lightning doesn't like to travel around corners or through loops, which is why the grounding electrode conductor or bonding jumper must be run as straight as practicable.

(6) Physical Protection. The bonding conductor and grounding electrode conductor must not be subject to physical damage. If installed in a metal raceway, both ends of the raceway must be bonded to the contained conductor or connected to the same terminal or electrode to which the bonding conductor or grounding electrode conductor is connected.

Author's Comment: Installing the bonding conductor or grounding electrode conductor in PVC conduit is a better practice.

(B) Electrode. The bonding conductor or grounding electrode conductor must be connected in accordance with (B)(1), (B)(2), or (B)(3):

(1) Buildings or Structures with an Intersystem Bonding Termination. The bonding conductor for the primary protector and the metallic sheath of communications cable must terminate to the intersystem bonding termination as required by 250.94. Figure 800-7

Note: According to the Article 100 definition, an "Intersystem Bonding Termination" is a device that provides a means to connect bonding conductors for communications systems to the grounding electrode system, in accordance with 250.94. Figure 800-8

Author's Comment: Bonding all systems to the intersystem bonding termination helps reduce induced potential (voltage) differences between the power and the communications systems during lightning events. Figure 800-9

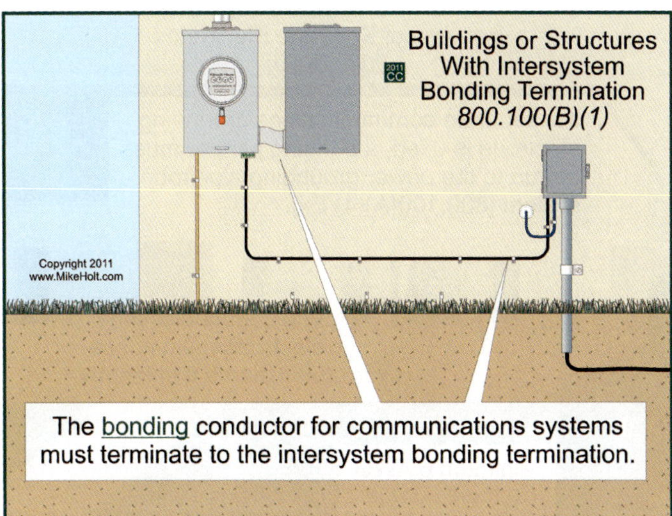

Figure 800-7

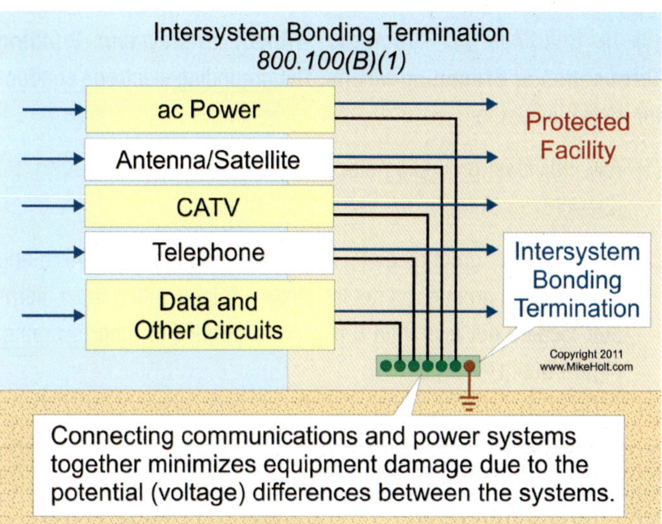

Figure 800-9

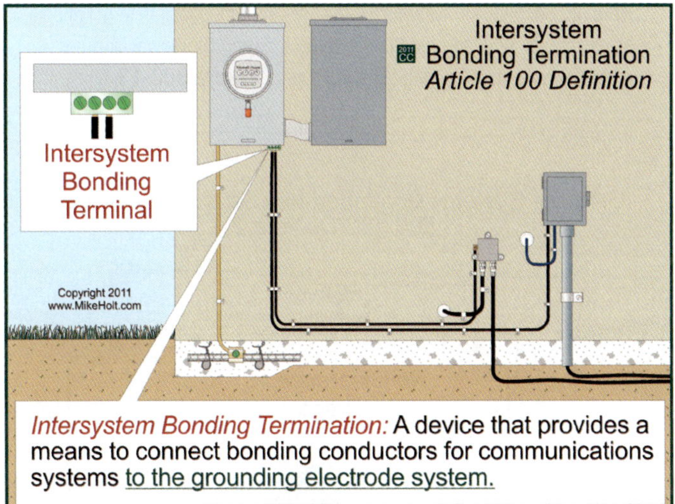

Figure 800-8

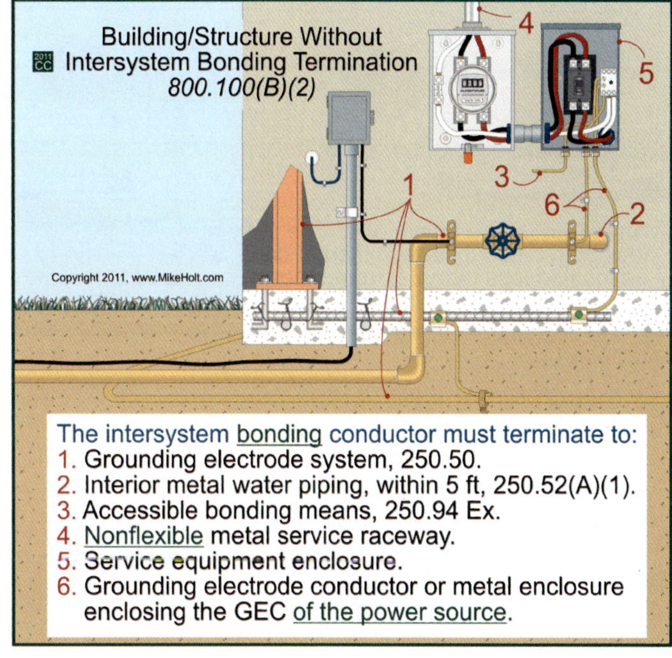

Figure 800-10

(2) Building/Structure Without Intersystem Bonding Termination. The bonding conductor or grounding electrode conductor must terminate to the nearest accessible: Figure 800-10

(1) Building/structure grounding electrode system [250.50].

(2) Interior metal water piping system, within 5 ft from its point of entrance [250.52(A)(1)].

(3) Accessible means external to the building, as covered in 250.94 Ex.

(4) Nonflexible metallic service raceway.

(5) Service equipment enclosure.

(6) Grounding electrode conductor or the grounding electrode conductor metal enclosure of the power service.

(7) Grounding electrode conductor or the grounding electrode of a remote building/structure disconnecting means [250.32].

The intersystem bonding termination must be mounted on the fixed part of an enclosure so that it won't interfere with the opening of an enclosure door. A bonding device must not be mounted on a door or cover even if the door or cover is nonremovable.

(3) In Buildings or Structures Without Intersystem Bonding Termination or Grounding Means. The grounding electrode conductor must connect to:

(1) Any individual grounding electrode described in 250.52(A)(1), (A)(2), (A)(3), or (A)(4).

(2) Any individual grounding electrode described in 250.52(A)(6) and (A)(7), or to a ground rod not less than 5 ft long and ½ in. in diameter located not less than 6 ft from electrodes of other systems. Figure 800-11

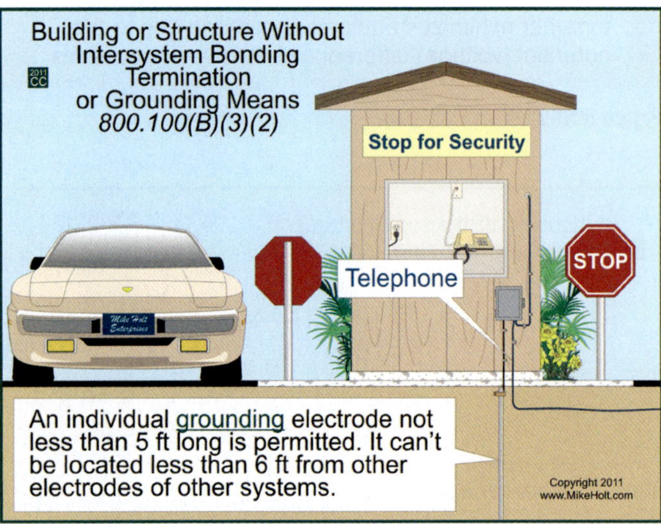

Figure 800-11

Author's Comment: The reason communications ground rods only need to be 5 ft long is because that's the length the telephone company used before the *NEC* contained requirements for communications systems. Telephone company ground rods were only 5 ft long because that's the length that would fit in their equipment trailers.

(C) Electrode Connection. Terminations at the grounding electrode must be by exothermic welding, listed lugs, listed pressure connectors, or listed clamps. Grounding fittings that are concrete-encased or buried in the earth must be listed for direct burial [250.70].

(D) Bonding of Electrodes. If a separate grounding electrode, such as a ground rod, is installed for a communications system, it must be bonded to the building's power grounding electrode system with a minimum 6 AWG conductor. Figure 800-12

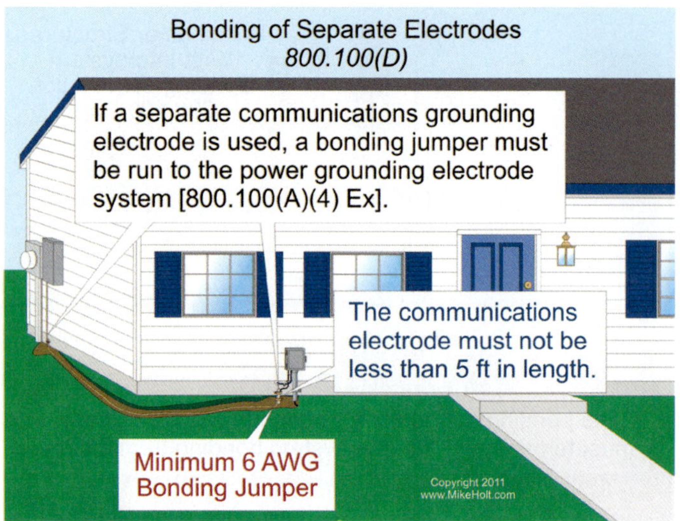

Figure 800-12

Note 2: Bonding all systems to the intersystem bonding termination helps reduce induced potential (voltage) between the power and communications systems during lightning events. Figure 800-13

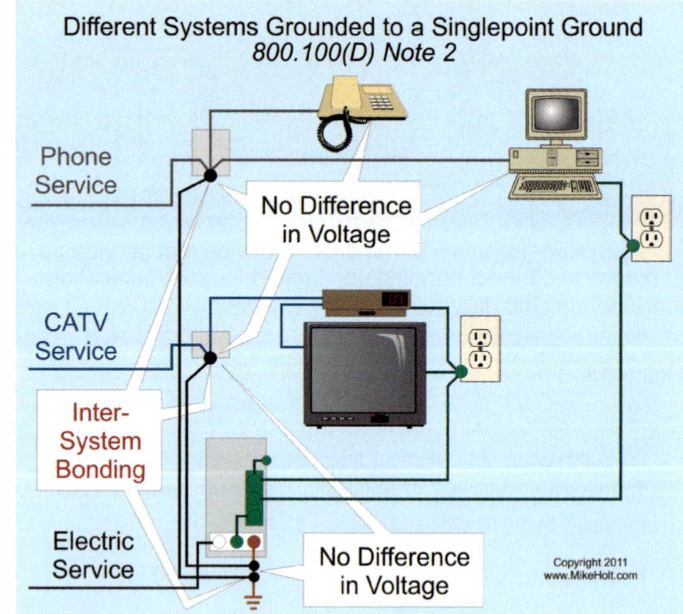

Figure 800-13

ANALYSIS: In previous editions of the *Code*, the grounding electrode conductor was required to be insulated. Because this makes no sense from an electrical theory perspective, this requirement has been revised to allow any type of conductor—insulated, covered, or bare, provided that the conductor is listed.

The size of the grounding electrode conductor has also been revised. Previous editions of the *NEC* have required it to be not smaller than 14 AWG, and this edition retains that text. New to this edition, however, is a requirement for the conductor to have a current-carrying capacity of not less than the grounded metallic sheath member or protected conductor of the communications cable.

Extensive changes in this section were also made in response to the deletion of the term "grounding conductor." As a replacement for it the *Code* user will see either "grounding electrode conductor," "bonding jumper," or both. Similar changes were made throughout the article, mainly in 800.90, 800.100, and 800.106.

Lastly, a new Informational Note was added to (B)(1). When a defined term is used in Chapter 8, a new Informational Note is typically added. This time the note refers the *NEC* user to Article 100 for the definition of "intersystem bonding termination."

800.110 Raceways for Communications Wires and Cables

The provisions for raceways containing communications cables and conductors have been revised, mainly for clarity and usability.

800.110 Raceways for Communications Wires and Cables.

(A) Types of Raceways.

(1) Chapter 3 Raceways. Communications cables can be installed in any Chapter 3 raceway in accordance with the requirements of Chapter 3. **Figure 800-14**

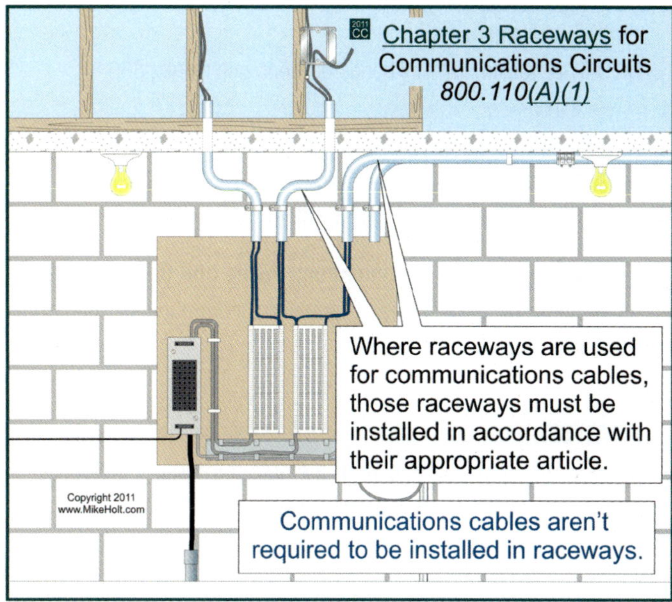

Figure 800-14

(2) Other Permitted Raceways. Communications cables can be installed in a listed communications raceway. If communications cables are installed in a listed communications nonmetallic raceway, the raceway must be installed in accordance with 362.24 through 362.56. **Figure 800-15**

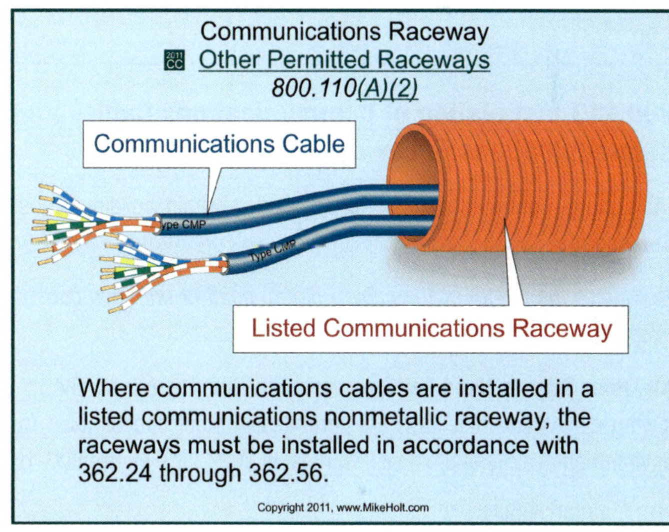

Figure 800-15

Author's Comment: In other words, listed communications raceways must be installed according to the following rules for ENT:

- 362.24 Bending radius
- 362.26 Maximum total bends between pull points, 360 degrees
- 362.28 Trimmed to remove rough edges
- 362.30 Supported every 3 ft, and within 3 ft of any enclosure
- 362.48 Joints between tubing, fittings, and boxes

(B) Raceway Fill for Communications Wires and Cables. Raceway fill limitations of 300.17 don't apply to communications cables installed in a raceway.

ANALYSIS: Previous editions of this *Code* section contained many provisions in the form of a single paragraph, including one sentence with an incredible 66 words! The provisions of this section are much easier to read and understand now that they've been broken up and formatted into a list.

800.113 Installation of Communications Cables and Communications Raceways

This section has been extensively revised to incorporate all of the requirements for the installation of communications cables and conductors, communications raceways, and cable routing assemblies.

800.113 Installation of Communications Cables and Communications Raceways.

(A) Listing. Communications cables installed within buildings must be listed.

Ex: Unless the length of the cable from its point of entrance doesn't exceed 50 ft as permitted by 800.48.

(C) Other Spaces Used For Environmental Air (Plenums). The following cables and raceways are permitted in other spaces used for environmental air (plenums) as described in 300.22(C): Figure 800-16

(1) Type CMP cables

(2) Listed plenum communications raceways

(3) Type CMP cables installed in plenum raceways

(4) Types CMP cables and plenum communications raceways supported by open metallic cable trays or cable tray systems

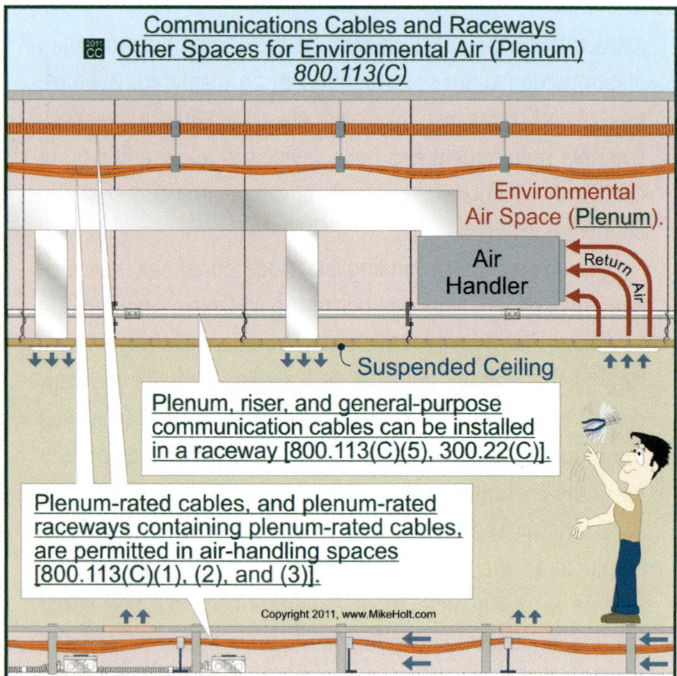

Figure 800–16

(5) Types CMP, CMR, CMG, CM, and CMX cables installed in raceways in compliance with 300.22(C)

(G) Cable Trays. The following cables and raceways can be installed in cable trays:

(1) Types CMP, CMR, CMG, and CM cables

(2) Communications raceways

(3) Types CMP, CMR, CMG, and CM cables installed in communications raceways

(I) Other Building Locations.

(1) Types CMP, CMR, CMG, and CM cables

(2) A maximum of 10 ft of exposed Type CMX cable in nonconcealed spaces

(3) Communications raceways

(4) Types CMP, CMR, CMG, and CM cables installed in communications raceways

(5) Listed communication wires and Types CMP, CMR, CMG, CM, and CMX cables and installed in a Chapter 3 raceway

(K) One- and Two-Family Dwellings. The following cables and raceways can be installed in one- and two-family dwellings in locations other than the locations covered in 800.113(B) through (F):

(1) Types CMP, CMR, CMG, and CM cables

(2) Type CMX cable less than ¼ in. in diameter

(3) Plenum, riser, and general-purpose communications raceways installed in compliance with 800.110

(4) Types CMP, CMR, CMG, and CM cables installed in plenum, riser, or general-purpose communications raceways

(5) Listed communication wires and Types CMP, CMR, CMG, CM, and CMX cables and installed in a raceway of a type included in Chapter 3

ANALYSIS: One need only glance at this section of the *Code* to understand the extent of the revisions to this section. While there seem to be many new requirements at first glance, a many of the changes involved moving existing requirements out of another section and into this one. Section 800.154 has long provided the installation requirements for communications cables and conductors, and communications raceways, but due to its location, the requirements were difficult to find.

800.133(A) Separation from Power Conductors

Provisions for cable routing assemblies, and enclosures, have been added to the separation requirements included in this section.

800.133 Installation of Communications Cables.

(A) Separation from Power Conductors.

(1) In Raceways, Routing Assemblies, Cables, Cable Trays, and Enclosures. Figure 800-17

(a) With Optical Fiber Cables. Communications cables can be in the same raceway, cable tray, cable routing assembly, or enclosure with conductors of any of the following:

(1) Optical fiber cables in accordance with Parts I and IV of Article 770.

(2) Coaxial cables in compliance with Parts I and IV of Article 820.

(b) With Other Circuits. Communications cables can be in the same raceway, cable tray, cable routing assembly, or enclosure with conductors of any of the following:

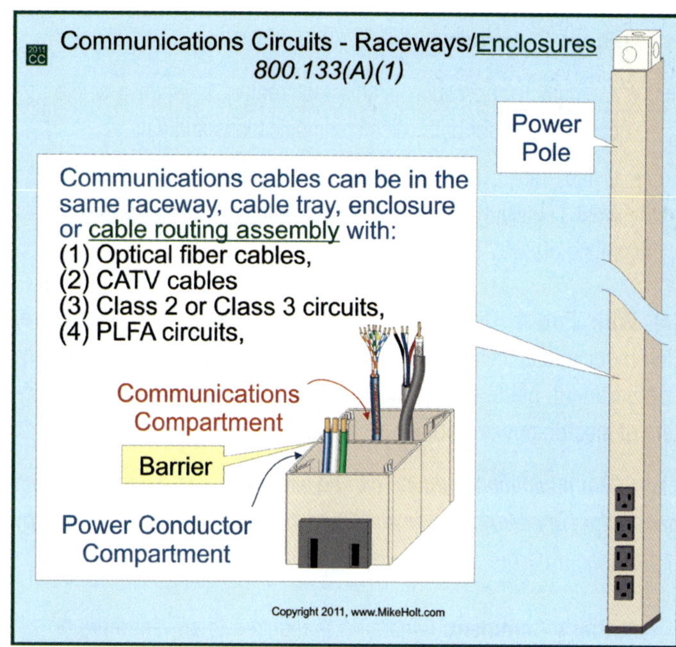

Figure 800-17

(1) Class 2 and Class 3 circuits in compliance with Parts I and III of Article 725.

(2) Power-limited fire alarm circuits in compliance with Parts I and III of Article 760.

(c) Class 2, and Class 3 Circuits. Communications conductors can be within the same cable with Class 2 or Class 3 conductors, provided that communications cables in accordance with Article 800 are used [725.139(D)(1)]. Figure 800-18

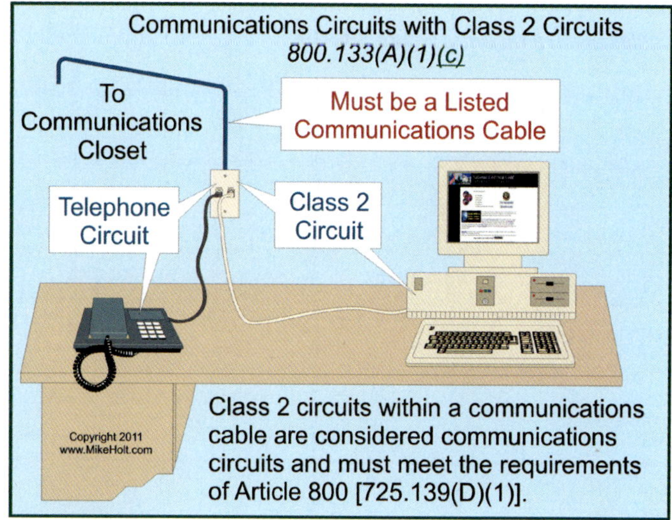

Figure 800-18

Author's Comments:

- A common application of this requirement is when a single cable is used for both voice communications and data.
- Listed Class 2 cables have a voltage rating of 150V [725.179(G)], whereas communications cables have a voltage rating of 300V [800.179].

(d) With Power Conductors in Same Raceway or Enclosure. Communications conductors must not be placed in any raceway, compartment, outlet box, junction box, or similar fitting with conductors of electric power or Class 1 circuits.

Ex 1: Communications circuits can be within the same enclosure with conductors of electric power and Class 1 circuits, where separated by a permanent barrier or listed divider.

Author's Comment: Separation is required to prevent a fire or shock hazard that can occur from a short between the communications circuits and the higher-voltage circuits.

Ex 2: Communications conductors can be mixed with power conductors if the power circuit conductors are only introduced to supply power to communications equipment. The power circuit conductors must maintain a minimum ¼ in. separation from the communications circuit conductors.

(2) Other Applications. Communications circuits must maintain 2 in. of separation from electric power or Class 1 circuit conductors.

Ex 1: Separation isn't required if electric power or Class 1 circuit conductors are in a raceway or in metal-sheathed, metal-clad, nonmetallic-sheathed, or underground feeder cables, or communications cables are in a raceway. **Figure 800-19**

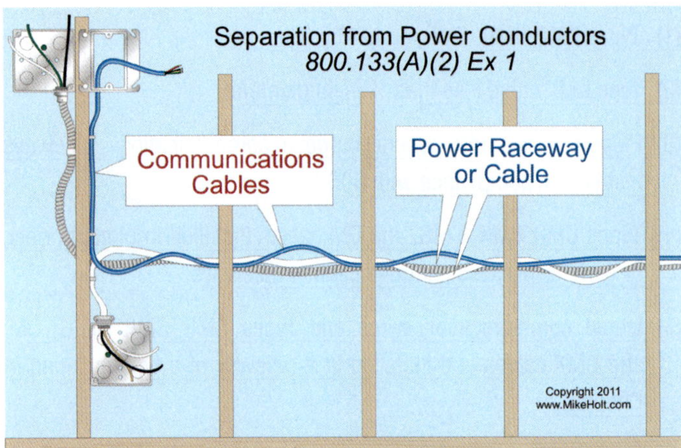

Figure 800-19

ANALYSIS: New to this *Code* cycle are "cable routing assemblies," as defined in 770.2. With this addition to the *NEC*, this section has been revised to clarify that the separation requirements for communications cables and conductors apply to cable routing assemblies as well as raceways, cable trays, and enclosures.

This section was also revised to add Part numbers to the references of Articles 725, 760, 770, 820, and 830—a change that enhances the usability and consistency of the *Code*.

800.154 Applications of Listed Optical Fiber Cables and Raceways

This section has been revised (and greatly reduced) due to other changes to this article.

800.154 Applications of Communications Cables and Communications Raceways. Listed communications cables and raceways can be installed as indicated in Table 800.154(A) as limited by 800.113, and cable substitutions in accordance with Table 800.154(B). **Figure 800-20**

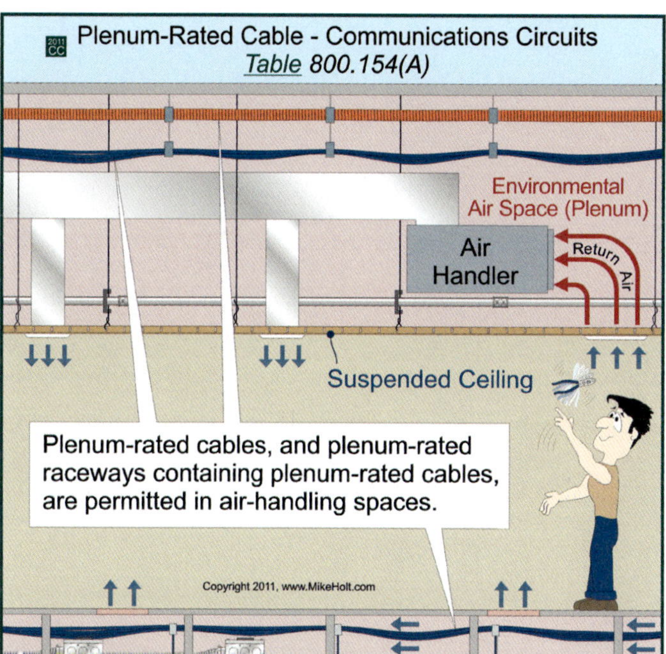

Figure 800-20

ANALYSIS: Most of the text that was found in this section in previous *NEC* editions has been relocated to 800.113. No technical changes have been made, but editorial changes referring the *Code* user to 800.113 have.

A new table has also been added, highlighting the permitted uses of the cable types discussed in this article.

800.156 Dwelling Unit Communications Outlet

The required dwelling unit communications outlet must now be installed in a readily accessible area.

800.156 Dwelling Unit Communications Outlet. One communications outlet must be installed in a readily accessible area within each dwelling unit and cabled to the service provider's demarcation point. **Figure 800-21**

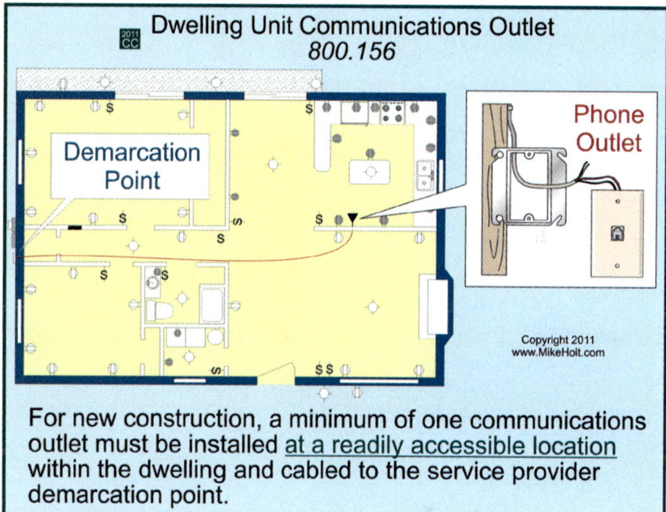

Figure 800-21

ANALYSIS: The 2008 *NEC* added a requirement for at least one communications outlet in every dwelling unit. As is often the case with new requirements, accidental oversights occur. While it seems rather unlikely that a dwelling unit would be constructed with only one communications outlet, installed in (for example) the attic, the *Code* allowed it. This change eliminates that possibility.

NOTES

Radio and Television EQUIPMENT

INTRODUCTION TO ARTICLE 810—RADIO AND TELEVISION EQUIPMENT

This article covers transmitter and receiver equipment—and the wiring and cabling associated with that equipment. Here are a few key points to remember about Article 810:

- Avoid contact with conductors of other systems.
- Don't attach antennas or other equipment to the service-entrance power mast.
- If the mast isn't grounded properly, voltage surges caused by nearby lightning strikes can destroy it.
- Keep the bonding conductor or grounding electrode conductor as straight as practicable, and protect it from physical damage.
- If the mast isn't bonded properly, you risk flashovers and possible electrocution.
- Keep in mind that the purpose of bonding is to prevent a difference of potential between metallic objects and other conductive items, such as swimming pools.
- Clearances are critical, and Article 810 contains detailed clearance requirements. For example, it provides separate clearance requirements for indoor and outdoor locations.

Article 810 Radio and Television Equipment

A new Informational Note was added to address changes to defined terms in this article.

Note: The term "Grounding Conductor" previously used in this article has been replaced by either "Bonding Conductor" or "Grounding Electrode Conductor (GEC)" where applicable to more accurately reflect the application and function of the conductor.

ANALYSIS: With the deletion of the term "grounding conductor," the terms "grounding electrode conductor" or "bonding jumper," or both, are new to this article. This new Informational Note is intended to alert *Code* users to this fact.

PART I. GENERAL

810.1 Scope

Changes made in the scope of this article incorporate citizen band (CB) radio transmission into the article.

810.1 Scope. Article 810 contains the installation requirements for the wiring of television and radio receiving equipment, such as digital satellite receiving equipment for television signals and amateur/citizen band radio equipment antennas. Figure 810-1

Author's Comment: Article 810 covers:

- VHF/UHF antennas, which receive local television signals.
- Satellite antennas, which are often referred to as satellite dishes. Large satellite dish antennas (often about 6 ft in diameter) usually have a motor that moves the dish to focus on different satellites. The smaller satellite dish antennas (18 in. in diameter) are usually aimed at a single satellite.

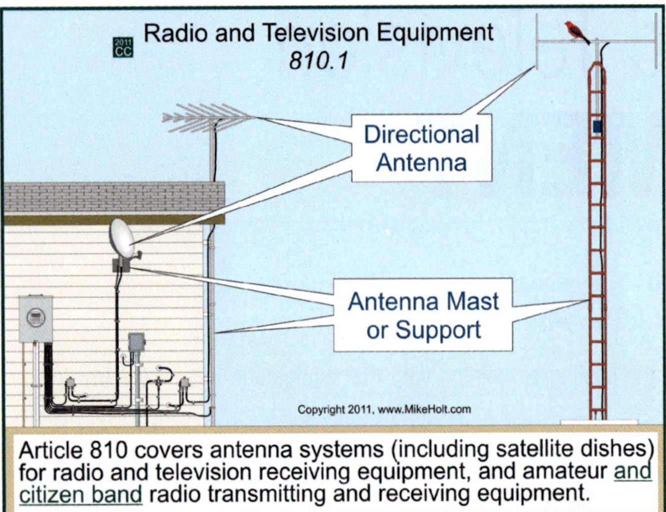

Article 810 covers antenna systems (including satellite dishes) for radio and television receiving equipment, and amateur and citizen band radio transmitting and receiving equipment.

Figure 810-1

- Roof-mounted antennas for AM/FM/XM radio reception.
- Amateur radio transmitting and receiving equipment, including HAM radio equipment (a noncommercial [amateur] communications system).

ANALYSIS: Citizen band (CB) radio antennas are very similar to amateur (HAM) radio antennas. They're both exposed to the same environmental and atmospheric conditions, such as lightning, wind loading, and clearance to overhead conductors. Due to these similarities, it makes sense to incorporate these systems into Article 810.

The title of Part III of this article was also revised to reflect this change, as were the titles of 810.51 and 810.58(A).

PART II. RECEIVING EQUIPMENT—ANTENNA SYSTEMS

810.21 Bonding Conductors and Grounding Electrode Conductors

This section has been revised extensively to provide consistency with changes made to grounding related terms.

810.21 Bonding Conductor or Grounding Electrode Conductors. The antenna mast [810.15] and antenna discharge unit [810.20(C)] must be grounded as follows. Figure 810-2

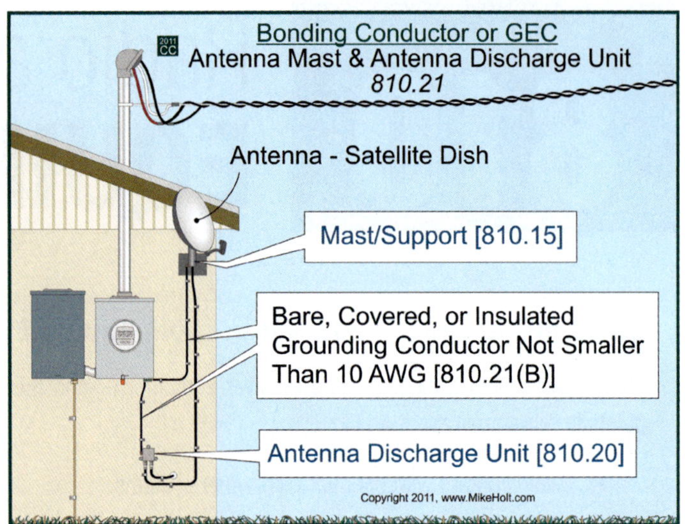

Figure 810-2

Author's Comment: Grounding the lead-in antenna cables and the mast helps prevent voltage surges caused by static discharge or nearby lightning strikes from reaching the center conductor of the lead-in coaxial cable. Because the satellite dish sits outdoors, wind creates a static charge on the antenna as well as on the cable attached to it. This charge can build up on both the antenna and the cable until it jumps across an air space, often passing through the electronics inside the low noise block down converter feedhorn (LNBF) or receiver. Connecting the coaxial cable and dish to the building grounding electrode system (grounding) helps to dissipate this static charge.

Nothing can prevent damage from a direct lightning strike, but grounding with proper surge protection can help reduce damage to the satellite dish and other equipment from nearby lightning strikes.

(A) Material. The bonding conductor or grounding electrode conductor to the electrode [810.21(F)] must be copper or other corrosion-resistant conductive material, stranded or solid.

(B) Insulation. Insulated, covered, or bare.

(C) Supports. The bonding conductor or grounding electrode conductor must be securely fastened in place.

(D) Mechanical Protection. The bonding conductor or grounding electrode conductor must be mechanically protected where subject to physical damage, and where installed in a metal raceway both ends of the raceway must be bonded to the bonding conductor or grounding electrode conductor. Figure 810-3

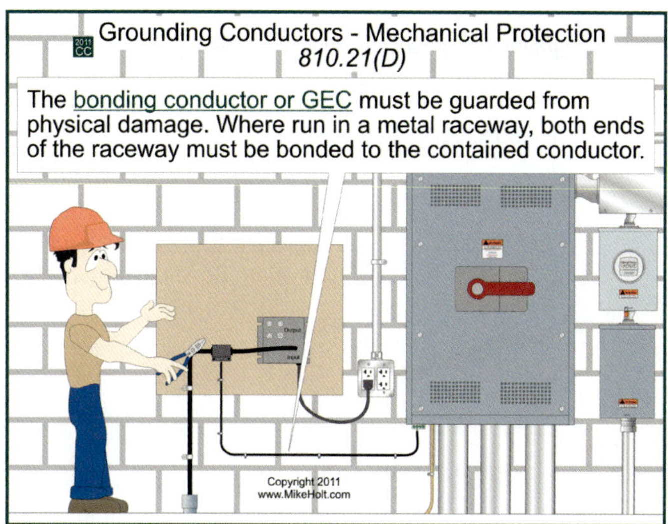

Figure 810-3

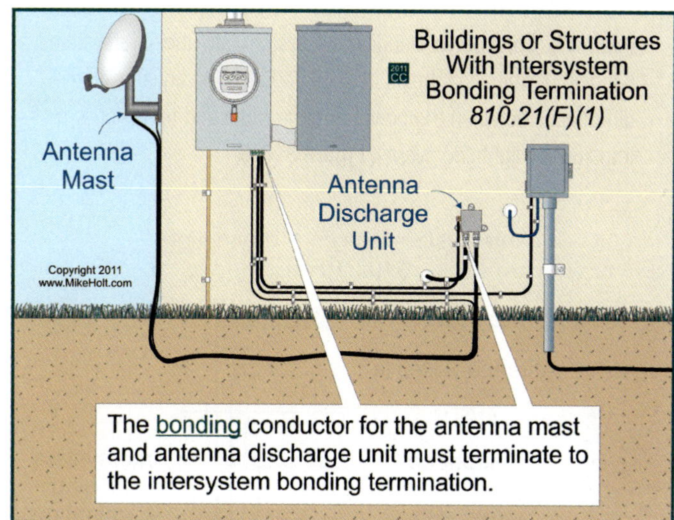

Figure 810-4

Author's Comment: Installing the bonding conductor or grounding electrode conductor in PVC conduit is a better practice.

(E) Run in Straight Line. The bonding conductor or grounding electrode conductor must be run in as straight a line as practicable.

Author's Comment: Lightning doesn't like to travel around corners or through loops, which is why the bonding conductor or grounding electrode conductor must be run as straight as practicable.

(F) Electrode. The bonding conductor or grounding electrode conductor must terminate in accordance with (1), (2), or (3).

(1) Buildings or Structures With an Intersystem Bonding Termination. The bonding conductor for the antenna mast and antenna discharge unit must terminate to the intersystem bonding termination as required by 250.94 [Article 100 and 250.94]. **Figure 810-4**

Note: According to the Article 100 definition, an Intersystem Bonding Termination is a device that provides a means to connect bonding conductors for communications systems to the grounding electrode system, in accordance with 250.94. **Figure 810-5**

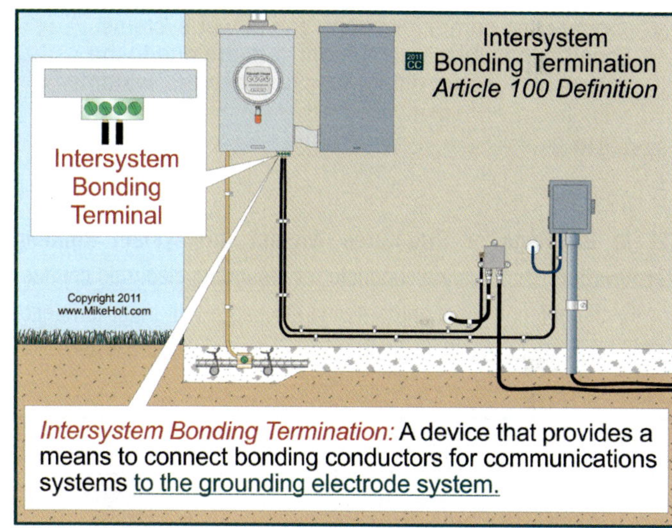

Figure 810-5

Author's Comment: Bonding all systems to the intersystem bonding termination helps reduce induced potential (voltage) differences between the power and the radio and television systems during lightning events. **Figure 810-6**

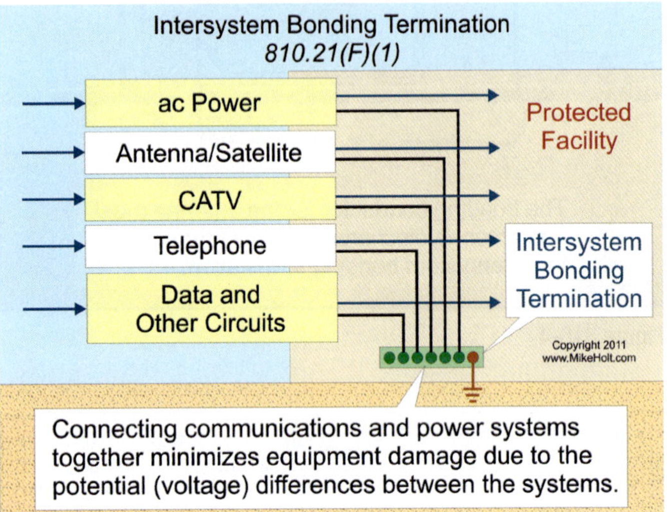

Figure 810-6

(2) In Buildings or Structures Without Intersystem Bonding Termination. The bonding conductor or grounding electrode conductor for the antenna mast and antenna discharge unit must terminate to the nearest accessible location on the following: **Figure 810-7**

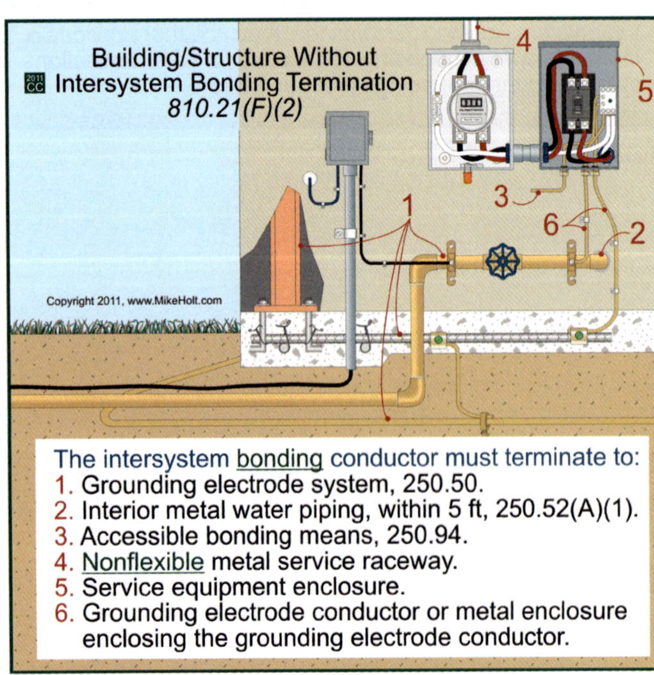

Figure 810-7

(1) Building/structure grounding electrode system [250.50].

(2) Interior metal water piping system, within 5 ft from its point of entrance [250.52(A)(1)]. **Figure 810-8**

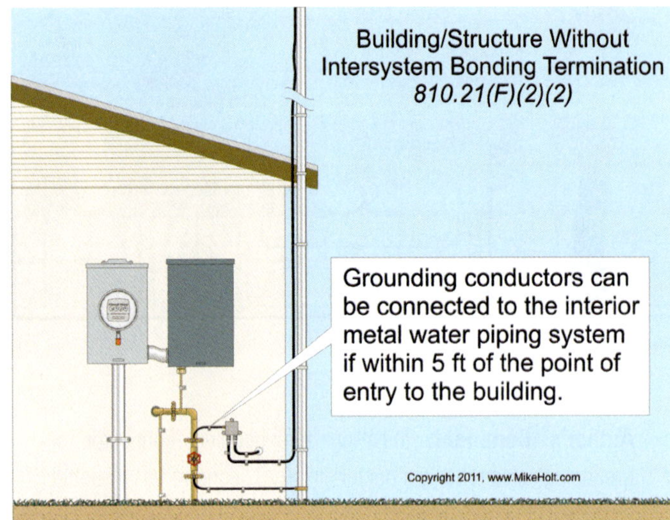

Figure 810-8

(3) Accessible means external to the building, as covered in 250.94.

(4) Nonflexible metallic service raceway.

(5) Service equipment enclosure.

(6) Grounding electrode conductor or the grounding electrode conductor metal enclosure.

(3) In Buildings or Structures Without a Grounding Means. The grounding electrode conductor for the antenna mast and antenna discharge unit must be connected to any grounding electrode as described in 250.52.

(G) Inside or Outside Building. The bonding conductor or grounding electrode conductor can be installed either inside or outside the building.

(H) Size. The bonding conductor or grounding electrode conductor must not be smaller than 10 AWG copper or 17 AWG copper-clad steel or bronze.

Author's Comment: Copper-clad steel or bronze wire (17 AWG) is often molded into the jacket of the coaxial cable to simplify the grounding of the lead-in conductor from an outdoor antenna to the discharge unit [810.21(F)].

(J) Bonding of Electrodes. If a ground rod is installed to serve as the grounding electrode for the radio and television equipment, it must be connected to the building's power grounding electrode system with a minimum 6 AWG conductor. Figure 810-9

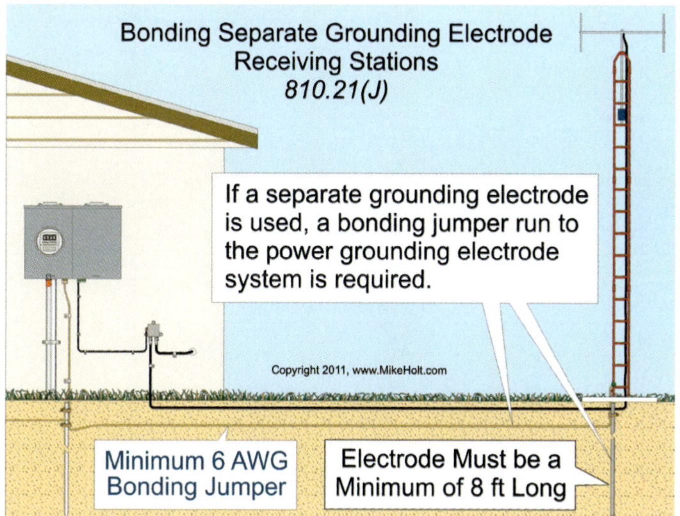

Figure 810-9

(K) Electrode Connection. Termination of the bonding conductor or grounding electrode conductor must be by exothermic welding, listed lugs, listed pressure connectors, or listed clamps. Grounding fittings that are concrete-encased or buried in the earth must be listed for direct burial [250.70]. Figure 810-10

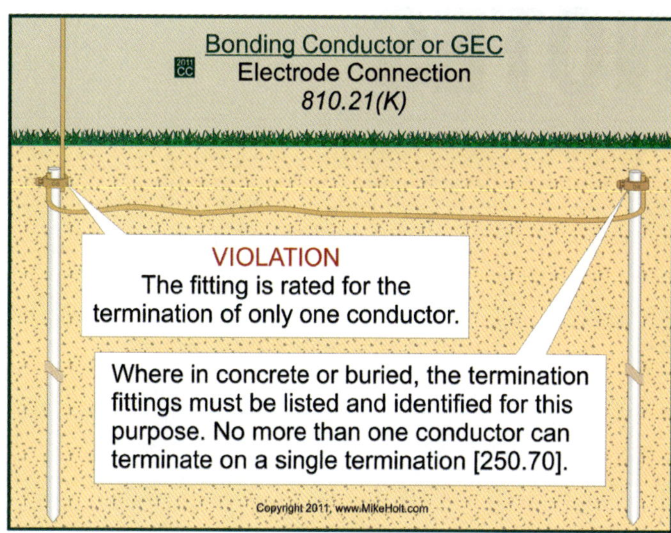

Figure 810-10

ANALYSIS: Extensive changes in this section were made in response to the deletion of the term "grounding conductor." As a replacement for it the *Code* user will see either "grounding electrode conductor," "bonding jumper," or both. Similar changes were made throughout the article, mainly in 810.58 and 810.70.

A new Informational Note was also added to (F)(1) which refers the *NEC* user to the definitions in Article 100. When a defined term is used in Chapter 8, a new Informational Note is typically added. This time the note refers the *Code* user to Article 100 for the definition of "intersystem bonding termination."

NOTES

Community Antenna Television (CATV) and Radio DISTRIBUTION SYSTEMS

INTRODUCTION TO ARTICLE 820—COMMUNITY ANTENNA TELEVISION (CATV) AND RADIO DISTRIBUTION SYSTEMS

This article focuses on the distribution of television and radio signals within a facility or on a property via cable, rather than their transmission or reception via antenna. These signals are limited energy, but they're high frequency.

- As with Article 800, you must determine the "point of entrance" for these circuits.
- Ground the incoming coaxial cable as close as practicable to the point of entrance.
- If coaxial cables are located above a suspended ceiling, route and support them to allow access via ceiling panel removal.
- Clearances are critical, and Article 820 contains detailed clearance requirements. For example, it requires at least 6 ft of clearance between coaxial cable and lightning conductors.
- If the building or structure has an intersystem bonding termination, the bonding conductor must be connected to it.
- If you use a separate grounding electrode, you must run a bonding jumper to the power grounding system.

Article 820 Community Antenna Television and Radio Distribution Systems

A new Informational Note was added to address changes to defined terms in this article, and the existing Informational Note has been removed.

Note: The term "Grounding Conductor" previously used in this article has been replaced by either "Bonding Conductor" or "Grounding Electrode Conductor (GEC)" where applicable to more accurately reflect the application and function of the conductor. **Figures 820-1 and 820-2**

ANALYSIS: With the deletion of the term "grounding conductor," the terms "grounding electrode conductor" or "bonding jumper," or both, are new to this article. This new Informational Note is intended to alert *Code* users to this fact. A similar change was made to Article 830.

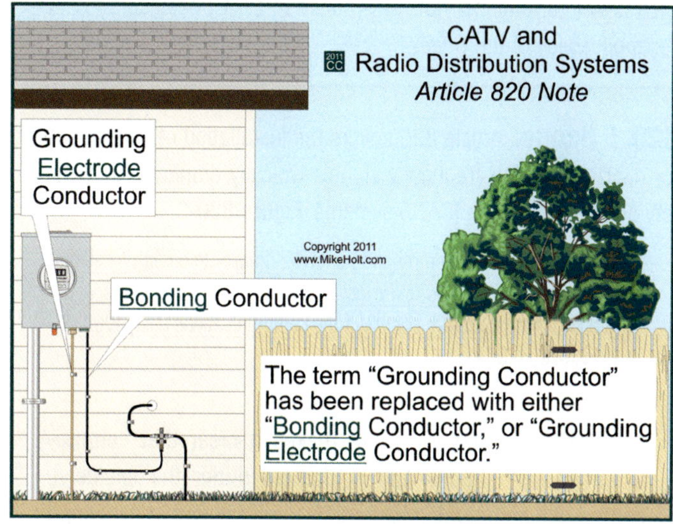

Figure 820-1

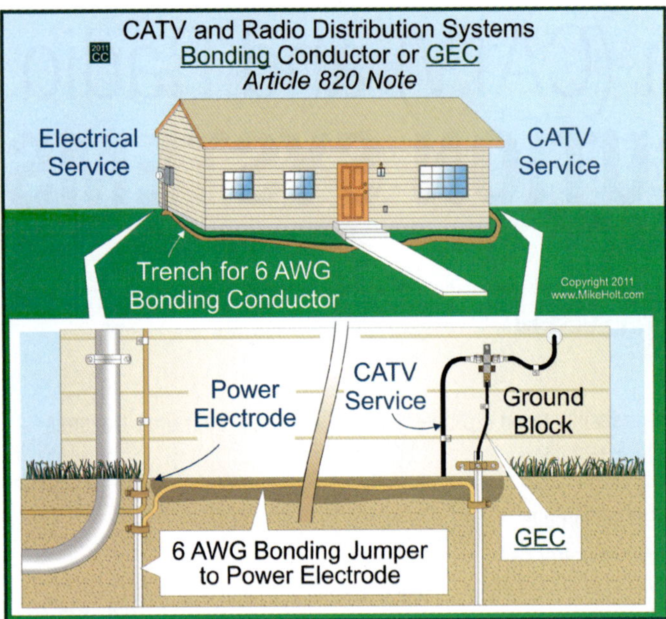

Figure 820-2

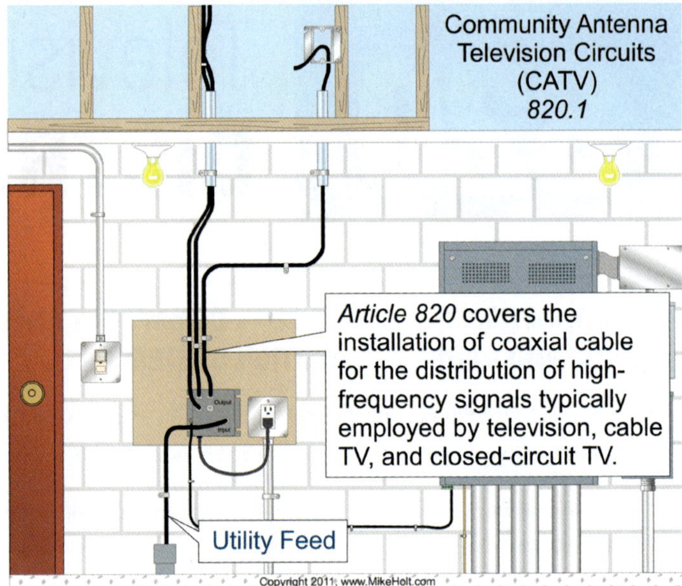

Figure 820-3

820.1 Scope

A new Informational Note was added to alert *Code* users to the applicability of the *Code*.

820.1 Scope. Article 820 covers the installation of coaxial cables for distributing high-frequency signals typically employed in community antenna television (CATV) systems. **Figure 820-3**

Note: The *NEC* installation requirements don't apply to communications utility equipment, such as CATV located outdoors or in building spaces where under the exclusive control of the communications utility [90.2(B)(4)]. **Figure 820-4**

ANALYSIS: Section 90.2(B)(4) makes it clear that communications installations and equipment under the exclusive control of a communications utility don't fall within the scope of the *NEC*. Many *Code* users, unfortunately, don't take the time to read and fully understand the provisions of Article 90. Due to this, confusion often results when it comes to installations under the exclusive control of a utility. While this isn't a change that brings any new requirements, it will probably help many users of the *Code* by reminding them that the *NEC* doesn't apply to certain communications equipment.

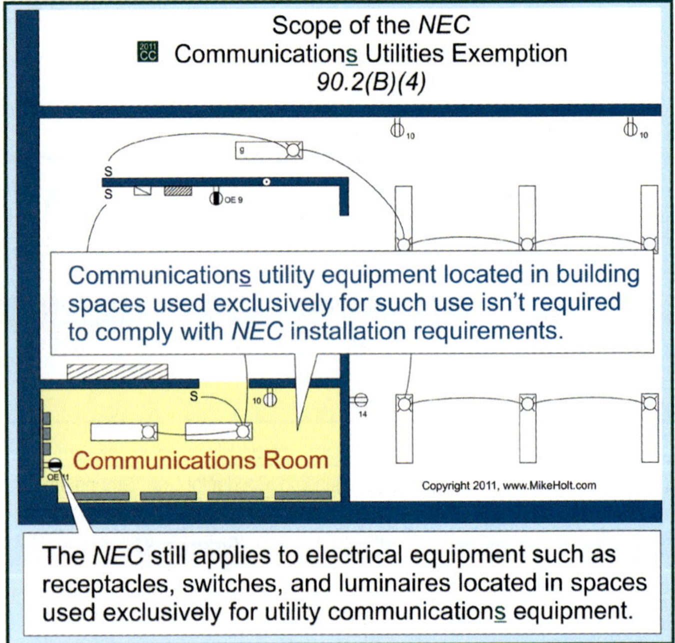

Figure 820–4

820.3 Other Articles

A new subsection has been added to address cable routing assemblies. A previous section addressing wiring in ducts, plenums, and air-handling spaces was removed.

820.3 Other Articles.

(B) Installation and Use. Equipment must be installed in accordance with manufacturer's instructions [110.3(B)].

(C) Optical Fiber Cables. Optical fiber cable must be installed in accordance with Article 770.

(D) Communications Circuits. Twisted-pair conductor cable used for communications circuits must comply with Article 800.

(H) Cable Routing Assemblies. The definition in 770.2, the applications in 770.154, and installation rules in 770.113 apply.

Author's Comment: The requirements for CATV and Radio Distribution Systems aren't subject to the general requirements of Chapters 1 through 4, or the special requirements of Chapters 5 through 7, unless there's a specific reference in Article 820 to a rule in one of those chapters [90.3].

ANALYSIS: New to the *Code* in 2011 is the concept of "cable routing assemblies." The definition and provisions for these systems are all found in Article 770, so a new subsection was added here to recognize them.

820.48 Unlisted Cables and Raceways Entering Building

The requirements for unlisted cables entering buildings have been revised.

820.48 Unlisted Cables and Raceways Entering Building. Unlisted coaxial cable is permitted in building spaces, other than other spaces used for environmental air (plenums), if the length of the coaxial cable within the building from its point of entrance doesn't exceed 50 ft and the coaxial cable terminates at a grounding block. Figure 820-5

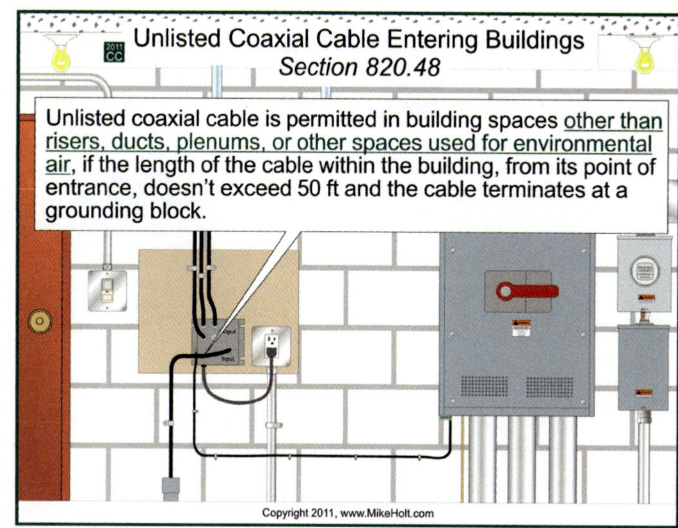

Figure 820-5

ANALYSIS: This subsection allows for an unlisted coaxial cable in a building, provided that the length doesn't exceed 50 ft. Although other sections of the *Code* already cover the requirements for cables installed in ducts used for environmental air, plenums used for environmental air, and other spaces used for environmental air (plenums), they've been reiterated here. The unlisted cables entering buildings discussed in this section aren't allowed in these ducts, plenums, and air-handling spaces.

820.93 Grounding of the Outer Conductive Shield of Coaxial Cables

Changes to this section have been made to provide consistency with other grounding terminology changes in the *Code*.

820.93 Grounding or Interruption of Metallic Members of Coaxial Cables.

(A) Coaxial CATV Cables Entering Building. Coaxial CATV cables entering the building or terminating on the outside of the building must have the metallic sheath members grounded as specified in 820.100. Figure 820-6

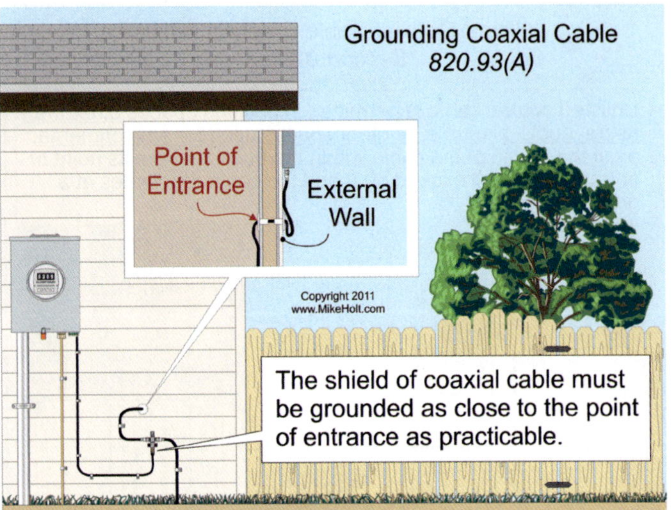

Figure 820-6

Note: Limiting the length of the bonding conductor or grounding electrode conductor helps limit damage to equipment because of a potential (voltage) difference between communications equipment and other systems during lightning events.

ANALYSIS: Extensive changes were made in response to the deletion of the term "grounding conductor." As a replacement for it the *Code* user will see either "grounding electrode conductor," "bonding jumper," or both. Similar changes were made throughout the article, mainly in 820.100 and 820.106.

820.100 Bonding and Grounding

The requirements for the insulation of the grounding electrode conductor have been relaxed, and the sizing requirements have been increased. A new Informational Note has also been added.

820.100 Bonding and Grounding. The outer conductive shield of a coaxial cable must be bonded or grounded in accordance with the following:

Ex: Coaxial cable confined within the premises and isolated from the outside cable plant can be grounded by a connection to an equipment grounding conductor. Connecting to an equipment grounding conductor through a grounded receptacle using a dedicated grounding conductor and permanently connected listed device is permitted. Use of a cord and plug for the connection to an equipment grounding conductor isn't permitted.

(A) Bonding conductor or grounding electrode conductor.

(1) Insulation. The bonding conductor or grounding electrode conductor must be listed and be insulated, covered, or bare.

(2) Material. The bonding conductor or grounding electrode conductor must be copper or other corrosion-resistant conductive material, stranded or solid.

(3) Size. The bonding conductor or grounding electrode conductor must not be smaller than 14 AWG with a current-carrying capacity of not less than the grounded metallic sheath member or protected conductor of the communications cable, but not required to be larger than 6 AWG.

(4) Length. The bonding conductor or grounding electrode conductor for CATV systems must be as short as practicable. For one- and two-family dwellings, the bonding conductor or grounding electrode conductor must not exceed 20 ft. Figure 820-7

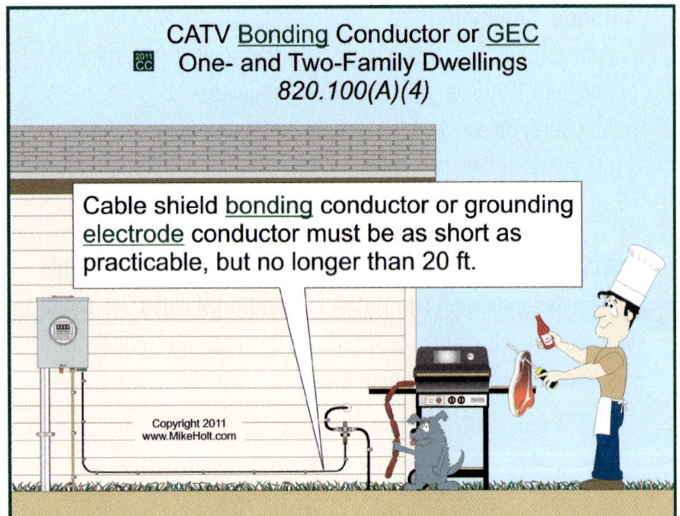

Figure 820-7

Note: Limiting the length of the bonding conductor or grounding electrode conductor will help to reduce potential (voltage) differences between the building's power and CATV systems during lightning events.

Ex: If it's not practicable to limit the coaxial bonding conductor or grounding electrode conductor to 20 ft in length for one- and two-family dwellings, a separate ground rod not less than 8 ft long, with fittings suitable for the application [250.70 and 820.100(C)] must be installed. The additional ground rod must be bonded to the power grounding electrode system with a minimum 6 AWG conductor [820.100(D)]. Figure 820-8

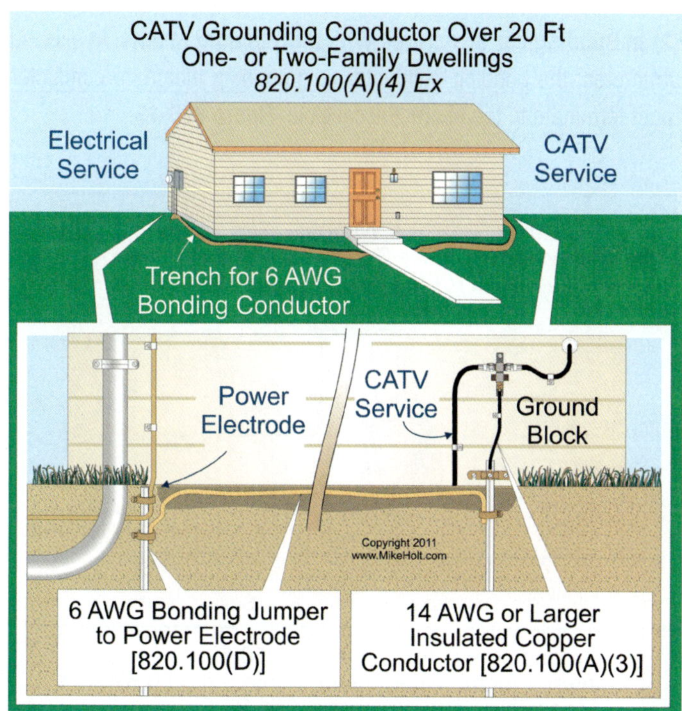

Figure 820–8

(5) Run in Straight Line. The bonding conductor or grounding electrode conductor to the electrode must be run in as straight a line as practicable.

Author's Comment: Lightning doesn't like to travel around corners or through loops, which is why the bonding conductor or grounding electrode conductor must be run as straight as practicable.

(6) Physical Protection. The bonding conductor or grounding electrode conductor must be mechanically protected where subject to physical damage, and where installed in a metal raceway both ends of the raceway must be bonded to the bonding conductor or grounding electrode conductor. Figure 820-9

Author's Comment: Installing the bonding conductor in PVC conduit is a better practice.

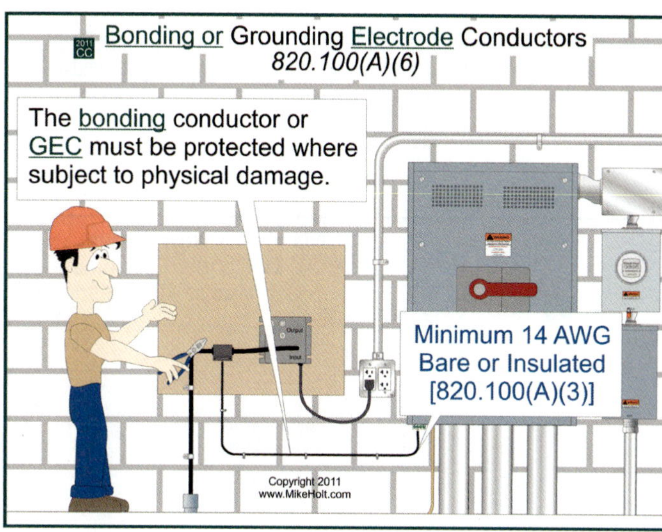

Figure 820-9

(B) Electrode. The bonding conductor or grounding electrode conductor must be connected in accordance with (B)(1), (B)(2), or (B)(3).

(1) Buildings or Structures with an Intersystem Bonding Termination. The bonding conductor or grounding electrode conductor for the CATV system must terminate to the intersystem bonding termination as required by 250.94. Figure 820–10

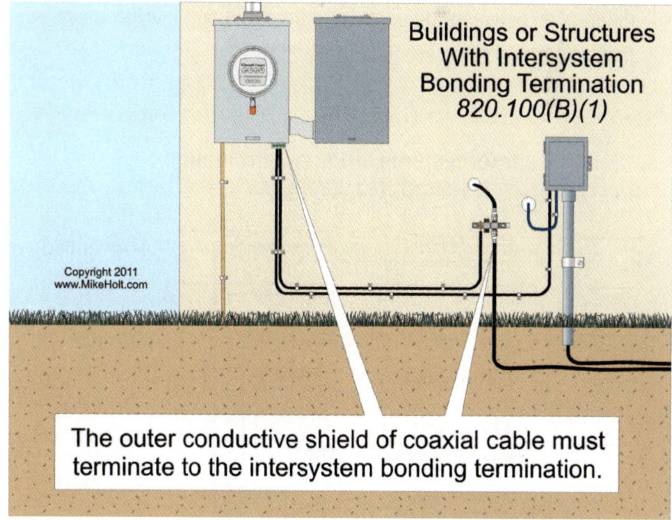

Figure 820-10

Note: According to the Article 100 definition, an "Intersystem Bonding Termination" is a device that provides a means to connect bonding conductors for communications systems to the grounding electrode system, in accordance with 250.94. **Figure 820-11**

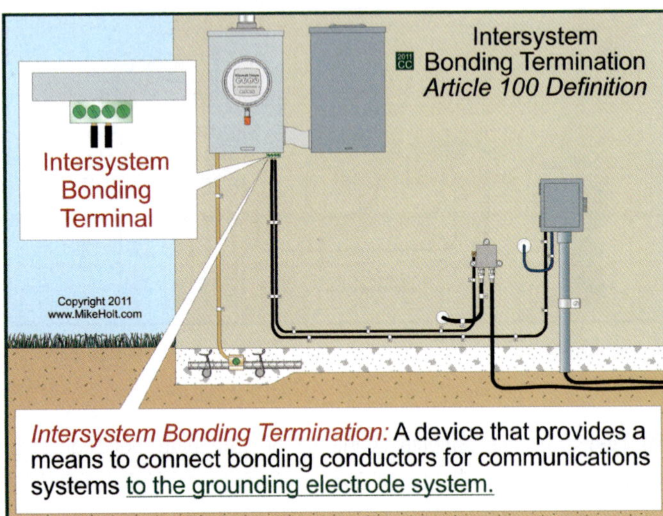

Figure 820–11

Author's Comment: Bonding all systems to the intersystem bonding termination helps reduce induced potential (voltage) differences between the power and the radio and television systems during lightning events. **Figure 820-12**

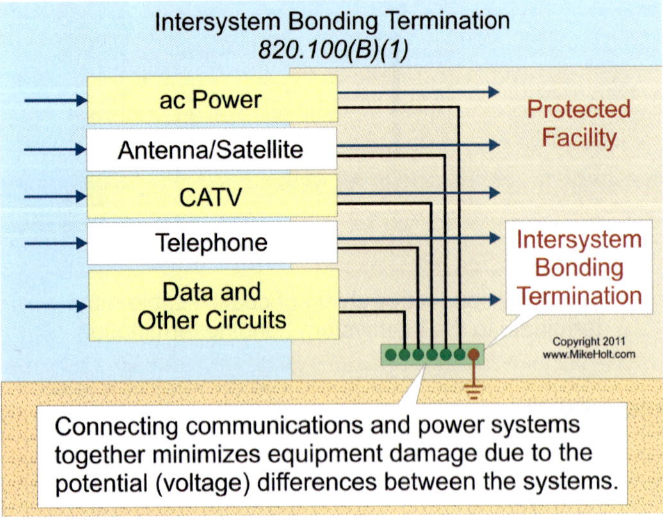

Figure 820-12

(2) In Buildings or Structures With a Grounding Means. At existing structures, the bonding conductor or grounding electrode conductor must terminate to the nearest accessible: **Figure 820-13**

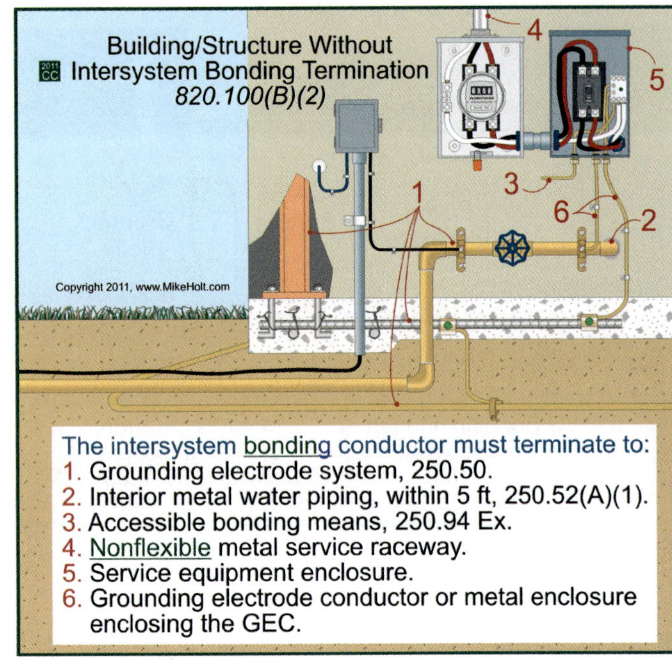

Figure 820-13

(1) Building/structure grounding electrode system [250.50].

(2) Interior metal water piping system, within 5 ft from its point of entrance [250.52(A)(1)].

(3) Accessible means external to the building, as covered in 250.94 Ex.

(4) Nonflexible metallic service raceway of the power service.

(5) Service equipment enclosure.

(6) Grounding electrode conductor or the grounding electrode conductor metal enclosure.

(7) The bonding conductor or grounding electrode conductor or the grounding electrode of a remote building/structure disconnecting means [250.32].

The intersystem bonding termination must be mounted on the fixed part of an enclosure so that it won't interfere with the opening of an enclosure door. A bonding device must not be mounted on a door or cover even if the door or cover is nonremovable.

(3) In Buildings or Structures Without Intersystem Bonding Termination or Grounding Means. The bonding conductor or grounding electrode conductor must connect to:

(1) Any individual grounding electrodes described in 250.52(A)(1), (A)(2), (A)(3), (A)(4), or

(2) Any individual grounding electrodes described in 250.52(A)(5), 250.52(A)(6), and (A)(7). **Figure 820-14**

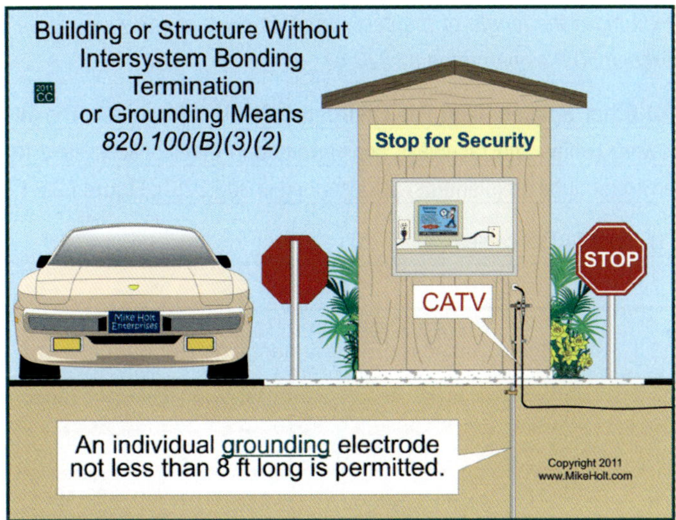

Figure 820-14

ANALYSIS: Coaxial cable systems that originate inside of the premises are becoming quite common in newer cable systems (such as where optical fiber cable is routed to the dwelling). The grounding of these cable systems, which are totally isolated and confined within the premises, shouldn't involve lightning induced currents. Therefore, grounding of the coaxial cable shield of such isolated systems to the alternating-current receptacle ground is proposed as sufficient to eliminate any stray potentials that might be present on the ungrounded coaxial cable shield due to cumulative leakage currents from connected equipment on the network.

In previous editions of the *Code*, the grounding electrode conductor was required to be insulated. Because this makes no sense from an electrical theory perspective, this requirement has been revised to allow any type of conductor—insulated, covered, or bare, provided that the conductor is listed.

The size of the grounding electrode conductor has also been revised. Previous editions of the *NEC* used the phrase "approximately equal to that of the outer conductor of the coaxial cable," a vague phrase that's all too subjective. With this change, the phrase "approximately equal" has been replaced with the more enforceable phrase "not less than."

When a defined term is used in Chapter 8, a new Informational Note is typically added. This time the note refers the *Code* user to Article 100 for the definition of "intersystem bonding termination."

820.110 Raceways for Coaxial Cables

The provisions for raceways containing coaxial cables have been revised, mainly for clarity and usability.

820.110 Raceways for Coaxial Cables.

(A) Types of Raceways.

(1) Chapter 3 Raceways. Coaxial cables can be installed in any Chapter 3 raceway in accordance with the requirements of Chapter 3. **Figure 820-15**

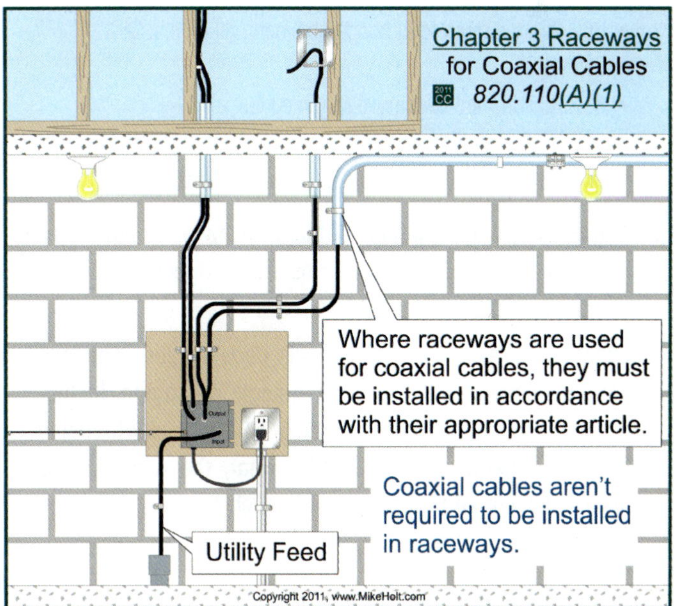

Figure 820-15

(2) Other Permitted Raceways. Coaxial cables can be installed in listed communications raceways. If coaxial cables are installed in a listed communications nonmetallic raceway, the raceway must be installed in accordance with 362.24 through 362.56. **Figure 820-16**

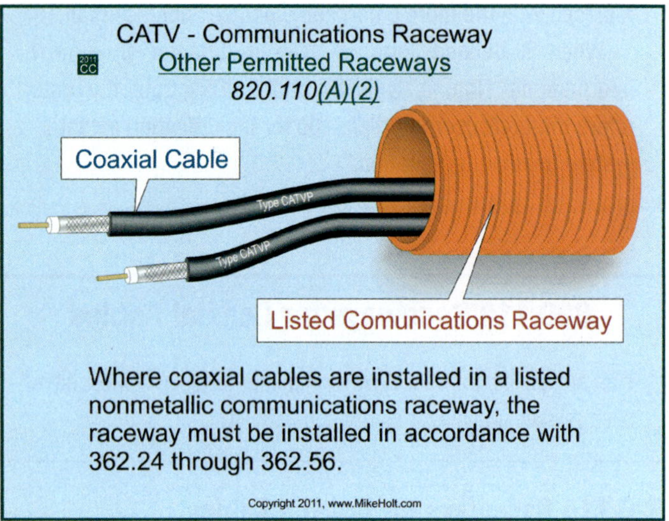

Figure 820-16

Author's Comment: In other words, listed coaxial raceways must be installed according to the following rules for ENT:

- 362.24 Bending radius
- 362.26 Maximum total bends between pull points, 360 degrees
- 362.28 Trimmed to remove rough edges
- 362.30 Supported every 3 ft, and within 3 ft of any enclosure
- 362.48 Joints between tubing, fittings, and boxes

(B) Raceway Fill for Coaxial Cables. Raceway fill limitations of 300.17 don't apply to coaxial cables installed in a raceway.

ANALYSIS: Previous editions of this *Code* section contained many provisions in the form of a single paragraph, including one sentence with an incredible 61 words! By breaking the requirements up into a list format, the requirements and allowances of this section are much easier to read and understand.

820.113 Installation of Coaxial Cables

This section has been extensively revised to incorporate all of the requirements for the installation of coaxial cables and cable routing assemblies.

820.113 Installation of Coaxial Cables.

(A) Listing. Coaxial cables installed within buildings must be listed.

Ex: Unless the length of the cable from its point of entrance, doesn't exceed 50 ft as permitted by 820.48.

(C) Other Spaces Used For Environmental Air (Plenums). The following cables and raceways are permitted in other spaces used for environmental air (plenums) as described in 300.22(C): **Figure 820-17**

(1) Type CATVP cables

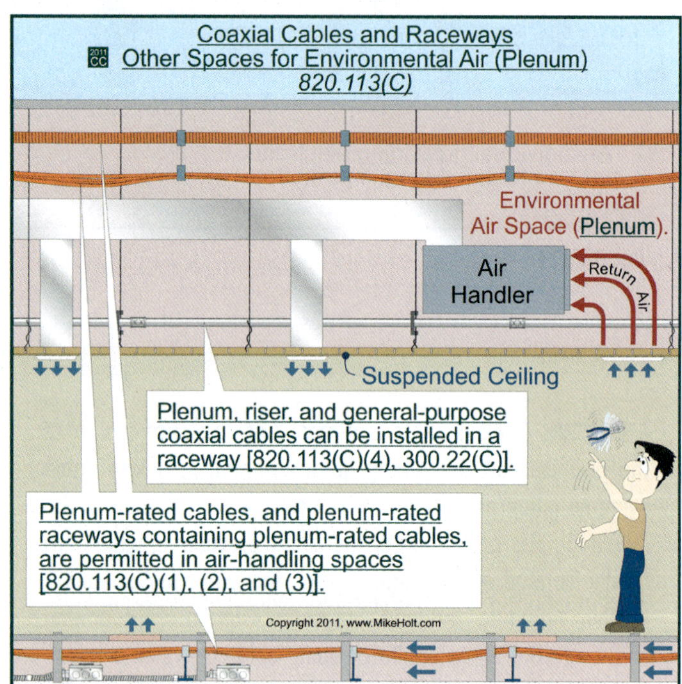

Figure 820-17

(2) Type CATVP cables installed in plenum raceways

(3) Type CATVP cables supported by metallic cable trays or cable tray systems

(4) Types CATVP, CATVR, CATV, and CATVX cables installed in raceways in compliance with 300.22(C)

(H) Cable Trays. The following cables can be installed in cable trays:

(1) Types CATVP, CATVR, and CATV cables

(2) Types CATVP, CATVR, and CATV cables installed in plenum riser or general-purpose communications raceways.

(J) Other Building Locations. The following cables can be installed in building locations other than the locations covered in 820.113(B) through (H):

(1) Types CATVP, CATVR, and CATV cables

(2) A maximum of 10 ft of exposed Type CATVX in nonconcealed spaces

(3) Types CATVP, CATVR, and CATV cables installed in plenum, riser, or general-purpose communications raceways

(4) Types CATVP, CATVR, CATV, and Type CATVX cables installed in a Chapter 3 raceway

(K) One- and Two-Family and Multifamily Dwellings. The following cables can be installed in one- and two-family and multifamily dwellings in locations other than the locations covered in 820.113(B) through (H):

(1) Types CATVP, CATVR, CATV cables

(2) Type CATVX cables less than 0.375 in. in diameter

(3) Types CATVP, CATVR, and CATV cables installed in plenum riser or general-purpose communications raceways

ANALYSIS: One need only glance at this section of the *Code* to understand the extent of the revisions that have been made. While there seem to be many new requirements at first glance, a great deal of the changes involved moving existing requirements out of another section and into this one. Section 820.154 has long provided the installation requirements for CATV cables and conductors, and communications raceways, but due to its location, the requirements were difficult to find.

New to the *NEC* are provisions for distributing frames and cross-connect arrays. These provisions can be found in 820.113(I).

The requirements for riser-rated cable have been clarified in 820.113(D) as well. Previous editions of the *Code* required riser-rated cables whenever "more than one floor" was penetrated. This led to arguments about whether a cable extending from one level to another (penetrating one floor/ceiling assembly) was required to be riser-rated. A clarification has been made on this issue to clarify that such a cable does need to be riser-rated. The requirement for riser-rated cables comes into play once the cable penetrates a single floor.

820.133(A) Separation from Other Conductors

Provisions for cable routing assemblies have been added to the separation requirements contemplated in this section.

820.133 Installation of Coaxial Cables and Equipment.

(A) Separation from Other Conductors.

(1) In Raceways, Cable Trays, Routing Assemblies, and Enclosures.

(a) With Optical Fiber Cables. Coaxial cables can be in the same raceway, cable tray, cable routing assembly or enclosure with conductors of any of the following: Figure 820-18

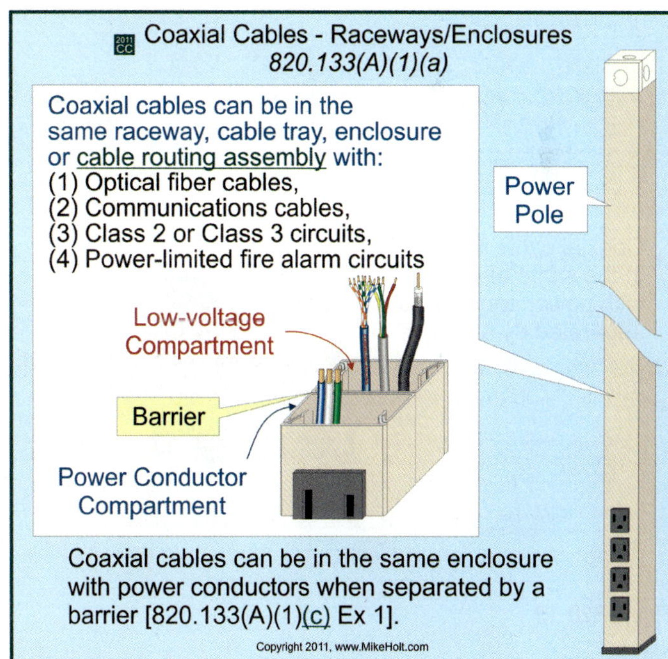

Figure 820-18

(1) Optical fiber cables in accordance with Parts I and IV of Article 770.

(2) Coaxial cables in compliance with Parts I and IV of Article 800.

(b) With Other Circuits. Communications cables can be in the same raceway, cable tray, cable routing assembly or enclosure with conductors of any of the following:

(1) Class 2 and Class 3 circuits in compliance with Parts I and III of Article 725.

(2) Power-limited fire alarm circuits in compliance with Parts I and III of Article 760.

(c) Electric Light, Power, Class 1, Nonpower-Limited Fire Alarm, and Medium-Power Network-Powered Broadband Communications Circuits. Coaxial cable must not be placed in any raceway, compartment, outlet box, junction box, or other enclosures with conductors of electric light, power, Class 1, nonpower-limited fire alarm, or medium-power network-powered broadband communications circuits.

Ex 1: Coaxial cables are permitted with conductors of electric power and Class 1 circuits, where separated by a permanent barrier or listed divider. **Figure 820-19**

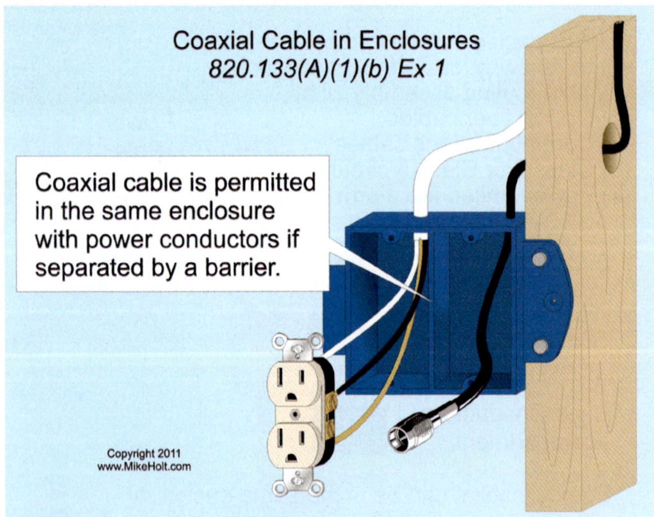

Figure 820-19

Author's Comment: Separation is required to prevent a fire or shock hazard that can occur from a short between the higher-voltage circuits and the coaxial cable.

Ex 2: Coaxial cables can be mixed in enclosures other than raceways or cables with power conductors if the power circuit conductors are only introduced to supply power to coaxial cable system distribution equipment. The power circuit conductors must be separated at least ¼ in. from the coaxial cables.

(2) Other Applications. Coaxial cables must maintain 2 in. of separation from electric power or Class 1 circuit conductors.

Ex 1: Separation isn't required if electric power or Class 1 circuit conductors are in a raceway or in metal-sheathed, metal-clad, nonmetallic-sheathed, or underground feeder cables, or coaxial cables are in a raceway. **Figure 820-20**

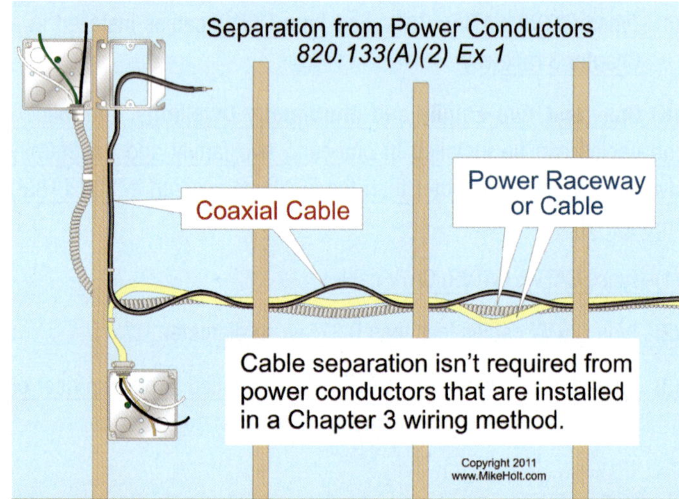

Figure 820-20

ANALYSIS: New to this *Code* cycle are "cable routing assemblies," as defined in 770.2. With this addition to the *NEC*, this section has been revised to clarify that the separation requirements for CATV cables and conductors apply to cable routing assemblies as well as raceways, cable trays, and enclosures.

This section was also revised to add Part numbers to the references of Articles 725, 760, 770, 800, and 830—a change that enhances the usability and consistency of the *Code*.

820.154 Applications of Listed Coaxial Cables

This section has been revised (and greatly reduced) due to other changes to this article.

ANALYSIS: Most of the text that was found in this section in previous *NEC* editions has been relocated to 820.113. No technical changes have been made here, but editorial changes referring the *Code* user to 820.113 have.

A new table has also been added, highlighting the permitted uses of the cables types discussed in this article.

820.154 Applications of Coaxial Cables. Listed coaxial cables can be installed as indicated in Table 820.154(A) as limited by 820.113, and cable substitutions in accordance with Table 820.154(B). **Figure 820-21**

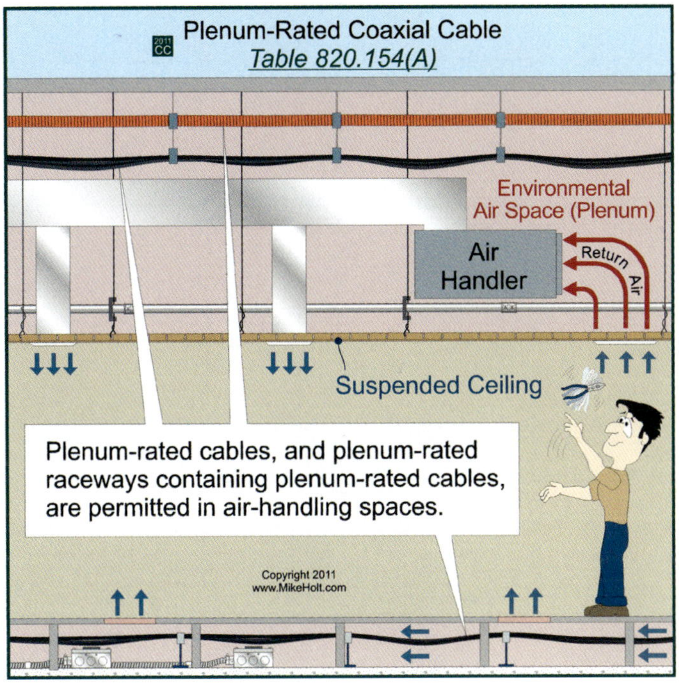

Figure 820-21

NOTES

Premises-Powered Broadband COMMUNICATIONS SYSTEMS

INTRODUCTION TO ARTICLE 840—PREMISES-POWERED BROADBAND COMMUNICATIONS SYSTEMS

Article 840 covers premises-powered optical fiber-based broadband communications systems. The systems use optical fiber cable to the premises supplying a broadband signal to an optical network terminal that converts the broadband signal into traditional telephone, video, high-speed internet, and interactive services.

Article 840 Premises-Powered Broadband Communications Systems

A new article covering premises-powered broadband communications systems was added.

ANALYSIS: Broadband services are offered that are outside of the scope of Article 830, due to the fact that they aren't network powered. Two solutions to this problem could have been made: add exceptions to existing *Code* sections, or add a new article. The *Code*-Making Panel opted for the second of these by creating a new article. Most of the provisions in it can be found in other areas of the *NEC*, but by adding a new article, all of the applicable provisions are now centrally located.

NOTES

Tables–Conductor and Raceway SPECIFICATIONS

INTRODUCTION TO CHAPTER 9—TABLES—CONDUCTOR AND RACEWAY SPECIFICATIONS

Chapter 9 consists of tables that are applicable as referenced.

Chapter 9, Table 1 Notes

Note 5 has been revised to account for flexible cords and cables, as well as optical fiber cables.

ANALYSIS: Although it could easily be argued that this table already addressed the flexible cords and cables discussed in Article 400, and the optical fiber cables discussed in 770, this change was made to solidify the fact. With this added text, the argument is removed, and it becomes quite clear that Note 5 does in fact pertain to these cables and cords.

Chapter 9, Table 5(A) Compact Copper and Aluminum Building Wire Nominal Dimensions and Areas

Changes have been made to provide for Types RHH, RHW, and USE Compact Copper and Aluminum Building conductors.

ANALYSIS: Types RHH, RHW, and USE are manufactured in the "compact" variety, yet this table hasn't provided dimensions for these conductors. With this change, users of the *Code* can now calculate raceway fill when these conductor types are employed.

Chapter 9, Table 10 Conductor Stranding

A new table was added to Chapter 9, addressing finely stranded conductors.

ANALYSIS: Although finely stranded conductors are not entirely new, the hazards associated with them are starting to manifest themselves. In an effort to educate *Code* users about the dangers involved with the terminations of these conductors, several changes to the *NEC* have been made. One of these changes is the inclusion of this new table, which provides information on conductor stranding, borrowed from UL 486A-B—Table 14.

NOTES

Recommended TIGHTENING TORQUES

INTRODUCTION TO ANNEX I— RECOMMENDED TIGHTENING TORQUES

Informative annexes aren't part of the requirements of this *Code* but are included for informational purposes only.

Annex I Recommended Tightening Torques

A new annex was added to provide recommended tightening torques for terminations.

ANALYSIS: Because the *NEC* doesn't mandate tightening torques [110.14], proposals to add new tables to Chapter 9 were rejected. These proposals contained useful information, however, so they were added as a new annex in 2011. It consists of two tables, each of which is borrowed from the UL standard 486A-486B. The tables recommend torque values based on the types of terminations and conductor sizes.

NOTES

NOTES

NOTES

NOTES

NOTES